The Barbed-Wire University

The Real Lives
of Allied Prisoners of War
in the Second World War

MIDGE GILLIES

First published 2011 by
Aurum Press Limited
7 Greenland Street
London NW1 0ND
www.aurumpress.co.uk

Paperback edition first published 2012 by Aurum Press Ltd

Maps on pp. xxvi-xxix by Reginald Piggott

A catalogue record for this book
is available from the British Library.

ISBN 978 1 84513 777 9

3 5 7 9 10 8 6 4 2
2012 2014 2016 2017 2015 2013

Typeset in Dante by M Rules

Printed and bound by CPI Group (UK) Ltd, Croydon, CR0 4YY

The Barbed-Wire University

MIDGE GILLIES has written six books including highly acclaimed biographies of the record-breaking pilot, Amy Johnson, and Edwardian music hall star, Marie Lloyd. She has written for a range of publications including the *Guardian, Financial Times, Independent* and *Los Angeles Times*. Her father was a prisoner of war in Europe. She is married to the prize-winning crime novelist, Jim Kelly and they live in Cambridgeshire with their daughter, Rosa.

'Enthralling'
Ian Jack, *Guardian*

'These astonishing tales of improvisation, ingenuity and courage are so enthralling. Every fact of this epic story is covered with sensitivity, restraint, and a leavening humour'
The Spectator

'Midge Gillies has tackled a colossal subject with calm professionalism and a lightness of touch which makes it a great joy to read. An outstanding piece of scholarship which is as readable as it is informative'
BBC History Magazine

'Midge Gillies's engaging *The Barbed-Wire University* . . . is a breezy, edifying history which knits together compelling tragi-comic tales'
Guardian

'What the reader is most likely to take away from this rich and well-researched book is a sense of the extraordinary ingenuity and resourcefulness so many POWs displayed'
Sunday Times

To Donald Webster Gillies
POW, husband, father, grandfather.

Contents

PART III EUROPE

PART IV THE FAR EAST

PART V FREEDOM

PART VI EX-POWS

List of Maps

Author's Note

Many languages were spoken along the Thailand–Burma Railway including English, Dutch and Japanese. As a result place names often have a variety of spellings, indicating a foreigner's attempt to pronounce a Thai word phonetically.

In most instances I have adopted the form commonly used by historians of the railway, for example, Ban Pong, Chungkai, Hintok, Nakhon Pathom, Nong Pladuk, Tarsao, Wampo.

Preface

You see the point is, if you've got a very restricted supply of food and opportunity, and a continual danger ... [you] tended to think you can do what you like when you get out of this lot; you must do what you like, because nothing could be worse, or as bad ... So it gives you a kind of, perhaps, a false hope in a way ... you think the world's going to be all right when you get out and that you can do what you want to do. So I think I had made my mind up that I wanted to be a painter, because if you were, as I was doing, painting things perhaps a lot better than most people ... then perhaps you would be able to do that when you get out.

Sir Terry Frost, artist and former Prisoner of War

My father could never sit still, never keep quiet. Watching *Match of the Day* on television with him meant enduring an agony of leg twitching and head jerks as he willed the ball into the back of the net. A missed opportunity was followed by a howl of exasperated disbelief as his fists thumped the wooden armrests of his battered armchair. When he wasn't striking the armrests he would casually drum his fingers on them so that over the years the chair's extremities gained a smooth patina. As a former footballer he had no sympathy for a striker who booted a ball over an open goal or – much worse – resorted to the 'continental' practice of lying prostrate, apparently in agony in order to win a free kick.

He was all-or-nothing. He gave up smoking overnight and when the cravings became too great would retire to our Morris Minor to savour the plastic-nicotine aroma that lingered there. And when he started to pile on weight after abandoning cigarettes he instantly gave up his two spoonfuls of sugar in tea and coffee and took up cycling until he regained his fighting weight.

He had started in middle age to look like two of the most talked-about men in our household – Eric Morecambe and Jim Callaghan. Like them he was balding and wore thick-rimmed glasses. Like Eric Morecambe he developed a habit of pushing his glasses up the bridge of his nose with his forefinger when he wanted to emphasise a point. And like the comedian he would adjust them from the side with thumb and forefinger in a nervous shuffle if he said something that he suspected might be slightly risqué.

His way of dressing was much more like a Labour prime minister's – neat but not ostentatious. On his days off he wore a tie, V-necked pullover 'to keep away the chill' and sober suit. As he grew older the clothes loosened – both literally and metaphorically. The grey woollen socks my mother knitted for him gathered in pools round his ankles and her Arran jumper expanded into a thigh-length tunic. Daringly, he once asked for a flowery shirt from the Boden catalogue but instantly rejected it because he said it made him look like Nelson Mandela – whose politics he admired but whose fashion sense he knew he could never match. He always wore his heart on his sleeve but the sleeve was never more exotic than a perfectly pressed, navy blue blazer.

So when he fell silent in front of the television, it was usually ominous. In the early 1990s there were several occasions when television images stopped him in his tracks, when the fingers gave up drumming on the armrest and instead gripped it hard. The pictures of Terry Waite, Brian Keenan and John McCarthy, all held hostage in Beirut for several years, arriving confused and startled on British soil stirred up uncomfortable memories that I could not place. My father grimaced at the screen, as if acknowledging some common bond, and then looked away. My mother and I both sensed not to ask questions.

The photo of RAF pilot John Peters was too painful for him even to look at. Peters was shot down over Iraq at the start of the Gulf War in January 1991 and images released by Saddam Hussein's regime showed him with a heavily bruised face and swollen eyes. His hands seem to be shackled and he is slumped forward, too angry or ashamed to confront the camera. Despite his khaki flying suit, the British flag just visible on his right shoulder, he looks as vulnerable as a young boy caught playing soldiers when he should be doing his homework. My father tutted at the TV screen, with a mixture of regret and recognition.

That my father had once been a prisoner of war was one of those undisputed facts that I grew up knowing as surely as I knew his country of birth – Scotland. But *prisoner of war* was a label, just like one of his many job titles – *shipyard joiner, semi-professional footballer, grocer, security guard, double glazing salesman, telephonist* – which I didn't really understand.

As a small child I remember being bitterly disappointed to discover that he had been a prisoner of war, not a convict. I so badly wanted him to have committed some heat-of-the-moment crime for which he had to pay by spending years in a high-walled Victorian prison and from which only the love of a good woman (my mother) had rescued him. It came as a grave disappointment to discover that it was merely misadventure that allowed the Germans to capture him and meant he spent eighteen months, as I saw it, tucked up in a stalag somewhere in the German Reich.

When I was about ten we would regularly gather round the black and white television set to watch *Colditz* with its cast of stereotypical officers: Robert Wagner as the handsome Flight Lieutenant Phil Carrington and Jack Hedley as the stern senior British officer, Lieutenant-Colonel John Preston. *Colditz* was a period drama as removed from my father's own experience as our other family favourite, *Upstairs, Downstairs*. He was equally happy to cheer on Steve McQueen every Christmas in *The Great Escape* as he sat astride his motorbike in his chinos that never picked up any dirt, revving his motorbike in an attempt to outwit the Nazis. My father was always the first to start whistling the film's theme tune.

If I had been looking harder I might have spotted clues to what it meant to be a POW in the spattering of German words he regularly reverted to: *Raus!* (to get me out of bed or his armchair), *Brot* (bread), *Kartoffeln* (potatoes), *Gute Nacht* (good night), *danke* (thank you) and *bitte* (please). And then there was the box of provisions that my mother packed up for me at the start of every university term. It usually contained supermarket Brie tightly wrapped in cellophane, a jar of Nescafé, and chocolate Brownies made from the 'favourite family cakes' section of the garishly illustrated *Hamlyn All Colour Cook Book*. My parents both referred to this box as my 'Red Cross parcel'.

But the biggest clue as to how being a POW shaped him was his indefatigable optimism. Hyperbole came easy to him. He had a way of wheedling out information from strangers and the most private of people and then inflating a minor success into a major triumph. Within minutes of my brother-in-law mentioning – in a self-deprecating way – that he had once won a school tennis tournament, my father was telling a neighbour how as a boy John had narrowly missed out on Wimbledon. My niece wasn't just pretty; she was supermodel 'Naomi Campbell'. When he learnt that a friend's father had been a Flying Officer in the war he immediately promoted him to Flight Lieutenant and on each subsequent meeting took his rank up a notch. The last time they met he had become a Squadron Leader. This compulsion to exaggerate was, I think, borne of a need to see the best in everyone. Optimism was part of his survival strategy.

George Haig, the 2nd Earl Haig and son of the First World War Commander, Field Marshal Haig, wrote that POWs could be divided into one or more categories: escapers, creators, administrators, students and sleepers. This book is not about the escapers. Their stories have already been told in countless ways – from the slew of first-hand accounts that emerged in the decade after the war to the more recent and distant stories written by survivors. I have every admiration for the tunnellers and forgers, for the men who bluffed their way across Europe wearing dyed blankets made to look like civilian suits and who, if caught, simply began the whole process over again. But, for me, their bravery is of a different sort from the more mundane courage of keeping going through the day-to-day boredom and uncertainty of life as a POW. I am far more interested in mental escape, the men who stole back time from their captors through creativity. Those who turned the contents of a Red Cross parcel into a cooking stove, a barometer or a stage set; men who discovered a talent for painting or foreign languages, or who took exams that might help their career when they got home; others who organised sporting fixtures or elaborate theatrical productions or who saved lives on a makeshift jungle operating table.

Of course there was considerable overlap. A noisy band practice could cover the sound of digging, Terry Frost painted a portrait of a man who was positioned directly over a tunnel entrance, and a beekeepers' club appeared so esoteric that no German guard would guess they were actually discussing an escape plan. The crafts that POWs used to alleviate boredom could equally well be used to help men leave their prison. The artist who designed stage scenery could forge documents; the tailor who made theatrical costumes could also run up a pair of 'civvy' trousers.

Learning German or French passed the time and might improve career chances but both languages would be useful for anyone on the run.

I know that a whole generation of boys (and they do seem to be mainly boys) grew up on the gung-ho tales of escape portrayed in books like Pat Reid's *The Colditz Story*, Paul Brickhill's *The Great Escape* and Eric Williams' *The Wooden Horse*. But their long passages of clipped, remarkably well-remembered dialogue leave me cold; the experiences they recount seem so far removed from the quiet desperation experienced by men like my father. This book is an attempt to find out what it was really like to be a POW – day in, day out, not just during those periods when someone was trying to escape.

As I grew up I learnt that there was a hierarchy of POW suffering. If captivity for some men in Europe had at times been tough, particularly at the end of the war when prisoners including my father faced starvation and the coldest winter in fifty years, it was nearly always universally grim for a POW in the Far East. In his job as a security guard at a local factory that made plastics my father got to know a former prisoner who had been held in the Far East and who regularly went through the dustbins for scraps of food. When a group of Japanese businessmen visited he had to be locked in a room for fear that he might attack one of them.

I wanted to find out how the experience of being a POW could change someone's life. How did it alter their personality, their relationship with their family and friends, their ambitions for life after captivity? The Second Earl Haig found a release from the weight of his own father's reputation by taking up painting while he was held at Colditz and other camps. Most European POWs – my father included when he became an escaper – resorted to one of Haig's categories – or to a sixth category of sport. In the Far East, POWs had far less chance to escape or to sleep but, with limited resources, they still managed to study, to create and to administer. It could be argued that the Far East POW (FEPOW) showed a much greater creativity because of the limited materials available to him and, for those engaged in heavy manual labour, the lack of free time.

I never knew my father when he was not an 'ex-POW' so I cannot fully judge how the experience changed him. But as well as the fear and despair, which he later recognised in the face of RAF pilot John Peters, being a POW marked him for life in a positive way, not least because he knew he was lucky to have survived. He was a storyteller and a teaser – talents that would have been valuable skills in the boarding school atmosphere of the camps. He had learnt that playing to the crowd and buoying other people up helped him to keep his own spirits high. He loved to spin yarns – about the war, about growing up in Scotland or about working in Persia (now Iran) just after the war. He hated to be alone which is why he loved crowded places – sitting with a passenger either side of him on a packed aeroplane flight, chatting with strangers on a football terrace, making friends with other parents and grandparents on the tightly packed rows of plastic chairs at his granddaughter's school carol service. He loved to make people smile – particularly if they looked ill at ease. In a doctor's waiting room he was oblivious to the fact that the English don't normally speak to strangers – especially in situations where they might be harbouring germs or unmentionable diseases – and my father would scan the room for a likely victim. If he couldn't immediately catch someone's eye he would home in on a toddler – unaware of the taboo now attached to an elderly man striking up a conversation with a small child. He was quite happy chatting to them in exaggerated tones, his playdough features working overtime to amuse them, but inevitably the parent would be drawn into the conversation.

Cashiers or anyone in a checkout queue were sitting ducks. He would stand softly whistling or humming under his breath until he spotted a way into the conversation. The whiff of a foreign accent usually provided an opening. 'Where do you come from?' he would say with unabashed curiosity, assuming his own Scottish accent gave him the right to probe. If the person came from north of Carlisle he had hit gold. 'Renee, Renee,' he would say to my mother who was from Balham and never got over the embarrassment of her husband's need to chat to complete strangers, 'you'll never guess where this woman comes from'. I often wonder whether his need to engage with strangers grew out of his POW days – particularly when he was on the run – when the ability to make friends was a life-or-death talent.

People usually responded well to such un-English behaviour – possibly because my father was so physically unthreatening. Babies chuckled back at him as if they recognised a mirror-image in his moon face with its chubby cheeks and twinkling, unwavering gaze; perhaps they sensed someone else who had still to grasp the rules of who you were or were not supposed to speak to.

The men whose stories I tell – both officers and the ordinary soldier – not only survived being a POW but also used the experience to change their lives in ways they could not have imagined before the war. They took captivity and made it their own. They set up universities, became experienced actors and musicians, devised life-saving medical gadgets from little more than bamboo and bits of old rubber, sat exams, studied birds, wrote books and poetry and made lasting friendships that crossed class and nationality.

By learning new skills or uncovering talents they stole back some of the months and years that the war had robbed them of. Few would have wished to be a POW but for a fortunate and resourceful group it changed the course of their lives. For my father being a POW taught him a lifetime skill – a genius for living for the moment.

North Sea

SWEDEN

DENMARK

Copenhagen

Baltic Sea

• Heydekrug

Kiel

• Barth

Danzig

Gross
Tychow

Hamburg

Stettin

Hammerstein

■ Marienburg

NETHERLANDS

Sandbostel ■
Marlag und
Milag Nord ■
Fallingbostel

Bremen

R. Elbe

Berlin

Schubin

■ Thorn

R. Vistula

Hanover •

Brunswick

Magdeburg

Lückenwalde

■ Posen

Warsaw

Warburg ▲

Spangenberg ▲

Furstenberg

Mühlberg •

Sagan

POLAND

R. Oder

Cologne

Hadamar ▲

Rotenberg ▲

Leipzig

Dresden

Lansdorf

■ Bankau

Limburg ▲
Frankfurt ▲

Oberursel

Bad
Sulza

Colditz

Blechhammer

Luxembourg

Bad Orb

Hammelburg

Prague

Mährisch
Trubau ▲

Teschen

Cracow

Metz

Wurzburg

Nuremberg

Nuremberg ▲

Hohenfels ■

CZECHOSLOVAKIA

Strasbourg

R. Rhine

Eichstätt ▲

R. Danube

Stuttgart

Biberach ▲

Moosburg ■

Munich

Tittmoning ▲

Gneixendorf

Vienna

FRANCE

Basle

Laufen ▲

AUSTRIA

HUNGARY

Budapest

SWITZERLAND

Wolfsberg ■

Gruppignano ☆

R. Danube

Milan

R. Po

Veano ☆

Fontanellato ☆

Venice

Belgrade

Turin

Gavi ☆

Modena ☆

YUGOSLAVIA

Genoa

Chiavari ☆

Florence

Vintigliata

R. Tiber

Corsica

Chieti ☆

Rome

Sulmona ☆

Adriatic Sea

ALBANIA

Capua ☆

Bari ☆

Naples

Padula ☆

Taranto

BRITISH & AMERICAN POW CAMPS
IN GERMAN TERRITORY, AND
BRITISH POW CAMPS IN ITALY

Camps in Germany (British & American):
▲ Oflags ■ Stalags • Air Force
Camps in Italy : ☆ (British)

THE EXTENT OF JAPANESE
OCCUPATION BY JULY 1942

MONGOLIA
Vladivostok
Hakodate
CHINA
JAPAN
Dairen
Hankow
Fukuoka
Tokyo
Shanghai
Shikoku
Yangtze Kiang
Chungking
Okinawa
Iwo Jima
Midway
INDIA
Formosa
PACIFIC OCEAN
BURMA
Haiphong
Hong Kong
FRENCH INDO-CHINA
LIMIT OF JAPANESE EXPANSION TO JULY 1942
Marianas
Wake I
Moulmein
THAILAND
South
China
Sea
PHILIPPINES
Bangkok
Saigon
Sandakan
Mindanao
Caroline Islands
Marshall Islands
MALAYA
Kuching
BORNEO
SUMATRA
CELEBES
NEW GUINEA
Gilbert
Islands
INDIAN
OCEAN
Batavia
Bandung
JAVA
DUTCH EAST INDIES
Bismarck Archipelago
Port Moresby
Ellice
Islands
Guadalcanal
Darwin
Fiji Islands
Alor Star
Ipoh
MALAYA
Kuala
Lumpur
Johore Bharu
Singapore
Alice Springs
AUSTRALIA
0   500   1000 miles
0   500   1000 1500 km

Johore
Bharu
Johore Strait
MALAYA
Kranji
Seletar
Airfield
Changi Village
Selarang Barracks
SINGAPORE   ISLAND
N
Bukit Timah
CHANGI ROAD
Keppel Harbour
Singapore
City
SOUTHERN AREA
Kitchener Barracks
Changi Village
India Barracks
Roberts
Barracks
Selarang
Barracks
SINGAPORE 1942
Changi Gaol
0   5   miles   10
0   5   10   15 km

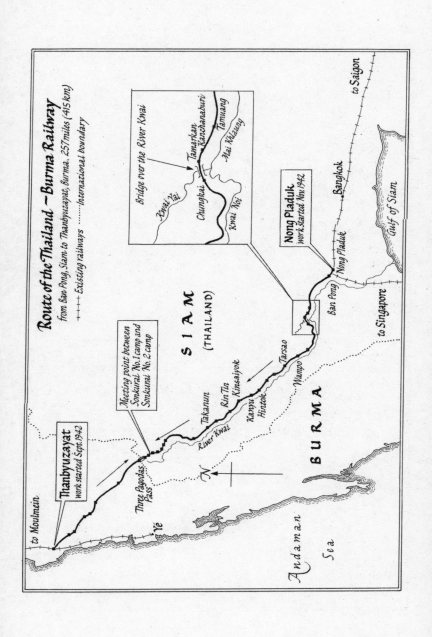

Route of the Thailand–Burma Railway
from Ban Pong, Siam to Thanbyuzayat, Burma. 257 miles (415 km)
++++ Existing railways ······ International boundary

Thanbyuzayat
work started Sept. 1942

Meeting point between
Sonkurai No.1 camp and
Sonkurai No.2 camp

Nong Pladuk
work started Nov. 1942

Bridge over the River Kwai

SIAM
(THAILAND)

BURMA

Andaman Sea

Gulf of Siam

to Moulmein
Ye
Three Pagodas Pass
Takanun
Rin Tin
Konsaiyok
Kanyu
Hintok
Wampo
Tarsao
River Kwai

to Saigon
Bangkok
Nong Pladuk
Ban Pong
to Singapore

Zwai Yai
Chungkai
Tamarkan
Kanchanaburi
Tamuang
Mai Mlung
Kwai Noi

PART I

Europe

I

Becoming a POW

Every soldier, airman or sailor who becomes a prisoner of war loses his liberty in a slightly different way. Capture might be a quiet surrender that comes almost as a relief: he is not required to fight on, the game is up, the struggle over. Or perhaps it is the conclusion to a bloody battle that has left him injured and traumatised: his over-riding concern is how – or whether – his wounds will be treated. Or perhaps he is smarting from feelings that capture was avoidable, that his officers were at fault, or, conversely, that he let his men down.

Sergeant George Booth, a twenty-nine-year-old observer with the RAF's No.107 Squadron, is usually credited as the first Briton to be taken prisoner in the Second World War. Booth's war ended the day after it had officially begun when his Bristol Blenheim was shot down over the German coast on 4 September 1939. The pilot was killed but the Wireless Operator, Air Gunner Larry Slattery, survived and, together with Booth, spent the next six years in captivity. They were among an estimated 170,000 to 200,000 British, Commonwealth and Empire men who were taken prisoner in Europe during the Second World War. This compares to the 90,000 Allied prisoners who were held in around a thousand camps around the Far East after Japan entered the war in late 1941.

Booth and Slattery left behind a country that was just embarking on what became known as the 'Phoney War' – when the population held its breath, waiting for a bombing onslaught that failed to appear. The first major influx of British POWs into German camps began nine months later in June 1940 when that phoniness gave way to a Blitzkrieg – or lightning war – as the Nazis swept down through the Low Countries into northern France. As the British Expeditionary Force (BEF), which had been sent to defend France, was evacuated from Dunkirk and other ports it was forced to abandon over 50,000 men who would spend the rest of the war as POWs. They entered captivity knowing that Britain faced the threat of invasion and that, if Hitler was successful, they were unlikely ever to see their homes again.

Each major Allied defeat made more men POWs. Germany's invasion of Greece and Yugoslavia in April 1941 was followed by the battle for Crete after which 11,370 Allied troops were captured in May 1941. The next big wave of POWs arrived from North Africa where Rommel was notching up significant victories. When he finally managed to break the siege of the Libyan port of Tobruk in June 1942, the garrison's 35,000 men, many of whom were South Africans, lost their freedom.

Since America did not enter the war until after Japan bombed Pearl Harbor in December 1941 only 62,000 of her soldiers became POWs in Europe. Most American POWs before D-Day were airmen. Soldiers began to be taken in large numbers when the Allies landed in Italy in 1943 and Normandy in 1944 and began to claw back parts of occupied Europe. The Germans captured over 6,000 men in September 1944 as a result of Operation Market-Garden when the Allies tried to establish a bridgehead across the Rhine at Arnhem; Hitler's surprise attack on the Ardennes (also known as the Battle of the Bulge) in a bitterly cold December 1944 led to around 23,000 Americans becoming POWs.

Most prisoners were soldiers. The nature of sea battles meant that few men serving in the Royal or Merchant Navy survived to become prisoners or internees – about 5,500 from each category. Around 13,000 British and Commonwealth airmen and 33,000 US airmen became POWs but their experience was very different from the other services. Of the 10,000 members of Bomber Command (about eight per cent of its total) who became POWs, many started their day with a British breakfast on British soil, and ended it in a cell where the enemy was keen to extract as much information from them as possible. The RAF did not suffer anything like the military setbacks of Dunkirk or North Africa and the peak year for Bomber Command was 1943-44 when 3,596 of their members became prisoners.

Becoming a prisoner in 1944 or 1945 felt quite different from becoming a POW in the early days of the war. Although the later prisoners had a sense that the war was drawing to a conclusion and that the Allies were winning, they still faced an uncertain future. Would they become hostages or even suffer execution at the hands of an enemy who felt he had nothing to lose?

Battery Sergeant Major Andrew Hawarden of the 53rd Field Regiment Royal Artillery (RA) was one of the longer serving POWs. He was forty-five in 1940 and the French landscape he was speeding through on his motorbike on the afternoon of 29 May 1940 was horribly familiar. He had first visited France during the Great War – which had also taken him to Egypt. This time round he was married and had a daughter, Sandra, who was less than a year old when he had last seen her in January. For his Second World War he was a mature soldier whom men looked up to – not just because of his status as a veteran but because he was also a sporting hero. As a teenager he had worked in a Bolton cotton mill but between the wars he had played professional football for Southend United and Tranmere Rovers, where he played alongside the future footballing legend – Dixie Dean.

The 53rd Field Regiment was a perfect home for him because it included the entire first team of Bolton Wanderers Football Club. In the 1930s, the club was a *Boy's Own* team, a young side of individual sporting heroes in their baggy shorts, thick, woolly socks and sleek Brylcreemed haircuts. At Easter 1939 their captain, Harry Goslin, had stepped in front of the microphone at Bolton's home ground of Burnden Park before their match against Sunderland. He urged everyone in the ground to do what he or she could to protect their country: whether that meant joining the Territorial Army or becoming an auxiliary nurse. A week later he marched into the TA's recruitment office with the entire first team. Hawarden became their coach and arranged matches against other regiments. By the time they landed at Cherbourg on 19 April 1940 he had formed a strong bond with them and he felt their absence keenly during his years in captivity.

He spent his first night as a POW sleeping in a field near Dunkirk. Although he had no way of knowing it, his comrades were inching their way towards the beaches in an exhausting loop of attack followed by retreat until they reached the sand dunes where men queued amid the smoke and burning oil hoping for their turn to be hauled onto one of the assorted boats that would make the perilous journey home.

He arrived in his permanent home at Thorn in Poland on 12 June 1940. Torun, as it is now known, is a medieval, walled city that sits on the wide, sweeping River Vistula. Its geographical position, wedged uneasily between Russia and Germany, explains why for centuries it has been batted backwards and forwards between different powers. After Napoleon's defeat in 1814 Prussia took control of it for a second time and in 1870, French prisoners of war built a chain of forts around the city to protect it from attack. By the time Hawarden arrived the central fortress and its string of crumbling and dank forts built by an earlier generation of POWs had become Stalag XXA.

The main fortress carried out the central administration of the camp, while the various satellite forts each had their own special functions: Fort XII was dominated by Polish POWs; Fort XIII was made up mainly of Scots; the hospital was at Fort XIV and Fort XV included mainly NCOs (Non-Commissioned Officers), New Zealanders and Australians; Fort XVI was the punishment camp and Fort XVII held mainly British POWs. Over the next two years Hawarden was to get to know each building well.

David Wild, the chaplain to the 4th Battalion Oxfordshire and Buckinghamshire Light Infantry, who was also captured at Dunkirk, describes crossing the bridge over the dry moat that surrounded Fort XV and being marched through a huge steel door. Inside the camp, which occupied several acres, men lived in two-storey barrack rooms leading off endless corridors that formed a figure of eight enclosing two deep grassy bowls where prisoners could exercise.

> Above it all was a thick layer of earth and vegetation, including many shrubby trees. From outside and from above, no building was visible except the barrack section facing the moat . . . A walk around the top of the fort amounted to about a third of a mile. All the barrack-rooms and corridors were brick-vaulted, like sections of underground railway, and the rooms, like Nissen huts.

Hawarden's first home at the nineteenth-century fortress of Stalag XXA, with its sprawling chain of satellite buildings, is a long way from the common image of a POW camp. But Germany's military successes left it with the huge logistical problem of what to do with the men scooped up as it surged through Europe. Prisoners were not just British,

Commonwealth and American but French, Polish and Dutch and – as countries changed sides – Italian and Russian. After Germany invaded the Soviet Union in 1941, the Germans took nearly three million soldiers prisoner in the first four months of fighting; by the end of the war she had nearly six million Russian prisoners. After the Italian Armistice in September 1943, Germany sent 600,000 of her former ally's troops to POW camps. Russian POWs were treated particularly badly and many British POWs are still haunted by memories of the starved and broken bodies they glimpsed through the barbed wire that separated the compounds. Like the Japanese, the Soviet Union had no sympathy for soldiers who had allowed themselves to be taken prisoner and these men (and some women) became non-persons. The Soviet Union had not signed the Geneva Convention and Russian prisoners could expect no assistance from home. While German captors felt a cultural connection with the British men they captured, they had only distrust for the Russians. It was left to other POWs to lob their own precious supplies over the wire to help the starving Russians.

At the start of the war Germany had thirty-one POW camps; by 1945 this figure had risen to 248 – of which 134 housed British and American men. After Mussolini joined forces with Hitler in June 1940, men who were captured in North Africa were usually held in Italy and by the time Mussolini was overthrown and an armistice declared in September 1943 there were nearly 79,000 Allied prisoners in the country. By the end of the year, 50,000 had been taken to Germany and more, like the future travel writer, Eric Newby, who had spent some time on the loose, were later rounded up.

There was a huge diversity of architecture among camps that varied dramatically depending on the prisoner's rank, his escape record and whether or not he was made to work. Andrew Hawarden's first camp of Stalag XXA does not conform to either of the two most common stereotypes of a POW camp – the barbed wire, barrack huts and sentry posts of somewhere like Stalag Luft III, near Sagan, (now Żagań) one hundred miles southeast of Berlin, which Paul Brickhill made famous through his book, *The Great Escape*, and Colditz, the glowering castle which many people still cannot think of without recalling the ominous music which accompanied the TV series of the same name.

Most POW camps were nearer in design to Stalag Stalag Luft III, which was run by the Luftwaffe. In 1940 the German air force decided to build and control separate camps but they were quickly overwhelmed by the intensity of Allied bombing raids and many POW airmen ended up in military camps, albeit in separate compounds. My father's first camp, Stalag IVB, at Mühlberg, near Dresden, was built to hold 15,000 men but at its peak housed double this and included a large RAF contingent.

At first, naval and merchant-sailor prisoners were held at Stalag XB near the North Sea coast at Sandbostel until the German navy took control in 1942, when they were concentrated at a purpose-built site nearby at Westertimke. Naval POWs were held at two compounds (one for officers and the other for petty officers and senior ratings) at Marlag (an abbreviation of *Marine Lager*). Merchant seamen were held nearby at the larger camp of Milag (*Marine-Interniertenlager*).

Paul Brickhill, an Australian who worked as a journalist before he became a fighter pilot, describes being taken to the North compound of Stalag Luft III where fifteen bare wooden huts were arranged in three rows next to 'a patch of stump-studded, loose grey dirt for recreation and appell'. The compound was about 300 yards square and surrounded by two 9 feet high barbed wire fences, with further thick coils of barbed wire sandwiched in between and a low warning wire which, if transgressed, was liable to attract a scattering of gunshots. Every 150 yards or so sentries looked down from their wooden towers, or 'goon-boxes'. The hospital, coal store and 'cooler' – the punishment block where in the film of *The Great Escape* Steve McQueen plans a new bid for freedom as he rhythmically bounces a baseball against the wall and floor – were situated between the two main fences at one end of the camp. Outside 'gaunt pines with skinny, naked trunks, packed close together in the dry, grey earth. They were everywhere you looked, monotonous barriers that shut out the world and increased the sense of Godforsaken isolation'. The only bare patch was immediately outside the camp where the trees had been felled so that escapers could not use them for cover.

As well as these purpose built stalags (an abbreviation of *Stammlager* meaning permanent camps) the Germans adapted existing buildings such as the fortresses of Stalag XXA, but also schools, barracks and more grandiose castles or even palaces. Oflag IVC (Colditz) is the most famous example of a castle prison – a sinister presence that dominates the surrounding countryside from its rocky outcrop. But there were other grand

Oflags (short for *Offizierslager* – officer camps). Oflag VIID at Tittmoning was a medieval castle on the Salzach river in southeastern Bavaria and prisoners taken to Oflag IX A/H crossed a drawbridge to arrive in the cobbled courtyard of the thirteenth-century castle that overlooked the medieval town of Spangenberg, near Kassel.

Colditz was in a class of its own, a fortified prison which held persistent escapers – the bad boys of the POW world. In *The Colditz Story*, Pat Reid's bestselling account of his time as 'Escape Officer' which was published in 1952, he describes his first impression of the castle:

> We arrived at the small town of Colditz early one afternoon. Almost upon leaving the station we saw looming above us our future prison: beautiful, serene, majestic, and yet forbidding enough to make our hearts sink into our boots. It towered above us, dominating the whole village: a magnificent castle built on the edge of a cliff. It was the real fairy castle of childhood's story-books. What ogres there might live within! I thought of the dungeons and of all the stories I had ever heard of prisoners in chains, pining away their lives, of rats and tortures, and of unspeakable cruelties and abominations.

Colditz was a *Sonderlager*, a special camp for men who were particularly troublesome – which usually manifested itself through their eagerness to escape – and *Prominente* – important or well-connected prisoners who could be used as hostages. The castle also contained an unusual mixture of nationalities – Poles, French, Dutch and British. It was this heady cocktail of international and determined officers set in a deliberately hostile setting that gave Colditz its unique atmosphere and set it apart from all other POW camps. The castle had once been a lunatic asylum and it often felt as if some of that mania had been released into the atmosphere. Prisoners who arrived for the first time – or returned after a failed escape bid – were introduced to Colditz's distinctive personality in the raucous greeting they received. When John Chrisp turned up with a group of naval officers in September 1942, amid the customary bugles, drums, shouting and singing, a miniature parachute floated down from a top window. It landed at their feet to reveal a white mouse with the message, 'Welcome to Colditz' on a label round its neck.

As the network of POW camps spread through the German Reich a nomenclature developed to help identify each one. A Roman numeral denoted the military district whose jurisdiction it fell under, followed by a letter attached to a particular camp – so Colditz was Oflag IVC. 'H' stood for *Hauptlager* (the main or administrative camp). As the war progressed and the number of camps increased, additions were given Arabic numbers. So, for example, my father was taken first to Stalag IVB and then to Stalag 357, which was originally in Poland, but later moved to south of Hamburg.

It was nearly a year before Robert Dunn settled in to a traditional POW camp at Stalag XVIIIA in Wolfsberg, south Austria. He was one of thousands of British soldiers captured in Greece where he was serving in the 4th Hussars. Clive Dunn, as he is now better known, will for many people always be Corporal Jones, *Dad's Army's* excitable veteran of imperial wars, but in 1941 he was just twenty-one and a stretcher-bearer and orderly for Captain Eden (cousin of Anthony). He had been on the run for weeks and was frail and suffering from dysentery when he was captured. Although the Germans who caught him were friendly, even sharing their last packet of cigarettes with him, he and thousands of other British, Indian, Yugoslavian and Palestinian prisoners were then taken to barracks in Corinth, 50 miles south of Athens, where SS guards punished anyone who failed to salute them properly. During the day he sought out slit trenches to escape from the searing heat and at night he shivered in the icy dormitories. Daily rations consisted of two or three bits of water biscuit and a quarter of an inch of olive oil; his friend who had managed to hang on to his gold engagement ring exchanged it for part of a loaf of bread.

Their clothes were baked for one or more hours in huge ovens delivered to the camp. Then they were ordered to march naked several miles to the sea, past women who pulled their gawping children inside. 'For some, this was probably the most degrading moment of their lives,' Dunn wrote later. At the beach a hose fired liquid carbolic at their groins and they ran into the sea to relieve the discomfort. The only sign of defiance left to them was to sing 'Tipperary' as they marched back, still naked, to their tattered clothes. The heat had weakened the seams of Dunn's uniform and the sleeves immediately fell off, making him feel 'more ridiculous than ever'.

From Corinth they were moved back to Salonika. One day they

'staggered' thirty miles in the blazing heat and a soldier Dunn had been treating collapsed and died; three guards died from heat exhaustion. They left Greece in cattle trucks, taking it in turns to stand or sit, and relieved themselves in one petrol can; a second can contained a small quantity of water for drinking. Light and air crept in through one small, barred window near the roof bringing clues as to their whereabouts – the cool mountain air and smell of pine trees – and the time of day.

'The surrendering of physical privacy became a habit – everyone suffered from diarrhoea and the petrol tin was continually full to the brim with germ-laden liquid faeces.' Emptying it out of the window was a hazardous operation that usually left the men below soaked by its noxious contents.

The travel writer, Eric Newby describes feeling like a 'traitor' after he was captured off the east coast of Sicily on 12 August 1942. In the preface to his memoir about that time, *Love and War in the Apennines*, he writes, 'I find no difficulty in remembering being captured. It is something, as most people who have been captured would agree, that is such a disagreeable experience that one remembers the circumstances for the rest of one's life'.

For my father, Donald Webster Gillies, capture was more than 'disagreeable'. Although a man who lived to talk and who looked back fondly on his days in the army, he was reluctant to speak about the day he was taken prisoner. His account of his life as a POW usually started on an overcrowded cattle train that rattled its way north from Italy to Germany with my father standing all the way. He made it sound no more uncomfortable than a student's experience of Inter-railing.

In reality, capture came after a gruelling twelve months. Before he enlisted at the age of nineteen he had played semi-professional football for the Vale of Leven and trained as an apprentice joiner, learning how to make and fit the wooden parts for ships at his home town of Dumbarton on the River Clyde which, when he was a young man, was still a thriving centre of shipbuilding, its skyline dominated by cranes. In March 1943 he left Europe for the first time in his life and arrived with the Scots Guards in a heavy rainstorm in Tunisia. His introduction to fighting came with the Battle of Sidi Bou Zid, a confrontation that became infamous for the intensity of shelling which went on for thirteen days.

'How I hate shells,' one officer from the Scots Guards wrote of the desert fighting.

I have seen strong courageous men reduced to whimpering wrecks, crying like children. Some arrive with a long screeching crescendo giving one time to take cover; others come faster than sound and burst without warning. And when one has nothing to do, the fumes and dust and echoed cries of 'stretcher-bearer!' strain one's nerves almost to breaking point. Yet if one goes to ground how incredibly hard it is to get out into the open again to do a job of work! I would sooner have a thousand bullets or even dive bombers than a day's shelling.

After the intensity of these 'stonks' (an onomatopoeic army word for bombardment by mortar, rather than guns) my father enjoyed the more humdrum soldier's life around Tunis after North Africa was secured for the Allies. In his free days he swam in the Mediterranean, dived off the half-submerged wrecks near Hammamet or passed the time by hurling water melons at the local boys – a piece of innocent horseplay he later felt ashamed of.

By early January 1944 he and his mates were living in schools and a factory near Pompeii in Italy. A visit to the ancient ruins left him shocked by the debauchery of ancient Rome where the statues displayed flesh that was too naked and virulent for his Presbyterian sensibilities. On the starry night of January 22 the first battalion boarded a ship bound for Anzio and an attack designed to break the enemy supply line between Rome and Cassino. The ship was bristling with Bren guns and wireless sets; the men, weighed down with primed grenades and fully loaded rifles, shifted frequently from sitting to standing positions to relieve cramp. They reached the beach from small landing craft thirty minutes after the first assault and, such was the element of surprise, took the area with ridiculous ease – as if it had been merely an exercise. On a day that might have seen a massacre the casualties were limited to a few men who stumbled into a minefield.

But if the landing had been easy – too easy – pushing inland was slow and dangerous. A fortnight later my father was less than ten miles away at Battalion Headquarters in Carroceto Railway Station. A German tank was systematically spraying each window with tracer fire that sent bullets ricocheting around the building with terrifying unpredictability. At 5.30 a.m. on 10 February it was decided that they must leave the station and make their way slowly along the railway track. I can not be sure exactly where my father was at this point but he said later that he spotted a light glimmering from somewhere in the rubble and followed it to find a group of women and children cowering in a shelter, dimly lit by candles. The older women, dressed in the traditional black dictated by their age and widowhood, clutched rosaries. My father tried to reassure them with hand gestures but the sudden appearance of a dishevelled foreign soldier who was barely less frightened than them must have been even more terrifying than imagining what was happening outside their shelter. Their fear escalated when they heard German voices above them. As the voices transformed into guns and battle-hardened faces, it became obvious that if my father did not surrender he would place the Italians' lives at risk. I will never know whether his time as a POW began with the words, 'For you the war is over' but it was a phrase that Germans favoured. Its stark simplicity made it clear that any resistance was pointless.

Settling In and Getting By

Some weeks after my father had boarded a cattle train for Germany his parents received a telegram saying their son was missing, 'presumed killed in action'. I remember my grandparents in their dotage as two little salt-and-pepper figures clad in matching Fair Isle cardigans, like the couple from Raymond Briggs's *When the Wind Blows*. As middle-aged parents they made a more robust couple. My grandfather, Alex, was an emotional man and probably wept at the news of his eldest son's death; my grandmother, Agnes or 'Aggie' was more pragmatic and may have hidden her grief for the sake of their two daughters, a younger son who was serving in the Commandos and my father's fiancée. The couple ran a corner shop in Dumbarton, near Glasgow, and their terrible, but far from unusual, news would have spread quickly through the neighbourhood.

My grandmother discovered that they had been misled when she attended a fundraising morning for the Red Cross. Handing over her sixpence she let one of the women who had 'the second sight' gaze at the tea leaves marooned in the bottom of her cup. 'Donald's not dead, Mrs Gillies,' she pronounced confidently, 'He's a prisoner of war.' My family, like many working class Scots at that time, held a deep-seated belief in the supernatural which sat comfortably with a devotion to the Kirk and my grandparents must have allowed themselves to hope that the 'old wifey' was more accurate than the telegram. News that a neighbour had heard my father's name read out on Vatican Radio, which broadcast from Rome, among a list of men taken prisoner reinforced their optimism. I suspect that at a time of religious sectarianism they placed more faith in the tea leaves than the Holy See.

My father remembered local Italians booing at the cattle trucks of POWs as they made their way slowly north on their long journey to Germany. It may have been the threat of retaliation that prompted such venom, or maybe they felt angry at the part the soldiers had played in reducing their homes to rubble. Other POWs experienced small kindnesses from local people – old women who rushed to give them a glass of fresh water, or who risked being beaten by German guards to push food into their hands. Lieutenant R.G.M. Quarrie, who was captured in Crete, was cheered by waving Greek crowds who enthusiastically gave the thumbs up and V-for-Victory signs until German guards quelled their enthusiasm by firing shots over their heads.

POWs taken in North Africa usually faced a dangerous and cramped sea crossing back to mainland Europe; others endured long marches or standing for days on packed cattle trucks that took them by train to the camps where they would be held.

Quarrie enjoyed a flight over the Acropolis but this incursion over enemy lines brought home the reality of defeat. His first rations as a prisoner had obviously been taken from British stores and as he looked down at Athens he was aware that the airport was now a busy Luftwaffe base.

Airmen and sailors had a different experience of capture. The enemy might have rescued them from a burning ship or aeroplane, plucked them out of the sea or saved them from a crowd of angry civilians who hurled venomous alien words which described them as pilots who brought terror, killed children and were murdering pigs: *Terrorflieger*, *Kindermörder* and *Mörderschwein*. And, after capture, RAF men had their own demons to grapple with: the horror of bailing out of a plane, of seeing their comrades enveloped in flames or of suffering terrible burns themselves. New POWs experienced searingly vivid dreams in which they leapt out of their flaming cockpit only to wake on the floor of a prisoner of war camp. These were the men who quickly earned their place on the bottom tier of a bunk bed.

Since the Germans concentrated their efforts on those men most likely to know anything of strategic importance – high-ranking officers or airmen – POWs such as Clive Dunn, Andrew Hawarden and my father were probably spared too gruelling an interrogation. Quizzing the enemy also became less of a priority when the Germans were struggling to cope with large numbers of prisoners, as in the summer of 1940.

A typical RAF prisoner, however, was whisked off to a special transit camp, *Durchgangslager Luftwaffe – Dulag Luft*, for short. If he were unlucky, the Gestapo might question him or he might be threatened with such an ordeal. Some airmen were given bogus Red Cross forms to complete in the hope that they might reveal more information than was strictly necessary: the type of aeroplane and where they had set off from were particularly useful. All prisoners should have been aware that they were only required to provide their name, rank and number – a holy trinity that my father, given the correct prompt, would fire off with bullet-like speed decades after he had left the army. The Ministry of Information produced a film called *Information, please* that warned the RAF what to expect should they end up in enemy hands. The narrator spoke with a thick German accent and described, from the enemy's point of view, the sort of details that would be most useful and the tactics used to obtain them. The film showed the POW arriving in camp and being interviewed by a series of German stereotypes who might easily have secured bit parts in the action films that were later made about the war. Some airmen were equipped with silk scarves with maps printed on them and miniature compasses and a few, but by no means all, received lectures on escape tactics, including advice that they should try to give their guards the slip before they reached their POW camp, rather than wait until they were behind barbed wire, deep in enemy territory.

Navigator Cy Grant was unlikely to evade the enemy for very long after he bailed out over Holland in July 1943 for the simple reason that he was black. The crew had already reached their target in Germany and were heading home during one of the shortest nights of the summer when a German fighter attacked them from below. They appeared to have seen it off but as they neared Haarlem it became apparent that part of the aeroplane had caught fire. They dived to try to stifle the flames but when they returned to the horizontal they realised that the fire had spread to a dinghy below the starboard wing. They dared not jettison it in case the slipstream swept it back towards the aeroplane. Next a wheel fell away. Their options were narrowing – they could no longer ditch over the Channel because they did not have a dinghy and by the time they reached the coast both wings were on fire and the pilot was struggling to control the aircraft. He turned back over land and one by one they bailed out. Grant had never practised a parachute jump and it was only his third operational flight.

As he made his muddy landing at 2.38 a.m. the dawn was already breaking. Above him, his plane had exploded and one of the Lancaster's engines had hurtled through the roof of a nearby farmhouse, killing the farmer's wife. He stuffed his parachute into a canal bank and then hid in a field of oats, listening to the everyday sounds of a farmyard waking up – dogs barking and buckets clattering. His first glimpse of the countryside gave him a jolt of déjà vu. He had grown up in British Guiana (now Guyana) where early settlers had imprinted a Dutch flavour on the architecture of their home-from-home. But the farm workers whom he approached for help knew that he could never pass as a local and that they would be shot if they did not hand him over.

When Cy Grant was handed over, after a farmer's wife had fed him and tended to his head wound, he was taken to Amsterdam for questioning. It was here that he was reunited with his crew's mid-upper gunner who told him that the tail gunner and engineer had both been killed. He was held in solitary confinement for five days and interrogated every other day but he was never threatened. One day he was dragged out, pushed onto a chair and photographed. It was not until he reached Stalag Luft III that the German Commanding Officer showed him a newspaper cutting in which his photo appeared. Before he was captured Grant was a dashingly handsome airman in his RAF uniform; here, his shirt open at the neck, he looked bedraggled and glowered at the camera through the beginnings of a moustache. The image is similar to the television image of John Peters who was shot down in the Gulf War and both are blatant pieces of propaganda. The caption underneath Grant's photo reads: *Ein Mitglied der Royal Air Force von unbestimmbarer Rasse* (A member of the RAF of indeterminate race). The implication is clear: the RAF has reached such a low point that they had to rely on men of uncertain racial origins. But the camp's Commanding Officer was unmoved by the Nazi propaganda. He warmed to Grant once he heard that he was from British Guyana, which he had visited as a boy and made a point of saluting Grant when he was doing his rounds of the camp.

POWs were fingerprinted and photographed holding a board with their number chalked on it, given an official ID disc which they were meant to wear at all times but rarely did, preferring to use it to cut bread. The guards would note down a few cursory scraps of information such as next-of-kin, home address and any distinguishing features, such as scars. They might ask whether there were any Jews in the group and study each face for clues as to ancestry. In most camps British prisoners vigorously resisted any attempts to separate Jewish servicemen from their comrades and in several cases the Germans were forced to back down when they tried to discriminate, for example, by withholding Red Cross parcels. Some Jewish prisoners threw away their British army identity disc, which gave their religion, while others stated they were Church of England (indeed, in some parts of the armed services, such as the Commandos and Special Operations Executive, men were ordered to do this and to adopt non-Jewish names for their own safety). A great many Jewish POWS, though, were brave enough not to disguise their religion.

For men like Andrew Hawarden the process that marked their initiation into the life of the *Kriegie* began when they were given a cardboard box with their name on and told to empty their clothes into it. Their heads and bodies were shaved to remove any hiding place for lice, which thrive in the warm crevices of the human body, and they were handed a bar of green antiseptic soap embossed with the letters, 'RIF' (*Reichsstelle für Industrielle Fettversorgung*, a government agency responsible for distributing cheap washing products). Sam Kydd, a small-time variety performer who was held at Stalag XXA, remembers its texture as gritty, 'like solidified Vim'. Then they were marched to a concrete bathhouse with metal pipes crisscrossing the ceiling. After their hot shower their clothes were returned, 'all lovely and warm, but smelling of cyanide fumes'.

Most men underwent delousing at least once, but usually several times, as each new arrival of POWs brought a fresh infestation. As late as February 1945 Andrew Hawarden grumbled in his diary that the Germans were incapable of carrying out the procedure properly, maintaining that clothes should be baked at 180°C, not the 90°C favoured by his captors, to kill off the bug and its eggs. The Germans had a pathological fear of lice because they can carry typhus; for the POW they represented a persistent irritant. Night-time scratching provided yet another deterrent to sleep, both for the sufferer himself and his neighbours. Men desperate to be rid of their constant companions would run a lighted candle down the seams of their battledress where the insect was known to lay its eggs. To be free of lice, if only fleetingly, was a release of sorts and, despite the degrading aspects of delousing, to have a hot shower, particularly in mid winter, clean towel and clean clothes were longed-for luxuries.

The first weeks after capture gave Andrew Hawarden a chance to reflect on what had happened to them. His wife and daughter, Sandra, who was less than a year old when he had last seen her in January, must have been uppermost in his mind but he must also have been wondering what plans the enemy had for him.

For most men capture was their first close encounter with the enemy and they were often surprised by the experience. Some British soldiers felt the nudge of a rifle butt in the back or a sharp kick that brought them to their knees; others had their watches looted or lost other trinkets that were taken as souvenirs. Some troops were held by nervous, 'trigger-happy' Germans, while others like Hawarden experienced the mental torture of being lined up for a mock execution. But for many POWs the harshness of their capture was limited to a shove and an abrupt *Raus*! to shake the stunned prisoners out of their torpor. A few soldiers, particularly officers, were surprised by the civilised manner in which they became POWs.

Andrew Hawarden was captured on the road to Dunkirk when he was trying to weave his motorbike through roads choked with refugees, military vehicles and soldiers with a message that his regiment were awaiting orders. He described what happened in an account entitled, 'How it all came about':

> I noticed that it was funny there was no-one knocking about and then I saw the horses which hadn't been hit by bomb or bullet were still standing, hooked up to their vehicles. There were many horse-drawn ambulances less drivers, with the sick and wounded lying inside. Gerry was still making himself a nuisance with his low-flying aircraft, dropping a kind of hand bomb and using his machine guns. The drivers had left their vehicles and some of the stationary traffic was already burning. I was thrown off my bike two or three times by some near blasts, but I did find time to unhook several horses.

Looking to his right across the fields he could see British and French troops, 'making their hurried and scattered way in the direction of Dunkirk'. He thought he might be able to follow them and started:

> Weaving a way between the stilled vehicles for what seemed to take a long time but was only a matter of minutes and as I got through the clearer part of the road, it was here that it happened: I heard a voice saying, 'Tommy, Tommy, for you the war is over.' I looked and found

myself gazing into a Tommy Gun held by a Gerry Tank Commander who was standing up in the Turret look out of one of the large Gerry tanks. I had bumped into one of the Gerry Tank Units.

Once he was captured the scene on the pock-marked road assumed a razor-sharp focus. He noticed six large tanks lined up in the field, their tops level with the road. Another six smaller tanks squatted at a right angle to the road. The German commander told him to lay his bike on the verge but when Hawarden asked if he could take his haversack and water bottle from the back of it, he consented. Two groups of soldiers – one French, one British – emerged with their officers; the French carried twigs with white hankies tied to them. Two other British soldiers stood a little apart from them. 'On a sudden impulse one of them decided to make a dash for the other side of the road, but unfortunately, he never made it. He was ripped by a Tommy Gun from the Tank.'

The commander ordered the body to be placed on one of the tanks. Moments later they were assaulted by German machine gun fire and mortar some five hundred yards away. Both captors and prisoners of war – as they now were – crouched behind the tanks until the commander managed, after several minutes, to stop the attack by waving a large orange flag.

He did not record his emotions in those first hours of captivity. But he was on the edge of a battlefield and he must have wondered about his comrades and the consequences of each crunch of explosives and whine of dive-bombing aircraft. In the days that followed he slowly found the measure of his guards and learned that not every German was as accommodating as the commander who had allowed him to take his haversack and water bottle:

30 May 1940

We were messed about quite a lot today with searches etc. At one period quite a number of us were lined up against a farm wall, then a Gerry with a machine gun took himself into a position about twenty yards away and facing us. We must have been there for more than an hour, then we were marched back in the field to join the prisoners. Later that evening, as it was getting dark, we were moved to West Cappel Churchyard, where we slept that night, amongst the gravestones.

Most families heard that their loved one was a POW after he had been officially registered and his name given to the Red Cross who passed it on to the British Government and it to the next-of-kin. After a very public military disaster, such as the evacuation of Dunkirk, this could produce an agonising wait until families knew a man was either dead or captured. The Red Cross also forwarded postcards from POWs to relatives at home. Under the Geneva Convention a prisoner should have been allowed to send a post card within a week of arrival in a camp; he was then permitted a certain number of letters and postcards a month. This depended on rank and varied throughout the war but Other Ranks (that is the 'Rank and File' soldiers) were generally allowed to write two letters and four postcards a month. These brief missives were as much a relief for the POW to send as they were for their family to receive and reassured the prisoner that their relatives knew they were safe.

Once family and friends were aware of a POW's whereabouts they were encouraged to write to them and the ritual of handing out the mail in camp became as important as the arrival of the Red Cross parcel. Many found the ordeal of waiting to know whether they had received any post unbearable. To walk away clutching a letter caused elation, to leave empty-handed could plunge a POW into a dark depression. Officers' families, accustomed to the separation of boarding school and university, were more familiar with letter writing but corresponding with a POW meant following different conventions. The Red Cross was particularly anxious that letters should be uplifting and not cause a POW to imagine unsettling situations that were beyond their control. It used its magazine, *The Prisoner of War*, which was sent to next-of-kin, to steer the writer towards topics that would raise morale. Under a heading, 'I must write to-night' the magazine urged:

What to tell him	What not to tell him
Film you saw	Dinner you ate
Book you read	Cold you caught
Sermons you heard	Bomb you dodged
Flowers you grow	Fright you had
Skirt you made	Pound you lost
Money you've saved	Vase you broke
Words baby's learnt	Ration book loss

The magazine suggested keeping a notebook in which to jot down points that might amuse or interest the POW. Other advice was contradictory. In one issue it urged letter writers to keep a carbon copy so they did not repeat themselves, but a later edition said it was good to repeat news in case a previous letter had gone astray. Confusingly, the magazine said that letters should be numbered in case they arrived in the wrong order but pages should not include numbers in case the German censor misinterpreted them as some sort of code.

This did not stop friends and families from using words or references that would have a specific meaning for the person they were writing to, or which could be interpreted by a British POW. 'Uncle Joe', for example, usually referred to Russia and was the writer's way of conveying war news that they thought the POW might have missed. W.H. (Bill) Murray, a bank clerk from Glasgow who joined the 2nd Battalion Highland Light Infantry (HLI) and was captured in North Africa, used a code when writing to his mother that relied on a sequence of letters. It allowed him to tell her that his boots had been taken and that they had no suitable footwear for the bitter winter months at the Italian camp where he was being held. She informed the Glasgow branch of the British Red Cross who arranged for two thousand boots to be delivered. Clive Dunn's grandmother, by comparison, paid no attention to the censor (either British or German) and only four words of the one letter she sent survived the censors' pencil so that her correspondence was reduced to: 'Dear Buddy . . . Love Nana'. Dunn said the hilarity the letter provoked was more valuable than any news the original may have contained.

Other POWs concentrated on passing on information that would be of use to MI9 – the intelligence service responsible for POWs. Robin Hunter, who served in 75 New Zealand Squadron, was held at Stalag Luft III but, on his own admission, did not have the temperament for escaping. Instead, he contributed to the war effort by weaving messages in to letters he wrote to certain addresses in London using the commonplace pocket Collins dictionaries (English-German and English-French) to construct a code both reader and writer could use. He used his messages to tell London why recently arrived RAF crews believed they had been brought down – whether it was due to a fault in the plane or to the Germans 'using any new wrinkles' (presumably technology or tactics).

*

A few POWs exchanged letters with their bank manager, ordered books or conducted other business. Tom Swallow, a twenty-six year-old motor-cycle enthusiast from the Midlands, learnt when he was held in Stalag IVB, 80 miles south of Berlin, that his local motorbike shop in Oldbury had closed. Swallow, who had competed in the 1938 24-Hour National Rally on a 250cc Coventry-built Rudge motorbike, was not willing to let captivity rob him of such a good opportunity and wrote to the Birmingham Small Arms Company (BSA), a well known motorbike manufacturer, to ask whether they would consider him as their agent when he opened a dealership after the war. Although BSA was busy making armaments and vehicles for the war effort the company still managed to reply that they would consider his application when the time came.

Some prisoners received regular letters whilst others might go for months with nothing until an avalanche of mail arrived; letters could turn up in the wrong chronological order so that a man might learn that his mother had died before he was told she was unwell.

The other main source of bad news was the 'Dear John' letter in which a sweetheart or wife confessed that she had found someone else. This could be devastating for a POW, especially if the thought of a fond reunion had been the only thing keeping them going, and unsettling to everyone in the recipient's immediate circle. My father received one of these letters from his fiancée in Dumbarton. As soon as the hut found out, he was made to pin the letter to the noticeboard and, with his mates hovering at his shoulder, forced to write a cheery reply agreeing that they were not compatible and wishing her well with her new sweetheart. These brutal tactics were not meant to be unkind, but merely a strategy of coping with a setback over which they had no control.

While my father was writing words he did not believe to someone he knew very well, my future mother was composing letters to a POW she had never met as part of a Red Cross scheme in which British families or individuals 'adopted' a prisoner. The family at home wrote to them or sent donations via the Red Cross. Very occasionally this led to romance, or even marriage.

My mother wrote to her POW 'about everything and nothing', careful not to say she was having too good a time or going to dances with soldiers who were not trapped behind barbed wire. At the time she was working as a typist for the Ministry of Supply and living in Kent in an area that

became known as 'Bomb Alley' because the Luftwaffe would often jettison their loads there on the way home from a raid over London. She had
met my father at a Scots Guards dance but the relationship had yet to grow
in to anything serious. When she wrote to her POW she may even have
included a photo, perhaps one of her wearing the pillbox hat she was so
fond of. For her POW, these letters were a lifeline and after the war, he was
quick to visit her. But by then my mother had moved on and her mother
was left to break the news and console the returning soldier with a cup of
tea.

John Phillips was twenty-three and a lieutenant in the Argyll and
Sutherland Highlanders when he started to write to an old family friend,
Philippa Cook, who was two years his junior. His first letter is dated
November 1941 after, as he told her, 'being fairly effectively laid out in an
argument with German parachutists' – a veiled allusion to his capture after
the airborne invasion of Crete. What he could not say was that whilst on
the island he had briefly captured the former world heavyweight boxing
champion, Max Schmeling, when he parachuted into an orchard occupied
by Phillips's men. Nor could he tell her that he had been wounded on
Crete – where he was eventually taken prisoner – but managed to escape
in Athens, after which he spent some months with the Greek Resistance
before he was recaptured while trying to sail an open boat to Turkey. He
was threatened with execution but saved when a German cousin, who
happened to be serving on the other side, spoke up for him. As a great-
great-nephew of General Gordon perhaps he took such adventures in his
stride.

By the time he was free to write to Philippa he was held in the lower
camp at Oflag IX A/H in Spangenberg, in the heart of Germany, north of
Frankfurt, from where he could look up at the medieval *Schloss* which held
the rest of the POWs. While John's war had compressed his life into the
walls of a remote camp in Hesse, Philippa's life had begun to expand. She
had already obtained a two-year diploma in horticulture at Reading University after which she moved from her family home at Storrington in West
Sussex to live with an aunt who had a house in what seemed the much safer
area of Wales. To relieve the tedium she joined the ATS (Auxiliary
Territorial Service) where she became a plotting officer for an anti-aircraft
battery. The work was like nothing she had done before and brought the
excitement of trying to protect Swansea steel works from aerial attack.

John had only an inkling of her new role and wrote on February 25, 1942: 'I'm glad you're finding your job interesting. I shall be a little afraid of you I think when I see you; officers of the other sex have, in my experience, been *formidable* (French).'

But he could not appreciate the drama of her night-time vigils as she helped to pump anti-aircraft missiles into the night-time sky with a ferocity that shattered some of the windows of the town they were trying to protect. He, by comparison, passed the time with a '*get fit campaign* ... hand ball, hockey, soccer, skipping and Highland dancing are some of the recipes', a bridge tournament and spelling bee. The war had interrupted his studies at Oxford University, where he had won a scholarship to read Classics, and now he took advantage of the skills of the men around him to learn modern languages. In the same letter to Philippa, he wrote: 'My Arab tutor, an officer from Haifa, called Faisoun, has been making me write Arabic letters lately. Last week I tried to tell him a risqué story in Arabic; we got a bit muddled & I had to revert to English as I couldn't remember the Arabic word which gave the story its point. Rather a flop.'

By the end of the year, though, the men were so bored that they were running a 'beard sweep' and he was timing how long it took to sew on a button – '12 minutes: 5 for threading the b-y needle, 2 for putting iodine on my fingers and 5 for sewing the button so that it stays on for about a week'.

Throughout their four-year correspondence he wrote about the life of a POW with the jauntiness of someone who has just started boarding school or university:

I'm in a very cheery room – known as the 'House of Lords', because it contains one Irish baron and the future Duke of Argyll, who was in my regiment; as a result the general line of conversation and behaviour is exceedingly vulgar ... I sleep in the lower half of a two-tier wooden bunk with a very hefty New Zealander in the upper one; two nights ago the boards collapsed and there was a frightful shindy as we tried to get sorted out – searchlights were turned on by the guard and we were generally pretty unpopular.

They were later joined by an Irish peer who received cigars from home that he shared with the other seven men in his mess.

Even when he was ill he managed to make a joke of it, as in October

1944 when he wrote: 'I'm still feeling rather unwell as a result of being jabbed in the arm with a needle as a precaution against rabies, scabies & for all I know babies.'

Of the surviving twelve letters and one card to Philippa only two attracted the censor's disapproval. One and a half lines were blanked out after a reference to the 'Dieppe boys' no longer being tied up and the title of a film the Germans showed appears to have been crossed through. The censor, however, seemed untroubled by a reference to 'reprisals' and to an escape attempt in July 1943 that was followed by a period in solitary confinement:

27 July 1943

My friend, Robert MacGill (7th Hussars) and I are waiting sentence for a daylight break on Saturday in the course of which we damaged German property & in general behaved rather badly. We got just over a mile dressed as workmen in dyed pyjamas. We were downed 200 yards from the forest by 5 soldiers, about 30 children, two Alsatian dogs & a car. I'll drop you a line from 'durance vile'. Love from John

14 August 1943

Dear Philipa. Thank you so much for two more letters last week. I am writing from 'Durance vile' where I'm doing 7 days solitary for getting about a mile on the road to England, Home and yourself. It is really very peaceful in here but they will drive me out for exercise, of which I have had quite enough recently. I hope I shan't have to use those warm gloves you sent for another winter in the Fatherland. The sentry outside the door has got a face and figure very much like old Chalmers who used to umpire cricket matches at Storrington 'when we were very young'. I've got a pea-shooter with me. Love John

As the years of incarceration passed, his feelings for his distant pen friend deepened. In his first letter he addressed her as 'Dear Philippa' but this soon became 'My dear Philippa' and his tone developed a flirtatiousness. He pinned two photos of her to his cupboard door – 'a reminder that another sex does exist beyond this world of wire and stone' – and regularly asked for more snaps. At the end of December 1942 he wrote appreciatively of one photo: 'Incidentally you're showing a satisfactory (was that the wrong word?) amount of leg!'

But he soon began to worry about the competition that he was incapable of seeing off:

> I get news of you from home as well; my last letter but one said you looked dazzling as an officer. This must surely be rather bad for discipline because in A/A you have to deal with men, don't you? Or perhaps I'm hopelessly out of date and it may be that women even fire the guns now! One of the biggest worries of a POW is the thought of all the eligible young men of every nationality who must be kicking about in England while we're caged up in monastic seclusion. Please don't go and lose your heart to an American. Or anyone else for that matter.

In early 1944 he reminded her: 'For yourself, Philippa, avoid Americans, shun Englishmen, rebuff 'Free' Frenchmen – in fact take the veil, till the war is over.' A few months later he urged her to, 'Watch your step with the Welshmen, likeable but ardent.'

Philippa was the perfect correspondent – sending him cheery news as well as practical treats like 'a topping pair of leather gloves' and cigarettes. But not all friends and family judged their content so finely and POWs resorted to humour as a way of dealing with the tactlessness of some letters from home. Several logbooks and memoirs include examples of thoughtless comments which, given the frequency with which they crop up and the fact that they were addressed to *someone else*, must surely be apocryphal. They were sometimes known as 'Mail bag splitters' and, unusually in POW literature, reveal a bitterness and helplessness, a worry that the outside world did not understand their plight.

Flight Sergeant Edward Charnock, who was held in three different camps including Stalag XXA, recorded in his logbook the following examples of lines supposedly written from home:

> Can you buy beer over there or do they only sell wine?

> I sent you a parcel last Thursday so you should get it by next Friday.

Put in some lovely mince pies, but the Red Cross [sent] them back.
    I asked the Red Cross, but can't send you a radio.

Darling, I'm so glad you were shot down before flying became dangerous.

Darling, I hope you are staying true to me.

Letter from best girl: 'Darling, I married your father. Love, Mother.'

Flight Lieutenant Bennett Ley Kenyon DFC's logbook, which he hid in one of the tunnels (known as 'Tom', 'Dick' and 'Harry') used to escape from Stalag Luft III, included more examples:

I have married your brother. I am so happy to be in your family, as I will be able to see you often.

From a wife:
You have just bought me a Silver Fox fur – aren't you glad?

I have had an affair with a Canadian airman & he is having cigarettes & parcels sent you from Canada.

Keep your chin up – it won't be long now. (September 1940)

Do you get out to do much shooting?

I have read that you have a beer garden in one corner of your camp.

Do you see the latest moving pictures?

From a complaining wife:
Here I am working myself to death and you are leading a life of luxury.

It must be lovely living in a fine forest.

It surely must be grand to lie around all day.

After all – Freedom is only a State of Mind!

These examples may be extreme but as some family allegiances started to crumble the camaraderie of the POW camp became even more important.

Uses for a Red Cross Parcel Number 1 – String

> Crump used the time to make new ropes for the trolleys [which transported the dirt from the escape tunnels], as the old ones were rotting. Williams had been saving up string from the parcel store, and Crump took on the exasperating job of making three hundred feet of four-ply plait, the long ends constantly tangling so that he had two men standing behind him clearing it.
>
> Paul Brickhill, *The Great Escape*

For most POWs the Red Cross parcel was their first tangible link with home. It provided a visible reminder that they had not been forgotten but also practical assistance that went far beyond the bare nutrients contained in its carefully packed tins of food. A parcel that had been assembled with the sole practical aim of delivering nutritious food safely was dismantled by its recipients with equal care so that every scrap of packaging could be put to good use after the contents had been consumed. The brown cardboard container, about the size of a tall shoebox, played a part in every major activity that took place in a POW camp. The string that held it together pulled the trolleys in the catacomb of tunnels under Stalag Luft III, the food tins became the main components for brewing up a cup of tea or ersatz coffee on a homemade stove or *stufa* and the packaging went towards elaborate stage sets or barrack hut furniture. The staggering organisation that allowed the Red Cross to send millions of parcels to POWs undoubtedly saved lives in a purely practical sense of providing calories and vitamins but the supply of other materials helped to raise morale in a way that the packers back at home could never have imagined.

The parcel carried a Red Cross logo in the top right hand corner and the circular, black Order of St John's emblem below. It was 31cm wide, 17.5cm tall and 11.5cm deep and was stamped with official black letters in three languages. 'Comité International de la Croix-Rouge, Genève – Transit, Suisse' described the route it had taken and the German *Kriegsgefangenenpost* pointed out that this was a POW parcel. Thick string was twisted tightly round the package like a barbed wire twine.

The British Red Cross, which was formed in 1870 to help the sick and wounded of the Franco-Prussian war, had joined forces with the Order of St John of Jerusalem to support the victims of the First World War and the two resumed their relationship in 1939 by becoming the War Organisation – known abroad as the British Red Cross. The food parcel was the most famous of the packages that the British Red Cross dispatched to POWs but it was also responsible for 'next-of-kin parcels' (made up of carefully monitored items supplied by a prisoner's family); educational parcels (books, exam papers and other aids to learning); 'medical comforts' (dressings, nearly 2,500 pairs of spectacles, false teeth, materials for making artificial limbs, etc.); and a wide selection of sporting, theatrical and musical items – anything from cricket pads to bagpipes.

Speculation about when the next Red Cross Parcel might appear and what it would contain could fill hours of conversation. Confirmation of its arrival produced a rare moment of pure joy for a POW. One elderly major was so overcome by the sight of the butter he found in his parcel that he fell off his stool and broke his collar bone; another man compared receiving his parcel to the thrill of finding a train set under the Christmas tree when he was a boy.

The first British Red Cross parcels were sent via the Swiss Legation's bag in Britain to RAF prisoners in Germany in October 1939. So long as the number of POWs remained low, packing and distributing the parcels operated like a cottage industry. Parcels were addressed to individuals and at the very start of the war packers grew to know the idiosyncrasies of their charges – the sailor, for example, who preferred soft food because he had lost his false teeth overboard when his ship was torpedoed.

The British Red Cross experimented with sending fresh bread to camps and there was even talk of using bakeries in Denmark as a distribution centre because they were known to use British ovens. However, it quickly became obvious that the parcels were taking too long to arrive for bread to be a sensible constituent. By April 1940, Germany had invaded Denmark and the fall of France, two months later, meant the British Red Cross suddenly had thousands of captured soldiers to consider. During the six years of the war it sent over twenty million food parcels to POWs. In the peak year of 1942 five and a half million were delivered.

These parcels, in all their various forms, captured the public's imagination in a way that other aspects of the Red Cross's humanitarian work failed to. Just as, years later, Julie Andrews sang of 'brown paper packages tied up with string' as one of her favourite things, so the idea of the Red Cross parcel pulled at the collective memory of birthday presents and mysterious bundles. Unlike a letter or telegram, a parcel usually brings excitement, rather than sadness and this potent symbol helped the British Red Cross to raise funds from flag days, cinema collections and special events. A poster, which showed a POW behind barbed wire gleefully clutching a parcel, summed up the impact for both donor and recipient in the caption: 'A bit of home'.

Fundraising made the ordinary person in Britain feel they could help someone in a helpless position. From her home in Barrow-in-Furness Nella Last kept a diary for Mass Observation, an organisation set up in 1937 by three young men with the aim of creating an 'anthropology of ourselves'. Nella's younger son, Clifford, was in the army and she became involved in running a shop for the Red Cross Prisoners of War Fund. She threw herself into knitting cotton dish-cloths and repairing and sprucing up other items for sale. The mayoress opened the shop in August 1942 and on its first day streams of shoppers stripped it of nearly all its goods and raised close to £50 (worth about £1,766 today).

'Such a happy worthwhile day, it makes up for all the thought and planning, all the hurry and tiredness of the last three hectic weeks,' Nella wrote on 26 August, 1942.

There is no sweetness like success of effort. There will be a lot of thankful hearts as a result of today: the poor prisoners of war will get a lot of parcels out of even today's efforts. The Red Cross said a little prayer at the opening, and asked for a blessing on the 'willing, tireless workers who had created the shop.' I felt it had been granted from the start, for everyone had been so kind and helpful, and no one has refused or been curt when I've asked for help.

In its first week the shop raised £100, which Nella described as, 'a marvellous thing – two hundred parcels of hope and comfort to heartsick men. Who knows who will be the next man to need a parcel? *Any* of our menfolk who have gone overseas.'

The next day she glanced at a poster of a POW clutching a parcel and the image encouraged her to pencil 'fantastic' prices on the toys and other items for sale.

A year later she wrote:

We put the wireless on, to listen to 'Trans-Atlantic Call', and heard a P.O.W. speak about Red Cross parcels. I felt the tears gather and slide down my cheeks. I knew it all, but again I felt the privilege to be able to think, 'This will be another parcel.' I felt a blessing on our efforts, and on the wee tatty shop. I feel that as long as it is needed – and we work hard – we can keep all going. I looked at my little cuddly toys, and thought of all the dollies sold . . . After tea, I sat and finished the nightdress-case and put it in a cellophane bag, and it is really lovely – for those who like doodads and blue ones! She will grace some 'new rich' bed, no doubt – but never mind, and that type *throw* money round. They may as well throw it in the P.O.W. direction.

Other people raised money in a way that suited their skills. Darts players contributed the largest sum from any one sport – £200,000 – and several POW camps managed to make donations from events such as arts and crafts displays and prisoners who did well in camp exams often showed their gratitude with financial gifts. These donations probably took the form of IOUs to be met after the war or by relatives, or deductions arranged from their bank accounts. In a pleasing irony, Hitler boosted funds when his UK publishers, Hutchinson, handed over the £500 royalties from the English edition of *Mein Kampf*. By the end of the war the British Red Cross had spent £52 million without incurring any debt. This figure seems even more remarkable given the fundraising efforts that went in to raising £20,000 to build a bomber or £5,000 for a Spitfire.

Although the parcels were assembled with scrupulous regard for what the prisoner most needed – the food parcels squeezed the maximum calories, nutrients and vitamins into the smallest space – and what the enemy would allow, both public and POW nevertheless regarded the parcels as a kind of hamper prepared by a loving matriarch or a doting nanny. 'They might have been packed by some wise and kindly mother,' wrote one POW in Stalag 383, 'for who else would pop bull's-eyes amongst the solid foodstuffs, or think of sending pancake mixture to prisoners of war?'

This description may give the impression of someone cramming last-minute items into a bulging suitcase but every ounce of the eleven-pound food package had a reason to be there. Rather than a 'kindly mother', a committee made up of representatives from the British Red Cross and dieticians from the War Office and Ministry of Food scrutinised reports from the International Red Cross Committee and the Protecting Power on the nutritional values of rations in German and Italian camps. The British Red Cross aimed to send a parcel to each POW every week but this was rarely achieved and camps quickly established their own systems of sharing food among groups, or syndicates, of men so that no one was left out. By the end of the war it was sending out seven different food parcels that varied slightly in contents. A few items, such as chocolate, tea and sugar, appeared in each package because they were universally popular and could be bartered for other goods, particularly chocolate which became a currency of its own. Sweets appeared in one of the most common packages, while pancake batter cropped up in the rarest; Indian POWs had their own parcel that included atta (a wheat flour used in South Asian cooking), curry powder, dhal and rice but no tinned meat. A capsule of fifty cigarettes or tobacco was sent separately.

The first packing centre was opened at St James's Palace on 11 November 1939 but the suggestion that more might be needed was controversial since it implied that many more prisoners would be taken. Despite objections from the Army Council a second centre started in Hove on the south coast and the disaster of Dunkirk forced the British Red Cross to make use of a range of accommodation – factories, drill, church and town halls, department stores, a rectory and a private house – so that by the end of 1940 there were fourteen centres around Britain. There were two types of packing centres – one that was staffed by a mixture of volunteers and paid workers and the second by an entirely paid workforce at a site, such as a factory, where packing was the normal, peacetime activity. The latter was often used when the British Red Cross needed to build up a supply of parcels in case transport problems made it harder for parcels to get through. There were also emergency sites at packing places used by famous names such as Lyons in Kensington, Selfridges in Paddington, Harrods, Peek Frean in Bermondsey, and Nestlé at Ashbourne. In the final year of the war, of the 2,700 staff, four-fifths were volunteers. It was heavy, physically tiring work, frequently carried out during air raids and carefully scrutinised by supervisors.

Packers unloaded tins and took them to the open shelves where around eighteen items were put into parcel lids and placed on a trolley. The trolley was wheeled to the packers who sat at benches where they made sure that every object fitted snugly in the box, any spaces were plugged with paper shavings which also formed a final top layer before the box was passed to the 'stringers' who had, perhaps, the hardest job. They worked with the three-stranded sisal that was so tough that after ten minutes unprotected hands were covered with blisters; even with gloves it was uncomfortable, fiddly work. Andrew Hawarden reckoned that each parcel used about 10 feet of string.

In the early months of the war the parcel was shipped to Belgium but when the Low Countries were over-run the route grew circuitous. Parcels travelled through neutral Lisbon or the South of France (once it became part of the puppet, Vichy state) and then via the International Red Cross's offices in Geneva to POW camps. Once the package arrived the string was carefully untied and the lid ceremoniously lifted off. It was then that the cord began its second life.

While at home, housewives like Nella Last were being urged to 'make do and mend' POWs were following the same mantra. Materials at the start of the war were in such short supply in POW camps, and boredom was so acute, that one stalag even held an exhibition of articles made from Red Cross string. These included: shoes, bags and 'breakfast sets'. One prisoner commented that the string was, 'Very hard on the fingers, but it helps to pass the time.'

Its toughness made it ideal for many other, less artistic, tasks. Hawarden recorded that it was used to make brushes and hammocks; the latter were particularly useful when POWs were moved from one camp to another in cattle trucks. In the final, bitter winter months of the war when fuel was scarce POWs burnt every stick of wood they could find, including table legs, and Red Cross string was used to suspend what was left of the table from the ceiling where it swung 'dizzily' while men tried to eat their soup from it.

At Marlag und Milag Nord near Bremen, which held men taken prisoners from ships, the string was used to improve the quality of theatrical productions. The camp already had considerable talent including the professional actor, Henry Mollison (whose cousin was Amy Johnson's husband, the record-breaking pilot James Mollison), and Robbie Robinson, a rating and former docker from Liverpool, who became known for the beautiful dresses he made. Mollison had worked in London's West End theatres and appeared in several films before the war. He was captured after the ship he was taking to Australia was sunk and he helped to produce fourteen variety shows and plays for the Marlag and Milag Theatre (MMT). But, in spite of convincing frocks, good actors and fresh-faced youths, long hair for POWs playing female parts was always a problem. One solution MMT used was to make wigs by steeping string in boiling water to soften it before attaching it to a skull cap made from material donated by Sikh POWs and originally intended by the Red Cross for making and repairing turbans.

At Stalag XVIIIA (Wolfsberg, in south Austria) Clive Dunn was eager to resume the beginnings of a theatrical career in which he had attended the Italia Conti Theatre School followed by small parts such as 'Slightly Soiled' in a touring production of *Peter Pan* and the ticket collector in *Brief Encounter* at Abergavenny. His youth and slight frame made him an obvious candidate for female roles and the theatre group created a wig out of a tail snipped from the horse that pulled the wagon used to suck up the excrement from the latrines. A figure-hugging dress made from dyed army pullovers and stuffed with breasts moulded from socks completed the illusion. When he took the lead of the gypsy princess in Ivor Novello's *Glamorous Nights*, his opening lines of 'I'm not really beautiful, I only make you think I am' dared anyone to challenge him.

String was put to all sorts of sporting uses. At Milag, merchant seamen made a cricket ball by winding it round a pebble and other camps used it to make tennis and cricket nets. Hawarden noted that the POWs had made football nets by tying together some 3,000 pieces of string using sixteen hundred knots; laid end to end the cord would have been three miles long. They also made a rope for the tug-of-war competition at the camp sports day but the guards confiscated it in case it was used in an escape attempt.

The Germans, too, had their own uses for the string. In the autumn of 1942 the High Command retaliated after it discovered evidence that German POWs had been bound and blindfolded. They demanded an apology and, when none appeared, started the practice of shackling the hands of around 1,300 British and Canadian prisoners between the hours of 9 a.m. and 9 p.m. The British Government took similar action and the tit-for-tat game continued when the Germans increased the numbers of those who now found it difficult to eat, smoke or go to the toilet without assistance. The British backed down in December but the Germans continued to shackle some prisoners until November 1943, although after a few months many guards were simply leaving it up to their charges to apply the chains or string.

Denholm Elliott, a wireless operator in the RAF who was shot down on his third mission and who was to become a professional stage and screen actor, was one of those POWs at Stalag VIIIB (Lamsdorf) who had his hands bound in front of his body using Red Cross string. After a few weeks the string was replaced with manacles but as the months passed guards and prisoners reached a working arrangement. For Elliott, who appeared in many POW plays, this meant waiting until he was due to go on stage before turning to his guard and saying: 'I say, would you mind, old boy?' At the end of his scene the chains would be replaced.

Other POWs found ways of slipping their chains off and would lie on their bunk with them dangling from a hook behind the door; often the guards knew what was going on but chose to ignore it. A sardine tin-opener from a Red Cross parcel proved the ideal implement with which to unpick the lock.

The Red Cross parcel also played an important part in encouraging budding golfers at Stalag Luft III's East Compound where players made balls by winding wool and cotton round a carved pine cone or stone. As the sport became more popular they used string to stitch together balls wrapped in old shoe leather, a tobacco pouch or rubber from gym shoes. Black shoe-polish helped to waterproof the ball. It was a matter of pride that the ball had a diameter of 1.62in, rather than the 'larger' size (1.68in) preferred by American players. These homemade balls were essential in what was to be the brief – if gloriously madcap – life of Sagan Golf Club.

Some of these golf balls still exist and one is on display at the Royal and Ancient Golf Club of St Andrew's – its weight and size exactly match the dimensions of a factory-made version. After the war, veteran Pat Ward-Thomas persuaded two professionals to try out the balls that had taken him six hours each to make. Both travelled an impressive 200 yards.

4

Friendships and Feuds

As friends and family at home began to feel more and more remote so POWs formed intense friendships based on their shared experience of being 'in the bag'. For officers, POW life could resemble boarding school, university or even a gentleman's club without the leather armchairs and brandy. Men asked fellow POWs to 'pop in about 10.30 for a brew' or issued invitations to attend formal dinners. Tradition dictated that army-minded families, schools and regions formed strong links with one regiment and it was not unusual for POWs to be reunited with school friends and neighbours, brothers and cousins. And, although logically such reunions should not have been surprising, they always caused a frisson of excitement. A father and son were held together at Lamsdorf and in the same camp a man captured at Dunkirk was reunited with his brother, who was taken in Crete – although the camp was so big that it was a year before they realised they were in the same stalag.

Whether 'circuit-bashing' – strolling round the perimeter fence – or lying on the grass or a bunk bed after a day's work, talking was an important way of passing the time. Many conversations focussed on what the POW would do when he got home – which restaurants he would go to, what his first meal would be, the pub he would take his friend to. Business plans were hatched and alliances forged. Ray Beal, who was a sergeant with the Royal Army Service Corps when he was taken in France, was held at Stalag XXA and later 383. He wrote in his diary in 1943:

January 3rd (Sunday) No Mail.
Walked around the football pitch this afternoon with John Hooper,
where we talked of the possibility of his moving out of the smoke to
work after the war – a very, very interesting conversation.

For several POWs it was their first exposure to men who came from a different class, believed in another religion, or voted for another party. The
capture of men from South Africa, Australia and New Zealand, and then
America, added yet another dimension to conversations, as Ray Beal's
diary shows:

January 5 (Tuesday) 1 letter Bulk issue Red X
Had a long chat about Psychology this evening with an Aussie schoolmaster – most interesting and it would appear that from the point of
view of practical work with School children they are far in advance of
us.

January 12 (Tuesday) No mail
In bed again till dinner time! What a life! The afternoon was spent in
walking and then painting some model aeroplanes for Basil. The conversation and arguments we have here are rather interesting ... We
had a heated debate today on whether a cold bath makes you warmer
than a hot one! 3 years is such a beastly long time to be isolated from
the world.

As with any long-standing group of people, cliques emerged and began
to niggle those who stood outside them. Eric Newby describes one that
emerged in Fontanellato, near Parma in Italy, where he was held in a converted orphanage surrounded by the Apennine hills:

In the camp the members of the coterie moved easily in a mysterious,
almost Edwardian world and when they addressed one another they
used nicknames, just as the Edwardians had been so fond of doing,
which were completely unintelligible to anyone else, and they knew
who was who so far down the scale of the aristocracy to a point at
which one would have thought that any blue blood corpuscles would
have been non-existent. They alone knew that 'Bolo' Bastonby was the

nephew of the Earl of Crake, that 'Jamie' Stuart Ogilvie-Keir-Gordon was the youngest brother of the Master of Dunreeking and that 'Feathers' Farthingdale was the third son of the Marquis of Stale by his second wife.

Other cliques were based around age, rank, whether a man had volunteered for service, been called up or was a career soldier, which camps he had been held in, how many escape attempts he had made, or how long he had been a POW. At Fontanellato, officers who had been captured early in the war had managed to dodge the Italians' strict rules on what could be worn and were marked out by the elegance of their dress, 'pigswhisker pullovers, scarves and socks from the Burlington Arcade secured with gold pins, made-to-measure Viyella shirts and corduroy trousers'.

Gatherings based around regional allegiances provided entertainment, food and drink and a sense of belonging. Many of the hundred or so clubs at Stalag 383 grew out of these geographical loyalties – the Sussex, Liverpool and Gaelic clubs and the St Andrew's Society, for example. At Stalag Luft VI, Yorkshiremen set up a 'White Rose Club', which recorded 174 members at one meeting, and which produced a handwritten 'house journal', which they called *Yorkshire Post*, '*Kriegie edition*'. A bound copy with the title carved into plywood stained with brown shoe polish was sent home to the original, daily regional newspaper, *The Yorkshire Post*, so that a version could be given to members' relatives. In a foreword, the camp leader, James 'Dixie' Deans, who as a Scotsman was a member of the Caledonian Society, explained the appeal of such clubs: 'The meeting together, the talks of home, the sound of the familiar dialect, and the uniting of common memories, all help to strengthen the ties with home, and bring a soothing influence. Home does not seem so far away, when men of one place get together and talk about it.'

Freemasonry flourished in Stalag 383 and was practised at some level in thirteen other camps in Europe. There were also active Freemason POWs in the Far East. In one sense, though, it was more dangerous to be a Freemason in Europe because the Nazis, fearing a conflict of allegiance and claiming it was a Jewish-led conspiracy, had banned the organisation. Many camps were simply too overcrowded for meetings to be held in private although larger camps sometimes had more than one group but, such was the secrecy under which they operated, they might be unaware of the other's existence. At one a Masonic group was known as 'The Chess Club' which led to confusion among the genuine players; others met in a room behind a stage, a dentist's surgery or in a chapel where the padre was a Mason. Someone was always stationed outside and would shout 'Goon up!' if a guard appeared. At the warning, the Master delivered a lecture on the first subject that came to mind 'be it theology, town planning or pig breeding'.

New members had to be approached with great care and the cryptic phrase 'too much caution cannot be exercised' was dropped into the conversation as a password. Records of meetings were usually written in code in exercise books and hidden. One stash of records in a cardboard box with a false bottom survived three Gestapo searches. The symbols of the Masonic order – the compass and square and regalia – were made from pieces of bunk beds or odd scraps of metal, such as a coin or a piece of reinforcing rod from a bombed building, and concealed in a hollowed-out loaf of bread, a bar of soap or a chimney breast. Some were small enough to fit into a matchbox and provided the owner with a talisman of defiance. My father, who belonged to a lodge in Dumbarton, was never aware of any Masonic activity in the camps he was held in and was shocked when I told him that many groups existed and were attended by members from his own Scottish lodge.

At 383, Masons held meetings on Saturday evenings in the former stable known as 'The Den' because it had once been occupied by a troop of German Boy Scouts and was now used by different clubs, and as a study and library. The Masons called themselves 'The International Group' and paid their dues in cigarettes that they used to 'buy' tea, sugar and milk; the surplus was held in a charity account. At Christmas they distributed stockings.

'Brothers' from a range of different nationalities attended meetings at 383 that continued until the end of the war, by which time it had eighty-two members and an average attendance of sixty. Strictly speaking, these were not Masonic lodges because members were not able to follow the correct procedure that would allow them to create a lodge from scratch. As well as a lot of toasting from a strange assortment of tins and pots, members listened to lectures on subjects with a Masonic theme. A Hungarian prisoner gave a talk on how Freemasonry had influenced Mozart and illustrated it with the use of a portable gramophone, and a

German-speaker translated an article in a Nazi newspaper on the installation of the Earl of Harewood as Grand Master. Although the newspaper was intended as propaganda, and pointed out that both George V and President Roosevelt were Masons, the newspaper nevertheless reported the king's address to the Grand Master in full.

There is no doubt that belonging to a secret society gave Masons added succour. Hoodwinking the Germans brought a delicious sense of satisfaction and being part of a select group also gave some a feeling of privilege, a reason why they pressed their threadbare trousers and replaced the habitual scarf for a tie when they attended meetings. When Col. D.P. Iggulden went to his first meeting at Oflag 79 he 'anointed' his hair with margarine, although he warned, 'I don't recommend it as a general habit as after a day or so it has an unfortunate tendency to go rank'.

Freemasonry could have an unsettling influence if, for example, a POW's position in the brotherhood gave him theoretical superiority over someone who held a higher position in the armed services. But usually being part of a closed fraternity was reassuring. F.S. Payne, who was held at Stalag XVIIIA (Wolfsberg) and Stalag 383, felt that being a Freemason put him in a select group:

> Without exception they represented the better class of man who had maintained that certain dignity under the appalling conditions of the past year. A feeling of pride to be associated with this group of men was not out of place. So many of these were of senior rank who had by very hard work done so much to organise the camp on decent lines and were therefore not always the most popular for their efforts with the lower element brought into prominence by the living conditions.

The ritual provided a comforting familiarity and the spiritual aspects helped many through their ordeal. It is true that Masons looked out for each other first but, as was their practice at home, many also tried to help the wider community – in one camp undertaking all the washing for the hospital patients.

Often it was a petty argument, rather than a clique, that led to a breakdown in the camp's harmony – as in this instance from Ray Beal's 1943 diary:

January 9 (Saturday) No mail

Discussion today hinged on the interpretation of Revelation which is supposed to foretell this war. Its length and end! – All Bosh! Tempers are getting somewhat 'Edgy' now. I suppose this is inevitable, and really it is surprising that things are not much worse than they really are. However, every now and then we get a flare up, usually over nothing at all and a most personal argument, coupled with really foul language takes place, no-one has gone for the throat yet.

January 14 (Thursday) No Mail

This week has appeared to drag, a direct result, I suspect, of the celebrations over Xmas. As I write, there is a heated debate going on as to whether parcel lists come round in the afternoon or the morning! No one thinks to go and see from the PO. They just gradually lose their tempers over a stupid thing like this.

The internal hierarchy of the POW camp was supposed to squash squabbles before they got out of hand. In oflags it was normal for the highest ranking officer – the Senior British Officer (SBO) – to assume overall command of the POWs. Among Other Ranks the most senior NCO was usually in charge, or the men voted for their leader. In some camps he was known as a *Vertrauensmann* (Man of Confidence); occasionally this title was given to a German-speaking POW who liaised with the enemy and supported the camp leader. Clive Dunn took the role of 'Man of Confidence' until he found the pressure of dealing with the Germans too much.

Oflags also contained men from the Other Ranks who were assigned to perform minor tasks, such as fetching and carrying, or shining buttons for officers. They were known as orderlies or batmen and were an accepted tradition in the course of day-to-day army life. Officers and orderlies frequently built up a close relationship based on mutual respect within the well-defined confines of military discipline. However, this relationship came under strain in POW camps when orderlies were allotted to officers without the bond that builds up over several years; in some cases the orderlies were even interned civilians.

Within the walls of an oflag the contrast between the apparently indolent officer and the skivvying orderly became most pronounced. It was a rift that the Germans did their best to encourage and which led to a strike of some orderlies at Colditz in the spring of 1941. Class divisions were exacerbated by the wilful character of the officers who, after all, had been sent to Colditz for the very reason that they were the 'bad boys'. It takes a unique personality to become someone who cannot stop tunnelling or counterfeiting; the key character trait required is gumption, but arrogance may not be far behind. Wing Commander Douglas Bader, the pilot with two artificial legs who was shot down over France in 1941 and ended up in Colditz, had both. When, in 1943, his batman, Alec Ross, was offered the chance of repatriation Bader is reported to have said: 'He came here as my lackey and he'll stay as my lackey'. Although, some POWs have claimed that Bader is unlikely to have said this, or that he said it only in jest, Ross remained a POW for the rest of the war.

The other factor that led to simmering resentment between ranks was that, under the 1929 Geneva Convention, officers did not have to work – and few did. The Convention emerged after the experience of the Great War had shown there was no uniformity in the way in which POWs were treated. The International Committee of the Red Cross thus drew up a draft convention that it submitted to the Diplomatic Conference at Geneva in 1929. The revised convention prohibited reprisals, addressed the issue of prisoners' work, the appointment of a POW representative and the role of the 'protecting powers'. POWs received *Lagergeld* or *Lagermarks*, specially printed slips of paper which they could, in theory, exchange for poor quality items such as toothpaste, soap or shaving gear in the canteens and which had no value outside the camps. Mostly, though, the *Lagergeld* were used as gambling tokens to be redeemed after the war.

In theory, NCOs from the rank of corporal up were only required to supervise work but as Germany struggled to find manpower this rule was often broken. My father, who held the rank of War Substantive Sergeant at the time of capture, obstinately maintained that he was not obliged to work in a factory and was sent to a *Straflager* (punishment camp). If his captors followed the normal procedure of asking him about his peacetime occupation I think my father – who was never a convincing liar – would have found it difficult to offer one of the standard facetious replies that British soldiers goaded their guards with. I cannot imagine him suggesting that he had been a food taster or brothel keeper. If he gave a truthful answer the Germans would have found his trade of joiner or carpenter extremely useful.

Clive Dunn considered claiming that he was a farmer, butcher or 'food sorter' in the hope that he might be put to work somewhere that offered the opportunity for snacking, but eventually he told the truth. His vocation did nothing to slow his immediate transformation into the role of peasant who was set to work building a road in the side of a mountain.

Under Article 31 of the Geneva Convention, the Germans were not supposed to force POWs to carry out work that might have a 'direct connection with the operations of the war' and, specifically, they should not be put to work 'in the manufacture or transport of arms or munitions of any kind, or on the transport of material destined for combatant units'. The Germans did not follow this rule too assiduously.

At Stalag XXA Sam Kydd worked in a variety of jobs – many of which were blatantly helping the German war effort, although he did his best to sabotage the work and to leave with something useful: sugar from a barge he was unloading or tobacco from parcels he was piling onto trucks at Thorn Railway Station and which were destined for German troops on the Eastern Front. The work was physically demanding and in the winter months made worse by the freezing weather. He unloaded telegraph poles from barges on the River Vistula, often in the driving snow, in shifts that lasted from 6 p.m. to midnight; he helped to unpack lorries stacked with signalling equipment, coils of telephone cables, porcelain knobs for telegraph poles and boxes of screws, nuts and bolts. He was forced to tear down a Jewish cemetery, to help build a theatre for Nazi rallies and to work on an Autobahn linking Berlin to Danzig. When he complained that clearing an airfield's runway of snow must surely be in breach of the Geneva Convention, he was brushed off with the excuse that the strip was principally for civilian use but that the Luftwaffe occasionally landed there too. Other POWs at Stalag XXB were made to repair railways and workshops damaged by RAF bombs. In Austria, some of Clive Dunn's fellow POWs went on strike when they were ordered to work in an armaments factory. They were threatened with execution and made to work at gunpoint until the Germans abruptly moved them to a different type of work.

Work had its compensations: the opportunity to earn money, the prospect of larger rations of better quality food, the chance to mix with the opposite sex, or simply a release from the monotony of prison life. Although labour left a prisoner tired and with little time for other pastimes some men preferred it to hours of lying on a bunk with the twin parasites of hunger and boredom gnawing away at them.

Clive Dunn's first spell of work was in a gang of twenty-four men in shifts that lasted for eight or nine hours. His job was to hack away at the mountainside to create a path wide enough for a cart to use. His new home was a long wooden hut next to a noisy stream near the village of Pruggern in Obersteiermark, Austria. He was given a pair of clogs, strips of cloth to tie round his legs and ankles, blue breeches, a dark green tunic and a grey side cap that made him feel like a peasant. They ate mainly potatoes which sent him scurrying to the latrine, a wooden plank with two holes cut in it that teetered over a trench. That winter was one of the coldest for forty years; two men suffered from frostbite and Dunn's clogs filled with snow within minutes. 'I was up a mountain, there was snow on the ground and Britain was doing very badly. I thought, "I could be here for forty years". But when you're young you can't be miserable for too long.'

The arrival of army boots from the Red Cross helped to raise his spirits and, remarkably, Dunn felt sorry for the German guards who, unlike the POWs, were unable to move around to take the edge off the cold. Although the POWs played pranks on the guards they felt sympathy for many of them – particularly the older ones. Dunn acknowledges that most of the Austrians were decent people caught up in a political hubris beyond their control. When the guards locked them up at night in their wooden hut they would call out, 'Gute Nacht' and the POWs would echo the sentiment: 'Gute Nacht, goodnight, sweetheart.'

When Dunn left the wooden cabin for an old school building next to a church in Liezen, he moved even closer to his captors. He was one of twenty men held in two rooms while a guard slept in the room above them. There was no exercise compound and they were locked up at the end of each day's work – building new apartments or a slaughterhouse – and from midday on Saturday to Monday morning. The barred window, which looked over the village street and across to the baker's house, provided the one link with the outside world. However, they quickly discovered a way of becoming 'latchkey' POWs.

When the guard marched them back from their meal at the cookhouse he got into the habit of slinging the key over the men's heads so that the man in front could catch it and open the door. Once everyone was inside the POW would return the key to the guard. But that was as long as it took for him to make an impression of the key in a soap mould and to use this to make a duplicate out of metal traded for cigarettes from a Polish worker. The spare key allowed POWs to steal out at night. They were let back in when they knocked on the door. A whispered 'Fuck off!' from inside meant a guard was on the prowl.

These night-time flits came to an end when a POW returned from a visit to his local girlfriend whose husband was fighting in Norway. He happened to knock just as the guard was in the dormitory but was too drunk to take in the urgency of the command to try again later, and the guard opened the door to find one of his charges waiting to be let in. The men bribed the guard with Red Cross cigarettes not to tell his superiors but, although he kept quiet, the locks were changed immediately. The episode might easily have been a scene from a sequel to *Dad's Army* in which the Germans won the war.

Male camaraderie could never replace the intimacy of a relationship with a girlfriend or wife. Prisoners could go for months without glimpsing a woman so that when a female entered the camp – perhaps the wife or daughter of a German guard who had been invited to a concert or display of craft work – they were gawped at like an alien. Eric Newby writes of the torment that the local girls in Fontanellato inflicted every Sunday when they walked past on their way to the town cemetery. Some of the men had not spoken to a woman in three years and – expressly against their captors' orders – would hang out of the windows desperate for a glimpse of brown, bare legs and short skirts. The guards were torn between taking pot shots at the faces that appeared at the orphanage windows and turning their backs on their charges to gaze at the beauty parade. The prisoners' only other contact with women was via the neighbouring convent where their laundry was sent and which occasionally returned with little notes tucked into the clean sheets or shirts informing the men that the nuns were praying for them.

Newby was highly unusual in that he met his future wife, the Yugoslavian-born Wanda, while he was at Fontanellato. He had first spotted her cycling to the cemetery, a startlingly rare blonde among the dark-haired gaggle, and got to know her after he broke his ankle running up and down the grand steps of the orphanage to improve his fitness before an escape attempt. When news of the Italian Armistice arrived he hobbled out of his prison with the help of two other POWs but had to be smuggled into a hospital for his foot to be treated – which was where he met Wanda.

Medical appointments provided a rare opportunity to talk with members of the opposite sex. Clive Dunn was sent to hospital for several weeks suffering from chronic colitis, which was exacerbated by his poor POW diet. Here the nuns gave him his first bath in three and a half years, put him in a bed with clean sheets and fed him semolina. He got to know an Austrian girl who was having her appendix removed and a young Polish woman who worked in the kitchen.

Allen Graham, a doctor from Toronto who joined the Royal Canadian Army Medical Corps (RCAMC) and was held in Italy and various camps in Germany, remembers hearing a story about a British pilot who managed to seduce a female radiologist when he was taken for an X-ray in Germany. 'I think that's the only time I ever heard of heterosexual activity,' he said later, adding that he thought that it was probably 'in his mind and not an actual fact'. But another doctor, William E. Tucker remembers a POW who became friendly with women outside the camp: 'I know that . . . when he came back he had a little difficulty with his wife because . . . he'd got this woman and I think she'd got a child. You see, a lot of these German women's men were on the Ost [Eastern] Front, and they were just as starved as some of the prisoners.'

POWs who worked at a farm or in a factory often came across women who were curious about them, although many were too frightened of the consequences to pursue that curiosity. Females who came into the camp to work frequently became the focus of sexual fantasies and some bestowed favours in return for Red Cross bounty. Sam Kydd remembers one POW claiming he had had sex with a woman who worked in the laundry and Kydd himself had a crush on one of the Finnish censors whose job it was to check their letters home. He managed to snatch a kiss in the Education Reference Library but she was so terrified of being caught fraternising with the enemy that the relationship never moved beyond this. Otherwise, men assuaged their desires through what Eric Newby terms 'pulling our puddings', although this was severely curtailed by lack of privacy.

Communal living, together with the taboos of the time, also made homosexuality problematic. Doctor Allen Graham was aware of the possibilities: 'it wasn't private there. There were a few [homosexuals] amongst the men ... The large sergeant had his boyfriends and a couple of these were well known, but it wasn't very widespread. There was no real incident of anything untoward sexually. I mean any gross abnormalities.'

POWs who might have had gay tendencies tended to sublimate their urges within a camp, just as they would have done at home. Others experienced feelings towards pretty young men, especially those who took female roles in plays or who assumed the female role during dances. These unexpected feelings were difficult to deal with but may have been driven by something other than homosexuality. In an environment in which men had too much time to think it was all too easy to make a fellow prisoner the focus of feelings that were essentially heterosexual. Even if there was no sexual undercurrent POWs were often drawn to someone who demonstrated a quality they longed for – the gentleness they might have found in their mother or sister, as much as their girlfriend or wife, and which was missing behind barbed wire.

'Homosexuality? I think one fell in love,' airman Robin Hunter remembered.

> Certainly I fell in love with a gorgeous youngster. I never touched him, I don't suppose he ever knew I was in love with him, other people obviously fell in love with other people – whether there was any overt homosexual contact or not, I couldn't say; I wasn't ever aware of it. Certainly in our mess I don't think there was. But sex, by and large, only became a problem when the food was sufficient. Otherwise it was all food.

Denholm Elliott played several female parts while he was a POW at Stalag VIIIB (Lamsdorf), including Eliza Dolittle in George Bernard Shaw's *Pygmalion*. His slim hands and features, made slimmer on POW rations, transformed him into a convincing girl and he had a keen following among the guards. Elliott himself developed a special affection for one of the younger Germans that he expressed through small gifts of chocolates or cigarettes until the guard was transferred to another camp. Elliott's second wife, Susan Elliott, described the relationship in his biography: 'What they shared was a warmth, a compassion. It certainly was not sexual. In any case, the low calorie count at Lamsdorf ruled out any possibility of sex for almost all prisoners.'

His first wife, the actress Virginia McKenna, believed that Elliott's later homosexual forays were directly related to his wartime experience: 'In truth, I suppose I thought it was the result of being in a prisoner-of-war camp and would no longer be a problem [after the war].'

For Dan Billany captivity brought its own special torment when he fell in love with a fellow prisoner who refused to see their relationship as anything other than the arm's length affection of one army buddy for another. Billany, a teacher from a working-class family in Hull, had just had his first novel published when he joined the army in the autumn of 1940. *The Opera House Murders* was the sort of detective story that was popular at a time when readers were looking for a distraction. A review in the *Sunday Times* described the novel, published by Faber and Faber, as 'definitely guaranteed to take your mind off anything but a direct hit'. T.S. Eliot, his editor at Faber, was keen for Billany to make the book one of a series but the war intervened before he could realise this ambition.

Billany was captured in North Africa in June 1942 and taken first to Camp 66 at Capua, 20 miles north of Naples, where he met David Dowie. Billany quickly emerged as a loner, a quiet and studious prisoner. He gave lectures on *Wuthering Heights*, *King Lear* and Shakespeare's *Sonnets*, wrote 'Mrs Unbeeton's cookery column' for the camp newsletter *Clickety-click* and sketched the other prisoners and the Italian hills. He devoted the rest of his time to writing a novel called *The Trap* that portrayed his own experience of war in an unusually unsentimental and frank way. Dowie was much more 'clubbable'. He had grown up in southeast London, the youngest of nine children and before the war worked in the local government town-planning department. As a POW he played rugby, took French and German lessons and studied sanitary engineering with the help of books from home and presumably with an eye to improving his career prospects after the war.

At first Billany tried to hide the attraction he felt for his friend; instead he wrote to his sister, who already had a boyfriend, suggesting that she should marry Dowie (who was engaged). When Billany revealed his true feelings, Dowie was embarrassed. Any sort of one-sided declaration is painful; in the cramped, joshing atmosphere of a POW camp it must have been excruciating. But, while Dowie appears to have distanced himself briefly from Billany, he was incapable of abandoning their longstanding friendship altogether. In May 1943, when they were both held in the orphanage at Fontanellato, he agreed to collaborate on a book about their experiences as POWs to be called *The Cage*. For Billany it offered the chance to be physically close to Dowie and, although some names have been changed, Billany's longing for his friend seeps out of the original manuscript. The lined ledger-like book, which is now part of the collection at the Imperial War Museum, includes the usual portraits of fellow POWs but there are other illustrations that hint at a personality trying to escape from the pages. A series of cut-out figures leap and cavort from page to page; they turn in the air, stand on chairs waving a flag or playfully hide under a table. Faceless men with lean limbs like Oscar statuettes queue for the latrine or stand self-consciously in the shower. A doctor armed with a huge syringe charges towards a man who bears his buttocks ready to receive the injection. The uneasy mixture of form and content gives the manuscript a strange feel – part homoerotic, part stylised Italian Fascist.

For men like Andrew Hawarden, who coped with captivity by trying to make it as near normal life as possible, any relationship that appeared to be careering away from the norm was unsettling.

'During our concert last weekend,' he wrote in Wednesday 8 October 1941, 'one of the lads was dressed as a waitress. During the evening, "Angela" would offer herself to be kissed by the highest bidder. It was a little unsavoury to me, although the proceeds were put into the Entertainments or Welfare Fund. From the pleasure (?) of kissing Angela the Welfare fund was 400 marks better off.'

So long as the physical boundaries were clear he was less troubled by cross-dressing, especially if it could be attributed to an army tradition of amateur dramatics. The following diary entry, for example, appears to describe a ceremony in which a French POW married his fiancée by proxy. Although it is unusual enough for Hawarden to record in his diary he does not seem too unsettled by the event – perhaps because it involved the French, rather than his fellow countrymen:

The French contingent had a ramadam [sic] tonight – one of them got married today. They held it in fine style – one being dressed as a woman. The usual wedding ceremony was followed by a feast and concert – really it was a skit of the marriage. The actual ceremony was one of proxy. This is the only case I've heard of whilst being a prisoner of war. [October 30, 1941]

A fancy dress ball was also a bit of innocent fun, with no hint of sexual tension:

Several of the lads dressed as girls and made a very good job of it. Prizes were given for the best character. 'Chocolate Box' won the first prize . . . It's quite amusing to see all the lads dancing – size 10s or more army boots being no handicap. During the dance one can hardly see his partner for dust. Collisions are common but you don't see many pardons being begged – give and take is the motto. [November 9, 1941]

And if there was any hint of impropriety in the following unusual sporting fixture Hawarden was unaware of it, or refused to recognise it:

We started with a fancy dress parade of the basketball teams. We had two matches played today. I don't think these games could have been played anywhere but in a prisoner of war camp. Some of the players had all their clothes pulled off, less bathing drawers. Perhaps it was a good job that they played practically naked when one considers that one character was a sweep, complete with his large bag of soot. Didn't he use it on the others and they on him. The games finished off with all niggers. [Saturday May 23 1942]

Certainly, Clive Dunn found that he was never laughed at for dressing up as a woman when a role in a POW production demanded it. At Stalag XVIIIA, near Wolfsberg, a sort of clearing house for work camps throughout Austria where Dunn spent part of his captivity, dressing up was taken very seriously. The camp's most ambitious production was a spectacle showing the Romans invading Britain. It took six months to stage and included POWs as Julius Caesar, Cleopatra and Brutus and produced the startling sight of lines of centurions marching past

prisoner of war huts and a smiling camp commandant buying a programme from a POW.

Andrew Hawarden felt more comfortable with the affection many men
lavished on animals. Rabbits and chickens were kept as much for food as
company and even cats and smaller birds could find their way into the
cooking pot if rations became particularly short. But cats were amongst
the last to be sacrificed as they kept the rodent population at bay and
eating them represented a line over which many POWs could not bring
themselves to step. John Phillips wrote to Philippa that the 'lager cat' Tom
looked as though it was about to have kittens: 'The only feminine thing
here is the cat, & even this changes its sex as there is one school of thought
which holds it to be a castrated Tom. In trying to establish its sex once &
for all I was very properly bitten on the thumb thus joining the ranks of
the Martyrs in the Cause of Science.'

Birds made undemanding pets that could survive on scraps. Perhaps,
too, cosseting an animal that was the personification of freedom gave
POWs a sense of control in their otherwise emasculated lives. Hawarden
knew of two or three lads who had trained jackdaws to land on their
shoulder when they shouted 'Jack!' and one of the birds appeared to be
happiest when it was hopping around with a cigarette in its beak. At
Liezen the men found a wounded young crow in a field and nursed it back
to health. Two POWs fed it morsels from their Red Cross parcel and the
bird became a sort of camp mascot. Dunn was among those who chatted
to it and dreaded the inevitable day that it would remember how to fly. Just
when they thought it had made a permanent home on the windowsill the
crow made its escape.

Bill Murray, a Scottish soldier with the 2nd Battalion Highland Light
Infantry (HLI), claimed that the best-fed prisoner at Moosburg (Stalag
VIIA), near Munich, was a tame kestrel that a subaltern had brought with
him from North Africa tucked inside his battle dress. The soldier shared his
rations with it and supplemented its diet with rodents. The two of them
earned a room at the end of a corridor because of the ripe smell of its
droppings. The bird survived the attention of the Gestapo since birds of
prey fitted the Nazi ethos; Hermann Göring enjoyed hunting and was
photographed with a falcon. This official approval extended to the camp
commandant who each day would dangle dead mice from his finger for it.

Birds were a potent symbol for POWs. Glimpsed on the other side of the perimeter fence or flying overhead they represented freedom and a vivid reminder of home; who knows, they might even have come from Britain or been on their way there. Hawarden found the sound of the nightingale as he strolled outside his hut in the evening, or the cuckoo's call in the morning, or even the sight of the unEnglish stork, made him think of what it must be like to go where you pleased. He became more conscious of nature and noted in his diary spotting a swallow's nest.

He does not say what happened to the pets that the men had nurtured when, in October 1942, they left Thorn in Poland for Stalag 383 (formerly Oflag IIIC). The only bird he mentions is a 'canary' – code for an illicit wireless set – which was stuffed inside the band's big drum and travelled with them to Bavaria.

Friendships in a POW camp were usually intense but, conversely, a combination of boredom, hunger and frustration could turn petty annoyances into a blind hatred. Long after the war my father felt deep shame about the time he 'nearly lost it' in a POW camp. It was his job to cut up the thin slices of heavy 'black bread' for his hut. Every day the loaf was carefully measured and divided into precise sections; a rota was established so that everyone took their share from a different part of the loaf at each mealtime and no one could claim they had had the crust too often. But on one occasion a prisoner started to grumble about his slice. My father was insulted, and exhausted by the man's petulance. He fell on him and grabbed him by the throat, trying to strangle him until he was hauled off by the other men. My father was convinced that if they had not intervened he would have killed a fellow soldier over a slice of black bread.

Sport

Sport was an effective way of relieving aggression and one that the Germans were usually happy to endorse. As well as taking the edge off frustration that might easily escalate into violence, physical exercise, like theatrical performance, was a useful lever – something that the Germans could remove if they needed to inflict punishment. And, like plays and concert parties, sporting fixtures were also events that the guards, who were often just as bored and frustrated as their prisoners, could enjoy.

Competitive sport in a POW camp offered one huge advantage – the potential for endless combinations of teams: the Camp versus the Fort, an inter-room five-a-side football competition, Thames versus Merseyside, Spurs fans against Chelsea supporters, Welsh versus Scots, one battalion against another, or, in Milag, where merchant seamen were held, officers versus ratings and the Engine Room against the Deck. Organising games was a natural part of service life; the only restrictions were energy and the risk of serious injury. If rations were low exercise used up dangerous amounts of calories and became unthinkable when food was so short that climbing stairs left some men breathless and sparked blackouts in others.

I still have a flimsy certificate that my father was awarded as a member of the Barrack 88 team who were runners-up in the inter-barrack, seven-a-side, rugby tournament held at Stalag 357 in May 1944. The team's names are carefully handwritten in black and there is a drawing of a red seal in the bottom right-hand corner. I wonder how my father felt about the irony that, despite having time on his hands, the calligrapher still managed to misspell his surname.

As the Red Cross became aware of the importance of sport in prisoners' lives they sent out cases of kit and equipment that they hoped would meet the needs of a hundred men. As well as bats and balls for different games the box contained a repair kit, lacing awl, extra bladders, pump adaptors and waxed laces. Each item was chosen for its durability and versatility: athletics slips could double as 'bathing drawers' and soccer style shirts were specially designed to be 'tough enough to stand the mauling of Rugger'. The Red Cross was also aware that POWs were adapting traditional games to suit their circumstances or whim; one camp played a game called 'Roccer' or 'Sucker' which was loosely based on football and rugby but, in reality, represented a 'free for all'.

Games had to be modified to suit local circumstances. At Oflag VIB in Warburg the parade ground doubled as the football pitch but, because it was made of fine cinders, players soon learnt that a sliding tackle would skin their legs. At Stalag XXA two teams played a game of cricket at the Sports Platz, a playing field that had been built by the POWs less than a mile from the Fort. Spectators were allowed but each team was permitted only forty-five minutes batting; the players had no gloves or leg guards but, nevertheless, Andrew Hawarden deemed it a success. 'I think a decent team could be selected from the lads who took part.' Players eventually secured pads and gloves but had to play in their slippers.

For the Hon. Terence Prittie, who had been captured at Calais in 1940, cricket made captivity just about bearable. During his five years in POW camps he made six escape attempts but as each of these failed his love of the sport kept him going, as he wrote in January 1944 in an article he submitted to *The Cricketer* whilst still a POW: 'Cricket has been one of the chief compensations in the prisoner of war's life in a vacuum ... Whatever we are missing, we might, after all, be worse off, for with a cricket bat in his hands, the prisoner of war is rather nearer home than at any other moment of his existence.'

At some camps, grounds were so cramped that batting had to be restricted to one end, and in his article Prittie explained that at Oflag IX A/H the officers had to fit a pitch into the setting of a medieval castle perched on a hill. They ruled out the inner courtyard because the tall buildings shut out the light and the floor consisted of protruding cobbles. It was overlooked by windows that would not have survived even a brief 'knock-about'.

The moat, which was 40 feet wide and full of old tin cans and other rubbish, seemed barely any better but in March and April 1942 they levelled it and built a series of flowerbeds and a raised path around it. In places a four-feet-high grass bank sloped down to the lower level and a section of this became the camp cricket ground. 'Imagine yourself to be the batsman at wicket,' Prittie wrote.

> Your view will be as follows: along the whole length of the leg side stretches the outer wall of the moat, 30 feet high and bending round behind the bowler's arm, until it disappears from view behind an out-jutting bastion of the outer wall of the castle itself, and roughly in a line with extra cover. Above this leg-side barrier is the sentry's walk, and beyond that again, flower and vegetable gardens running to the very edge of the small plateau on which the castle system is sited. This outer, or leg-side, wall is no more than eight to ten feet from the wicket; but so gradual is its curve, that from wicket to the straight boundary is over 45 yards. Part of this straight boundary is marked by the built-up line of a vegetable garden, surmounted by a low fence and running out from the buttress ... From half-way across the moat, where the garden comes to an end, a white line prolongs the bound-ary up a slight grassy slope, across a path and through four feet of flowerbed to the opposite wall at a point just behind the protruding bastion. This point, where the boundary line meets the inner wall of the moat, is roughly where deep extra-cover would stand, and from here back to wicket 'A' the lay-out is rather more complicated.

The men started to use the moat even before the flowerbeds had been dug and the raised path finished. At first they used plywood boards propped up with stones for the wickets. They had proper bats but only a limited number of tennis balls and the creases were scratched in the ground. The wicket was made of a three-inch cover of earth levelled over the rubble.

Players soon made wooden stumps with fixed bails and the tennis balls, which tended to bounce very high, were tempered with a covering of Elastoplast which made them easier for the bowler to grip, reduced their bounce and made them more receptive to spin. The covering also pro-longed the life of the tennis ball. They received bats, balls and pads from Holland but it soon became evident that because they had no bat-oil, or similar substitute, the cricket balls would not stand up to continued use and they were forced to revert to a soft ball. Life became easier for the umpires when the POWs found some lime that they mixed with water and used to mark the creases. Teams were forced to wear rubber-soled shoes to protect the ground.

At the start they played a form of cricket called 'tip and run'. As the pitch was so small it was extremely difficult to score runs and only the striker could be ruled out. In order to give as many men as possible a game, an innings was limited to half an hour. Games were played between two and four in the afternoon to cater for men who ate either a late lunch or an early tea.

The usual rules for scoring also had to be adapted for a game played in a moat. It was decided that the flowerbed at third man was out of bounds and, in order to appease the enraged gardeners, one run given for any hit into it. Prittie wrote that a 'slight slice' became the most popular stroke because it avoided the risk of a hit over the castle wall. Teams learnt to hone their tactics as one end favoured left-handed players who struggled at the other because of the angle of shots needed to avoid hitting the castle. The ancient walls kept fielders on their toes as the tennis ball was liable to bounce off it at crazy angles or become lodged in a hole – in which case it was deemed to be 'dead'.

The pitch was used daily in 1942 and 1943 from April to the end of October. Over three quarters of the camp played and half regularly. NCOs, who worked during the week, played an officers' side on Sundays. A team score of 50 was average; 90 was reached often, but never a hundred.

Golf started in a small way at Stalag Luft III, Sagan in Poland in the summer of 1943 when Sidney Smith, a *Daily Express* journalist, received a women's golf club (a wooden-shafted five iron known as a 'mashie') from the Red Cross and started to chip pebbles between the huts. Another enthusiastic golfer, Pat Ward-Thomas, challenged him to a competition to see who could take the fewest shots to hit a tree-stump. The spectacle was enough to ignite interest from other POWs and Sagan Golf Club was born.

The guards lent a spade to help the POWs dig out the roots and stones to make the first 'green' which was covered with sand and which became known as a 'brown'. The holes were between fifty and seventy yards long and a full-time 'brown' keeper was appointed to keep the course clear and the sand smooth. He swept the dirt and sand using a handmade string broom to remove footprints.

Golfers aimed at tins sunk into the ground or tried to hit objects that took the place of the hole – tree stumps, poles for supporting washing lines and electric cables, an incinerator door and an eighteen-inch fir tree. There was much debate over whether hitting the fir's slender trunk counted, or if a glancing blow to a leaf was acceptable. The bunkers were never allowed to be deep enough for an escaper to lie low in and evade search-lights. The first course was 1,220 yards with a par of 55.

The game attracted novices as well as veterans and the club had to pro-duce rules and notes on etiquette. Ward-Thomas started to write accounts of matches for the camp newspaper and in doing so wondered whether he could make a career from sports journalism. He wrote a 14,000 word account of the Sagan Golf Club which the German censors passed and allowed him to send home to the journalist, Henry Longhurst. Although he was unable to get it published an article called 'Extracts from the story of the unique golf club at Stalag Stalag Luft III, Last Summer, by a Flight Lieutenant who was one of its founders' appeared in the Red Cross mag-azine, *The Prisoner of War*, that was sent to next-of-kin. After the war Ward-Thomas became golfing correspondent for the *Guardian*.

As the sport grew in popularity players had to make their own clubs; some melted down lead water jugs or silver cigarette foil to form the head that they attached to a shaft made from the branch of a tree or an ice hockey stick. One Canadian named his club 'Abort Annie' and a musician who was desperate to play but needed a left-handed club made a shaft from the lid-support of a grand piano. (It is surely more remarkable that he had a grand piano, which the POWs may have bought or borrowed from out-side the camp, than that he wanted to use it to fashion a golf club.)

A Danish pen-friend sent Ward-Thomas ten clubs and in the autumn of 1943 he wrote to the Royal and Ancient Golf Club at St Andrew's in Scotland to ask for clubs and balls. The club sent a steel-shafted driver that was too powerful to use with a genuine golf ball in such a confined space and was only used for practice swings. 'I used to feel it longingly and wonder whether I would ever hit a shot with it,' Ward-Thomas mused. He finally had a chance on a winter's day when the camp was deserted and he stole out for a clandestine swing. The ball sailed over the kitchen building and through a hut window where the occupants were so startled that they believed they were being attacked by a sniper and threw themselves on the floor.

Golf tried the patience of both the guards and those of the 700 airmen who preferred other pursuits such as gardening or sunbathing. Although there were no serious injuries at least one tomato plant was beheaded by a low-flying golf ball and the Germans found the activities associated with the sport worryingly similar to another popular activity at Stalag Luft III – escaping. First there was the movement of sand and then there was the habitual problem of wayward balls that frequently strayed into the strip between the inner and outer fences where many golfers risked being shot at rather than wait for permission to retrieve their ball. The guards eventually allowed a system whereby anyone wishing to get their ball from this area would wear a white jacket as proof of 'parole' – that they would not try to escape. 'Germans became used to seeing golf balls sail over the wire; they were very helpful, and it was not an uncommon sight to see a guard using his field glasses to guide some erring golfer to his ball.'

In August golfers bowed to pressure and reduced the course to nine holes – a total of 850 yards with a par of twenty-nine and a longest hole of 140 yards. Within ten days of it opening 300 golfers had been round it. The course record was fifty-seven – presumably taken by someone playing two rounds to make eighteen holes.

But while the golfers were striving to improve their game, Eric Williams and his two companions were hard at work between the wire and the 'sixth brown'. Under the cover of a wooden vaulting horse they spent 114 days digging their way out of the compound. When they escaped at the end of October 1943 the golf course was flattened because the guards assumed the golfers had been in on the plan. The three escapees got back to Britain safely and eventually the Germans were persuaded that Sagan Golf Club had not been involved and it was reinstated. By the winter of 1944 one golfer was already looking back with nostalgia on the club's early days. 'A few mounds covered in snow are the sole evidence that not long ago there was what we liked to call the Sagan Golf Club, where for seven months during a strange summer we found entertainment, exercise, and something akin to happiness.'

At Colditz the football ground, which was outside the castle, provided the means for escape when six Dutch inmates hid under a manhole and slipped away at nightfall. Prisoners got round the lack of exercise space at the castle by inventing their very own game, 'stoolball', a no-holds-barred, madcap contest inspired by public school tradition in which the architecture, anything from jutting out bits of masonry to stone steps, became part of the 'court'. Players could run with the ball or bounce it off the granite wall. A goal was scored when someone from one team (there could be as many as thirty aside) managed to touch the ball on their opponent's stool which was guarded by a goalkeeper at either end of the courtyard. There were no referees, no touchlines and no rules about physical intimidation. Pat Reid described stoolball, played on the unforgiving Colditz cobbles, as 'the roughest game' he had ever experienced.

Andrew Hawarden lived for sport and he only really started to settle into life as a *Kriegie* once it became possible at Stalag XXA, Fort XVII. In the early months of captivity he recorded in his diary the formation of a camp orchestra – a ragbag of instruments including a piano accordion, mouth organ, mess tins and spoons. By the end of September 1940 a thousand men were squeezing into a room that should have held three hundred to hear a concert by the band, which now included a guitar. But, as far as Hawarden was concerned, the most important distraction arrived on Saturday 21 September 1940:

> The football which came from the YMCA has come into service with quite a number of lads just enjoying a 'kick about', not having a suitable piece of ground to play any matches on. So, we shall just have to be content with just kicking the ball about. If it takes on I wouldn't be surprised if we didn't ask the Germans to take us to a suitable piece of ground outside the camp where we could enjoy playing a few games in between the companies, under guard, of course.

At first, sporting equipment was scarce. He told the Red Cross representative when he visited Stalag XXA in November 1940 that they were sharing two footballs between 23,000 men and, after watching a game in March 1941, he noted: 'They would all have played much better, had they possessed football boots and something like a decent strip.'

As the YMCA and Red Cross began to send a variety of sporting implements, bats, different types of balls, boxing gloves, fencing foils and other equipment *Kriegies* across Europe started to play an astonishing range of games from hockey and rugby to softball (a version of baseball played with a larger ball) and volleyball.

POWs at 383 played sports with a brio that worried the Senior British

Officer who was constantly trying to assess whether the morale-boosting effects of physical activity outweighed the risks. In some camps contact sports were banned because of the strain injuries put on medical supplies. In March 1943 Hawarden reported that the rugby league at Stalag 383 had been suspended after a catalogue of broken limbs and one dislocated shoulder. Medics were kept so busy that they put up a sign at the entrance to the treatment room that read 'Rugby injuries this way'. But, despite the risks, all kinds of sports thrived at 383 including violent pastimes such as boxing, wrestling and judo, as well as more temperate games like basketball and hockey. Terry Frost favoured the high jump. Those who did not like team games could keep fit in the gym, where a vaulting horse was constructed from a barrel, palliasse covers, the string from Red Cross parcels and odd pieces of wood, or use the pool, which stood ready to douse fires, for swimming. It was twenty-two yards by eleven and six feet deep which made it suitable for international galas, swimming lessons and water polo. Over 200 men put their names down for lifesaving classes and in the summer some men took up residence in the pool, staying there from five in the morning until eleven at night. In winter it became an ice skating rink (the Red Cross provided skates), while water was sprayed on to the basketball pitch so that it froze and could be used for ice hockey.

The type of game played at 383 was limited only by the imagination of the players. On June 1, 1944 Hawarden wrote: 'Take a walk round our Sports Platz when the organised games are on any evening and you will be lucky if you get away without being hit by a football, cricket ball, golf ball or soft ball (not too soft when one gets hit quite unexpectedly).'

As a former professional, Hawarden's overriding passion was football but his sporting tastes were eclectic. The different nationalities of his fellow POWs allowed him to observe new sports, like soft ball introduced by the Canadians, and provided the impetus for different contests including a Highland Games and Anzac Day Sports Day. 'Our lads just got the better of an exciting game [of netball against the French]', he wrote in 1941, and a homemade table tennis table, which was not quite the regulation size, led to a tournament between the French, Poles and British in which some 'v decent players' showed their talent. In the summer, traditional rivalries among New Zealanders and Australians added a frisson of excitement to cricket matches and when, during the winter months, they tobogganed down slopes on bits of wood and upturned benches it was the first time many Antipodeans had seen snow. The spectacle became even more sur-real when a chain of twenty men squatted to slide down the one-in-ten gradient on their shoes, while others perched on broom handles like sledg-ing witches.

Hawarden was also very interested in cricket and his men sometimes called him 'Ranji' – the popular, shortened form of Kumar Shri Ranjitsinhji, one of the most famous cricketers of the early twentieth cen-tury and the first Indian to play cricket for England. He probably earned the nickname through his ability to mimic Ranji's famous 'leg glance' shot or another movement of similar economy but there were other similari-ties. They both had piercing eyes, thin lips and a long nose – although the Indian had the addition of a dandyish Edwardian moustache. The first Ranji was a dapper dresser with a charisma that could draw people from shops to any street that he walked down. Hawarden, who was fascinated by sporting records, would have been more impressed by the first class cricket statistics next to his name: his ten centuries and 2,780 runs in 1896, his five double centuries in 1900 when no one had previously scored more than two in a season and his unprecedented two centuries in the same match on the same day.

Hawarden spent much of his time as a POW filling exercise books and scraps of paper with sporting statistics, league tables and the results of the fixtures he helped to organise, or which he attended as a spectator, and which became more and more ambitious. On St Patrick's Day, 1941 an Irish football team drew 4-4 with a Scottish side; a sports day later that year pro-duced a torrent of statistics and he noted down the times for each type of swimming stroke and distance in the Empire Aquatic Sports Day of July 1944.

While other POWs were finding solace in writing poetry he turned his mind to the beautiful game and how other countries interpreted it. Under the title 'Some football facts which are rather interesting' he wrote: 'Smaller ball used on Continent; No Chipping goalkeeper; Substitution.'

His diary took the place of the man who might have been standing next to him in a football crowd at home or sharing a pint with him in his local pub. It became the place where he chewed over performances and behaviour; a substitute for the genuine terrace talk denied him. Refereeing was something he felt particularly strongly about: 'A football match at the Camp, between the Camp and a combined team from Fort and Camp – a very good game which was inclined to be spoiled by an inefficient referee. The camp won 4–1. They were the better team. The military band played for an hour before the start and again during the interval.'

The topic cropped up again on Sunday, April 5 1942:

This is my impression of basketball: – First and foremost those people who complain at home of too much Referee's whistle at soccer matches have never seen a basketball match refereed by a Frenchman. In both games there was never a period of seven seconds played without the whistle going for something or another. The more he blew the whistle, the better the Referee enjoyed it. To me, he was out to draw attention more to himself than to the game. He dressed in a pink and light blue striped jersey, light khaki stockings, light blue knicks, and kind of cycling boots with red ribbons around the tops with a broad white belt. Frenchmen say he's a good ref ... I seem to think that France will be the eventual winner, especially if this ref. takes charge of all the matches.

This particular fixture had a tragic postscript, a reminder that, despite the pretence, this was sport behind barbed wire. The Polish entry was cancelled at the last minute because, 'Unfortunately, eleven of them were taken to Danzig for trial [accused of killing a German guard]. Three of them got shot and the other eight got five years each.'

The attack on the German was a rare incident; as Hawarden commented: 'A notable thing being mentioned by several men on the working parties is the good camaraderie between the German guards and our lads ... It's a common thing to see a Tommy pull a photo out of a Polish or German girl.' He added that many of the guards were extremely short and were equivalent to Germany's Home Guard, rather than the Nazis' crack fighting troops, and perhaps that made them less intimidating and easier to befriend. Occasionally, the war appears to have been forgotten altogether, as happened during a Sunday football match when Hawarden noticed that one of the 'Gerries', who was watching the game, was called over by another guard who was 800 yards away, outside the camp. A POW grasped the situation instantly and helpfully pointed out a gap in the barbed wire where the guard could pop through, rather than walk the long way round.

David Wild, a padre at Stalag XXA, reported a similar example of POWs rushing to the aid of their captors. In June 1944 he was taking a party of medical orderlies for a dip in a large quarry pit a mile and a half from the fort. Suddenly their guard, who was quite elderly, staggered and appeared to be unwell. The POWs were reluctant to miss their swim and decided to help him along; one man carried his rifle for him while the local Polish people looked on in amazement. Once they reached the quarry they made him comfortable in the shade while they swam.

The Germans regularly attended concerts, theatrical productions and other events put on in the camp and the POWs respected the Commandant who had served in the Great War and had had an arm amputated while he was a POW in Manchester. When he brought his daughter with him to a camp concert and boxing exhibition, Hawarden noted how strange it was to hear the compere say, '*ladies* [my italics] and gentlemen'. Several German soldiers invited their wives to the stalag band competition and the females 'made the day look more cheerful'.

Hawarden's passion for football provided a potent link with home that was reinforced by the results he garnered from a hidden wireless. Other fans inundated their clubs with requests for news of their favourite players; Arsenal Football Club in particular was swamped with letters from POWs in Germany. But in their absence, professional football had become a very different game. In order to accommodate the loss of men who had been called up, teams could use 'guest players', men who found themselves stationed near a club other than their own, and petrol rationing meant leagues were based on geographical regions, rather than meritocracy, so that teams did not have to travel far. It was not uncommon for players to arrive late for a game because their train had been delayed. These new arrangements led to odd pairings – Arsenal versus Aldershot, for example, and outlandishly high scores (such as West Ham's 11–0 trouncing of Hawarden's old club, Southend United in October 1940) as strikers and defenders alike, perhaps freed from the threat of relegation and feeling a duty to entertain, produced double digit goals.

My father remembers how the routine of Saturday afternoon games played on muddy Scottish pitches haunted one of his fellow prisoners. In peacetime he had worked for a newspaper where his job was to transcribe all the football results as they flooded in. At roughly the moment when the deluge would have started in the newspaper office, so my father recalls, the man would suffer blinding headaches as the tension of another life returned to torment him.

Hawarden felt the absence of the Bolton Wanderers players keenly and when, at the end of December 1940, a staff sergeant told him that two players were among the POWs held at Fort XIII he persuaded the Germans to allow him to visit. It was a depressing experience. He arrived under armed guard, a few days before his wedding anniversary, and harbouring the beginnings of bronchial pneumonia. As they waited outside the fort he knew as soon as he saw the soldier that he was not to be reunited with any of the team:

> I asked him who he was and why he was impersonating this player. He said he had played as a part professional. He came from Atherton. I asked him about the person who was supposed to be Ray W. and he said he was a cousin of Ray. Apparently, these two have been kidding the troops that they are two of the present Bolton Wanderers' team. Unfortunately, the guard at the gate was getting a bit windy and, in other words, he asked us to close the conversation.

It seems that at least one of the men may have continued the deception because in June 1944 David Wild noted in his diary meeting someone who had played for Bolton Wanderers. Given the extremes to which some men went to in order to stand out in the anonymity of a POW camp, the appeal of impersonating a sporting hero is, perhaps, understandable. There is no doubt, too, that playing side-by-side with professionals provided a thrill for the ordinary *Kriegie*. When else in life would they have the chance to compete with, or against, top class sportsmen such as Queen Park Rangers' goalkeeper, Reg Allen, who was held in several camps after his first escape attempt, and the Norwegian Johnny (Jan) Staubo, who was at Stalag Luft III and later played tennis for his country.

Although Hawarden spent several months in the sick bay at Stalag 383, when he was fit enough he poured his energy into improving facilities and organising competitions of his beloved soccer. In March 1943 there were only two sets of soccer kits, minus the boots, to share among 4,000 men and many games were held in which the opposing sides were distinguished only as 'skins' and 'vests'. Dubbin and laces were hard to come by and teams had to use margarine to grease the ball. Hawarden wrote to Bolton

Wanderers and his local newspapers to ask for any spare kit. He also persuaded the guards that they needed picks and spades to convert the outside parade ground into a pitch. The Germans were naturally suspicious that they would be used for tunnelling. They had already banned darts because the board might conceal maps or tools and had confiscated the rope for tug-of-war in case it was used for escape purposes. However, once the POWs had cleared the ground of stones the Germans provided a roller to level it and became regular members of the crowd. The final touches were made by whitening the goalposts with German toothpaste, which Hawarden pronounced 'about the best use for it'. Finally, someone risked being shot at by climbing onto the ground one night to erect a board that declared the name of the pitch – 'Burnden Park', Bolton Wanderers' home ground. The England–Scotland game was always a 'thriller' and bagpipers piped the two teams on to the pitch to intensify the sense of occasion.

If, as in the case of mountaineering, being in a POW camp meant that a prisoner could not indulge in his particular sport he talked about it instead. As a young man Bill Murray had developed a passion for climbing; as a POW he found solace in his memories of those days of freedom in the Scottish mountains and in the bond he felt with other climbers. That bond had even helped him when he was first captured.

In June 1942 he was crouched in a slit trench in the North African desert with the 2nd Battalion Highland Light Infantry (HLI). The HLI had lost 600 men and Murray had seen, too closely, the horror of warfare. At one point, he turned to speak to his 'runner' only to find the man's lower trunk perched on his legs, what was left of the body smoking at the waist, no sign of his trunk or head. He had not heard the blast that reduced his comrade to a collection of body parts.

His company had twice been hit by friendly fire and he was surrounded by burnt-out vehicles and charred human remains. He had been told to delay the advance of the German 15th Panzer Division to allow British artillery to withdraw east in a bid to save Egypt but his commanding officer had been blunt about his chances, telling him: 'Murray, by tonight you'll be either dead meat or a prisoner.'

As he waited in his slit trench he went through his personal belongings destroying anything that might be of use to the enemy: his prismatic compass, ID card, notes and his address book. The names of fellow mountaineers conjured up memories of climbs he had made in Scotland and may have prompted his reply to the German tank commander who approached him early next morning. The officer walked towards him nervously, a pistol shaking in his hand, and asked him if he was cold. Murray's response instantly changed the tone of the encounter: "'It's cold as a mountain top." He looked me straight in the eye, "Good God, do you climb mountains?"'

When the German discovered they were both mountaineers he relaxed, put his gun away and gave Murray a coat, some bully beef, biscuits and a slab of chocolate. They talked about the Alps, Scotland and climbing on rock and ice. They toasted 'mountains' and 'mountaineers' over a bottle of beer. When the Italian infantry arrived to relieve the German they tried to take the Rolex watch Murray had bought in Cairo but the German ordered them to give it back.

As a POW he again turned to climbing and when he was moved to Stalag VIIA at Moosburg, near Munich, he set up a mountaineering club, which he advertised through the camp noticeboard; the only requirement for joining was that new members had to be able to give a talk about mountains. Alastair Cram, whom Murray had first encountered on Glen Coe, was one of the first members; Cram was to make a total of twenty-nine escape attempts and clearly the mountaineering club was another bid to leave the prison behind. Their camp was surrounded by dense forest but beyond that were the snow-capped foothills of the Bavarian Alps. Other club members came from England, New Zealand, Canada and South Africa and delivered lectures that Murray believed were all the more vivid because they had to rely on their memory.

Sport provided a source of endless discussion. It cropped up as a topic in the debating society meetings that became popular in many camps. Hawarden recorded themes that ranged from 'Has Youth too Much to Say for Itself ?', 'Country versus Town Life', 'Is Capital Punishment Justified?' and 'Theatre versus Cinema?' and included two subjects close to his heart: 'Are We too Fond of Sport?' and 'Amateurs v Professionals'. Arguments over rules and sporting trivia were batted backwards and forward between bunk beds after lights-out in frustrating exchanges that rarely reached a conclusion. The POWs were like a group of holidaymakers who argue over the meaning of a word or a country's capital city and whose curiosity will only be sated once they find a good library. In May 1942, the FA received a postcard from Stalag VIIIB, north west of Krakow, in which POWs asked them to settle a dispute over how many times Arsenal had met Walsall in the FA Cup. The British Red Cross reported a constant demand for rule books for several different sports and that the Football Association's Referees' Chart was hugely popular among POWs who wanted to settle debates over what was or was not a goal.

At school and university Terence Prittie had always enjoyed the mental exercise of 'team-picking'– indulging in the fantasy of selecting the best possible cricket side – but when he was captured in June 1940 it proved the most valuable 'mental stand-by'. In the early months when he had no books to read and very little to do, he and some other keen cricketers would pick their 'World XI', all-time England, Australian and South African sides. Next they moved on to first class counties and then universities that they sub-divided into ten-year periods from 1880 onwards (which was as far back as their knowledge would allow). Finally, they chose teams based around the letters of the alphabet.

Ray Beal, who was at Stalag XXA at the same time as Hawarden, remembers an argument over the cricketing question of whether a man who was stumped after a no-ball when he was out of his ground was stumped or run out. Another vexing question was whether a drowned man floated down the river on his back or his stomach. One POW remembered from somewhere that Mark Twain's opinion was that the corpse faced down (he may have been thinking of a scene in *Huckleberry Finn*). These sorts of conundrums summed up camp life. While at home they were entertaining diversions over which to pass an hour before someone turned up with the *Wisden Cricketers' Almanack* or more pressing concerns intervened, in a camp such unanswerable questions had an insidious way of highlighting the distance between captivity and freedom.

6

Uses for a Red Cross Parcel
Number 2 – Cigarettes

The power of Allied cigarettes in central Europe during the war was
staggering – they became a currency. A non-smoker could save up his
Red Cross cigarettes and become a clean-lunged tycoon.

Clive Dunn, *Permission to Speak*

Smoking was ubiquitous among Allied servicemen during the Second
World War; it helped to pass the time and many friendships began over a
hand cupped round a shared match. 'Let it suffice to note that anyone in
the services who did not smoke cigarettes was looked on as a freak,' wrote
the American historian and Second World War veteran, Paul Fussell.

In the 1940s smoking was a pastime uninhibited by health concerns but
in a POW camp it was an addiction that gave men who could not shed the
habit another layer of vulnerability. For these men craving tobacco was as
painful as craving food and in some instances, such was their desperation,
they would trade food for cigarettes. They scoured the ground for discarded cigarette butts (although throwing away any part of a cigarette
came to be seen as a sign of decadence) and offered to empty enemy ash-
trays in order to salvage titbits to roll up for a second smoke. When
Andrew Hawarden was in hospital during a particularly lean period for
smokers he noticed patients turning their beds upside down and banging
the hollow metal frame on the ground to extract fag ends discarded there
in less straitened times.

POWs in both Europe and the Far East (where shortages were more
severe) fashioned ersatz cigarettes from whatever was available. Pages

from the Bible or reference books such as *Pears Encyclopaedia* were popular because the paper was particularly thin. Recipe pages or descriptions of food were the last to go up in smoke because POWs derived a quasi-pornographic pleasure from reading about something that they spent so long dreaming of. In the absence of tobacco, smokers stuffed their roll-ups with dried leaves, coffee grounds, grass, peppermint or even manure. Hawarden often saw POWs prepare 'smokes' from dried tree bark that had been ground and then wrapped in a page torn from a prayer book. While these homemade efforts may not have produced a tobacco-induced 'high' the POW could at least pretend that he was holding a precious cigarette.

The British Red Cross was quick to recognise the needs of smokers and aimed to send each man a weekly supply of fifty cigarettes (or 2oz tobacco); double this at Christmas. From the beginning of 1941 until the end of March 1945 it sent 6,129,504oz tobacco and almost 1.5 billion cigarettes to Italy and Germany through the International Red Cross Committee at Geneva. At first, both the British Red Cross and its American equivalent included cigarettes in the main parcel but the British Red Cross soon switched to a separate delivery in tins. Family, friends, former work places and military units also sent cigarettes to POWs via tobacco companies who held special permits.

On 14 February 1944 (presumably the date was significant) John Phillips wrote to Philippa:

My dear P Thank you so much for sending me my biggest cigarette parcel to date (500 PM de luxe): at the same time I must rebuke you for spending so much on me. They must cost a small fortune nowadays. My friend, Robert MacGill (7th Hussars) and I pool our cigarettes, etc., and your parcel came at a most opportune time when the stock was low – we're both very grateful.

Occasionally other sources helped out (the British Community Council of the Argentine included cigarettes among the items they sent to POWs) but prisoners were creatures of habit and preferred familiar brands like Woodbine, Players and Craven A rather than foreign alternatives. It was only as a last resort that a POW might accept a Polish or French cigarette from another prisoner.

For anyone who was not a committed smoker the cigarettes represented a regular bonus, as Canadian doctor, Allen Graham remembered:

I didn't smoke cigarettes very much. I smoked a pipe. In the British parcels there was some very good pipe tobacco, Players . . . and I feel guilty about this too. I had a stack of them about two feet high, of tins of Players, and I can't remember whether I smoked it all myself – it all disappeared – or I gave some away or not. Cigarettes, of course, were worth their weight in gold. The Germans wanted them. You could get stuff in the black market, they would smuggle stuff – silk stockings were a great thing. They actually were, the silk stockings were in great demand. If you had a pair you'd get quite a lot for them. Food we're talking about.

Unlike *Lagergeld*, most things could be bought with cigarettes and most Germans could be bribed. A POW at Stalag 383 confidently asserted that it was possible to buy a Luger for 500 cigarettes. Andrew Hawarden described how cigarettes were offered as prizes in competitions and that Father Christmas gave them out to sick POWs. Ten cigarettes bought an advert in the 'wanted and for sale' section of *The Yorkshire Post – Kriegie edition* which had a 'guaranteed circulation of 350'.

The value of cigarettes rose and fell depending on their availability and the economist R.A. Radford, who was a POW in Italy and Germany, studied the part they played in the business of a camp. After the war he published an article called *The Economic Organisation of a POW Camp*, which is still occasionally quoted by academics today. In it he describes how in permanent camps a sophisticated 'Exchange and Mart' usually evolved in which items were marked up on a blackboard and crossed off after deals were done. Other POWs were willing to offer services in return for a smoke – laundrymen charged two cigarettes a garment or would scrub and press battledress and hire out a pair of trousers in return for twelve cigarettes; a good pastel portrait cost thirty cigarettes. A coffee stallholder sold tea, coffee and cocoa for two cigarettes a cup and employed someone to gather fuel and stoke the fire. He even had an accountant but finally overreached himself and collapsed with debts of several hundred cigarettes.

Every POW knew the market rate for a cigarette and as the war progressed only food and cigarettes held their value. When in March 1945

Allied bombing was making it difficult for supplies to get through, Hawarden noted that 2,000 cigarettes cost £380, a watch was worth thirty cigarettes, a gold ring twenty. One cigarette could buy a safety razor, boot polish or toothpaste. A few weeks earlier the going rate for a cigarette tin full of salt was ten cigarettes. At Stalag VIIIB, Lamsdorf a sunny Whitsun carnival in 1944 produced 'takings' of 61,000 cigarettes; the profits were spent on the camp comforts fund for hospital patients, new prisoners and musical instruments.

But cigarettes were not always used for altruistic causes. Gambling was a popular way of relieving boredom and cigarettes provided the most obvious 'chips'. Despite their confines POWs became adept at finding reasons to place a bet.

'Some of the lads have got gambling fever', Andrew Hawarden wrote on 29 June 1941 before describing a 'horse race' in which riders moved along a course depending on the roll of the dice. There were bookmakers and a quarter of wagers went to the Fort Welfare Fund. Australians would sit on top of the Fort so that they could gamble on the direction of the next train to arrive at Thorn railway station. POWs would bet on anything and everything. At Fontanellato some of the inmates, who were part of the upper class coterie, raced corks down a tiny stream that trickled through the exercise field or put money on other POWs in a mile race. Many bet on Eric Newby to win but he miscounted the number of laps and came third. At a camp in Germany, Terry Frost, who became famous after the war as an abstract artist, acted as bookie for a competition to see who could eat their potatoes fastest.

Football pools operated in a similar way: the number from the first shake of the dice denoted the home team's score, the second shake related to the away club; a matching number meant a draw. POWs bet on sporting events held in the camp and German guards frequently joined in. In some camps jockeys raced round on human horses; in animal versions mice, earwigs, beetles and frogs were urged round the course, although they rarely did as they were told and sometimes attacked each other. At the camp in Barth, men bet on how long bluebottles with loads attached by thread to their tiny bodies could stay airborne. In other camps prisoners built miniature racetracks on tables and moved wooden horses on the throw of a dice. Stalag Luft VI's '*Flieger* Jockey Club' employed horses cast in lead and painted in bright colours. The meeting was part of a Gala Day which produced 76,000 cigarettes for the communal Cigarette Fund.

Developments in the war were usually worth a punt. The most talked-about date was, of course, the end of hostilities and men usually bet on a period of less than six months. For Cy Grant, the black airman who was held in Stalag Luft III, this was 'Long enough to maintain reasonable hope but not too long a period to endure'. There were other milestones – an Allied landing in Europe, or when a certain country would enter the conflict or change sides. On 24 February 1945 Hawarden bet fifty cigarettes that Turkey would appear on the Allied side on 1 March 1945. As POWs dared to hope that the end was in sight they placed bets on who would liberate them – the Russians, British or Americans?

At Hawarden's second camp, Stalag 383, bookies would accept bets on most sports and advertised their odds on brightly coloured posters. Australians introduced 'two-up', a game played either with coins or dice, and the main camp square was given over to the event. More esoteric games flourished in oflags where POWs had more time. The rattle of dice and the shuffle of pieces on a backgammon board provided an almost constant soundtrack to life at Fontanellato. In the cellar, members of White's Club cleared the big table used for meals and set it up for baccarat. They used the letter cards intended for their next of kin as cheques and sent them to each other's bankers on settlement day.

Most camps had several packs of cards – sent by the Red Cross – and played a range of games from bridge and gin rummy to poker. One camp in Italy produced a set of playing cards out of Craven A cigarette packets. Cards were popular because they were portable, and contract bridge, in particular, could use up a whole day. They were also used by MI9 to insert maps that might be useful for escapers. Some chess sets and the board game Monopoly were also tampered with to a similar end. 'An Ajax Chessman' set that carried the words 'Patent Applied for', together with a large full stop on the box, indicated the game concealed escape aids.

Just as in real life, gambling was not always a harmless distraction. Some POWs ran up huge debts of cigarettes and others wrote IOUs for financial sums that could be collected after the war. According to family tradition, Jock Hamilton-Baillie, an inveterate escaper who ended up in Colditz, 'won' his future wife, the sister of a fellow POW, in a game of cards.

'Stalag Happy' – Imaginary Worlds and Other Ways of Escape

Terry Frost first came across the power of a POW's imagination at Stalag 383 when someone asked him, 'What do you think of my duck?' . . . 'He hadn't got one at all . . . you had to play along.'

This was not an isolated incident of a POW who had decided to escape the harsh reality of captivity by stepping into an invented world. Later Frost came across someone who was convinced he was riding a horse around the drab setting of Stalag 383. Perhaps it was this very drabness that made invention so necessary.

Stalag 383 had none of the grandeur of Colditz or the idiosyncratic charm of Fontanellato. It sat in a hollow with a few pine trees in the distance; in winter a thick layer of snow covered the ground and swirls of white smoke hung over the clusters of grey buildings. The huts, which squatted uneasily in the mud, looked as if they were about to collapse under the weight of the clothes lines strung between them, although their precariousness was more likely to stem from the careful filleting of wooden planks from walls and ceilings. Stovepipes peeped out of each roof at a jaunty angle against a backdrop of barbed wire. Men lent against the huts or sauntered down the dirt walkways with their hands deep in their pockets, most of the year wearing thick jumpers or various assortments of clothes to protect them against the bracing Bavarian air.

But while Stalag 383 *looked* like a drab shanty town it was alive with all sorts of activity driven by an energy that teetered on the edge of, and occasionally tipped over into, insanity. Stalag 383 was for NCOs who refused to work. Technically they were not obliged to work, although the

Germans tried very hard to make them. These POWs came from other camps in Poland, Germany and Austria and included among their number were professional actors, musicians, sportsmen and journalists each keen to show off their talents. It was as if the threat of boredom released a special kind of creativity and bred an unusual form of confidence among the 6,000 or so men who lived there.

'This is a queer gaol, this Hohenfels', a German censor was said to have commented. 'The French walk about as though they own the place. We Germans like to think that *we* own it. And the British don't give a damn *who* owns it. They just run it how they like – and *patronise* everybody.'

Another POW writing in *Behind Barbed Wire*, a collection of reminiscences about Stalag 383 compiled by journalists and sold after the war, claimed that some guards had 'assumed the status of attendants at a holiday camp' and were busy shopping, carrying out chores and fetching cricket balls for the inmates who made them click their heels and 'Heil Churchill' before handing over cigarettes. 'The whole camp went absolutely what they call 'stalag happy' ... finishing up with a big hunt which went through the camp and the hunting horn was blown, and ... the fox went through the pool, which was the fire pool, so the riders went straight through full-dressed, out the other side.'

An even more elaborate charade followed in which they set up a regular, twice daily, train service to England. Departure times were announced throughout the camp and POWs were warned to be on time and to have their tickets ready. At the appointed hour, whistles were blown, men pushed their way through carrying their kitbag or suitcase, tickets were handed over at the barrier and passengers jostled for a window seat, some craning their necks to watch the late arrivals and urge them on with shouts of encouragement. Frost polished his cap badge, put on his best clothes with a sharp crease in his trousers and ordered a taxi. Two men arrived with a blanket over their backs and he climbed on to be taken to the imaginary train. A man in a straw hat leaned out shouting, 'Goodbye, goodbye'. 'It was wonderful to go to Blighty,' Frost remembers. These imaginary excursions seem particularly poignant because they indicate a desperate, communal homesickness.

The train was just one feature of what became known as 'Crazy Week' at Stalag 383. German guards were treated to men dressed as Napoleon, a cock-hatted Nelson gazing through a telescope and painted North American Indians whooping their way round the perimeter fence. Other POWs appeared on a stifling parade ground in coats and balaclavas. How much this behaviour was a genuine sign of instability and how much was simply prompted by boredom and a wish to unsettle the guards is debatable. The Germans were worried enough to consult one of the POW doctors. However, the Australian had been given advance warning and did his best to confirm that he too had succumbed by playing marbles under the table with his assistant before starting a game of imaginary table tennis. 'It was wonderful stalag happiness,' Frost remembers.

At Stalag 383 and other camps men retreated to a make-believe world of their childhood. They got dressed to walk an imaginary dog on a string that they pulled along behind them, herded imaginary sheep, rode a make-believe bike, marched to a band that was nowhere to be seen or played imaginary marbles or snooker with such a convincing air of authority that bystanders would be drawn into the game, while the guards stood by muttering 'verrückt' (mad). Airmen ran with their arms outstretched, swooping and diving and imitating the sound of an aeroplane engine. Others pretended to be small boys squabbling over a kite who kicked each other until one finally collapsed in tears.

But many POWs were keen to avoid such strange behaviour. Ray Beal recognised the importance of filling every waking hour and after a day of rehearsals and studying for his salesmanship and office management exams wrote in his diary on 4 February 1943: 'I am becoming more and more busy, as days go by I am glad. I am mentally far more healthy and have come to the conclusion that the best way to escape "Barbedwireitus" is to have as much to occupy your mind as possible.'

In a very few cases POWs feigned insanity as a way of securing repatriation but this carried the risk that the pretence might become second nature. At Stalag Luft III Paddy Byrne succeeded in convincing his guards that he was mad and instructed others in the deceit at a 'Lunacy School'. The Stalag 383 Commandant certainly believed his charges were slipping towards insanity and sent for the Senior British Officer to suggest walks under parole outside the camp in an attempt to alleviate the symptoms.

Occasionally a genuine psychological problem assumed a physical form and doctors drew on their own imagination to solve the problem.

Robin Hunter, for example, was walking round a camp with a Canadian rear gunner who confided that he was suffering from a mist in front of his eyes:

> It was just driving him squirrelly because he found he couldn't read, though he had all the time in the world. I looked at him and saw he had a very long proboscis indeed, and it was very keeled over to one side. I took my finger and pushed it in the mid-line. The mist disappeared. He was enormously grateful. Well of course it had been there all his life but he never noticed it.

When an eye specialist from Liverpool, Major David Charters, arrived at Kloster Haina, a camp which held blind POWs, he discovered that two men were not technically blind but that some psychological trauma had robbed them of the ability to see. Both had lived as blind men for a year and a half. Charters decided a mock operation might jolt them back to normality. He told the Germans he was going to perform surgery and put the two patients through the very painful procedure of injecting them in the side of the eye with water. When they came round they were told the operation had been a success but that they had to lie on their back for ten days. Gradually their sight returned.

Although a few desperate men committed suicide by goading the guards into shooting them for breaching the trip wire, clinical depression was rare. However, it was a constant worry among POWs that they might be 'going round the bend'. My father told me how one man sat for hour after hour with his arm in the air for no apparent reason, as if constantly asking for an unseen teacher to answer his question. Others re-lived battles and felt guilty that they had survived, as Hunter remembers: 'There was an enormous amount of guilt floating around over how it happened that one came to be a prisoner. You know the dirty side of the war. People aren't always brave or strong or any of that crap. Some guys didn't get there in ways that they'd want their parents to know about.'

Camaraderie helped to pull most through but occasionally one strong personality could crush a less robust man. 'There were some pathological people, very pathological – psychopathic a lot of them, including Douglas Bader, who was a menace,' Hunter recalls.

He drove a friend of mine crazy, actually psychotic, and he had to be repatriated through Geneva. This was a sensitive fellow ... But Bader gave him orders to fill a bucket with night soil and put it in such a way over the doorframe that when the guard opened the door at night this thing descended upon him, and to my friend it was such a humiliation – he was a very well-bred and well-brought-up Englishman. He couldn't stand it, he just went bonkers and became delusional and started to hallucinate and they repatriated him through the Swiss.

Most men, though, avoided anything more serious than mild depression by pouring their energy into one activity that absorbed their thoughts. A Guards' officer whom Hunter met survived by concentrating on outward appearance, while at the same time imagining the Germans away.

He was always spruce and dapper, and I made a friend of him because I was always curious about him. One day we were walking along the perimeter and I said to him, 'Bill, you know it's very noticeable that you're beautifully turned out, your Sam Browne [belt] is polished, everything is just perfect. How do you do it?' He said, 'Frankly old chap, I refuse to admit the existence of the bloody Hun.'

Uses for a Red Cross Parcel
Number 3 – Tins

> The pumps weren't any good without air pipe lines, but the engineers had been making these out of powdered milk tins from Red Cross parcels ... The tins were about four inches in diameter, and the engineers peeled off the bottoms, leaving a clean metal cylinder. Where the lids had fitted, the tins were a shade smaller in circumference, and this section fitted very neatly into the base of the next tin. The joint was wrapped tightly with paper and was strong and airtight enough because once the pipelines were laid they were never touched. They made yards and yards of the piping and smuggled it down the shafts.
>
> Paul Brickhill, *The Great Escape*

The average Red Cross parcel might contain as many as eleven tins of various shapes and sizes, plus cigarettes or tobacco that arrived separately. The tins of biscuits, vegetables, puddings, margarine, sugar, jam, dried eggs, condensed milk, sardines or herrings, processed cheese, meat roll and cocoa powder were potent reminders of home. Brand names like Spam, Nestlé, Rowntree, Peek Frean, Crosse & Blackwell and Colman's evoked slightly different memories for each man – perhaps of high tea or tiffin, picnics in the park or Sunday school outings. Indeed, some POWs found the labels, which might show a leaping salmon or a slab of luncheon meat, so enticing that they stuck them in their logbooks to drool over in quiet moments.

The tin only came into its own once every last slither of food had been scraped out and enjoyed. It was one of the few sources of metal available to the POW and its durability and malleability were put to good use in a huge range of products. Metal cut from a cocoa tin made the ferrule on Terry Frost's brush; he mixed oil from a tin of sardines to produce paint and when he was allowed outside the camp he returned with flowers that he arranged in a red and white Canadian butter tin and then painted. The British Red Cross produced a helpful leaflet written by The Metal Box Company, who had produced the containers in the first place, called *Useful Articles from Empty Tins, Hints on How to Make Them*. The thirty-one page booklet offered tips on techniques including lacquering, soldering, punching holes and cutting tin plate and suggestions about how to use the tins. It urged POWs to try making kitchen utensils such as a multiple frying pan, drinking mug, coffee pot, pastry cutter and spoon and personal effects like a shaving mug, comb case, letter rack, picture frame, and clothes peg. Tins could be used for planting seeds and watering thirsty plants like tomatoes, for making seed markers, trowels or even a sundial. They were useful in stage productions – for shading lights, making artificial trees or armour plating for costumes. They could be fashioned into dominoes, chess pieces, skittles or quoits, or a xylophone. Tins were the ideal material from which to make a mousetrap, ashtray, brooch, spectacles case, candlestick, soap tray or even a handwarmer.

POWs took out their frustration on tins that they hammered and bent into plates, cooking pots, holes for the golf course at Stalag Luft III and the ubiquitous metal mug. At Clive Dunn's camp, Stalag XVIIIA, the theatre spotlights were made from flattened tins and in Stalag Luft III they were essential in the ventilation system that allowed the Great Escape tunnellers to breath. The most coveted receptacle was the tin sent by the Canadian Red Cross which, when stripped of its yellow and brown label and fitted with a handle, could hold more than a pint of liquid. The tins originally contained powdered milk and were called Klim (milk spelt backwards). At Stalag 383 the Klim tin was even used to make clogs. Men like Frost's roommate, 'Smudger', became skilled at converting tins into homemade stills or stoves. A particularly popular device that appeared in several camps was a 'blower' (or *stufa*) which was used primarily to boil up water for a cup of tea and might include as many as five different types of tin, plus some Red Cross string. Tins became an intrinsic part of camp life, as Frost points out:

There was nobody who wasn't wanted, like Smudger Smith, who spent more time in bed than anybody, was the greatest manufacturer of [a] kitchen stove to boil the water to cook the meals in and to make the booze. And he was a great character. He could put tins together so nothing leaked and nothing but pure alcohol came out at the other end.

Smudger, who had been a dentist before the war, was also able to pick the locks on the shackles they were forced to wear because they were Commandos. A bugler played if an SS guard was spotted and they would replace the – unlocked – shackles and walk around 'looking abject' until the SS had gone.

But tins were not simply utilitarian objects. Camps held craft exhibitions of objects made from them that ranged from the crude to the elaborate. One technically-minded POW used them to make a barometer; another, at Stalag Luft III, made a clock which earned the grudging praise of a fellow prisoner who said it, 'kept horrible time, but it did work'.

John Worsley, an official war artist for the Admiralty, was surrounded by Red Cross tins at Marlag O near Bremen. He used a chain of them to construct a rudimentary heating system that helped to keep him warm while he painted. A sardine tin also played a key part in Worsley's most famous work – a dummy prisoner called Albert who was constructed during the weekly trips to the shower house. His head was fashioned out of painted newspaper and his eyes were ping-pong balls that could be made to blink using a pendulum made from a sardine tin. He had a wig made from strands of human hair donated by other prisoners and his torso was a collapsible wire frame covered by a naval greatcoat. Albert, held up on either side by other prisoners, took the place of Lieutenant Mewes who hid in the bathhouse until the others had marched back to their huts. For four days Albert stood in for Mewes in the thrice-daily count of heads. Mewes was finally recaptured at Lübeck and the story was made into a stage play and then, in 1953, a film, *Albert R.N.* (released in America as *Break to Freedom*), for which Worsley made a second dummy.

POW Artists

Under normal circumstances Adrian Heath and Terry Frost would never have met. Frost was from a working class family in Coventry; Heath was a privileged son of the British Empire. But their unlikely friendship was to affect both their lives.

Heath was born in 1920 in north Burma where he was the only child of a rubber plantation manager. When he was five he was sent back to Britain to live with his grandmother before boarding at a school in Kent. He was mischievous, causing havoc in the classroom, but a good athlete despite suffering from blackouts which were probably caused by a form of epilepsy. After leaving school he went in 1938 to Newlyn in Cornwall to study painting with Alexander Stanhope Forbes and from here he entered the Slade School of Fine Art, moving with the school when it was evacuated to Oxford in 1940.

His social background and class made him obvious officer material but Heath never did what was obvious. He shunned the responsibility of a commission and felt that his absentmindedness and lack of empathy for mechanical objects ruled out becoming a pilot. Instead he joined 101 Squadron RAF as a gunner, a position which in terms of vulnerability, it would be difficult to match.

On his fifth sortie, on a January night in 1942, he squeezed his short, muscular body into the aeroplane turret, the loneliest seat in the aircraft, cold and draughty and a sitting duck for German fighter planes who usually attacked from behind. It had been known for a bomber to arrive home apparently unscathed only for the crew to find that their rear turret had been sheared off by enemy fire. Heath's Wellington took off from Oakington, just north of Cambridge, and flew over the flat Fens towards Germany.

As they neared their target the tension was compounded by a sudden change in the engines' register as one began to splutter and then fell silent. Heath suspected that it had iced up due to the high altitude. The young pilot's voice crackled over the intercom, asking the crew members what they wanted to do: should they drop their load on the railway station and try to limp home, or should they turn and head for Denmark which, although under German occupation, would give them a better chance of reaching neutral Sweden? In what sounded more like a good-natured discussion about whether to continue to the seaside through a cloudburst or to head home, the crew voted five to one to drop their bombs; only the observer, whose wife was expecting a baby, wanted to abandon the raid.

As they started to lose height over the River Elbe they could smell the flak in the air. Heath shifted backwards and forwards in his seat waiting to see how the struggling plane would react as the pilot eased the nose into a dive. The crew broke into hunting songs as the bomber swooped down and released its load over the station. Miraculously, at 2,000ft the engine revived and the aeroplane pulled up and away. But as it started to climb searchlights picked out its silhouette and a wave of shelling followed its retreat. They headed for the North Sea but as soon as they were over water the first engine failed again and then the second cut out, leaving the cumbersome plane caught in an uneasy glide. Seeing what they thought was a beach, they attempted a crash landing, their descent buffeted by guns fired from a nearby island.

As they drifted down over the coast it became obvious that they were heading, not for the mainland, but for another island. This unscheduled landing was a 'very boring and alarming experience' Heath said later with his usual talent for understatement. It became more alarming when he realised as the ground raced towards them that one of the levers on his turret door had jammed. He was trapped. The fore-gunner scrambled through with an axe and was desperately hacking away at the door when they bounced on to the shore. Heath had just enough room and time to scrabble away from the out-of-control plane. As they hit the ground they realised the plane might burst into flames at any moment and they knew the enemy had watched their arrival.

They decided to split up and Heath went with a Canadian crew member. As dawn broke they found a 'Van Gogh peasant gathering firewood' who spoke Walloon, a language that neither of them was 'up in'. He showed them on a map where they were and, using sign language, made it clear that the islands were swarming with Germans. It was not long before they ran in to some. When the two men, still wearing their RAF uniforms, were challenged the Canadian adopted a childlike attitude to the situation. 'Take no notice, pretend we haven't seen them,' he told Heath. But the if-I-close-my-eyes-they-won't-be-able-to-see-me tactic failed. The Germans fired shots over their heads; Heath and the other airmen looked up in mock surprise and were quickly arrested.

They were taken to a prison in Amsterdam and then to a *Dulag Luft* (transit camp) near Frankfurt for a week's interrogation. From here, Heath went to Stalag VIIA at Moosburg near Munich, where he was held with French and Russian POWs in long barrack rooms until September 1942. He painted portraits for the French using six tubes of paint he received from the Red Cross and tried several times to escape: he 'had a go but never got very far and always paid for it'. As an airman he had been lectured on escape and evasion at Lossiemouth in Scotland and made a total of seven attempts during his time as a POW for which he was punished by several spells of solitary confinement.

Terry Frost had flirted with art before he became a prisoner of war but it was never a talent to be taken seriously in a working class family in Coventry – especially during the Depression. It was the only school subject at which he was any good but was viewed as 'for the ladies over the road'. When he was on the dole he was forced to attend an evening class in order to qualify for benefit and remembers creating a plaster cast of a sheep in an art lesson. But when he was seventeen other interests took over – girlfriends, soccer, cricket, table tennis, cycling. He lurched from one job to the next: the youngest on the payroll was usually the first to go when orders dried up. He worked in Curry's cycle shop as a window dresser, where he sketched designs to entice shoppers through the door. Then he assembled radios at a factory in Warwick until he lost that job and worked as a baker's boy. He joined the Armstrong Whitworth Aircraft factory just as Prime Minister Neville Chamberlain was hooraying 'Peace in our time'. Here, in temperatures of around 90°C, he made tea for the draughtsman who painted the roundels on the aircraft. Later he progressed to dipping metal tubes in lead paint, followed by varnish, and eventually he was allowed to paint the electrical wiring for the highly secretive bomber that was being developed there. The intense heat and the fumes from the 'dope', used to seal the plane's outer skin, were so great that the workers were given two pints of milk to drink a day.

He joined the Territorial Army so that he could ride horses; the annual fortnight's camp became the holiday he could never have afforded. But when war was declared it was a shock to have to wear the uniform of the Warwickshire Yeomanry every day. Worse followed when he had to endure a sea journey to Palestine during which many horses were taken ill and had to be thrown overboard. He patrolled the border looking for hashish smugglers but soon grew impatient to see some real fighting and volunteered for the Commandos.

'Never having had any real action with real bullets I thought that I was quite brave, I suppose, until I actually got into action.'

Now a corporal, he was sent behind the Italian lines in Abyssinia (modern-day Ethiopia). Africa sharpened his senses and gave him a new landscape: the palm trees and lake mirages; chattering, colourful birds; crocodiles; gazelles and the fish in the Blue Nile; tall, elegant Abyssinian guides with caste marks on their faces and bright bands of cloth wrapped round their waists. He got used to covering his plate of stew with his tin hat to prevent the hawks from swooping down to steal his food and to seeing the dense jungle-like forest from a different perspective.

> I think that something quite permanently gets into your mind, ... walking through the jungle ... because you are walking through things that are higher than you ... You're absolutely lost or enclosed in this stuff ... So that it's a different kind of space sensation to what you get walking about in a street ... And then when you break out into a clearance, apart from being scared that you'll be seen, it seems to be a new kind of silence or a new kind of space. And I think these things have always stayed with me from that experience of walking about in that jungle and being always on your toes and aware of every sound. You see, you get to recognise the sound of every sort of animal and birds and that because it's a different sound from somebody's foot being put down – which is what you're listening for really.

He learnt to be wary of the man who coughs when the patrol is creeping forward in dead silence. He realised, too, that, with his poor eyesight (he wore glasses) and habit of breathing loudly when he was nervous he could easily be the person to give them away. His subconscious logged the beauty and the buffoonery of battle, ready to return to it when inspiration arrived. One night they were sleeping naked on the banks of the Blue Nile under their 'mosy nets' when a sentry reported that there was someone moving about on the other side of the river. They threw on their great-coats, which flapped open at the back, and rushed down to the river.

'There were these beautiful bare arses which are the two shapes I always use still now [in my paintings] . . . And this big moon and these beautiful white bare arses shining out . . . I thought, "Well, what a lovely sight".' A family of baboons had been responsible for the noise, although it seems it was the men's arses, not the monkeys' that so fascinated Frost.

From here they were 'whipped back' to 'Alex' where, 'The Crete job came up'. The intention was to take Maleme Aerodrome, near Chania, and prevent the Germans dropping their parachute corps there. But it was a hopeless task; Frost and his fellow soldiers were surrounded and dive-bombed by Stukas. Their commanding officer walked down the road towards the Germans with a white flag while his men emptied their rifles of bullets and dumped their gear down wells to stop it falling into German hands.

They were taken prisoner and put in the hold of an overcrowded ship bound for Salonika where the heat, boredom and brutality of the guards confirmed their status as POWs. To pass the endless hours the Australians started playing two-up, betting on whether coins would land heads or tails, while Frost and others gathered round to watch. Some fifty men used the game as cover to escape down a manhole and into the sewage system. Frost was about to take his turn when the Germans spotted one man emerging from the drain. 'And they just machine-gunned the whole bloody lot that was in there . . . I mean, they had no time for you at all in those days. They were definitely trying to demoralise you because you'd just been taken prisoner, you see. And that was our little spell in Salonika.'

It was the only time he came close to trying to escape. From here, Frost was taken to Germany to spend six weeks in a camp where the sheer bore-dom started to wear him down:

And we found one of the hardest things was to just hang around. It wasn't even the limited rations that worried one so much . . . We could always moan every day about the slice of bread and one potato and all that stuff. But the thing was having no books, no news, no nothing to do at all.

A few blokes had got a bit of the Bible left. And I think I read Acts several times until we smoked it, you see, when we got little bits of tobacco . . . It was good rolling paper. So we'd got nothing to read and nothing to do. I remember the only thing we did, we got lice. So we used to sit in the afternoon catching these lice out of the seams of our shirts which was a great entertainment, not realising how serious such things were. But the actual boredom of your mind is terrible. And it does reduce your morale quicker than anything. It seems that everything's a waste of time. It's quite a punishment to have nothing to do at all and nothing to think of and no books and no communication.

They started to perform some drama in a small way but this was cut short when they were forced to lay railway tracks, work that became particularly difficult when temperatures fell to nearly thirty degrees below zero centigrade. Frost was unaware of the frostbite that had started to attack his face until a passer-by rubbed snow on it to try to alleviate it. After six months of heavy labour they moved to a camp in Poland and then to Stalag 383 where he began to take a greater interest in art.

One of the men in his hut, 'Hobo' Challis, whom Frost described as a 'professional tramp', was a gifted caricaturist. He tried to teach Frost but, while he never mastered this skill, he found that he could draw a convincing likeness and was soon in demand as a portrait painter. To begin with he used old bits of cardboard or paper discarded by the Germans after they had blacked out the hut windows against air raids.

He met Adrian Heath for the first time when he was drawing the back of a seated figure. He was using tentative strokes when an incongruously upper class voice demanded: 'Why don't you *put it* on?' Heath invited him to his hut to see his figure studies and still lifes (bowls and tins). He was the first person to talk to Frost seriously about painting and he urged him to concentrate on 'getting his tone values right'. Until then, Frost's exposure to art had been limited to the brightly coloured railway posters that had adorned his classroom at school. Frost's ribald humour and Heath's playful understatement and rebelliousness, together with their shared sense of social justice, made a neat fit. 'And that was the start of our friendship, and [he] also encouraged me to carry on painting for ever.'

In their unlikely pairing of drawling upper class accent and flat Midlands voice, they discussed Frost's emerging style and Heath described the work of artists such as his friend Victor Pasmore. The first art book Frost ever read was Irving Stone's fictional biography of Van Gogh, *Lust for Life*, which Hobo obtained for him through the Red Cross.

Heath introduced him to six other men who together formed an art school. They invited Frost to be their model and he polished his buttons and regimental badges in preparation for the first sitting but as he watched them working he became conscious of an emerging critical faculty. 'I thought, "They don't draw that well."' Soon after he was invited to join the class as an artist.

He also met Basil Marin through Heath. Marin had studied at Madrid University and knew a lot about the history of art. He showed Frost a book about Velasquez and explained his use of angles and geometry that Frost found a 'revelation'. In return, Frost supplied him with lines from Keats and Shelley that he could drop into the letters he wrote to a pen friend in England.

Frost later described the camp as a 'university' where he found a pleasure in reading and listening to music and poetry. Painting portraits introduced him to men he might not otherwise have spent time with and who assumed that, because he could paint, he would enjoy other art forms. One customer invited him to listen to Beethoven on a Red Cross gramophone the evening after he had sat for his portrait. He went to poetry readings and all kinds of plays, and listened to different kinds of musical instruments ('the bagpipes, my dear, they used to drive us mad at times').

Hobo read out loud books sent by the Red Cross, anything from the classics to an autobiography of Henry Ford. Frost absorbed geography through a map on the wall that showed the positions of the Russian, German and British troops and he soon found he knew the capital of every European state. All around him men were studying and it was impossible not be sucked into the process. As he lay on his bunk he listened to someone reading *Paradise Lost*, while he tested a man in the bed behind him on his German verbs and answered questions from a third man, who had worked on the railways, and was now studying geography. And in the background, there was the constant sound of men gambling.

Frost's first portrait was of a man called Workman who had a big chest and was lying down. The only colours he had were Prussian blue, yellow and white.

> I got the big toe in my eye like that, and his chest coming up over the big toe, that was my point of view, and I didn't know at the time but of course it was about the worst perspectival [sic] problem you could have possibly had, and as I had never heard of the word 'perspective' or anything like that at that time, I was actually copying every shape, and it didn't work out too badly actually but if I had been worried about perspective I might have got it all messed up you see, because you have to know it properly to use it. And so I did it by eye, and it didn't work out too badly, except the colour of course was outrageous really. But then you have to use the colours you've got, which is quite an interesting lesson.
>
> You can do it in anything if you get it right. And I didn't know about that at the time, but I was using just the colours that I had been given, because they were the colours they didn't want, and so, they weren't flesh colours you see, they're not flesh colour at all. So, that probably was a very good lesson.

Frost painted around 200 portraits and these, in turn, gave him the means to experiment with other forms of art. As payment he would ask for the sitter's pillow – two pieces of Hessian stuffed with grass – which provided him with a pair of 'canvasses'; one for the subject's portrait, the other for his own use. Or he would be paid in cigarettes. As he did not smoke much himself he would barter them for paint from the German guards or from Mick Moore, a well-connected POW at the heart of the camp's commercial life whom Frost described as 'king of the camp'. He ran a swap shop and wrote the value of items on a blackboard; for example, a pair of socks could be bartered for a tin of bacon. 'Mick Moore would get you anything from an elephant to the map of the German defences if you could pay him enough.'

Occasionally, the Red Cross would send paints but one German guard, who had attended an art school in Munich, provided tubes of oil from Kharkov in Russia that he had bought for his own use but gave to Frost in return for his portrait.

A POW who had been a commercial artist made excellent brushes by snipping hair from the fetlocks of the horse that pulled the latrine waste truck. He then fixed the brush to a ferrule cut from a cocoa tin. Other sitters gave Frost the oil from sardine tins which he mixed with his paints. He treated his canvas with 'glue' made from the residue of boiled barley that the Germans made their soup from and which became very sticky once it was boiled.

Art became his profession. He worked every day, painting sportsmen, illustrating club dinner menus and Christmas cards. He designed posters and programmes for plays and concerts and in this role was allowed to attend dress rehearsals. 'I used to come back and tell all the boys in my room that so-and-so had got a new bra and so-and-so a new wig. Cor! . . . And they'd all lie on the bed waiting for me to come back from the dress rehearsal.'

He learnt to use woodcuts and watercolours and to study the landscape with an artist's intensity. Every day he stared out through the barbed wire at the 'strange' place beyond and watched how the seasons changed the colour of the distant pines, the grass and the few isolated trees near the perimeter.

> I used to write little poem things about the way in which it had gone through into gold and the way its arms seemed to spread out towards me and all that kind of lark, which was very sentimental for a soldier to do I'm sure. But anyway, the point was that a blade of grass became important. And every leaf became important. And when the leaves fell off I was most distressed . . . I remember going out one morning and the last leaf had gone off in the night. And it was about six o'clock in the morning. I was going along towards the latrines. And I stopped dead because the last leaf had gone. And it absolutely shattered me. I was in tears to think that I'd missed that last leaf, which was my friend, on the particular tree.

When, after Crazy Week, he was allowed to walk in the woods he gathered flowers to paint. But the taste of freedom was too painful and he only went once.

> I couldn't take the going out and coming back, particularly as the flowers and things were so beautiful. I never realised how beautiful they

were. So it had certain things in that hunger and deprivation of various kinds [that] make you more spiritually aware, I think, than one has ever been. At least I was more spiritually aware of nature then than ever. And I'm sure that made me make my mind up to paint those kinds of subjects and to be always interested in landscape. And I always have been since.

The atmosphere of the prison camp gave Frost the freedom to experiment without the fear of being accused of pretentiousness. He was also encouraged by the interest shown by 'the thirteen other blokes' in his room who all wanted to know what he was doing, although they were quick to say if they did not like a portrait.

Fred Mulley, who was also from the Midlands and was captured at Dunkirk, was a particularly useful critic of the art shows put on in the camp. He was tough but knowledgeable. Mulley was himself studying and obtained a B.Sc. (Economics) from London University and became a Chartered Secretary while a POW. He later became a Labour cabinet minister.

Frost had his first public exhibition of landscapes and portraits when he was at Stalag 383. A group of men who were suffering from TB were sent home and a sergeant major agreed to take a collection of his paintings with him which were shown near his home at Leamington Art Gallery. He was not the only POW to achieve this peculiar honour while they were still in captivity. George Milne, an accountant and son of a baron, was held in the much grander Oflag IX A/Z at Rotenburg where he set up an art club. His mother supplied him with materials via the Red Cross and in 1944 he sent home a package of portraits on strips of cardboard. Two were accepted for the Royal Academy summer show and two were displayed in the *Daily Telegraph* Prisoners of War exhibition at Clarence House to raise funds for the Red Cross. John Worsley's sketches at Marlag O became so famous that visiting German admirals came to view his work.

Other POWs poured their artistic talents into camp newssheets and magazines. The most rudimentary were no more than typed sheets of paper while the most sophisticated took advantage of the camp's artistic talents and focussed on a particular interest or hobby. *Flywheel*, the magazine of the Mühlberg Motor Club, at Stalag IVB near Brandenburg was a perfect example of the latter.

Tom Swallow and five other car enthusiasts set up the club and membership quickly grew to two hundred. Swallow suggested producing a magazine to help POWs to keep up-to-date with technical developments and new car models; it would also educate men who had learnt to drive in the army but who had never owned their own vehicle.

The magazine used every scrap of expertise at the club's disposal. Pat Harrington-Johnson, a journalist from South Africa, became editor and Swallow was 'staff reporter'. Other POWs assumed roles that chimed with their civilian expertise: a truck driver held the position of 'Diesel Expert', someone else specialised in sports cars. Swallow used up one of his precious monthly letters to write to the Isle of Man TT winner, Graham Walker (father of motor racing commentator, Murray, and then editor of *Motor Cycling*) who sent copies of *Road Tests Recalled*. These were bound in hard covers and became part of the club library. Swallow's mother provided magazine cuttings that showed the prices of secondhand bikes and cars, and reports of motoring events. As the men were miles from the nearest showroom, they discussed the cars driven by the German officers – models such as a DKW, Wanderer and Opel Admiral.

Flywheel had a circulation and production manager but what is most striking about it is the quality of its colour illustrations that show sleek cars driven by elegant motorists who might have stepped out of a 1930s issue of *Vogue*. 'Cocktail bars and vanity sets are frequently found in the 7-passenger Cadillac on the 142-inch chassis. It has a V8 engine developing 160 bhp. Priced at $2,000 in 1941,' *Flywheel* told readers who lay reading it on their rickety bunk beds.

The magazine was lubricated by nostalgia – men described their favourite journeys or what it was like to drive in their home country – but a desire to educate fuelled the editorial of a publication whose motto was: 'Keeps the works going round the idle strokes.' The articles, which were handwritten, covered subjects such as 'Laying up or riding on?' (Should you continue to ride your motorbike in winter?), tips on the correct alignment of tyres and tappet adjustment, histories of various cars and a piece about 'your dream car'. One copy was circulated among members, whilst a supplement was pinned to a noticeboard and loaned to each hut for half a day. Many camps produced this type of 'wall' newsletter (so called because they were pinned to a wall), which were typed or written by hand and tacked to a noticeboard to be passed round until they were dog-eared and stained. They usually contained general news about camp activities and were sometimes glanced at by bored guards.

What makes the quality of *Flywheel* all the more remarkable is the meagre materials available to its editorial team. During the two months it took to produce the first issue, the production team borrowed a pen-holder and nib, bought ink with *Lagergeld* and exchanged cigarettes for paper. They stole quinine tablets from the German sick bay to mix colour and set aside part of their rations of millet soup that they fermented until, after a few days, it became gooey enough to use as a glue with which to stick illustrations into a school exercise book and which remained in place for over forty years.

Both Sam Kydd and Ray Beal worked on *Prisoner's Pie*, a fortnightly journal produced at Stalag XXA and printed outside the camp. The magazine was free, although it carried a nominal price of 20 pfennig, and had a print-run of 480 copies. It featured the usual mix of short stories, drawings, camp news and cartoons, although contributions from professional journalists such as the Scottish reporter, E.W. Reach, and K.C. Robb, who had worked on the *Daily Sketch*, elevated it beyond the standard of a camp 'rag'. In its early days, as Andrew Hawarden noted, it also organised events such as dance competitions but it struggled when paper became difficult to find and had to cut production to every three months until it eventually closed in 1944.

Prisoner's Pie contained cartoons by James Woolcock, a sign writer from Barry in Wales who also used his artistic talent to produce convincing copies of German documents for escape attempts. But this was one skill Terry Frost never mastered. He tried copying German travel documents in Indian ink and pen but his efforts were never convincing enough. And, while Heath was an inveterate escaper, Frost preferred to take a backseat. Frost's hut was in the last row nearest the wire and once he was asked to lie in the grass below the sentry box pretending to read and sunbathe while beneath him men, including Heath, were tunnelling their way out of the camp. Frost's job was to watch the German and if he appeared to show any signs of suspicion he was to drop his handkerchief, as a signal for the men in the hut to stamp on the floorboards to warn the tunnellers to stop. The team were a yard or so away from the point where they could have broken through on the other side of the wire when Frost noticed the guard hesitate as if he had heard something. Frost immediately raised the alarm.

But the message did not get through and the guards burst into the hut firing guns. The British started yelling and waving their arms, running backwards and forwards to distract the Germans and give the escape team a chance to hide their tools. 'And Adrian was still left down there you see, right to the end, and when they put their white coats on to have a look along the tunnel, their overalls, Adrian was sort of curled up, hanging up on something, and he just barked like a dog and frightened them to bloody death.' It was this sort of behaviour that convinced Frost that 'Adrian was the bravest man I have ever known'. Heath spent the next twenty-one days on bread and water.

On another occasion, Frost acted as an unwitting stool pigeon when he was tricked into helping the resistance movement, formed to protect POWs when the end of the war seemed near. He was given a mug of cocoa to drink and some chocolate to munch and told to paint Mick Moore's portrait. What he did not know was that he was positioned above an ammunitions dump where POWs were training for the final showdown.

Although they were not able to attend, Terry Frost and Adrian Heath both exhibited at the *Daily Telegraph*'s POW exhibition of May 1944. Heath contributed an interior of the camp, a portrait and landscape in oil and a line portrait and Frost showed watercolours of the inside of the camp and a look-out post.

Discovering his artistic talent was to change Frost's life after the war; it also transformed the way George Haig, son of the famous First World War commander, saw himself. As a child he had enjoyed drawing but being a prisoner gave him the time and a reason to paint. In his early days as a POW in Italy, he read books on the history of art and bought watercolours on the black market because oil paints were forbidden in case the tubes contained maps. His bed was surrounded by drying paintings. Later, his sister sent him paints and he received canvases, oil and brushes from the Red Cross. At Colditz where he was sent as a *Prominente* – someone with valuable connections – he painted portraits of his fellow inmates, large snowscapes and self-portraits that he achieved by sitting in the toilet which had the only available mirror. 'For myself I was able to shed the burden of the responsibilities of living up to my father's great reputation as a soldier. Now suddenly fate had liberated me. I could slink away into the shadows of a prisoner of war camp to cultivate the resource of painting. This new purpose was to save my morale during my time as a prisoner.'

PART II

The War in the East

Surrender

Modern visitors to Singapore usually land at Changi International Airport, a shiny temple to consumerism on the very eastern edge of the island. Passengers glide along air-conditioned, artificially lit walkways beneath ceilings tall enough to accommodate small clusters of palm trees. Fragrant flowers and ponds of koi carp present a sanitised, hushed version of what sits outside the glass windows; but, as seasoned travellers like to remind novices, Singapore is not the real thing; this is 'Asia lite'. Tourists who arrive in this comforting cocoon are usually shocked if they ever discover that Changi Airport was built on a gritty reality, its foundations dug by Allied prisoners of war labouring in temperatures of over 30°C, wearing little more than rags and using only primitive tools like the Asian hoe, or *changkol*.

Japan started the twentieth century as Britain's ally against Russia but when, in 1937, she turned her attention to China, the war that followed changed the West's image of Japan, not least through what became known as 'The Rape of Nanking', a bloody orgy in which hundreds of thousands (the figure remains disputed) were massacred and countless women raped. Japan in its turn became virulently anti-Western. American fashions, from hemlines to hairstyles, which had once been *de rigueur* became *infra dig*. Kimonos and jujitsu made a comeback and cinemas, theatre and radio adopted a militaristic soundtrack. Japan, which had been badly hit by the Great Depression and which had few natural resources of its own, began to suffer from trade embargoes designed to punish her aggression. The US held back petroleum, while bans on scrap metal from Australia and tin from Malaya helped to bring a simmering anti-Western sentiment to the boil. In 1940 Japan signed a treaty with Britain's enemies – Italy and Germany – and the following year the Imperial Conference in Tokyo formed the Greater East Asia Co-Prosperity Sphere, a Japanese-led alliance that aimed to undermine British colonialism in the region.

When Japan entered the Second World War, Britain's military resources were already stretched to breaking point as they struggled to turn the tide in Europe. Defending her colonies on the other side of the world could never be a priority.

Britain had considerable power in Malaya (a collective name for the states of the Malayan Peninsula and Singapore) through the Crown Colony of the Straits Settlements, which included Singapore and Penang Island, and – to varying degrees – groups known as the Federated and Unfederated Malay States. British planters and managers of mines drove the region's commercial cogs: Malaya produced thirty-eight per cent of the world's rubber, which became an increasingly valuable asset as the motor industry emerged in the early twentieth century; its mines produced fifty-eight per cent of the world's tin.

Singapore's size – it is usually compared to the Isle of Wight – was less important than its position. It sits at the tip of the Malayan Peninsula where ships pass on their way to the East and from where 'Fortress Singapore' could protect British interests in India and Australia. Although it is true that most defences were geared towards an attack from the sea, the old chestnut that the guns were 'pointing the wrong' way is not quite true. Heavy guns, nearly all on swivel mountings so that they could turn to fire at invaders coming from the north as well as from the sea, were put in place but there was inadequate ammunition and other equipment to counter a land-based attack.

On the night of 7 December 1941, Japanese soldiers invaded Thailand and started to fight their way down the Malayan Peninsula towards Singapore with a zeal and technical ability that astounded their opponents. It was a huge psychological blow for Britain when, after fierce fighting, Lieutenant General Arthur Percival, who was in charge of the defence of Malaya, surrendered Singapore on 15 February 1942 and 14,000 Australian, 16,000 British, and 32,000 Indian troops became POWs.

The Netherlands East Indies (NEI), a sprawling colony that included Java, Sumatra, Dutch New Guinea and western Timor, was pulled into the conflict when Japan attacked Dutch Borneo, the Celebes and the Moluccas on 20 December 1941. The colonies were rich in oil and tin, as well as other minerals, rubber and foods such as rice and sugar. Dutch soldiers, helped by Australian, British and American forces, tried to stem the Japanese tide but, on 1 March, they landed on Java. A week later, the Dutch surrendered and around 93,000 of the Royal Netherlands East Indies Army became prisoners of war.

America entered the war after Japan's surprise attack on its base at Pearl Harbor in Hawaii, 3,400 miles from Japan, on the morning of Sunday 7 December 1941. Most American POWs became so when the Japanese conquered the Philippine Islands in the winter of 1941–42. Overall 25,600 Americans were held in the Pacific theatre.

The war in the Far East covered a huge geographic area and POWs were held in about a thousand camps in a range of exotic places from as far north as the Thai border with Burma, Japan itself, Hong Kong, Formosa (now Taiwan) and Indonesia. They were moved around more than POWs in Europe as their captors used them as slave labour – to build railways, load and unload ships, or to work in mines. Conditions varied from the heat and humidity – as well as the monsoons and mud – of Thailand, where they worked in appalling conditions to build a railway, to the freezing winters of Japan's northerly conquests. The climate of Java, with its backdrop of volcanoes and lush rainforests, could be enervating but at Bandung (also known as Bandoeng), in the centre of the island, the local weather tended to be more benign. Their living quarters ranged from army barracks, schools and civilian prisons to canvas tents and huts made from bamboo and palm fronds. The hostile terrain, their distance from home and the fact that most POWs were white made escape much rarer than in Europe and explains why the majority of POW camps in the Far East lacked the high, bristling banks of barbed wire, the searchlights and the watch towers typical of a German stalag. It also partly explains why, in some camps, prisoners had greater opportunities to trade with local people. A cursory glance at a photo of the neat rows of bamboo huts at Tamarkan camp on the River Kwai in Thailand, for example, shows a scene that might appear in a holiday brochure for western tourists keen to experience the *real* Thailand – until one considers that each hut held over 300 men who were ravaged by a battery of tropical illnesses, who slept on platforms made unbearably hard by the fact that their appalling rations had turned them into skeletons whose bones hurt every time they shifted in their 'bed'.

The other big difference between POWs in Europe and the Far East is their survival rate. The Germans were relatively benign captors – at least when dealing with non-Russian POWs and people whose race they approved of. Only four per cent of their prisoners (excluding Russians) died in captivity. The Japanese, by comparison, viewed being taken prisoner as the ultimate humiliation and had no sympathy for their charges.

The figures speak for themselves. A quarter of the 50,000 British service men captured in the Far East died as prisoners – most from disease and starvation, exacerbated in many cases by forced labour and instances of unimaginable brutality. Of the 94,000 Americans held in Europe, only one per cent died in captivity – mainly from wounds sustained in battle. This compares with the 10,650 American POWs who died in the Far East – nearly forty-five per cent of the total of 25,600. The contrast for Australian POWs is even sharper. While only 265 Australian prisoners died in Europe around 8,000 (almost thirty-five per cent) of Australian prisoners held by the Japanese died in captivity – almost as many as were killed in action in the Pacific War. The carnage among Australians, together with the fact that the war against Japan was much closer to home, explains why their experience has always been near the top of the Australian people's collective memory.

These figures mask individual stories of great hardship. Between 7,000 and 10,000 out of 78,000 American and Filipino POWs died during the Bataan Death March of April 1942, when they were forced to walk sixty-five miles to the prison camp near Cabanatuan in the Philippines. They were already weak from illness and starvation and were allowed only tiny amounts of food and water; many were bayoneted or clubbed to death by guards. Of the 61,000 Australian, British and Dutch POWs who were made to work on the Thailand–Burma Railway, about 12,000 perished.

Many of the British soldiers who were taken prisoner at the fall of Singapore had left Britain in the autumn of 1941 unaware of where they were heading – although the fact that the guns and vehicles on the ships transporting them had been painted sand-coloured and packages were marked 'Basra' suggested the Middle East. The 18th Division of the British Army – around 15,000 men who came mainly from the Cambridgeshire, Norfolk and Suffolk regiments – had weaved their way across the Atlantic to Halifax in Nova Scotia, down to the West Indies and across to Cape Town in a bid to outwit lurking enemy submarines. But Japan's invasion of Thailand and the attack on Pearl Harbor persuaded Winston Churchill that they were needed more urgently in another part of the world. Many arrived just a month before the fall of Singapore.

Those soldiers and airmen who were already based at Singapore were witnessing the last gasp of a privileged, colonial lifestyle. While friends and family back home grappled with rationing, blackouts and bombs, Singapore's ruling elite – the businessmen and civil servants and their families – were more concerned with the price of rubber (originally fuelled by the growth of the car industry and now supported by rearmament) and tin, their next glass of *stengah* (whisky and soda) or game of tennis and golf. Wives supervised servants and planned well-tended gardens of emerald lawns and purple bougainvillea or donned their white gloves in the stifling heat to visit the Victorian cathedral, St Andrew's, which looked out onto the grassy Padang, a convincing substitute for an English provincial park. Husbands talked business over cocktails sipped at Raffles Hotel or one of the many clubs that allowed them to mix with the right class and race. Cigarettes and alcohol were cheap; servants cheaper and less obtrusive. In the 1930s, Singapore had attracted writers like Somerset Maugham and Noël Coward, Hollywood stars and royalty who swept through and left a sheen of glamour in their wake. The ruling elite saw no reason for this to change.

Ordinary soldiers, airmen and sailors could also find a good time in Singapore – often at one of the dance halls that carried hedonistic names such as 'New World' or 'Happy World'. Here a 'Taxi Girl', a dainty Chinese woman with a painted doll's face, would dance with them for a price and keep them company while they drank Tiger beer. Then, as J.G. Farrell described in his novel, *The Singapore Grip*, they 'staggered outside into the sweltering night . . . to inhale that incomparable smell of incense, of warm skin, of meat cooking in coconut oil, of money and frangipani, and hair-oil and lust and sandalwood and heaven knows what, a perfume like the breath of life itself'.

For British soldiers the sights and sounds of Singapore were exquisitely exotic. Len Baynes, from Cambridgeshire, breathed in 'a mixture of garlic, fish, joss-sticks, frying oil, charcoal and probably much more' and observed the wealthy Chinese men followed by wives who 'appear to move forward in a series of jerks'. Alistair Urquhart, of the Gordon Highlanders, from Aberdeen, noticed the 'heady mixture of tamarind, cinnamon, nutmeg, wisps of incense, frying fish and rotting vegetables'. He was struck, too, by the ethnic variety of the population and how their ways of living brought exoticism to the island – from the clattering of the mah-jong tiles to the sight and smell of men frying green bananas or cracking open coconuts with machetes.

Perhaps, as an Australian, Russell Braddon was bound to be less enchanted by his first impressions of Singapore:

> There were the vivid colours of tropical flowers in parks: the incred-
> ible stenches of fish drying on the pavements – each fragrant morsel
> the target of a million flies: the bamboo poles slung out from each side
> of the street, on which was suspended much native washing rather
> indifferently laundered: and in the streets, everywhere, contemptuous
> of death and traffic laws alike, a bedlam of fowls, rickshaws, and
> natives, through which all vehicles careered as fast as possible.

Despite the secrecy which was meant to accompany their arrival, a huge banner in the Lavender Street red light district announced: 'Welcome to the AIF' (Australian Imperial Force). The pugnacious Argyll and Sutherland Highlanders, who were well established on the island, were less friendly, and several fights erupted as the two nations worked out a peck-ing order. The disapproval of the resident British ladies in their white gloves was subtler and confined to supercilious glances directed at the Australian troops.

As British troops neared Singapore they switched to 'tropical kit'. Jack Chalker, a gunner in the 118th Field Regiment, R. A., described their large solar topis as 'reminiscent of something worn at the relief of Mafeking' and noted how the lighter, more flexible bush hats worn by Australian sol-diers were to prove so much more suitable for jungle warfare. In India dhobi wallas had washed and pressed British uniforms but no amount of laundering could prevent the 'let-down shorts' from appearing, as Jack said, 'idiotic'. The razor-sharp creases, blancoed belts and gleaming boots were to appear all the more ridiculous when they finally came face-to-face with the Japanese in their comfortably baggy uniforms. To complete the decep-tively amateurish image, the enemy often rode rickety old bikes. Although the Japanese were, on one hand, rekindling ancient notions of what it meant to be a warrior and to live by this Bushido creed, this spiritual reawakening was matched by a stark appreciation of the realities of modern warfare.

British commanders made the mistake of assuming that the enemy would share their limitations: if they found the Malayan Peninsula impassable then so would the Japanese. But the jungle did not hold the same fear for the Japanese.

'We were fed ridiculous propaganda to the effect that the Japanese were all half-blind and ill-trained,' according to John Lowe, Lance Bombardier, 5th Field Regiment, RA (11 Indian Division). 'Instead of the ridiculously heavy studded boots issued to us (ideal perhaps if one were performing guard drill in front of Buckingham Palace), the Japanese soldier wore split-toed rubber boots which meant that he could shin up a rubber tree, and drop his grenades on the enemy passing below.'

Some soldiers may have been taken in by the propaganda simply because it was more comforting to believe that the enemy was a lower life form but others challenged the assumptions. Charles Fisher, a Second Lieutenant in the Royal Engineers, attended a lecture in which an RAF officer confidently told his audience that their slit eyes meant that Japanese airmen could not use a bombsight properly and were unlikely to hit their target. In addition, their reactions were slow because of their abnormally low body temperature and they were thus ineffective at hand-to-hand fighting. When Fisher pointed out that the Japanese had invented jujitsu, the officer countered that it was exactly because of these weaknesses that the Japanese had been forced to develop the martial art.

Racism extended to the view of Japanese pilots. A British newspaper reported that they had an appalling sense of balance because as babies their mothers had carried them on their backs like monkeys. The importance of balance may also have led to the theory that Japan's lack of a cavalry tradition was another severe drawback – after all, air aces such as the Red Baron (Manfred von Richthofen) in Germany were usually skilled horsemen. It was believed, too, that the Japanese suffered from an inner-ear defect that made flying at high altitude extremely painful.

An intelligence officer confirmed this view of the Japanese as small and myopic in a lecture to Australian troops. One of his audience, Russell Braddon, remembers: 'Nor was this all. They had aeroplanes made from old kettles and kitchen utensils, guns salvaged from the war against Russia in 1905 and rifles of the kind used by civilised peoples only in films about the Red Indians. Also, they were frightened of the dark.' Another Australian soldier, Billy Young, was told that the Japanese's equipment was substandard because it was made in Japan.

The Japanese air force was perhaps the area in which the Allies were most guilty of underestimating their enemy's equipment and expertise. This delusion was exemplified in the fighter plane that became known as the 'Zero'. It could take off from both land and ships and was as fast as a Spitfire, highly manoeuvrable and had an astonishing range of 1,000 kilometres. The pilots who flew the Zero had become 'battle ready' through Japan's long battle with China.

By comparison, one of the more modern planes used by the RAF in the Far East was the Brewster Buffalo, an aeroplane as ungainly as its name. One military historian has said that flying a Buffalo after flying a Spitfire or a Hurricane was 'like driving a pick-up truck instead of an Aston Martin'. The men in the cockpit tended to be inexperienced pilots, many from New Zealand and Australia, as more seasoned pilots were busy defending Britain.

One of the first things Jack Chalker noticed when his ship docked in Singapore on 29 January 1942 was a huge sign that read: 'BEWARE OF THE SHARKS'. He arrived to the sound of wailing air raid sirens and a harbour congested with people desperate to leave, among them many women and children. Cars and suitcases were abandoned as space on departing ships grew more precious; one car was dangling over the side of the quay as if it were considering a swallow dive to freedom. 'No matter how much training you do nothing can prepare you for the sheer noise of battle – the shells and bombs and air raids,' Fergus Anckorn, also a gunner in the 118th Field Regiment, remembers.

Mass shelling and bombing of the naval base's oil tanks left a thick pall of smoke that blotted out the sun. The air was acrid with a cocktail of burning rubber, smouldering ruins and myriad minor blazes. The heat and the smuts that floated down left the soldiers blackened and slippery with sweat, as Percival said, like exhausted miners emerging from the coalface.

Jack Chalker has two distinct memories of the fighting – one an unexpected flash of beauty that appeared in the horror of battle; the other a vivid revelation of what war means to the ordinary person caught up in it. As he was on his way to an observation post on the outskirts of

Singapore Town, he took a shortcut through a bombed house that was on fire. As he dodged through the building a rainbow of colour caught his eye in the smoke and dust and, despite the danger, he paused for a closer look. A small chest had been blown apart and scattered skeins of Chinese embroidery silks and pieces of canvas on to the floor. He lingered momentarily to admire their exquisiteness before wrapping some of the silks in the canvas and stuffing them into his pockets.

His other memory is from the last stage of the fighting when he was returning to his gun position with a Canadian soldier. Looking down from a high bank they could see a small saloon car burning brightly on the road. A young Malay woman in tears was running distractedly backwards and forwards. Someone was trapped in the burning car. The two men scrambled down the bank to help but before they could stop her she had hurled herself into the vehicle. The heat was so intense that they were left as helpless bystanders. 'After a while the car hulk shuddered and settled onto the road with a shower of sparks and a small blackened arm appeared sticking out from a side window among the flames. We were near to tears at the sight of the funeral pyre and at our own helplessness.'

On 15 February 1942 General Percival surrendered. There are many theories about why Singapore fell a mere seventy days after the Japanese had first invaded Malaya; Percival is often blamed for the defeat and his physical appearance makes him ideal material for a scapegoat. He met his opposite number, General Tomoyuki Yamashita, at the Ford Motor Company Factory, where the car manufacturer's distinctive handwritten name sat proudly atop the Art Deco building, a beacon of Western capitalism. The contrast between the two men seemed to sum up the differences between the opposing forces. Percival, buck-toothed beneath his moustache, appeared scrawny in his shirt sleeves and twitchingly indecisive, like a rabbit stunned by the speed of events; Yamashita, by comparison, was stolid in his thick army tunic, impatiently bullying his opponent into a final submission.

But defeat was about more than one man. The Japanese troops and airmen were well trained, experienced and more adaptable; their equipment – whether tank or bicycle – suited the terrain. The Japanese could communicate with each other more effectively and, as the attacker, had the element of surprise. And, unlike the British, they were not constantly looking over their shoulder, gambling on how many ships, troops and aeroplanes they could afford to send to the other side of the world. They were a homogeneous group, whereas the British, Australians and the Indian Army, and perhaps, most tellingly, their leaders were driven by different motives and lacked the ruthless sense of purpose of the Japanese.

Jack Chalker remembers the silence of the ceasefire as both strange and a great relief. Like many other Allied soldiers he was shocked by the appearance of the enemy who had beaten them to a standstill.

After hours of hanging around, those who were fit enough were made to walk the fifteen or more miles – depending on where they were when they surrendered – in the blinding heat to a sprawling cantonment of army buildings and prison at the northeast tip of the island. Before the war the well-planned colonial buildings and beach views gave Changi a reputation as one of the most attractive and well-run military bases in the world. After the war, Changi became synonymous with a particular kind of prison degradation. But neither reputation is quite accurate. Individual camps change depending on who is in charge, the prisoners and conditions outside. Changi was no exception.

Changi

Marching to their new home – whether it was in Java, Hong Kong, Kuching or Singapore – gave the men time to reflect on what had happened to them and on their new status as prisoners of war. Stephen Alexander, a 22-year-old subaltern in the 135th Field Regiment R. A., found it difficult as he marched to Changi to revert to 'walking upright and careless' after days of crouching behind a gun.

Singapore's once heady mix of architectural styles was now reduced to rubble and chaos. Everywhere were signs and smells of the carnage: charred and mutilated corpses, unexploded bombs. Sometimes high-ranking Japanese officers would sweep past in their cars, occasionally with an official photographer leaning out from the running board to snap the bedraggled prisoners. Local people lined the streets to gawp at them, in amazement and pity rather than with any sense of exultation. Many were in tears and some offered the prisoners water to drink, or bananas and coconuts to eat.

Although many POWs passed through the island, Singapore was only one of many outposts established by Japan as she swept through South East Asia and the Pacific, overturning long-established British and Dutch colonies as she went. Four days after the capitulation everyone in Singapore had been forced to put their watches forward by one and a half hours so that the island was operating on Tokyo time and the Japanese referred to the island as 'Syonan'. By March, the Imperial Japanese Army (IJA) had imposed a strict order to the day: reveille at 8 a.m., breakfast at 9 a.m., 13.30 lunchtime, work 14.30 –18.00, evening meal at 18.30, roll call (or *tenko*) at 21.30 and lights out at 22.15.

British soldiers, many of whom had been brought up in the damp fens and waterways of East Anglia, were trying to get used to Singapore's exoticism. They were startled by strange noises, flashes of colour and darting movements caught out of the corner of the eye – geckos which scuttled behind picture frames or up tent poles; black snakes that sometimes slithered indoors and set the dogs barking; frogs, their hooting calls magnified by the storm drains; the chattering mynah birds and insistent cicadas. Sudden thunder boomed like distant mortar; lightning cracked the sky and then the rain fell in great droplets that cleared the air before the humidity started its inexorable rise. Nightfall was sudden, like a switch being tripped, and brought forth a cacophony of other unexplained noises, as well as fireflies that glowed and flashed in the gloom and bats that looked like flying dogs.

Changi is frequently used as a catch-all term for the camps where the Japanese held POWs and civilian internees after Japan entered the war in December 1941. In reality, there were some six camps on the Changi Peninsula, which covered an area of about twenty-five square kilometres, as well as Changi Gaol itself. The Changi Military Cantonment included three well-built barracks: Selarang, Roberts (where the camp hospital was based) and Kitchener, which was part of the Southern Area camp and from which a POW could look out towards the clear blue sea – a vista that was both inspiring in its beauty and depressing in its confirmation that their chance of escape was negligible.

Changi Gaol was on the south of the peninsula and initially held only civilian prisoners who had been unable to flee Singapore before the island fell, or who had made the decision to stay. The building was just six years old and benefited from an efficient sewage system that included flushing toilets. But even this modernity could not withstand the strain placed on it by the influx of internees. The gaol was built to hold 600 men but around 2,400 internees lived behind its tall walls. Most were white, male civil servants or tin and plantation managers, but there were also 400 women and children who were kept in a separate wing until all internees were moved in 1944 to a camp at Sime Road.

In the first few months in jail, some of the women passed the time by working on what would become known as the Changi Quilts. Every woman who helped to make the three quilts embroidered a patch made from a scrap of bed linen or a sack of flour with her name and 'something of themselves' – an illustration that held some meaning for the individual woman. Some chose symbols of freedom – a flower or butterfly; or defiance – 'GR' (George Rex) or 'V' for victory; or a message that would only hold meaning to a husband – a mother rabbit with her baby wearing a blue collar to indicate that a son had been born in prison, or a reference to a family dog. The women also made a quilt for the Japanese wounded and this clever ploy may have been what persuaded the Japanese commandant to allow the quilts to be passed to the military hospital where they not only raised morale among the POWs but provided cheering proof for the local 'volunteers' – men who were not professional soldiers but who had permanent homes on the island – that their wives were still alive.

When the women and children moved out in 1944, some 11,700 Allied POWs took their place, squeezing into the jail and its surrounding grounds. It is this grim period in the prison's history – when rations were pitifully small and POWs were allowed few diversions such as concert parties or lectures – that has often been depicted as the true 'Changi' – a word synonymous with brutal incarceration, as depicted in *King Rat*, a novel based on the experiences of its author, James Clavell, as a POW.

The other factor that shaped a prisoner's experience of the Changi area was when exactly he was held there. In the first few weeks after the surrender the POWs were left to themselves. The men were forced to erect a fence at the beginning of March but this was mainly to stop them wandering into Singapore town. It made it harder to move between different camps, although some men continued to break in and out to barter goods with local people. The fence was one of many changes that made them feel more like prisoners.

Immediately after the surrender 45,562 POWs lived on Singapore. The number would ebb and flow over the course of the war but camps on the Changi Peninsula were the key holding areas in South East Asia and many men passed through them before they were spun out into a more permanent setting such as Formosa (modern-day Taiwan), or Japan itself, or to meet the need for workers on the Thailand–Burma Railway. Demand for labour in the autumn of 1942 pushed numbers at Changi down to 15,744 and by the following June the number had fallen to a wartime low of 5,359 when a newly accelerated 'speedo' period on the railway sucked in ever more workers in a drive to finish the line. After the horrors of jungle camps some POWs came to view Changi as 'home' and returning to it after a spell in some even worse camp as 'coming home'.

The hiatus between capture and the imposition of tighter rules had given most of Changi a chance to establish its own routine. A newsletter produced by the Cambridgeshire regiment, called *The Fenman*, gives some idea of how the soldiers had 'shaken down and sorted ourselves out', as Major P.T. Howard put it in 'general notes'.

CLASSIFIED   ADVERTISEMENTS

※   ※   ※

WANTED

A reliable WINNOWING-MACHINE for sorting Brigade Messages and separating the wheat from the chaff.▼...price no object.. send all particulars to the Adjutant.

※   ※   ※

A RICE-CONVERTOR guaranteed to produce unlimited supplies of bacon and eggs requiring little or no maintenance; hire purchase or cash; free trial requested....Apply H. Cotton & Co., The Changi Restaurant.

※   ※   ※

A large quantity of ALE; must be genuine.

FOR SALE

TWO TINS of genuine 1939 BULLY. Owner compelled to sell at a great sacrifice...$.300. the pair...worth double....Box 242.

※   ※   ※

YOU WANT the best rumours; WE HAVE them. Apply for our latest Easter selections............ 18 Div. Signals.

※   ※   ※

15 INCH GUN part-worn. Make ideal souvenir. What offers? Apply 53 Bde Gardens Committee.

BANKRUPTCY   NOTICES

To be sold at Changi on May 1st by order of the Official Receiver the stock-in-trade plant equipment and assets of FERNIE'S LTD. haulage contractors (in liquidation). Large stock of 412s to be disposed of.

BOOKSELLERS   ADVERTS

Secondhand books for sale. Real bargains. To-day's special snip.. Fine old first edition of "Brigade Standing Orders for M.T." Author's signed copy..(8vo. bound in old rope) practically unused.

┌──────── TO-DAYS BEAUTIFUL THOUGHT ────────┐

"GRIND YOUR RICE

AND NOT YOUR MOLARS"

└───┘

The newsletter's tone – jocular with the occasional lapse into maudlin poetry – is remarkably similar to the tenor of 'wall newspapers' produced in European camps. Its cover shows a drawing of Ely Cathedral – a potent reminder of home for many of the men who served in the regiment – and it contains a 'classified' section that tried to find comic relief in their predicament.

Major Howard, by comparison, used his article to stress how living conditions were improving. It is easy to imagine him pacing up and down, his swagger stick tucked neatly under his arm, as he searches for words to present their situation in a positive light:

> One thing does loom up in our minds nowadays, and that is FOOD, and in this connection I think we have a lot to be thankful for – our Q.M. and C/Sjt. [Company Sergeant] Stubbings (who, laying aside the soldier's rifle and the lawyer's quill, has reverted to Bakery) have really done their stuff, and it may not be generally realised that we are one of the few Bns [battalions] who are able to produce bread regularly; also we still use the original issue of yeast, a fickle growth requiring much care and attention to keep it alive and multiplying.

Digging a vegetable patch had been one of the first jobs the Cambridgeshires tackled when they arrived in Changi. An old Chinese garden of around four acres was immediately revived, although men who had been keen gardeners at home had to adapt to the different soil, crops and climate.

The battalion had already started to organise whist drives and talks on travel and subjects 'of general interest'. Speakers from the Federated Malay States Volunteer Force, including senior members of the MCS (Malayan Civil Service), who had been billeted with the Cambridgeshires, were particularly popular. Seven POWs agreed to form a 'Brains Trust', or quiz panel who would answer within five minutes questions put to them by the audience in the Brigade Church. They answered a total of twenty-nine questions – with varying degrees of success and conviction. They hazarded a guess that the reason why men's clothes buttoned on the right was to keep their sword arm free but made no reference to the part of the question that asked why ladies' clothes fastened on the left. The team appeared on safer ground when answering questions about the size of the Swiss navy (a trick question – they had three small gun boats, according to the Brains Trust), whether Napoleon and Wellington were born on the same day (the same year, but not the same day) and the year in which Columbus discovered America (1492).

POWs from the battalion had played several games of football and cricket against other units but more sport was dependent on being allocated ground and adequate rations. For the first three weeks they were allowed to bathe in the sea and enjoyed swimming off Telok Paku, where there were few rocks. Like other POW camps in both Asia and Europe, they named the buildings they lived in after places at home – whereas London POWs chose 'Piccadilly' and 'Mayfair', the Cambridgeshires used street names local to Ely – such as 'Fore Hill' and 'High Street'. Other men took comfort in daydreaming about home. *The Fenman* contains an essay on wildfowling in which one soldier remembers hunting birds in the snowy darkness outside Yarmouth; remembering the icy conditions must have offered some pleasure in the clammy Singaporean heat.

An anonymous poem, *Exile*, is all the more poignant when read with the hindsight that its author still has another three years to wait until he can return home – if he did indeed return home.

> Do you remember how the Mill
> Half way to Downham, on its hill
> Points on with moving finger where
> Haze-dimmed with distance, strong yet fair
> In proud magnificence the fane
> Of Ely rides above the plain;
> Where friendly clustered houses lie
> Beside the Ouse slow wandering by?
> I wonder, does the Mill still stand
> And beckon to that Promised Land?
> I would give all the golden sand
> From Singapore to Samarkand
> And all the glowing Eastern scene
> If I might stand on Palace Green
> And feel the kindly English sun

Beside the Old Crimean gun.
There sit those folk who never seem
To have much else to do but dream;
While see, amidst a reverend throng
The Bishop goes to evensong ...

Such were the numbers of POWs taken and the speed of the ceasefire, that it was several days – sometimes even weeks – before many soldiers had a chance to study their captors and when they did they were shocked by what they saw. Most of the Japanese, Charles Fisher noted, were: 'So small that they seemed to us to be mere boys rather than grown men, and the extreme shortness of their legs had the effect of turning their marching style into a strut which to us appeared both insufferably arrogant and excruciatingly comic.'

This, together with their lack of 'spit and polish' and inability to march in step, 'created among our own well-drilled troops a sense of contempt which served only to intensify our feeling of humiliation at having been defeated by what appeared to us as a rabble rather than an army. Roman citizens in the days of the barbarian invasions must have felt much as we did in February 1942.'

Jack Chalker remembers how he felt when he saw a Japanese soldier for the first time:

I think I was frightened, like everyone else. You were very, very anxious – to say the least of it because a lot of us had known what had happened in the Rape of Nanking and all the other things that had happened. There were quite a few massacres and we knew the fact that they thought that to be a prisoner was a complete dishonour and that we were then expendable so we thought, 'What the hell's going to happen?'

Eric Lomax, who after the war wrote *The Railway Man*, a moving account of his time as a POW and his later attempts to come to terms with the torture he endured, spent his first days in captivity in a bungalow with tranquil views out to sea. But this 'odd kind of normality' was shattered when Colonel Pope, a senior signals officer in the Southern Area of Changi, addressed the men. He was concerned that because many of them had not seen a Japanese soldier yet they were in danger of drifting into a false sense of security. In a bid to avoid this complacency he told them about statements he had taken from POWs who had witnessed the Alexandra Hospital atrocity in which the Japanese had killed an estimated fifty staff and patients on 14 February 1942 and another 150 the following day. He also passed on accounts from men who had arrived from Sumatra and other islands and who had heard of the fate of a ship that was carrying sixty-five Australian nurses and over 200 evacuees – among them women and children – and which had been sunk off Bangka Island, which lies to the east of Sumatra in Indonesia. The survivors who had turned themselves in to the Japanese were lined up on the beach and shot as they were forced to wade out into the sea; the injured were bayoneted to death as they lay on stretchers. Only one nurse and one English soldier survived. For Lomax and the other men, the story of the beach killings was particularly chilling because so many of the victims were nurses – a figure of veneration among soldiers. If anyone doubted the veracity of these reports they were soon presented with proof of how the Japanese dealt with dissenters.

Bored with the routine of Changi, Lomax volunteered to join a working party at Kranji, on the northern side of Singapore. One morning as they set off to march to the site, he saw six severed Chinese heads skewered on poles by the side of the road. Lomax describes them as looking, from a distance, 'like Hallowe'en fright masks'. But, even though the POWs passed 'this display of medieval barbarity' daily, they felt immune to it because they assumed it was a purge of suspected plotters from the Chinese nationalist Kuomintang party. Such brutality, they believed, must be reserved for those who continued to oppose Japanese rule.

When Jack Chalker left the camp to join work parties around the island he, too, came face-to-face with similar barbarity. He saw the heads of civilians left on tables where they accumulated a mask of flies and he witnessed children and old people being struck down by impatient guards. But, of all the horrors he encountered during his captivity, one particular incident remains seared into his memory which, even in old age, is capable of reducing him to tears.

One day he was in a group of men sent to the docks to shift bodies, clear up the godowns (warehouses) and stack cans of petrol. As they marched along the road an old Chinese lady appeared carrying a cardboard box that she had packed with delicate porcelain cups, each containing a small sponge cake that she handed out to the POWs. The first time she did this their guard seemed untroubled by the act of kindness but when she tried the next day a different guard turned on her, beating and kicking her until she was barely alive, 'just a mangled black thing on the road'. What he found heart-breaking about this outburst of cruelty was that the POWs were powerless to help. 'We were so angry. We couldn't do anything at all because we had two or three guards with us – if we had attacked him we should have been shot anyway and everyone else would have been.' The following day they passed the same spot – but with a different guard. The old lady, 'all bruised and damaged', was there again, undaunted, with her cakes.

When he was held in Roberts Barracks he lived in a pantry in what had once been the married quarters. He and a friend slept on the concrete floor and used the shelf above their tiny sleeping space to store their few possessions. The irony of making their home in a kitchen cupboard, while their rations dwindled, appears to have been lost on them. They lived off one or two hard biscuits a day, stale rice mixed with lime that had once been used as fertiliser and would make up for some of the many vitamins they were lacking, and a watery sort of slop.

The sick were laid on and under the beds and on the floor where the intense humidity and shortage of water added to their discomfort. He remembers one of the 'camp fatigues' was to collect bundles of blankets soaked with blood and faeces and to carry them to the nearby, idyllic beach, where he waded out into the water with the rags to rinse off as much of the dirt as possible and then lay them in the sun to dry. He found this sort of stark contrast between the natural beauty around him and the ugly aftermath of human conflict particularly disturbing. On another occasion, when he was sent to gather wood, he came across a well-kept bungalow set in beautiful gardens that swept down to its own beach. The home had a Mary Celeste stillness to it but the sound of buzzing flies and stench of rotting flesh alerted him to two blackened figures whose dug-out had become their grave. He could see that the home had been ransacked and through the open door he glimpsed a pile of magazines and books strewn across the floor. Among them he spotted a copy of his old school magazine; inside was an item about his brother's marriage earlier that year. He tucked it inside his shirt before rejoining his working party.

Turned Out Rice Again:
Food and Cooking

During the battle for Singapore, fighting had disrupted the normally efficient supply of army food but adrenalin and fear had kept hunger at bay.
Food was simply not a priority, as magician Fergus Anckorn recalls:

> That's another thing I learnt – there's no such thing as first and second
> course. I remember in action, when we were actually fighting, one day
> a little truck came down with food on board in a hay box. They said
> get out on the road with your mess tins. We hadn't eaten anything for
> two days and along comes this. I hadn't got a mess tin, I had no pos-
> sessions. If I was lucky, I would eat off a banana leaf, if not, out of my
> hand. I remember standing at the side of the road like that. They put
> in a sausage, mash potato, pears and custard, all in there [his cupped
> hands]. I ate them, who cares – in ten seconds it's all down there. If
> you want to eat something just down it, in any order you like, it's
> down there doing its job.

But once he became a POW there was more time to dwell on the gnawing hunger that crept over his body. He realised that he could use his magic
to obtain food, and later, when he performed in front of the Japanese
guards and high ranking officers, he always chose tricks that needed eggs,
fruit or other food. He was usually allowed to keep the prop to eat later,
or share with friends because the Japanese considered anything that had
been touched by POWs as contaminated.

One of Jim Swanton's most vivid memories of the early days in Changi was the feeling: 'for the first time in one's life of being absolutely paralysingly hungry'.

As in European camps, POWs feasted on lavish literary descriptions of food or luxurious settings; a description of a feast in Kenneth Roberts' *North-West Passage* was particularly popular. When books like *Pears Encyclopaedia* were plundered for their tissue-thin pages to make roll-up cigarettes, it was always the recipes that were the last to go up in smoke. Officers would relive sumptuous dinners at the Café Royale or other grand restaurants. In the early days of his captivity in Pudu Gaol, Kuala Lumpur, Russell Braddon dreamt of 'chocolate éclairs mixed with steak and served heavily garnished with egg'.

The Japanese paid Braddon and other POWs ten cents a day for the work they did. They received three dollars for a whole month's work (with no time off) and this bought a small handful of dried fish, a little coconut oil in which to fry it, and possibly one or two bananas. POWs were particularly keen to eat bananas because they had heard that they were rich in vitamin E, which they believed protected against infertility – something that many soldiers had an obsessive fear of. Most of the men donated twenty-five cents of their pay to a kitty that Noel Duckworth, the Cambridgeshire Regiment's padre who had coxed Cambridge University's boat before the war, took into town where he bought soap and food for the sick. From the end of 1942, officers were, as a standard, operating to Geneva Convention procedure, being paid a rate equivalent to IJA wages in local currency. In reality, POWs received only a fraction of what they were due. The Japanese held back part to cover lodgings, food and clothes (what became known as the 'rent, rice and rags' deduction) and part was placed in a bank for repayment after the war. Unlike Other Ranks, officers usually received pay when they were sick.

After the war, rice became the source of uneasy jokes among former POWs who had spent over three years with the grain as their staple diet. Tales are told of the doting mother who saved up her ration coupons so that she could present her boy with the meal she thought he would most enjoy – rice pudding. Take a POW out for a meal today and he will often choose a Thai or Chinese restaurant – and josh about how the rice is not as good without a garnish of weevils. Perhaps years of staring at the same colourless grain, chasing the last morsel round a plate, or wondering how the cooks might try to disguise what they were serving up, gave them a grudging affection for it. Or maybe humour, no matter how uncomfortable for fellow diners, is the only way of banishing horrific memories.

Rice soon featured in the Cambridgeshire Regiment's newsletter, *The Fenman*: 'For a few days British Army rations were lived on, with the rice-element gradually creeping in until one day it burst on us in all its glory! Rice for breakfast, rice for dinner, rice for tea, (it is learned on good authority that some people have actually discovered microscopic portions of meat, fish, and even pine-apple in their helpings of rice!!)'

Food Notes – The food and standard of cooking have been much improved in the last 10 days or so, and there can be few legitimate causes for grousing. There are three meals, which may be classified as follows (according to the Chinese fashion): 0930 (Morning Rice); 1330 (Midday Rice): 1830 (Evening Rice). Although rice is naturally the predominating item on the menu (17oz. per man per day), it is sufficiently well blended with such things as meat-rissole, bully-stew, fish-cake and curry, with the addition of little delicacies like jam-pastry, rice-cake or biscuit, and bread roll and butter, occasionally to make it both palatable and interesting. May we have nothing worse to put up with.

But there was a lot worse to put up with – especially for men who were sent to work on the Thailand–Burma Railway. Even for those who stayed behind on Singapore, 17 ounces per man per day, would later seem like a feast and protein would be even rarer.

One of the major challenges of the early days of captivity was how to cook rice for large numbers so that it did not end up as an unappetising ball of glutinous matter. Pre-war Britain was still a place of meat and two veg. where potato and bread were the king and queen of carbohydrates. Rice was a foreign commodity that few people knew how to cook properly and which Western digestive systems struggled to accommodate. Eating so much rice made men urinate frequently, which often led to dehydration and then constipation. At home most men would have poured milk or cream over rice and eaten it with sugar and tinned peaches or prunes; they rarely thought of it as anything other than a pudding.

The library at the modern Changi Museum in Singapore contains a copy of *The Changi Cookery Book* in which an anonymous Mrs Beeton-style author offers tips for anyone faced with the challenge of catering for around a hundred men at one sitting. In the handwritten section, the author explains in careful detail that there are two ways of cooking rice – boiling and straining off, and steaming (the usual native and IJA way). If boiling, the cook should use five parts water to one part rice and preserve the remaining water for soups because it contains useful nutrients. While steaming produces the most 'appetising and attractive looking rice' it is not recommended for POWs 'in that a burnt crust is left as a sort of skin covering the whole of the inside of the pot which is wasteful when every grain is precious.'

Cooks had to put up with snide remarks about their lack of culinary skills or hints that they were keeping food back for themselves. Stanley Chown, a chef at Pembroke College, was among the soldiers taken prisoner on Singapore but it is unlikely that life at Cambridge University could in any way have prepared him for serving up rations to POWs. Others, however, discovered hidden culinary talents. In Bandung, Laurens van der Post became proficient at making a type of marmalade. Other POWs devised ways of doing their own cooking by making little stoves out of scraps of equipment. Eric Lomax used a 44-gallon drum with a door cut in one end as an oven in his early days at Changi and then, after his return to Singapore, helped to boil sea water to extract the salt using an army mess tin and an old electric fire element twisted to form a ring that linked up to the mains.

James Wakefield, a 2nd Lieutenant in the Royal Engineers, was equally ingenious at Shamshuipo camp in Hong Kong where he had been taken after its surrender on Christmas Day 1941. As in Singapore, fighting had been fierce. He had time to lay only one minefield before he found himself in a trench cut into a gulley close to the main high road facing a bombardment that came in salvoes of sixteen shells a minute. Like most soldiers he knew the old saying that you never hear the shell that kills you and he listened intently for each one as it followed its trajectory before exploding. 'We were counting the shells and saying whether it was behind us, before us or where and as the next one came in – it was the thirteenth – I shouted: "This is ours!" and it landed right over the top of my head, killed a man in the little slit trench where we were. His head was blown off; the other man, a Portuguese from the battery, he had a big hole in his back. They were both dead.'

The blast covered him with dirt and left him with a permanent hearing problem. Stunned by his lucky escape and the death of his comrades, he and three other men somehow made their way back to Head Quarters: a Salvation Army building at Shushon Hill in the Deep Water Bay area. From here, he and a small unit of about twenty Royal Engineers were ordered to The Peak, a normally quiet and well-to-do residential area of Hong Kong. They found a deserted bungalow very close to a place known as Jardine's Lookout. The bungalow was owned by Hong Kong Electric. Its General Manager, who was a member of the Hong Kong Volunteer Defence Corps, lived there but was fighting in another part of the colony.

The soldiers discovered some turkeys in the yard, chopped their heads off and took them by army truck to be cooked at the nearest barracks. That night they had a roast; since the meat had not been hung it was rather tough but it was one of their final meals as free men. On Christmas Day they heard that the British had surrendered Hong Kong. Once they knew their fighting days were over they scoured the bungalow for anything that might be of use in captivity. Wakefield found three big cakes of Yardley's lavender soap. 'Well, I thought, that's a good thing to take into camp. At that time a cake of soap was a huge thing and they virtually lasted me two years.'

They first saw their captors in front of the Hong Kong & Shanghai Bank before, back on the mainland, they were marched four miles to Shamshuipo camp along streets strewn with dead bodies and soldiers' helmets, boots and uniforms. The Japanese flag fluttered from doorways and windows. Among the prisoners was the general manager whose bungalow Wakefield had stayed in. He was not one of the most optimistic of men and Wakefield soon assessed him as a member of the 'doom and gloom squad'.

Shamshuipo had previously housed British soldiers. Since then looters had ripped out toilets, taps, basins and baths; the doors, windows, furniture, even woodwork had disappeared. It looked, to one eyewitness, like a typhoon had hit it. The POWs were forced to dig latrines and Wakefield slept on the bare floor in a room with about ten other men.

Before joining the army Wakefield had worked in a design office and studied structural engineering at a night class in Manchester. His innate interest in how things worked was put to good use in a POW camp. 'It was surprising how many men, officers, went into camp with a [tin] box of Jacob's Crackers.'

The POWs used the boxes, together with bits of asbestos that the looters had torn from the walls and chicken wire, to rig up a primitive stove. They unwound the wire and wrapped it round a pencil to make an induction loop that they connected to the mains. 'You got this wire lovely and hot and you could boil water.' The problem was that the device got through fuses very quickly; each time one blew they resorted to a bigger one until they had all been used.

Cigarette containers proved a useful alternative to the Jacob's Crackers box and were the nearest the POWs could get to the Red Cross tins that prisoners in Europe put to such good use. In the Far East, cigarettes were packed in tins to protect them from the humidity; two of the most popular brands were Garrick and Players. Jim found that the Players tin would fit snugly inside the Garrick container and could be arranged in a similar way to the crackers box. The device could boil a bucket of water in ten minutes.

In his diary, 'Weary' Dunlop estimated that soldiers performing duties needed between 2,400 and 3,000 calories a day but by May 1942, POWs at Bandung Gaol were struggling on around 1,800. Ernest Edward Dunlop was an Australian army medical officer who gained a reputation for ingenuity and courage that was reinforced by the publication of his diaries after the war. His nickname of 'Weary' came from the boundless enthusiasm with which he played rugby and fought as a heavyweight boxer when he was a medical student at the University of Melbourne. Like the advertisement for the Dunlop tyre, a product with which he shared a surname, he 'never wore out'.

On 28 April 1942 he wrote: 'Nobody feels much like exercise. There is a tendency to slight giddiness and stars flash at times when one rises to the vertical.' By 2 July 1942, daily calorific intake had increased slightly to 2,173. In the UK today the government recommends that men should consume 2,500 calories a day. In other camps, and particularly later in the war when the Japanese, too, were suffering from food shortages, many POWs were subsisting on a starvation diet whilst at the same time being forced to take part in hard physical labour.

But it was not simply the lack of calories that led to suffering and illness. The *type* of food, and in particular the lack of certain minerals and vitamins, caused medical problems. Most POWs' diets were desperately short of animal fat and of anything sweet. Recipes in *The Changi Cookery Book* include sugar as an ingredient but also alternatives such as sweet potatoes or 'sugar' made from palm or date trees. As the war continued POWs' lives turned sour. Looking back on a point in his captivity when there were very few diversions Fergus Anckorn remembers: 'Do you know what we missed more than anything? Well, sex that's way down the list somewhere. The first thing was music – I used to imagine orchestras; I could see them playing. And the next thing was sugar.'

Overcrowding, poor sanitation and bodies weakened by a meagre diet allowed debilitating diseases such as malaria and dysentery to creep into the camp and spread through the men. Weeks, and then months, of low-fat, low-protein meals which were little more than piles of rice ushered in other, strange-sounding illnesses which seemed to have escaped from the pages of a journal of tropical medicine. Young men who joined the army at the peak of their physical fitness found themselves diagnosed with exotic troubles such as beriberi or pellagra. A whole nomenclature evolved around the growing list of terrible complaints that the POWs fell victim to. 'Happy feet' (or 'electric feet' as it was also known) was an ironic term for a condition associated with beriberi that sent hot, stabbing pains through the soles of the feet that burnt, itched, throbbed and ached; sufferers found some small relief by stamping their feet. 'Rice', 'Java', 'Changi' or 'Bandung balls' were all names for the same problem: a sort of scrotal dermatitis which left the skin raw and itching and which was usually caused by a shortage of vitamin B2 (Riboflavin). A lack of vitamin B12 caused nutritional amblyopia, or 'camp eyes' in which POWs developed a blind spot that, if left untreated, could lead to total blindness. Fergus remembers that the only time he received any Red Cross supplies in Singapore, the package contained Marmite. His friend who was suffering from beriberi and could barely see, hear or move was miraculously restored after a four-day diet of the spread. Many POWs at Changi were tormented by 'dhobi itch', a fungal infection of the groin, which resulted in incessant scratching and was particularly irritating when the sufferer was trying to get to sleep.

Each of these terrible illnesses changed the outward appearance of the POWs, forcing them to move in different ways and making them more conscious of what their body was going through. As an artist, Jack Chalker could not help but observe these changes and the drawings he did as a POW reflect both his sympathy for the sufferings of others but also a medical eye for illness and how it was invading the body. Before the war he had secured a place at Charing Cross Hospital and was particularly interested in orthopaedics, but he had also won a scholarship to the Royal College of Art in London in the School of Painting. He chose the latter but had to abandon his plans when his call-up papers arrived at the end of September 1939.

In the case of tropical ulcers, amputation was often the only hope of saving the patient but dietary solutions were found for many other illnesses. As the camps became more established, POWs devised ingenious ways of extracting vitamins from unexpected sources such as the tall lalang grass with its feathery white heads and the hibiscus bushes, whose red, white or purple flowers look like neatly folded hankies, and which are rich in vitamin C.

As well as learning how to cook rice and other unfamiliar foods so that they were palatable, cooks had to understand that the way they prepared meals was also vital to the men's health. They improved both the flavour of the rice and replaced salt lost through tropical perspiration by adding salt extracted from seawater, or boiled the rice in seawater. They learnt, too, to retain the fine flakes of rice called 'polishings' (the external layers of the grain that are usually removed by the modern, commercial form of milling) which are rich in vitamin B1 (Thiamine). The dangers of using polished rice had been well known in the region since the second decade of the twentieth century when the link with beriberi, which can affect the cardiovascular and nervous system, became clear. Pork and eggs are both rich in thiamine and protein, and eggs in particular became a much sought-after commodity when bartering with local people. Duck eggs, which were high in protein, vitamins and fat, were particularly prized.

The shortage of vitamin B caused most problems. Today the developed world takes B1, B2 (Riboflavin) and B3 (Niacin) for granted; they appear as a commonplace litany on the side of our breakfast cereals or crop up in school biology lessons. In the Far East their absence added to the battery of illnesses attacking the POW.

Beriberi, caused by a deficiency of vitamin B1, was quick to appear in the camps. Those who had been heavy drinkers were among the first to exhibit signs – probably because alcohol can inhibit the absorption of B1. Beriberi is thought to derive from the Sinhalese word 'beri' meaning weakness – the repetition serving to stress the severity of the affliction. It is a telling etymology since the illness causes an underlying weakness that takes many forms. A long period of under-nourishment can lead to beriberi heart in which the organ is damaged, although there appear to be few outward signs of illness. The most obvious indication of wet beriberi is oedema – swelling caused by water retention – that begins at the feet and legs and spreads upward through the body. Dry beriberi leads to tender and painful muscles, eventually making it difficult for the sufferer to walk. It is this last form that suggests the alternative etymology of beriberi: from the Malay word for sheep, recalling the abrupt, stumbling gait of the patient. After the war, the experience of POWs in the Far East helped scientists to recognise a cerebral form of beriberi whose symptoms can include hallucinations and memory loss.

The POWs' bland diet led to cases of pellagra, an illness that usually starts with redness around the neck, or other areas exposed to sunlight, a sore throat and difficulty swallowing. If left unchecked it can escalate into diarrhoea, paralysis of the lower limbs and suicidal tendencies. The Australian soldier and entertainer, Sydney Piddington suffered at Changi and was taken to Roberts Barracks where he was given hibiscus and boiled grass. What he needed was vitamin B3 that is found in animal foods such as meat, eggs and milk.

A shortage of dairy foods and their meagre rations left the POWs lacking in vitamin B2. This deficiency caused cracks at the corner of the mouth and a sore tongue that made it painful to eat – thus locking the sufferer into a vicious circle in which their vitamin-related illness made it difficult to consume enough Riboflavin (which cannot be stored in the body but must be ingested regularly). The deficiency also led to the scrotal problem of 'rice balls' and sensitivity to light. A spoonful of Marmite often helped, and yeast, which contains many B-complex vitamins, was used when available. In late April 1942, the camp medical authorities at Changi started to issue a daily two-ounce dosage to each man; the yeast was grown specifically for this purpose. Other camps found ways of bringing in supplies. Every fortnight at James Wakefield's camp in Hong Kong, prisoners lined up with their mugs to receive liquid yeast supplied by a chemist who worked in a sugar refinery.

A lack of vitamin A led to problems with eyesight but this could be corrected fairly quickly by red palm oil which was used in cooking. Many artists, without realising it, captured the ocular damage caused by this and other vitamin deficiencies as their sitters stare out of portraits with red-rimmed, scarred and bulging eyes. In James Wakefield's camp the prisoners made shades out of cardboard to protect them from the sun's glare.

Vegetable patches helped to boost both calories and vitamin intake and establishing gardens was one of the first tasks POWs performed at Changi although, to begin with, it was classed, with other pursuits such as education and entertainment, as something to keep the men busy in their spare moments. But as rations dwindled gardening assumed greater importance. Eight hundred men from the AIF set to work digging out the once sweeping lawns of Changi and by the time POWs had settled into camp life, market gardens had spread to most parts of the peninsula. The Cambridgeshires were quick to start planting in an old four-acre Chinese garden. According to 'Garden Gossip' in *The Fenman* newsletter, 'football committees' of officers began to meet in the gardeners' hut but it seems their purpose may have been to raid the beds, rather than discuss tactics as they became known as The Cadgers Club and 'after several pointed remarks ceased to function'.

The gardeners, often advised by men who had lived in the region and were part of the volunteers who joined the fighting, were amazed at what they could cultivate and how fast it grew. They planted exotic foods such as *ubi kayu* (more commonly known in the West as cassava) for its fleshy tuberous root that they grated onto tapioca, sweet potatoes, chillies, ginger and aubergines. Ceylon spinach, amaranth and *kangkong* (water spinach) were all eaten for their leaves which are rich in minerals, vitamins A, B6, Riboflavin, K and C and protein but which stained the soldiers' teeth green. Sergeant Hyde, who was in charge of the Cambridgeshires' garden at Changi, tested various flowers, fruits and vegetables to see whether they were edible and whether the leaves could be smoked. When the gardeners started to use human manure and urine as fertilisers on the vegetable patches, tending them became less pleasant as the smell grew overpowering in the heat.

At home Britons were being forced into a similar culinary ingenuity. As Germany did its best to starve the country into submission, the British Government was encouraging its citizens to grow their own and 'dig for victory'. Like the anonymous author of the *Changi Cook Book*, the Ministry of Food urged housewives to experiment with ersatz substitutes, replacing apricots with carrots in apricot jam or disguising mutton as goose in 'mock goose', and to gather herbs and fruit from the hedgerows.

The 'hedgerow' in the Far East had much more to offer than the black-berries, wild garlic and sloes of rural Britain. Ingredients in the *Changi Cook Book* include coconuts, peanuts, green ginger, chillies, papaya, sweet potato, tapioca root, *tow gay* (a sort of bean sprout) and black beans. Lalang grass was frequently added to soup as a way of countering eye problems linked to nutrition. In some parts of Changi it was compulsory to drink it once a week and when Eric Lomax returned to Singapore after working on the Thailand–Burma Railway he was told to down a pint every day as a restorative. The prisoners cut the grass, which harboured rats, with scythes and used some of it as compost on their vegetable gardens. They also made a crushing machine so that it was easier to add to food. POW cooks were also incorporating Asian mainstays into their repertoire: sambal (a highly seasoned condiment), *gula melaka* (palm sugar) and *tempeh* (a soya bean product similar to tofu). It is impossible to know whether the author of the *Changi Cook Book* meant to change the traditional Malaysian dish of *nasi goreng* to 'Nazi Goering', or whether his version was an act of defiance.

The rest of the book is devoted to typed recipes that range from cakes and biscuits to condiments and jam. Rice is a feature – if not the main ingredient – of nearly every dish and often the recipe is a triumph of imagination over availability. 'Surprise bread' contains four pounds of boiled rice, 5 pounds of rice flour, a pound of sago flour, salt, cooking oil, limes and sugar – but no yeast. Small, afternoon tea cakes 'can be deco-rated to be pleasing to the appearance and enhance their value'. Pink glaze, for example, could be made from water in which red spinach had been boiled. Lemon duff pudding contained no lemons, but a quarter pound of limes; 'fresh meat sausage rolls' included the hopeful ingredi-ent '8–9 pounds fresh meat (day's issue)'; a final apologetic note reveals the challenge cooks faced: 'This method forms a fine large sausage roll, pleasing to the eye which after all is half the art of cooking.' The author admitted in his recipe for jam tarts and jam flans, 'A jam flan is where the jam contents are more in the form of a sago jelly into which some jam has been mixed to give it a flavour.'

The *Changi Cookery Book* does not mention the less appetising ingredients that desperate POWs sometimes chewed on to take the edge off their hunger, or to provide some welcome protein – dogs, cats, mice, rats, frogs,

birds, snakes, cockroaches, grasshoppers, snails, even strips of army blanket.
According to Stephen Alexander the change in diet led to extreme
constipation, when the outside privy 'assumed the air of a maternity ward'.
Sydney Piddington found snails difficult to cook because of the slime they
exuded. Sometimes a new food was the result of opportunism. At Bandung,
a working party marched back to camp with a 12-foot long Java lizard in tow.
They secured it with rope and it provided about 150 pounds of fresh meat.

POWs had an ambivalent attitude to animals. For some, dogs, cats,
ducks and rabbits were pets – creatures that they could cosset and over
whose life they had some control at a time when their own existence was
entirely in the hands of their captors. Len Baynes had kept ducks at his
home in Cambridgeshire and built an elaborate duck house and run at
Changi out of wire netting, attap palm and bamboo. He thatched the
house with grass and their home drew POWs who came to marvel at it.

> That night I hardly slept, thinking about my dear little ducks, and plan-
> ning their future! So exciting was it to have something constructive to
> do and some little lives dependent on me.

He caught frogs and 'creepy crawlies' for them to eat and worried about
their every need.

> How different life now seemed with my little charges. I built my work-
> ing day around them, and even dreamed about them at night. They
> were now my substitute family.

However, disaster struck when he let them out of their pen and they were
swept down a storm drain and into an underground culvert. The loss of
his adopted family left him feeling bereft.

Pets were only ever a glance away from the cooking pot or the guard's
bayonet. While they may have given their owners great comfort they also
left them vulnerable to the pain of further loss. Fergus Anckorn adopted
a spaniel at Changi and when rations became desperately low he trained
it to walk on its hind legs so that when the men were queuing to buy
peanuts it would beg for food. When he was invited to the Dutch sector
to perform some magic his audience treated him to delicious fried meat
rissoles. When he asked where they got the meat they admitted that he

had just eaten his pet. The news came as something of a relief as he was struggling to feed it.

Stephen Alexander remembers how Bobby Greene, a partner in a Singapore law firm, kept his dachshund puppy with him in Changi and always fed it before he fed himself. As it became increasingly unlikely that his wife had survived the evacuation of the island, the dog assumed greater importance in his life and his fellow POWs helped him to hide it. They were probably concealing it as much from their captors as hungry prisoners. Slim de Grey, the Australian concert party member, writes in his memoirs of starting a 'Dog Lovers' Club' in Changi and how its six members supplemented their diet with canine meat. On one occasion they smuggled a Labrador in to the camp in a double bass to serve for Christmas lunch and masked the barks coming from inside the instrument with a burst of *Jingle Bells*. As a fully-grown Labrador would not have fitted easily into a double bass perhaps this macabre tale is an example of the black humour that some POWs thrived on.

Rabbits, ducks and pigs were easier than some livestock to rear because they could live off scraps; they also offered the welcome addition of animal protein and fat. However, their survival became more precarious when the calorific intake of those tending them dipped below their charges. Laurens van der Post found that at Bandung eventually both the pigs and the rabbits' requirements were too great – not just the food they needed but the material for pigsties. The swill, though, had been handy for local people to hide food for the POWs in and some men had become so attached to the 400 rabbits they kept there that when they were moved to a new camp the owners wrote their name and rank on the animals' ears after the Japanese promised to send the animals on later. The guards, of course, did not keep their word.

Caring for three piglets provided a turning point for Fergus Anckhorn. By this time he was working on the Thailand–Burma Railway. The guards had said that if they fattened them up they could slaughter them for Christmas.

'It was monsoon and when you're in the monsoon for three months you forget what the sun looks like and you're up to your knees in water and mud.' The pigs, by comparison, were dry and snug. The prisoners built them a little shelter out of bricks and gave it an attap roof to protect them from the rain. Of the 60 grams of rice they received a day the men gave one spoonful to the sick, who because they could not work were not paid, and one spoonful to the pigs.

When a high-ranking Japanese general was due to visit the camp, the guards ordered them to make everywhere spick and span.

I was given the job of cleaning the pigs, scrubbing them. I had a bucket of hot water and a scrubbing brush. We never had hot water so I had to scrub these pigs until they were pink – just like you get on a cake. I scrubbed these piggies – they resented it – all in the pouring rain and I got them all nice and pink and then I had to chase them around in the mud so that they couldn't sit down and get dirty because if the Jap general had found even dirty pigs the commandant would have got beaten up. So I had to move them around all the time and then suddenly the retinue turns up and I have to be got out of the way so that the pigs are there on their own. So the pigs are standing there; they could scarcely breath because I'd had them on the run for half an hour and the Jap general just walked past – as they do – and the pigs went in to their little shelter and lay down out of the rain and I said to myself, 'God, I wish I was a pig.' And then I said to myself out loud, 'Fergus Anckorn you've just wished you were a pig.' The only way is up.

Private Albert Nuttall of the 2nd Battalion, Loyal Regiment had a very different experience of rearing livestock when he was held in Mukden, Manchuria, where, during the winter months in particular, food was scarce. Many of the men were forced into heavy manual work in the half-built Ford factory but Nutall kept quiet about his expertise as a mechanical transport fitter (a mechanic) and instead said he was a farmer (he had, indeed, been born on a farm). He started off with six pigs and a sow in the factory and within two years, and with the help of an elderly man – probably a local – had produced 6 tons of dressed pork. He finished the war with 106 pigs, including two pedigree Hampshire and Yorkshire boars and a Hampshire gilt. The two men built a fine pigpen, mainly from stolen goods, and installed electricity so that the sow could see her farrow at night and not smother the piglets or step on them by mistake. Nuttall was able to keep a share of the pork and managed to slip some of it to the canteen but after the old man was replaced he was only allowed to keep the pigs' heads.

The pen doubled as a clearing house for stolen goods – mainly machine tools such as hacksaw blades and electric motors that fetched good prices on the Chinese black market but also shoes and clothing. In an account given after the war, Nuttall said an American supervisor from a rival gang who was disappointed at not getting 'an out' in a deal he felt he was entitled to had informed on him. When the Japanese searched the pen they found 120 pairs of shoes. Nuttall was one of eight men arrested and tried. They were beaten and clubbed and then sentenced to thirty-six days solitary confinement in a cage measuring 3 metres cubed. As he was such an expert in pig husbandry he returned to his old job after he had served his sentence – and continued to hide stolen goods.

POWs in the Far East became skilled farm hands, ingenious cooks and wily thieves because they could not fall back with such certainty on the Red Cross parcel which saved so many lives in Europe. The International Committee of the Red Cross (ICRC) simply did not have the infrastructure within the Pacific region; individual guards were slow to hand out parcels and many had no qualms about consuming the contents themselves or selling them. There are several accounts in which guards were found to have been stockpiling Red Cross packages or supplies that could have saved lives and which were only handed out when the war had tipped in the Allies' favour. Some POWs went for years without receiving a parcel and when they did, had no option but to divide the contents between several men. Henry William Sherwood, a sergeant in the 35th Light Anti-Aircraft (LAA) R. A.,who was known as 'Johnny', had to share his Red Cross parcel with twenty-nine other POWs, 'which of course meant we got almost nothing'.

The ICRC could not draw on its experience in the First World War when attempting to help men in the Far East; it also faced a different perception of the prisoner of war. The Japanese government had not ratified the Geneva Convention concerning POWs and a report by the ICRC after the war revealed the 'most serious difficulties' it had faced were in the Pacific. 'These difficulties were doubtless due chiefly to the survival of certain ancestral ideas, according to which the status of prisoner of war is degrading.' When a soldier left home in Japan, the report said, he was, as far as his relatives were concerned, dead. They had no desire to hear from him and he had no wish to write to them. He was only alive again when he returned as a conquering hero.

The Japanese government, therefore, had no sympathy for the efforts of the ICRC to help POWs and were suspicious of the foreigners whom the Committee tried to establish as their delegates in the region. These representatives were mostly neutral businessmen who had stayed behind and who bought food and other provisions locally with money sent by the ICRC. One representative, Dr Matthaeus Vischer, who was a missionary in Borneo, was beheaded – as was his wife. Other delegates found it extremely difficult to visit camps and when they did, the visits were brief and they were not allowed to speak to POWs alone.

There was no regular supply route for Red Cross parcels and the parcels that arrived by sea came on ships used to exchange diplomatic and civilian personnel. A pitifully small number of around 225,000 parcels, which were divided between Allied POWs and internees, reached the Far East in this way.

The unreliability of supplies meant that the POW in the Far East did not have the basic materials of string, tins and packing that his European counterpart put to such good use. He would have to look elsewhere when making stoves, constructing theatrical sets, finding materials for drawing and the myriad other uses the POW found for a Red Cross parcel.

Vitamin deficiencies combined to form a cast of illnesses that were difficult to distinguish from the habitual feelings of fatigue, the stomach cramps and the endless visits to the latrines. Even a man's skin took on a new identity as it revealed the outward signs of malnutrition exacerbated by the extreme heat, the perspiration, the inability to wash properly and the tattered remnants of uniform. But food was at the heart of the problem. Not only did starvation leave the POWs vulnerable to disease but it made every second of living an effort. It also left deep mental scars. Men who had spent years fantasising about food brought back attitudes that were out of place in a country that would soon be able to put rationing behind it. Some insisted on stockpiling cans of food to ensure that they were never without, others could not resist searching through dustbins for left-over food; normally doting fathers and grandfathers might fly into a rage if their children or grandchildren failed to clear their plates, ate noisily or made throw-away comments about being 'starving'. Others became obsessed with their bodies and despised couch potatoes who slumped in front of the television.

Thankfully, very few people in today's developed world know what it means to be genuinely starving. POWs returning from the Far East did – and that knowledge set them apart forever.

Make Do and Mend

In Europe, POWs had a regular supply of Red Cross parcels that not only provided sustenance but whose tins, packaging and string formed the raw materials for countless gadgets. In the Far East, Red Cross parcels were a rarity and had to be shared between a much larger group of prisoners. Often guards helped themselves to them or only handed them over when it was obvious that the Allies would win the war. Instead, POWs had to rely on what they already had with them – a bit of gas cape here, some webbing there; what they could 'scrounge' or 'find' (POW euphemisms for theft), barter or buy, or the natural largesse of the tropics.

Men who had lived in Asia before the war came into their own in a POW camp because they knew how to make the most of their environment. British and Australian POWs who had sniggered at the Dutch when they took a small bottle of water with them to the latrines eventually conceded that, in the absence of toilet paper, the Asian approach to ablutions was an effective way of slowing the spread of disease and saving pages of precious books. POWs who had made their homes in Asia could reveal the hidden medicinal properties of a flower or grass, or give horticultural advice to help make the most of a climate where fruit and vegetables grew at a spectacular rate.

Many of the men with this specialist knowledge came from the local 'volunteer forces'. In Singapore and the Malayan Peninsula, for example, members of the Malayan Volunteer Forces were a huge help to other POWs who had spent their life in Europe – and may only have arrived in Asia a matter of weeks before being captured. The British Empire had a long tradition of local volunteers dating back to the Crimean and Boer wars and the outbreak of hostilities in Europe persuaded many men in British Malaya to join. They came from a range of ethnic backgrounds: Chinese, Malay, Eurasian, as well as European, and from a wealth of jobs. Some held positions in the civil service, others were planters or worked in tin mines; there were doctors and religious ministers and men involved in commerce. The Volunteer Forces were similar to the Territorial Army in Britain and were organised in three geographical groups: Straits Settlements (S.S.), The Federated Malay States (F.M.S.) and The Unfederated Malay States (U.M.S.).

Several of the volunteers spoke Asian languages, and knew which local people might be sympathetic to their plight and the best way to approach them. Having lived in the tropics they knew ways to avoid certain diseases and how to treat them once they were contracted. Planters were knowledgeable about one of the region's most prized natural resources – rubber, although that expertise had been gathered at arm's length. They knew about the life cycle of the rubber tree, the price the material fetched worldwide and the effect international politics could have on its market, but few had the practical experience of how to make the perfect incision in the bark – not too deep and not too wide – to coax the milky white sap out of the tree. Now, far from the neatly planned and cosseted plantations that had provided their livelihood, they wondered whether the ravaged gum trees in and around their camps could be put to work.

Before he became a POW John Clemetson had worked for the Kinta Electrical Distribution Company, a subsidiary of British GEC (General Electric Company), in Ipoh. The town in north west Malaya had grown rich from the tin that lured colonial mining companies and attracted banks and bureaucrats in their wake. John, his wife and young son lived in a typical, large timbered house and he became a captain in the Federated Malay States Volunteer Force (FMSVF). When the Japanese invaded, his family managed to find a place on one of the last ships leaving Singapore, from where they reached Freemantle in Western Australia. As they headed for exile he began his life as a POW in Changi.

He was keen to find a pastime that would keep the troops busy and offer a practical benefit. Repairing and making shoes did both. Feet were particularly vulnerable because cuts were slow to heal among sick and malnourished men and, in the tropics, often led to life-threatening ulcers. Clemetson and his team started to use scraps of leather and bits of old boots, belts, lino, fire hose, kit bags and tyres to patch footwear. They made wooden clogs – more like the modern-type of Doctor Scholl's shoe with a single strap over the front of the foot than the traditional Dutch clog or sabot – and the corridors of Changi Gaol later rang with the noise of men clip-clopping along. Russell Braddon said it was possible to recognise one's friends by the sound of their footfall and this was particularly helpful to POWs whose sight was failing.

Rubber would have been perfect for repairing boots but the Japanese were hoarding sheets of treated or 'smoked rubber' and it seemed unlikely that the gnarled old trees that had grown-up haphazardly in Changi would be of much use. Duncan Paterson, a planter from the Ipoh area who was also in the FMSVF, agreed to experiment. Initially, they succeeded in tapping about a dozen trees that yielded half a pint of latex a day. To this they added virtually anything they could find from sand, soot and sawdust, to hair clippings and coconut fibres. After five months they discovered that the red laterite clay, which is soft when dug up but hardens on contact with the air, proved effective as both a filler and a coagulant and they were able to present a rubber sole to Lieutenant-Colonel E.B. Holmes at POW Head Quarters who agreed to allow them more time to continue their work.

Their first 'factory', in a broken-down building in Changi Village, close to the beach in the north of the peninsula, opened in October 1942. When it collapsed they used the debris to build another workshop nearby. Changi Industries Inc. – as the enterprise became known – moved with its workers to Changi Oil Store in December 1942, Selarang Barracks in April 1943 and finally to Changi Gaol in May 1944. Staff included thirteen 'tappers' and ten other workers. With the exception of one soldier from the Dutch army, they were volunteers; all were classed as 'unfit' and unable to work on Japanese construction projects.

The tappers had been either managers or senior assistants on rubber estates in peacetime when they left the tapping to an experienced local man, usually a Tamil, who knew how to prolong the tree's productive life for as long as possible. The seasoned tapper used tried and tested equipment with which to gather the latex. At Changi Industries the process was much less subtle. The trees had not been planted with a view to harvest but were self-sown, which meant the bark was very hard to cut into. The latex dripped out of spouts made from bits of galvanised iron and was collected in old tins and coconut shells hung on bamboo pins hammered into the trunk. Cartoons drawn later show a bemused POW squatting in his tattered shorts next to an ancient tree from which an insipid substance drips. Whether consciously or not, the tree, with its low-slung white belt of sap, looks as though it is wearing a form of 'jap-happy'– the loin cloth that many POWs wore when their uniforms were in tatters.

The best, grit-free clay was about 12 feet below the surface so that whenever a team of POWs dug a 'borehole' (where human waste was buried), someone from Changi Industries was on hand to collect the red laterite. The clay was then either dried in the sun or in an oven before being ground into a fine powder. This was done by hand until someone 'found' a small electric motor and this became part of a Heath Robinson style contraption constructed from an old bicycle wheel and a belt made from rubberised rope.

The mixture of clay, cement and latex was sticky and awkward to handle so that a production line of three men took on the different roles of mixing the latex, cement and clay, and pouring it into the moulds. The shoes were pressed in their moulds under inverted car jacks to extract moisture and then left in the sun for a few hours to dry before being tidied up with a pair of scissors, put in the sun again and then baked in an oven, sometimes built into the ground. Once Changi Industries had mastered this moulding technique, shoes were custom-made for men whose battle injuries had left them with deformed feet. Later they made covers for old cricket balls.

Latex met a whole range of DIY needs. It was used to hold dressings in place when bandages became scarce and as a replacement for thread when cotton ran low and clothes needed patching (darning needles were made from old bicycle spokes and sold in the canteen so that soldiers could repair their socks). POWs glued rags together which they covered with sand or ground glass to use as sandpaper. Latex gave rotting beds a longer life and offered the unexpected bonus of keeping bugs at bay.

Changi Industries never stopped experimenting. It made boot polish from bad eggs, sugar and wood alcohol until even bad eggs became hard to find. It produced 250 pounds of soap a week from palm oil, wood ash and caustic soda. When a chemist who had worked for the Rubber Research Institute of Malaya arrived in January 1943, experiments became even more sophisticated. He helped to build a still from an old fire extinguisher and used it to transform scrap rubber into an oil to make rubber pliable enough to make and repair false teeth. His team also concocted a substance for making dental moulds after plaster of Paris was in such short supply that it was only permitted for setting broken bones. Changi Industries mixed amyl acetate, a bottle of which they had 'found' in the early days of captivity, with celluloid to repair around 1,400 spectacle frames.

By April 1944, the IJA at last agreed to give Changi Industries smoked sheet rubber so that they could make more durable shoes. By the time the factory closed, it had produced a total of 21,736 shoes and repaired a further 20,889, mainly from latex they had tapped themselves. Their handiwork was of such a high standard that the Japanese guards brought their shoes and boots to them for repair.

While Changi Industries concentrated on making and repairing items that were essential to everyday life, helping men to walk, see and eat, other POWs produced objects that appeared to be non-essential, even frivolous. In some cases they were breathtakingly beautiful.

For Frank Bell, who had studied French and Spanish at Cambridge University where he obtained a first class degree before becoming a 2nd Lieutenant with the 48th Light Anti-Aircraft Regiment RA, being able to write was a visceral need as important as having shoes to wear or glasses with which to see. Occasionally he even sacrificed food in return for paper. He was captured in Java and spent most of his time in Borneo. When he arrived at Batu Lintang, in Kuching, in August 1943, it was his sixth camp and he had only thirty quarto sheets of lined paper and two large notebooks left. He began to eye up any scrap of material as a potential paper substitute: the flyleaf of a book, an official form, a discarded soap wrapping (decorated with the word 'LUX') or toffee paper (if he was lucky sugar ants would clean up the paper and make it easier to write on). As he did not smoke he was happy to trade tobacco for the large, yellowish sheets covered on one side with red Chinese characters that it was wrapped in. A letter from home offered the double thrill of contact with loved ones and a blank sheet on the reverse since the sender was only allowed to write on one side. Envelopes once carefully unstuck could be flattened out and written on. The men learnt to make the most of their materials by writing in tiny script and using the same sheet over and over again; one officer battling with his French lessons rubbed out his work so that he could use the same piece of paper thirty times.

Lifting the lid, in the domed reading room of London's Imperial War Museum, of the sturdy, brown cardboard box which stores many of his notes and textbooks is like breathing in the rainforest of Borneo: its contents smell dark and damp and fusty, although of course they have been preserved with the utmost care. Perhaps the contrast between the notebooks inside – bound in a range of exotic coverings from once colourful scraps of material to airmail card bearing the familiar blue and white Basildon Bond signature – and the minute, painfully neat handwriting that fills them conjures up this olfactory image of clandestine learning amidst the heat and humidity of Borneo.

The box records his efforts to carry on learning and teaching. Every item is well-worn and looks as though it has been pored over: an official red ledger; a slim, homemade book about the size of a packet of cigarettes filled with irregular verbs; and a notebook covered in a batik-style material that would not look out of place in a modern, upmarket stationer's. These books became the key teaching aids when, in autumn 1943, he set up 'Kuching University' at Batu Lintang. One of his students, Donald Yates, kept the Spanish grammar book for years. It was bound in bits of old pyjamas and when he visited Spain in 1989 he took it with him and found it helpful despite its age and the limited resources under which it was produced.

Batu Lintang was built on the site of a former rubber plantation and a few trees remained near the army barracks to offer some shade and the chance to extract latex that was collected in earthenware pots. As in Changi, the prisoners used it to resole shoes, patch up cricket balls and protect ulcers. Frank Bell also used it to ant-proof his shelves and thus protect his precious books. It was vital in binding and he took great pride in the books he made with it. He would smear latex up and down the book's spine, making sure that it was not too damp to soak through and spoil the appearance of a cover made from scraps of sarong, the sleeve of a worn-out shirt, or denim from army overalls. It acted as a glue to hold together what looks like a gentleman's portable writing case bound in a checked material and which he made from a section of cigar box and a piece of elastic from a garter. Inside he stored documents such as the exercises he set his language students and a form he had devised to help him jot down interesting facts from the books he read. The form was made from old drinks chits used by Naval Warrant Officers. After the war he had this prototype form printed so that he could use it in his peacetime reading.

A cigar box with a painting on it of a dark-haired woman who looks as though she might be part of a late eighteenth-century tobacco family stored his index of about 2,000 cards made from army forms for repairing vehicles. Most of the cards related to French grammar, his thoughts on education and extracts from the Bible. The rest contained the 'meat' of his books and his thoughts on education. These cards, together with the university's records and sections from the New Testament were buried in a thermos flask for safe keeping.

He made five notebooks of over 300 pages each from sheets of yellowish 'tobacco paper'. The first, a trial run made from the borders of tobacco paper, was used to make an address book. He saved the better quality paper for a German vocabulary book, a book of Dutch grammar and phrases and Russian exercises, and *Miscellaneous Jottings on the Most Important Subject of Food* and *Notes on an Attempt to Study the New Testament with an Open Mind*. Many of his fellow POWs had similar notebooks in which they tortured themselves with descriptions of food and recipes. Bell's included restaurants recommended by his friends and arranged by geographical area, a list of organisations that specialised in different foodstuffs, ideas for sandwiches and a long catalogue of recipes. Collecting recipes became a craze and one man had at least seven hundred. Most were gleaned from two magazines that were so well-thumbed that they had to be rebound, whilst others were mined from memory or invented from scratch. As the years in captivity lengthened, the obsession with food grew.

As well as rubber, palm trees and bamboo grew in many camps and were used as building materials. Men who were not fortunate enough to live in barrack blocks or other fixed buildings often slept on bamboo platforms in attap huts. In Changi, POWs stripped the hard spine from the palm frond leaf and bunched several together to make brooms. The same technique was used to make nail brushes for doctors and medical orderlies so that they could scrub up before examining patients. Fastidious POWs manufactured toothbrushes. In one version, the handle and head were made from bamboo and the bristles from coconut fibres stuck together with untreated latex. An Australian doctor, Captain Les Poidevin, made his by boring holes with a dentist's drill in a piece of flat wood which he then threaded pig's hair through. As Fergus Anckorn had lost most of his possessions during the fighting he made himself some chopsticks out of bamboo and taught himself how to eat with them. He still uses them today as they save on the washing up.

Others became expert at plaiting attap to make screens round showers and latrines. In the early days at Selarang, POWs rigged up a system whereby one man pumped rainwater into tanks that fed showerheads while clean prisoners dried themselves on bathmats made from bundles of lalang grass. Bamboo was used to make traps for animals such as lizards or, together with wire netting and attap, houses for poultry.

While these objects had an obvious practical use, other items were both practical and aesthetically pleasing. Chess became an obsession in some camps and a few men enjoyed carving beautiful sets – even if the board was only a piece of cloth with the squares pencilled on. One POW created a bone chess set using a small hand lathe he had made himself but the Japanese general, Saito demanded it and after that he stuck to making util-itarian items: medical instruments and parts of artificial legs. Others transformed old green filing cabinets into mugs and spoons or engraved 'Rolex Waterproof' onto watches to inflate their wealth on the black market.

Whittling or carving could have a palliative effect and passed the time without expending too much energy. Some men carved ornaments from Perspex salvaged from crashed aeroplanes, others used bone or wood, or bashed bits of soft metal into a pleasing or useful shape. The act of cre-ation gave the maker a sense of achievement and owning something at a time when most men had few possessions because they had lost them through battle, pilfering or simple wear and tear, boosted esteem.

Regimental Sergeant Major Kenneth Davey was also thinking of his family when he persuaded his fellow POWs at Changi to carve a series of thumb-sized shoes as a present for his wife. The tiny footwear includes boots, women's high-heeled shoes and Thai sandals. 'I have a whole lot of boots for you dear carved by the men in their spare time,' he wrote to her.

POWs in the Far East, who could not rely on the Red Cross to send them musical instruments, clothing or even packaging that they could transform into theatre scenery, became scavengers and inventors. When the Japanese refused to give the prisoners in Changi paper, one prisoner who was a chemist used rice sacks to make a sort of ersatz sheet music.

Major Denis Houghton, who played the flute in the camp orchestra, went to even more trouble and made his instrument in the camp workshop. It took him five months to complete and was made up of 175 separate pieces, including parts from stirrup pumps, fire extinguishers, naval guns, bicycle spokes, a watch spring and a packet of sewing needles. To the casual observer it looks like the real thing; there is no hint that it was put together from an unlikely collection of odds and ends.

Kenneth Trigg, a gunner in 21st LAA RA who was captured in Java, spent his spare time when he was not working in the hospital at Batu Lintang making musical instruments to play for the one hour every Sunday evening when they were allowed to sing and make music. He built the main body of what he called a banjo-mandolin, but which was known in the camp as a 'plinkertina', out of a circular Dutch Army aluminium mess tin. For the instrument's wooden neck he risked extracting a piece of camphor from the top rail above the door of the rickety hut in which he slept. He shaped this using a Taylor's Eye Witness penknife that his brother had given him as a Christmas present in 1940 and which had a Sheffield steel blade. The sounding board was made from a tea chest that, after much persuasion, the Japanese quartermaster at the hospital agreed to relinquish. This was wedged into the rim of the mess tin using the wrappings from Chinese tobacco – a huge sacrifice since the paper was in demand among smokers who used it to roll their own cigarettes. He made the tuning pegs from scraps of lignum vitae or ironwood, nuts from the handle of an old toothbrush and frets from copper wire stolen on a working party to an airfield. He made a case for it out of plywood that he lined with the blue paper wrapping from a packet of cotton wool that he had treasured for some time. This was glued in place with latex; scraps of gas cape helped to make it waterproof. A piece of sock suspender became a handle which he attached using the brass 'D's from webbing equipment; he fastened the case using the strap and press stud taken from a water bottle. Finally, he engraved 'Kuching, May 1944' on the side using a penknife. Trigg played the plinkertina to accompany several songs that the POWs were ordered to perform when important Japanese visited the camp. Another man had made a stringed instrument using half a coconut shell for the body.

Trigg adapted his technique to make a violin, using 'hair' from the stem of a banana plant for the bow. But after all his hard work he was unable to coax a sound from the instrument. Eventually he realised that he had forgotten to apply the rosin that helps the bow hair to grip the surface of the string so that it vibrates. Incredibly, another POW found a pot of rosin at the bottom of his tattered bag. He was not a musician and had no idea why it was there.

Concert parties went to great lengths to create convincing scenery and costumes from everyday objects. Perhaps the most sumptuous example of this is the dress that Gunner Charles Woodhams wore in numerous revues at Changi and at camps on the Thailand–Burma Railway. The gown – dress does not do it justice – is made from mosquito netting. This may not sound very grand but 'in the flesh' the ankle-length costume with its delicate straps becomes a fairy-tale outfit that many small girls – and several women – would long to wear. The material looks more like tulle than mosquito netting and is a glamorous champagne colour – perhaps as a result of ageing. This is a gown that is more debutante than drag queen. Seeing it on a shapely mannequin makes it suddenly obvious why female impersonators like Woodhams could transport their audience several thousand miles home so that they could easily imagine they were sitting on red plush seats in a gilded West End theatre, rather than under the stars in the noisy jungle or some equally uncomfortable makeshift auditorium. Imagination was the only form of escape for most POWs in the Far East and it rarely failed.

Entertainment: 'You'll Never Get Off this Island!'

Once the camps had established a cooking regime, organised sanitation and set up basic hospital wards, entertainment became a priority. And although they lacked the musical instruments, costumes and basic materials for building sets available to most European POWs, plays and variety performances became as important – if not more so – for raising morale. The theatre producer in a stalag or oflag might have to share his scenery designer with the escape committee who wanted the artist to concentrate on forging documents; the camp tailor might be dyeing and fitting clothing for an escape attempt – as well as a production of *Who Killed the Count?* – and the Red Cross packaging might have to be shared between someone who wanted it to make a theatre set and someone who needed it to make a false suitcase when they were on the run. In the Far East, entertainment was the purest form of escape because there was usually no alternative.

As a magician, Fergus Anckorn was an ideal performer for straitened circumstances because all he needed was his hands and he was fortunate to survive the battle for Singapore with both intact. He was the divisional concert party's magician, where he was known as 'Wizardus', and had entertained troops on board the *USS West Point* on its way to Singapore.

He started conjuring when he was given a box of tricks at the age of four, and for the next few years he performed for his parents who never let on that they could see through his sleight of hand. His family lived near Sevenoaks in Kent and his father was a journalist on the *Dundee Courier* which had an office in Fleet Street. In his spare time he wrote novels and mixed with authors such as A.A. Milne, whose son played with Fergus so that he could later claim that he grew up with the real Christopher Robin. Fergus's mother was an expert secretary who won awards for her typing speeds. By the time he was in his teens a local magician gave him a brutal assessment of his abilities. He impressed on him the need to be able to work equally well with both hands and not to rely on props. The older magician allowed him to take his place at less lucrative bookings and by the mid 1930s Fergus Anckorn had became the youngest member of the Magic Circle.

He was twenty-four when he was thrown into the mayhem of war on Singapore: 'No matter how much training you do nothing can prepare you for the sheer noise of battle – the shells and bombs and air raids.'

By the time the fighting had closed in on Singapore Town he had twice managed the improbable trick of emerging unscathed from situations in which men next to him had died: once at the docks and once at Seletar Aerodrome. The third time he was not so lucky. He was towing a 25-pound gun on the Thomson Road, which runs through the centre of the island, when the truck was caught in a bomb blast and burst into flames. The door jammed and when he looked down at his right hand he saw it was attached to his arm by nothing more than a flap of skin and bone. He lent back and kicked the door open with all his might; then he hurled himself out of the seat but as he left the vehicle he felt a bolt of searing pain as he was hit through the kneecap. He staggered through the smoke and dust and collapsed into a storm drain where he passed out. Soon afterwards he was discovered, a mess of bone and blood, by another gunner who turned him over and decided he was dead. He removed both dog tags – one should have been left with the body so that it could be identified – and headed for the docks where he escaped by boat.

When Anckorn came round, he was dimly aware of being dragged away to a lorry and tied to its wing; he was paralysed from the waist down. They hurtled through the streets at 40 mph, every bump in the road jarring his broken body. In his last lucid moment he remembers the surgeon, Colonel Julian Taylor, warning him that he would have to remove his hand. Anckorn was lying on the famous polished post office counter in the grand Fullerton Buildings which – at 100 metres – was credited as being the longest in the world. By now he was past caring and told him to 'Just get on with it'. But a medical orderly, who was preparing the gauze and ether to put him under, peered into his face and recognised 'Wizardus' from a performance in Liverpool. He told the doctor that Anckorn was a magician and urged him to save the arm. As he floated out of consciousness he heard the doctor say that he would do what he could.

When he woke up in the Alexandra Hospital the first thing he did was to ask the man lying on a stretcher on the floor next to him whether he still had two hands. By way of reply the man gently tugged at each of the fingers in the tightly swathed boxer's glove of bandages, 'This little piggy went to market . . .' until Fergus knew he had a full set of digits.

Occasionally the noise of bombs woke him or the clatter of orderlies scurrying to fit blackout boards in the windows which instantly crashed to the floor after the latest blast. The morphine he had been given to kill the pain allowed him to inhabit a surreal world in which nothing much mattered. What exactly happened that day remains disputed but it seems that outside in the normally tranquil grounds of the modern military hospital a brief but fierce battle was raging between Japanese soldiers and members of the Indian Army who were retreating towards the building. Medical orderlies and doctors had rushed to display every Red Cross flag they could find as a way of reminding the Japanese that they were approaching a hospital.

Anckorn was still living in a morphine-induced twilight world. Once he woke to see Japanese soldiers in the ward and asked his neighbour what they were doing there. He replied that they were taking patients onto the front lawn and killing them. 'Oh, I see,' Anckorn said before passing out again. The next time he woke the Japanese were going from bed to bed with fixed bayonets in a macabre parody of a sick parade. As the soldiers plunged their weapons methodically into the helpless patients Anckorn was overcome by a wave of tranquillity. He was unable to move and was therefore relieved of any hope that he could save himself. He felt no fear. 'I remember thinking to myself, "I suppose I'm dying" and I thought of home. Once you realise you're dying there's no fear, no anxiety, nothing. Even when they were all being bayoneted. You realise it's over, you've got nothing to worry about. It's all done.'

As he waited for his turn he put his head under the pillow so that he would not have to witness his own disembowelment. When it became necessary for him to raise the pillow and gulp air there were only four men left alive in the ward but the Japanese had gone.

He has two theories about why he managed to survive what became one of the most notorious massacres of the war in the East. It may have been that the Japanese simply did not notice him lying with his head under the pillow. But it seems unlikely that the soldiers would have passed an apparently empty bed in a crowded ward without giving the bedclothes at least a cursory prod with their bayonets. It is more probable that they passed over Fergus because they thought he was already dead: his injuries had left him deathly pale and his bandages were soaked in blood; the head under a pillow also pointed to someone who had already been dispatched – rather than to a patient braced for the end.

He does not know exactly how he was transported from Alexandra Hospital to the floor of a Chinese girls' school where he lay for about three weeks, barely exchanging a word with the other wounded. From here the Japanese took him to the hospital in Roberts Barracks where he eventually found a sergeant major who would help him. By now his arm was gangrenous. He was taken to the gangrene ward where the smell of rotting flesh was overpowering. The medical orderlies used maggots to clean up his wound and within eight to ten days it was 'all nice and clean'. The doctor, however, was unable to extract a bullet from behind his left knee using pliers. The injury had damaged the nerves so that his foot became a dead weight which he could only move using a rope that he tied to its front and operated using his left hand. In this fragile state he stumbled on the uneven ground and broke the same foot; it was reset as he lay on the concrete floor with his foot braced against the wall.

While he waited for his right arm to heal he started to practise magic tricks with his left. This was a laborious process, like starting to learn magic from scratch, but it gave a purpose to the day and helped to entertain his fellow POWs. But he knew that ambidexterity would give him a great advantage as a magician.

The British troops of the Southern Area of Changi camp put on reviews such as 'Hellsabuzzin' in an old open-air cinema. The bill usually consisted of a mixture of sketches – many of which poked fun at the 'top brass', a comedian or double-act and musicians who played a range of songs, usually with several sentimental numbers. Puns played a big part. 'The Optimists', a concert party from the 18th Division in which Fergus performed, produced a topical revue called 'Rice and Shine'; another group put on a play with the title, 'Turned out rice again'. Both reflected the POWs' monotonous diet and their growing obsession with food.

John Lowe was also a keen entertainer when he was living in an attap-roofed hut on the Changi Peninsula. He was twenty-three and from Islington, North London. Before the war he had run errands for Clarion Studios which, from their slightly shabby premises in King's Cross, produced glitzy advertising displays – promoting the Ballet Russe from the windows of His Master's Voice (HMV) showrooms in Oxford Street or offering shoppers a hint of the glamour through the perfume and cosmetics of the houses of Lentheric and Helena Rubinstein. Here he met exotic business people and performers from Europe and America and in the evenings he played the piano in a dance band trio.

His battery had been ordered as far north as Alor Star before the Japanese forced them to retrace their steps. In the period immediately after the surrender he felt a nagging worry that they might be shot. This fear was reinforced by the 'lorry loads of dead Indians and Chinese ... driven past us, stiff arms and legs waving grotesquely as the vehicles bumped along'. But the worst that happened was that he was arrested by an officer called Windy Forbes for refusing to serve as a mess waiter in the biggest hut which had been designated an 'officers' mess'. He escaped with a 'severe reprimand'.

At some point his details – including his name, nationality, date of birth, rank and unit, place and date of capture, parents' names and 'destination of report' (effectively the address of his next of kin) – were added to a pre-printed record card. Around 50,000 of these are held in the National Archives in Kew, South London. A diagonal red line indicates when a POW has died. On John Lowe's card the unnamed Japanese official has described his occupation as 'Display Man' – a reference to the advertising firm he worked for in Islington but an apt title for someone who loves to entertain.

He supplemented his rations by occasional trips through the wire to a local village where he bartered what little money he had for tins of food. Once he managed to bring back two small turkeys in a pillowcase; he planned to fatten them up but, like everyone else, they shrank. They were eventually eaten on a POW's birthday. On a more official trip he joined a gang looking for bits of furniture. One of them carried a Japanese flag as proof that they had permission to wander away from their camp. The most prized possession they brought back was a piano which they had found in a grand villa that was now deserted; it was still in good condition and provided the focus for a concert party of about eight men who performed on a small outdoor stage they had built themselves. Lieutenant Morrison, who had been a professional stand-up comedian but whose jokes John found 'pretty awful', was in charge. He was more impressed with Jim Brennan, a former waiter at the Criterion and Café de Paris in London where he had learnt off by heart many of the numbers sung by the cabaret acts. The two of them performed duets such as *Tiger Rag* and accompanied songs written by Harry Berry, a POW who had been a journalist and who called himself 'Beriberi'. Danny Goldberg, a tailor by training, was able to make costumes but he also played the violin well and teamed up with another member of the concert party, Frank Brimelow, as a comedy double-act. They were occasionally joined by a professional actor from the Australian POWs called John Wood, 'a quiet, most unassuming man, he transformed himself on stage into a quite wonderful woman' using a long, blonde wig made from a sporran.

One of John Lowe's and Jim Brennan's most popular songs was a fast-paced skit called 'Romanov, Dumbenough, Tallenough, Smallenough' which Jim had seen an act called the Four Yacht Club Boys perform at the Café de Paris. The lyrics were inspired by the fate of the more distant relatives of the Russian royal family, the Romanovs. Although the immediate family were executed during the Russian Revolution some members managed to escape to America where they started new lives – often working in less than royal occupations. They performed it wearing loose shirts and belts, in a modest attempt to imitate a Cossack style. These lines from the second verse give a flavour of the jauntiness of the lyrics:

We're working in the cloakroom of the Hotel Waldorf Bar
We were considered pretty hotski, until Trotski put us on the
  spotski,
But now, we're better off than Trotski, Trotski's notski even got a
  potski.

Chorus: I'm Romanov, I'm Dumenough, I'm Tallenough, I'm
  Smallenough.

Between four and five hundred British and Australian troops watched the performance sitting on the grass or on the trunks of palm trees.

Most POW camps in the Far East had a concert party, although their size and sophistication varied depending on the health of the performers and the strictness of the Japanese guards. In Changi, the most lavish productions were staged towards the end of 1942 – just before thousands of men were dispersed to other parts of the Japanese empire – and eighteen months or so later when an influx of troops returned from working 'upcountry' on the Thailand–Burma Railway. When Russell Braddon arrived in Changi he was shocked by: 'The rash of concert parties and theatres – dozens of them playing each night: everything from *Androcles and the Lion* to Army 'smoke-ohs'.

There was fierce rivalry between the British and Australians as to who could produce the best entertainment. The Australians were among the first to present a divisional concert party in Changi; the Eighth Division formed theirs two days after arriving at Selarang Barracks. To begin with, it put on variety shows that relied on what would now be known as an 'open mike' approach (although, of course, there was no microphone): anyone who thought they had an act was welcome to try it out. Gradually, though, the organisers became more discerning and established a troupe of about twenty performers (among them dancers, singers and comedians) and fifteen musicians. The concert party included several professionals and some very good amateurs. Sydney Piddington was a twenty-four-year-old magician who would later explore the possibilities of a mind-reading act that would make him world famous. John Wood's personae included 'a beauteous female'; Keith Stevens specialised in 'fearful old bags' and Ray Tullipan sang a range of sentimental and comic songs with titles such as 'You're Sweeter than all I Know', 'Just a Bungalow Called Home' and 'Out of the Army'. Harry Smith, known as 'Happy Harry' because of his relentlessly lugubrious demeanour, provided the antidote to this saccharine offering with his catchphrase, 'You'll never get off this island!' It always made his audience laugh.

Slim de Grey, who wrote many of the songs as well as playing the funny man, had a very long career after the war, including the part of the priest in the film *Crocodile Dundee In Los Angeles* when he was in his early eighties (no one was quite sure exactly how old he was). As a POW he became expert at writing parodies of sentimental songs and at using *double entendres* to hit back at his captors. When he was made to take part in a propaganda film he adapted the words of *The Prisoner's Song* so that the POWs sang about how the Japanese gave them the 'Edgar Britts'. When questioned by a guard he avoided the truth – that 'Edgar Britts' was rhyming slang – and instead reassured him that it was a fine breakfast cereal. He also wrote a ribald parody of the romantic song, 'Remember Me'. De Grey's version aimed to take the sting out of one of the most humiliating events in a POW's life – the ritual in which all men had to line up, drop their shorts and wait for a Japanese medical orderly to shove a glass rod up their backside. The swabs were analysed for signs of dysentery and other diseases. The experience was made worse by the fact that it was communal, but De Grey's words may have helped to lessen some of the feelings of violation.

The concert party put on a new show every fortnight. At first they performed on the back of abandoned trucks but Val Mack, who had run a travelling show called 'Mack's Follies' during peacetime and had an eye for spotting promising venues, found an amphitheatre-shaped space by the barrack square. Eventually they moved to garages where they could rig up lighting and offer night-time shows which allowed them to double their audience numbers. When staging was at its most sophisticated they used seven backstage technicians. As well as the traditional variety fodder, they produced musicals, pantomime and serious drama. Their instruments included two guitars, a fiddle, a double bass made from an old tea chest and a pump organ they had 'scrounged' – probably while working at the docks. Terai, an Anglophile Japanese interpreter who had taught English at a university before the war, helped by providing violin strings, make-up and costumes.

Designing and painting sets, or producing props provided another outlet for stifled creativity. 'Joey' was the product of such inventiveness – a sort of Changi version of John Worsley's 'Albert' at Marlag but designed without the hope of escape. He is now part of the Australian War Memorial Collection. Gunner Thomas Alfred Hussey who served with the 2/10 Field Regiment AIF and was a member of the Australian Concert Party owned, and probably made, Joey. He picked up his skills as a ventriloquist from an old music hall performer in Queensland and performed in an amateur group called The Snap Company. Its male members enlisted in 1940 but Hussey lost his original dummy when he was captured; he managed to produce three replacements in Changi. The one he came home with has the traditional, unnerving stare of a ventriloquist's side-kick. Joey's blue eyes, the right slightly higher than the left, bulge out of his wooden head which is painted a ghostly white; long cracks or joints run through his raised eyebrows and down his red cheeks so that he looks as though he is crying. Red hair peeks out from a white cotton cap that has been nailed to his crown. He wears a double-breasted, yellowing suit with a crossed black tie, like a judge might wear and a cardboard collar fastened with a press stud. His feet have been painted black to give the appearance of shoes. On careful inspection the faint pattern all over his suit assumes the form of signatures, presumably autographs left by fellow POWs.

The concert parties were so important to morale that officers did their best to keep performers together. Piddington was keen to join his friend, Russell Braddon 'up country' and John Wood and Keith Stevens also wanted to go with their mates to a new camp the Japanese had told them would be more salubrious than Changi. But Lieutenant-Colonel F.G. ('Black Jack') Galleghan, the senior officer of the AIF POWs, was so concerned that their departure would deplete the concert party that he refused to let them go. His decision to keep the concert party members at Changi might well have saved their lives.

Looking back from a peacetime perspective, Sir David Griffin, an Australian POW at Changi, agreed about the role of the concert party: 'You can't exaggerate the importance. They kept people alive. They kept life moving.'

The lack of women meant that some POWs had to assume female roles in the many plays – serious and comic – staged in different camps. At Bandung in Java, where the writer Laurens van der Post was held, POWs built a stage with a proscenium arch and orchestra pit in a hut they called 'Radio City'. Douglas Argent, an RAF navigator and former bank worker, took part in many shows. After the war he became a successful producer of TV classics such as *Fawlty Towers*. The POWs found plays such as *The Importance of Being Earnest* and Somerset Maugham's *The Circle* in the library of a local Dutch school. Their captors were invited and usually enjoyed the performance – except when one guard was enraged by Lady Bracknell whom he assumed must be a woman who had been smuggled in (as Dutch civilians were interned nearby this was a reasonable suspicion). The part was played by Ian Horobin who after the war became a Conservative MP.

Theatre groups avoided anything likely to depress their audience and favoured whodunits or romantic comedies. The 18th Division, for example, chose to put on A.A. Milne's *Dover Road*, which had been a Broadway hit in the 1920s. Although it is rarely produced today it was an inspired choice. An eccentric millionaire kidnaps an eloping couple and holds them in his mansion for a week so that he can decide whether or not they are really compatible. The theme of captivity was all too familiar to the audience but the actors made them laugh at the situation.

Charles Fisher was impressed by *Dover Road* and by the 'serious' music produced at Changi. Standards were kept high by a scattering of professional musicians and several highly talented amateurs. The pianist Eric Cliffe did not always have either a piano or sheet music but was able to play other homemade instruments and to remember or compose and arrange a startling range of classical music from memory – both at Changi and in the Thai jungle. He managed to produce versions of 'Finlandia', the 1st movement of Schubert's *Unfinished Symphony*, three of Elgar's *Enigma Variations*, the *Peer Gynt Suite*, *Eine Kleine Nachtmusik* (without the wind section), the slow movement of the Mendelssohn's *Violin Concerto* and some Handel and Purcell – all from memory. Dennis East, a professional musician from London, lost his violin in the Battle for Singapore but had a replacement made. By the end of 1942 he was playing in a band called The Nitwits.

Sport

In normal circumstances sport, like entertainment, was a pastime that the upper ranks of the armed forces approved of. Both provided a safety valve through which to release tension and frustrations and both had long traditions within the armed forces. But sport was only viable when the men were physically strong enough to risk the extra physical exertion and when their captors would allow them to express themselves in this way.

In the early days at Changi, educational classes or organised games usually took place in the afternoon and men could choose from a range of sports that included basketball, throwing a medicine ball, hockey, boxing and quoits. One POW who found two old volleyballs managed to stitch them up and use them to start a competition but was frustrated when two of the twelve teams were suddenly sent away on work parties.

Football and cricket were popular at the start of captivity but demanded a degree of stamina that evaporated as rations dwindled and disease took hold. When that happened, or if they did not have the equipment or space, the men would talk endlessly about sport or write about it, for example in *Sportsman's Paper*. Battered rule books provided the starting point for an absorbing discussion – even if it related to a sport they had never played – or the basis for a quiz. As in Europe, such volumes sparked memories of leisurely weekends and past triumphs. One book, more than any other, was passed round like an Aladdin's lamp, its pages pored over with the absorption of men trying to retrieve a past life from batting averages and talismanic names such as 'Lord's', 'Trent Bridge' and 'The Oval'. There may have been several copies of *Wisden Cricketers' Almanack* among the Far East POWs but the one that must have seen the most service was the 1939 edition owned by E.W. 'Jim' Swanton.

Swanton was a thirty-five-year-old officer in the 148th Field Regiment, R.A., at the fall of Singapore and a walking sports compendium. He had gone straight from public school (Cranleigh) to work as a reporter where he indulged his love of sport – particularly cricket. After twelve years on the *London Evening Standard* and the publication of *A History of Cricket* (which he co-wrote) in 1938, he was just edging into a second career in broadcasting when war was declared. He carried his treasured copy of *Wisden* with him throughout his captivity and used it to recreate famous cricket matches through mock commentaries. A purple official Japanese stamp at the front shows the book has been classified as 'non-subversive' but the condition of the 958 pages reveals the religious devotion with which its contents were consumed – to the extent that it has been rebound with rice paste and sackcloth. When he took it with him to the Malay jungle it was so popular that a time limit of twelve hours had to be imposed on each of its readers.

In an article entitled 'Cricket under the Japs' in the 1946 edition of *Wisden*, Swanton remembered how discussing the game 'filled countless hours in pitch dark huts between sundown and the moment that contin- ued to be euphemistically known as lights-out. And it inspired many a daydream, contrived often in the most gruesome setting, whereby one combated the present by living either in the future or the past.'

After the fall of Singapore he remembered:

A certain amount of play on the padangs [fields] of Changi camp that really deserved the name of cricket . . . It is true that one never seemed able to hit the ball very far, a fact probably attributable about equally to the sudden change to a particularly sparse diet of rice and the con- scientious labours of generations of corporals in charge of sports gear, for whom a daily oiling of the bats had clearly been a solemn, unvary- ing rite. These Changi bats must have reached saturation point in the early thirties, and I never found one that came up lighter than W.H. Ponsford's three pounder. However, the pitches were true – matting over concrete – and there were even such refinements as pads and gloves.

A series of test matches were organised between Australian and English teams as a sort of unofficial Ashes series which Swanton acknowledged as 'Cricket de Luxe' compared to later efforts. Ben Barnett, the former international test wicket keeper and left-handed batsman, captained the Australian Imperial Force (AIF) in the five matches that were held on rest days in which each side had a set number of overs. The marl surface meant the ball's bounce was unpredictable – and probably added to the excitement of the four to five thousands spectators. Although many cricket games were played with balls made from moulded latex, the test series were fortunate enough to have a cricket bag that had survived the battle for Singapore and which contained stumps, bails, bats and a new ball. England won the series 2-1 (the other games were drawn) – mainly due to Len Muncer of Glamorgan and Geoff Edrich. The latter, who came from a famous family of Norfolk cricketers and would later play for Lancashire. However, England was soon to lose their prolific batsman.

There were also professional footballers among the POWs: Albert Hall from Spurs, Billy James from Cardiff City and Johnny Lynas, who had played in the 1920s and 1930s and was working as Blackpool's assistant trainer when war broke out. Johnny Sherwood had signed for Reading Football Club in June 1938 and scored in its 3-2 win over Brentford in the 1941 London War Cup final at Stamford Bridge. The competition plugged the gap left after the wartime cancellation of the FA Cup and, although it was called the London Cup, teams from all over the South competed.

Football had been Sherwood's escape from poverty. His father ran a pub in Reading and Sherwood was one of eleven children. By his own admission he was a bit of a tearaway as a teenager: when he was not kicking a football around he usually got into fights or amused himself by throwing stones at lampposts. His chance came when a talent scout spotted him and signed him for his local side. In the season before his battalion was sent overseas he was allowed to play for Middlesbrough Football Club every Saturday afternoon. He also married Christine, a former 'Miss Reading', in 1939.

Changi was not his first experience of the Far East and – even more unusually for an ordinary British soldier – he had visited Japan. Soccer gave him the opportunity to see the world – at a time when footballers rarely went abroad. His chance came early in his career when, as an amateur, he was selected to play for the prestigious Islington Corinthians on their international tour of 1937–8. They played ninety-six games in fifteen countries across Europe, Asia and North America. Sherwood could play at right wing and centre forward and was the tour's top scorer with seventy goals. The team won two games in Burma and played at Kuala Lumpur and Alor Star before visiting Singapore, where he would later start his life as a POW. They even played one game in Yokahama where they lost three nil before continuing their tour in America. They were feted wherever they went: the King of Egypt and Hollywood stars turned out to watch them. His return visit to Japan later in the war could hardly have been more different.

One of his first tasks as a POW was to clear up the bodies that littered the roads of Singapore. He dug holes and buried the corpses, many of whom were women and children. As a fit young man, Sherwood was slow to recognise the illness that crept over him during his first days as a POW and assumed that what he was experiencing were hunger pangs. It was almost certainly dysentery.

Dysentery is a debilitating illness that strikes with a two-pronged attack: it batters the stomach with shocking violence and then saps the sufferer of all their energy through raging diarrhoea. The Nobel Laureate Doris Lessing experienced a bout of it as a child in Rhodesia and described the symptoms in the first volume of her autobiography, Under My Skin: 'Those who have never had it will not believe the intensity of the intestinal gripes, like jabbing beaks or hands wringing.'

The disease, which is spread through contaminated food and water, became a huge killer among POWs in the Far East and particularly in the jungle. In August 1942 there were forty-five deaths at Changi – nearly all from dysentery. The illness reduced men to spectral versions of their former selves who haunted the latrines, or who were too weak to move and suffered the further humiliation of soiling themselves. It was vital to clean cooking utensils in boiling water but this depended on the supply of firewood which could only be collected if there were enough fit men to gather it and transport to deliver it. Officers attempted to combat it by declaring all-out war on flies. They used whatever mosquito nets they had left and urged POWs to make their own fly swats – even offering cigarette bounties for numbers killed (at one time in Changi the going rate was ten cigarettes for every five hundred dead flies). Encouraging recovering patients to swat flies helped them to believe they were contributing to camp life and gave them a sense of control.

'Not knowing or realising how very serious this was,' Sherwood wrote later, 'I kept it to myself and just wandered about Changi Camp with the pains getting worse and worse, and my visiting the latrines more and more often.'

When he finally decided he should seek medical help he 'almost rolled' in to see the doctor who told him he was just a few days away from death. He was carried by stretcher to the barracks hospital where, at that early stage in their captivity, there were drugs to help him. After ten to twelve days of 'absolute agony – virtually sleeping outside the lavatory door', he was taken off the seriously ill list. Without enough of the right sort of food, though, his recovery was slow and he spent most of the day just sitting or lying, too weak to move. In the cool of the evening two friends would take him for a 'steady walk'. Left by himself he suffered frequent blackouts when, without warning, he would crash to the floor. He felt 'down in the dumps' and started to go to the church services that were held every two days. 'I must admit that even at this very early stage I looked just a shadow of the young Sherwood, who only a few weeks earlier had been playing professional football with Middlesbrough football club.'

He had heard that one of the Japanese guards (it was more likely to be a local Chinese man) was throwing down tins of food from a tower to the POWs waiting below at a certain time in the evening and decided to try his luck. The first night he joined the crowd of five to six hundred men he came away empty-handed but on the second occasion he and a friend managed to catch a tin of bully-beef and one of jam.

Increasing their calorific intake became vital when the Japanese made the POWs carry out heavy manual labour. As petrol and oil were scarce, they were tethered like horses to four-wheeled tractors and other vehicles; even the slightest incline made pulling their load almost impossible. Like John Lowe and other POWs, Sherwood started to break out of the camp at night to barter with the local people who would give him food in exchange for clothes, rings and watches. He knew that if caught he faced execution but since he had already lost two stones in weight he was willing to take the risk.

As he was now classified as 'fit' he was moved with around 1,400 other men to a camp at Havelock Road near the docks at Singapore City. An officer who knew he had been a professional footballer and that he had a football with him asked Sherwood to take a party of men to clear some rough ground and to organise games. It took him and a dozen 'light sick' men a few weeks to make a pitch and some goalposts so they could play in the evenings. During the day they were marched to work – clearing up the debris and damage left from the destruction of Singapore. They had to be on parade by 7 a.m. The first time they marched out of the camp they were confronted by the heads of five local people stuck on spiked railings. Under each one the guards had placed a placard explaining their crime – such as stealing, or obtaining food for prisoners. Blood from the heads lay in sticky pools on the pavements.

The prisoners were not allowed to talk while they worked. If they were caught chatting they were made to hold a heavy piece of wood or a large stone over their head, arms outstretched. Whenever the strain became too much and they began to lower the burden, the guards would beat them. Every ten days they were allowed a day off and they arranged football matches with nearby River Valley Road Camp where ex-Spurs player, Albert Hall, was held. 'It was something both camps looked forward to, and it certainly boosted the morale of the boys, and funnily enough – we had one "Pro" on each side,' Sherwood said later.

After a ten-hour day the prisoners were given a bowl of watery pumpkin stew, rice and sometimes a piece of hard dried fish. The diet was lacking in so many ingredients vital to the proper working of the body but one of the first signs of vitamin deficiency appeared with the onslaught of beriberi. The men's legs ballooned in size and it was possible to push a finger deep into the spongy flesh where the indentation remained after the digit had been withdrawn. Their diet was also causing diarrhoea so that they needed the toilet ten or twelve times a day. The medical officer at Havelock Road was so concerned about Sherwood's health that he ordered him to stop playing football, warning him that if he continued while he was riddled with beriberi he was in effect committing suicide. He added that if he found him on the pitch he would court martial him and that any charges would be confirmed upon his release. Perhaps this last threat was a show of bravura designed to boost his morale, since the idea of a world where the British army held sway seemed remote.

The Allied POW authorities eventually banned soccer and boxing because of the high number of fractures. It seems remarkable that both pastimes had been allowed to persist for so long. Instead of playing football Sherwood switched to giving night-time talks about his pre-war tour with Islington Corinthians. One evening he was addressing a hut full of officers when he strayed off the point to talk about a beautiful young Eurasian school teacher called Eileen whom he had fallen in love with on his visit. When he had finished his lecture an officer took him to one side and shook his hand before revealing that he was married to Eileen and that she had told him all about her romance with a British footballer called Sherwood. 'Well what a shock it was – Thank God I only spoke and said good things about her,' he remembered later.

Recording Captivity Through Art and Photography

Just as writers feel the need to write so, throughout his captivity, Jack Chalker, Ronald Searle and other artists felt compelled to draw. After the war, when he had become one of the world's most celebrated graphic artists, Searle said that he deliberately set himself up as an '(albeit self-appointed) participator-recorder'. He maintained that the POW drawings were not a means of catharsis, 'Circumstances were too basic for that. But they did at times act as a mental life-boat.'

> During my captivity I had, in a somewhat unimaginative and already ambitious way, convinced myself that my mission was to emerge from the various camps, the jungle and finally prison with a 'significant' pictorial record that would reveal to the world something of what happened during those lost and more or less unphotographed years.

In his review of Searle's book, *To the Kwai and Back: War Drawings 1939–1945*, Graham Hough, who had also been held in the Far East, commented in the *London Review of Books*:

> Life as a prisoner of war is an indeterminate sentence, and for that reason nothing you say about it afterwards can ever be quite true . . . While it is going on, no one knows whether it is ever going to end, and the absent ending colours every moment of every day. Once it has ended, if you are still alive, you know it was always going to. The basic premise of POW life has disappeared, and no effort of retrospection

can make it real again. Notes taken on the hoof are no good: too many words are needed to flesh out the experience, and there is never time for them. But there is an art, more rapid and more immediate, that can bring back that lost eternal present. One would hardly believe it if it had not actually been done. But it has been done, in Ronald Searle's wartime drawings.

Searle was twenty-one when he began his captivity. Before the war interrupted, he had experienced less than a year as a full-time student at Cambridge School of Art and was contributing cartoons for his local newspaper, the *Cambridge Daily News* (now the *Cambridge News*) and for the university magazine, *Granta*. Just before he became a POW he experienced a strange brush with his previous life when he was fighting in a Singapore street and happened to glance down at a copy of the magazine, *Lilliput*. In the heat of battle he saw his cartoon of five schoolgirls gathered anxiously round a noticeboard. Most are wearing boaters and are armed with hockey sticks but they are plumper than Searle's later creations; their hair in neat blocks, rather than the spidery pigtails of his postwar drawings. Perhaps the only clue that this group would evolve into the devilish harridans synonymous with rebellious schoolgirls is in the daring gap between the top of their stockings and the bottom of their tunics. The caption below the cartoon reads: 'Owing to the international situation the match with St. Trinian's has been postponed.' Although, of course, the girls looking at the noticeboard must have belonged to another school this is always credited as the first 'St Trinian's' cartoon, despite the fact that, with hindsight, the cartoon's humour now seems to rely on knowledge of the school's future reputation. Searle had not seen the cartoon in print before.

At first the Japanese did not impose restrictions on keeping a record – whether visual or written – but after several months they began to enforce strict rules about drawing or keeping a diary. While the guards still took a relaxed attitude to art, Jack Chalker drew a mural in pastels on the concrete wall of the small room that the officers used as a quasi lounge. 'Of all things I did a strip of country scenes with cricket going on!'

Captivity gave men the chance to consider how the war – brief and bloody as it had been for men like Chalker and Anckorn – had been waged and often this gave rise to bitterness and recrimination. Chalker used his skill as an artist to make a point about a British colonel whom he describes as 'a very pompous, nasty little man who loved self-importance. He was terribly concerned about the way you laid your kit out and if there was anything out of place that was far more important than war or training for it.'

Chalker placed the colonel at the centre of a battle scene he drew on the kitchen cupboard where he slept; it showed the colonel inspecting a man's kit while all around him soldiers were dying. There was no doubt who the central figure was meant to be because he depicted him holding a riding crop with a large loop identical to one that the colonel always carried, although he had never ridden a horse. When the colonel came to inspect their cupboard he studied the mural and obviously realised the point Jack was making but simply left with much harrumphing.

It was while he was at Roberts Barracks that Chalker met Ronald Searle for the first time when they were both involved in a small concert party. Chalker also listened to a friend who had been a concert pianist entertain his audiences with recitals of Grieg and Mozart on an old upright piano in a shelter made from bamboo supports and thatched with palm fronds. He remembers Searle sketching cats and kittens, creatures that seemed incongruously playful and plump compared to the POWs who were physically dwindling. A programme of talks and lectures was also being organised, card schools were flourishing and a radio set was hidden underground among the latrines.

Murray Griffin was in his late thirties and an experienced painter and art teacher when he arrived in Singapore as an official war artist from Australia. He had to wait several months after the island's surrender for a working party to find his art supplies; when they ran out POWs scrounged new materials or made replacements for him. He retained his rank as an officer and was not sent 'up country'.

Compared to Ronald Searle and Jack Chalker his style is considered Modernist. He finished 230 works of art while he was a prisoner and, to begin with, he depicted POWs in intimate moments, a naked man showering under water as it dripped from the eaves of a house, men frying rice cakes or debugging their beds. But as the starved and diseased men returned from Thailand and conditions worsened on Singapore he pulled back from the individual to concentrate on the mechanical or religious: a man working a machine to spin thread from hemp twine, his face partly obscured, or a chapel in Changi. As his paints ran out the pictures become both figuratively and literally darker.

George Aspinall, a farmhand from Wagga in rural Australia, recorded his time as a POW through another medium – one that had started as a peacetime hobby but which became a dangerous obsession. He was just eighteen when he arrived in Singapore having borrowed his older cousin's birth certificate to join the army the year before. When he left home his uncle gave him a folding Kodak 2 camera as a going-away present and he soon found an addictive pleasure in taking photos, snapping portraits of his fellow soldiers and capturing the bustle of Singapore's city life: the rickshaws and the local people squatting to cook meals by the roadside.

He became friendly with a Chinese photographer, Wong Yeow, who ran a camera shop in Changi Village. Aspinall's mates asked him to deliver their photos for processing and he became fascinated by the magical process through which a picture of a grinning Australian soldier could emerge from a dull negative. His initiation into the dark art of photography came one day when an order had to be rushed through in time to catch the mail home to Australia and Yeow asked for his help in developing and printing the photos. He started to spend two nights a week at the studio, staying from 6 p.m. to as late as 11 p.m. – although he was meant to be back in barracks by 8 p.m. By the time his battalion moved to Batu Pahat on the Malaya mainland he was known as 'Changi Aspinall'.

During his first few weeks of imprisonment he was able to take photographs with an abandon that would have been unthinkable a few months later. In those early days, when the Japanese guards spent most of their time on the other side of the perimeter fence, he was more concerned that his own officers would disapprove of what he was doing than that the Japanese would punish him for his hobby.

I didn't have any grand design in mind for making a documentary record or anything like that. It was just something to keep my mind occupied more than anything. I thought it would be good to get the photos back to Australia and perhaps show them to my mother or relations or anybody that was interested. They were just general photos, as I'd been taking earlier, of my trip to Malaya. I suppose it was my photographic diary.

Aspinall's camera was a slim model – about 5 inches long and 3 inches wide with a depth of an inch and a half. To take a picture he had to pull out the front part that looked like a pair of bellows and which concertinaed back after use. One of the riskiest shots he took in the first months was through a hole in an iron wall of a warehouse where he was working. The photo shows a guard standing in front of a 6-inch naval gun; eerily, the man is looking straight at the camera.

As security tightened he began to worry that his camera would be discovered. His solution was to make a canvas belt with a secret pocket at the rear that fastened down with two press studs. The camera sat snugly in the small of his back and he was careful to cover it with his shirt. It would not have survived even a cursory body search but he was lucky enough never to be wearing it when this happened and he noticed that the Japanese seemed to find close physical contact with the POWs distasteful. Sometimes he wrapped it in a scrap of gas cape and hid it in a pipe in the ground but this carried the risk that one of his fellow soldiers might unearth it by mistake.

He began to worry about developing the photos as he was aware that the film would not survive the tropical heat and moisture. He even considered breaking out of camp to visit a photographic shop but eventually he found the answer when he was working at the docks. Here he discovered boxes of negative film, bottles of developer and other chemicals designed for use in X-ray equipment. He shoved the film down the front of his shorts and smuggled it back to The Great World amusement park where the POWs lived in a tented village. Under a staircase in one of the nearby park buildings he made a dark room using an old globe (presumably one that lit up) wrapped in a piece of bunting he had found lying around to provide a low light in which he could work.

Developing and processing the photos was a matter of trial and error. He decanted X-ray developing fluid from a large jar he found at the godown into a Tiger beer bottle and sealed it with a rubber cork. As not all the bottles were labelled it was harder to spot the 'hypo', or fixing solution, but he recognised the smell from his evenings with Wong Yeow. In his darkroom under the stairs, he put the developing fluid in an old enamel kidney dish that had probably once belonged to a hospital. At first he poured the hypo into half a coconut shell but it rocked wildly from side to side and he switched to a bamboo trough. He had no thermometer and had to guess the ambient temperature and count the seconds as he dunked the film in the various chemicals. When he was not using them he hid them in little medicine bottles around Selarang and buried the original chemicals under the building to keep them cool, occasionally pouring water over them to prevent them warming up.

As he exhausted his stock of spools he had to devise a method of fitting individual sections of film in the camera – one shot at a time. Using his Gem razor blade he cut the ten by eight sheets of X-ray negatives to fit his camera with an inch border so that the film could be stuck in behind the frame using dabs of latex to hold it in place. He stored the film in a flat, four by three inch, 'Town Talk' tobacco tin which he wrapped in water-proof gas cape and sealed with sticking plaster. The film lasted him for nearly two years – when other considerations forced him to stop taking photos.

'At that time I regarded the whole thing as a hobby. It gave me an inter-est in doing something apart from the everyday chores. It wasn't until later years that I realised how important the photos were. But I realised right from the beginning how important it was to keep my camera hidden and to take photos secretly.' He fell into a pattern of fitting the film at night and then waiting for a suitable subject. Friends helped by gathering round to hide him while he took the shot, or he would rest the camera on some-one's shoulder while he pretended to be engrossed in conversation. Sometimes he would kneel behind two men and aim the camera between their bodies.

One of his photos shows men sleeping on low, makeshift beds called *charpoys*. These were built around four posts and a mattress woven from coconut husks. Washing is hung above them from the high ceiling; sheets and clothing suspended like ghosts. He also captured men eating their bland rice meals and later he photographed confrontations between guards and POWs. Some of his photos were kept in the false bottom of a water bottle – a common hiding place for forbidden objects such as parts of wireless sets.

Over the next two years he managed to take a hundred photographs behind the backs of his Japanese guards and his Australian officers. What makes his work so haunting is that it is rare to see a photo of the day-to-day life of a POW in the Far East. Since German captors frequently allowed photos of prisoners and their guards it is possible to look the

European POW straight in the eye, to see their boredom and frustration, the rickety hut where they lived or the game of football or the concert party that alleviated their mundane life. The Far Eastern POW has largely dodged this scrutiny: the soldier or airman enters the war well-fed in their neatly pressed uniform and, if they are lucky, emerges to be snapped by liberating forces, half-starved and wearing native 'G-strings'. Aspinall's snatched photos offer an insight into the period in between, how the over-crowding, terrible rations and cruelty led to the skeletal and haunted man at the end of more than three years in captivity.

He captured Changi from different angles and heights. He climbed a water tower to take aerial shots and the photos from this early period show Changi as a scrubland with a few trees dotted here and there. Many POWs were living in once grand houses near Selarang that had been damaged by bombs and robbed of all their furniture. Aspinall also recorded the camps the Sikh soldiers lived in where washing was hung out to dry between palm trees and among the attap huts, like some ill-disciplined Scout jam-boree.

By the end of March the Japanese had managed to cajole some Sikh sol-diers from the British Indian Army into joining the renegade Indian National Army (INA). Captain Mohan Singh, who had been captured when the Japanese invaded Malaya, led the recruitment drive with the vague promise that they would later help to dislodge the British from India. The Japanese were happy to encourage this racial realignment and posted members of the INA around the boundaries of Changi. POWs were ordered to salute the Sikhs – a final insult that many found degrad-ing, while others felt sympathy for the Indians whom they believed had been coerced into changing sides.

Jack Chalker remembers the tension these Sikhs, whom he describes as 'changelings', caused when they guarded the Havelock Road labour camp in Singapore Town. He was marched there in early May 1942 and made his home in an attap-roofed hut where each man had a sleeping and living area about a yard wide on one of two platforms – the lowest just above ground level, the other reached by a ladder. His bed was on the upper tier. His pen-and-wash sketch from the time shows a ramshackle dormitory; the men biblical with their long hair and beards, many stripped to the waist and wearing only loincloths. He made the sleeping space his own by join-ing forces with a friend to scrounge old bits of canvas and a battered car seat they found on a dump. They raised the attap above their beds and fitted a bamboo ladder to make it easier for them to reach the cooking area behind the hut. A car wheel-hub, which they had discovered when they were out with a working party, became a useful frying pan.

The arrival of the Sikh guards caused immediate tension, particularly as a few began 'homosexual assaults' on the men when they visited the latrines at night. 'The whole camp rose up in anger' and from then on, anyone who visited the toilet in the dark went in 'small fighting groups' and the Sikhs learnt to keep their distance. The changing role of the Sikh soldiers was to play an important part in what became known as the Selarang Barrack Square Incident.

Before the war the parade ground was bordered on three sides by seven, three-storied glittering white colonial buildings, a few palm trees standing neatly to attention and well-kept gardens. It was here that the proud Gordon Highlanders wheeled and turned in their precise parade ground drill. Events at the end of the summer of 1942 would make the square, previously a symbol of British rule, unrecognisable.

On 30 August the Japanese ordered that all POWs should sign a form giving their word that they would not escape. On one hand the order was ridiculous; on the other it was an insult. It was ridiculous because although some POWs might fantasise about escaping they knew that trying to flee was suicidal. The sea provided a constant reminder that they were on an island surrounded by inhospitable waters patrolled by sharks. Unlike European POWs, a 'home run' was impossible because they were so far from home. A tiny minority of Allies spoke a few words of the local languages and, although some brave local people helped POWs, the rewards for handing over an escapee were too tempting and the threat of retribution for harbouring one too horrible for anyone on the run to expect help. In Europe the Resistance's lifeblood was a bitter resentment at Nazi occupation; in the Dutch and British colonies of the Far East local people had yet to experience their independence. And, most telling, while a POW in Europe might be able to blend into a crowd in France, Germany or Poland, in Asia most had Western features which would instantly set him apart.

But, if POWs knew logically that escape was foolhardy, they still saw it as their duty to try and they resented being made to acknowledge the hopelessness of their position in writing. Nearly all refused to sign and on

1 September the Japanese ordered between 14,000–17,000 POWs to make their way to Selarang barrack square where they joined around 1,800 Australians who were already living there. Over the next four days the two-acre site took on the appearance of a Hieronymus Bosch painting as hordes of soldiers, many still suffering from their battle wounds, were forced into a compound that in peacetime had accommodated a single battalion of between 600 to 800 troops. They arrived in a raggle-taggle procession, loath to give up what few comforts they had established in their temporary homes. They pushed handcarts, hand-made sledges, bits of old bikes and other vehicles loaded down with their meagre possessions. They brought animals – chickens, dogs, a herd of goats, even a monkey. The parade ground began to look like a late twentieth-century refugee camp. Men sat on the flat roofs, in the stairwells or clung to the crumbling barrack buildings that had been damaged by shellfire and now looked more like the Colosseum than a symbol of the British Empire. It was so cramped that the men had to take it in turns to sleep on the floor. The seriously ill – although such terms are relative – were allowed to stay at Roberts Barracks but the very sick were put in a tented section of the parade ground where tarpaulin and bits of material protected them from the worst of the heat. The standard of sanitation was appalling. The Japanese had cut off the main water supply so that the toilets no longer worked and the men had to dig latrine holes by breaking into the hard surface of the parade ground. Major Gunther, an Australian doctor, was in charge of digging the latrines and stood on the spoil that was extracted from the ground and which got higher and higher and became known as 'Mount Gunther'. The stench of these toilets, together with the mass of sweating bodies in the tropical heat, was unbearable – even after they built wooden boxes to cover the latrines. Water was in such short supply that the men were ordered not to wash their clothes – which added to the fetid atmosphere. George Aspinall spent some of the time spread-eagled on the top of the AIF barracks from where he snapped the scene below. Of the eight photos he took one shows a black cloud hovering over the square. The mark is water damage caused when the photo was hidden in the bottom of a water bottle but the stain looks like an avenging angel observing the wretched scene. Ronald Searle sketched the scene from the roof of one of the barrack blocks. His depiction looks like a very overcrowded market place with a sea of tent roofs, a few vehicles and a mass of tiny figures.

The troops marked the third anniversary of the start of the war on 3 September with a concert organised by the Australians. Illuminated by oil lamps, a choir stood to one side of the parade ground and sang the haunting 'Waltzing Matilda'. Other voices around the ground joined in and then more blatantly patriotic songs followed – 'There'll Always be an England' and 'Land of Hope and Glory'. The waiting was reminiscent of the queues that formed on the beaches of northern France that some men had also endured. But then they had known what they were waiting for; now they had no idea of the outcome of this first, big standoff with their captors.

The mood became subdued when a rumour started about the fate of four men who had been caught trying to escape as long ago as May. Corporal Rodney Breavington and Private Victor Gale (both members of the AIF, although Gale was born in Southend) had got furthest – having rowed 200 miles to a small island where they were arrested. But for most of the time since their capture, they and two other escapees – Private Harold Waters from The East Surrey Regiment and Private Eric Fletcher from the Royal Army – had not been earmarked for special punishment. All POWs were aware that the penalty for trying to escape was death but so far it had been no more than a threat. What happened at the beginning of September showed a change in their captors' attitude.

A new officer in charge of the POWs, Major General Shimpei Fukuye, insisted that the men must die. Despite pleas and protestations he remained immovable and senior commanders were taken from Selarang to the beach to witness their execution. As details of the firing squad spread, it was not so much the fact of their deaths that proved most shocking but the barbaric ordeal of their final minutes. According to most accounts the execution was a botched affair in which ineptitude added to the suffering of the condemned and the anguish of those who witnessed the event. Breavington pleaded for the life of his young friend, Gale, whom he claimed he had dragooned into joining him – but to no avail. The four men refused a blindfold and returned a salute from the POW witnesses. When the Indian soldiers fired, all four fell backwards. But some twenty seconds later, according to an eyewitness account, Breavington raised himself up on one elbow and managed to say: 'For God's sake shoot me through the heart. You've shot me through the arm'. At this the squad started firing 'indiscriminately' until the four men lay limp in the sand. Even then the executioners made quite sure they were dead by moving to within a yard before firing several rounds into each corpse.

News of what had happened on the beach added to the tension at Selarang, especially as many of the guards surrounding the parade ground were INA and the Japanese had also trained machine guns on the men in the square. On 4 September General Fukuye threatened to move Roberts Barracks Hospital to the square; such a move would undoubtedly have killed many of the patients and added another contagious ingredient to the already foul mix of illnesses that included diphtheria and dysentery. Although it seemed that, at this point, the Japanese held all the cards the POWs managed to extract what they saw as a face-saving compromise that allowed them to sign the 'no-escape' form. By changing the Japanese's *demand* to sign to a *military order* the POWs felt morally justified in complying. Galleghan climbed onto the back of a trailer to address his men, telling them that it was up to them if they signed but that the water shortage and the spreading disease meant that more of them would die if they stayed put for much longer. If they signed they did so under duress. Colonel Holmes issued a similar order. They lined up near the clock tower to sign a pile of forms. Among the Australian POWs, 'Judy Garland' (the nickname of a female impersonator) appeared several times – as did the Australian prime ministers 'Jack Lang' and 'Bob Menzies' and the outlaw and folk hero Ned Kelly. Ronald Searle signed his but adorned the form with sketches of two Japanese guards.

For Eric Lomax, Selarang was a 'watershed', 'an important twist in the spiral of capitulation and cruelty'. For many, the executions on the beach and the standoff at Selarang marked the end of the phoney captivity during which being a POW had been a harsh life but never as brutal as it would be over the next three years. For others, the Selarang incident helped to unify the Allies and went some way to patching up the relationship between the British and Australians that had been strained by recriminations over the fall of Singapore. Some POWs felt strangely heartened that they had managed to put up a resistance in what some called 'The Black Hole of Changi'. Just as the evacuation from Dunkirk assumed a sort of quasi heroic status, so Selarang became significant to a defeated army with no victory in sight.

POW Doctor

The tropical illnesses, limited diet and harsh living conditions produced a battery of illnesses for the doctors who were held in the Far East to deal with and made their experience of captivity vastly different from their counterparts in Europe. Many treated patients who were suffering from diseases they had never seen before with limited medicines and few instruments so that by the time the war ended they were living off their wits as much as their medical training.

Flight Lieutenant Nowell Peach, a doctor from Bristol, arrived in Singapore in September 1940 having joined the RAF the October before. He had spent the years after qualifying in 1937 in the usual assortment of medical roles, working in a hospital and as a GP, before he made up his mind that he wanted to be a surgeon. The anatomy course he signed up for was due to start at the Middlesex Hospital on 4 September 1939 but the announcement of war meant it was postponed indefinitely. After a brief spell with Bomber Command near Grantham, he was posted to the Far East. At first he was based at Seletar, Singapore's main aerodrome, and then Kallang, an elegant Art Deco aerodrome close to the city which welcomed seaplanes and which had a swimming pool nearby. 'I just did an hour's sick parade a day and was on call for anyone who happened to crash their aeroplane. That didn't happen very often – not in peacetime.'

Then, early in 1941, he was posted with the Blenheim Bomber 62 Squadron 'up country' to Alor Star, the most northerly of the seven main RAF airfields in the Malayan Peninsula, close to the west coast and near the border with Thailand. On the morning of Monday 8 December he was doing the rounds of the sick when he heard a low humming. He rushed outside and counted twenty-seven bombers. 'I thought they were ours until suddenly I noticed the Japanese roundels underneath.'

He dashed back into the sick quarters and alerted the ward but they were already under attack. He helped patients and staff through the back door and into a slit trench. Within minutes bombs were leaving craters all around them. 'It was pattern bombing, fairly small bombs, but lots of them.'

The attack was part of Japan's assault on the Malayan Peninsula that had started on the north east of the peninsula at Kota Baharu, about an hour and a half before Pearl Harbor. Canadian pilot, Bill Bowden bailed out of his Blenheim after his plane was caught by anti-aircraft fire at Kota Baharu. Bowden clung on to the tail wheel for twenty-four hours before a Japanese destroyer rescued him from the sea, making him the first Allied airman to be taken prisoner by the Japanese.

After the raid on Alor Star most of the staff were moved in the surviving aircraft to an airfield further south. Peach's Commanding Officer asked him to stay behind with medical orderlies to support the handful of men who would remain to keep the airfield operating as a refuelling and bombing base. Over the next two days the enemy attacked repeatedly until the Japanese were only about three or four miles away. When the base was evacuated Peach took a Ford V8 motorcar he had bought from a Chinese man in Singapore. 'It went like a train. I did 400 miles in that in a day.'

He was constantly aware that he might be attacked from the air at any moment but, by sheer luck, he managed to avoid the Japanese, although at least once he arrived after a raid had battered an RAF base. At Kuala Lumpur, about half way down the peninsula, he allowed himself to pause long enough to have lunch with the wife of a Malaysian police officer and to shower. From Singapore he was sent south to Sumatra, the 1,100 mile-long island which was then part of the Netherlands East Indies and which produced most of the colony's oil. After three weeks the Japanese landed and he was on the run again, this time by ambulance to the southern tip of Sumatra where he joined the crowds jostling for a place on board one of the ships heading for the next place of safety – Java.

I had a hair's breath escape at that time. I was waiting on the quay with my luggage near this little steamer and one of my RAF orderlies who was already on board called out, 'We're leaving' by which time we had already cast off at the stern but there was a rope leading up to the bows – most probably the height of about eight feet – and with my haversack on my back I started swarming up this rope, got two hands on the rail and with the weight of my haversack and my fingers slipping, suddenly I was gripped by both [the orderlies] and pulled on board. I don't know what would have happened to me if I'd fallen back in to the water – probably drowned or eaten by a shark or something. That was a very close one.

At first he was in charge of a hospital in Batavia (modern-day Jakarta) but then he was posted to No. 1 Allied General Hospital at Bandung, about 160km inland, where the Australian surgeon Weary Dunlop was Commanding Officer. Peach worked as his assistant as they tried to save men who had suffered terrible battle injuries.

'Then the Dutch capitulated on 8 March 1942. They [the Japanese] left us more or less alone in the hospital for about six weeks and we just went on doing our work. They supplied us with rations, but apart from that they didn't interfere at all.' His first encounter with the enemy came when some Japanese troops marched past 'all very smart' and one of their officers approached and said he thought they should take down their British flag. 'We duly did that and then we had one of two visits from Jap medical officers.'

Weary knew of Peach's medical ambitions and managed to find the one book that every aspiring surgeon needs at his fingertips and which, although he could not have realised it in 1942, was to give a purpose to the next three and a half years of captivity. Weary found the 23rd edition of *Gray's Anatomy* in a secondhand bookshop in Bandung and Peach set himself the task of memorising a section every day. He did not need to make notes; nor was it difficult to concentrate – even when rations were meagre. Studying the 1,216 engravings of veins, arteries and tendons that converged in cross-sections of the human form, like a road map of a congested city centre, took his mind off the uncertainty of his daily life and within three months he had memorised the book's 1,381 pages of detailed drawings and dense text. He carried the 5-pound, dark green tome with its golden title embossed on the front with him as he moved from camp to camp. In 1943 the censor at Batavia stamped the title page with what was known as his 'chop' – a dark blue oblong and red circle that ensured Nowell would not be made to surrender his most treasured possession.

The Japanese closed the hospital at Bandung with just twenty-four hours' notice and the staff and 'walking wounded' were sent to a jail at Lands Opvoedings Gesticht, which the British referred to as 'The Landsop'. Nowell stayed here for six weeks. Overcrowding was very severe: the jail was built to hold around 500 men but there were at least 2,000 Australians, British and Dutch crammed into it. All of the six latrines were blocked.

'But of course most armies have got people who could do almost anything. The Royal Engineers soon got it all unblocked but it was still very insufficient for the number of people.'

He shared a room that measured about 20 feet square with sixteen other people. There was no furniture or beds but they found a rug to spread on the tiled floor. 'It was pretty hard but you got used to it.' They were sustained by their shared belief that they would be liberated within three months.

Captivity hadn't sunk in. One just went on with it and thought it would all come well in the end. I didn't get any post for two and a half years. My parents didn't get any news of me for 18 months, just 'missing believed taken a prisoner of war'.

It was pretty strict. If you passed the lowest of the guards you had to bow to him and on one occasion we were called out on parade and a little Japanese officer turned up and started reading out some kind of rules and regulations and the interpreter misinterpreted something Weary Dunlop said. This Japanese officer took out his sword and advanced on Weary. We thought he was going to chop his head off and lots of people started going forward but fortunately it was just a gesture. He didn't do anything and nobody was hurt but it was pretty alarming. It was a foretaste of what you could look out for.

Over the next three and a half years he was held in a variety of different Javanese camps. He spent two weeks in Tjimahi – a barbed wire camp of big wooden huts surrounded by mountains. It was 'quite pleasant', although it was his first encounter with bedbugs.

We were given some boards to sleep on, on a slight slope, and a mosquito net. I woke up in the middle of the night to find these wretched bugs crawling all over me – it was a nightmare. Every morning we used to get them out of the corners of the mosquito net and squash them. There was a horrible stink.

We had several parades in which people were bashed about, for some reason they didn't do quite what the Jap guard wanted them to, but it was fairly peaceful in that camp.

From here they moved to a three-bedroom brick 'under officers' house' that was part of the 15th Infantry Barracks at Bandung where Dutch NCOs had once lived and where they now slept in the comparative comfort of three to a room. 'I got on very well with some of the Dutch doctors. They had a separate compound through some barbed wire and I was able to get through to them and I was sometimes entertained by Dutch doctors to a meal because they had contacts outside where they could get some quite decent food. I had a very good Nasi Goreng.' But good food was rare.

In the first two months I lost nearly two stones. We had practically nothing except rice and very coarse vegetables and developed diarrhoea but people were still reasonably fit. As far as we were concerned if we found a piece of beef the size of a sugar cube once a day in our stew we were lucky and people fought over it as the chap was ladling it out. We got practically no protein. The rice was full of maggots but that was probably a good thing because at least it was a source of protein but very soon people started to develop deficiency diseases, particularly skin conditions, such as eczema of the scrotum – 'Java balls'.

Boredom was a constant problem. In one camp he passed the time by carving the head of a native man out of the teak wood banister. When they still had sufficient energy – at Bandung – they held football, athletics and boxing competitions against Dutch sides who, because they were well-established in Java, had good contacts with the locals and could smuggle equipment in.

People started all sorts of classes. I gave a lecture on bird photography, although not illustrated with slides as I did after the war. There were all sorts of colleges and educational subjects that people studied. And I, having a table and a chair – we still didn't have any beds – was fondly imagining that since I'd be out in three months I must work for my primary fellowship so I spent three hours every morning on the anatomy book and three hours in the afternoon writing on the physiology book which was lent to me by an Australian doctor.

He made notes in five Dutch school notebooks and managed to finish studying the physiology textbook a week before he was moved to a new camp and had to return it to its owner. He carried these notes with him for the rest of his imprisonment.

From Bandung he was sent to the Bicycle Camp in the suburbs of Batavia. The camp, which had once been a major Dutch barracks, housed around 5,000 men of all ranks in high-ceilinged brick buildings with red tiled roofs. It was obvious that this was a transit camp from which POWs were being sent to other parts of the Japanese empire – mainly Thailand. But they had no idea that these men would be used as slave labour to build the Thailand–Burma Railway. Fortunately, after two weeks he was moved to Tandjong Priok, a camp by the port of Batavia 'where life really was quite reasonable'. The site covered about six acres and was divided into thirteen sub camps and surrounded by barbed wire. There was a football pitch where the Welsh rugby international and cricketer, Wilfred Wooller became a star player on a pitch that was too hard for rugby. They were also allowed to swim in the sea.

Peach carried out minor operations such as treating sebaceous cysts, varicose veins, in-grown toenails and amputating a finger. He noted each with meticulous care in his record book. He also helped a young Australian doctor, Captain Les Poidevin, carry out more complicated surgery. Poidevin, who was twenty-eight, had been captured in Timor, which at around 500 miles from Darwin, was frustratingly close to the Australian mainland. Here coral proved one of the biggest problems. It ripped into men's skin, leaving it susceptible to ulcers, and made digging latrines or burying the dead extremely difficult. It was on Timor that he performed the first of many amputations in an operating theatre with an attap roof and a suspended cloth for a makeshift ceiling. Although he was confident of his own technical ability he always found the decision about whether or not to amputate agonising without the confirmatory evidence provided by X-rays.

Like so many POWs with medical training he learnt to harness what few resources were available. In the storeroom on Timor he found ampoules of quinine urethane – most commonly used to treat varicose veins – and gave it intravenously to malaria patients who had drifted into unconsciousness and whom he feared might not survive. The effect was 'miraculous' and they regained consciousness within minutes. 'This was a great experience in experimental clinical medicine; no microscope, no laboratory, just a bit of initiative and many lives were saved,' he wrote later. 'Some finished with clotted veins, a small price for a life.'

It was while Poidevin and Peach were both carrying out sick parades at the end of November 1942 at Tandjong Priok that they came across a patient who was suffering from something neither of them had encountered before, although Poidevin remembered a professor who had served in the First World War describing a similar injury. At first the pulsating cricket ball-sized tumour in the man's left arm was a mystery. He had been shot during fighting on Timor but until now the injury had caused him no discomfort. Poidevin found the case 'most exciting'. Knowing that he had suffered an early battle injury allowed them to diagnose traumatic aneurysm of the left brachial artery. The bullet must have scratched and weakened the arterial wall but the damage only became apparent when the patient started to carry out heavy work that drove up his blood pressure and inflated the arterial wall.

There was no operating theatre at Tandjong Priok and any POWs who needed surgery were sent to a Japanese hospital, from which they seldom returned. Poidevin pored over Nowell's copy of Gray's Anatomy to remind himself of the relationship of the left brachial artery with the ulnar and median nerves and worried about his ability as a surgeon. A team of doctors set up an operating theatre at one end of an open veranda at the back of the main hospital hut and hung sheets over its thatched ceiling to catch the dust. Nowell assisted in this delicate vascular surgery as Poidevin tied the brachial artery with parachute silk in two places and did the same to the brachial artery below the tumour which stopped it pulsating. He opened the aneurysmal sac and cleaned it before inserting a drain and closing the wound. After the operation the patient's temperature shot up to

102° F but a medical orderly assured the doctors that he was *only* suffering from malaria and that this was not an indication that the operation had failed. The man made a full recovery and survived the war.

Although he never lost sight of the human suffering endured by his patients and which he strove to alleviate, Peach's intellectual curiosity was, nevertheless, piqued by the range of illnesses he came across and the medical solutions available. He was particularly interested in the phenomenon called 'burning feet'. He interviewed fifty sufferers and observed how the Dutch brewed up alcohol from fermented beans and fruit and used it as a good source of vitamin B.

He helped to set up the Tandjong Priok Medical Society at which doctors presented case histories – sometimes supported by laboratory reports – or gave talks on subjects such as the difference between being a GP in Britain and Australia. Medical officers and orderlies attended meetings every fortnight and lecture notes were typed up. Poidevin found preparing for the presentations 'not only a stimulus but a time-killer as well' and the society helped 'to convince ourselves that we were leading as normal a life as possible'.

Study could help to assuage the feeling that they were being left behind. This was the case with Captain Andrew Atholl Duncan of the 2nd Battalion Argyll and Sutherland Highlanders who had been studying mechanical engineering at St Andrew's University in Scotland when war was declared. He joined the ill-fated British Expeditionary Force in France and was evacuated from Cherbourg in the summer of 1940. He was captured in Java (where he was working as a cipher officer) and held at Tandjong Priok, before being shipped to Honshu Island, Japan, and the Motoyama coalmining camp, in October 1942. It was here that he started to worry that he was in danger of falling behind with the subjects that he once knew so well. In February the POWs tried to buy some books and he showed an interest in chemistry, physics and maths textbooks 'so that I shall not lose touch altogether with these subjects'.

A year later, on 28 February 1944, in Zentsuji Camp, Shikoku Island in Japan, he wrote:

Making good progress with the maths these days and feel that I am really getting somewhere. It is often said that opportunity does not knock twice, but I think that this is my second chance and am not going to let it slide as I did when I went to University. To my mind, George Blakey [a POW who taught him Maths] is heaven-sent, as it means that I can get hours of individual tutoring which would have cost a small fortune anywhere other than in a POW camp. The only drawback is that it is very difficult to concentrate in a room where about 27 others are all talking or walking about, but tho' my progress may not be meteoric, it is at least steady and I do understand all that I have covered. George says that it will take about a year to cover the 2nd BSc. course, which is just about right if my estimation of the duration of this war is correct; however, the news has been quite reassuring of late and there is a slight possibility that I may not 'graduate from Zentsuji' but this will not worry me overmuch!

His studies extended to lessons in physical chemistry and calculus using textbooks salvaged from the American Embassy. But it was the miraculous work carried out by the POW doctors who managed to alleviate suffering with very little medicine or equipment that brought about the biggest change in his life. He was so impressed by their skill and dedication that when he finally returned to Scotland he decided to study medicine instead of engineering. He qualified as a doctor in 1950 and he, and later his wife Elizabeth, worked as doctors in Moreton, Wirral, for almost 30 years. His daughter, Meg Parkes, is now chair of the Researching FEPOW (Far East Prisoner of War) History organisation and has been gathering oral testimony from survivors as part of a major research project into the long-term effects of captivity led by Professor Geoff Gill at Liverpool School of Tropical Medicine.

Peach faced the same dilemma about signing the 'no escape' form that POWs had been confronted with at Selarang in Singapore.

I had quite a trying incident when I first arrived at this camp with about 20 medical orderlies (there were two other officers but I was the senior one) and before we got there the camp had been made to sign a document saying that they would not attempt to escape which of course is against all honourable instinct. Everyone had to resist this very strongly but in the end with machine guns trained on you

people gave in but I was one of a party of eight [including] a US merchant seaman who had been torpedoed by the Germans and
decanted at Java. He and I and one or two other officers who'd
arrived recently were lined up in the road with machine guns and
told we had to sign this thing. Everyone refused. Actually, I had a
trump card up my sleeve because I could have given in at any time
because it was my duty not to try to escape – it was my duty to stay
with my patients. So I could sign without any loss of honour anyway
but we all stuck our neck out and said we wouldn't and the Japanese
officer said that if we didn't sign we'd be very severely punished. So
the senior one of our party said, 'Well, what would that punishment
be? Would it be death?' and he said, 'Yes,' so we said, 'Alright, then
we'll sign – under duress.'

After Tandjong Priok he was sent for a year to the Mater Dolorosa
Hospital in Batavia where the main illnesses were dysentery, malaria and
a few cases of TB.

We had nothing to treat them with except magnesium sulphate [a lax-
ative] which seems a rather peculiar treatment for dysentery . . . and
after that a matter of diet.
    Rations [were] still pretty awful, just rice and jungle stew rather like
a very coarse spinach. We started the day with a cup of tea minus milk,
what the Dutch called rice pap – just a sort of porridge made out of
rice, without any sugar, and for lunch we had steamed rice and coarse
vegetables and the same again in the evening. For about two thirds of
the time I suppose we had canteen facilities where you could buy an
egg for instance and also bananas and another bit of fruit. The other
ranks were paid a pittance if they went out on working parties which
most of them had to do. The doctors got paid I think 10 guilders a
month; you could buy an egg for 3 cents which was quite useful. We
gave about a third to a general fund for the other ranks.

He again carried out minor operations such as circumcisions of men with
infected foreskins. Many POWs had infections of the outer ear that he
swabbed with gentian violet. 'I remember one awful, stressful thing – it
was an army officer, Dutch, and he had a terrible abscess in his upper arm

where he'd had an injection that had become infected and I had to open this abscess without any anaesthetic. It was awful for him and for me. For me it was relative. I managed to let the pus out. It must have been terrible agony for him.'

From here Peach was transferred to the bigger hospital of Saint Vincentius that was tucked away among the backstreets of Batavia. The faded brick two-storey building retained some of the presence of a religious refuge. It had a red tiled roof with wide verandas and a central, grassed courtyard and patients slept in real beds. But it was also surrounded by an 8-foot fence topped by a barbed wire apron and guarded by armed sentries. The Dutch doctors were already well-established at St Vincentius and one of them had even managed to produce ether using alcohol and sulphuric acid extracted from lorry batteries by men on working parties. This allowed Poidevin to perform longer operations such as appendicitis cases and perforated gastric ulcers. In his spare moments he also wrote a long dissertation on acute appendicitis.

Peach, who still had six artery forceps, scalpels and other forceps that he carried in a hold-all a fellow POW had made for him and which he had brought from the Number 1 Allied General Hospital, was able to assist. The hospital workshop had a lathe that helped POWs to make a range of items from brooms, mops and garden tools to surgical retractors made from motor vehicle springs. The herb garden produced sixty different plants that were used to treat patients and the hospital became part of a cottage industry making soap in collaboration with Glodok Gaol, on the other side of Batavia. POWs in Glodok collected tallow when they were on working parties, but needed an alkaline solution. Men at St Vincentius were able to help out by contributing drums of urine. The process was so successful that the Japanese sent batches of the soap to Singapore where it was hard to come by.

Doctors like Peach and Poidevin, who in their peacetime professions lived by a strict code of hygiene in which they scrubbed up using soap and hot water and protected the patient on the operating table by donning masks and gowns and by discarding their tools after just one use, learnt to improvise. Their theatre had no running water and they were forced to reuse skin clips and swabs over and over again; parachute silk took the place of catgut. In the tropical heat and tension of an operation Poidevin perfected a technique of flicking back his head at the crucial moment to avoid sweat dropping into a wound – although if this happened it never seemed to cause any problems.

They struck up a good relationship with a Japanese doctor who was keen to learn English and who arranged for medicine, food, clothing, books and even gramophones to be sent to St Vincentius. He also helped them to get an X-ray machine but, like everything else, the barium meal had to be recycled and they reckoned they could recover about 700gm of the original 800gm each time.

Poidevin found himself in demand among the guards to perform circumcisions which were seen as conveying kudos and which he carried out at a rate of two or three a week. He 'charged' an ampoule of local anaesthetic and a pack of cigarettes for the operation and sometimes received chocolate for lancing a boil or treating an ingrown toenail. Although he worried that he was helping the enemy, the padre reassured him that his conscience should be clear.

In early 1944 he performed the first tendon lengthening operation. His patients were men who had been confined to the holds of ships and had spent so long curled up in a foetal position that their tendons had contracted. The emaciated condition of the patients made it difficult to know how to treat them: it was too painful to try to straighten their legs manually and their skin was too thin and the bodies too light for traction to work. Surgery proved successful in several cases.

Taking Flight: Escape Through Birdwatching

For Peach, birdwatching and concert parties provided two forms of escape from the suffering he witnessed. About 400 species of birds live in Java and Peach, a life-long ornithologist, became absorbed in watching and drawing them using crayons the Dutch gave him. At Bandung he climbed to the attic to take a closer look at the swifts' nest there and studied the birds through a pair of binoculars he found. He held on to the binoculars for a year and a half until they were confiscated – the only item he ever lost in this way. He kept a record in an old school exercise book of the nests he discovered. One of the most unusual was built by the tailorbird, a green-coated wren-like warbler with a call of *cheeup-cheeup-cheeup*. The bird's name comes from its ability to create an outer pouch for its nest by piercing the edge of a large leaf with its sharp bill and sewing it up with gossamer or plant fibre. At Tandjong Priok he spotted a black-winged kite; the next time he saw this bird of prey was twenty years later in Portugal. While at Mater Dolorosa he sketched the scarlet-headed flowerpecker as it nested in the hospital grounds.

As in European camps, birdwatching provided a satisfying distraction for POWs – with the added bonus that they were likely to spot colourful creatures that would never appear on the well-tended lawns and bird tables of Britain. For men who had already embarked on this hobby, birdwatching in captivity offered a sense of continuity amid a life now marked by uncertainty and over which they had very little control.

Ronald John ('Jack') Spittle was, according to his son, Brian, already 'an inveterate note taker' when he arrived in Singapore aged twenty-seven as part of the Royal Army Medical Corps. He had been jotting down observations about the wildlife he saw around his Buckinghamshire home since he was a teenager and began a census of herons nesting in a small wood between Henley and Marlow which he first visited when he was fourteen.

In Singapore he began by writing in high quality notebooks but as he exhausted this supply he switched to school exercise books. When he was moved from Changi to Kranji (in north Singapore) paper became very scarce and in his final year as a POW he wrote on loose scraps of paper, backs of envelopes, pages torn from books and the insides of cigarette packets. His son believes these notes were a vital defence mechanism: 'No doubt my father's note taking at Changi and Kranji became a survival strategy; a way to ward off both the boredom of captivity and an apprehension, that seemed to increase as time dragged on, about what the future would hold. If there was to be a future, that is.'

Judging from the dates in his notebooks, it seems that he did most of his bird-watching between July 1943 and May 1944 when he was held at Selarang and before he was moved to Kranji. He may have been allowed more freedom to roam at Selarang and a letter written after the war from a fellow POW, E.K. Allin, mentions the walks they took together to study birds. Brian remembers his mother saying that one of the Japanese officers was a keen ornithologist and as a result may have allowed him to indulge his passion.

He recorded his observations in pencil, often adding a sketch of the bird he had seen in pencil or crayon. His handwriting rarely rests on the page's lines – perhaps because he was studying the bird as he wrote and sketched. This entry for a magpie robin is typical of his style: '12.V.43. One seen perched on roof of Chinese house by gate leading to Selarang area. Another in vicinity of Headquarters Malaya Command buildings. Both in 18th Div. Sunset.'

He began to write up his bird notes soon after he arrived back in Britain and had finished a long draft by 1947. He was still in touch with E.K. Allin who was living in North Wales and who had introduced him to Carl Alexander Gibson-Hill, Assistant Curator of Zoology at the Raffles Museum and a noted ornithologist. Gibson-Hill, who had worked in Singapore's Health Department, had arrived on the island four days before its fall and had himself been interned at Changi Gaol and Sime

Road camp, where he tried to study birds he could see from within the camp boundary (he and two others spotted a hundred species and twenty 'doubtfuls').

In 1950 Jack Spittle's article 'Nesting Habits of Some Singapore Birds', based on notes made by him and Allin, was published in the *Bulletin of the Raffles Museum;* it is still cited today. Although the tone of the article is one of scientific objectivity it is possible to catch a glimpse of the author as he scours the flame trees, bougainvillea bushes, and coconut palms for signs of nests. His descriptions capture an island ravaged by fighting: the house swifts who made their home in the six-inch gap between the ceiling and beam of a bomb-damaged building, the colony of blue-throated bee-eaters who had settled into an over-grown sandpit near Changi Village and the yellow-vented bulbul who moved into a shrapnel hole made in a coconut tree. It is hard not to draw an analogy between the birds building nests out of pieces of old newspaper, scraps of bandages, brightly coloured darning wool (as in the case of the tailorbird), sloughed-off snake skin and lalang leaves and the POWs foraging for remnants to make their equally temporary homes more hospitable. Was the keen birdwatcher able to limit his thoughts purely to the satisfaction of observing a creature he would not have encountered at home, or did he allow himself to linger on the image of the cosy families living amid 'fluffy nest-lining' where the adults did their best to meet the demands of their youngsters who clamoured for food? If his mind did wander from the purely ornithological it must have been difficult not to conclude that the birds were much better off.

Survival Teams

I had at this moment in time made friends with an Australian boy, his name was 'Roly-K-Hull' and I believe he came from St-Arnaud, and we had become very good friends, and as a survival team, we did very well.

It was amazing how he would suddenly turn up with food he had stolen from the Japs, and he would always share it with me, he proved a real lifesaver to me at this time, and helped me through a very bad period

I always seemed to have plenty of friends, and as fast as they died I found new buddies, and that's how it went on right through the campaign.

Johnny Sherwood

Friendship was a matter of life and death to the Far Eastern POW. As in Europe, a buddy would lift your mood when you were down and help you to pass the hours of boredom. But in the Far East friendship offered practical benefits. A good mate would bring you food when you were too sick to move, coax you to eat and make sure the medical orderly did not forget about you. He would support you to the 'borehole' and know which memories would lift your mood – whether that meant talking about your football team or your 'best girl'. It helped to be part of a gang: a group of three was too small; five was the optimal number. Being a loner meant you did not have this safety net to fall back on but for some POWs, like the photographer George Aspinall, friendship was too dangerous or made you vulnerable.

The friendships POWs forged in Europe and the Far East often lasted a lifetime. But the difference for Far Eastern prisoners was that many saw their friends die – not in battle but through starvation or some terrible disease or a combination of both, plus despair. It was not unusual in the Far East for someone to watch their friend simply turn over on their sleeping platform and give in to death. POW camps in Europe held funerals for men who had died of battle wounds, in attempts to escape or from illness – which often took hold among older men – but these ceremonies never occurred on the industrial scale of some Far Eastern camps, particularly during the construction of the airfield at Haruku in the Molucca Archipelago and the Thailand–Burma Railway.

Friendships – and feuds – became part of the rhythm of camp life. POWs celebrated each other's birthdays with elaborate ritual that might include a handmade card signed by friends, a singsong or an invitation to a special dinner or party, or perhaps bigger rations for the person whose birthday it was. Men exchanged gifts such as grated coconut or a handmade trinket on these and other important days such as Christmas. When Russell Braddon and his fellow Australians left Pudu Gaol for Singapore in November 1942, those who remained, led by Padre Duckworth, gathered to wave and shout. Some of them even gave each other gifts: Braddon received a small lump of *gulah malacca* (a brown sugary substance).

Battle revealed men at their most basic. The indignity of illnesses such as dysentery, when men often could not help but soil themselves or had to rely on their mates to hold on to them as they leant out of a moving cattle truck to defecate, meant that prisoners saw each other at their most vulnerable. The heat and illness removed barriers – real and psychological. As clothing disintegrated POWs displayed more flesh and, sometimes, exotic tattoos that presented a different side to their character – a visual pun or a hidden devotion to something or someone. The terrible tropical ulcers, too, literally stripped away flesh to expose a man's naked bone.

Conversations circled around recurring topics and one of the most common was what they would do 'when they got home'. This included the short-term – their first meal – and the long-term – whether they would change jobs, start up their own business, travel, go into politics. And in the absence of any real news much time was taken up with chewing over rumours, many of which were generated at the latrines and became known as 'borehole rumours'. News – for example snippets passed round from hidden radios – was referred to as 'griff'.

There were the inevitable grumbles and gripes about whether officers were receiving special privileges but it is difficult to know whether there was more dissent than in peacetime or freedom. The historian R.P.W. Havers suggests that, in Changi at least, there were complaints of this nature during the period May 1944 to September 1945 when POWs were moved into Changi Gaol. This may have been because prisoners had less opportunity to scrounge and were contained within the gaol and its immediate surroundings.

Certainly, in the early days of captivity there were some camps where officers clung to the perks of their rank. The officers' mess at Bukit Timah in Singapore, for example, had a mosquito-netted verandah with a view over the golf course. Russell Braddon, an outspoken critic of the officer class, felt that the official insistence that officers and Other Ranks should be divided by privileges was hard on both sets of men. He describes lower ranks giving up their clothes for officers in Changi and those officers eating first, being allowed to keep poultry and having fuel to cook light snacks.

A cursory reading of Stephen Alexander's description of conditions in Sime Road, Singapore, might give the impression that officers were attempting to continue a Raj-like existence despite their incarceration. However, there is a strong element of irony in his account of the 'Sad Case of the Disappearing Cocktail'. He describes how they had 'acquired' a fridge and were 'eager to exploit its scope for gracious living'. While his group of friends had brewed and bottled beer from old fruit, rice water and yeast the senior mess had secretly assembled a cocktail whose key ingredient was old brandy. Both concoctions were kept in the fridge. Just before dinner the mess waiter was told to decant the beer into a jug but picked up the cocktail by mistake so that the would-be beer drinkers tasted something more potent and the other group was disappointed. Words such as 'decant', 'cocktail' and 'mess waiter' sound as though they belong in Sandhurst rather than Sime Road but it was this sort of hyperbole that bolstered POWs who had lost everything.

It was usual for officers to sleep and eat in different huts or even different camps and not to have to work. But in some parts of the Far East they were forced to labour, for example, during some periods of construction on the Thailand–Burma Railway. By the start of 1943 all British officers below field rank (except those involved in administration and tending the sick, as well as elderly officers) were labouring on the railway. It was common, although not universal, for higher ranks to make a contribution to a fund to help the very ill and lower ranks.

At Tamarkan camp, on the Thailand–Burma Railway, Colonel Philip Toosey broke with army tradition to order officers to sleep in the same hut as their men in a position by the door so that they could keep an eye on everyone. He dispensed with the idea of an officers' mess and made sure that all POWs shared the same food. The historian Sibylla Jane Flower also suggests that as very few first hand accounts have been published by officers or men who held responsibility perhaps it is too easy to criticise the upper ranks.

The stripes on a man's arm immediately put him into a certain category. Freemasonry was a less obvious subgroup and one that, since it relied so heavily on clandestine ritual, would seem destined for failure in a Japanese POW camp. But the secret society thrived and, just as in Europe, one group of Masons was often unaware of the existence of another.

In 1942 H.W. Wylie, a former rubber planter, asked General Percival for permission to hold Masonic meetings in Changi because he felt they would help to raise morale. Percival agreed with the proviso that they should avoid talking about politics, the conditions in which they were held and – to avoid argument – religion. They met each week in an empty barrack block on top of the highest hill in the camp. Four rings of six lookouts kept watch. If they had been discovered they would have claimed they were holding a religious service. Another group started, without knowledge of the first, and held meetings at the Old Garrison Church. Wylie wrote later of the psychological benefits:

> The peace and tranquillity of those meetings stood out in great contrast to the turmoil and irritation of the day. Although it was very hot and most of the time all the men were in rags, ill, hungry, tired and dirty, yet it was possible during these meetings almost completely to forget the normal conditions of their lives as prisoners of war. To sit quietly among proven friends and listen to the ceremonies took one's thoughts very far from a prison camp and lifted the mind above the reach of petty annoyances, restored one's balance, and demonstrated the possibility of the victory of mind over matter – a very important factor at such a time.

Around twenty masons, mostly Australians, met on Sunday afternoons in the clock tower at Selarang Barracks. Another eight met in a bombed house and a third group called the Selarang Study Group held meetings in a depot. At Roberts Barracks' hospital, British and Australian Freemasons gathered in a storeroom, while in another part of the camp Dutch members actually initiated a candidate – although their British and Australian brothers refused to acknowledge the authenticity of this ceremony. The Changi POW Masonic Association (a mixture of Australian and Southern Area masons) held its first meeting in December 1942 when forty-seven men met in the old theatre at Roberts Barracks before deciding in future to meet in the bomb-damaged barracks' church which was screened by trees.

Freemasons usually managed to continue to meet when they were moved to different camps: in a storeroom at Changi Gaol and at River Valley Road POW camp. Elsewhere they made their identity known to each other. On one occasion a POW in a jungle camp in Thailand realised that a Dutch officer was a fellow Mason because of the distinctive white squared carpet he was using as a sleeping mat and which he had carried with him from Java. A Masonic association was formed at a camp in Tamuang near Kanchanaburi in Thailand.

These tight Masonic groups offered the bond of security and the practical advantages of a few extra perks – cigarettes for the sick and gatherings at which small amounts of food (often stolen during work parties) and drink ('coffee' made from grains of rice burnt to charcoal on a heated steel sheet) were served. One POW wrote how a team had quizzed an officer for several hours before they decided that he was an impostor. 'Many men, indeed many officers, tried to "muscle in" under these unique conditions, and I have spent many interesting hours checking and cross checking on words from the ritual.'

But, while it is easy to see the advantage of being a Mason, it is not so obvious why Masons took such great risks in accumulating documents that would certainly have incriminated them. Most groups kept detailed 'visitors' books' in which they recorded members' names, rank, lodge and country of origin and handwritten or typed minutes of their meetings. They made beautiful artefacts to help them conduct their rituals. At Changi Gaol, the internee J.R. Skipper fashioned what masons refer to as 'Jewels', but which look like charms from a bracelet – silver swords, keys, birds, an open book – from scraps of metal salvaged from a bombed bus. Elsewhere, Masons used pieces from a Japanese shell case, a wrecked aircraft and brooms to make other artefacts. When an Australian Mason died his comrades built a coffin for him from scraps of wood and cut the Masonic emblems of a square and compasses from an aluminium fan blade with his name and number etched into it.

The Changi POW Masonic Association stopped meeting after the Kempeitai (the Japanese equivalent of the Gestapo) began to show an interest in their activities in early 1944. Several Masons were interrogated and one man was severely beaten up after regalia were found amongst his possessions. As a precaution Masons buried many of the minute books and 'working tools' in a tin box. After the war several attempts were made to find the box but it is now lost under a modern building.

Conversation and debate helped to pass the time, even if subjects were banal. Officers in Java discussed whether red-headed women perspired more than other females and Laurens van der Post recorded in his diary how, in early 1943, a group of men debated whether it was preferable to be held in Bandung for a further six months with the certainty of release or to face three weeks desert fighting with the chance of being killed. The chance to rejoin the battle won the day. He wrote, too, of a 'camp giggle', a 'sort of helpless, eye-watering chuckle with an air of – well, here I am properly caught, what a fool I have been . . . it is astonishing how many people have been affected by it . . . It is involuntary and, I am sure, a more pleasant manifestation of hysteria.'

Given his passion for learning it is hardly surprising that Frank Bell spent much time discussing intellectual subjects at Kuching: the relationship between Nature and Art and how Western values compared to Eastern culture. Whenever someone remembered a literary quotation they seized on it as an 'intellectual link with the world from which we were separated'. But Frank was not entirely removed from the real world. A topic that provided a prolonged and heated debate was whether single or double beds were preferable in married life. Frank was adamant that, as a restless sleeper, he would prefer not to share a bed with his future wife. (In the event he changed his mind).

Throughout the camps there were POWs who could give a talk on almost any subject – from ski-ing to crime and big game hunting, to scents and perfumes, 'A Holiday in a Lunatic Asylum', 'Hollywood' and 'Murder and Robbery in Shanghai'. In Changi two English Indian Army Majors, called Bartram and Dart, gained a reputation for their outrageous 'Poonah' yarns. They told stories about hunting tigers, spying in Afghanistan and sniping in the Kyber Pass. Bartram usually ended his tale with words that became a catchphrase: 'Now you may doubt this, gentlemen, but I know it's true because I was there-ah!'

Laurens van der Post found an eager audience at Bandung. He wrote a column for the camp magazine, *Mark Time*, under his pen name, 'The Walrus', and worked on the adventure story that was to be published in 1955 as *Flamingo Feather*. His biographer, J.D.F. Jones believes the experience was pivotal to his development as a writer. When Jones wrote his biography he uncovered many instances in which his subject had exaggerated his role, stoked up myths about himself or just plain fibbed:

> Evidently this [his time as a POW] was also the period when Laurens discovered his gift as a storyteller in front of an audience: *Flamingo Feather*, for example, was apparently conceived as a serialised tale of African adventure with which Laurens entertained his men in the long depressing evenings of captivity. There may be a clue here to his future career, as he found that in camp his stories worked well (like telling a tale to put a child to sleep, when the storyteller is permitted any and everything, however fanciful). Maybe he never entirely made the necessary transfer into the peacetime world when literal truthfulness once again becomes a moral imperative.

The creation of imaginary worlds does not seem to have been as prevalent as in European camps such as Stalag 383 where whole groups of men entered into elaborate charades. Perhaps this sort of organised make-believe simply required too much energy or a level of good humour that could not exist amid so much death. There were a few POWs, though, who escaped from the jungle into a parallel universe – either to amuse themselves and their friends or because they could not cope with reality. Fergus Anckorn remembers a man called Pinkie who developed a talent for impersonating the sound made by both animals and inanimate objects. He was able to reproduce with uncanny accuracy the 'voice' of a duck, cat or dog, as well as more ambitious noises such as a car, lorry and motorbike, eggs frying in a pan, a gong sounding or a hinge creaking. After a while he added mime to his impersonations: firing an imaginary Bofors gun at the all-too real vultures, hammering a fictitious nut into a motorbike that existed only in his dreams. When he headed for his hut at night he would go through an elaborate routine in which he stepped over invisible wires and dodged make-believe clothes lines until he made it to his bed.

Jack Chalker knew a man he met at Chungkai in Thailand who lived a 'Walter Mitty existence'. One day he was a cowboy brandishing guns and riding an imaginary horse, the next he was revving up the engine on his imaginary motorbike. At first they thought he was only pretending to be mentally ill but it became evident that he had lost his mind. One morning he escaped, swam the river and was lost in the jungle beyond. The guards found him, naked, wet and laughing, still brandishing his imaginary pistols.

Having a mental haven to retreat to was particularly useful during hard, but monotonous labour. When Russell Braddon was helping to dig out the runaway at Changi's new aerodrome, he dealt with the mind-numbing tedium of the ten to twelve hour shifts by trying to remember the second movement of Bruch's violin concerto or struggling to prove Pythagoras's theorem as he shovelled the white earth in the blazing heat. He never did prove the theorem despite using the blade of his *changkol* to sketch out his workings in the dirt – an exercise that led to his arrest when guards were convinced the drawings were plans for a radio.

Atholl Duncan 'gave the old memory a good spring clean' by revisiting good times he had enjoyed in the past: caravan holidays, games of golf, walks and dances with his fiancée Elizabeth, evenings with the old folks, fishing trips, rags at university. But the trouble with these mental excursions was that 'sooner or later you must come back to earth, the jolt of this being pretty terrific'. But he also spent some time in the future and he and his fellow American POWs drew up lists of items they would exchange after the war, a sort of hopeful auction of promises. For example:

Angus M. Morris wishes haggis and information about tweeds.
Will exchange maple syrup for haggis.

Erwin W. Lasher Desires: tweeds
Will send: pina cloth table sets, manilla cigars in cabinet, hardwood carved cruet and salad bowl.

He recorded foods he craved which included steak and kidney pie, liver and kidneys, 'mother's ginger cake', toad in the hole, treacle pudding, fish and chips, mealy puddings. Later he had a longing for a particularly Scottish snack – a sausage in a 'morning roll' (a floury bap). He made a list of the tasks he had performed as a POW, such as planting sweet potatoes, and a list of the things he longed for. Many of the items would have appeared on most POWs' wish list – to have clean, well-fitting clothes, a proper bed, to feel free from the shouts of 'Kora' [Hey] and 'You!' Others met deeply felt needs in him – the urge to go for a picnic, to sit in a comfortable chair by a log fire with the rain and wind outside, to eat at a neatly laid table a 'civilised meal with civilised materials', to fish for yellow trout and to see a neatly laid-out garden and to smell flowers, to read and study in comfort.

Frank Bell's list of 'The Things that Annoy Me' offers an insight both into camp life and his own personality:

1) Coming to the end of a bar of peanut toffee and realising he had been thinking of something else all the time (he was determined to savour every mouthful);

2) Reading in a book a list of virtues and finding he possessed none of them;

3) Books placed upside down on a shelf;

4) The fact that it is only ever possible to see one side of the moon;

5) That there are so many books in the world and so little time to read them all;

6) Double-jointedness;

7) Hearing someone telling someone else that they *ought* to know a particular fact;

8) 'The fiendish clatter of Rolls Razors vying with each other in the morning';

9) Reading in a novel that someone 'scarcely touched his meal'. This made him want to throw the book in the fire or tear it to pieces;

10) Watching a praying mantis's 'slow, deliberate, ghostly movements' gave him 'the creeps'.

11) The triple three-noted rising call of the mocking bird. He found it impossible not to stop what he was doing and wait for the final note.

Very often friendships formed in the Far East remained cast-iron after the war. Indeed, some POWS found they could only be themselves with men who had gone through a similar experience; while it was impossible to explain to their family what they had endured, this group remained one for whom no explanation was necessary.

Escape Through Study

Jack Spittle and Nowell Peach gained their knowledge through observation and a mixture of private and public study – Jack's companionable walks with other bird enthusiasts and Nowell's membership of the Tandjong Priok Medical Society. As in Europe, study fulfilled several very important roles: it kept boredom and depression at bay and it offered a hope that the years of captivity would not be entirely wasted – especially if a new skill could be learnt or valuable knowledge assimilated. Many POWs picked subjects with an eye to life after the war, or in the phrase that became a constant refrain: 'When we get home'.

Many POWs who craved learning found that their greatest resource was the men around them, together with a few textbooks garnered from an abandoned library, college or house. Weary Dunlop set up a prison university at Landsop camp in April 1942 and this continued when he moved to Bandung where Laurens van der Post was Senior Education Officer while also teaching Afrikaans and basic Japanese. Other men lectured in subjects in which they had a degree or whose career had given them specialist knowledge: a squadron leader taught navigation, an Oxford don lectured in Ancient History, another graduate who would later became a head teacher in Wales provided French lessons. Subjects ranged from the purely intellectual, such as art, architecture and Homer's *Odyssey*, to more practical skills like book-keeping, English law and reading and writing. By September 1942 1,200 students were engrossed in thirty subjects, many taking notes or writing exercises on toilet paper which the Japanese supplied in abundance because they believed it helped to limit the spread of disease.

Charles Fisher describes two POW 'universities' at Changi, each with its own distinct flavour that allowed many young men to continue their education for at least three successive terms. The 18th Division, which included the Cambridgeshires, started in March 1942 and was staffed by men whom Fisher compared to the sort of senior schoolteachers who would normally be found at a British evening class. The Southern Area (which housed more British troops as well as local volunteers in the Changi Village area), by comparison, offered courses that Fisher, who lectured there, believed to be 'at least comparable to that of a typical British redbrick university'. Indeed, while he was at Changi he continued to work on what he hoped would be a PhD thesis and which he had started before the campaign. When prisoners were ordered to hand in all written documents he parted reluctantly with his manuscript, which he reckoned represented twelve months' hard work. He was told he would be given a receipt for it but later found it had been thrown on a fire.

Their postwar careers suggest that he was not entirely right about the 'senior school teachers' at the 18th Division's university. One of its founders, Ian Watt, had already shone at Cambridge and won a scholarship to the Sorbonne. After the war he became a respected literary critic, the first dean of the influential School of English Studies at the University of East Anglia and Professor of English at Stanford. He also wrote the seminal work, *The Rise of the Novel* (1957). Another founder, Guthrie Moir, was an officer in the 5th Suffolk Regiment and graduate of Peterhouse College, Cambridge, who went on to a postwar career in broadcasting. At Changi he lectured on literary subjects such as Oscar Wilde.

Stephen Alexander's experience at the 18th Division's University of Changi was certainly more Cambridge college than evening class. He attended lectures on English Literature in a small mosque and was impressed by Ian Watt's insistence that literature was not to be enjoyed unthinkingly but should be put in the context of the writer's – and reader's – social background. S.C. Irons of the Cambridgeshire Regiment attended the same course and remembers it began with Watt's lecture on 'The structure and growth of the English language'. They were given copies of Keats's poems 'Ode on a Grecian Urn' and 'Ode to a Nightingale' to criticise and one afternoon he read *The Napoleon of Notting Hill* by G.K. Chesterton. Their library was in a small hut; membership was offered in return for the donation of a novel or collection of poetry. There were occasional moments when the setting had echoes of a rarefied Oxbridge education: as Irons waited in the courtyard of the mosque for his English lecture to start he caught snatches of a Latin lecture by a 'brilliant' academic. According to Stephen Alexander it was mainly second lieutenants and lieutenants who supplied both lecturers and students at the 18th Division's University, although occasionally a few senior officers came along to see what was going on. It has been suggested that, at its peak in March 1942, as many as 9,000 POWs out of a population of 45,562 were attending some sort of class at Changi.

The Fenman newsletter acknowledged the impact of the classes:

There are, it's true, several fellows wandering around muttering 'J'ai – tu as – il est –nous nous – what the deuce comes next?', and others burbling about pistons, gears and other weird and wonderful contraptions, but far out-numbering these are the would be 'artists'.

These disillusioned fellows sit in odd corners feverishly measuring this, that and the other with a pencil stuck at arms length, then scribbling away on a somewhat muddy piece of paper – of which – for some vague reason – they are terribly proud.

Seriously, though, I'm sure we all sincerely hope these classes continue, and even grow larger, because we all feel the need for something to occupy our minds as well as our hands – and what better way could we have?

The Southern Area had two big advantages: it had more academics and more books. Several professors and senior staff from Raffles College (which later became the University of Malaya and is today known as the University of Singapore) were held there. They included Alexander Oppenheim, a brilliant mathematician originally from Manchester who had taken a first at Oxford University before settling down as Professor of Mathematics at Raffles College. 'Oppie', as he was known, was a lance-bombardier in the Singapore Royal Artillery; his wife and young daughter had escaped just before the fall of Singapore. He was known for his witty conversation and the POWs elected him Dean of the University.

Other former colleagues from Raffles College, representing several different subjects, joined him in the university. Graham Hough, a member of the Singapore Royal Artillery, lectured in English; Donald Purdie, an expert in metallic compounds, taught Chemistry; Prof. T.H. Silcock's sub-ject was Economics and Dr Charles Webb lectured on Physics. Most continued their glittering academic careers, apparently without hitch, after the war. Hough became a professor at Cambridge University and wrote several books such as *The Last Romantics* (1949), which became a classic in the study of English literature. His book on D.H. Lawrence, *The Dark Sun*, led to him appearing as a defence witness in the Old Bailey trial of October 1960 in which Penguin was accused of breaching the Obscene Publications Act by publishing *Lady Chatterley's Lover*. He rarely spoke of his experiences as a POW but the scholar and critic Antony Easthope, whom Hough supervised when he was an undergraduate at Christ's College, Cambridge, remembers that Hough once rebuked him over his inability to decide which of Yeats's poems were the best saying: 'You don't know anything about it. You soon find out which are the best when you are in a Japanese concentration camp with dysentery and the only paper you have is *The Collected Poems Of W.B. Yeats.*'

Oppie and some of the other lecturers persuaded a Japanese officer, Lieutenant Okazaki, to provide them with a truck that they piled high with several hundred books from their old university. They also encour-aged POWs to donate their own books to the new POW library. The university was able to offer most subjects – except classics and modern lan-guages – in the small block allocated for its twelve classrooms. The selection board interviewed applicants who had to have passed a 'school certificate'. As far too many applied for the 600 places, preference was given to younger men whose education had been interrupted by the war. Oppie found himself in the uncomfortable position of having to inform a brigadier that his application had been unsuccessful. By the end of the third term Oppie, and most of the fitter men, had been sent 'upcountry'.

The Australians had their own Education Unit that provided classes in a wide range of subjects such as agriculture, medicine, engineering, debat-ing and art. Its lecturers included Oxford-educated Alec Downer, who went on to become Minister for Foreign Affairs in postwar Australia, David Griffin, who had graduated in law before joining the army, and John Carrick, who was later knighted and became Australian Minister for Education (1975-1979). Captain Leslie Greener, who had worked as an artist for the Sydney-based magazine, *Pix*, became the university's Dean.

As well as teaching esoteric subjects the university offered the chance for POWs to learn practical skills. Griffin lectured on English poets and read verse to men who had never heard a poem before but he also taught men to read and write. Although he was inexperienced in this particular aspect of teaching he and other teachers helped an estimated 400 Australians to acquire these two basic skills. He later acknowledged the importance of building an alternative world within the prison camp: 'each man created for himself a microcosm into which he could crawl: flowers, hobbies, poultry, painting, writing, what you will. And the most contented prisoner was he who could build the most perfect microcosm and disappear most effectively within it'.

Griffin was one of three Australian POWs behind *The Happiness Box*, a story he wrote for the interned children held with their mothers at Changi Gaol. Other POWs made presents – model cars, trains and ships, dolls, animals and a miniature theatre with cardboard actors for the children's first Christmas behind bars. The book was completed within thirty-six hours. Griffin wrote the story on Gordon Highlanders' paper and handed each page to Bruce Blaikey to type up before passing it to Greener to illustrate. It was bound and added to the display of toys that General Saito was to examine. *The Happiness Box* tells the tale of three characters, a monkey called Martin, Wobbley the frog and the wise little lizard Winston, who live together in a house in the jungle. But even in this children's story the POW's preoccupation with food is obvious. The trio live off the north, south, east and west winds that Winston catches in a trap he has set in the very highest tree and which Wobbley serves up with rice and vegetables. But the wind trap is the only one in the jungle and they are forced to share their meals with hundreds of other creatures that turn up at their door. Their happy existence is rocked when Wobbley finds a strange wooden box in a rice field.

But Griffin had made a fatal mistake in choosing 'Winston' as a name for the main character. When Saito spotted it he assumed it referred to the British prime minister and that the book contained a coded message that would be passed between the POWs and the internees. He ordered the book to be destroyed but it somehow escaped and was buried in an ammunition container somewhere in the camp grounds.

Griffin, together with Downer and Tony Newsom (who had been a senior sales rep for a toothpaste company in Southern Australia), helped to run the Australians' library in a small room in the former Gordon Highlanders Officers' Mess at Selarang. According to one estimate, it contained around 20,000 volumes. Most were gathered from Raffles Library after 'Black Jack' Galleghan persuaded the Japanese to allow him to send lorries in to collect what books they could find. A pen and ink drawing produced by Murray Griffin shows Australians, many wearing their 'slouch' hats, queuing at a window to borrow books while a librarian sits on the other side of the counter – still managing to look officious despite his bare chest. The library was such a valuable resource that the AIF set up a workshop when they moved to Changi Gaol to repair books ravaged by the heat and constant use. In the bindery POWs became skilled at using latex, rice paste, stewed bones, banana leaves, bits of blinds and old hosepipes to restore much-loved volumes; old prison records and charge sheets for wayward Indian privates helped to strengthen books that were wilting in the humidity or under attack by insects that sometime also bit the reader.

The supply of books was one of many areas in which the Far Eastern prisoner was at a distinct disadvantage. Whereas European POWs could order books from home, it was not until March 1945 that the British Red Cross even began planning to send books to the Far East. Fifteen units of 500 books each were ready to send by the end of June – a month after the end of hostilities in Europe. POWs for whom reading was essential developed a keen nose for sniffing out books. J.G.B. Millns, a subaltern in 18th Division Troops Company, Royal Army Service Corps (RASC), was allowed to take a tin trunk full of personal belongings, including a dozen books, with him into captivity. Later he stumbled across a stash of books when he was sent to a polo club in Singapore Town to supervise a hundred or so Other Ranks who were repairing a range of vehicles from Cadillacs to ambulances and small cars before they were shipped to Japan. The men managed to sabotage several vehicles by driving them without oil in the sump. When Millns investigated a club building which looked run-down and had broken windows he discovered that one room was full of books. A friendly guard allowed him to take as many as they could carry and he filled fifty sacks. This formed the basis of a library he started at his next camp. New members had to provide one book and he soon had several hundred. After the war Millns returned to work at his family papermaking business. For other POWs the role of librarian was a natural progression in what became exalted academic careers. Lieutenant David Piper was librarian at Shirakawa in Formosa camp in Japan and went on to become an internationally respected art historian and director of the National Portrait Gallery, the Fitzwilliam Museum in Cambridge and the Ashmolean Museum in Oxford.

POWs were usually forced to hand over their own books to the censor shortly after capture. The Japanese could be as unpredictable as the Germans when deciding what the prisoners were allowed to read. Some books were banned for the sole reason that they contained maps which the guards thought might be used in escape attempts – even if they depicted biblical Palestine or, in the case of a tourist book, modern-day Wales. Frank Bell found that any religious books were returned immediately and that the censors tended to approve the Russian, Spanish, French or German books first because they did not want to lose face by admitting they did not understand them.

At Batu Lintang, Kuching, Bell used a library made up mainly of books picked up in various camps; a few came from the civilian library in Kuching Town and a few were owned by private individuals. Several belonged to one of the internees, Herbert Johnson, who had a large stock of scholarly books. Many of the POWs were so impressed by his personal library that they determined to buy their own copies of certain books after the war but then found them impossible to obtain because of the publishing austerity throughout the war.

Once the libraries became established and POWs started to swap books with each other, these two resources meant that, no matter where they were, most prisoners had an eclectic selection to choose from. To begin with, in Changi, Stephen Alexander read Siegfried Sassoon's *The Old Century* and vivid journalistic reports of the war such as William Shirer's *Farewell to Berlin* and John Gunther's *Inside Asia*. Others preferred fiction and authors such as A.J. Cronin, J.B. Priestley, Daphne du Maurier and Richard Llewellyn were in demand, but bored men would read whatever they could get their hands on – even if it appeared wildly inappropriate, as in *114 Proved Plans to Save a Busy Man Time*.

POWs took books with them to the jungle of Thailand – although, in most cases, they did not know that was where they were heading. Ronald Searle hung on to his for as long as possible until, forced to march in temperatures of 105°F, he lightened his load by discarding his least loved books or ripped off the covers of his most treasured volumes. In some Thai camps, books were in such short supply that they were dissected, page by page, so that twelve men could read one volume at the same time. Even in the worst possible conditions POWs sharpened their powers of literary criticism or discovered new interests. While he was working on the Thailand–Burma Railway at Kinsaiyok camp, Stephen Alexander read *Gone with the Wind* – which he found rather humourless – and when he was recovering from cholera in the officers' hut of the hospital camp at Kanburi he immersed himself in *The Forsyte Saga*, *The Works of Oscar Wilde*, *War and Peace* and *What is Art?* Guy Coles, a keen cellist, lent him *The Musical Companion*. 'To my surprise I found it exciting reading, like drinking after a long thirst, yet I had never before read books about music or even reviews of concerts.'

When he was moved to a large, relatively healthy camp at Tamuang in Thailand, he resumed the literary studies he had started at Changi. He still had James Boswell's *The Life of Samuel Johnson*, *Eothen* by A.W. Kinglake, *The Knapsack*, *The Golden Treasury*, *Letters to Malaya I and II* and St John's Gospel. His fellow invalid, Ian Watt's selection was just as broad: the *Faber Book of Modern Verse*, Émile Legouis and Louis Cazamian's *History of English Literature*, some Dante, a selection of Yeats, an *Oxford Book of English Verse* and John Lehmann's *New Writing*. Another patient, Terence Charley, preferred poetry, art, history and *Teach Yourself Russian*.

The Knapsack, an anthology of verse and prose extracts chosen by Sir Herbert Read, famous for his poem *To a Conscript of 1940*, was designed with the serviceman in mind and published in 1939. It measured four by six-and-a-half inches and its hardwearing, camouflage-green cloth cover overlapped to form a case secured with a stud that protected its 622 pages of India paper. The book could fit neatly into a uniform pocket or kit bag and was designed to offer inspiration and comfort. Stephen Alexander described its contents as 'on the solemn side with a strong whiff of Fabianism', but nevertheless enjoyed its eclectic mix. Americans had their own anthology called *As You Were* which had similar dimensions but which was slightly less earnest and more nostalgic.

When Frank Bell was recovering from diphtheria at Jesselton in Borneo he competed with one of the doctors to learn by heart poems from Palgrave's *Golden Treasury*. He read aloud all of *Gone With the Wind* and several books that featured Simon Templar, a detective also known as 'The Saint', to patients, taking 'vicarious pleasure ... from Simon Templar's wonderful physical agility and the luxurious conditions he lived in'. At a poetry reading he chose Matthew Arnold's *The Scholar Gypsy* because of the descriptions of the countryside they longed to see again.

Some sought comfort in childhood favourites. When Jack Chalker reached the Kanyu River camp he still had with him a paperback copy of *The Wind in the Willows* and a pocket edition of Rupert Brooke's poetry that he had brought with him from England. Russell Braddon read *Winnie the Pooh* three times at the River Valley Road camp on Singapore. At first his friends were dismissive but then started to dip into it surreptitiously and the book went round both tiers of his overcrowded hut. *Alice's Adventures in Wonderland* was very popular in the hospital at Tamarkan Base where Colonel Toosey arranged for officers to read it out loud to men whose diet and illnesses had reduced them to little more than shadows. As they lay exhausted and starving in their makeshift huts, Alice's transportation to a world of shrinking bodies, summary executions and exotic creatures from which there appeared to be no escape, must have seemed less of a flight of fancy than their own transformation from guardians of one empire to slaves of another.

University of Kuching

Frank Bell felt an equally urgent need to teach and to learn wherever he was held. His first prison, Koan, Batavia in 1942, had once been a day school for Chinese children. Some 1,300 POWs crowded into the building whose internal windows were strung with barbed wire. They were allowed to use its library of mostly English books and they set up an *al fresco* classroom with desks and a blackboard. Each student had his own notebook, paper, pen and ink. In later years he would look back to this first classroom as the height of luxury but at the time his mind was still whirring with the realisation that he was a POW; amid this inner turmoil most men found it extremely difficult to focus on learning. Just as they were starting to settle in they were moved to a new camp about a mile away; it was built as a prison for civilians and was called Boei Glodok. Frank had yet to adopt the mindset of the POW and in his second camp regretted that he had not stolen the French dictionary he had consulted so often at Koan. Although they had been ordered not to remove any books from the school, several POWs arrived at Boei Glodok laden with them. In both camps the men were sent out on working parties that made it difficult to offer a regular timetable of lessons but at Glodok they managed lectures, debates and evening discussions.

From here Frank was taken to Changi.

[It was the] nearest approach to good conditions that we were ever to see. There was even a fully organised university, with flourishing classes in every conceivable subject. There were well-stocked libraries, ample room, a fair number of well-qualified teachers, and quantities of stationery. It was all there, making it a place such as I had dreamed of. Courses under expert tuition, inviting study; theatres in full production, and complete orchestras presenting symphony concerts.

After three weeks he was shipped to Jesselton, a port in North Borneo where eight hundred POWs were squeezed into a jail built for seventy. It was hardly surprising that an epidemic of dysentery broke out. Officers were taken to a small camp nearby where they were given the duty of recording the deaths of those who succumbed to the illness.

The forty officers organised a series of talks on general subjects of practical interest but their small numbers and the uncertainty of their situation again made it hard to concentrate. Frank studied French and Spanish by himself and began to learn shorthand using some books he found buried underneath an old oven. Much later he discovered that a large stash of tinned food and money had also been buried nearby. He gave up the shorthand after a few weeks because he was too physically weak and his hands shook. Instead, he planned a bookshop. 'I envisaged it as the cultural centre of some provincial town, with its own lecture rooms, reading rooms, discussion groups and so on.'

Daydreaming about 'Bell's Bookshop' fed his passion for books and stationery. He designed invoices and labels for 'the high class booksellers' and drew up an imaginary stock list. When he was not busy in his make-belief bookshop he would join another POW who had built a potter's wheel in one of the outbuildings and make rudimentary pots from the abundant clay.

Over the next few months Frank became dangerously ill with diphtheria. Just as he started to recover from this, beriberi and ulcers took hold, leaving him so weak that he could barely move. As he lay in the sick ward (an attap hut), he memorised poetry and read out popular novels to the other patients. The padre organised lectures, debates and discussions and Frank gave a talk on Blaise Pascal, the seventeenth-century French mathematician and religious philosopher who had been the subject of a thesis he had started to work on in England. One has to wonder how the other patients responded to this highbrow topic but it is difficult not to admire his ambition. He was honest enough to describe his audience as 'small, but select'.

He was barely able to walk when they were taken by ship 500 miles east to Sandakan and his condition meant he was one of the few POWs allowed to travel the final stretch by lorry. As he recovered he started to worry about the education on offer in the camp. The Japanese banned 'stationeries' – as they called pens, pencils, ink and paper – but the POWs managed to hide enough materials to allow them to continue lessons in secret. During this period he and another officer copied out the whole of *Otto's German Grammar* (an edition which dated from around 1880) into a blank notebook using a pen that escaped one of the guards' searches; it was to prove very useful when they finally got down to serious study. Then suddenly on 14 August 1943, when he and his friends were rehearsing a sketch in which he played a lunatic, all but ten officers (who were to stay behind to perform administrative duties) were told to prepare to move. They spent ten days at sea before arriving at Batu Lintang POW Camp, Kuching in Sarawak, a camp that held just over a hundred officers and twenty-five Other Ranks. Of the 700 British men who had stayed behind at Sandakan none survived.

The British officers lived in three huts next to the Australian and Dutch officers' compounds and separated from the British Other Ranks by the civilian internees' camp and garden and a sentry path. Prisoners were forbidden to communicate with the other camp inmates and the Japanese guards ruled with a strictness that came close to paranoia. When a choral sextet was hauled into the Guard Room for interrogation it eventually became apparent that the Japanese were suspicious of the conductor's flamboyant gestures and believed he was signalling to the internees' camp.

Studies were already underway but the standard of teaching was basic and led by an officer who agreed to teach anything – so long as his pupils knew less about the subject than he did. Frank joined the French class and found it 'such as I had never met before!' As they had few chores and he had a feeling that they would be at Kuching for some time he started to organise a programme of study 'to make this period of captivity into some advantage to us'. He may have been encouraged by an article he read in the *Nippon Times*, 27 July 1943, (published in English in Tokyo) which described how German POWs in Britain were allowed to study and sit exams and he knew that British POWs in Europe were given similar privileges.

After obtaining the permission of his Commanding Officer he asked each of his fellow officers what they would like to learn and what they would be willing to teach. All but four POWs – who said they were either too old or 'too far gone in mental decay' – said they wanted to study. 'General commercial knowledge' – which offered lectures on subjects such as the structure of companies, the stock exchange, banking, patents, how to read accounts, advertising and selling – proved the most popular and attracted forty students. Civics came next with thirty students; then poultry and pig farming (twenty-one and twenty respectively); public speaking (seventeen students); history (sixteen); chess (eleven), navigation, military law and bookkeeping (seven or under).

French and German were the most popular languages but five students also enrolled in elementary Urdu which was taught by an officer who had worked for a firm of jute planters in India. One young student, who wished to join the church, learnt Greek. The course ended after six lessons – much to Frank's relief as it had been ten years since he had studied the subject and he was struggling to remember enough for the lessons to be worthwhile. Classes in chess also lasted just a few sessions as it was found that the game did not lend itself to formal teaching. But, once the teacher had explained the general principles, many POWs, including Frank, played it with passion and several officers carved chess sets out of wood. The officer who had started the class died of dysentery in 1945.

Frank despaired at the lack of linguistic knowledge among the hundred or so officers. Later, when he was in a position to compare Kuching with other camps, he was convinced that the officers at Batu Lintang were less well educated. The only areas in which they had any expertise were practical subjects such as mining, mineralogy and commerce. He was equally harsh on himself, acknowledging that, while he had a 'reasonable' knowledge of French and Spanish, he had not spent any length of time abroad and was not fluent in either. It was particularly galling to realise that they were living next door to an internment camp where prisoners spoke perfect French, Italian, German and Spanish.

He posted a list of classes with names next to each subject in the canteen, adding a note that there was not enough demand for art, English, maths and shorthand and that individuals should arrange private tuition. Roman History, Portuguese, Pashto, Latin and Russian had to be abandoned due to a lack of teachers. Farming was thought to be impractical but would be reconsidered at the end of the pig and poultry courses. He urged would-be students to think hard before signing up to too many courses in case they ran out of time and energy. He kept a register of those who turned up, devised syllabuses and drew up a new timetable for each term – including exams. Once or twice a week lessons were disrupted without notice by 'wood parties' when officers – who otherwise were not made to work – had to leave the camp to collect fuel. When rations hit rock bottom many men secretly welcomed the excuse not to study – even if it meant the physical exertion of chopping up logs.

The guards soon challenged the POWs about the classes and they presented a doctored list of subjects – military law and navigation were not included – but the Japanese were alarmed at the level of organisation and ordered them to stop. They decided to continue in secret but to keep classes small. They were careful not to date their notes so that, if challenged, they could claim that they had been made before the ban. To begin with Frank taught in the shade of the rubber trees but the secret classes had to take place in the corners of their raised, bamboo huts or the canteen. Here conditions were cramped and noisy and some POWs were reluctant to make way for the students.

> To be at a desk with a blackboard beside me, pupils in their places, each with his own book, pen and paper – that was the stuff of dreams! Instead – just imagine trying to teach French with the rain rattling down on the attap roof, with cooks no more than a yard away banging and chopping, with the batmen whistling, calling, hammering their beds, and my pupils uncomfortably perched on stools well beyond shouting range.

The stools were handmade or carried from previous camps. Frank made himself a canvas folding chair but could not find enough wood with which to build a table. Instead he learnt to write on his knee.

Many classes such as 'General Commercial Knowledge' and language conversation were held outside in the humid dusk or darkness. The British officers' three huts were arranged around a square at the bottom of a 150-yard path which gave them some warning if a guard approached unless – as happened on one occasion – he crawled in under the perimeter barbed wire. Originally, anyone who spotted an intruder would shout, 'Nip in camp' but this evolved to 'Nip in the air' and then simply 'Cold'. The code took on a surreal air when in the sweltering humidity (frequently a hundred per cent), which made any movement an effort, men would whisper, 'It's cold. Very chilly in this hut.'

A lack of paper was a problem right from the start and students struggled to protect their material from desperate smokers. Supplies were so critical by the time they sat their 'finals' in November 1944 that Frank could only provide one copy of each exam paper and students took it in turns to answer the paper under a strict promise of secrecy. Stocks of ink ran so low that it had to be either diluted – which made it turn a faint grey – or homemade from indelible pencil lead. 'In my dreams, I was even buying notebooks and pens and ink; and even now,' he wrote after the war, 'though I can walk past a cake-shop without my mouth watering, I cannot pass a stationer's without longing.'

As well as making notebooks out of tobacco wrappings, scraps of material and card, Frank and his students used slates for exercises, quizzes and temporary notes. As they broke they were repaired with latex and bits of old rag.

He had three of what he described as 'pukka notebooks'. The first was the only surviving volume of his thesis on Pascal's *Pensées* that he had brought from England in the belief that he would be able to work on it in his spare moments. He had lost most of it in Java and the surviving section contained parts of the original in French pasted on to the left-hand pages with his English translation on the right-hand side. In the years that followed he surrounded Pascal's original work with an eclectic mixture of literary and linguistic notes on a range of subjects such as Thomas Carlyle, Baudelaire's poems, jottings about the historicity of Christ, English comic drama 1700–50 and a selection of quotations in German, French, Greek and Latin. While his body shrank, from eleven stone (one stone off his 'fighting' weight) to under eight stone, so his handwriting diminished from its initial bold form to minute lettering that scurried around Pascal's paragraphs.

The second pukka notebook was the remnants of the diary he had burnt in Jesselton and which rose out of the ashes to provide grammar and lists of vocabulary in German, Spanish, Italian and Russian. *Language Notes* was in constant use – especially since the only other Italian grammar was transformed into cigarettes. The final notebook was made by a friend as a birthday present in September 1944 and was designed for use as a diary as soon as freedom allowed him to resume this habit.

In addition to these pukka notebooks, he had a few made from good quality paper such as airmail paper (whose transparency meant he could only write on one side), government notepaper and paper he had bought in Woolworths before the war. He covered each with Javanese sarong material of vivid blues, oranges, reds and browns, many decorated with floral designs and tessellated circles. He wrote in heavily diluted ink that had been 'pepped up' with powdered charcoal and filled these books with 'Quotations and Thoughts', games and puzzles and foreign language vocabulary. Towards the end of his captivity, when his energy was low and he was incapable of anything more taxing, he compiled an index to his notes in one booklet.

But the three notebooks he cherished most were made from a bundle of old American racing newspapers that turned up unexpectedly in the camp. The print had failed on one side of several pages and he used these pages to produce notes on literature, Greek grammar and the New Testament. The mishmash of material kept the reader on his toes. A page of handwritten notes on Russian literature, for example, might be followed by two closely printed lists of horses and the races they had won or lost.

More serious still than the shortage of notebooks was the dearth of up-to-date textbooks and Frank reckoned that their entire supply would have been easily accommodated on a two-foot shelf. Dutch was the only language in which students had anything close to a good supply of reference books: three pocket dictionaries and 'one large and excellent dictionary'. Those wishing to study French had to share one pocket dictionary, while German and Spanish students had just two but anyone interested in learning Italian or Russian had to make do without a dictionary. The pocket dictionaries brought their own frustrations. Although they were helpful in reminding someone of a word they had once known, Frank found them 'highly dangerous' to students with little previous knowledge. As anyone who has ever grappled with a phrasebook in a foreign country will know, pocket dictionaries offer a bewildering choice of quite different meanings for the same word. How could a POW know which to pick?

The Italian students used a version of *Hugo's Italian Grammar*, which included exercises and vocabularies. Four of the first POWs had copied it in pencil on to the backs of forms from a Dutch motor firm in Batavia that had probably been gathered on a working party. Although there was much interest in learning Russian the lessons took a year to get started simply because of the lack of teachers and textbooks. A few officers had picked up a handful of words such as 'beer', 'eat' and 'drink' while in China but this was not enough to start a class. The real breakthrough came in October 1944 when a POW who was keen to learn the language discovered that the internees' camp had a Russian grammar – another version of the familiar *Hugo* series. He negotiated a week's loan and it was smuggled the 300 yards into Frank's camp where he and three other POWs chopped it into quarters and spent the next days furiously copying their section including index, vocabularies and exercises on to the Dutch motor chits that had been used for the Italian book.

One of the biggest challenges was copying a sample page of Russian script. Frank's knowledge of Greek helped and the other scribes tried to break the monotony of transcription by dictating sections. They did this by giving some of the most ornate letters nicknames such as 'spider' and 'Buzz'. It was only after the war that they discovered that, although 'Buzz' had a legitimate place in their 1916 version of *Hugo*, it had since become obsolete. They rebound the book and returned it to the internees' camp – Frank believed – in better condition than they had received it. Later, a Russian-born Australian who was fluent in the language managed to smuggle a list of modern words into the British camp – an exercise that carried considerable risk. However, they never actually *heard* Russian and had to rely on *Hugo's* guidance on pronunciation. The book, for example, likened the sound of one particular vowel to the noise made when a team took the strain on a rope during a tug-of-war. Whenever the POWs came across this vowel they would put down their pencil or slate and adopt a tug-of-war stance. Frank later discovered that this was the only vowel that they had badly mispronounced.

The lack of reference books forced him to adopt a teaching method in which he concentrated on what he knew. He was honest with his students and never tried to gloss over areas of his own ignorance. If he was unsure of something he would urge them to keep an open mind and check what he had said when they were in a position to consult 'a proper book'. This honesty extended to the certificates he handed out to those who asked for them when they left Kuching. The diplomas were printed on larger sheets of handmade paper and presented after repatriation. The University's motto, 'Artes in Arduis' was added to the top. A typed note at the bottom read:

It should be understood that the standards given above represent my own carefully considered opinion based on limited experience and with no relevant official test papers and syllabi to assist me. A + sign indicates that the standard mentioned has been reached with a comfortable margin; no symbol indicates that the standard has been fairly attained, and a – sign that the standard is doubtful. F.E.B.

The certificate gave details of how long the POW had studied which language and the standard they had reached – 'higher certificate', 'university honorary degree' or 'school certificate'. The 'instructor's remarks' often revealed the conditions under which the student had studied; the comments were equally honest about the teacher – and how his limitations might have affected the student's progress. Lieutenant P.G. Lovely RA, for example, was awarded a Higher Cert + in French. He had studied the language for eighteen months but, although he was 'intelligent' in class, interest in other languages had prevented him from devoting enough time to private study. However, he excelled in Spanish that he had studied for twenty-two months and for which he was felt to have reached the level of a university honours degree. His progress in Italian was severely limited by the availability of textbooks – just the 'Hugo Course' – and his instructor's own knowledge. Despite studying for twenty months he was deemed to have reached the level of school certificate. However, during this time Lovely had also been dabbling in Dutch, Malay and geology and teaching an outline of the history of England and lecturing in elementary Spanish.

Frank judged that two students reached degree level in French and three in Spanish. Seven students attained a level equivalent to higher certificate in French, four in Spanish and three in German. Seven students reached school certificate level in French, three in Dutch, eight in Spanish and four in Italian. He preferred not to guess at the standard he and his friend mastered in Russian.

In the book he published about his experiences, *Undercover University*, Frank admits that most of the 'useful' work was done in the first year when, although students complained of hunger, they had yet to experience the deprivations of the final months of the war and he even managed to put on a little weight. When the university closed only six students in each language had stayed the course while in most other subjects teachers and pupils had run out of materials and energy. German was one of the university's biggest success stories in terms of the progress made and, unlike French, classes continued until the very end. When the class began no one, including Frank, was able to read a word of the language; by the end they could follow a German novel. Four students sat their 'finals' in November 1944 and wrote essays on: *'Das Lesen'* (Reading), *'Die Kleider'* (Dress), *'Der Amerikanische Geist'* (The American spirit) and *'Hunger is der beste Koch'* (Hunger is the best cook). Limited rations hit the conversation class and when they tried to hold a German dinner 'the food was not conducive to lively repartee in a foreign tongue'.

The standard of writing was highest in Spanish and students were capable of producing essays of a thousand words on literary subjects written in competent Spanish. Frank himself wrote an imaginary dialogue between George VI and the ghost of Henry VIII and more serious appreciations of the work of Cervantes and Dickens.

His experience of teaching and learning was to have a profound effect on his choice of career after the war. One of the most popular titles in the camp library was *The Importance of Living* by Lin Yutang, which the men spent hours discussing and which chimed in perfectly with their plans for the day when they would be free. Books such as Yutang's, and others like H.G. Wells's *Wealth, Work and Mankind*, helped Frank to formulate his own views on education. In terms of how he spent his postwar career, Kuching University was to prove as significant as his three years at Cambridge.

Languages and Communicating with the Outside World

Although textbooks were often scarce POWs in the Far East had much greater opportunity to *hear* a wide range of foreign languages than their European counterparts. Their guards spoke Korean or Japanese and local people – and some POWs –were fluent in various Chinese and Malaysian dialects. They also heard European languages, other than English. The many bureaucrats, businessmen and planters who had been caught up in the war spoke languages such as Portuguese, Russian, Dutch and French and it was usually possible to find someone who could offer conversational German, occasionally even Italian and Spanish. Fergus Anckorn realised he could understand much of what the Dutch POWs were saying – simply because their language had provided a constant soundtrack in Singapore. Most POWs learnt a few basic Japanese words, if only terms of abuse, commands such as *speedo* (fast) or essentials like *benjo* (toilet). Russell Braddon believed it was possible to learn any language known to man in Changi – including Esperanto. Even at the Thailand–Burma Railway camp of Kanburi, Eric Lomax studied Hindustani, making 'neat columns of vocabulary and tenses' on green scrap paper.

Jim Wakefield learnt he had an affinity for Asian languages even before he became a POW. On the ship taking him to the Far East he became friendly with an airman who could read and write Chinese. He was captivated by the elegance of the characters combined with the sophistication of the ideograms. Until then his exposure to foreign languages had been limited to schoolboy French and Latin. When his RAF friend taught him the basic principals behind Chinese writing the experience failed to awaken

Top left: John Lowe arrived in Singapore after a relaxing sea voyage. As a POW he looked back fondly on the time when he wore a well-pressed uniform. *John Lowe, Private Collection*

Top centre: Most families of men captured in the Far East endured an agonising wait before they learnt whether their loved one was alive or dead. *John Lowe, Private Collection*

Top right: Doctor Nowell Peach led a carefree life in the months before the outbreak of hostilities in the Far East. *Nowell Peach, Private Collection*

Right: Fergus Anckorn's fiancée, Lucille, wrote to him while working as a nurse. In one hand she holds a gas mask; her glasses are hidden behind her back. *Courtesy of Fergus Anckorn*

Bottom left: Fergus Anckorn relaxes. *Courtesy of Fergus Anckorn*

Bottom right: For Harold Montgomery Belgion captivity provided the chance to indulge his love of literature and to write what would become a surprise bestseller. *Churchill Archives Centre, Cambridge*

Top: Huts, like this one at Changi, Singapore, were made from bamboo and attap-palm and could hold several hundred prisoners. Men's clothes quickly disintegrated in the heat and humidity.
Cambridgeshire Collection, Cambridge Central Library

Right: For part of his time as a POW Clive Dunn was held in an old school building in Austria. The men soon found a way of breaking out at night.
By kind permission of Clive Dunn

Right: Terry Frost painted this guard tower at Stalag 383 in 1943 using watercolours. He also produced about 200 portraits in paint supplied by the Red Cross. © *Beaux Arts London and the Terry Frost Estate*

Left: The Australian official war artist, Murray Griffin, used pen and ink and wash over pencil on paper to depict Changi Gaol and the surrounding area in 1945. *Australian War Memorial*

Right: This modern photograph of Bankao in Thailand is close to the area where Dutch POW H.R. van Heekeren uncovered significant prehistoric finds while working on the railway in 1943. *Raoul Kramer*

Above: William Lawrence, a Warrant Officer in the RAF, took several clandestine photos showing the everyday life of POWs. Here they are playing football at Stalag VIIIB (Lamsdorf). *IWM*

STALAG 357
Certificate of Merit

Awarded to

BARRACK 88
RUNNERS - UP
IN THE INTER-BARRACK
SEVEN-A-SIDE
RUGBY TOURNAMENT

GILLIS D.	LOTTER F.
MICHAEL J.	BERRY C.
SMYTHE C.	McLEAN W.
WILSON J.	
(CAPT.)	

CHAIRMAN

CAMP RUGBY COMMITTEE

Above: The author's father, Donald Gillies, was awarded this certificate at his second camp, a few months after capture. His surname has been misspelt. *Midge Gillies*

Above: Andrew Hawarden (in uniform, seated, third from right) was a former professional footballer and lived for sport. At Stalag 383 he spent most of his time organising fixtures. *Andrew Hawarden*

Right: Officers play cricket at Oflag IX A/H (Spangenberg). Terence Prittie wrote articles describing how the game had to be adapted to suit the setting of a medieval castle. *British Red Cross Museum and Archives*

Above: Ice hockey staged on a frozen pond (here at Stalag Luft III, Sagan) was one of the many sports played in Europe. The Red Cross provided skates. *IWM*

Right: Despite the risk of serious injury, boxing was popular in European camps and the British Red Cross supplied gloves. *British Red Cross Museum and Archives*

Below: Swimming was particularly popular during the summer months, here at Stalag Luft III. The pool, which stood ready to douse fires, was often used for recreation. *IWM*

Right: Golfers at Stalag Luft III used Red Cross tins for holes, but bunkers had to be shallow so that an escaper could not use them to hide in. *oldgolfimages.com*

Right: During the course of the war the British Red Cross sent over 20 million food parcels to POWs. Transporting them across occupied Europe proved a logistical nightmare. *British Red Cross Museum and Archives*

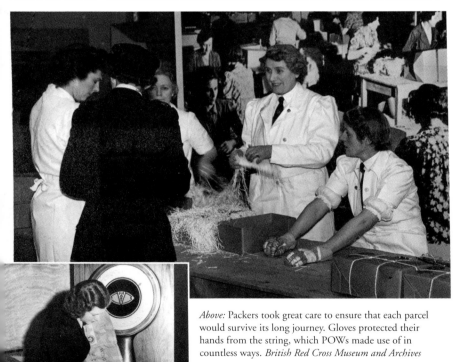

Above: Packers took great care to ensure that each parcel would survive its long journey. Gloves protected their hands from the string, which POWs made use of in countless ways. *British Red Cross Museum and Archives*

Left: Medical supplies were also sent to POWs in Europe. A new pair of artificial legs is weighed before being dispatched to Wing Commander Douglas Bader at Oflag VIB (Warburg). *British Red Cross Museum and Archives/ Science & Society Photo Library*

Above: Miss Ethel Herdman (seated, front), director of the Educational Books Section of the British Red Cross, worked tirelessly to supply distant POWs with books and study aids.
British Red Cross Museum and Archives

Left: Paper shortages at home meant books were hard to come by and the Red Cross relied on public donations to send thousands of books to bored POWs.
British Red Cross Museum and Archives

Below: The delivery of Red Cross parcels was a moment of pure joy and excitement. Once the contents were consumed every scrap of material was put to good use.
British Red Cross Museum and Archives

PRISONERS OF WAR
NEED BOOKS FOR STUDY
WILL YOU HELP THEM!

RED CROSS & ST. JOHN WAR ORGANISATION

Left: Stanley Gimson's drawing shows a prisoner's possessions at Chungkai, Thailand: a 'Jap Happy' loincloth, boots without laces, a blanket of rice bags and waterproof cape. *IWM*

Below: Although bamboo could inflict terrible wounds, it was also a hard-wearing and versatile material, as Stanley Gimson's sketch of a dentist's chair made by Captain J. Spalding shows. *IWM*

DENTIST'S CHAIR
CHUNGKAI 1943

Gimson

Below: A well-stocked pharmacy in a European POW camp shows the extent to which medical supplies reached Germany, depending on the progress of the war. *British Red Cross Museum and Archives*

Left: Doctors in the Far East camps performed remarkable medical feats, such as blood transfusions, in the most basic conditions using improvisation and ingenuity.
Cambridgeshire Collection, Cambridge Central Library

Below: Jack Chalker's drawing shows one man helping his sick mate at the dysentery latrines, Kanyu River Camp, Thailand. (Pen and brush and ink on paper, drawn in Bangkok, 1945). *Australian War Memorial with kind permission from Jack Chalker*

Above: 'And this is Rachel – our head girl'. Many of Ronald Searle's St Trinian's cartoons are distinctly macabre. *By kind permission of Ronald Searle*

Right: The horrific scenes Ronald Searle witnessed as a POW (such as here in a Singapore street) obviously influenced his development as an artist. *By kind permission of Ronald Searle*

Left: The Red Cross sent out a mixture of instruments to cater for the range of musical talent available in POW camps. *British Red Cross Museum and Archives*

Below: Musical instruments were made from bamboo, tins, tea chests and other scraps. A POW brought the drum pedal for this percussion set with him into captivity. *G.S. Gimson, Chungkai, IWM*

Above left: Probably the most ambitious POW musical performance was held at Eichstätt (Oflag VIIB). The festival lasted for thirty-three days and included a piece especially composed by Benjamin Britten. *Courtesy of the Britten-Pears Foundation*

Below: Most European camps had at least one band; some had several with an astonishing range of instruments, as shown by this open-air concert at Stalag Luft III. *IWM*

Left: Concerts and plays could have a miraculous effect on both audience and performers, as at Chungkai in 1944. *Sketch by Stanley Gimson, IWM*

Below: Performances were advertised using elaborate posters such as in *Thai Diddle-diddle* at Chungkai. The revue was banned – probably because the Japanese felt the title was offensive. *IWM*

Above left: The cast of *Wonder Bar* performed at Chungkai in May 1944 with professional actor Leo Britt as producer/director and two celebrated female impersonators. *Cambridgeshire Collection, Cambridge Central Library*

Below left: An actor prepares for a show at Stalag Luft III. The Germans sometimes provided make-up or POWs bought it locally, concocted their own or the YMCA sent supplies. *IWM*

Below right: Gunner Thomas Hussey waits to board a ship home. He is holding 'Joey', the last of three ventriloquist's dummies made in captivity. The doll's suit is covered with autographs. *Australian War Memorial*

Left: The library at Stalag XXA (Thorn, Poland). By the end of the war most medium-sized camps had several thousand books. *British Red Cross Museum and Archives*

Below: Australians queue up to borrow books from a library in Changi, 1943. At first they relied on their own books but later added titles from Raffles Library. *Murray Griffin, pen and blue ink and brown wash over pencil on paper, Australian War Memorial*

Above: A POW's bunk provided a rare space he could call his own and where he could pretend he had some privacy. Self-portrait by unknown artist at Stalag Luft III. *IWM*

Right: Jack Spittle kept detailed notes about the birds he saw on Singapore and their nesting habits. His findings were published after the war. *Courtesy of Brian Spittle*

Above, left to right: W. H. Murray wrote the first draft of *Mountaineering in Scotland* on Italian toilet paper, leaning on a Red Cross parcel. Later it was destroyed by the Gestapo.

John Buxton's book, based on his painstaking study of the Redstart when he was a POW, was published as part of Collins's prestigious *New Naturalist* series.

When he was not playing cricket at Oflag IX A/H Terence Prittie wrote about his sporting memories in a series of essays later published as *Mainly Middlesex*.

Below left: H.R. van Heekeren spent much of his post-war career in the Far East and discovered evidence of an extinct form of pig that was named after him.

Below right: The copy of *Gray's Anatomy* that Nowell Peach studied during captivity and the head of a Javanese man he carved from a wooden banister. *Midge Gillies*

Above: A man launches a model ship made by a fellow POW at Stalag Luft III. *IWM*

Left: A POW concentrates on the intricate task of assembling a clock. Such time-consuming hobbies played an important part in the battle against boredom. *British Red Cross Museum and Archives*

Below: Men spent much of their time dreaming about food. Preparing meals took on greater importance and led to unlikely lessons, as at Stalag Luft III. *IWM*

Above: Boot repairing was an important way of protecting legs from deadly tropical ulcers (drawn here by Stanley Gimson at Chungkhai in Thailand). *IWM*

Above left: Rabbits, such as this one at Stalag 383, made popular pets that often ended up in the cooking pot when rations dwindled. *British Red Cross Museum and Archives*

Above: Gardening could supplement rations and bring colour to the camp. At Stalag Luft III, shown here, it was used in 'The Great Escape' to disperse earth from tunnels. *IWM*

Left: A diagram of the vegetable patch at Stalag Luft III in 1943, recorded by Squadron Leader C. Rolfe in his logbook. *IWM*

Below: George Aspinall used a hidden camera to record the stand-off during which the Japanese confined around 18,000 men at Selarang Barracks after they refused to sign a no-escape clause. *Australian War Memorial*

Above left: The author's parents, Renee and Donald Gillies, outside the first home they owned together in west London. *Midge Gillies*

Above right: Frank Bell in September 1945. His experience of captivity was to change the course of his life and career. *By kind permission of Elisabeth Bell*

Below left: Fergus Anckorn at the Researching FEPOW History Conference in 2008. © *Julie Summers*

Bottom left: Doctor Nowell Peach with the copy of *Gray's Anatomy* that helped him to resume his medical studies on return to Britain. *Midge Gillies*

Below right: Sir Terry Frost became one of the most distinguished abstract artists of the twentieth century. *Alamy*

Bottom right: John Lowe celebrated his ninetieth birthday by dancing in Ely Cathedral. *Graham Diss*

Design: www.timpeters.co.uk

any dormant linguistic talent but his engineer's mind immediately warmed to the sheer structural cleverness of the written language. When they went their different ways at Singapore the Chinese lessons came to an abrupt halt. Wakefield stayed for a fortnight in a tented camp before continuing to Hong Kong.

He remembers Hong Kong in the summer of 1941 before the Japanese invasion as 'paradise'; 'There was no war; life was going on just as usual.' For the half a million Chinese refugees who had fled there after Japan's capture of Canton, Hong Kong was a haven from which to organise resistance. For Wakefield there was plenty of free time for swimming and to resume his Chinese studies. As he was in charge of Chinese soldiers it seemed the ideal moment to learn how to speak their language.

In April 1942 Jim Wakefield and around 500 other officers moved to Argyle Street, a hutted POW camp surrounded by a high electrified fence and six guard towers adorned with mounted searchlights and machine guns which was much closer to a European POW camp than most in Asia. It was here that he became acutely aware of the cosmopolitan nature of his fellow POWs. Many of the local volunteer force were married to Chinese or Portuguese women (Portugal remained officially neutral during the Second World War) and several POWs were White Russians. Compared to some Japanese camps the guards kept their distance and relatives (usually the wives of men who had joined the local volunteer force) were allowed to bring food parcels. 'The Japanese were quite good – they would see that it went to the individual concerned,' Wakefield remembers.

They allowed family members and POWs to exchange shouted messages and requests across the barbed wire. The distance caused problems for one Russian who had been a medical student at the Hong Kong University when war was declared. He wanted his wife to bring him some needles and shouted out his request but she could not catch what he was yelling and called back: 'Noodles?' He failed to make her understand and the whole camp starting shouting: 'Needles, noodles!' From that moment he became known as 'needles-noodles'.

It was much harder for POWs to communicate with family members held at the Stanley internment camp at the southern tip of Hong Kong Island. But Wakefield found himself unexpectedly in a position to pass messages between the POWs at Argyle Street and their wives who were held there. The Japanese ordered the POWs to clear the mines they assumed the British had laid before the occupation and a British general told him:

> 'Wakefield, you're the one who laid them. You go out!'
> Well, the capers that I got up to! I cleared one minefield and I was able to take the little trip mechanism and the copper wire that joined it to some post that might be stuck in the sand, twenty feet away, and I just kept them in my pocket.

He was not searched when he returned to camp and hid the debris he had picked up. When the Japanese told him to continue to clear the mines he convinced them that he had laid some at Stanley Fort. To reach this spot involved driving through the internment camp. 'I had a whole wad of letters and as we went round a corner I saw some internees and I was sitting at the back of the Japanese covered wagon and I dropped these down by the feet of these people and when I'd finished my operation I actually got replies to a lot of those letters to take back with me.'

He attempted to repeat this subterfuge by telling the Japanese that the beach near the old prison officers' quarters, where many of the internees were living, was mined and he needed two sappers to help him clear it. But, although the Japanese fell for the ruse, his plan was almost scuppered by the very people he was hoping to make contact with. When he arrived at the beach he was confronted by a group of internees led by a very tall man, Colonial Secretary F.C. Gimson, who had arrived in Hong Kong the day before the invasion and who insisted haughtily: 'There are no mines here, never have been mines here.'

No amount of pointed looks could alert him to what Jim was trying to do and the exchange between them started to make the Japanese suspicious. 'He wouldn't get the message and he said, "There's nothing there" and I said, "I'm not going to argue with you." And went down to the beach.'

When they returned he produced the bits and pieces from the genuine mine clearance as evidence that they had been making the area safe. 'The Japanese were very suspicious, *very* suspicious, but we'd got the little bits of stuff in our pockets and we'd got long trousers on –which was unusual. We'd all got holes in our pockets, and as we marched around [we shouted],

"Look, look! We found these little bits of wire." We got a laugh on Gimson. But we saved our own skin as well.'

Although Argyle Street camp was for officers, they were allowed to take 100 soldiers with them as batmen. The local volunteers – as opposed to the regular soldiers from Britain – often chose their friends and even employers to fulfil this role because they thought they would be better treated at an officers' camp. This distorted the normal class divisions in the relationship. 'Two or three of the batmen were really well off. They were sort of taipans'.

But the old-fashioned army types found it difficult to adjust to this more relaxed relationship and many clung furiously to their rank and the divisions it maintained.

It wasn't done for you to speak to a major or for a second-lieutenant to speak to a colonel. And there were some of the officers in camp who took that attitude, even when we were prisoners of war. My colonel got very annoyed with me but he didn't tell it to my face, no, he told his adjutant to come and tell me that I wasn't to associate with a brigadier. But the brigadier and I got on fine. We had a little workshop [that we worked in together].

Then there was another man there who was a wing commander or a group captain – quite senior in the RAF. And, again, I was on very friendly terms with him and my colonel just did not like this at all.

Humour, particularly through cartoons and sketches, offered one way of hitting back at this insistence on hierarchy. Colonel Shaw was an obvious target. He demanded any perks he felt he was entitled to and always insisted on having more blankets than men of lower rank. In one cartoon a POW asks for a pile of blankets; the man handing them out is incredulous.

'Five, are you sure?'

'No, I'm only a Second Lieutenant.'

It was at Argyle Street that Jim heard that a Hong Kong civil servant was offering Chinese lessons. Inevitably among a group of POWs, K.M.A. Barnett's initials provided the nickname 'Kiss My Arse' – although his given name was 'Ken'. He first came to Hong Kong in 1932 where he quickly demonstrated a talent for languages and a phenomenal intellect.

He could write and speak several Chinese dialects – some of them quite obscure – liked cryptic crosswords and composing poetry. While he was a POW he passed the time translating and learning off by heart Chinese poems from the Tang and Sung dynasties. At the time of his death – forty-four years later – he was still trying to improve on his wartime interpretations of these thousand-year-old lines. His other hobby was chess – which he learnt to play in his head. His friend, Solomon Bard remembers that when the guards called one of their surprise night-time roll-calls the two men would contrive to stand next to one another so that they could pass the time by whispering chess moves to each other. Solomon struggled to hold eight or ten moves in his head, at which point KMA carried on playing for both of them.

'He was a great chap but needed somebody to look after him. He just couldn't look after things himself. His head was in the clouds,' Wakefield remembers. KMA's affinity for languages was put to practical use. When Japanese guards came to the POW doctors asking to be treated for VD (an illness for which they would have been severely punished), the prisoners pounced on this opportunity for blackmail. In return for anonymity they demanded various items, including Chinese newspapers that KMA translated. As he sat on his bunk with the paper hidden inside a book, another POW who had learnt shorthand in the camp would sit next to him and take down his translation of the news.

He was also extremely brave. Every six months the Red Cross's representative, a Swiss businessman called Rudolf Zindel, was allowed to visit Argyle Street but not permitted to speak to any of the POWs. The men looked starved but the Japanese claimed that their poor physical state was due to their reluctance to keep fit. During one visit the POWs were lined up on both sides of the passage and just as Zindel was about to pass him KMA stepped forward and called out twice in French: 'Nous mourons de faim.' Six guards rushed him and demanded a translation. When he replied, 'We are dying of hunger', he was knocked down, dragged away and beaten so severely that he spent several weeks in hospital. Zindel did not intervene because he thought this might encourage other men to join in and would make KMA's ultimate punishment much worse. In addition to Zindel's limited knowledge of the true conditions, the reports he sent back to Geneva were heavily censored and many never arrived. By 1944 his flat and office were being searched weekly.

Wakefield was not forced to work for the Japanese but he had duties in the camp, such as organising wood chopping, and his studies had to be fitted in around these chores. He would turn up at KMA's bedside when he had a spare minute and ask to be taught. Four other men started the class with him but dropped out after a few weeks. His first lesson was to translate the label on a can of Amoy soya source; he quickly discovered that it was extolling the product's virtues.

'Barnett said: "Really, if we want to study properly you've got to get some books."' Wakefield knew of a Swedish woman who had not been interned and who had sent him a parcel of provisions and told him to let her know if he needed anything else. 'So Barnett made a note of quite a lot of things. And lo and behold she brought the whole lot to camp.' The books included a Chinese dictionary, which Jim still has with the official Japanese stamp in it; a collection of writings by the early Chinese philosophers Mencius and Confucius; *The Spring and Autumn Annals*, a history of the ancient Chinese state of Lu usually attributed to Confucius; and several books of poetry. In between his lessons with KMA, Jim read these classics of Chinese literature and studied the language, making little pencil jottings in the margin and learning whole sections off by heart.

At the same time he took Japanese lessons from an RAF officer who had acquired the language as part of his training. There were few formal lectures but men banded together to discuss their hobbies or pass on their knowledge. Wakefield learnt Old English and navigation and developed a fascination for fly fishing after listening to the reminiscences of a band of men who were known as the huntin', fishin', shootin' group. He had never fished but their tales of lazy days spent by the river was the start of a lifelong passion. After the war he visited Connemara in Ireland to fish with one of the members of the group and in his retirement he set up a fly fishing factory with his son in China which made use of two branches of knowledge he had first acquired at Argyle Street POW camp: fishing and knowledge of Cantonese. His familiarity with the language of Mencius and Confucius gave his spoken Chinese a unique charm.

It was almost like talking biblical English in comparison to the slang of the man in the street and I never did descend to that sort of language. I was always very respectful. I would say: 'What is your honourable name?' or if I asked them about their children I would give

them the special honorific form for a little girl or for a precious little
boy – 'a precious thousand pieces of gold'.

He had no difficulties concentrating on his studies in the camp. Although
his diet was low on protein and fat he did not lose as much weight as men
in other camps. When he joined the army he weighed around 115–120
pounds but dropped to 104 pounds as a POW. The only interruption to his
studies was when the alarm went up that the Japanese were approaching
the huts. Whenever this happened the POWs would warn each other by
starting to sing the traditional children's song made popular by Ella
Fitzgerald in a swing version just before the war, 'A-tisket, a-tasket, a green
and yellow basket' – except that in their version they sang, 'A-tisket, a-
tasket, A little yellow bastard'. He also spent three or four months in
isolation because he was found to be carrying diphtheria. The illness
caused many deaths in the autumn of 1942 until the Japanese recognised
its seriousness and sent in an anti-epidemic unit to isolate carriers and provide enough serum to stem the disease.

Hidden Wireless Sets

Like most Far Eastern POW camps Argyle Street had a secret radio, although very few POWs knew of its existence. The set was put together in the summer of 1943 from pieces found in a bombed-out house and valves stolen from a Japanese wireless. The radio allowed them to pick up news from London, San Francisco, New Delhi, Sydney and Chungking in China about four times a week. It was hidden in an old biscuit tin and buried when not in use. The news bulletins were written in a style that would allow them, if challenged, to convince the guards that they had been gleaned from official Japanese newspapers.

Some POWs in Argyle Street were also passing messages out to the British Army Aid Group (BAAG), an organisation based in China and led by Colonel Ride who had escaped from Shamshuipo. BAAG aimed to help POWs escape and to pass on any information that might be useful to the Allies. It made contact through the regular wood deliveries that arrived by truck in Argyle Street. The Chinese driver would give a warning cough and then drop a cigarette packet. A colleague of Jim Wakefield's from the Royal Engineers, Lieutenant Harris, picked it up and a scrap of paper inside, when held up to a piece of smouldering charcoal, revealed a message. Information about shipping and military information were passed back when a captain from the Punjab regiment, who spoke Hindustani and occasionally worked in the vegetable garden next to the Indian POW camp, was able to tap into the Indian intelligence network. Medicine and other items such as compasses were smuggled into Argyle Street.

News from outside was vital in maintaining morale but building and hiding a wireless, or 'canary', 'Old Lady' or 'The Pipe' as a set was often referred to, brought with it the terrible risk of torture or execution if it was discovered. The radios even moved with them from Changi to the Thailand–Burma Railway, at least one packed in a bully beef tin. Charles 'Lance' Thew showed astonishing bravery in building a primitive crystal set to hear the news from All India Radio broadcast from New Delhi. He hid the nine-inch-long, four-inch-wide device in a coffee tin that had a false top filled with ground nuts and kept it with him from February 1942 to its discovery at Kanburi in Thailand in August 1943. In the first of many punishments he was made to stand to attention in the 100°F heat and then repeatedly to swing a sledgehammer at a block of wood; he was beaten and forced to stand to attention for two days and nights. Brothers Max and Donald Webber were equally brave and ingenious in managing to transport a wireless set and batteries along the railway in Thailand and then to disseminate the vital news bulletins.

Several other sets in various camps were hidden right under guards' noses – in a broom head, a water bottle with a false bottom, a sack of rice, a pair of clogs, a xylophone, an accordion or under the stage. Mosquito netting and pieces of clothing concealed aerials, hollowed-out bamboo hid batteries and the toe of a spare boot held an improvised earpiece. At Bukit Timah on Singapore, where POWs were made to build a Shinto shrine in memory of the Japanese soldiers who had died capturing the island, two men from the 2nd Cambridgeshires smuggled in various radio components in the grass box of a lawnmower and disguised other parts as bits of an old fridge. George Aspinall stole a set from a building where all the confiscated wirelesses were housed and kept it in the ceiling; later he hid a radio in a water tank. Another set was bricked up in the wall cavity at Changi Gaol where the POWs listened to it with a kind of stethoscope. Other radios were hidden where they knew the guards would not venture – down a borehole, in the cholera ward, or under the boilers in the sweltering heat of the cookhouse of Changi Gaol where a few drops of sweat splashed from a POW's forehead on to the receivers and cracked its valves. The set was out of action until someone stole some replacement parts. POWs found it slightly easier to listen to the BBC broadcasts in the Far East because the Japanese insistence on Tokyo time meant it was prematurely dark for the evening news. There are countless tales of moments when the radios came perilously close to being discovered and the POWs could only watch in horror as a guard sat on a chair in which a set was concealed or as parts were skilfully passed down a line of prisoners as they were searched – the components just one step ahead of the guard. Sydney Piddington, the young Australian magician, enhanced his reputation as a conjuror when he appeared to make two radio valves disappear just before the guards reached him. He had skilfully flicked them into a hedge but the story soon became inflated to the extent that he was believed to have made a large wireless set, equipped with seven valves and an aerial, vanish.

But news was a dangerous commodity. If a guard recognised that a prisoner knew something he should not have he might assume there was a radio in camp. As a precaution, news was disseminated a fortnight after it was received and if a guard overheard a POW talking about something they should not have know they would say they had picked it up from 'an educated Thai on a ration-detail' in the local town.

Fergus Anckorn recalls: 'We knew about the Dieppe raid and that it was a complete fiasco and that everyone had been killed. One of our officers relayed that to us so they must have got it with a radio. That was the only truth that we got. If you had information you didn't dare tell anyone. If the Japs got you they would torture you and torture everyone.'

It was safest to disseminate the 'griff' by word of mouth, rather than writing anything down. Radios were rarely mentioned in diaries. At Batu Lintang in Kuching a professional actor who was used to learning his lines was given the responsibility of memorising the news. At Chungkai on the Thailand–Burma Railway POWs told guards that they were lecturing men on the danger of flies when in fact they were passing on snippets of news. At another camp, the code for asking whether any news had been received was the cryptic question: 'Have you had any icecream today?' Often as a precaution the news was disguised by 'larding' it with ninety per cent false information.

Wakefield intuitively stayed clear of clandestine attempts to build radios, although he was once asked if he could supply copper through his workshop. 'So I took the ballcock off one of the loos, tied it up so that it could never be used again and then I cut it and beat it out all flat and I said, "Well, there's your copper." And I never asked any questions and I never knew what happened to it. But obviously it was used for something.'

By the summer of 1943 a wave of arrests made it clear that the BAAG network in Hong Kong had been infiltrated. On 21 September the wireless was discovered. Captain Bird, who had helped set up the original message network and whom the Japanese believed to be the ringleader, was arrested and tortured. His hands and arms were bound and he was put in a coffin-shaped box and his head was placed under a tap. His mouth was covered with a rag and the tap dripped on to it so that his lungs slowly filled with water. After a week he had not revealed the names of any other POWs and he was released. Colonel L.A. Newnham from Argyle Street, Captain D. Ford and Flight-Lieutenant H.B. Gray of Shamshuipo and an Indian officer, Captain M.A. Ansari, were also tortured and also refused to give away information about their fellow POWs. They were executed after summary trials. Each was given the posthumous award of the George Cross.

Religion

In Far Eastern POW camps religion was put to the test in a way that was missing from Europe. Although the horror of battle may have prompted some men in Europe to question the existence of a god, most found comfort in the routine of church services and the support of army chaplains.

In the most brutal camps in the Far East it was easy to feel that they had been abandoned in a type of hell. For others, witnessing acts of barbarity confirmed their belief in God and provided spiritual comfort that strengthened their will to survive. Some men took extreme risks in order to observe their faith, stealing tin from the mines they were working to fashion a communion chalice; others used precious reserves of energy to build elaborate bamboo altars in the jungle or to paint religious murals. The cricket commentator Jim Swanton, who had been accused by some POWs of using his rank to dodge hard work or danger, was severely beaten up at Kinsaiyok on the Thailand–Burma Railway for helping to organise a harvest thanksgiving service in the open air. A few Korean guards, who had told him they were Christians, gave him eggs and bananas for the service but the Japanese were furious at what they saw as a test of the guards' loyalty. Swanton's trenchant support of Anglo-Catholicism also led to some bitter argument among his fellow POWs who objected to his proselytising stance.

Padres were not universally popular but sometimes they inspired respect among their fellow POWs – not just believers. Noel Duckworth, the chaplain to the Cambridgeshire Regiment, won over cynics like Russell Braddon because of the bravery with which he stood up to the Japanese and because, unlike some padres, he took an active part in both the official and underground life of the camp.

Duckworth was a small, rosy-cheeked man. He had coxed the winning Cambridge rowing crews in 1934, '35 and '36 and taken Great Britain's eight to fourth place in the Berlin Olympic Regatta. As a POW he employed a similar mixture of cajoling and, if needs be, verbal castigation in dealing with his guards. His torrent of abuse directed against the invading Japanese is widely believed to have saved many of the injured from summary execution, although he suffered a beating as a result. In Pudu Gaol he lectured on his rowing tour of Europe and transformed a cell into a chapel where both believers and atheists could contemplate God or home. He was also adept at 'working the system'. He established a black market in which he sold items such as gold fillings, signet rings, cigarette cases, watches and fountain pens to the Japanese and used the takings to buy food from local people. He delighted his fellow POWs by abusing the Japanese – who could not understand him – by delivering insults in tones so gentle and wheedling that they were mistaken for flattery. He berated the Japanese in his sermons and on other occasions would engage guards in conversation so that another POW could remove the bolt from their rifle. He was a spectacular liar when it came to boosting morale. When he returned from burying the dead he would relate how he had met a mysterious well-dressed Eurasian man who had passed on news of the Allies' unstoppable progress.

Captivity was a testing time for padres. Not only did they have to adjust to the privations of life as a POW but they also had to grapple with their own doubts in the face of terrible cruelty and to watch some men turn away from God. On the practical side, the high mortality rate in some camps – particularly during some periods on the Thailand–Burma Railway when a camp might suffer six deaths in a day – meant they were constantly in demand to visit patients, offer final prayers and conduct funerals. Occasionally there might be as many as fifteen funerals in one twenty-four hour period.

Many adapted well to their reduced circumstances. A British padre at Tamarkan used cold tea in place of Communion wine; another made alcohol for a Christmas celebration and kept it under his bed so that, if it was discovered, he could claim it was for the Eucharist. Others, though, were unable to adapt their beliefs for different circumstances. When Fergus

Anckorn was at Nong Pladuk camp in Thailand, working on the Thailand–Burma Railway, the camp, which was right next to a yard and railway sidings, was bombed by Allied aeroplanes. Several POWs were killed and Fergus was given the job of carrying the dead – many a jumble of body parts – on stretchers made from rice sacks and bamboo poles to a mass grave a mile away. A Roman Catholic priest dressed in white lace vestments appeared to take the service but demanded that the graves were divided into those who followed his faith and those who did not. A mound was dug for him to stand on and face the Catholics with his back to the others. 'I was disgusted with him but I could see that he genuinely meant it, his conscience wouldn't let him do it any other way.'

Colonel Toosey believed that religious belief helped many men: 'One thing I discovered was that those men who had the benefit of a religious background, even though they may not have been actively practising Christians, curiously enough survived much better than those who were atheists, who had no belief or faith in anything.'

The Bible was more readily available than many books but not always used for the purpose for which it was originally intended. American POWs who were captured after the fall of Bataan in the Philippines found the pocket-sized brown, mock-leather copy of the New Testament they had been given extremely useful for making roll-ups. It measured three by four and a half inches and included The Ten Commandments (despite the inconvenient Thou Shalt Not Kill), and a selection of psalms, prayers and songs such as 'America the Beautiful' and 'The Star Spangled Banner'. British POWs asked Noel Duckworth for permission to use Bible pages with which to roll their cigarettes; he agreed – with the proviso that they read them first. More devout prisoners swapped different translations of the Bible: for example, an authorised version for the Moffatt edition of 1926. Russell Braddon read a copy of the Bible that he found in a Pudu execution cell – twice – but preferred the 'cynicism' of George Bernard Shaw – whose complete works he came across when he was ordered to repair the beds of a Japanese brothel. Frank Bell witnessed a similar interest in the Bible at Kuching. When the Japanese removed non-religious books for censorship, men would turn to it and *The Book of Common Prayer* for recreation. Their interest, however, usually evaporated when they were given a monthly quota of secular books.

Religious belief helped to sustain Frank Bell and he filled one of his handmade notebooks with 'Notes on an Attempt to Study the New Testament with an Open Mind'. He was also part of a small group that met every morning (except Sundays) before roll-call to discuss the New Testament, which they read in chronological order. The rest of the camp referred to them as 'God Botherers' but Frank saw this as friendly tolerance. He had lost both his copies of the Bible in Java but an Australian who managed an oil drum factory where they worked at Tandjong Priok Harbour procured a replacement for him just before they left for Borneo. At Kuching he marked the passages that held special resonance for him with the abbreviation, 'P.P.' (purple patch) and later buried these for safekeeping.

Others turned to religion after the war to help them make sense of their ordeal. Louis Zamperini, an American airman and Olympic athlete who survived on a raft for nearly seven weeks after his aeroplane was shot down over the Pacific, was beaten, tortured and experimented on in various POW camps. He survived, but turned to alcoholism to help him deal with the flashbacks and nightmares. It was not until Billy Graham converted him to Christianity in 1949 that he found peace.

For others who watched their comrades die with hideous regularity, the barbarity of their situation made religion irrelevant. As Charles David Griffin (later Sir) said later: 'Religion comes up against a very tough barrier when something real is happening.' At Kanyu River camp Jack Chalker saw the bamboo crosses that marked a prisoner's grave multiply daily. He helped to place the bodies of emaciated soldiers sewn into rice sacks in shallow graves and noted that, 'formal religion had little appeal in our camps as few could associate any divine providence with the unending daily carnage'. Fergus Anckorn's many brushes with death made him less willing to believe in divine intervention. 'Another thing people often say, because of my various escapes, is "Someone up there was looking after you" or "God was looking after you." I say, "Well, he didn't do much for my mates."'

25

The Magic of Letters from Home

The speed and efficiency of the *Kriegsgefangenenpost* – POW post – in Europe allowed prisoners to maintain a tangible link with home. It was also vital for families and friends. But a regular postal service was something POWs in the Far East could only dream of. Some families never even received official confirmation that their 'boy' or 'husband' had been captured and most had to be content with the official cards the Japanese allowed prisoners to send home. These cards provided very little scope for the POW to say how they were. They were simply permitted to complete by hand the typed line: 'I am interned in . . . ' and to cross out either 'My health is excellent' or 'I am in hospital' and to indicate whether or not they were working for pay. A few lucky relatives received letters.

The knowledge that someone was waiting for the POW was an immeasurable form of succour; sometimes the only way a fellow prisoner could help a dying man was to talk to him about his 'girl back home' and, while the conversation might not save him, it would ease his passing. Fergus Anckorn was fortunate in that he had his parents, a brother, a sister and a sweetheart waiting for him. He fell in love with Lucille Hose, a nurse, on the first day he was admitted to hospital in Dartford, South London, with pharyngitis. An outbreak of scarlet fever among some of the other patients kept him in quarantine and gave him the chance to woo her. They were engaged in 1941 – the night before he was due to leave the country.

Over the next four years Fergus had a spasmodic correspondence with Lucille and his mother, Beatrice, but a bit of cunning on both sides allowed them to extract more from their letters and cards than either the Japanese or British authorities realised. Beatrice was in her early sixties when on 17 March 1942 she received notification that her son was missing:

> Dear Madam
> According to the records in this office your [blank to be filled in by hand] son 947556 Gunner Fergus Gordon Anckorn Royal Artillery, was serving in Malaya when the garrison of Singapore capitulated on 15th February 1942. Every endeavour is being made through diplomatic and other channels to obtain information concerning him and it is hoped that he is safe, although he may be a Prisoner of War.
>   Immediately any information is obtained it will be sent to you, but in the meantime it is regretted that it will be necessary to post him as 'Missing'.

Over the years that followed she wrote to her 'darling boy', for months not knowing whether he was alive, or whether her letters were reaching him – wherever he was. Occasionally her letters sound as if she is talking to herself – and maybe the lack of replies made her feel this way. She admitted that she envied other mothers who had received news and that she was jealous of a woman whose son had been reported safe in Australia. She wrote about the routine of her everyday life, of bottling fresh produce and making jam – oblivious to her son's battle against starvation.

But she also has the mother's instinct for what might be worrying him and what news might buoy him up. She constantly reminds him of his fiancée, Lucille or 'Luce'. In one letter she describes how Luce is gathering her trousseau and comments, 'I think she wants me to teach her housekeeping, so that's significant, isn't it, dear?' (24 June 1943).

In October 1942 she signs her note 'V loving mother' – the 'V' an oblique reference to Churchill's 'V for victory' rallying cry; in another letter she incorporates a shorthand message that appears to be part of her signature but which reads 'Russia is through in 4 places and winning'. Since Fergus had learnt Pitman's before the war, when he was considering a career in journalism, he was able to decipher her code and although he did not receive this for over a year – by which time he would almost certainly have heard the news from a hidden wireless – he still found the coded message thrilling.

Luce was determined to present an irrepressibly optimistic veneer, even though her work had taken her to a part of London that was being battered by German bombers. In 1942 she was at Lambeth Hospital in South London where she was preparing to sit her exams to become a State Registered Nurse. The area was hit several times, although in her letters to Fergus she was careful to avoid any mention of the bombing – probably to avoid the censor's pencil but also so that she did not worry him. It was only later that he discovered just how difficult a time she had had. After one raid she emerged dripping with shards of glass, a newborn baby under each arm.

While she waited to hear, she wrote to a void, not knowing whether she still had a fiancé or whether she had assumed the awkward status of someone who had narrowly missed out on widowhood. Her letters, though unanswered, are bright and breezy, full of titbits of family news but they read like someone groping their way through a room that is pitch black. She sent her first at the end of July 1942.

My Dearest
Pop has just told me that I can at last write to you, so Darling at long last I am doing so. Mum I believe has written to you twice, Beryl [his twin sister] also, so I expect when you receive the two letters you'll think I have forgotten you, far from it. I assure you that I haven't not for one second even!

At this moment I am in your room at home writing this in bed. I seem to have adopted your room these days – hope you don't mind!

The little family here is just the same as ever. I expect you will already know that Beryl is still at home with Stewart or 'Stewpot' as we call him. For the past four months I have been on night duty, and as usual have spent all my spare time here.

Darling, Mum & Dad and everyone have been marvellous to me, many many times I have wondered if I could even have existed without them, I don't think I could somehow. God knows I've been lonely, but they've helped so much. Stewpot is the sweetest little boy, fair as are all the Anckorns or perhaps I should say 'Andrews', always laughing. I always consider that he's half mine as I've looked after him such as lot.

I'm still supposed to be studying (my usual cry). My 1st exam is August 24th and my state is Sept 22nd so it's not far off. I shall be glad when its all over. Mum has been playing tennis just lately, jolly well too I think she's marvellous.

Pop's sense of humour seems to be improving, he's quite fun these days, I believe he told you that I sometimes meet him for lunch, not often though.

Robin is still the same as ever, he has just paid one of his usual visits.

Gordon [Fergus's brother] is fitter than ever! I expect its being down this part of the world.

I haven't changed a bit Darling, except for being much thinner its quite funny seeing myself with a thin face. I hope you haven't although it doesn't matter two hoots if you have.

Well Darling mine, one page is all that seems to be allowed, so where ever you are, God bless you & keep you well to return to your ever loving Luce xxx

Fergus received this letter eighteen months later, on 14 March 1944.

Luce threw herself into her studies, passing her 'blue belt' exam with distinction. Fergus's parents bought her a belt and 'lovely silver buckle', saying that they were only doing what their son would have done if he had been there. Her letters to him were fond and reassuring: 'Don't forget, I seem to love you more than ever these days so don't worry.' But by December 1942 a note of despair had crept in.

Dearest

Since I have had almost every letter that I had ever written to you returned I haven't had much heart to write, but I felt that I must share my good news with you however far away you may [be] darling.

My results came through on Saturday and I am now State Registered!!

Mum was just as thrilled as I was, both she & Pop were marvellous to me.

I know that without the Anckorn family I could never have succeeded. Bless 'em. Each day I hope that we shall hear something about you, I'm sure we shall very soon, I feel it somehow.

Stewpot is marvellous at the moment he's a grand little boy, we have lots of fun together.

Everyone at home is quite well, Andy is at present home on leave.

*I'm just the same, perhaps a little older with a few more grey hairs
but my heart is just the same. Half of it is with another little boy,
somewhere!*

   Perhaps he'll bring it back with him someday.
   All my love, Darling
   Yours ever, Luce xx

This reached Fergus over a year later, on 9 January 1944.

On 25 January 1943, the anniversary of their engagement, she wrote:

My dearest,
*I wonder if you remember what day this is today. Two years ago, what
a lovely memory. How time has flown hasn't it?*

   *Last year I got a letter from you, this, I'm afraid I have nothing,
except happy memories and the faith & hope that you are alive and
well and that you will come back to me sooner or later Darling. I shall
still be here. Everyone at home is well, Mum & Pop especially. I am
shortly going to do my 'Midder' [midwifery training] so that'll be
something else in hand. Must go now Darling mine. All my love, yours
ever,*

   Luce xx

A week later his family heard that he had been wounded on 13 February
1942. When they learnt more about the injury his mother worried that it
might affect his conjuring.

Lucille could not resist writing to him on the eve of St Valentine's Day,
on London County Council Public Health Department notepaper during
the loneliness of the night shift:

Dearest,
*I feel somehow the urge to write to you, actually I have always the urge
but I lack courage 'cos I hate having them returned.*

   *I'm still on night duty at the moment, in Lambeth, in a few months
time my contract will finish and I will have to decide my 'fate'.*

   *Mother wants me to do my 'Midder' at Tunbridge Wells and be non-
residential so I could live at Three Corner Mead but I think it would
worry her rather, as I'm afraid I should always be out on call!!*

She's just the same as ever Darling. I still go to see her each week, if possible and if for some reason I'm not able to go, I feel that there is something missing.

Pop still potters about in his green house and argues with Beryl in his spare time.

Stewpot is growing very fast, he is now about fourteen months only and still very blond and very like you at times! We are trying to teach him to walk but he's lazy and just sits down after having walked about three steps. He's not an Anckorn is he Darling? Tomorrow is St Valentines Day or rather today is, I remember one two years ago I don't expect you do though. Oh, well, I have many, many happy memories to keep me hoping for a better future with you. Darling, no matter <u>what</u> may have happened to you.

All my love
Yours always
Luce
Have faith, Darling. God Bless, xxx

By the end of the month Fergus's mother had included another coded message that was wildly optimistic: 'The twins, Beryl & Gus, may be able to spend their birthday together, as the work Gus was sent to do is on the way to being finished.' Decoded this meant that the war Gus had been sent to fight was nearly finished and that he would be able to celebrate his birthday in December with his twin, Beryl, at home in Britain.

Finally, on 10 March 1943 – over a year after he had been captured, there was good news:

My dearest
Today is a day and a date which I shall remember all my life. This morning Pop 'phoned the hospital to tell me where you were, the first news of you for thirteen long weary months!! Three hundred and ninety four days!!!

In spite of my faith and hope, it was a long, long time, darling.

Thank god my prayers have been answered. I remember in one of your many letters to me, your saying that prayers were usually answered, in a round about way sometimes though.

You must have known, darling.

At the moment I am on my ward but I don't know what I'm doing, I'm quite 'Bats in the belfry'.

I wonder how you are? You'll find that in each of my letters. Perhaps one day I'll get a letter from you then I will know.

I wonder if you can imagine everyone's delight at the good news of you?

Darling, if only you could see mother now, she's tripping round the house singing and whistling, just like she used to do.

We've shared so many thoughts and yearnings for you Ferg.

There are many things which I must do once again, I stopped getting things for our home, but I'll start again.

Pop looks ten years younger than usual.

I'm still the same old 'Luce' thinner with many more grey hairs and a much thinner face. As soon as such things are allowed I will send you a photograph.

I still have the 'Poly' photographs remember?

Well darling mine (I hope you still are!) Look after yourself as far as possible and become well again. Yours always Luce

God bless you darling.

This letter arrived eighteen months later, on 6 August 1944.

In the summer of 1943 Fergus's mother sent him another cryptic message: 'Old Argent has now got his old Sunday job back again, regularly, every week. You will remember why he had to give it up, but the reason is non-existent now!'

Fergus knew very well that Argent's 'Sunday job' was a reference to bell ringing that the Government had announced in 1940 should be used exclusively to warn that German parachutists had been spotted. By 1943 the threat of invasion in Britain had receded and church bells were allowed to ring out once more.

26

The Changi Murals

It was the quiet as much as its religious nature that attracted men to the small room on the ground floor of the dysentery wing of Roberts Barracks in Changi. The white colonial building with its verandahs and shutters was riddled with death and disease but the chapel of St Luke remained still and calm. In the rooms around, men lay dying from dysentery and other diseases, a laboratory analysed their illnesses and the nearby mortuary dealt with the dead.

Sometimes as Stanley Warren, a Bombardier with the 135th Field Regiment Royal Artillery, was resting at the back of the chapel he would catch snippets of conversation from the men as they looked up at the bold religious murals that crowded in on the chapel. They gossiped about whether the artist who dragged himself up ladders despite his illness to paint these pictures of Christ must be a reformed sinner, perhaps a very violent man who now wanted to atone for his sins or someone who was offering thanks for being hauled back from the edge of death. Among the stories his favourite was how nuns smuggled eggs into the camp so that he could use the whites to paint with. These unfortunate women, so the story went, were captured and shot. Stanley said later that while he had no idea whether any nuns had been shot they were certainly not smuggling the eggs for him. He added that if he had been given any eggs he would have eaten them, rather than use them for painting.

He arrived at the hospital on 23 May 1942 suffering from amoebic dysentery and renal problems contracted on a working party that built roads to the Japanese shrine at Bukit Timah. As he grew stronger, one of the padres, Gilbert Chambers, who knew of his reputation as an artist asked him if he would paint a mural to decorate the rather drab room.

The chapel was an important part of the barracks – even to non-believers. It had a branch of Toc H, a charity started in the First World War to help fellow soldiers, whose members read to the patients suffering from failing eyesight and washed and mended their clothes. The choir sang religious music but also gave concerts of Gilbert and Sullivan, *Hiawatha's Wedding* and a skit on the film *The Dancing Years* called *The Dancing Tears*. The chapel was dimly lit with a high ceiling that allowed the air to circulate but its stark fittings made it appear gaunt. The men had filled it with church trappings – all of it made from salvaged material: brown benches from old pieces of window, a lectern, an altar rail and the altar itself with a backcloth made from hospital sheets that were so patched that they barely hung together.

Warren was twenty-five when he became a POW. He was born in North London, where his father ran a tobacconist's shop, and had studied at Hornsey College of Art before taking a job as a graphic artist. He had been very religious in his teens and still retained a strong faith. He started to read the gospels, looking for texts on which he could base a coherent series of paintings, although he was realistic enough to know that he could die before he finished even the first one. The scope of the project also depended on what colours the POWs could scrounge for him. The engineers who left the camp to repair generators and carry out other technical work brought back a turf-brown camouflage paint, a tin of good quality white oil paint, a very small tin of a violent red colour, six cubes of billiard chalk, a child's paint brush and some bigger brushes for filling in larger areas. The walls themselves were a golden-coloured distemper that could easily be used for skin colour or to depict animal hide. As Warren planned which scenes he would paint from the gospel he had to work out how long his material would last.

He began in August in the tense atmosphere of the Selarang Barracks incident and what he described as the 'slow motion execution' of the POWs who had tried to escape. Although he was shocked by the deaths, he was surprised to find that the first mural he painted displayed no bitterness but was gentle and humorous. He decided to paint a nativity scene for Christmas when POWs would be able to look up and see the Holy Family under a banner urging 'Peace on earth to men of goodwill'. The figures are almost cartoonish; the sort of characters you might see in a 1950s children's book of Bible stories. His mischievous humour appears in the face of the old shepherd who leans forward on his crook to coo at the baby, the red calf who, unlike the other adoring animals, turns to look at Jesus over his shoulder – as if as an after-thought – and Joseph who is throwing up his hands in utter amazement at the commotion around his wife and child.

Warren took most pains over Mary's face and drew her by using the minimum of line work on white. This Mary would be instantly recognisable to men used to the stained glass windows of British churches and is swathed in the traditional blue and white cloth garb of a typical European Madonna. She is a long way from the more severe, Malay representation of the Virgin which he adopted when he drew her as part of a nativity scene at the improvised chapel at Bukit Timah. Stephen Alexander saw this mural, and a second –'The Descent from the Cross' – after they had been moved to St David's chapel at Sime Road. Both are painted on asbestos panels using grey vehicle paint mixed with charcoal. Alexander found the images 'too institutional, not to say downright soppy, for our circumstances' but admitted they were 'well drawn'. In 'The Descent from the Cross' the figures, whose faces are modelled on POWs, are dressed in army kit – the Magi wear tin hats, ground-sheet capes, webbing and turned-up mosquito shorts and two Red Cross stretcher-bearers lift Christ from the cross by the light of a hurricane lamp while the grave-diggers stand by waiting with *changkols*.

By the time he came to paint the Magi at Roberts Barracks he deliberately chose three wise men to represent a more ethnically diverse mankind. One looks Slavic and wears a cloak trimmed with fur; a second has a turban to represent the Middle East and the third is obviously from the Far East. Stanley said later that if the Bible had allowed him he would have included a fourth king – from Africa.

The camouflage paint was oil-based but he was applying it to the wall's powder pigment distemper which was fixed with glue and which sucked up paint like blotting paper. In order to counter this absorbency he painted with strong sweeping lines and then used a dry brush technique on top. There was no room for error because any attempt to scrape off colour took the distemper with it and left a white patch of bare plaster. He was still very weak from his illness and lack of food so that he worked slowly.

Often he felt too faint to climb the ladder-and-plank scaffold which was about 18 or 19 feet long and 9 feet high, from which he painted the first scene.

Chambers and Warren had an uneasy relationship. Chambers had always wanted to serve abroad. He trained at St Augustine's College, Canterbury, which was set up for clergymen destined to work in the British Colonies, and he was ordained in Cape Town where he served as a vicar between 1926 and 1934. Immediately before the war he had a parish in Nutshalling, Hampshire. Chambers valued Warren's artistic talents and hoped that after the war he would paint some murals in his home church but he took no account of the artist's weakened state or of his artistic sensibilities when he argued with him about his choice of subjects and the captions that would accompany each mural. Warren wanted 'Glory to God in the highest' in the middle and 'On earth peace, goodwill to all men' because he felt this looked forward to a time when there would be no war and no divisions among mankind. The padre was adamant that the caption should state: 'Peace on earth to men of goodwill' which Warren interpreted as indicating that they could decide who the good men were. The two argued about which version to use until the vicar was finally reduced to tears and Warren gave way – although he said he had intended later surreptitiously to replace the words with the version from the Authorised Bible.

As Christmas neared, Warren was hit by another bout of dysentery and the stomach cramps became so severe that he had to lie down and rest behind the altar every 10 to 15 minutes. When it was finished he was taken to the ward above the chapel from where he could hear the carols being sung on Christmas Day 1942.

Once he recovered he started work on the Ascension mural in which Christ appears to the apostles and tells them 'Go and teach the nations I am with you'. He chose this episode so that if he died before painting any other murals, the chapel would have a picture on either side of the altar showing the beginning and end of Jesus' life. This mural took only two or three weeks to complete.

In his next mural, he depicted the Crucifixion but chose to show slaves in the process of pulling the cross up, rather than having it fully erect, so that the scale of the figures is in keeping with the other pictures. According to his friend, Wally Hammond, he felt elated when he was painting this mural and often lent his head against the wall to talk to Christ, asking him why he allowed himself to be captured and why he did not escape to the hills. In choosing slaves, rather than centurions, he felt the inference was quite clear: that the Japanese who had taken part in atrocities were acting under orders. Warren felt sure that the guards were aware of the point he was making. He never asked their permission to paint the murals but they were keenly interested in the progress. Often they would rest on the chapel benches where they leaned their rifles against the wall and removed their caps to mop their shaven heads.

By the time he came to The Last Supper he had nearly run out of blue paint and billiard chalk. Instead, he chose a predominately grey palette because he had a big drum of grey paint and consequently, this is a much more sombre painting. But the lack of colour forced him to depict Christ in a different way and he chose to make him tall, wearing a dark gown with a white shawl round his neck. The inspiration for the colour and dimensions came from the observation post he had once manned in a lighthouse at Pulau Pisang, a small island in the Strait of Malacca, and gave him the idea of painting Jesus with a broad base tapering to his head and the white shawl. In the foreground he painted his own *chappals* (sandals) and a three-legged table which belonged above the chapel in the quarters of the Royal Medical Corps.

The final mural brought him again into direct conflict with Padre Chambers. Warren wanted to show another scene from Christ's life but the vicar was set on featuring the imprisonment of Saint Luke since the chapel was named after the disciple who was known for his medical skill and for the time he spent with Saint Paul in a Roman prison. Warren thought the final mural should be full of movement – Luke raising a sick man from his deathbed, children pushing forward or a scene from Christ's life – to counterbalance the crucifixion scene which was dominating the chapel to the extent that the padre often took his services just below it. Of the five murals he was least happy with the final one, which he believed the men did not really understand.

The chapel became a place where the POWs could rest. They covered the altar with frangipani flowers to mask the stench from the dysentery ward and held night-time services by candlelight or lit by small electric lights with porcelain shades so that the murals were illuminated by a gentle glow. But whenever Warren walked into the chapel he found it hard to accept that Saint Luke had been the right choice and he felt that the battle had cast a shadow over his relationship with Chambers. But he also realised that Chambers was striving to maintain spiritual values at a time when death was so common that it was easy for men to become callous and when, in the absence of pain relief, death could be slow and excruciating. Sometimes when they talked the padre would tell him how it was often difficult to persuade men to carry on living.

The murals probably saved Warren's life because he was due to be sent upcountry on a party called F18 but Colonel Roberts called him in and told him he would not be leaving Singapore because he needed to complete the murals. Warren believes that, in his weakened state, he would not have survived the railway.

In 1944 both Warren and Chambers left for Kranji in the north of Singapore. When they had gone the Japanese knocked a hole in the bottom of the artist's least favourite mural, the drawing of Saint Luke's escape from his prison cell. The building was converted into an administrative block and the murals disappeared from view under a layer of distemper. They remained hidden – and largely forgotten – until long after the end of the war. It was not until 1958, when the RAF occupied Block 151, that traces of colour appeared on the walls that led the new occupants to wonder about the room's concealed history.

By 1945 the POWs at Kranji were digging foxholes and defensive positions as the Allies edged nearer. Warren remembers this period as an anti-climax when he turned inwards and concentrated on reading Herodotus and a book on anthropology and jotting down notes on ancient Greek history and mythology. He was deeply concerned by the mental breakdown all around him. Some men succumbed to psychological factors, others were affected by physical illness which attacked the brain. A talented actor who took the part of a man who murders his wife using an axe became deeply depressed by the play and was ordered to stop performing in it. Another POW threw himself into the latrine and would have drowned if a second POW had not rescued him.

Gilbert John Marion Chambers died on 13 July 1945, having undergone an operation for a perforated ulcer. He had been found to have been suffering from internal haemorrhaging, and it was obvious nothing more could be done for him. He is buried at Kranji War Cemetery. A month later, on 15 August, Emperor Hirohito made his first ever broadcast.

Although he did not say the word 'surrender' he intimated that the war was nearing its end.

Stanley was told that St Luke's had been destroyed by Allied bombing and preferred not to see the rubble before he returned home.

PART III

Europe

Reading for Profit

Prisoners of war shall be permitted to receive individually consignments of books which may be subject to censorship. Representatives
of the protecting powers and of duly recognised and authorised relief
societies may send works and collections of books to the libraries of
prisoners' camps. The transmission of such consignments to libraries
may not be delayed under pretext of difficulties of censorship.

Geneva Convention, Article 39

For many prisoners in the Far East simply staying alive was a priority.
They learnt to cook rice and built ingenious stoves because both were
vital to survival; doctors and medical orderlies became familiar with tropical illnesses and devised ingenuous ways of treating their patients. Men
read what books they could find, took lessons or taught, performed, or
studied birds because it took their mind off hunger or allowed them to
escape from a world that was a long, long way from home. In Europe,
boredom rather than brutality, starvation and illness proved the main
threat in the first years of the war – particularly among officers who were
not forced to work. Even for lower ranks there was always the danger that
frustration and the uncertainty of their fate – guessing when the war
might end and whether they would be held as hostages – would infect
their free time.

But POWs in Europe never had quite the same sense of isolation that
haunted prisoners in the Far East. Until the closing months of the war
POWs in Europe had regular correspondence with home and, even when
they became less frequent, the cheering arrival of a Red Cross parcel.

Every camp had at least one man like Andrew Hawarden who enjoyed organising sports fixtures, putting on plays or devising a series of lectures to stimulate bored POWs. If these organisers, impresarios and entrepreneurs had been held in the Far East they would have been fighting low levels of energy, as well as disease. They would also have lacked the encouragement – both practical and emotional – that came from organisations like the Red Cross, the YMCA and European Student Relief Fund, as well as the more intimate succour of a letter or parcel from a family member. Even writing to a distant organisation might lead to warm friendship with the person who wrote back. Andrew Hawarden's sporting fixtures would have been far less ambitious without the advantage of supplies sent by the Red Cross and his final months of captivity would have been bleaker without the letters he exchanged with the Football Association as he planned a Scotland–England game in which ex-POWs would take part after the war.

Harold Montgomery Belgion, who was captured in Greece in 1941, possessed the same organisational drive as Hawarden but for him literature, rather than sport, helped to see him through his years as a POW and brought advantages to the men held with him. Belgion's experience of captivity could only have happened in Europe because it relied on regular communications with home and on the indulgence of his captors. His years as a POW brought a tangible reward born of his own persistence and his pre-war network of contacts.

Belgion was a captain in the Royal Engineers and nearly fifty when he became a POW; he was just over five foot nine, a slightly-built man with a balding head, thick moustache and kind eyes. He was already a well-connected author and journalist and he was determined not to let the fact of his incarceration hold back his career or interfere with his passion for books. He must have been relieved that, as an officer, he was not condemned to manual labour, and as the months dragged on he managed to keep himself busy in a way that would transform his eventual homecoming. At first he went to Oflag VIID at Tittmoning, a medieval castle in southeastern Bavaria, then he was sent to the uncomfortably overcrowded Oflag VIB at Warburg. Finally, he crossed the drawbridge at Oflag IX A/H to arrive in the cobbled courtyard of the castle that overlooked the medieval town of Spangenberg. The castle was built on a crag and surrounded by a dry moat.

Although he had many of the trappings of an English gentleman – membership of the Athenaeum and the Savile – he had led an unusually international life in which he ping-ponged between Paris, London and New York. He was born in Paris in 1892 where his father worked for an American life insurance company. His maternal grandparents were Australian. Belgion was educated in France and became Editor-in-charge of the European edition of the *New York Herald*. He eschewed French citizenship and in 1916 joined the British Army as a private in the Honourable Artillery Company. In July 1918, he was commissioned as a Second Lieutenant in the Dorsetshire Regiment.

After the First World War he worked as a sub-editor for various publications in London, New York and Paris including the *Daily Mail*, *Daily Mirror* and *Daily Sketch*. He read prolifically – in English, French and Italian, mainly about philosophy and literature. His private studies provided the fuel for his first book, *Our Present Philosophy of Life*, which Faber and Faber published in 1929 and in which he attacked the influence of men like André Gide, George Bernard Shaw, Sigmund Freud and Bertrand Russell. He wrote two other books before war was declared and contributed regular articles and book reviews which appeared in Europe and America and which established him as a well-respected literary critic. He also began a life-long habit of firing off letters to national newspapers.

It was one of his reviews, published in July 1936 but unsigned, that led to a case of mistaken identity that wrong-footed a later generation of critics. The review, which was just 171 words long, appeared in T.S. Eliot's magazine, *The Criterion*. Its subject was *The Yellow Spot* with an introduction by Herbert Dunelm – an early account of the mistreatment of German Jews. Looking back with the hindsight of the twenty-first century and in full knowledge of the horrors of the Holocaust, the review appears cruel and peevish. The writer quibbles over words such as 'persecution' and 'extermination' and accuses *The Yellow Spot* of trying to 'rouse moral indignation by means of sensationalism'. Belgion, like many of his contemporaries, underestimated the plight of Jews in Nazi Germany and many literary scholars who believed Eliot had written it later saw it as proof of his anti-Semitism – until in the 1990s Belgion was identified as the true author.

Belgion seems to have adapted to life as a POW by treating each of the camps he was held in as rather drafty gentlemen's clubs – the food was a bit below par and the management needed cajoling but he could still write to his friends around the world, amend his entry in *Who's Who*, oversee his financial affairs and order food from the right shops and obscure books from dealers in Paris. After a few months he began to receive correspondence from home – one of the first pieces of mail to arrive was a postcard from the Athenaeum which informed him about their new lunch arrangements: in future a buffet would replace the usual à la carte service.

He wrote to the manager of the Midland Bank in Haverstock Hill, London asking him to send a list of all his bankers' orders, to pay certain bills and to find out whether the army had ever sent the £15 for his servant allowance. Over the years that followed he exchanged several letters with the branch about matters such as his income tax assessment and his claim for war damage after many of his books and correspondence were destroyed in an air raid. Most of the letters from the branch are purely official but occasionally a human element slips in. On one occasion the manager adds that former members of staff who are now dispersed (presumably into war work or the armed services) ask after him when they pop in; in another instance he scribbles a note telling him that the squash club is still open but that few people play and he hopes to take him out to lunch before too long. This was written in the summer of 1943.

Belgion was unmarried but had a vigorous network of friends who, as soon as news got round that he had been captured (helped by his appearance at the top of the 'Roll of Honour' in *The Times*, 16 September 1941) started to write to him regularly – although few could appreciate what it felt like to be a POW. He received around 240 letters during his three years of captivity. His friends addressed him by a range of affectionate names from 'Dear old Boy' to 'My dear Poge [or 'Monty'] to 'Dearest Pouge'.

Many would have benefited from *The Prisoner of War* magazine's advice on what to include and what to leave out when writing to a man in captivity. Nancy Lanchester was one of his most assiduous correspondents and in an early letter complained about the absence of domestic staff but a month later was honest enough to admit: 'It is difficult, impossible of course, to realise your life.' However, in September 1941, she was nevertheless tactless enough to write in another letter that she had celebrated his birthday, 'For old time's sake I opened a bottle of good claret hoping you too were able to indulge in something of the sort.'

Friends and relatives worked their way through the lists of warm clothing he asked for which reflected the bitter winter of 1941–42 and added extras 'as sanctioned by the authorities'. It was like preparing for a far-flung boarding school as they parcelled up a wind-proof coat, long camel-hair wool scarf, Viyella pyjamas, safety razor, shoe brushes, canvas kit bag, soles for mending shoes, a 'housewife' (mending kit), Librol soap, vests from Harrods, shaving brush. Mrs Lanchester asked the Red Cross whether his valise should be sent direct from Harrods. Another, male friend, wrote: 'I think perhaps if I ask Fortnum & Mason they will know what you would like'. Belgion kept a list of the 'outward' letters he wrote back and a record of the clothes, Red Cross parcels (including ones from the Belgian and American organisations) and books friends such as T.S. Eliot and C.S. Lewis sent him.

During the First World War many POWs had complained that it was difficult for families to send them parcels directly and in 1917 a Parliamentary Committee recommended that a special service should be set up to help relatives to communicate with their men. This proved so popular that the idea of 'personal' parcels – or 'next-of-kin parcels' as they became known from April 1941 – was readily adopted during the Second World War. Under the scheme a registered next-of-kin was allowed to send a quarterly parcel to a POW or interned civilian. Although the idea sounded simple it needed a highly complex operation in which the contents had to be checked to ensure families were not sending forbidden items or had hidden notes in socks and gloves. One estimate suggested that about ten per cent fell into this banned category, although few were as obviously inappropriate as the pair of underpants one family sent with an embroidered 'V' for victory on the back.

The list of banned items changed from time to time but the June 1944 version gives some idea of the limitations. It is easy to see why the Germans would not be keen on a POW receiving field glasses, sextants, compasses, torches, knives, tools and nail files; clothing such as complete suits, coloured or grey flannel trousers, sports coats and other civilian garb was probably refused because it could be used in escape attempts. Mrs Lanchester fell foul of the colour code and had to abandon the blue pullover and start knitting an Alpaca wool jersey in the correct army colour instead. She also arranged for him to receive a new pair of glasses in 1942.

Items such as soap flakes, mirrors, anything in glass containers and candles were obviously banned for practical reasons. Books, cigarettes, food (except solid chocolate with no fillings), and medical 'comforts' were probably excluded because the Red Cross distributed them separately and any printed material would have had to be censored. Perhaps wellingtons, bedding, and haversacks were too bulky. But it is less obvious why toilet paper and rubber soles and heels were banned.

The packers had to check every item and return anything that was prohibited. They made sure the weight of the packet (no more than 10 pounds) was evenly distributed and wrapped the chocolate in cellophane paper and then corrugated paper and placed it as far away as possible from the soap which they put inside boots or a sponge bag. They also added items of clothing to parcels that looked rather thin. The whole bundle was wrapped in a towel or a piece of clothing and then encased first in corrugated and then waterproof paper and tied firmly with sisal string.

The introduction of clothing rationing in Britain in June 1941 caused considerable hardship for poor families who, unlike Belgion's set of friends, did not have extensive wardrobes to plunder. Instead they had to buy clothes using coupons they needed for their own use before sending the receipts to the Prisoner of War Department of the Red Cross who issued replacement coupons. Eventually the Board of Trade allowed relatives to receive extra coupons. When soap and chocolate were rationed in early 1942, the Next-of-Kin Parcels Centre (the main depot was in Finsbury Circus in central London) held stocks of both and asked relatives to send in postal orders which could be used to buy their allowances. At its peak in the first two quarters of 1943, the centre was receiving on average 1,300 next-of-kin parcels a day. The centre's efficient production line continued throughout the heavy bombing that hit London between September 1940 and May 1941.

Belgion's many friends and business contacts in America were keen to help by sending him items through the American Red Cross. Harry Yoxall, chairman of Condé Nast publishing house, arranged for food packages to be forwarded each month from Macy's store. Other friends in New York wrote to apologise that they had not been able to supply everything he asked for. Just one can of the tinned fruit or vegetables he had requested would have used up too much of the weight allowance, one explained, and in their haste to send the package they had completely forgotten the tooth powder and toothpicks he wanted.

Although the friend was obviously anxious to help, his letter reveals just how little he understood of Belgion's predicament. America had yet to join the war and they could have no inkling that they were writing to a man who at that time (October 1941) was still living in an overcrowded camp in Bavaria. They could not be blamed for filling their letter with a description of the apartment they were renting in New York which had 13 feet high ceilings but *only* two bedrooms (for two people), or for telling him about the fortnight's holiday in Maine that had helped to make them feel less tired. There is no way of knowing how Belgion reacted to the accounts of their comfortable life. Perhaps he found a letter from a young boy in New York he had once sent stamps to more uplifting. The boy sent him a joke (in writing that was not yet joined up): 'A doctor and a skeleton are playing poker; a nurse comes in and asks what they are doing. The doctor replies, "Playing a game of strip poker – he over did it!"'

Another friend, Professor Allen Tate of Princeton, was shocked to receive Belgion's letter from Germany that brought home the reality of war. 'It is in perfect condition, white and smooth, as if you had just written it and handed it to me.'

Belgion had included a list of friends' addresses for the professor to contact, hoping they would send him items he badly missed – tinned vegetables, toothpaste, cigarettes and coffee. He told Tate that he was studying Greek – a fact that prompted the admission from Tate: 'Our state of mind, even so far from the war zones, makes it difficult to read anything.' Tate added a tantalising piece of literary gossip in his reply: 'Frank Morley tells me that Old Possum has had seven teeth taken out; I pass this news on because Eliot himself might omit it.'

The publisher Jonathan Cape sent him a typewritten letter on 13 August 1941 from 30 Bedford Square in London after he had seen the notice in *The Times*: 'This is the first news that I have heard of you. Bad luck.'

During the 1920s Belgion had acted as an *ad hoc* advisor to the publisher whenever he needed a second opinion on a manuscript. Now Cape wrote to him from a Bloomsbury transformed by war. The central gardens had been given over to trenches and shelters and much of the workforce had been called up and replaced with very young and inexperienced females whose work was often disrupted by air raids when they all trooped down to the basement. Thirty Bedford Square avoided any great damage beyond a few smashed windows and, unlike neighbouring squares, the railings were not carted off for the war effort after the occupants claimed their railings' special shape gave them a right not to be melted down. But the industry had lost some of its sparkle as publishers grappled with paper and manpower shortages. In the same letter Cape wrote: 'I do not meet many people these days, only those who come along to see me in the general way of business. Very occasionally I go as far afield as the Reform Club for luncheon, but most days I find it takes up too much time and I lunch nearby, sometimes at the Etoile which however is very expensive these days.'

Two months later, on 30 October 1941 he wrote again from London: 'The paper restriction limits very much the number of new books one can publish, as each day some book comes up which needs reprinting among our "bread and butter" titles. So it is a matter of holding a fine balance between the claims of books to be reprinted and new ones which seem to be worth publishing, under the conditions which exist.'

By 8 December 1942 he wrote to say he had lost his 'three readers' [who sampled manuscripts]:

> The days go by with nothing much to mark them, and then one wakes up and realises that a month has gone by which seems to be only a week! I often wonder how you feel as to the passage of time. Do the days seem long and endless, with boredom and ennui as their chief feature? Or do you find that you have employed the time with some sense of satisfaction because you have achieved something in the way of developing a thought or an idea? I know, of course, that you have been busy preparing and giving lectures on literary subjects.
>
> Margaret and David [his two children from his second marriage] are still in the United States as wards of Don Brace. They would like very much to come home and we would be very glad to have them, but for the time being it is best for them to stay where they are. They have been away now for nearly two and a half years. Margaret will be eighteen next March and has, I understand, grown miraculously tall. David is thirteen and a half.

He had failed to find any Players Number Three cigarettes to send Belgion but was posting him a revised copy of *Spain: A Modern History* by Salvador de Madariaga. His assessment of it was to prove prophetic: 'It is not a book that is going to please either the extreme Left or the extreme Right.

Madariaga's political standpoint being that of an enlightened Liberal really means that he is liable to be attacked on either side.'

Belgion was also in touch with another friend, C.S. Lewis, who was a fellow of Magdalen College, Oxford. He was not yet well known for his Narnia books (*The Lion, The Witch and The Wardrobe* would not appear until 1950) but *The Screwtape Letters*, an epistolary exchange between a senior demon and his nephew, was published in 1942 and Belgion wrote to congratulate him on it. Lewis sent a warm reply in February 1943, writing in neat black handwriting on a tiny scrap of paper. The note took nearly two months to reach Belgion and was filled with literary titbits and book recommendations.

> All you have done and gone through at an age when you might feel yourself excused has made a deep impression – in fact you are become rather a hero ... As for news – I suppose you mean literary news which is the only kind available – I don't know that I have much to tell. There seem to be very few good young poets: nothing to compare with last years's crop. Auden (I believe and partly hope) is ceasing to be a name to conjure with ... The outstanding Xtian [Christian] book of the moment is Midnight Hour by 'Nicodemus' but I haven't read it – you know I never have read the book of the moment. Novel-reading and writing appears to be in a v. bad state: music v. flourishing, ... Crocuses and snowdrops are showing in Addison's Walk, glad you liked Screwtape. Blessings, yrs, CS Lewis

Another literary friend, the editor and bibliographer John Hayward, who had been evacuated to Cambridge because he suffered from muscular dystrophy and was living as a guest of Lord Rothschild at Merton Hall, wrote him several letters of literary gossip. Hayward was a close friend of T.S. Eliot and may have been the inspiration for his 'Man in White Spats' in *Old Possum's Book of Practical Cats*. In August 1942 he wrote Belgion a very gossipy letter about Cyril Connolly becoming the new literary editor of the *Observer*: 'He is rapidly becoming a kind of seedy Grand Cham of Lit.! and is living in some state in Bedford Square with two devoted concubines.'

But what Belgion really wanted was books. The Fonds Européen de Secours aux Étudiants (European Student Relief Fund) in Geneva, which helped POWs who were trying to study, proved a useful source. It was part of an umbrella organisation, *Comité consultatif pour La Lecture des Prisonniers et Internés de Guerre*,whose members included the International Red Cross Committee, the War Prisoners' Aid of the World's Committee of YMCAs and the Service of Intellectual Assistance of the International Bureau of Education. Belgion began a long correspondence with its Assistant General Secretary, Yngve Frykholm, whom he treated rather like the proprietor of a shop that specialises in rare and secondhand books. Over the next two years Frykholm arranged for him to receive a range of titles – mainly French books such as Alfred Fabre-Luce's two-volume *Journal de la France* and the former French Finance Minister Joseph Caillaux's *Ma Jeunesse Orgueilleuse (Mes Memoires)*. Belgion was so well connected that he was able to suggest a Paris seller where Frykholm might obtain harder-to-find titles (the two volumes of Caillaux had to be sent in two instalments).

His knowledge made him a demanding 'customer', asking for books that were not allowed in Germany or for titles before they had been published. Frykholm, however, was always patient and enthusiastic in his replies. In September 1943 he wrote to Belgion:

> We are glad that these books could be obtained for you without our having to write to your friend in Paris, as this channel is unfortunately not very reliable under present conditions . . . [hardly surprising since it had been part of the Third Reich for three years]
>
> Looking forward to hearing from you soon again and hoping that we shall find the ways of keeping you well supplied for your remaining days of captivity.

Although from an enemy country, Professor Mario Praz of the University of Rome sent him other books he had asked for, wondering whether his knowledge of Italian was good enough to enable him to appreciate the contemporary Italian writer Antonio Baldini.

In the early days of the war, the Red Cross concentrated on supplying food and clothing and prisoners had to rely on books that they already had with them. The Red Cross and St. John Indoor Recreations Section (originally the Fiction and Games Section) was set up in autumn 1940 with the aim of giving each camp the beginnings of a library and also supplying games such as Monopoly, cards, chess, draughts and dominoes. By December 1941 it had sent out 71,000 volumes to POW and internment camps in Europe. When the war ended it had supplied 239,500 volumes either directly to POW camps or to a holding reserve in Geneva. The YMCA, which had distribution centres in Switzerland and Sweden, sent over a million books on behalf of the United States Red Cross.

Choosing the books was a tricky business. Few POWs had Belgion's lofty tastes and the Red Cross selected a broad mixture designed to appeal to the widest common denominator: classic novels, contemporary writers, thrillers, Westerns, and a mixture of non-fiction including history, biography, travel writing and books on art, music and literature. As men spent longer in captivity, history and biography grew in popularity. Descriptions of English country life proved very popular and there was a great demand for works of reference from men who were studying or who simply wanted to set quizzes or to find the answer to something they had been chewing over – such as what exactly the Football Association classified as a goal.

As early as October 1940 a representative from the Red Cross had visited Andrew Hawarden's then camp in Poland to ask whether the POWs needed any books. In fact, they had already started a library and by the autumn of 1941 it contained over 2,000 volumes. When they moved from Thorn they had to leave it behind, but by 1944, when he was held at Stalag 383, supplies had been replenished and the library was very well stocked; during wet weather, men would queue up for extra books to help them pass the time.

Belgion started to receive books via the Red Cross from at least February 1942. These included the prose writings of Jonathan Swift and Immanuel Kant's *Critique of Judgement*, which he had requested. He could also receive books via the permit system which allowed next-of-kin, other relatives and friends to send gifts for 'the comfort, pleasure and recreation of a prisoner' such as cigarettes, tobacco, books, printed music, games and sporting equipment by placing an order with a supplier who had a special permit and who sent the goods to the POW. Penguin Books also gave relatives the chance to order ten books at a reduced price and the *Prisoner of War* magazine offered advice on which books relatives should send; an article by A.A. Milne suggested a series of small books called *Britain in Pictures* that featured English villages, houses and sport.

For men of all ranks reading was a form of escape. In December 1944 Andrew Hawarden wrote in his diary: 'I'm sorry that I haven't kept a record of the books which I've read whilst being a prisoner. I'm sure it would fill a decent sized library. Whilst here, it's reading morning, noon and night.'

His fellow prisoner Ray Beal recorded in his diary finishing *The Small Dark Man*, a novel by the Irish writer Maurice Walsh, in bed one bitterly cold day in January 1943: 'Again this quiet of mind from reading this book. His descriptions are marvellous and his characters simply live.'

David Read, a chaplain with the 51st Highland Division, who was captured at Saint-Valéry in France in 1940, began his captivity by losing two of his most precious books – the Bible and a copy of Herbert Read's anthology for the armed forces, *The Knapsack*. He had stuffed both into his haversack that he had abandoned in a last minute dash across the beach at Saint-Valéry as he tried to reach a ship that was returning to England. The German who captured him was so delighted to find someone who spoke his language that he agreed to walk him back to the beach hut where he had left his rucksack. But when they got there he discovered that someone else had taken it. He was furious at the thought of being book-less and the German suggested he should help himself to a leather case that had belonged to a French officer. Read was hopeful that it would at the very least contain a volume of Proust or Stendhal but was disgusted to discover it held a pair of silk pyjamas, a bottle of eau de cologne, a manicure set and other male grooming tools.

As he trudged through Normandy towards the Rhine he remembered that a friend had given him a miniature Greek Testament and he spent his days on the road trying to memorise the Prologue to St John's Gospel in Greek. When he arrived at his first camp nine men shared one book and a strict timetable was drawn up for reading; if someone was not actually reading a book another man was entitled to take it.

It is hard to describe the effect of an almost entire absence of books on a community of 1,500 British officers, which included not only 31 chaplains and over 60 doctors, but dozens of school-teachers, writers, poets, lecturers, and other professional men, who depend more than they know on books both for the feeding and the recreation of their minds.

By this time his copy of *The Knapsack* was on its way to a stalag in Poland. When its new owner was taken to a hospital in Germany, he gave it to an officer who brought it to a big oflag in southern Germany. He happened to be reading it when an old college friend of Padre Read's recognised his name and handwriting in the front and took custody of it. He was forced to abandon it when the officers were marched out of the camp just before liberation. A year later the Red Cross recovered belongings from the oflag and *The Knapsack* was sent to Ayrshire where the padre was working.

Paul Fussell maintained that soldiers read in a different way from men in civilian life, that they paid more attention. Certain authors, too, were ideal for POWs. Anthony Trollope, he believed, was perfect because 'like the Dutch painters of the seventeenth century, [he] paid such leisurely attention to detail, to the textures and nuances of everyday life'. Eric Newby's experience confirms this impression that POWs read with alacrity. He remembers devouring books in Italy to the extent that he found his speech and thoughts were peppered with literary allusions. When he went into hiding in a cave, his friend Wanda brought him a parcel of what she considered essentials – maps, food and his two-volume edition of Edward Gibbon's *Decline and Fall of the Roman Empire* that she had rescued from the camp at Fontanellato.

Padre Read noticed how often food seemed to crop up in books:

> It was extraordinary how the hero and heroine could hardly emerge from chapter one without entering a Parisian restaurant and ordering the choicest food and wines. Autobiographies seemed to consist of little else than descriptions of gastronomic orgies, and even theologians appeared unable to resist drawing illustrations and examples from the culinary art. Many a time I have seen a book flung down in disgust by some starving subaltern with querulous demand why the author could not forget his stomach for at least a couple of chapters.

He believed that the experience of being a POW turned some men into life-long readers. Books became carefully guarded possessions that could be traded; lists of books read marked out time 'in the bag'. Many POWs had their own bookshelves which reinforced the territorial boundaries around their bunk. For Padre Read the sheer longevity of his time in captivity meant that, as a member of the William Shakespeare Reading Society, he had the chance to read all of his plays once and was well through a second round when his camp was liberated.

Pat Ward-Thomas, who helped build Stalag Luft III's golf course, viewed time in the cooler as the chance to read: 'One could settle peacefully to reading or writing and I managed the greater part of *The Forsyte Saga*. Five days in the cooler was pure holiday, ten a shade too long.'

As the war progressed the supply of books increased and libraries expanded. The best stocked libraries usually indicated an active educational system within a camp. Stalag Luft VI at Heydekrug, in what is now Lithuania, was the most northerly of all camps and had a library with around 6,000 books, partly to support the educational demands of its inmates where study was so intense that the camp became known as the Barbed-Wire University. By the end of the war, Oflag VIIB at Eichstätt, south of Nuremberg, had an incredible collection of 15,000 books, as well as 60,000 that belonged to individual POWs. Books were not so readily available to the lower ranks who worked and had less free time and if, like Clive Dunn, they worked away from the main camp books were less likely to reach them.

The other major problem was censorship – both in Britain and when the books arrived in mainland Europe. At home the censor was worried about any reading material that would make it easier for the Nazis to bomb or invade Britain. As a result any book that contained navigational charts, plans of wharves or docks, or any information about ports or inland waterways in any part of the British Empire was banned. Weather or current charts, atlases, navigational reference books, tide tables, nautical and air almanacs were also forbidden unless the Admiralty – which had been evacuated to Bath – gave express permission. Packers scrutinised every page of secondhand books and rubbed out any marks or underlining that might be construed as a code and put the entire package in jeopardy. Maps were carefully extracted – no matter what the book's subject – and newspapers were not permitted in the packing rooms in case a sensitive item of news inadvertently made its way into the package.

Censorship at the other end was unpredictable and could vary from camp to camp. The Italian Government did not allow any study courses to be sent to POWs, the Red Cross could only provide brand new books and these often arrived after long delays and with their covers ripped off. The Germans frequently took exception to books by Jewish authors, books that mentioned escaping or an interpretation of history that did not fit in with their plans for world domination. H.A.L. Fisher's *A History of*

Europe was banned because of its very first sentence: 'We Europeans are the children of Hellas.' Presumably the Nazis did not agree with the claim that Greece had founded modern Europe. Words like 'liberty', 'democracy', 'freedom' and 'totalitarianism' usually upset the censor who also frowned on writers such as George Bernard Shaw and H.G. Wells, whose politics did not square with Nazism.

There were also countless anomalies. John Buchan's two novels *Greenmantle* and *Mr Standfast*, which featured his hero Richard Hannay, were banned because they were set in the First World War but the omnibus edition *Adventures of Richard Hannay* slipped through. The American novelist Winston Churchill was not allowed because of his unfortunate name but censors failed to spot that *My Early Life* by Winston Spencer Churchill was written by the British Prime Minister. *Scouting for Boys* was ruled out because it was believed to be about the British Secret Service. German censors, who usually worried about POWs' morals, however, allowed *Lady Chatterley's Lover* (which was banned in Britain) in Stalag Luft III where it was passed round in units of ten pages.

In 1943 Belgion was having repeated battles with the censor who confiscated *Midnight Hour* by Nicodemus, which C.S. Lewis had recommended, and *Spain* by Salvador de Madariaga which Jonathan Cape had sent him. He was so furious about losing the books that he produced a six page memorandum for the Protecting Power regarding the German censorship of books sent to British Prisoners of War, written in ink in which he underlined the sentiments he wanted to stress.

> This immediate review is needed because the operation of the censorship gives rise to <u>much irritation and discontent</u> among prisoners. At a time when the German War Office has gone to the trouble of appointing special Welfare Officers to the camps in which British prisoners are detained, in order presumably to ensure that discontent shall be kept down to a minimum, it may be presumed that the German War Office can not regard this disturbing effect of the operation as satisfactory.

Censorship, he said, 'reflects a <u>misinterpretation of the English character</u>' but he was careful to praise the German authorities, 'In all camps of which prisoners of three or four years' standing have experience, the <u>censors</u> have always been found to do their work <u>courteously</u> & consciously and to wish to be as <u>lenient</u> as possible.'

But he pointed out that on some occasions the censor was taking his job too literally by banning a book that contained a character who hated National Socialism – even though the author ridiculed that character – and confiscating a book that criticised Franco, even though it also attacked parties that were opposed to Franco. A book of short stories about Japan had similarly been banned because the introduction included a reference to the fact that there were slums in Japan.

Some authors were doubly cursed. The censor had removed all books by the Nobel Laureate and American novelist, Sinclair Lewis from the camp library – presumably because he had written a satirical novel about the rise of Fascism in America called *It Can't Happen Here* and because, Belgion speculated, the censor believed that 'Lewis' was a Jewish name. The censor had taken exception to George Eliot's partner, George Henry Lewes's life of Goethe, which Belgion considered the finest biography of the German philosopher, because the censor was 'under the impression no doubt that G.H. Lewes was Sinclair Lewis and probably a Jew into the bargain'.

Belgion argued that this inconsistent approach was provoking more anti-German feeling than anything that the POWs might read in the books themselves and suggested a rather naive experiment in which books sent to officers were not censored.

> The abolition of the censorship would be in harmony with the policy at present being followed of granting to British prisoners of war a number of amenities previously denied and of conducting so called 'holiday camps' at Steinberg and Genshagen. <u>Why, in the face of granting of amenities and in the face of setting up holiday camps, allow such a source of irritation and discontent to subsist?</u>

These two 'holiday camps' – as they were commonly referred to, although their official name was 'Special Detachment' – were set up by the German Foreign Office in an attempt to persuade selected POWs either to switch sides or, at the very least, view their captors with greater sympathy. Officers were taken for short breaks of up to six weeks to Special Detachment 999 – an elegant villa in the quiet Berlin suburb of

Zehlendorf. Later officers spent their break at the Bavarian schloss at Steinberg that Belgion refers to. There was no blatant attempt to 'turn' the POWs – the approach was much more subtle: they had slightly more freedom, bigger rations, a swimming pool (at Steinberg), the chance to go for walks and more relaxed rules about routines such as when they got up in the morning. Other Ranks were sent to Special Detachment 517 at Genshagen, also near Berlin. There is no evidence that the holiday camps persuaded any POWs to change sides but Belgion's knowledge of them proves that their reputation was not confined to those who had enjoyed a break there.

His rant against the censor did not stem solely from his own desire to read. He needed books to help him deliver a series of lectures on English literature that he was giving to fellow officers, as he confided to Jonathan Cape who wrote back enthusiastically in March 1942:

> I am glad you are giving lectures on literature in the camp. This series might find a public if published here in book form: also it might find an audience in the United States. It will be a labour for you to copy them out, but perhaps that labour may have its satisfaction for you. I would certainly like to see them and will consider seriously the possibility of publishing them.

Books read at intense moments in life – whether they are particularly happy or sad – have a way of lodging in the psyche of the reader. This was often true of the POW. Men made lists of books they read and many would later look back on certain titles with special affection. Padre Read wrote later:

> I shall ever associate Gibbon's *Decline and Fall* with sitting on a patch of grass surrounded by other semi-naked bodies in a hot summer month of 1943; and Motley's *Dutch Republic* with crouching as near to the radiator as I could in the only heated room of the camp in that last winter when Rundstedt's final despairing push had cast an indescribable gloom over the camps of Germany; and Thackeray's *Newcomes* with a blissful fortnight in the camp hospital to which I had been rather flimsily consigned by my friend, the doctor.

Gardening and Birdwatching

Although POWs in Europe could not hope for a glimpse of vibrant plumage or the cry of an exotic bird that the prisoner in Asia enjoyed, captivity was still in many ways the ideal setting for the keen ornithologist. It was something both officers and men who had to work could enjoy, although, of course, officers had more time to turn a hobby indulged in snatched moments into a serious scientific study. When else would you have months – sometimes years – in one place to study the sky, only interrupted by roll-calls and meals? Camps, which were often far from a town and close to woodland, offered the ideal position from which to observe birds and many officers used captivity to produce data that made a lasting contribution to ornithology.

John Buxton realised the potential of his prison when he was lying in the sun by the river Salzbach idly watching a family of redstarts in the cherry and chestnut trees. He had no paper with which to make notes but by the time spring arrived he decided that he would study this particular bird. Before the war he had been a Fellow of New College, Oxford, where he studied English literature and wrote poetry, but joined the Commandos and was captured in the disastrous Norwegian campaign of 1940.

'I determined that these birds should be my study for most of the hours I might spend out of doors. It seemed to me that we prisoners might watch some birds together, and that several of us working on one kind might discover more than if we tried to make our notes on all the birds that should visit us.'

He was held first at Laufen in south-east Bavaria and Austria and then Eichstätt and organised his fellow POWs into a team of observers who began to keep watch systematically in April 1941. A report on the bird-watching group appeared in *The Manchester Guardian*, 29 August 1941, when readers learnt that the Germans had allowed the prisoners to turn part of the wood into a bird sanctuary and that the POWs were making nesting boxes. The task soon assumed obsessive proportions as they devoted around nine hours a day to the project. Between April and June 1943 the team spent a total of 850 hours watching just one pair of redstarts. He also wrote lyrics for songs performed by concert parties and wrote for the POW magazine, *Touchstone*, while at Eichstätt.

Buxton was enchanted by the migratory songbird, whose male has an orange breast and flanks and a rusty-red tail, because they 'inhabited another world ... They lived wholly and enviably to themselves, uncon-cerned in our fatuous politics, without the limitations imposed all about us by our knowledge. They lived only in the moment, without foresight and with memory only of things of immediate practical concern to them.'

He joined another study – this time of a drabber and more sinister bird. Peter Conder had begun to watch crows at Oflag VI, Warburg, and in thirty-nine days in March and April 1942 his team counted 39,000 of them. The men ate their meals in relays so that there was no gap in their obser-vations. Between 1942 and 1945 he and other birdmen, including Buxton, M.J. Waterhouse and George Waterston, studied the migratory patterns of rooks and jackdaws which left northeastern Europe in the autumn and headed for warmer parts and in the spring reversed their trip. Conder described conditions for birdwatching at Eichstätt as 'as near paradise as possible in a prison camp' and began a daily routine that filled nearly every waking hour. During the summer he scanned the skies between 6.00 and 8.30 a.m. with an hour off for breakfast and roll-call. He continued until lunch at 12.30 and then watched again until 5.30 p.m. when he had a thirty-minute break for tea. He resumed his observations until 9.30 p.m. when he retired to his bunk to write up his notes – some in a German school exer-cise book – and to read. As well as crows, he was fascinated by goldfinches and crested larks, which were common in mainland Europe but rare in Britain, and filled sixteen notebooks with observations about them, some-times recording the results on German toilet paper. Other birdwatchers also pursued their own special interests: George Waterston was captivated by wrynecks, Richard Purchon by swallows and John Barrett by chaffinches.

The crow study is as much about the life of a POW at Oflag VIIB as it is about migratory habits. Conder wondered in particular what prompted the birds to pause for a snack at Eichstätt and noted how they picked over the camp rubbish tip and dined on the fields 'newly spread with human excrement'. Sometimes the birders were interrupted by air raids or when the Germans insisted on searching their living quarters. On other occasions they were inconvenienced by a head count in which the guards tried to establish who had escaped and how.

Buxton was fully aware of how the non-birding POWs viewed their obsession. In the acknowledgements section of his book, *The Redstart*, which was published after the war in the prestigious 'New Naturalist' series, he reprinted a poem which had first appeared in Eichstätt's POW magazine, *Touchstone*, of May 1943. It was written by the future librarian of King's College, Cambridge, A.N.L Munby.

Birdwatching – The Song of the Redstart

Though this box is labour-saving
It necessitates the waiving
Of the right to any privacy of life.
All this peeping and this prying
Is particularly trying
To a sensitive and newly-married wife.

When your mind is set on mating
It is highly irritating
To see an ornithologist below:
Though it may be nature-study,
To a bird it's merely bloody
Awful manners. Can't he see that he's *de trop*!

How would Waterston or Purchon
Like a bird to do research on
The way in which they propagate *their* clan?
Thank the Lord, the bugle's callin'
And they'll have to go and fall in –
Now for twenty minutes' love-life while we can!

So long as it kept them quiet the guards were relaxed about what seemed like a harmless pastime. They allowed a German ornithologist, Dr E. Stresemann, to send Buxton books, rings and academic papers that a fellow POW translated for him. Conder became such a familiar figure, stationed around the camp with his pencil in hand, that it simply never occurred to the guards that his hobby made him an excellent lookout. But his birds could never entirely remove him from his position as a soldier held on enemy territory and he and his fellow bird-watchers agreed that the crested lark sounded very much like it was calling 'God Save the King!'

Although officers had more time to make a comprehensive study of birds, ordinary soldiers who had to work still found time for bird-watching. Robert Warren jotted down birds he spotted from the first place he was held, a film studio outside Rome in February 1944 where he noticed a pair of black redstarts, to Stalags VIIB in Moosberg, Bavaria and VIIIC in Upper Silesia. When he joined a working party at a brick and tile factory twenty miles southeast of Sagan his hobby helped him to forge a friendship with the camp commandant who had been a POW in England in the First World War, where he had been treated well. He invited the POW on a bird-watching trip to some woods in the Oder valley where he saw his first waxwing in a birch tree.

A few weeks later the German gave him some cigarette cards with pictures of birds and when he had to attend a meeting, took Warren by train to visit his brother who was a POW at Stalag VIIIC. He stayed overnight and returned to his own camp the following morning with the commandant. This overnight sojourn would not have been possible without the common bond of birding.

Warren's interest in natural history also strengthened friendships with his fellow POWs. One of his 'colleagues', as he referred to POWs who worked with him at the tile and brick factory, was interested in lepidopterology and during the summer of 1944 caught a swallow-tail butterfly and a Camberwell beauty. In the months that followed, Warren found a red underwing moth and a comma butterfly for him.

The men's sleeping quarters were inside the factory that was fenced with barbed wire and surrounded by woodland. Although he spent his days working he still had time to study the breeding habits of the sparrows and to draw a sketch of their nests. In his diary he noted corncrakes, storks, cockchafer beetles, sandpipers and a flock of rooks and jackdaws that he reckoned included between 1,000 and 2,000 birds.

During July, however, his particular interest in sparrows put him in a dangerous situation. He had noticed the birds entering the side of the factory roof through small holes and was determined to discover whether they were roosting there. During a nightshift he took a torch – a civilian supervisor probably lent him one – and climbed on to the roof where he discovered that the sparrows had built small nests in the holes for roosting (the holes were too small for breeding). While he was carrying out his research the factory manager, a fervent Nazi, decided to check the roof and discovered him. He could easily have been arrested on suspicion of sabotage or attempting to escape but his reputation for bird-watching was so well known that the manager accepted his story.

In the film of *The Great Escape*, lectures on birds provided an instant cover for a school of forgery. Gardening had an equally important role at Stalag Luft III and supplied one of the film's most lasting images of the 'penguins' – POWs who shuffled forward with their specially adapted trousers full of the tell-tale yellow sand produced by tunnelling. When they reached a vegetable patch they would discretely tug on a string and the sand would trickle down their leg and onto the ground where a diligent gardener would instantly rake it in with the grey topsoil.

In most other camps gardening was a more innocent hobby – and one that the Germans viewed as such. In some camps, POWs were allowed to grow tomatoes in disused greenhouses and at the naval camp of Marlag the Germans helped by giving prisoners seeds. Even at Colditz, where any kind of digging was a source of concern for the guards, prisoners were eventually allowed small vegetable plots on the castle slopes. At Andrew Hawarden's second camp of 383, POWs produced industrial amounts of lettuces and tomatoes which, although they did not contribute greatly to the prisoners' calorific intake, added variety and vitamins to the diet and gave gardeners a sense of achievement and power. The daily pattern of watering and fussing over plants offered a routine as comforting as counting crows. Just as a POW's bunk bed and the space immediately around it was a sacrosanct patch of territory so, as anyone who owns an allotment will know, tending a patch of land bestowed a special sense of pride.

However, gardening also represented an acknowledgement that release was a far-off dream.

Flowers brought colour to a drab world and a reminder of traditional British homes. POWs planted familiar types such as lupins and tulips; some even designed rock gardens and dug in herbaceous borders. Many camps held competitions that mimicked the traditional horticultural show or echoed an English fete. Experienced gardeners passed on their skills to novices who on their return to Britain continued to garden in a *Kriegie* fashion of improvisation and make-do-and-mend which they handed down to the next generation. After the sandy soil of some stalags they found British gardens surprisingly fertile.

The Royal Horticultural Society (RHS) took an early interest in gardening POWs. In the First World War it had sent flowers and rules for organising shows to the civilian camp which the Germans set up at a race course at Ruhleben. The internees were keen to establish their own horticultural society, partly to supplement rations, and nearly 1,000 members (roughly twenty per cent of inmates) joined. The society sold produce to the camp canteen, held competitions and even sent dahlias and chrysanthemums back to England. The RHS wanted to help again but at first the Ministry of Economic Warfare was worried that any gardening success might give the Germans an excuse to cut rations. The RHS persuaded it that the amount of seeds was too small for this to present a danger and the ministry relented, although it continued to keep an eye on the quantities sent to camps.

The RHS ran an appeal asking members of the horticultural trade to provide seeds free of charge; POWs also bought supplies from their guards or local people. Suppliers in Britain, Canada, Australia and South Africa sent a wide range of vegetable seeds, as well as forty different kinds of flower seeds and bulbs. By early 1943 the Red Cross had sent four hundred and fifty-six parcels of vegetable seeds and one hundred and ninety-six of flower seeds to sixty-seven camps. Individual camps sent the Red Cross details of the area they hoped to cultivate so that the organisation could supply the most suitable seeds. It was particularly important to avoid wasting seeds which were in short supply at home where the whole population was being urged to 'dig for victory'. Typically, camps were not built on good soil (gardeners at Stalag Luft III struggled with sandy conditions) and plants needed extra help. POWs often used manure obtained from the

Germans or scooped up dung from the horses who pulled carts and other vehicles which transported human waste from the camps.

The RHS sent horticultural textbooks through the Red Cross's Educational Books Section and allowed POWs to sit its exams. The first nine candidates took their papers in July 1942 and the exam grew in popularity so that by the end of the war the RHS's council faced the dilemma of whether or not POWs who had missed their chance to sit the exam because of repatriation should be allowed to take an equivalent exam back in Britain, free of charge. The council agreed that they should, so long as they applied within two years. Fifty candidates sat their exams, as the RHS's official history put it, 'in more conducive circumstances than at first expected'.

Study

Belligerents shall encourage as much as possible the organisation of intellectual and sporting pursuits by prisoners of war.

Article 17 of Geneva Convention

Belgion delivered a series of nine lectures to his fellow officers between the winter and spring of 1941–2 and the summer of 1943. He began when he was held in Oflag VIB at Warburg in north Germany. Desmond Llewelyn, who would later become famous as 'Q' – the inventor who supplied 007 with ingenious and lethal gadgets throughout seventeen James Bond films – remembers the camp as: 'in the middle of a plain and depressingly large with masses of blackened army huts enclosed by walls of barbed wire and German guards.'

Although it was a grim, uncomfortably overcrowded camp its sheer size meant that it was bound to include some talented POWs. Inmates could enjoy a wide range of theatrical productions, from a full-length musical, revues, pantomimes and more serious productions such as *Henry V* and *Corialanus*, although the theatre was closed for a week in February 1942, not long after Belgion arrived, when two RAF men were discovered under its floorboards – presumably preparing to escape. Llewelyn took part in a reading of *A Midsummer Night's Dream* which was preceded by a lecture on the play by Belgion which some POWs found a little too lengthy.

There was also considerable musical talent, encouraged by the arrival of a Red Cross parcel from America that contained violins, saxophones, clarinets and a sousaphone. This last instrument was a rarity and only one person was willing to try to play it. He was forced to practise as far away from his fellow POWs as was possible in a camp – the latrines. He mastered it to the extent that he could extract notes which he used to mock their German captors.

Education ranged from the informal, such as a spelling bee and Douglas Bader's talks on the Battle of Britain, the Luftwaffe's tactics and how the Royal Navy had been used to thwart an invasion, to more intellectual lectures such as Belgion's on English literature. He was one of several men who taught a range of some fifty subjects and by the summer of 1942 POWs who wanted to study in greater depth had set up six different faculties.

Belgion found an equally conducive audience when he moved to the thirteenth-century castle of Oflag IX A/H at Spangenberg where his fellow officers were already engaged in a wide range of intellectual pursuits organised with the help of Captain Charles Hamson, a Fellow and lecturer in law at Trinity College, Cambridge. Hamson said he had never seen such a thirst for education and believed it was 'a method of escape from the immediate circumstances of prison life'. A group even produced a collection of poetry, essays and coloured illustrations about their life called *Backwater, Oflag IX A/H*, which was published in Britain in 1944 in aid of charity. John Phillips, who was still writing to Philippa, contributed two poems.

Terence Prittie spent much of his spare time when he was not playing or watching cricket at Oflag IX A/H writing about Test and County matches between 1925 and 1939. 'Nostalgia is the Gulf Stream of the whole wide ocean of memory', he reflected in one of these essays, and his descriptions are warmly evocative, not just of the game, but of a halcyon version of home: 'In the evening light Lord's is a place of infinite peace and quiet friendly charm. Spectators (save when Big Jim Smith was at the wicket!) allow themselves to be lulled by the languor of the soft air and the mellow beauty of deepening sunlight on the white seats of the stands and the dark red brick of the Pavilion.' The essays were published in 1947 as a book called *Mainly Middlesex*.

Bill Murray, who had been captured in North Africa by a German officer who shared his passion for mountains, also found comfort in writing about his passion for climbing and the Scottish landscape. He started his first book when he was held at Chieti in Italy and wrote on coarse Italian toilet paper whilst sitting on the top bunk, using his Red Cross parcel as a portable desk. The first page remained blank for two days and he wondered how he would manage to remember his favourite climbs without the benefit of diaries or reference books but the effort of concentrating solely on his memory produced startling results. He wrote later: 'I came in the end to realise that diaries are a trap that I'd been lucky to escape. Too many expedition books, and other exploratory talks, stay dull because their author blindly copies from diaries – a temptation all too easy to fall into when time is short and distractions many. To bring a tale alive, he has to relive it in his own mind, which means to recreate.'

After the Italian Armistice he managed to take the nearly-completed manuscript with him but the Gestapo soon discovered it and, assuming that it contained coded military intelligence, destroyed it. The loss hit him hard but he eventually viewed the destruction as a blessing.

I no longer believed that I would climb mountains again, but felt impelled to get the truth of them on to paper. Nor did I want, as before, to write specifically about hard climbs, or to enlighten anyone about techniques and winter severities. I wrote because I must, shedding the twin humbugs of understatements of difficulty and exaggeration of danger and likewise of reticence about feeling for beauty. The whole mountain scene was vivid in mind and in detail. I had learned to ignore distractions of noise and movement, and to shut them out. I now had good paper and could write fast. I had a mind to say what I'd found of beauty and delight, effort and fun. I would try for truth only, and while knowing that it could never be said, still I would try.

He finished the book on his thirtieth birthday in March 1944 and spent the rest of the war 'polishing' his words. When he was moved to Oflag 79 at Brunswick he hid the manuscript under his tunic and then when they were finally liberated transferred it to a suitcase. At the last minute the American soldiers told them that their luggage would travel separately by plane and, not trusting them, he kept the manuscript with him. He never saw the suitcase again. The manuscript was to prove well worth saving.

Listening to a traditional ghost story must also have conjured up memories of home – particularly at Christmas. A.N.L. (Tim) Munby wrote 'The Four-Poster' for a festive edition of *Touchstone*, which was produced at Oflag VIIB on the Bishop of Eichstätt's printing press. He set out deliberately to imitate the classic Edwardian writer of ghost stories, M.R. James, in this and two other ghost stories, 'The White Sack' and 'The Topley Place Sale', which appeared in later editions of *Touchstone*. Another tale, 'The Alabaster Hand', grew out of an air raid alert when he and another POW took it in turns to compose alternate paragraphs of a story told in the style M.R. James, as they sat in the dark. It must have been an effective way of taking the men's minds off the danger they were powerless to avoid. Munby also lectured on English novelists and founded an antiquarian society known as 'Tim's Old Funnies'.

Belgion set out the guiding principles behind his lectures in the preface to his collected lectures that he called *Reading for Profit*:

> Most other ranks in captivity in Germany have been put to work. Not so officers. Theirs is a situation of whole-time leisure. And since the latter part of 1941 there have been plenty of books. So for reading British officers in German hands have an opportunity such as few of them can ever have had before. Indeed, not only have many never before had so much time available for reading; many have found themselves reading for the first time. Once the novelty of doing so wore off, they have been apt to wonder how they might go on reading to their own best advantage. And so it seemed appropriate, if there were going to be lectures on literature, that the contents of the lectures should correspond with some general title as Reading for Profit.

Conditions, however, were not always ideal for study. It was usually difficult to find a quiet spot and concentration was liable to wander if it was cold, rations were low or the camp was being bombed. Lighting was frequently a problem: there might be power cuts or students might have to confine their studying to the hours before lights-out. Some POWs made their own candles from tins filled with margarine or even boot dubbin and lit by a wick made from rags. At some stage most students had to contend with the upheaval of moving camp. POWs were also susceptible to a form of lethargy that Rev. Read described using the Latin word, '*accidie*', 'something different from sloth . . . a creeping paralysis of the mind and will, and emotions by which . . . nothing in the world seems really worth any effort whatsoever.'

But if POWs could rise above this ennui, study could have hugely restorative effects. Stalag Luft VI Heydekrug had its beginnings in Stalag Luft III-E where the first tutorials were held on the top of a three-tiered bunk bed and the only book was *Sesame and Lillies* by John Ruskin. In the summer of 1942 several camps were amalgamated into Stalag Stalag Luft III at Sagan where the first timetable included fifty-five lectures a week. Eventually 1,500 students were attending 220 classes each week and in spring 1943, one hundred students sat their City and Guilds of London Institute exams in the camp cinema with the help of the Germans who provided tables and chairs. When the camp moved to Stalag Luft VI in Heydekrug in Prussia the educational facilities continued to expand and in 1944 it had 3,000 registered students and one hundred men took their London Matriculation exam. The 'university' produced a beautifully hand written prospectus, decorated and illuminated in red, blue and black ink reminiscent of a monk's script. Its education officer, Sergeant Eddie Alderton viewed study with a religious fervour, describing the main value of the university as 'its power to provide a distraction from Boredom and an antidote to Mental Stagnation'.

Throughout Europe, POWs were studying and passing on skills. Sometimes they learnt through a formal system of lectures that covered deeply intellectual subjects; elsewhere learning was more relaxed. Camps encouraged students to sit exams – either those set by official boards at home or 'internal' exams devised and marked within camps – so that they could feel they had achieved something during their time behind barbed wire. The most optimistic education officers argued that captivity offered the first chance for men to pause and consider their intellectual needs without the distractions of a nine-to-five job, family life or temptations such as the pub or girlfriends. POWs could choose subjects in which they were interested – not just subjects they *thought* they ought to be interested in or which others forced them to study.

On 29 March 1942 Andrew Hawarden noted that syllabuses were available from the institutes of Civil Engineering, Electrical Engineering, Industrial Administration, and Chartered Insurance. In August 1943 he passed his St John's Ambulance Association test at Stalag 383 and the following summer several men took their life-saving tests. At the same camp Sergeant Ray Beal used his managerial background to teach classes in 'psychology and industrial administration' and received a hand-drawn certificate signed by the Senior British Medical Officer (SBMO), Principal of Education and Man of Confidence. On the back, the Principal described him as a 'capable and zealous instructor . . . during a most difficult period' and the SBMO added a comment that he had helped the camp medical services to carry out 'certain measures of psychotherapy'. He also took exams set by the Institute of Management with books sent from the New Bodleian, Oxford.

These educational efforts would not have progressed beyond the standard of an ill-equipped evening class without the help of the Educational Books Section of the British Red Cross POW Department, which sent out forms for POWs to use to request books to help them study. The form made it clear that it should not be used to ask for 'light literature'.

Towards the end of 1940 the headquarters of the Educational Books Section moved from London to the New Bodleian where there was more space and less risk of bombing. Miss Ethel Herdman became its director. In a photo of the time she appears as a rather gaunt, unsmiling spinster: her gaze avoids the camera as she sits at a desk strewn with books, behind her a team of women is armed with a battery of typewriters. Miss Herdman and her team worked tirelessly to find the books and study aids requested by their unseen customers to whom she wrote encouraging letters and who came to view her as a sort of distant but kindly aunt.

The Educational Books Section took its responsibilities very seriously and showered its POW students with a fantastic array of books. Few other students at the time, or since, can surely have been treated with such care and thought for their particular needs and circumstances. The level of thought that went into this early experiment in distance learning is all the more remarkable since the members of the Educational Books Section could only guess at the circumstances under which their students were working. To make sure it sent the most suitable books it drew upon the expertise of a panel of forty specialists in different fields who met regularly at the New Bodleian. They assessed each form filled out by a POW and recommended books and study courses depending on the POW's educational background and the camp's resources. Several members of the panel were eminent scholars. But, despite this high level of tutorial advice, the Red Cross was battling against paper and book shortages at home and relied on donations from professional bodies, publishers, authors and the public. It placed advertisements in the press for certain books and volunteers scoured bookshops. The Central Institute of Art and Design, for example, formed a Prisoners of War Fine Arts Committee and gathered a selection of books. The King and Queen sent 1,700 books as a Christmas gift in 1941; each carried a standard inscription from the royal couple.

By the end of May 1942 Miss Herdman and her team had received 15,355 requests for books and study aids and had arranged for 69,400 educational books and 3,542 study aids to be sent to camps. Books on languages and engineering were the most popular but POWs wanted books on a staggering range of subjects from nursing and medicine to fine arts and the installation of telephones. Many requests pointed to career ambitions after the war: a bus conductor was interested in 'light psychology' to help him become an inspector, a rabbit trapper wanted to be a gamekeeper, someone else wanted to know about the duties of a landlord. Other requests suggested greater ambitions or fuel for daydreams – POWs read about gold mining in Canada and farming in Australia, one POW wanted to research a future polar expedition. By contrast some students simply wanted to study for study's sake as, for example, the factory hand who wanted a book on the Poor Law. The Section set up a 50,000 book 'dump' in Geneva covering the seventy-six most popular subjects. There was also demand for foreign language books; Miss Herdman had to deal with requests for books written in Urdu, Hindi, Bengali, Turkish and Arabic. If a POW asked for a book because he had a specific exam in mind it was sent to him personally; otherwise the book was earmarked for him but went to the camp leader who made sure it went first to the camp library.

The idea of helping POWs to work towards examinations sprang from the Educational Books Section and pleas from the prisoners themselves. In 1942 the German authorities agreed (although the Italians did not) and scripts reached the camps via Geneva. The Germans could be astonishingly accommodating: sometimes allowing a man to miss work before an exam. Oflag V-A at Weinsburg had a full-time German education liaison officer – although it took him three weeks to produce twelve sticks of chalk, during which time the lecturers improvised by using charcoal on old newspapers.

The Section persuaded professional bodies to offer study aids and to recognise exams sat within camps. C.S. Lewis and J.R.R. Tolkien, Merton Professor of English Language and Literature, devised a special English course for which the university agreed to grant a diploma after it passed a resolution in December 1941. Academics marked the papers for free. C.S. Lewis said he looked forward to the task and suggested that candidates might actually benefit from the lack of 'bulky works on criticism'. It was the first examination held by the university outside Oxford. Twenty-one POWs sat it; three failed and two of the remainder received a first class mark. The university pointed out that, although the exam did not constitute an honours degree (which required, among other things, matriculation and residence), markers were looking for a similar level of knowledge. Unlike the normal Oxford degree, the second class was divided into an upper and lower section so that POWs had more information about how they had done. The university also set up special honours-standard exams for POWs studying economics and modern languages (French, German and Italian).

Eventually the British Red Cross approved 6,091 different papers from 136 examining bodies including Cambridge University, the Royal Horticultural Society and the School of Oriental Languages. Eleven POWs sat the ordination exam for the Church of England. Among the most unusual bodies to offer exams within POW camps were the British Bee Keepers' Association, the Institute of Brewing, the Chiropody Group Council, the Institute of Horse and Pony Club, the Royal College of Organists, the National Federation of Meat Traders' Association and the National Association of Swimming Instructors. Men studied most subjects offered by universities, as well as several more practical subjects such as flour milling, hotel management, occupational therapy, papermaking and stock exchange dealing. Many sat more than one exam and some undergraduates at universities including Leeds, Aberdeen and Sheffield resumed studies cut short by the war.

John Phillips studied Arabic and Urdu and told Philippa how he 'took' the *Frankfurter Zeitung* – which made it sound as though a newspaper boy delivered it every morning. In January 1944 he sat an Arabic exam and urged her to 'offer a prayer to Allah for my success'. At the end of August he wrote to tell her: 'I managed to fox the examiner in Arabic.' This newly acquired skill was to have an important bearing on his postwar career.

Bodies such as the Institute of Civil Engineers waived fees for exams and asked students to state whether instruments such as drawing materials, scales and slide rules were available in camps so that concessions could be made when marking exams. The Royal Institute of British Architects (RIBA) and the Chartered Surveyors' Institution sent out paper and instruments; other bodies provided microscopes and set squares. Stalag Luft VI asked the Educational Book Section for gold leaf with which to adorn its university prospectus and the British Red Cross, International Red Cross and YMCA sent rulers, mathematical instruments, drawing boards, black boards and chalk. Medical students received skeletons, pickled dogfish, frogs, and slides to help them prepare for their practical biology exams. Paper was extremely hard to come by and charities in Canada and Argentina sent donations; the Swedish Red Cross sent 40,000 exercise books. POWs taking accountancy exams asked their friends to spend the weeks before helping them to rule lines on plain paper. Although this helped they were still at a disadvantage because they did not know the up-to-date personal tax allowances.

Would-be students learnt to improvise and found intellectual outlets even with few books and study aids. At Belgion's camp at Spangenberg, a group of thirty officers (of whom only two knew some Greek) met in an old bathhouse to listen to Captain Hamson, who had studied Classics at Cambridge before switching to law, read the entire text of Sophocles' *Electra* in the original Greek over a period of thirteen one-hour sessions, offering a translation and comments as they occurred to him. At Oflag V-A officers put together a wall display called 'Bringing up Children' in which they lent photos of their own children to demonstrate the physical, intellectual, emotional and social aspects of child development.

The University of London provided 1,305 different papers – a fifth of the total – ranging from its matriculation exam to various diplomas and certificates of proficiency in all its eight faculties of theology, arts, law, music, medicine, science, engineering and economics. The university's External and Extension Registrar, Clow Ford, played a special part in making sure that no questions on any paper sent by the British Red Cross fell foul of either the German or British Censor. Examining bodies sent him their papers for checking eight weeks before candidates were due to sit the exam in Britain; papers that included extracts in languages other than Latin, French and German had to be translated. His role demanded the utmost secrecy; if any details leaked out they would have undermined the entire exam system. Ford was ideally placed because his peacetime job at the university involved arranging for students to sit exams overseas; he had also set up exams at Ruhleben camp where he was held as an internee in the First World War and knew just how vital they were to morale.

Ford maintained that it was harder to arrange such exams during the Second World War 'in view of greater suspicion and irritability of the Nazi mind'. And from time to time he came across exam questions that would certainly have irked the average Nazi: an English paper stated 'there is every chance that Rommel will be bustled through the gap to begin another Odyssey' and an examiner for a French essay set the title 'Londres, Quartier-General de L'Europe Libre'. At least two history questions were likely to inflame the Nazi censor – one asked the candidate to illustrate the statement that 'War is the national industry of Prussia'; in another, students were told to discuss the claim, 'For the past fifty years Italy has been regarded as a first-class power only by courtesy'. A question of comparative education asked students to compare 'the aims and development of the youth movement in any one totalitarian country with those in any one democratic country'. An exam on international law included a question about the legality of shackling POWs and a paper on the Old Testament compared the Jewish 'campaign' against mixed marriages with 'other antipathies' such as the theory of the Nordic race. Perhaps the most patriotically inappropriate question was one that was arranged in an acrostic that spelt out 'A SAFE RETURN'. Ford simply rearranged the letters.

Many merchant seamen and Royal Navy POWs were naturally interested in learning skills that would further their careers but these topics were particularly problematic because they required special instruments and because so many of these skills could equally be used for escaping or helping the enemy. Instructors found ingenious ways round both problems. As they were not allowed to teach 'signals', this subject was renamed 'seamanship' and 'wireless telegraphy' became 'electricity and magnetism'. One POW made a deviascope (a type of compass), a model mast and a derrick. Two other instructors built working models – a Hastie steering gear (used to steer a ship) and a Weir shuttle valve to show how the valves related to the pistons – and pinned up large-scale drawings of intricate machinery for students to study or copy.

The Red Cross aimed to have exam questions on their way to POW camps before candidates at home were turning over the papers so that there was little chance of leakage. Camp leaders or education officers were told to expect the papers about six weeks after they had been sent and were urged to hold the exam as soon as possible. Each package contained details of the conditions under which the exams were sat at home. In most camps it was a point of honour that they were run with as much – if not greater – strictness. However, the winter of 1944–45 was so bitterly cold that in some camps candidates were allowed breaks to warm themselves and temperatures were included in supervisors' reports. One POW remembers the Gestapo interrupting an accountancy exam to undertake a search; rather than complaining the candidate said the interruption came as something of a relief. At Oflag 79 at Brunswick in 1944 those who were about to take their exams agreed that they would continue during a normal air raid but if the building started to vibrate any one of the candidates could ask the invigilator to suspend the examination.

The completed scripts were returned to Miss Herdman who forwarded them to the examining bodies who then relayed the results back to her to send to the camps. Many camps complained about the time it took to receive the exam papers and then the results. Miss Herdman did her best to speed up the process but candidates sometimes did not know whether they had passed until they arrived back in Britain. The Educational Section sent exam papers to just under 17,000 candidates who took nearly 11,000 exams (including some which were sat at home). The pass rate was 78.5 per cent.

Sometimes an examining body allowed a candidate to take the theory papers and to postpone the practical or oral section 'until they got home' – words which in themselves must have been hugely heartening. Occasionally a camp leader put forward a foreign language speaker who was competent enough to conduct an oral exam – if he could convince the examining body. But men who passed medical exams could not qualify as doctors because they lacked the experience of hospital work and would-be teachers had to wait until after the war to fulfil the practical side of their teacher training. At Belgion's camp of Oflag IX A/H, Major C.H.R. Gee, a graduate of Cambridge University who had been a housemaster at Clifton College in Bristol where he had worked for over seventeen years, was keen to study for a Certificate in Education to help him to apply for a headmastership. Miss Herdman wrote to Mr Harvey, Secretary of the University of Cambridge's Education Syndicate, arranging for specimen papers to be sent to Gee and providing details of his background and experience. Clifton's headmaster was also willing to provide a testimonial. Gee sat the theoretical exam in June 1943 and Harvey wrote in October to tell him that he had passed but that his class would be decided after he had taken the practical exam. Miss Herdman conveyed the good news to Major Gee's wife and then passed on Mrs Gee's query to Harvey about whether he was required to write a thesis approved by a director of studies. 'We have several prisoners of war writing theses on various subjects, and we assume that the two candidates who have just completed their theory papers will be willing to write theses, should they be required,' Miss Herdman wrote. Harvey replied to Miss Herdman that, at Cambridge, the thesis was only necessary for the more advanced Diploma, not the Certificate that Gee had sat. However, Harvey went on to suggest subjects that Gee might like to consider for a future thesis, giving him details of the word length and including the regulations for a diploma for Miss Herdman to inform Mrs Gee.

The lengths that Miss Herdman and university officials like Harvey went to to encourage POWs, whilst still offering them honest criticism, is touching. Harvey, for example, arranged for men to sit previous papers and for examiners to give them feedback on their answers. Sometimes their comments could be brutally honest but always there was a flicker of encouragement. Captain P.N. Bartlett, who 'worked papers' in education at Oflag IX A/Z, received the following blunt comment on his Principles of Education I paper: 'The candidate seems not to have done any reading on the subjects dealt with in the questions but to be answering them out of his head. The thought is muddled and incoherent. He would not pass the examination.'

The response to his second paper on the Principles of Education II were slightly more encouraging: 'Answers thoughtful, sincere and original, but they were marred by being expressed in very slipshod English – very long rambling sentences, poor punctuation and informal grammar.'

Like Belgion, James Oswald Noel Vickers (known by his initials, 'JON' or to his close friends and family as 'Mouse') was using his spare time at Oflag IX to study two subjects that fascinated him. One would make him a useful member of the escape committee; the other would shape his post-war career.

Vickers was born in 1916 – the same year that his father was killed on the

Western Front – and brought up in London by his mother. He went to Stowe School in Buckinghamshire where his teachers included the novelist T.H. White and the historian George Rudé. He studied history and English at Queens' College, Cambridge, where he also won a boxing blue. He was deeply affected by a contemporary's death in the Spanish Civil War and by the time he had graduated in 1938 he was a committed Communist.

He was due to start studying for a diploma in education at King's College, London, when he was called up and posted to France with the 5th Division of the British Expeditionary Force. While on leave in February 1940 he married Winifred Lambert, a fellow Communist and Cambridge graduate. Two months later he was captured. During his first days as a POW a German doctor removed a bullet from his thigh without an anaesthetic.

Vickers was not the sort of POW who was prepared to drift through however many years he might be forced to spend in captivity. He started to learn modern languages and sat the University of London's Certificate of Proficiency in Russian. He also learnt Serbo-Croat and some Hebrew, the latter from Jewish POW friends, and took English literature. His talent for languages came in useful for planning escapes and allowed him to monitor broadcasts on a clandestine radio. But his Communist sympathies prompted the Germans to classify him as a subversive and he spent a spell at a *Straflager* at Stalag XXI D, outside Posen (Poznan). Much later a distant family connection to Winston Churchill attracted the Nazis' attention and Heinrich Himmler interviewed him personally.

But despite these many upheavals, by May 1943 Vickers was starting to think of his career after the war and he contacted Mr F.E. Harvey, Secretary of the Educational Syndicate at the University of Cambridge's Department of Education. Writing on an official POW postcard sent by *Kriegsgefangenpost* (POW post) he explained how the war had interrupted his studies. He wondered whether he could take the Diploma while he was a POW 'as it will, obviously, save a lot of time'. It was the start of a postal relationship in which Harvey, writing on the back of scraps of old bits of paper such as used exam papers and handwritten scripts presumably because paper was in such short supply, wrote Vickers letters of encouragement full of practical advice, sometimes with Miss Herdman passing on other information about Vickers' progress. Harvey sent his first reply six weeks later (on 24 June 1943), saying that he could not sit the exam because he did not have the necessary year's teaching experience in a school approved by the Syndicate. However, he threw him a lifeline by suggesting that he could 'work' the exam papers set the previous year, June 1942, and that examiners would assess his answers.

In November 1943 – under strict conditions – Vickers answered papers on the principles, history and practice of education. Although he would not receive a grade the invigilator (Lieutenant Colonel W.G. Chadwick, who was the officer in charge of Education at Oflag IX A/Z and a schoolmaster in civilian life) provided a signed affidavit to prove that examination conditions had been observed. Afterwards, on 11 November 1943 Vickers wrote to Harvey from Oflag IX A/Z on a long, lined and folded POW letter thanking him for his letters and for the papers. 'Although I have done a certain amount of teaching in prison camps, conditions are scarcely comparable!' He added that no one in the camp had sat an exam from Cambridge University's Education Syndicate and that there was a limited number of books so he must 'excuse a rather general approach to the questions'. He went on:

> I very much appreciate your kindness in making this concession to me, as I am extremely keen to teach after the war but it would not be financially possible for me to go back to a university as a pupil-teacher, and, to be frank, after three and a half years here I have had all I want of our institutional life!
>
> I would be extremely grateful if you could give me an idea of what prospect of a future I should have on these lines. If, in your opinion, I have left it too late to enter the profession, I should particularly appreciate being forewarned.

Harvey answered some of his concerns in a letter dated 14 January 1944:

> When you are in a position to take steps about your career, you may bear in mind that there is at present an acute shortage of teachers, and as you wish to adopt that profession you would be advised to seek a post of that kind. The possession of a Diploma or Certificate in Education is not yet essential to get a post in a secondary school, but the younger generation of headmasters like men on their staff who have this qualification. In your case you could get settled down first, and then read for the examination as spare time permitted.

He offered further careers advice, suggesting that the army might 'find a niche' where he could use his knowledge of Russian.

By March 1944 Harvey was ready to send the examiners' reports on Vickers' work to Miss Herdman to forward to Germany. The group of experts who read his scripts were obviously suffering from the pressures of living in a country at war. One apologised for the delay in sending his report: 'No secretary, almost no domestic staff, wife been laid up!' Miss Wilshire who read his paper on the teaching of history (possibly his weakest subject), confided in her covering letter of 28 February 1944: 'I have found the report a bit difficult because I don't want it to be too damping if it is being sent out to him. He is not very good as yet at really answering the question and it is difficult to know how much knowledge he really has: some of his statements seem to me wild in the extreme.' In the report that Vickers received she commented that he approached the subject in an 'independent and thoughtful way' while adding some mild criticism and a suggestion that he should use fewer parentheses. Another examiner said that 'Given wider reading' he would have 'produced a good result' in the history of education paper and the experts who read his scripts on the principles of education suggested his work would have merited a pass.

Vickers took the comments in good heart and sent a postcard on 23 April 1944 thanking Harvey: 'The criticisms of inadequacy of reading and experience are, unfortunately, more than justified, but conditions have not been ideal for remedying these faults! May I thank you again for the great personal interest and trouble you have taken on my behalf.'

It must have been gratifying for Mr Harvey when Miss Herdman wrote to tell him that Vickers had applied to become a teacher after the war and was also taking exams set by the School of Slavonic and East European Studies in Russian and Serbo-Croat.

In September 1944 Vickers wrote again to Harvey saying that he had heard that the University of London was offering POWs the chance to sit a Diploma exam. The university was sending him the current papers but Vickers commented 'under present conditions the papers are unlikely to arrive (if indeed they are able to be sent at all)' and wondered whether the papers he had completed might count towards this, adding, 'it would save a valuable year in peacetime'.

Harvey pursued the point on his behalf but the University of London was not willing to accept his scripts as there was no guarantee that he had not somehow seen the papers when they were set a year before. This decision was made in February 1945, by which time Vickers had more pressing concerns to deal with than any possible postwar career.

Captain John Colin Dennistoun-Sword of the 1st Battalion Gordon Highlanders was equally determined not to let his incarceration hold back his career. He was severely injured at St Valéry in 1940, when he was twenty-four, and after a period in hospital spent most of his captivity studying law. He was the son of a solicitor and had been admitted to Lincoln's Inn in 1935. At Oflag VIB at Warburg, he passed the 'elements of real property' examination (Class Two) and his name appeared with three other POWs from Warburg in the Bar Examination results announced in *The Times* in October 1942. Six months later he was awarded a Class One pass for Roman Law while at Oflag VIIB, Eichstätt. One of the idiosyncrasies of the English legal system requires candidates to eat a certain number of dinners at their prospective Inn of Court. In the 1930s it was seventy-two but during the war the Inns relaxed their rule on attendance for men serving in the armed services and he was called to the Bar *in absentia* in the summer of 1944. Although the *Gordon Highlanders' Regimental Journal* states in its obituary that his wife ate the dinners on his behalf, Lincoln's Inn has no record of this. After the war he practised law until his battle injuries affected his health to such an extent that in 1955 he turned to the less arduous profession of genealogy.

In many ways a POW camp was the ideal place for someone who today might be described as an 'over-achiever' and several passed exams as a POW that helped push them in a certain direction after the war. One direction was politics. Angus Maude, Aidan Crawley and Airey Neave were all POWs who became MPs in postwar Britain. A further three used qualifications they earned as a POW to shape their political careers.

Anthony Barber was evacuated from Dunkirk then transferred to the RAF as a photographic reconnaissance pilot but in 1942 he bailed out over France after running out of fuel. He made several attempts to escape and got as far as Denmark before being recaptured. Back 'in the bag', he studied for a law degree and secured a first. He attributed his success to the fact that the camp had 'no women, no drinks and no distractions of any kind'. After the war his degree helped him to obtain a grant to read Politics, Philosophy and Economics (PPE) at Oriel College, Oxford, and then to pass his Bar exams. Barber did not come from a political dynasty – his father was a confectionery maker in Hull – but he went on to become a Conservative MP and then, under Edward Heath, chairman of the party and Chancellor of the Exchequer between 1970 and 1974.

Fred Mulley, the son of a factory labourer, also obtained a degree in PPE from Oxford and became a barrister after obtaining a B.Sc. (Economics) from the University of London and becoming a chartered secretary while a POW at Stalag 383. Mulley later praised his German captors for their help in supplying him with books in English to help him study. His determination impressed the Reverend Dr John Lowe, the distinguished theologian and Dean of Christ Church, Oxford, who welcomed several ex-POWs on adult scholarships to the college in 1945. Mulley held several cabinet positions in Labour governments in the 1960s and 1970s, including Minister for Transport and Secretary of State for Education and Science and Secretary of State for Defence.

Peter Thomas already had a law degree from Oxford when the bomber he was flying was shot down in 1941 and he became a prisoner at Stalag Luft VI, and later Stalag Luft III. He quickly discovered a talent for acting and was held with Roy Dotrice, who would become a professional actor after the war, and Rupert Davies, who later played Maigret in the television detective series. Thomas resumed his law studies and used his knowledge to help fellow POWs by conducting long-distance divorces and representing an RAF man in a Hamburg court who was accused of sabotage during an air raid. The defendant was acquitted. He was called to the Bar after the war and took silk in 1965. He moved into politics and became the first Conservative Secretary of State for Wales and the party's first Welsh chairman. He ended his career as Lord Thomas of Gwydir.

Perhaps studying for professional examinations was so appealing because it offered the certainty of work after the war. This may have been why so many officers took accountancy and legal exams and why the pass rate of POWs taking the final exam of the Institute of Chartered Accountants in England and Wales was higher than the contemporary average.

There were two groups of men for whom education was not so readily available: those, like Clive Dunn, who were on work parties away from camps, and the inhabitants of Colditz. The Red Cross sent application forms to all working detachments and men asked for some 400 courses in

1944 alone – the most popular of which were diesel and auto-engineering – but many were too tired from their daily endeavours to contemplate academic study. There were also concerns that if the Germans thought the men had enough energy for study they would extend their working hours.

The enemy was naturally less accommodating when it came to helping the men of Colditz to enhance their educational credentials. POWs were not allowed ink in case they used it to make fake ID cards and drawing instruments were banned until late 1944. Students had only two small rooms and books were sent to Berlin to be censored. Anyone wishing to study also had to contend with the disruption of four parades each day and more frequent snap searches. Nevertheless, at least one officer qualified as a chartered accountant whilst at Colditz.

For men who had lost their sight during battle the chance to learn Braille proved an invaluable advantage and gave them hope in a desperate and bewildering situation. The War Organisation with the help of St Dunstan's, a charity that helped – and still helps – the blind, started to organise 'Braille comforts' in early 1941 and by the end of the year relatives and close friends could submit their letters to be transcribed into Braille which was then censored by the National Institute for the Blind. Each POW received a Braille watch and St Dunstan's gave advice and funds to provide special playing cards, domino and draught sets. In the latter the blind POW was able to feel his way round the board because one player's pieces were larger than his opponent's and the squares alternated in height.

From the start, the aim was to try to give men who found themselves doubly imprisoned hope by teaching them skills to use at home. This became easier when in the summer of 1942 the fourth Marquess of Normanby persuaded the Germans to move blind POWs into a former mental asylum at Kloster Haina, north of Frankfurt. The Germans had placed many precious paintings from the Kassel Art Gallery in the centre of the building but most of its new inmates were not in a position to enjoy them.

Normanby had been captured at Dunkirk and soon afterwards, at Obermassfeld near Meiningen, he was deeply affected by the hopeless conditions in which men who had been blinded in action were held. Although they were otherwise physically fit they were confined to bed. Normanby rounded them up and taught them Braille by translating a Larousse

Dictionary someone had found into a Braille version made from a card-board box lid with matches poked through. He also encouraged them to act by pushing four tables together to make a stage and reading a short play out for them to act. 'The real difficulty in the rehearsing, which was intense and took a long time, was to prevent them falling off the tables. Everything had to be done by numbers of steps. It was a great success and even the German chief doctor came. So we gradually evolved into being more of a body together and that kept them busy.'

At Kloster Haina severely injured, but sighted, POWs teamed up with blind men to guide them during walks in the grounds and to help them grope their way into a new life. Normanby convinced the Germans that he was high up in St Dunstan's (although, in fact, he had little knowledge of the organisation) and this helped him to procure items such as Braille typewriters from a nearby university. He started classes in business cor-respondence to teach skills such as how to set out letters and Braille shorthand. To begin with they only had one book of Braille so Normanby was forced to read it by sight, rather than touch, and upside down as he helped the blind student sitting opposite him. As the flow of books increased, the National Institute for the Blind sent records of 'talking books' every month. 'Then we really settled down to school work, because I was very anxious that they should go back, and indeed so were they, trained in some form of profession, possibly, but at any rate, knowing Braille fluently enough to read it, and this we achieved at the end of our time.'

A man who wanted to become a masseur received both practical and theoretical training in the camp hospital and eventually made a living from the profession in Bath. Another blind POW studied through the University of London; two men learnt about poultry farming and others became tele-phone operators after the war based on know-how they had accumulated at Kloster Haina. Others learnt bookbinding, boot mending and carpen-try. A man was spurred on by the fact that he was engaged to be married to a girl who was better educated. He had worked in the fishing industry in Hull but could neither read nor write. By the time he left Kloster Haina he could do both, had learnt some geography and history and played an instrument in the band.

Normanby also encouraged blind POWs to put on plays and concerts and the Red Cross sent musical instruments, scripts, carpentry and joinery outfits, gym apparatus and gramophones and records. The Swedish YMCA representative arrived with a rickety old piano. Eventually, in October 1943, Normanby and thirty blind men were allowed to return to Britain.

A year later, in September 1944, Belgion was in Sweden after he had been repatriated on medical grounds. His final year at Oflag IX A/H had been as busy as ever. He had acted as a moderator for the Institution of Structural Engineers' Associate Membership exam and had received cigarettes in lieu of the usual fee. In February 1944 Miss Herdman wrote to tell him that he had been awarded a second class honours degree in the special English exam devised by Oxford University. She went on to tell him that out of twenty candidates two had gained a first and four a Class IIA. 'Please accept our hearty congratulations on this result. Considering the conditions under which you have studied for it, and the high standard demanded, it was a magnificent achievement.'

But comments in a letter that Belgion received from the Red Cross in May 1944 showed that C.S. Lewis, who was one of the examiners, was not afraid to offer criticism – even to a friend held in a POW camp. Or maybe he did not realise Belgion would read them: 'H.M, Belgion. Began well & was often interesting, but knowledge tended to fail in the later papers & there was much irrelevance.'

Belgion completed the manuscript of *Reading for Profit* in January 1944. It included what must be one of the most unusual acknowledgements sections ever found in a book in which he thanked Miss Herdman and his friends in England for sending him books and other POWs for giving him exercise books and lending him novels. He ended with the final paragraph: 'Finally, let me acknowledge the courtesy of the German military authorities in enabling me to typewrite a portion of my MS. And in allowing me to send the whole of it home.'

Music and Theatre

To begin with, the soundtrack to Andrew Hawarden's daily life as a POW consisted almost entirely of human voices: commands in German or broken English and men squabbling, debating or cheering each other on at some form of competition. Then there was the night time medley of snores, the trumpeting flatulence produced by a diet heavy on cabbage and the grunts, moans, urgent chattering and screams of men who only really came alive in their dreams when they relived battle horrors or were reunited with loved ones.

Music was slow to enter the lives of POWs captured early in the war. As the number of POWs increased, so camps benefited from a smattering of professional musicians and men who, although not always talented, were keen to learn an instrument. By the summer of 1944, Stalag 383 was able to hold a four-day music festival and had five bands: two played dance music and two others Spanish music and mouth organs; the fifth was a pipe band. Novice Scots and Australians squeezed strangulated wheezes from their bagpipes, causing the German guard on duty in his watchtower to complain that the noise of the *doodle sacs* was driving him mad. Perhaps it was this dual ability to aggravate the enemy when played badly and to inspire the POWs with stirring patriotic music when played well that made the pipes so popular. At the enormous camp of Stalag VIIIB at Lamsdorf, a village now in South West Poland, one POW noted that there were *only* ten sets of bagpipes but that the Provost of Inverness had started a fund to buy drums to complete the Stalag's pipe band.

By the end of 1941 the Red Cross's Indoor Recreations, Fiction, Music and Games Section had sent out twenty-four sets of bagpipes, as well as fourteen instruments each to the eight largest camps so that they had the basis for an orchestra. Thousands of mouth organs, Tipperary flutes and ukuleles also arrived in this first flood of instruments and camps started to specify which instruments they wanted. The most popular were banjos, ukuleles, flutinas (a type of accordion) and ocarinas (an egg-shaped terracotta wind instrument) because they were relatively easy to master. Harmonicas were in such demand that the British Red Cross soon ran out of them. More expensive instruments such as violins, clarinets, flutes, euphoniums, cornets and trumpets were sent directly to professional performers or talented amateurs. One Red Cross worker complained about how hard it was to wrap kettle drums in brown paper and string. By the end of the war the Red Cross had provided one hundred camps with orchestral combinations and had sent out over 16,000 instruments for individuals. It also passed on instruments bought by friends and relatives and provided strings and other spare parts. POWs were able to buy instruments locally; some musicians had managed to hang on to theirs after capture whilst other camps relied on donations from home.

When Cy Grant, the navigator who bailed out over Holland, arrived at Stalag Luft III, music was one of the interests that helped him to settle into a daily routine. His mother had been a music teacher and he had learnt the piano as a boy:

> For me being a prisoner of war for two years was equivalent to having a University education. Not only did I have an opportunity to reflect upon my life, about who I was, what I was doing there and what had brought me into that situation, but I was in the company of men who were officers, well educated and above average intelligence. We were able to organise ourselves into a highly efficient community – Escape committees, recreation facilities, libraries, theatre groups, a jazz band, (in which I played) and music societies. I actually ran a music society for my block and in so doing increased my own knowledge of European classical music.

Stalag VIIIB at Lamsdorf, which at its peak held 10,000 British POWs (plus around 9,000 in satellite work camps) making it the biggest British camp, had probably the grandest theatrical and musical ambitions of any stalag. It had been a POW camp in the First World War and for some men it was their second stay there. At one time it had three large orchestras, a dance band of twenty-four instruments, a twenty-five piece military band and a string orchestra. Its theatre could hold 600 and often there were long queues for tickets. One POW remembers how 14,000 men wanted to hear a production of Beethoven's Fifth performed by a fifty-piece orchestra that included many professional players.

Lamsdorf proved a turning point for Denholm Elliott when he 'found a talent emerging that I hadn't really felt when I was at RADA [Royal Academy for the Dramatic Arts]'. 'Denny was totally engrossed in the theatre and did everything to ensure each show was a success,' one of his friends remembered. 'To make our way down to the theatre to see the latest show was the highlight of our miserable day-to-day existence at the thought of a couple of hours' return to a happier life.'

The Lamsdorf theatre was so successful that the Germans allowed its production of *Twelfth Night* to go on tour and even raided the wardrobe of Breslau Opera for costumes. Elliott took the part of Viola in a cast of around ten that visited camps in the area and the Farben oil refineries, which were under constant threat of air attack from the Allies. One POW who watched the performance found it captivating:

> They were so different from the rest of us hunger-hardened, predatory POWs that they could well have come from the other side of the cosmos. They had beautifully modulated voices, and elegant movements such as to embarrass us with our own uncomeliness and set us to wriggling on our bare benches and emitting oafish noises like the mindless work slaves we had become. But as the wonderful language began first to make sense to us, then became riveting entertainment, we were won over – especially by the lad who played Viola. Spellbound, we watched and listened as first he presented as a girl, then as a girl pretending to be a youth, then again as a girl.

Captivity also convinced Peter Butterworth and Talbot Rothwell that they wanted to spend their lives entertaining people. They met in Stalag Luft III where Rothwell started to write scripts for comic sketches which Butterworth took part in. Butterworth was also a keen tunneller and in the summer of 1941 got as far away as 27 miles before he was recaptured. During one performance it was later claimed that the noise of the audience covered the sound of tunnelling; Butterworth was also said to have been one of the vaulters over the wooden horse that covered another escape route. Rothwell had been an art student and then worked in Brighton Town Hall and Butterworth seemed destined for life in the military. After the war they would be reunited in the *Carry On* films where Rothwell helped to establish the films' saucy tone and Butterworth portrayed many of the hapless characters.

When Clive Dunn was held in an old school building in Liezen, Austria, the men put on concerts, cabaret acts or short melodramas with little more than an accordion. Music helped them through the claustrophobic evenings and the period from midday on Saturday until Monday morning when they were not allowed outside. Dunn specialised in comic skits and female impersonations. 'I pulled funny faces, told jokes – anything to make them laugh. They laughed – and cried – very easily.'

When he became so ill with chronic colitis that he could hardly digest his food he persuaded the guards to send him back to the main camp of Stalag XVIIIA at Wolfsburg in Austria near the Yugoslavian border. Dunn was the only professional actor and was allowed to 'go into the smoke' – that is his registration card was 'mislaid' and he effectively disappeared from the official records so that he could not be moved to a work camp. This system was used for POWs such as dental mechanics, watch menders and entertainers who had particular skills. Whenever there was a roll-call he hid in the rafters or the latrines so that the numbers tallied. Other POWs took more desperate measures to avoid hard manual labour and one of Dunn's jobs was to apply Vaseline to wounds to stop them drying and healing. One man tied his ankle to the top bunk and then repeatedly threw himself off in an attempt to break his leg; another whipped his knee with a wet towel until it ballooned in size. Perhaps the most unpleasant case was the man who injected his penis with condensed milk using a fountain pen filler to produce the symptoms of gonorrhoea. On this occasion the doctors were not fooled but the old short-sighted Austrian doctor who usually treated POWs and who had no love of the Nazis could often be persuaded to see injuries in X-rays that others could not. POWs lined up to try to persuade him that they were suffering from exotic complaints such as: 'Toss-the-Quack', 'Singapore Toe', 'Actor's Knee', 'Chinese Doldrums' and 'Mental Inertia'.

A professional musician, Lindo Southworth, who had somehow

managed to transport his viola from Corinth, ran the orchestra, 'The Hottentots', and practised his scales every day. Many of the guards believed he was really German and called him 'Fritz' – a nickname that his fellow POWs adopted. A particularly sympathetic guard took him off work duty so that he did not damage his hands. He was accompanied by a piano bought with stolen money from Wolfsburg. POWs removed its legs and covered it with a tarpaulin to transport it back to the camp on a horse and cart. The camp commandant, an elderly man who shouted a lot but was generally fair – although he would occasionally close the theatre by ordering guards to nail a wooden batten over the doors – was furious when it arrived but allowed them to keep it.

Professional musicians, like professional sportsmen, became minor celebrities whose fame spread from camp to camp. They inspired their fellow performers and audiences, both of whom could feel that they were gaining an experience they might not have had at home. By a strange quirk of fate many musicians and sportsmen began their POW lives in Italy.

POWs at PG21, Chieti, were fortunate to have two extremely talented musicians – one classical, the other an accomplished jazz player. Both were useful in boosting morale not just because of their talent at performance but because they could arrange music at a time when sheet music was hard to come by. The Red Cross sent out packages of what they referred to as 'mixed grills' – a selection of different types of music from orchestral arrangements of well known works to chamber music, solos for piano, music for dance bands, light operas, music hall songs and music for what one Red Cross worker described as 'Nebuchadnezzar's Band' (a distinctly POW combination of ukulele, piano accordion, guitar and a more conventional instrument such as a flute). They sent out carols in time for Christmas.

The Germans and Italians frequently banned sheet music if they suspected it was encoded with a secret message. In December 1944 the Germans also insisted that any music had to be by a German composer or a native of the POW's own country. This scarcity of printed music meant that anyone who could jot down arrangements from memory or from a record had the power to transform the scope of a prison orchestra. Tony Baines was one such musician. He arrived at Campo PG21 after he was wounded and captured in North Africa. He had studied chemistry at Oxford, where he also played the saxophone in dance bands and arranged jazz music, before winning a scholarship to the Royal College of Music. He played third bassoon and contra in the London Philharmonic Orchestra until the start of the war.

At Chieti he scored from memory an astonishing array of classical pieces for two violins, a bass, two clarinets, a tenor sax, two trumpets and a tenor soloist. The music he managed to conjure up from his memory included Mozart's Divertimento in B flat, Schubert's *Rosamunde* ballet music, three items from Handel's *Water Music*, Tchaikovsky's *Nutcracker*, Borodin's dances from *Prince Igor*, two tenor arias from *Figaro* and *The Magic Flute* and some of the last act of *La Bohème*. He also took down music by Beethoven and Mozart and Tchaikovsky's *Swan Lake* from records and other pieces from piano transcriptions.

Tommy Sampson made a very different noise at Chieti. Sampson grew up in Leith, a port near Edinburgh, where he spent his childhood playing the cornet for the Salvation Army. By the time war broke out he had discovered jazz and he arranged jazz sets while Baines provided a more classical alternative. They went their separate ways after Baines escaped. He was recaptured when the packet of Gold Flake tobacco poking out of his pocket revealed his nationality. From here he was sent to Oflag VIIB at Eichstätt, a castle camp whose inmates had musical ambitions to match his own.

Sampson's next move was to Oflag 79 at Brunswick, near Hanover, where he set up his own big band and performed in black tie at a POW nightclub called 'The Rum Pot'. He got to know Herb Perry, who in peacetime worked as a musical arranger for Walt Disney Studios and who after the war tried to lure him to Hollywood. The German guards were so enthusiastic about Sampson's jazz arrangements (at a time when Nazis viewed jazz as degenerate because of its associations with black music and Jewish performers) that they agreed to find the costumes Sampson said he needed for a camp play. The clothes went straight to the escape committee. On another occasion he played a trumpet solo on two valves so that the guards would not notice that he had replaced the third valve with a rolled-up map.

As with so many other POW pastimes, music-making provided an effective 'cover' for escape plans. Pat Reid hid a small saw in his guitar at Colditz and Douglas Bader used a baton to conduct a group of musicians as a way of signalling that the coast was clear. At Stalag Luft III a male voice choir and an accordion muffled the sound of the *Great Escape* tunnellers and dirt extracted from 'Harry' was hidden under the theatre through a trapdoor concealed by one of the seats in the back row of the auditorium.

The Germans were particularly suspicious of gramophone records – especially at Colditz where many were smashed to see whether they contained money, maps or other escape aids. In theory, camp leaders could ask for particular records to be sent and ENSA (Entertainments National Service Association) made monthly recordings that the YMCA delivered to the camps. When Hawarden was in hospital in late 1944 during one of the main bouts of ill health that started to creep up on him he could listen to records on a portable gramophone player. But it became harder to meet demand as the raw materials used to make them became scarcer.

There was no clandestine motive behind the Eichstätt Music Festival, which was held over thirty-three days from 28 February 1944 at Oflag VIIB, and which may have been one of the most ambitious musical productions to be performed during the war. The idea for the festival came to Lieutenant Richard Wood when he was shaving and represented the culmination of four years of making music behind barbed wire.

Wood had been a choral scholar at New College, Oxford, and on graduation became a professional singer. He was captured at Dunkirk and at first was too despondent to think of music but instead spent his days resting and reading Eastern philosophy. He returned to his peacetime passion when he was asked to coach a Mozart trio. Perhaps he was also inspired by his place of captivity, Oflag VIIC, the 'massively built palace of Mozart's Salzburg archbishop' at Laufen. Desmond Llewelyn and Michael Goodliffe, who had worked with the Royal Shakespeare Company, also resumed their acting careers at the camp after both were captured in 1940. But professional actors had standards and some refused to perform until their hair had started to grow back after that first brutal shaving following capture.

By October 1940 the YMCA had sent instruments from Geneva and Wood grasped what he might achieve with 1,600 men who had very few books to read and no other demands on their time. At Christmas 1940 he organised an evening of carols modelled on the famous service at King's College, Cambridge, which he organised with the help of Captain Robert 'Bobby' Loder. It must have been particularly poignant to gather round a

German Christmas tree lit with candles to listen to music and bible readings so strongly associated with family celebrations.

The Gala all-Schubert concert was another milestone as the musical group had just bought a grand piano from Salzburg and wanted to pay off the 2,000 marks it cost so they risked charging relatively high ticket prices. By February 1941 Wood had given up his own studies of Russian, German and botany and was coaching musicians in cello, violin, piano, lecturing twice a week on musical subjects and planning the *St Matthew Passion* for Holy Week.

He found even greater enthusiasm for the arts at Oflag VIIB, just north of the Danube at Eichstätt, near Nuremberg, where Goodliffe and Llewelyn were held. They were joined by other professional performers and Llewelyn, who stayed there for just a year, found his fellow inmates an up-market group who referred to the Savoy as their 'local'. He had contracted chicken pox at Laufen and was so badly nourished that his jaw kept dropping out of its socket but nevertheless 'threw' himself 'seriously into acting and reaped the benefit of working with several professionals'.

One of the first productions at Eichstätt, which Llewelyn took part in, was *Post Mortem*, a gloomy play written by Noël Coward in an attempt to counter claims that he was only capable of writing light-hearted pieces. Before it could go ahead, the German guards made the entire cast and backstage crew promise that they would not use any of the props or costumes to help them escape. The play had its world premiere in January 1943 and ran for ten nights, including a special performance for POWs in shackles. Many members of the audience found the subject matter too grim and Wood pronounced it 'a poor play, well-acted'. Goodliffe took the lead as an idealistic soldier who, as he lies dying in the trenches, is transported forward in time to 1930s England. Coward's biographer, Philip Hoare, later concluded: 'The play splutters to an end like a badly made firework, with bursts of sharp emotion,' adding that Coward never pursued its production, perhaps fearing that it might suffer by comparison with the highly successful *Journey's End* by R.C. Sherriff, which takes place in a dugout.

Over the next two years Eichstätt put on more ambitious plays including *Gaslight* (a favourite in many camps), a thriller called *The Case of the Frightened Lady* by Edgar Wallace and a shortened version of *Hamlet*. Box office returns show that most productions played to audiences of around

200 men. At the end of 1944 they staged a special Christmas version of *A Comedy of Errors* that included a ballet and grand finale. Looking at photos (taken by guards) of each of these productions, the sets, costumes and bearing of the actors all appear highly professional. Whether he is dressed as a First World War officer, or as an Elizabethan courtier in a ruff, tights and doublet, the POW actor has a quiet confidence. It is only in the occasional drawing room scene when, although the armchair, mantelpiece and paintings look authentic, the gauntly masculine face of the female part betrays the production's one weakness.

As Llewelyn pointed out, these POW productions were in many cases more lavish than at home, where theatre companies were struggling with rationing and shortages, the worry of bombing, and the constant threat of losing their performers to the armed services. Plays put on behind barbed wire had a captive audience desperate for distractions. The German authorities, too, encouraged anything that kept their inmates – and their own guards – happy. They seemed genuinely to have appreciated the POWs' theatrical efforts and helped them by providing civilian clothes, props, wigs and Leichner make-up. It was not unusual for an actor at Eichstätt to gaze down through the reflectors and spotlights hammered out of old Klim tins to see among the 200 strong audience the faces of expectant German officers in the front row – particularly if they were watching an 'improving' play like *Hamlet*. There was certainly a degree of respect between guards and actors. When POWs were forbidden to sing the national anthem the stage manager in many camps would stand in front of the curtain and announce, 'God save the King!' to which the audience would rise to their feet and bark: 'God save Him!' The Germans would often stand to attention and salute.

The theatre was also a useful disciplinary tool: as with a child and its pocket money it could be withdrawn as a punishment for bad behaviour such as theft or escape attempts. At Colditz the opening of an elaborate revue called *Ballet Nonsense*, which was based around a group of burly, mustachioed POWs prancing about in crêpe paper tutus and bras, and which was advertised by a poster campaign throughout the castle, was delayed by a month as a punishment after workmen who delivered the grand piano for the performance took off their waistcoats and jackets to haul it up the narrow stairs but returned to discover that their clothing had disappeared, although the contents of their pockets remained. The

POWs offered to pay for the loss and this gesture was eventually accepted.

It seems incredible that even at Colditz, which housed persistent escapers, the Germans were prepared to give POWs access to wigs and other forms of disguise. Jock Hamilton-Baillie took full advantage of these theatrical facilities in one of his many escape attempts. He was the main engineer behind the Eichstätt tunnel through which he and sixty-two other men escaped in June 1943. In this, his fifth escape attempt, all men were recaptured. In the 'Warburg wire job' he planned a mass break-out using ladders made from the huts to scale the barbed wire fences. Three men made it home – but not Hamilton-Baillie. In one of his final attempts at Colditz, his theatrical prowess tripped him up. He was caught wearing a tight-fitting black catsuit, long hair and lightweight shoes after guards recognised the star of the prisoners' production of Noël Coward's *Blythe Spirit* and called out excitedly: *Das Theatermädel!* (The Theatre girl!).

As productions, whether of a pantomime, opera or play, became more sophisticated they sucked in men whose talents were not obviously theatrical. Carpenters, electricians, artists and tailors worked with set and costume designers to coax, cajole and steal in a bid to maintain their high production standards. Sometimes ingenuity was enough. Red Cross parcel crates, for example, made excellent flats and the Marlag and Milag Theatre (MMT), where the company put on at least one show every month, devised their own make-up by mixing talcum powder, margarine and dyes from crêpe paper. MMT also created a special kind of head-dress for actors playing the part of Japanese girls in Gilbert and Sullivan's *The Mikado*. POWs dug up mud from the camp reservoir, smoothed it over the actor's head, carefully removed it and shaped it before baking it in an oven and then sticking thin pieces of paper on to give the appearance of hair.

At Stalag 383, Andrew Hawarden enjoyed many performances at the Ofladium Theatre, a long building named after the camp's original name of Oflag IIIC, which could hold an audience of 600. A sloping auditorium had been created from tons of earth that were stamped into place and there was also an orchestra pit. Each hut brought their own forms to sit on and the front row was reserved for the Commandant and his staff. Admittance was by cigarettes which helped pay for the sets, lighting, costumes and anything else that could not be obtained through theft or barter. A successful show usually ran for at least ten nights to give everyone a chance to see it.

'Jumbo' Brown, a former cathedral chorister, formed a choir and several army bandsmen accompanied productions of Gilbert and Sullivan operas including *The Mikado*, *HMS Pinafore* and *Madame Butterfly*. The Red Cross sent scores and librettos but the orchestral parts had to be written out by hand, most of which – together with the orchestration – was done by a graduate of the Royal Military School of Music at Kneller Hall. A song, 'Until the Dawn', was composed in the camp and sent home to be performed at the Winter Gardens, Blackpool. On a rather grander scale, the French musician, Olivier Messiaen, composed the *Quartet for the End of Time* while he was held at a POW camp at Görlitz in Silesia in the winter of 1940–41. It was first performed by a violinist, cellist and clarinettist who were also held there.

The Ofladium also put on plays; most, such as *The Importance of Being Ernest*, *French Without Tears* and *Hay Fever*, aimed to raise a laugh. Costumes for these, and more serious productions, were made from hankies, sheets, coloured shirts and pyjamas. The need for men to play female roles led to the surreal sight of actors washing their drawers amid all the male paraphernalia of the camp. Such was the dedication of one actor that a sergeant who broke his jaw playing football during the day insisted on continuing in his role as leading lady in a performance that same evening.

A POW set up Decoria Ltd, which dressed whole shows, including the elaborate costumes worn for productions of Gilbert and Sullivan. The Germans helped by converting cigarettes into marks to allow POWs to buy props and materials from shops in Munich. Their encouragement is all the more remarkable since, at home, the British Red Cross was turning down requests for wigs and costumes because they were too expensive and because they feared the enemy would not tolerate the arrival of such 'heavy disguises'. In reality, it was said that the State Theatre of Berlin lent costumes for a production of *The Merchant of Venice*, which starred a professional Australian actor as Shylock, because of its perceived merits as an anti-Semitic play. Other camps hired costumes from a professional costume company in Berlin and from the Munich Opera. At Eichstätt an *Unterführer* (subordinate commander) told the entertainment committee to mention his name when they approached the Munich State Theatre about hiring costumes – as they did for the *Babes Up* pantomime of

Christmas, 1942. The archive of material belonging to Captain Robert 'Bobby' Loder, who helped to organise entertainment at Laufen, Warburg and Eichstätt, includes a well-thumbed catalogue from the costume hire company of F. & A. Diringer, Munich, which specialised in historical costumes and uniforms. Someone has left a pencil mark next to illustrations including a male gymnast and women dressed in Spanish and Mexican costumes. The YMCA often provided make-up and lighting equipment.

But, although POWs were a captive audience, they still had strong views. Ray Beal recorded his comments about a play at Stalag 383 in February 1943:

> Went to see the show 'Someone at the Door' tonight. As a show and an evening's entertainment I enjoyed it very much. But looking at the thing from the point of view of a so called producer, it simply shouted for correction in parts, two at least of the actors were simply atrocious! The producing was very amateurish and showed no signs of polish at all. However the leading lady is one I have chosen for my show and he is simply great. This has cheered me immensely – but see how critical I am getting!

During the winter of 1942–43 records of Britten's *Seven Sonnets of Michelangelo* had proved popular at Eichstätt and their success prompted Wood to ask Benjamin Britten whether he would write a piece of music especially for the camp's music festival. He had met the composer before the war and his sister, Anne, had performed with Britten's partner, Peter Pears, for the BBC Singers.

Britten wrote to his friend, the German-born translator, Elizabeth Mayer, on December 8 1943: 'That brings us to the present, when I am quickly scribbling a short choral work for a prison camp in Germany where some friends of mine are, & where there is a choir & enthusiasm for my tunes!' He finished *The Ballad of Little Musgrave and Lady Barnard*, for male voices and piano, on 13 December at his home at Snape near the Suffolk coast and dedicated the eight to nine minute piece to 'Richard Wood and the musicians of Oflag VIIB – Germany – 1943'.

The *Ballad* arrived shortly before the festival was due to start, leaving very little time to copy out the parts and rehearse the piece. It is not known whether Wood made any suggestions about the type of piece that might have been suitable for an audience of POWs but what he received was a tale of courtly adultery and bloody revenge based on a traditional ballad. It was performed four times as part of the Eichstätt Music Festival that started in February 1944 and ran for thirty-three days. Each house held between 186 and 200 people. A printed programme with a stylishly illustrated front cover lists the performers and credits those responsible for stage direction, scenery, painting, props, lighting, wardrobe, box-office and publicity. Posters promoted the festival and a series of lectures about the music helped to build interest in the event.

The festival catered for a wide range of musical tastes and most of the time the organisers could flatter their hosts by including German composers who would naturally provide the mainstay of any classical programme. The three concerts of symphony (performed by a twenty-nine piece orchestra), choral, orchestral and chamber music included pieces by Mozart, Schubert and Bach. The light orchestral concert was more eclectic and included the overture to *The Barber of Seville*, Elgar's *Three Bavarian Dances*, ballet and piano pieces, and ended with an orchestral medley of tunes from Walt Disney's *Snow White*. However, the programme also included a piano piece by Mendelssohn, a composer who was banned in Germany because of his Jewish ancestry. It is impossible to know whether the organisers of the Festival slipped this piece in as an act of defiance or whether they simply felt it helped to provide the right balance of music. Whether consciously or not, the *Snow White* medley is also an interesting choice. The film, which was released in America in 1937, was the first feature length animated film and won an Oscar. The soundtrack must have evoked a range of memories and meanings for its audience: family outings to the cinema to watch the garishly painted seven dwarves, maybe coupled with a subconscious echo of the original Grimm tale of confinement in a forest and ultimately a glass coffin, perhaps even the irony that, as officers, it was not a case of 'Heigh ho, heigh, ho, it's off to work we go'.

A concert called *Round the World with Song and Dance* celebrated the different nationalities held at Eichstätt and included performances by a Russian orderly, French Canadians, a choir of Welsh singers and Spanish songs and dance, Scottish and Ukranian dances and traditional sea shanties. Seven Maoris sang and performed their traditional warlike welcome in the form of a haka dressed in authentic skirts made from rushes that grew near the camp.

A year later, on 2 March 1945, *The Times* carried a report of the Eichstätt Festival in its Entertainments pages, under the headline, 'Music in Prison Camp, Festival Behind Barbed Wire'. The account included a frank appraisal from Wood who had conducted *The Ballad*: 'The choir (35 to 40 voices) started by cordially disliking the work but finally they all thoroughly enjoyed it. It grew on us all the time and the audience took to it immediately or were at least brought up short by it.'

The Times report is warmly appreciative of the Eichstätt Festival. The only hint of criticism creeps in when the piece describes *Round the World with Song and Dance*, noting: 'There is something wrong here, if a camp containing enough men to raise so varied a selection cannot find one person who knows the immemorial dances of England to teach one of their own sword dances to his countrymen.'

However, the writer strongly approved of the grand finale in which all the company marched and sang to a version of the traditional folk song *High Germany* that had been renamed *Across the Narrow Sea*. The words to the final verse had been changed to appeal to a POW audience:

Oh Polly, love, O Polly, but I shall come again
And we shall be in England, and there we shall remain;
And you shall dress all in your best and come to welcome me
When I have done with fighting across the Narrow Sea.

PART IV

The Far East

'Upcountry': The Thailand–Burma Railway

Descriptions of the Thailand–Burma Railway usually include the fact that for every sleeper laid along its 420 kilometres (260 miles) a man gave up his life. This telling detail sums up the subjugation and despair of what became known as 'The Death Railway'. Not only does it give a sense of the scale of the deaths but comparing each POW to a block of hardwood hammered into place at the request of the Imperial Japanese Army conveys the systematic violence with which the slave labourers were treated. Those who survived were reduced to ossified creatures dressed predominantly in loincloths. Although such deprivation was not unique in the Far East, nothing in European POW camps came close to this level of physically demanding work endured in such gruelling conditions.

The other persistent, but much less accurate, image of the railway comes from David Lean's 1957 film, *The Bridge on the River Kwai*. In it Alec Guinness plays Colonel Nicholson, the domineering British commanding officer who initially takes a heroic stand against the Japanese but finally cannot bear to see *his* bridge blown up by Allied saboteurs. The film, which was based on Pierre Boulle's novel, is fiction and many ex-POWs accept it as such. Boulle himself was evasive about which railway bridge he had in mind but the obvious candidate is the one that crosses the river at Tamarkan and which POWs built. Several former POWs feel that the film belittles their experience and besmirches the reputation of Colonel Philip Toosey, who had been in charge of the men and who stood up to the Japanese. Many walked out of screenings and it still rankles today. Fergus Anckorn, who worked on both the wooden and the concrete and steel railway bridges, sees it as a 'travesty'. 'Alec Guinness saying to the Japs, "Let's discuss this over a cup of tea." Some chance. They didn't speak English, we didn't speak Japanese.'

Around 61,000 Allied POWs – about half of them British – and perhaps as many as 270,000 native labourers from Burma, Malaya, Thailand and the Netherlands East Indies helped to build the railway. Some 12,000 POWs and over 85,000 Asian prisoners perished during its construction between July 1942 and October 1943. Everyone who worked on it endured terrible hardship – at its worst the railway represented a type of hell – but as Sibylla Jane Flower, a long-term historian of the railway, has pointed out, the experience varied greatly from camp to camp. A base camp that was well run (both by the Japanese commandant and the Allied commander in charge), had decent rations and was built on more forgiving terrain was less hellish than a water-logged, disease-ridden camp deep in the jungle. Arriving by barge was not as arduous as tramping through jungle thick with razor-sharp bamboo, vicious insects and the threat of snakes in the undergrowth and trees.

Kanyu I and II were run by guards such as the sadistic Lieutenant Usuki whom the POWs christened the 'Black Prince'; food was scarce, there were no days off and not a single book in the entire camp. The Australians dubbed another camp Hellfire Pass because they had to gouge their way through sheer rock or risk being blown to pieces by explosives they were forced to detonate under the auspices of another guard, Sergeant Seiichi Okada, who was known as 'Doctor Death'. The camp at Chungkai, where men played sports, watched theatrical productions and received expert medical attention – albeit with improvised equipment – was, by comparison, a much more benign experience.

Despite the disparity in living conditions, all of the 118 or so camps between Ban Pong in Thailand and Moulmein in Burma had one thing in common: they made the POWs feel the furthest from home they had ever been.

The Japanese needed a direct route that would connect their empire in the east with Rangoon – from where they planned to invade India. A railway would allow them to carry troops and provisions across land, rather than making the slow and dangerous journey by sea around the Thai–Malay Peninsula where they risked attack by submarines. The new railway would begin in the south at Nong Pladuk and shadow the river Khwae Mae Klong until the river divided at Tamarkan, at which point the track would continue north west, with the Khwae Noi river by its side. This audacious route took in dense tropical jungle, wide rivers and limestone hills until it met the existing railway at Thanbyuzayat, south of Moulmein in Burma. Earlier in Thailand's history, engineers had investigated the idea of a railway but decided that trying to tame such inhospitable terrain in a climate of extreme heat, enervating humidity and sudden downpours of rain would prove too great a feat. And besides, where would they find the workforce to take on such punishing and dangerous work?

In September 1942 the former professional footballer Johnny Sherwood arrived back from working at the docks to be told by the Japanese interpreter that all the fittest men were being moved to a camp in Bangkok where they would be required to 'do a little light work' and where there would be plenty of food. As they were working ten-hour days on meagre rations, he and his friends agreed that this could only be a change for the better. Fergus Anckorn, who left Singapore in early 1943, had heard stories of recuperation camps built in pleasant hill stations. Other POWs in Singapore were fed fantastic stories: that they were being moved to well-prepared sites in beautiful countryside where they would have proper beds with blankets and mosquito nets; medical supplies would be plentiful and they would even be able to listen to gramophone records. In some cases, POWs were keen to make the trip to Thailand to accompany a friend who had been chosen.

When he knew he was leaving, Jack Chalker chose a selection of watercolours from his large metal box of Windsor and Newton paints and wrapped them in a bit of old army gas cape to protect them from the heat and rain. He chose white because he could use it as a wash, ultramarine and a selection of primary colours. He hid the package in his backpack under a false bottom.

As soon as they arrived at Singapore Central Station it became obvious that their living conditions were not about to improve. They were herded into windowless metal containers where, among the Other Ranks, thirty or so men were forced to share a space the length of three men lying down (except there was no room to lie down) and ten feet wide. The walls were red hot and started to slow-cook the occupants – many of whom were suffering from malaria and dysentery and who quickly became badly dehydrated. There were no toilets and they were forced to relieve themselves where they stood. One man died in the truck where Johnny Sherwood was held. For those 'lucky' enough to be in a truck where the door was open, men held each other out of the carriage to defecate. If there was room they took it in turns to sit down or to stand for a few minutes in front of the crack where the sliding doors allowed a breeze to waft in. There was little food and water and Jack Chalker occasionally managed to slake his thirst from the engine's outlet valve when the train stopped to refuel. When night fell the truck transformed itself from an oven into a fridge and its occupants shivered in their rags.

Some Volunteers wept as they caught sight of their former homes – well-tended bungalows that mocked their squalid cabins. Others, like Jack Chalker, managed to appreciate the beauty of their surroundings – despite the stench and degradation from which it was viewed. Alfred 'Tommy' Atkins, a Lieutenant in the RASC, wrote in his diary:

2 Nov. [1942]. . . Passed wallowing water buffaloes. Bridges look very rickety . . . Rice sawah getting a richer green as we go northwards. The zigzag irrigation channels make an intricate pattern on the landscape . . . We are only 26 but find the days hot and the nights cold, so I don't know how the men must feel about it – we have our kits bundled in with [us] too, of course.

From N. Johore, hills have been with us constantly and beautifully wooded too. The sawahs run longwise, often bordered by deep green trees which contrast pleasantly. Houses are mostly on stilts from N.J. onwards too.

Rubber tapping seems to be like the bridges, haphazard in what seems Jap fashion. Some native kiddies give 'V' signs & thumbs-up – although others Malay & Tamil mostly – give vehement thumbs-down. I wonder if it is a sign of the adult populations feelings on the subject.

The above mentioned hills stand out clearly but a defiant blue veil hangs between them and us, giving them a beautiful aspect.

Just outside Kuala Lumpur a boy of about eight threw bananas until a Japanese guard shouted at him and he assumed an innocent expression and saluted. Once the guard's back was turned he started to hurl the bananas at them again. In other places they bought cakes, eggs, pomolos (a large citrus fruit similar to a grapefruit) and bananas when the guards were not looking.

As we sat, filthy, unshaven, upon the station at K.L. [Kuala Lumpur] a Jap officer wandered along taking photos of us eating. They do this during the most distressing moments I find, such as the above instance where we could not, nor had not had the opportunity to make ourselves decent. Left K.L. at 2.35 p.m. The hills look glorious in the distance after leaving K.L. – the Cameron hills I suppose.

Further north they waited for about an hour at Prai, the station for Penang.

It was glorious to glimpse for this short period, the blue water, upon which motor launches, tonkeys, dhows, junks – all types of craft – were moored, or were moving along on their tasks – all unfortunately flying the red blob. Beyond the Straits rose the island of Penang, beautifully wooded, and tranquilly basking in the noonday sun. God, how Hugh Watts must feel as he gazes upon this vista of beauty!! His home has been on this lovely island for a number of years, he being the manager of an Estate here.

But Atkins, who was a fastidious man, was sitting next to the doorway when it started to rain heavily and as well as getting soaked he was covered with soot: 'I have about 1cwt in my hair and eyes at the moment'.

He watched the women who 'in their conical, vari-coloured hats look very picturesque as they paddle about in the paddy fields' and noted 'a bird like a crane' who seemed to 'wait in attendance upon the water-buffaloes'. As they moved north he caught glimpses of elephants and noticed the fields change colour as the young yellowy-green shoots of newly planted rice emerged. In Thailand the hills rose in 'peculiar formations'.

Thai troops look more like comic opera actors; they are quite indifferent excepting when trying to cadge clothing, but are armed with our rifles & bayonets. The natives in 'down' trains gaze at us as though stricken dumb at seeing such queer beasts as us wandering about.

The girls are rather comely, their breasts not being bound like Chinese girls which makes them look more like natural females.

1pm Passing through some lovely country, not unlike Surrey, all the hills being thickly wooded. It is very hot today, in contrast to last night's coldness. These Thai engines don't burn coal, only wood; this is quite a good thing from my point of view as I don't get the bits of soot in my eyes or hair as I did before.

When they arrived at Ban Pong, a cockney voice calling, 'All aht, viv yer kits' chimed with the dream he was having in which he was on leave in England. Waking up must have been a horrible shock.

We were fallen in outside the station in the dark, and inspected by a Jap General, after which we were marched off amid rain and awful smells. The roadsides were covered with garbage, with fowls, ducks, sows and all sorts feeding off it.

At 3pm, we were more or less settled in a beastly verminous camp, ankle deep in mud, with latrines filled to within 2'6" of the top with a maggot [sic]. Thai women are squatting all over the place selling cigarettes, peanut toffee, tobacco etc. Their lips are stained with betel nut, & every now and then they exude a large globule of the filthy stuff around their wares.

Some of the younger women are quite attractive and other POW [sic] tell me that these are prepared to do 'business' during late evening for anything up to $3. No thanks.

Nov 6 Staying here today, and move tomorrow. Took the men to the river for a swim this morning; two women were *dhobi*-ing when we arrived. At first they were rather confused, but got over it, stripped and came out of the water with their black smock affair hiding all they had from the view of the assembled spectators. They then walked off without the slightest embarrassment.

Nov 7 Left Bang Pong on hopelessly overcrowded trucks & lorries [unable to read due to water damage] I was squashed up . . . from this vantage point I saw a carcass on the side of the road – a bullock I think – and around it was a group of about 15 vultures, shuffling & jostling one another to get a piece of flesh. Occasionally one would come away from the group with a piece of dripping flesh in its beak.

The feathers of these rotten birds are a dirty dusty brown in colour, jaded and sparse; from the shoulders to the head they seem featherless from this distance and this part of them is of a raw blood-coloured appearance.

Jack Chalker had trudged on foot through the jungle, and finally by boat, to Kanyu River camp about half way along the railway. He remembers how the wildlife mesmerised him and offered an escape from the everyday drudgery of the hard manual labour. 'The jungle is full of lovely things: birds and the most exquisite butterflies and monkeys and so for me in the middle of all that carnage was a lot of delight. It was really quite beautiful. So I started doing some little notes up there but it was forbidden to make any records.'

Keeping a diary was strictly forbidden and Tommy Atkins buried his under the attap huts where he lived in a camp at Tarsao, and where it became mottled by the damp and humidity.

In May 1943 George Aspinall, 'the Changi photographer', was taken even deeper into the jungle, marching 190 miles in eighteen days to Songkurai camp where the Three Pagodas Pass – so called because of the Buddhist pagodas that sat on the highest point – carried the railway into Burma. Here cholera was rife and the camp had its own isolation area. Although he was suffering from dysentery and beriberi he continued to take photos. Among them he captured the bamboo operating theatre where doctors amputated legs eaten away by tropical ulcers and where patients begged to be separated from a limb that was causing them so much pain. He also recorded the subterranean cells covered with bamboo where the guards put POWs who had tried to escape. He developed the film at night, worrying that the starlight might affect the exposure, and crouching with a ground sheet over his head to work away with his chemicals before washing the film in a stream, wiping it with a hanky and hanging it on a bamboo shoot but never having enough time to wait for it to dry completely before placing it between blotting paper in his Town Talk tobacco tin and wrapping the negatives in a piece of gas cape. He hid his camera in the bamboo frame of his sleeping space so that if it were found, no one else would be implicated.

He became a loner, not wishing to risk involving anyone else in his dangerous hobby. By November 1943 their work on the embankment was finished and they were taken south, back over the track they had laid and the wooden bridges where they had planted termites in a hope that they would eat away at the structure – a defiant gesture which now seemed rather foolhardy. At Kanchanaburi, which the POWs shortened to Kanburi, he avoided a body search by the *kempeitai* because he was supporting an amputee. It was enough to persuade him that taking photos had simply become too risky. He broke up his camera and dropped it down a well. He hid the Town Talk tin in his belt, reasoning that he might have a chance to hurl it away if he heard of an imminent search.

Several of Jack Chalker's early sketches were ruined because he hid them in a hollow section of bamboo only to find when he pulled them out that termites and cockroaches had eaten away at the paper, leaving it perforated like a 'pianola roller'. He kept the insects out by fitting a 'good, hard stopper' made from wood and burying the bamboo in the ground under his bed space. When the monsoon rain came he had to check the sketches frequently to make sure they stayed dry. Later he found hiding places in the roof of the attap hut where he lived and even in a POW's artificial limb. Ronald Searle, who was also making sketches of the men on the railway, hid his work under the bed of men dying of cholera because he knew this was one place the guards kept well away from.

Art and Medicine on the Railway

Although he did not realise it at the time, the railway was shaping the way Jack Chalker worked as an artist and what he painted. Conditions on the railway also forced doctors, medical orderlies and even theatrical performers to adapt their skills and the way they did their job. It taught Chalker to work fast and in short bursts. At any minute he might have to stop if the guards burst in to search his hut and because he was toiling for eighteen hours a day on the railway he only had the energy to sketch for short periods at a time. Later, when he was ill, he had more time to draw.

The railway also shaped *what* he depicted during his time as a POW and immediately afterwards. He sketched the harsh bamboo and attap shelters where he lived amid the teak and kapok trees at Kanyu and his unbearably poignant pen and brush and ink drawings capture the quiet dignity of emaciated POWs – in one, a man supports a stick-like figure as he bends over the latrine; a bamboo pole has been placed over the pit to stop the weakest prisoners from falling in and drowning amid the maggoty filth. But he also painted delicate blossom, passion flowers, scarlet hibiscus and mauve ground orchids that grew in the subtropical forest. At home in England he had painted landscape; now he discovered nature. It is perhaps partly this opportunity, which he would never had found in England – and what he describes as 'the blessing' of being an artist – that enables him to look back with no apparent bitterness. Perhaps, too, focussing on the positive is an effective way of dealing with heartrending memories. 'I think it [art] was an enormous help to survival – an unconscious one – the fact that you could do that and not sink into hating everything.'

I was just incredibly lucky: the fact that a lot of people hated the heat and I loved the heat. The jungle was new to me, it was full of interest and some of them hated the sight of it. This carnage and this continuous illness, which we all had, but we were surrounded by these lovely things – beautiful butterflies, I love monkeys and the gibbons were always with us. Of course it was virgin jungle then, which it isn't now. I was just terribly lucky being an artist.

The one time he got caught was in the early days at Kanyu when the fact that he was suffering from dengue fever and dysentery may have meant he was slow to react to danger. A Korean guard burst in on him as he was tucking away a drawing but he caught sight of the forbidden paper and flew into a rage, beating him up and ripping his work to pieces. 'I was dragged off to the guard house and I thought this is the end of the line because if you had a radio or you were keeping records you had to go to the *kempeitai* and you just disappeared.'

Over the next two days he was badly beaten up. Again, with typical optimism, he believes he got off lightly. Others were tied to a bamboo pole with a large tin of stones or water round his neck, its jagged rim designed to lacerate the neck and chest. And all this in the blazing heat, with little, or no water. He believes he was 'lucky' because the Korean guard inadvertently destroyed most of the evidence by ripping up his drawings, rather than taking them to the commandant. When he returned to his hut, he discovered two small drawings under a rice sack that the guard, in his blind rage, had overlooked. One pen and ink and brush sketch, which shows a POW supporting a hollow-eyed figure bent over like an old man and leaning on a stick, his legs thin as pipe-cleaners emerging from cartoon-large boots, became Chalker's favourite of the work he produced at that time because it summed up the support men gave each other.

His brush with the guards made him very cautious about telling men what he was doing. He had to take some into his confidence, though, because he needed paper. POWs who worked in the commandant's office were able to 'knock off' paper for him and later, when he was working as part of the medical teams at Chungkai and Nakhon Pathom in Thailand, he was officially allowed a pencil and a little book with red Chinese figures on the front in which to make notes.

It contained softish paper similar to Western toilet paper and took colour well. He had stolen one or two brushes from the Japanese and had some mapping pen nibs. One of the older guards at Kanyu, who had been a bank clerk in civilian life and enjoyed art and music, gave him a small Chinese notepad and some Japanese stick ink. In return, Jack did some watercolours for him on Japanese Army postcards. Nevertheless, he constantly worried that he would run out of materials and this forced him to use colour with great circumspection. In retrospect, he believes these conditions made him more aware of what could be done with a limited palette, but at the time: 'You just fought to get these blasted things down.'

His years on the railway also gave him the chance to explore different forms of artistic expression. He painted portraits of men from different races such as an Anglo-Indian medical orderly, a Eurasian Dutch POW, as well as Australian and Dutch men. Not only did this expose him to different bone structures but, because he was working in watercolour, he had to be very accurate with his brush strokes. At Nakhon Pathom, a hospital camp set in the Bangkok Plains next to a golden, bell-shaped temple, where he was held between June 1944 and August 1945, he even managed sculpture.

'It was better there because either you were terribly sick and you got better or you died and there were gaps between in which you could have a laugh and quite a lot of fun.' During one of these gaps he had a mud fight with 'Weary' Dunlop's batman, 'Blue' Butterworth, that resulted in Butterworth running straight into the path of a Japanese guard riding a bicycle. Although the guard was knocked off, Blue avoided serious punishment and Jack discovered clay beneath the mud that he used to create a bust of Dunlop who recorded the event in his diary of 15 December 1944:

> I am rather amazed that Jack Chalker, one of our young artists with a head resembling Rupert Brooke, has asked to do a sculpture of my head. I did not have the necessary assurance to refuse. So he comes along and works at his model. I am being continually non-plussed by this three-dimensional art and being asked to turn this way and that. He is a very nice fellow.

As well as developing as an artist he was also able to pursue his other great interest. Whereas as a student before the war he faced the dilemma of which career path to follow – medicine or art – both collided on the railway.

In March 1943 he was laid low by a return of dengue fever and dysentery and was moved down-river with a party of sick men to the camp at Chungkai where he had a better chance of receiving medical treatment. Before he left he dug up the pieces of bamboo in which he had concealed his drawings. He transferred them to a new hiding place in the false bottom and sides of his haversack. The party of men were transported by bumpy Japanese lorries and arrived at their new camp in the early hours of the morning and after a downpour of rain.

He was dismayed by the state of the living quarters. The wind had blown away sections of the attap roof, leaving the rain to gush through the holes, and the bamboo staging on which the men slept with a central aisle down the middle was in a state of collapse. The habitual 'sweet-foul' stench of latrines and rotting limbs provided a backdrop to this wreckage. Typically, though, Chalker was able to see another side to his new home. The camp was set in a beautiful clearing by the river where they could wash and where he spent some evenings listening to a Javanese Eurasian friend playing his flute.

> Just before sundown each day white ibis would fly back up-river to their night roosts, their shapes reflected in the glassy, swift-flowing water, and hornbill might call. Sometimes at night flights of huge fruit bats would glide silently overhead, silhouetted against the velvet sky, and hang like black rags over a nearby mango tree. Gibbons gave an occasional whooping call or chattered intermittently as they settled for the night, and the large geckos would call from the bamboo supports of our huts. It was strange that these hauntingly beautiful moments could occur within a few yards of huts full of pitiful sights, stench, carnage and death.

Food was better and they were spared the crippling railway work. They could hear the sound of children in a nearby village laughing and watch Thai boats plying up and down the river. They seemed less cut-off from the rest of the world.

He spent his first few weeks at Chungkai in the dysentery hut where he made some pen-and-wash drawings of his fellow patients. One shows the scene from his bed space: the men are skeletons, most appear not to have the strength, or spirit, even to hold up their heads; one man is propped up on his bamboo bed by a bamboo support, next to him is a wooden commode and a pile of leaves. The tableau is like a tropical version of Belsen.

The patient next to him had been a university mathematics lecturer and when he had the strength would unravel some of the mysteries of his subject to Jack. One afternoon during the middle of one such 'lecture' he suddenly paused, chuckled and died. Although it seemed like a contented end, and death a daily occurrence, Chalker was still shocked by it.

Often there seemed no reason why one man should survive while another died; death could appear quite suddenly amid the daily routine – as these extracts from Tommy Atkins's diary show.

> Nov 20 [1942] – Hugh Watts has found a good spot for bathing & fishing & Sale [?] & I went there with him for a wash & a fish. Nearing the river, we came upon a little jungle clearing in the centre of which was a water-hole, the first think [sic] we saw was 3 peacocks which, as soon as they saw us, shot off, trailing their tails with a swishing noise like 3 trains into the undergrowth. Our attention was arrested by a water buffalo and her very young calf; she was giving us a very dirty look as we made a good detour around her. No fish but a good bath, only to get sweaty getting back to camp.
>
> Nov 21 Jungle clearing; the men are getting WOs 25c NCO 15c, men 10c per day, for soul-destroying heart-breaking labour.
>
> Nov 22 – We had some of the kit which we left at Bang Pong today; came by barge, which eases the clothing situation for the time. Caught 1 small fish today (1/2lb).

There seems to be a radio in the camp as he comments in his diary, on 25 November: 'L'Roi [sic] a dire quelque chose d'importance aujourdhui'. [This referred to the Allies' success in North Africa.]

> Nov 30 – On the Rly [railway] today working Southwards. We are meeting with great masses of bamboo; we set alight to it down below and after a while down it comes in showers of sparks and anything up to 80ft in height. It is vicious stuff, having spikes about 7" in length all

over its arms. The big trees are being blasted out of the ground, excepting where the Nips do not lay the charge properly, when the trees merely get a shaking – and this is not infrequent.

6 Dec Jungling Caught some snakes in one of the felled trees; a nip showed us how to cook them after beheading them & skinning them. They were grilled to a nice golden brown & then we ate them; they are quite pleasant, not unlike not-too-salty kipper. There were some lovely chameleons in this tree too; a Nip got hold of one & placed it on the red embers of the fire where it died slowly, being held on the fire by a stick of bamboo. The Nip delighted in this sickening sight; they are very sadistic people.

He and others suffer from the 'squitters' and his diary becomes a catalogue of his illnesses or those contracted by his fellow POWs – diphtheria, dysentery, appendicitis, malaria, ear ache (treated with a hot rice poultice which raised a laugh). At first he is shocked by the deaths – 'Nov 16 Doc's batman died today – sheer murder! Dec 10 "C" died at 8.45pm very suddenly. What a shock!! How will the men fare if it [the illness] kills [someone like] him?' – but as the deaths become commonplace his anger is transformed into a quiet acceptance. In one thirty-hour period at the end of April 1943 seven men died. Atkins had a need to record their deaths and kept lists of the men. In one version he has scribbled their names, address and army number on eight sides of paper, and placed an asterisk next to those who died and where they died. Sometimes he names a specific camp, others have simply 'died in Thailand', occasionally he gives the year. In a second version he has written the list in pencil in alphabetical order in tiny writing on the back of some Japanese forms.

Dec 22 MacDougall DK with malaria & dysentery, been with him most of the afternoon and it was a nightmare. He messed himself last evening & during the night & is still lying there with it all over him. He is covered with a fouled mosquito net over him, and is terribly filthy & emaciated. He was rambling something about his leave being due, going to the river to wash etc. but nothing of importance. A man was brought in from the jungle, a tree having fallen on his leg.

Dec 24 MacD died at 9pm last evening.

Jan 1st Here's to 1943!! It ought to happen this year. Everyone is saying how glad they are that 1942 has gone being so black especially for us.

In May 1943 Tommy Atkins became desperately ill with diarrhoea and vomiting. He drifted in and out of consciousness for six days. During this time he passed gallons of what looked like rice water and vomited a similar liquid. He was repeatedly sick – he lost count after thirty-six – and when he was helped to the latrines he passed out. His friends watched as his fingers and toes shrivelled to bone, skin and nails and his face sunk into gaunt hollows around the eyes, temples and cheeks.

I still maintained touch with an unearthly world, my only connection with it being to my ears which, to me seemed to be connected with a white hot piece of brain which recorded all that was going on around me. I was given an injection in my arm & I heard Pop V whisper 'Cholera I believe', then I was put on to a stretcher & carried to the death chamber of the dysentery ward – although the orderlies who carried me knew me well they didn't recognise me, I had changed so much.

He was taken to an attap shack where a 'feeble oil lamp flickered in the hands of the orderly'. Three doctors' faces stood out from the gloom. He was given a morphine pill and Major Cyril 'Pop' Vardy injected two pints of a saline solution into the elbow joint of his right arm. One doctor muttered something about 'bubbles in the blood' but Pop reassured him. Later he was given a 24-hour course of MB 693 tablets in twelve hours.

7 May My Javanese partner in the Death Chamber died while I was taking my morning fluids & was followed out by a Dutch Lieut. I am hoping to get out into the main ward today or tomorrow. Thank God for my recovery!!

9 May Feeling much better now & in the main ward 2 more men died last night 1 Dutch, 1 English. They were complete opposites, the Dutchy saying that he no longer wished to live at about 3pm & died accordingly at 11.30pm; the Englishman had been expected to die 3 days ago, but continues to talk to his wife 'Pat' & fights like hell in the hope of seeing her again. He died at 4.30am.

Owing to the bugs in here I have prevailed upon the Dr to allow me to go back to the hut, away from the contact & smell of death. Of course I am 'bed down'.

May 10 Had a grand sleep last night. Most of the chaps are amazed, but very decent to me, one saying 'You were at death's door a few days ago & here you are as good as new with some fattening up.'

May 11 Vomitting & squittering last night. I am on a strict diet from now on. Stronk [?] committed suicide last night in the Dip ward; he had won the fight too.

Once Jack Chalker was well enough to leave the dysentery ward he started to help the doctors and medical orderlies who worked at the camp. Captain Jacob Markowitz, a Romanian-born Canadian with jet black hair and brown eyes, became well known for remaining unruffled during the most testing surgical operations. Marko, as he was called, was a gregarious man who before the war had worked as Associate Professor of Physiology at the University of Toronto where he developed a form of blood transfusion for dogs and, in 1932, performed the first heart transplant from one warm-blooded animal to another. He was one of a small number of Jewish POWs held in the Far East.

Marko performed his first leg amputation in April 1943. He had been reluctant to carry out the operation, fearing that the lack of proper medical instruments and poor levels of hygiene meant the patient was unlikely to survive. But there was already a high mortality rate among men who had contracted tropical ulcers when their bare feet and legs were cut by bamboo or rocks. As Jack Chalker's drawing of their injuries shows, the ulcers stripped away the flesh to reveal bones and tendons, so that the men became living anatomy lessons.

Marko's first operation took place on a makeshift bamboo operating table but as the volume of operations grew the medical team set up a dedicated attap and bamboo theatre lined with bits of old green mosquito netting. Within nine months, according to Jack Chalker's estimates, Marko had removed over 120 legs, as well as performing other operations. He did not have a surgical saw but relied on an old tenon-saw, supplied by a British carpenter and sterilised by boiling, knives and bits of wire. Novocaine offered the only pain relief and the patients were conscious throughout and may have been dimly aware of the running commentary Marko provided for the benefit of the orderlies stationed around him in their shorts. Chalker made surgical notes and sketches as Marko worked.

He remembers one of the early operations:

Marko had sawn the leg off and we just put this aside. It was the end of a hut and two men walked by and were absolutely horrified, and Marko was sawing away, and were standing there for a moment and quite suddenly the tourniquet broke and a jet came out of his artery and went straight over them and Marko said, 'That'll teach them!' and I put the new tourniquet on and finished the job but I found that quite horrific. I'd never seen a leg taken off before and because you were helping and assisting you had to go through with it you couldn't just be sick or something. So that was a weird introduction to the whole thing. After that it simply became – not a routine – but you were much more prepared for it in your mind and also prepared for how you could help or not.

It helped one's survival because I wasn't just thinking 'Oh, have I got to go to the latrines yet again or when is the next bit of malaria going to start?'

Occasionally the Japanese would watch the operations. 'They didn't want to admit it but I think that they had some respect for this. Some came in and one went outside and fainted; another one was terribly sick. They'd never seen anything quite like it. They'd been murdering people all over the place but they'd never actually witnessed a leg leaving a patient.'

Chalker also removed the dead tissue from infected ulcers and one of his drawings from this time shows a hellish scene in which an orderly scoops out maggots and pus from a tropical ulcer with an old dessertspoon and surgical forceps. The patient gasps in agony, his mouth a black hole of pain.

Other drawings record the inventiveness of the medical care. The orderlies made dressings from scraps of mosquito netting, rags taken from dead POWs and soiled bandages that they scraped off, boiled and re-used. As in Europe, the malleability and strength of tins made them suitable for a range of purposes. An old can fixed to bits of stethoscope tubing produced a saline drip to help drain ulcers and the lid of a Dutch army mess tin was fashioned into a retractor for leg amputations. A condensed milk tin covered in gauze and fitted to a gas mask formed an anaesthesia mask and at Nakhon Pathom Hospital camp an old Ovaltine tin became part of a surgical suction pump. Patients were fitted with ileostomy and colostomy bags made from Dutch Army water bottles, which were more compact than British bottles. They were edged with rubber from lorry tyres and held in place with webbing. Distilled water was produced from stills made from old tins and bits of stolen pipes.

At Nakhon Pathom all sorts of Heath Robinson contraptions were constructed to help POWs recover from illnesses or to adapt to their changed bodies. The medical team built an orthopaedic bed from buffalo hide, ropes made from stolen hemp and bamboo lashed together with rattan. They even built a wooden exercise bike. The rate of what Chalker calls 'the leg off business' led to a high demand for artificial limbs. The simplest were made from split bamboo attached to 'buckets' stuffed with kapok from nearby trees and held in place with a belt. Wooden prostheses, which bent at the ankle and knee, gave the wearer more freedom because he could move without the aid of a crutch. This must have been so much more comfortable than an artificial leg made – with great ingenuity – by Royal Engineers in Singapore out of pieces of a crashed aeroplane. It weighed 7½ pounds and the metal must surely have heated up in the tropical sun. The leg is a curious Calamine lotion-pink colour – perhaps to mimic the man's skin tone – and has a brown and silver foot, as if he is wearing spats. The high number of amputations in the Far East may explain why POWs became so skilled at producing these artificial limbs. Similar examples in Europe appear basic by comparison. One made in Germany in 1940 looks like a grotesque shooting stick: the leg is a piece of wood with a rubber tip at the bottom and part of a jackboot at the top.

Ronald Searle has said that he decided to make himself an unofficial war artist as a way of recording the victims of the railway but Chalker was not conscious of making a pictorial record of the atrocious conditions under which men lived. He was keener to record the extraordinary medical feats that were performed daily. But without his art, and that of the other artists, there would be only a scant visual record of the camps. The range of his work – people, wildlife, medicine, landscape – was, as he says modestly, 'sufficient to give an overall sniff of the whole thing'.

Other artists made contributions that reflected their own distinctive style. George Sprod, a farm labourer from Adelaide who had lied about his age in order to join the Australian Artillery, had always wanted to be a cartoonist. In Thailand he produced cartoons and caricatures to amuse his fellow POWs. They show men coping with the trials of being a prisoner in the jungle: in a 'Jap Happy Christmas' cartoon POWs sing carols while sheltering from the monsoon; in another they look up from a vegetable patch and giant palm tree at a bomb heading straight for them. A collection of his work called *Smoke-oh* helped lift the mood on the hospital wards. Later, in Changi Gaol, he worked with Ronald Searle on the magazine, *Exile*.

Stanley Gimson, who was from Glasgow and a lieutenant in the 1st Indian Heavy Anti-Aircraft Regiment, Indian Artillery, was a fine draughtsman who, like Chalker, showed everyday life as well as medical scenes in pen and ink. His panorama of Chungkai shows huts behind furrowed fields and, in the distance, mountains. In another drawing he takes a spectator's view of the open-air stage during a performance at the same camp. Harsher drawings show the scaffolding supporting the bridge at Tamarkan (more commonly known as the bridge on the river Kwai), a surgeon performing an appendectomy in a bamboo operating theatre at Chungkai and the gloomy interior of Kanyu Riverside Camp dysentery ward.

Chalker also gave massages to the invalids, particularly the amputees who had lost the movement of other parts of their body due to sitting or lying for so long in one position. He had learnt something of this skill from an army friend who was a trained masseur and this, together with his growing knowledge of anatomy – through drawing and talking to the medics about physiotherapy – helped him to bring life back to torpid bodies by gentle massage of parchment-thin skin. One case that brought him particular satisfaction was a man who was suffering from a neurological problem in his lower face similar to lockjaw. He was unable to open his mouth and, as a result, could not eat. The doctors had tried everything and had even brought in a spiritualist to summon help from 'the other side' but nothing worked. The man was starving to death.

I was sure this was a muscular thing and we had a bash at his face and it might have been sheer auto suggestion or whatever, I don't know, but his jaw started to come open and he started to eat and again I'm not telling that because it was me, I'm just saying how lovely it was that by some fluke something could happen because he was well on the way and that's why I think massage is so invaluable.

He passed on his knowledge of massage and anatomy through lectures he gave to other POWs who, though ill themselves, were helping the medical orderlies. Instead of a blackboard he drew on the emaciated backs of his fellow POWs with coloured chalk. 'We had these kind of skeletal creatures and you could see *everything*.'

By this stage in their captivity most men's uniforms were reduced to rags or they wore a 'Jap-happy' loincloth. Being a POW had robbed them of all their inhibitions. Most had suffered the indignity of losing control of their bladder and bowels at some point – for many this had become a way of life. Death, too, was all too familiar. Lines that were taught in childhood and strictly observed in the armed services were crossed daily. A black, gallows humour thrived.

'Something terribly funny – in a sick way – happened,' Chalker remembers.

I was very badly beaten up and I had a big hole between my eyes and they couldn't close it and I couldn't see out. I thought I'd lost the sight in my left eye. But never mind, damn it, there were people dying all over the shop and I was lying next to an Australian in the ulcer hut who'd just had his leg off that afternoon. I think there must have been 150 people in there, and lying on one of these bamboo racks in the middle was a man in my own regiment who wasn't very bright. He wasn't off his head but he was just pretty thick and very dim-witted and he had a bad ulcer which had granulated very, very well and he was one of these people who was in a reasonably fit state and could have made it quite well.

But anyway I was lying there feeling a bit odd and there was this Aussie with me who'd just had his leg off and this man in the middle and it was dark, at night, and during the night this man was sitting up – the ulcer patients used to sit up and just rock to ease the pain – and he was doing this and he was saying [in groaning voice], 'I'm going to die, I'm going to die.' And he was the last person in that hut [who was going to die] and then this Aussie next to me said, [in thick Australian accent] 'If you're going to die, mate, for Christ sake bloody well hurry up and bloody do it cos I want some sleep.'

That's verbatim, I've never forgotten those words and within two hours this man had died and the Aussie was nudging me, course I couldn't see him. He said [ashamedly], 'poor bastard, that's the last thing anybody said to him.' And in a way, it was funny.

At Chungkai, an ear, nose and throat specialist successfully grafted a piece of skin over the hole between Chalker's eyes that had refused to close up. He recovered from the operation in a hut where a man had tried to cut his own throat four times. Mental illness was a big problem on the railway and several diarists write about how some men surrendered the will to live. Those who had given up would fix their attention on the roof in a gaze that became known as the 'attap stare'. Men whose mental illness took a more violent form would lash out at other prisoners. In one camp, the Japanese allowed the POWs to build two six-foot square cages as a sort of bamboo asylum for the worst cases. In Jack Chalker's final camp at Nakhon Pathom Hospital camp, men who had suffered mental breakdowns were kept in a separate secure compound where he would visit them to encourage them to do some sort of physical exercise. Most sat silently weeping, some with rags over their heads. Only the Walter Mitty character whom he had known at Chungkai when he enjoyed taking the role of a Wild West cowboy showed any inclination to move and would enjoy playing hide and seek around the latrine.

Mental illness could take several forms. Alistair Urquhart remembers that most POWs on the railway talked to themselves. Every morning he would repeat the mantra, 'Survive this day' and he often experienced flashbacks to funny moments in his childhood. His eccentric Auntie Dossie regularly featured in these scenes and the memory of her would make him burst out laughing to the extent that tears would tumble down his face in a display similar to the 'camp giggle' that Laurens van der Post observed in Java.

The appearance of mental instability could even work in a POW's favour as two privates in the Argyll and Sutherland Highlanders discovered. They recognised that the Japanese and Korean guards found any inkling of madness deeply unsettling and calculated that any apparent signs of it would help to keep them at arm's length. To feign lunacy they created a phantom dog which they took everywhere with them. They threw sticks for him and praised him as a 'Good dog' when he brought them back. They gave him drinks of water and imaginary food and paused while he relieved himself against posts. As a result the Korean guards gave them both a wide berth.

As Chalker lay recovering from his operation, the mentally ill patient in his hut decided to make a fifth attempt to kill himself. He jumped off his bed covered in blood as a nearby patient groaned: 'God, he's done it again!' Obviously, his latest bid had failed so he ran the length of the hut and hurled himself into a pile of red-hot wood ash outside the cookhouse. As he hurtled into the fire he sent sparks into the air like a 'great firework display'.

But he had failed to notice that the fire was on a steep bank on the other side of which was the river. He shot through the cloud of ashes and right into this water. The cooks jumped in to rescue him and because he had been running so fast, he had avoided major burns. This last desperate attempt to die by his own hand provided a shock treatment that saved him. He started to learn Dutch and became interested in what was on offer in the camp.

'He went home a more intelligent, searching person and it all came out of this performance, this firework display that we all laughed at.'

Archaeologist on the 'Death Railway'

Survival was as much about finding a mental release as physical endurance. Ronald Searle compared his psychological state after sixteen hours of dragging rubble in the oppressive Thai heat to a drug-induced or religious trance. 'On many occasions there would come a bizarre moment when the mind liberated itself from the body and went off independently into the most incredible flights of fantasy.'

Some prisoners burrowed into their memories for comfort; others like Jack Chalker derived pleasure from the wildlife around them. A few, despite their desperate situation, studied the unusual butterflies, birds and insects around them. One POW in particular discovered a reason to keeping going in the very earth that the men were excavating to build the railway.

H.R. van Heekeren, who was more commonly known as Bob, was born in 1902 in Semarang, central Java, but spent his childhood in Rotterdam where he enjoyed the circus, boxing, football, sailing and adventure stories such as James Fenimore Cooper's *The Last of the Mohicans*. The tobacco plantations of the Dutch East Indies allowed him to fulfil those early dreams of adventure and in 1923 he boarded a Dutch steamer for Java. Much later he distracted his fellow POWs from the bitter cold of a Japanese mining camp with the story of what happened when he met a young French archaeologist on the ship who relieved him of his virginity and taught him how to read hieroglyphics. Madeleine was on her way to the Far East to investigate the migration route of the Tartars whom she believed had reached Java because of two small bronze statues of riders that had been found there. When they parted she asked van Heekeren to find another one for her to study.

This romantic quest led to a passion for prehistory. 'I threw myself with enthusiasm into Java's grey past, collected a mass of literature, studied the history and began tentatively to hunt around [for Tartar stones],' he wrote later in his memoir.

Over the next eighteen years he used all his spare time as a tobacco planter to study the region's geology and natural history. He was nearly killed when he climbed to the top of a volcano and it started to erupt; he excavated caves where he found human skeletons and bone tools and collected Javanese manuscripts for an established philologist. And eventually he found a little bronze rider and sent word to Madeleine, only to discover that she had died.

He recorded his findings and wrote papers for academic publications. He read about the latest excavation techniques being used in Europe and picked up tips when a palaeontologist from the Dutch East Indies Department of Antiquities arrived to investigate sites he had identified. He used his leave to visit archaeological digs in the Netherlands, England and Kenya. But despite his enthusiasm and knowledge he had no official connection with an academic organisation and was only ever, as he said later, 'an enthusiastic, competent amateur'. Being a POW was to change his status and his career.

He was held at a camp in Malang, East Java, and his wife and two sons were interned. From the start of his imprisonment he found unlikely ways to stimulate his mind and began to study beetles by catching them in jars to observe their breeding habits before releasing them. This came to an abrupt end when the area where the beetles' food grew was dug up to create a vegetable patch.

When he left Malang on 9 January 1943 he had no idea where they were going but the Japanese commander told them it would be a better camp and they supposed it would be somewhere in East Java. After a train and sea journey they arrived at Changi where after a week they were woken in the middle of the night and half of his group were herded into a goods wagon. Two of his best friends who were not chosen rushed to say goodbye and they managed to press hands. They never met again.

He arrived at the base camp of Nong Pladuk on 9 February 1943 and went straight to a village called Taroewa, some eight miles upcountry, where he became part of the 'nail-shift' which dragged the heavy wooden sleepers into place and nailed the rails onto them. They had to meet a target of four kilometres a day and their exposed bodies began to sweat profusely in the blinding sun, attracting wasps and other insects which, if disturbed, stung them.

The gang of POWs who were working ahead of them, cutting a rough track through the forest and building temporary bridges, brought back tales of the terrible conditions ahead. But despite his daily exertions and the worries about where the railway track would lead them, van Heekeren was nevertheless aware of the opportunity to look for prehistoric relics in an area that had never been studied before. He also collected insects and butterflies.

He knew that if prehistoric tribes had ever wandered through Thailand they would have followed the course of the river that would provide food, drink and a passable route. The POWs were shifting tonnes of earth each day in the low, flat country beside the river and he began to peer into the recently disturbed earth. One of his first finds was some shards of a clay pot decorated with rope impressions that he recognised as probably Neolithic.

When they moved north to Bankao, between Wampo and Chungkai, he noticed a change in the landscape. While most POWs were unable to see beyond the agony of each long day, his knowledge of geology and archaeology told him that the wide gravel bank about ten metres above the river had been deposited in a period of increased rainfall during the middle Pleistocene era. The river terrace's height meant it was the oldest along the river. In order to flatten the ground, the POWs had to excavate the bank and his attention 'sharpened'. 'There was something in the air,' he wrote later. And sure enough he uncovered what, to the untrained eye, looked like a large stone with chippings on one side. 'I took it in my hands and inspected it from all sides, all Japanese guards forgotten.'

He immediately identified it as a quartzite hand-axe. Similar objects had been found in the Punjab, on the terraces of the Irrawaddy in Burma, in Malacca and northern China. In each case they had been found with the fossilised remains of a now extinct world. He had just uncovered a hand-axe that was about 3,000 years old. He found three more within a five-metre radius. 'I felt immediately that here in Siam I had filled an important gap in a culture that had covered a large part of South East Asia during one of the oldest phases of man's development.'

Encouraged by his success, he started to look in the caves that they occasionally passed in 'fleeting, superficial visits, snatched if I could briefly escape the attention of the Japanese guards'. Sometimes he would swim across the river and in a cave north of the village of Wampo he found more stone tools – this time dating from the Middle Stone Age. A few weeks later he found more beautifully polished stone axes from an earlier period in excavated ground beside the railway. He studied the area from Wampo as far north as the Three Pagodas Pass, where the railway chugged into Burma. He hid his finds or carried them with him, aware that he had to preserve what he referred to as 'important documents' until the end of the war – which might be years off.

The rains began in April when they were deep in the jungle and everything turned to mud. They tried to keep their spirits up by telling stories at night or during the day finding optimistic signs in nature – birds flying in a V formation which they took as a portent of victory. By now the sun had blackened their skin, they wore loin clothes and had long beards. 'Slowly we were falling back into the Stone Age lifestyle.' They became adept at spotting plants, making snares to trap lizards and gathering mussels from the river and berries, tree roots and birds' eggs from the forest.

His finds were repeatedly confiscated or thrown away but his passion for the old stones had become so well known among POWs that there was always someone to pick them up and return them to him. When the railway was finished, they were taken back to Nong Pladuk before being sent in a party of fitter POWs to a mine in Japan. Their beards and hair were cut off which led to such a dramatic change in appearance that for a while they could only recognise each other by their voices.

On the day they left for Singapore his entire collection of stone tools was confiscated during a general inspection. Several officers who asked the Japanese to return them were beaten up. 'Lots of people had done their best, and for more than a year I had carried the stones around with me, but now it seemed they were lost again forever. I accepted the inevitable and put it out of my mind.'

But during an inspection on the quay at Moji in Japan a Dutch doctor told him that his stones had been found in a Korean guard's luggage. Without hesitation van Heekeren stole the stones back and for the first time ever he was overlooked during the inspection that followed. Only one stone was missing – a beautiful polished shoulder axe that he had last seen on the table of a Japanese commander in Nong Pladuk where it was being used as a paperweight.

Entertainment and Ingenuity
in Thailand

Like Jack Chalker, Fergus Anckorn found himself in a bamboo sick ward at Chungkai. But, although he was now wearing just a blue cotton 'jap happy', a banana leaf hat that had once belonged to a native and nothing on his feet, he had so far avoided the deadly ulcers. Instead, he was suffering from burns sustained when he was perched high up on the wooden viaduct at Wampo. Here he had found himself suddenly gripped by a bout of vertigo that froze him to the spot. A Japanese guard, furious that he had stopped working, tipped hot creosote over him. His hat had protected his head and face but his body was badly blistered. The injury allowed him to 'escape' from the drudgery of the railway to what he later viewed as his 'salvation' at Chungkai.

He had arrived in Thailand a few months before the start of the 'speedo' stage of the railway construction. In May 1943 the Japanese demanded an even greater effort to finish the overland link with Burma because of the Allies' success in mining strategic ports such as Rangoon and Moulmein from the air, making it more perilous for the Japanese to take the long journey by sea. The deadline for completion of the railway was brought forward from December 1943 to August. To meet what was already a punishing schedule they shipped in POWs from the Dutch East Indies, reinforcements from Singapore and local Asian men. Not only was the work even more physically demanding during the 'speedo' period but the influx of labour meant there was less food and fewer medical supplies and, as the working parties pushed further into the jungle, the huts were poorly constructed. Then, in May, the monsoon and cholera hit.

Before he was sent to Wampo, Anckorn had been given one of the standard postcards to send home from Kanburi. It offered little chance for expression and was merely a matter of crossing out what was least accurate or likely to worry relatives.

> I am interned in [here he wrote] 'No. 1 POW CAMP THAILAND'
> My health is excellent
> I am in hospital [he scribbled this out]
> I am working for pay.
> I am not working. [he scribbled this out]
> Please see that . . . . [he wrote] 'your health + Luce' is taken
> care
> My love to you [signed] Ferg

It was usual for POWs to cross out 'I am in hospital' and he also scribbled through 'I am not working for pay' but the marks that he used to obliterate these phrases were actually Pitman shorthand which his mother, who was a skilled secretary, could decode as 'Kanburi Camp' and 'Don't worry'. He also added a flourish to the 'F' in his signature which meant 'still' and extended the 'g' to incorporate the shorthand for 'smiling'. His nickname at home was Smile and one of the last things his mother had said to him before he left Liverpool was to 'keep smiling'.

As the Japanese were painfully slow at censoring the cards, the commanding officer had persuaded them to let him do the job and Anckorn felt he had to warn him that his contained a code since he would have been punished too if the guards had discovered it. But, Toosey reasoned, as he could not understand the code he felt able to let it through.

At Wampo he felt the full force of the 'speedo' order. They worked all day and sometimes into the night, with only about six hours in which to eat, wash and sleep. Some men had to make 3 feet deep holes for dynamiting using a 7-pound hammer and steel bar that numbed their whole arm. As the POW became exhausted his aim grew less accurate and accidents happened. Others dug with primitive *chungkols* and removed the earth in baskets passed along a human chain. The guards, too, whether because they were being harassed by their superiors or because they were simply sadistic, were easily roused to violence. The *yasume*, or rest day, that was allowed every ten days in most camps was forgotten in this 'speedo' period.

As stories started to spread about men forced by the Japanese to dig their own graves Anckorn become concerned that, if this proved to be his fate, his family would never know what had happened to him because he had lost his identification tags. A Dutch friend, who had been a jeweller in peacetime, offered to make a dog tag for him. He used a sharpened nail to engrave Anckorn's details onto a piece of aluminium mess tin that he fitted onto a bangle made out of wire. The object looks like a grand label that might hang from a carafe to announce its contents as port or brandy but the bangle is so small that it could be a child's. He remembers that it dangled loosely from his emaciated wrist. 'I was so pleased with that because I thought if I do end up in a grave and I'm found one day they'll know that I'm in it.'

A friend of his wore something similar, as well as a chain with his sweetheart's name on it. He would kiss it before he went to sleep every night. Anckorn wrote later of his own 'code for living': 'shave daily, wash well, walk from one place to another fixed in my mind, as opposed to meandering . . . I always used to try and go to sleep with a smile on my face.'

Anckorn became adept at finding new uses for damaged objects. When he was looking for firewood in the jungle he came across the bezel of a watch. It had lost its glass face and strap but it was about the right size to hold a photo of Luce. On the day of their engagement she had gone to a Polyfoto kiosk (the 'Poly' photographs she mentioned in one of her letters), which were all the rage before the war, and had a series of around forty-eight miniature portraits taken in quick succession. The one she gave to Gus fitted snugly into the watch's frame and he made a strap for it out of a collar of an old shirt, adding a buttonhole and button so that he could wear it on his wrist.

By November 1942 Tommy Atkins was based at Tarsao, a camp just north of the Wampo Viaduct. As a young boy growing up by the coast at Dartmouth in Devon, fishing had always been a favourite form of escape. Now it provided both a reminder of home and a vital source of food. His diary entries are peppered with references to fishing and fishing competitions. Occasionally, when the Japanese used explosives to clear some of the rocks, the fish had merely to be gathered from the riverbank.

The jungle was both fascinating and fearsome to him and he became attuned to its sounds and colours – a forest fire set the monkeys 'swinging and chattering', a 'Jap' took a shot at a crocodile 'close enough to scare the beasty off in a lather of foam'. The jungle ruled his daily life and became both verb and adjective. When they cut through the vicious bamboo they went 'jungling'; the elephants that arrived to help carry the great logs of teak wood, to shift rocks and push over boulders were, like their keepers, 'jungli'.

The mahouts sat astride the elephants' necks and controlled them with a stick. Occasionally they lost control and would run amok, scattering terrified POWs. At one camp a man was flung into a ditch and only avoided being trampled to death because the elephant's foot was too wide to reach into the crevice.

POWs waged constant war against rats. Professional footballer, Johnny Sherwood remembers being 'invaded' by them at night. 'Where they all came from I don't know, but they would come into our hut, and simply run over us, it sent shudders through you, and some of these rats were as big as half grown cats.'

He would jump out of bed and frighten them off but some of his friends were too ill or too weak to do the same. 'Some of these rats had the time of their lives, this was of course something we had to learn to live with. What most of us did was to wrap ourselves completely in our blankets, and try to ignore them but it really was an awful sensation.'

A few POWs caught them, skinned them and stewed them but, although Sherwood would eat almost anything, he did not think he could keep the food down and he knew he had to avoid vomiting.

In July 1943 a man in Atkins's camp devoted much of his spare time to making 'snooses' (a cross between a noose and snare) to catch the vermin that swarmed through the hut at night. 'Damned things nibble anything eatable that isn't in a tin & run over us keeping us awake,' Atkins wrote. 'To crown it all, they leave their droppings wherever they feel disposed – on blankets, plates etc.'

They were still a problem in February 1944: 'Commenced a war against rats about a week ago.' They laid poison and caught about a hundred in one day. Post mortems on four 'proved several possible plague symptoms'.

On 19 July 1944 Atkins recorded what he described as a 'partial eclipse of the sun up to 50% being hidden. The light was only about the strength of a normal English summer's day.' At Kanburi, J.G. Brian Millns remembered 'one hot sunny day we were surprised by a creeping darkness. So also were the monkeys as total silence fell on the jungle. We were witnessing a total eclipse of the sun.' This sudden disappearance of the blinding light that made their days so uncomfortable and the way that jungle creatures reacted to it must have been particularly unnerving.

Fergus Anckorn's burns recovered surprisingly well at Chungkai and he started to help out at the ulcer ward and to perform magic tricks to cheer up the other patients. He volunteered to help prepare corpses for burial in a small hut where he sewed rice sacks together to make a sort of body bag. He slept in the hut with stacks of bodies around him that made unearthly noises during the night as the emaciated frames continued to expel gas. He was untroubled by his sleeping companions, merely thankful that he was out of the mud.

The arrival of Dutch POWs brought a welcome surprise. He was working in the jungle one day when he heard a British POW arguing with a Dutchman. He immediately recognised the foreign accent as belonging to Frans Bakker, a young man whom he had first met in the swimming pool near his home in Kent when he was taking a break from selling trees and shrubs for his father's horticultural business. Anckorn lost contact with him when he went to work on a tea plantation in the Dutch East Indies. Although British and Dutch POWs did not always get on well, he found it easy to resume his pre-war friendship and discovered that through his contact with the Dutch at Singapore he could understand quite a bit of their language.

His newly found expertise at sewing gave him the chance to earn a little cash by repairing clothes which were constantly drenched by sweat and ripped by bamboo. Bakker also had a racket which involved collecting the slivers of soap left after the men washed themselves. He put them in a pillowcase and used it to clean their clothes. The humid weather dried the clothes quickly and allowed him to offer a 'same-day' laundry service; he even 'pressed' them by sleeping on top of them. Anckorn pointed out that he could offer a mending service and they went into business together.

Occasionally the guards recognised that particular POWs had certain skills that could be useful to them. Back home in Paisley, near Glasgow, Lieutenant John McCallum had worked in a family-run dye business. On the railway he managed to create a red-brown dye from wood-chips and pale green from leaves, and from these 'a dark khaki'. In a letter home in September 1945, he wrote: 'We did nip clothing mostly, but it was more interesting than doing the ordinary coolie work!' They also had a soap and paper plant, a spinning mill which used banana tree fibre and a laboratory where he spent most of his time when not dyeing. The Japanese commandant was particularly interested in chemistry and encouraged these ventures to try to impress his senior officers. Despite a lack of chemicals the POWs managed to produce alcohol for the hospital, ether, acetic acid, carbon paper, waterproofing agent and clove oil. McCallum gave a talk to his fellow prisoners about the process of dyeing and the paper they made was used for drawing cartoons.

J.G.B. Millns, who had set up a library using books he found at a polo club at Singapore, managed to take his camp bed and his tin trunk with him to Thailand. The tin trunk was to prove the key to the cottage industry he established 'upcountry'. By his own admission he was very fortunate to avoid the worst horrors of the railway work. At Kanburi he had an administrative job for a year, lost *only* a stone in weight and, apart from a scorpion bite, was generally in good health. When the Japanese started to find extra jobs for the officers – working in the cookhouse and canteen, manning the water pumps or digging slit trenches in case of Allied air raids – he began to think of more productive, and less arduous, ways of keeping them busy. 'It was this useless occupation that gave me the idea that perhaps I could make toilet paper, a much needed material, as we had none. Having spent some months learning the basic principles pre-war in the family business in our paper mills at St Paul's Cray, I at least knew what was needed.'

It took him several weeks of experiments before he produced something that looked anything like paper. A fellow POW entertained him while he worked by whistling his way through every Mozart opera until he managed to produce a suitable pulp from rice straw – a commodity used in the camp for food and packing. He needed a hut big enough for the twenty-five POWs ('mostly old friends') who would carry out the work and arranged for an interview with Captain Noguchi ('the dreaded Nogoochi'). To his surprise, Noguchi was fascinated by the project and gave Millns 'every encouragement, which later became an embarrassment'. As well as the workshop, they were allowed a hut with four *kaulis* (large cast iron pots), which were normally used for cooking rice in, on open fireplaces where they boiled the rice straw.

Millns collected wood ash from the cookhouse, sifted it into a fine powder and rinsed it in a perforated forty-gallon drum of water. This formed a clear potassium carbonate in which the rice straw, which had been cut into one-inch strands, was boiled for six hours. The team of POWs beat the resulting pulp in buckets using wooden clubs for about half an hour and finally rinsed it to remove dirt or alkali. A jolly Dutchman made 12 x 6 inch frames covered with a gauze of mosquito netting nailed tightly over them. Millns poured a layer of the pulp into them which when dried in the sun formed a sheet of paper. His officer's trunk made an ideal vat for reducing the straw pulp to the right consistency for forming a sheet of paper. As this was the most skilled part of the process he took this over himself and was soon making three sheets a day.

At first they concentrated on making toilet paper but then expanded into thick board for repairing books that had lost their covers. Jim Swanton, the cricket commentator, took charge of this. Millns remembers he 'permanently wore a sling on one arm for no good reason except to fool the Japs and be regarded as a light duty case'. When the Japanese discovered the board they demanded it for their loose-leaf record books but Millns pretended that it was difficult to dry and that only a few sheets could be made – and only when the weather was right. 'The paper factory soon became the star show piece in the camp and frequent visits by high ranking Japanese officers had to be endured with much bowing, followed by curious grunts of approval from the heavily be-medalled Jap visitors.'

Early in 1945 he was ordered to salvage bags of salt, cement and alum from a railway siding that had been bombed by the Allies. The alum allowed him to make paper that would take ink and he started to produce it – presumably for making cigarettes and for writing and drawing on. This type of paper was dried on a tin plate to give a smooth finish to one side. When it was perfectly dry, the other side was smoothed out with a glass bottle.

The Japanese guards were just as impressed by Fergus Anckorn's conjuring skills. Distracting the guards by making pebbles disappear or other tricks was a useful way of extending rest periods or deflecting attention from the other POWs.

We got every hour ten minutes to boil some river water and drink it and these guards I would start doing tricks to and they loved it. The

Chinese and the Japanese are real suckers for magic and sometimes it would go to 45 minutes before they realised and during those 45 minutes and friends of mine like Jack Chalker would be pinching potatoes from the jap stores and it really paid off and in some of the camps the Japanese really liked me. Some would even salute me so I was quite safe with them.

News of his conjuring reached the Japanese Sergeant Major Teruo Saito. 'Whenever he couldn't sleep he would summon me to do magic until he would fall asleep but the best part of it was that he gave orders for me not to be moved out of that camp while he was there.'

Fergus made sure that his tricks always involved food or cigarettes.

Well, I would borrow a coin off him and vanish it and then point to a tin of fish on his table and open it and find the coin in there. I got to eat the fish. Then I would get him to take a card. I remember on one occasion he took the four of hearts and there were bananas there so I picked up the bananas and broke one off and got him to peel it so it fell out in four pieces as he peeled it and I got to eat the banana. Every trick I did with food I got to eat it because they wouldn't touch anything we'd touched because they considered us verminous and foul so I would touch anything I could that was in there that was edible or usable because I ended up getting it.

He was treading a fine line between entertaining the Japanese for the POWs' benefit and risking accusations that he was 'jap-happy' – that is *too* willing to please the enemy. When he was told to perform at a special show in front of important generals he asked permission of his commanding officer, who agreed that there was no danger of him appearing 'jap-happy'. He made sure that he did not have to drag along the official interpreter who had been working hard all day and who was frequently beaten for delivering translations that offended the Japanese. He asked the interpreter to tell him the Japanese sounds for a magician's stock phrases, such as 'pick a card', 'look at it' and 'shuffle the pack', which he took down in shorthand and was able to read back. He became so adept at jotting down phrases in Japanese that the guards sent him on errands, although he often did not know what he was saying. Once he was sent to deliver a message that he innocently read out and which meant, 'Give me a beat-ing'. The Japanese met his request.

His proficiency at mimicking the Japanese sounds backfired when he performed in front of the generals who assumed he was fluent in their language.

The generals were very pleased and they all clapped afterwards. One of them gave me a cigarette, another one gave me a little rice ball and then he started to speak to me so I said, 'I don't understand you.' So he knocked me down and kicked my head in and both eyes were blacked and I know that my top lip was out here somewhere and the reason of course was that they'd heard me speaking Japanese and when he speaks to me I says, 'Sorry, mate'. So they thought I was being absolutely arrogant. So I got really beaten up and I found my way back to the camp. Colonel Toosey was waiting for me and he said, 'My God, Anckorn, what's happened to you?' I said, 'They didn't like the show.' We both laughed about it.

Anckorn much preferred concerts for his fellow POWs. At Chungkai, 300–400 men attended, many 'reserving' their seat by putting a little mat with their name on it in the hut where the performance would take place. A more sophisticated concert party started to perform at a custom-built open air theatre at the end of 1943 but by then he had left Chungkai for the southern tip of the railway at Nong Pladuk, near Bangkok.

The audience of around 2,000 men sat on the ground in a natural basin surrounded by hills in front of a bamboo and attap stage built on an earth mound. It was an elaborate affair with wings and dressing rooms and an orchestra pit in front. The commandant and guards attended regularly in a specially reserved area.

There was fierce rivalry between the Dutch, British and Australian per-formers which helped to keep standards high. One English musician still had his violin, another his trumpet. Other instruments were put together with the usual detritus – a double bass made from a soap box and strung with telegraph wire, guitars from scraps of wood and animal gut, a drum kit from pieces of tea-chests and teak. A few instruments had arrived from the Red Cross at Bangkok. Tom Boardman, from Howe Bridge, near Atherton in Lancashire, who served in the Royal Army Ordnance Corps, played requests on his ukulele that he made after studying instruments played by local boys. He used a South African Red Cross packing case to make the body and telegraph wire for the strings and performed it mainly at Chungkai Base Camp. The instrument, which took two months to make, is now part of the collection at the Imperial War Museum North.

Audiences at Chungkai could watch a wide range of ambitious and sometimes unlikely performances, the words and music either written from memory or composed from scratch and advertised by beautifully drawn posters that showed glamorous women in exotic costumes. *The Circle*, a social satire set in a country house and written by Somerset Maugham in 1921, was put on in April 1944. Leo Britt, a professional actor, directed one of the most successful musicals called *Wonder Bar* in May 1944. His audience was astonished by the costumes, some of which men had brought with them from previous army concerts, and the bamboo stage that had been transformed by whitewash and natural earth dyes. Britt wore a pink loincloth.

When Dutch POWs staged Bizet's *The Pearl Fishers* at Chungkai, the curtain rose to a view of the Grand Canal in Venice painted on coconut matting. The scenery painters had made red from powdered bricks and green, yellow and brown from bullock and buffalo dung.

Usually the Japanese members of the audience enjoyed the perform-ances. At a Christmas concert at Tandjong Priok POW camp in Java the guards laughed 'more than we knew they could' and in Hong Kong they supplied chalk to use as make-up. But occasionally there were misunder-standings. A review called *Thai Diddle Diddle* that followed *Wonder Bar* was banned for no apparent reason, although POWs suspected that an inter-preter may have looked up the word 'diddle' and jumped to the conclusion that the title was a veiled insult aimed at their captors.

Charles A. Fisher, who watched these performances, believed such spectacles had:

The ability instantly to make an entire, and very diverse, audience sud-denly feel transported from its surrounding squalor, filth, and drearily monotonous diet of rice and watery stew, into a totally different – and yet more real – world of beauty and sanity. Even those who had come only for their weekly ration of bawdy jokes went back to their huts almost in a trance. It was the most powerful demonstration of the uplifting powers of genuine art and sheer artistry that I have ever witnessed.

Jack Chalker enjoyed taking part in the entertainment at Chungkai and at Nakhon Pathom hospital camp, where he moved in June 1944. Although the setting was not as beautiful, the theatre at Nakhon Pathom, built on one side of the assembly ground, had bigger wings, a bamboo drop-curtain and 'flies' operated by ropes made from stolen hemp. As at Chungkai, there was a wealth of professional and amateur actors and musicians. Chalker took part in two plays written by the Dutch humorist and playwright, Wim Kan, whom he describes as a 'sort of Peter Sellers of Holland'. His full name was Willem Cornelis Kan and he had been touring the Dutch East Indies with his wife and their highly successful cabaret act when war was declared and he was taken prisoner. He wrote five plays at Nakhon Pathom which were produced first in Dutch and then in English. Chalker appeared in both versions. All scripts had to be submitted to the Japanese Commandant for approval. The actors wrote their individual parts on scraps of paper, sometimes sewing them together to make a booklet. They rehearsed after work at night and at one point, Chalker was rehearsing four shows at the same time.

At a hospital camp actors could only use material that was of no use to the medical staff, who were carrying out complicated surgical procedures including a craniotomy on an American pilot with a brain tumour and blood transfusions in which blood was continuously stirred with a wooden whisk and then filtered through layers or gauze before it was given to a patient. Performers had to be content with materials that were plentiful – bamboo, copra matting, animal and snake skins, feathers and wood, and bits of string and mosquito netting which were more sought after. Professional tailors made needles out of pieces of soft metal taken from army equipment and used them to sew with thread pulled from rags. They stuffed bras with kapok from trees for men like Chalker who took a mischievous delight in their cross-dressing adventures. Bamboo combs helped to tease out stolen hemp that was sewn onto caps to make wigs and then dyed using soot, wood ash, or clays mixed with tapioca flour. The production team concocted make-up and dye for costumes by grinding clay from ponds dug to collect rainwater. This gave them terracotta, grey, yellow and black that they mixed with animal fat. Soot, burnt cork, chalk and betel nut offered a further colour range and boiled bark produced a dark brown.

Although men's possessions had been stripped to the bone it was remarkable how the prospect of a show could magically produce hidden treasures. Far Eastern POWs still talk fondly of a P.G. Wodehouse play that required two women to appear in their underwear. After a mass appeal to the camp two pairs of silk cami-knickers were surrendered (different items of women's underwear appear in different versions of this story). After the play was over the knickers were returned to their owners – no questions asked. Chalker remembers a similar request for a woman's handbag proved successful.

As well as lack of materials the players had to contend with the heat and humidity. Both caused a problem when Chalker helped to make an elephant costume for two men to wear in a review called *The Raj of Coconut*. It was constructed from woven bamboo and tapioca flour boiled to make an adhesive paste and coloured grey with wood ash. The central joke hinged on the elephant being fed a huge tin of baked beans which emerged from its backside after its stomach had gone through a series of convulsions. 'But the trouble was that, almost immediately, the man in the hind legs was completely suffocated. First he was too hot, the ash was coming off, he could hardly breathe and he passed out, so the back legs suddenly collapsed and the front legs walked him off. I mean we were rolling about, it looked as though it was meant to be.'

In an exclusively male environment, female impersonators frequently stole the limelight and performers went to great lengths to appear feminine. Working this magic proved a source of inspiration for both the spectator and the star. Charles Fisher remembers how the prospect of an evening performance could revive starving and sick men who had dragged themselves through a day weighed down by heat and humidity and physical intimidation on the Thailand–Burma Railway. At the weekly open-air concerts at Chungkai camp, 'it was astonishing to see how so many of the least impressive-looking prisoners managed to transform themselves into remarkably glamorous creatures with the aid of locally improvised theatrical make-up and elegant dresses which many of them, who had previously been active in army concert parties, had brought with them into captivity'. At Nong Pladuk, further south on the Thailand–Burma Railway, the concert party members inserted shallots into their bras to give the appearance of nipples.

As in European POW camps, the appeal seems, in most cases, not to have been sexual; rather, they provided a fleeting reminder of a softer element that had been expunged from the POWs' lives. Certainly, some men did succumb to homosexual urges which, in less harsh circumstances, they might have felt compelled to repress. Memoirists tend to be coy about this side of POW life. Fisher, for example, ends his description of the female impersonators: 'Clearly some of our leading ladies seemed to be as intensely sought after by their respective fans as were their real-life counterparts in London's theatre-land, and more than a few wells of loneliness apparently changed overnight into fountains of desire.' Stephen Alexander noticed how flirtatious banter between men was directly linked to diet. Once the POWs on the railway hit the 'egg belt' and food wavered above starvation level, libidos began to twitch back into life.

Of all the female impersonators, two names still have the ability to produce an affectionate smile from Far East POWs. When Bombardier Arthur Butler of the 122nd Field Regiment Royal Artillery transformed himself into Gloria D'Earie *she* became 'exquisite'. She made all her own costumes and moved and spoke just like a woman. Butler was a professional female impersonator and widely regarded as the best in Changi. His act was so convincing that some men found it too painful: they would rather not be reminded of what a woman looked like as it made their separation from wives and sweethearts harder to bear.

Anckorn remembers Bobby Spong as the best drag artist he had ever seen. 'He was a very, very nice chap who worked hard in the hospitals, always on the go but on the night there he was. He was really absolutely just like a woman. You couldn't tell. He was I suppose what you'd call gay now.'

The Japanese guards were fascinated by his act and at Chungkai the camp commandant sat in the front row of the audience, his eyes fixed on Spong. At the end of the show he marched back stage and lifted up his skirt to make sure that the performers had not smuggled in a female performer.

The following description almost certainly refers to Spong:

It was he who played the part of the Jungle Princess in the entertainment at our first Christmas as prisoners [in Changi]. Little did I think then that he and I would be orderlies together in an ulcer ward. He was an extraordinary fellow and so completely feminine in his habits that I often found him most embarrassing. He carried a full set of lady's attire with him and for his stage appearances would wear a complete woman's rig-out, roll-on corsets and all. The Nips would crowd round to see his dresses. He would spend hours over his teeth and hair, talked like a girl – 'Oh dear! Mother's tired' being a favourite phrase – and was a dab-hand at mending clothes. He kept a folder of cuttings which told of his own appearances on the stage and for every show made out a programme with his own name on top of the bill. He would do individual turns in the ward – 'I'm an old Norman castle with a ruined Tudor wing' is the one that sticks in my mind. When he had shaved his hairy chest and legs and was dressed as a woman it was difficult to believe he wasn't the genuine article. I've known him sit on patients' beds looking so much like a woman that they would blush and attempt to cover their nakedness. I could understand their feelings for I myself, who knew him so well, often felt most awkward in his company. The poor chap died at sea and I have often felt since that had he not been so embarrassingly womanish we should have shown more gratitude for his attempt to cheer the most dismal stretch of our time as prisoners.

The shows at Nakhon Pathom and Chungkai were among the most sophisticated on the railway but smaller scale performances took place in many camps outside the 'speedo' period – even if they consisted only of a singsong of 'Green Grow the Rushes, Oh'. Some stagehands worked wonders with hurricane and kerosene lamps and were able to dim the lights and vary their colour.

For Chalker, entertainment was vital for both the audience and the performers. 'It played an enormous part for those of us who had something in it because there was an intent all the time; there was something to look forward to, something to struggle with. And I do think that was terribly important psychologically for some of the desperately ill patients.'

Christmas and New Year were always poignant for POWs when they remembered their families and friends at home and wondered whether this would be their last year in captivity. Performers planned special productions, including pantomimes such as *Babes in the Wood*, which a cast of mainly British POWs performed on a river sandbar at Takanun for

Christmas 1943 where POWs had built a proscenium arch and their audience watched from a terraced slope.

Tommy Atkins spent his first Christmas Eve on the railway in 1942 helping to make an altar from green wood and then fishing: 'I hooked a whopper today – 10lb at least I should think, but my new hook – Norwegian size 12 – straightened out, after about 5 min fight.'

The Japanese allowed 'festivities' to continue until 11 p.m., but they were all in bed by 10-10.30 p.m. A colonel gave a talk on Gallipoli and Atkins ended the day hoping that his family were having a good time. On Christmas Day he wrote:

Dec 25 – Seasons Greetings. Nearly broke my hips this morning, falling from one rock to another about 6ft below, and landing on my hip. A bad bruise but no worse thank God!! The man two away from me won the fishing comp this afternoon with a 3lb approx caught a 2½lb this evening. There was a concert this evening 8.30 pm. which I thought was poor but the men liked it which is the main thing. We had a rice duff made with peanut toffee to celebrate Xmas. Auck's altar was very successful. Many happy returns Lena – the only date I can remember!!

Dec 26 Jungling

Dec 27 Held a Gen Knowledge contest this evening, giving $1 prize. The men seemed to thoroughly enjoy it too.

A year later he was spending Christmas at Tarsao, (also known as Tha Sao). One of the POWs had been 'a guest of the *kempi* [kempeitai] for some days' and an air of tension had descended on the camp, which the celebrations and entertainment – no matter how contrived – went a long way to lift. 'I threw a feeble party to Auck & Col Dunlop & the setting with the moon etc. was best of it,' he wrote.

Jim Swanton was also at Tarsao where he helped to entertain sick POWs with talks about cricket. His audience sat on the slopes of a dip in the ground that made a natural amphitheatre to hear lectures on a range of subjects. Swanton's talks were particularly popular. The Australians and British would fire questions at him and barrack as if they were on 'The Hill' at the Sydney Cricket Ground.

He also helped to produce the weekly 'Radio Newsreel' in which a team of entertainers simulated a live broadcast of documentaries from behind a huge wireless set made from bamboo and matting. The set, which was 9 feet tall and 7 feet wide, stood on a stage made from similar materials. A rectangular section had been cut out of the set about 2 feet from the top and lamps burning peanut oil had been set on a ledge behind and below the gap to give the impression of an illuminated wireless dial. A large hole covered with hessian represented the radio's 'speaker'. The actors who produced the broadcast, and their assistants who produced sound effects, were shielded from the audience by wings of bamboo matting that fanned out from each side of the set. One of the most memorable 'broadcasts' was Swanton's talk on the life of the Australian cricketer, Don Bradman. He was introduced with the words: 'Good Evening. This is the Allied Broadcasting Corporation transmitting from Tarsao and tonight Radio Newsreel brings you a cricketing feature about the world's greatest batsman.'

Weary Dunlop's diary describes how each battalion did something special for their men that Christmas of 1943 – whether giving them a gift, cigarettes or money – and that an extra 25 cents was to be spent on the Christmas meals. The festive entertainment started on 22 December when Dunlop dressed up as Boadicea with a trident and helmet to take part in a balloon debate with Christopher Columbus, Nell Gwynne, Florence Nightingale, cricketer W.G. Grace and comedian Will Rogers. The Christmas Eve pantomime was cancelled due to worries about air raids but a combined Japanese and Allied memorial service for the dead in Thailand was held at 7 p.m. when two wreaths were laid on a cross.

On the afternoon of Christmas Day both POWs and Japanese officers watched *Cinderella* on a small bamboo stage. There was a gasp as the curtain swung back to reveal women and 'elegantly costumed men'. Dunlop was amazed at what could be done with mosquito netting, scraps of cloth, silver foil and tinsel but was amused to spot the tell-tale scabies and ulcer scars on the 'ladies'' legs.

In the evening Doctor 'Pop' Vardy dressed up as Father Christmas and toured the wards with a 'crazy gang' of doctors dressed as maids-in-waiting and clowns. They decked the ward masters as sisters with tin bras and sackcloth hoods with red crosses and gave them a shepherd's crook and a bottle with a teat. Each ward had a lottery in which men won small amounts of money (one or two Thai ticals) or a bar of soap. The parade finished in the concert area where some of the higher ranks were given presentations in front of the 'up patients': Tommy Atkins came off worst when someone put a thunder-box over his shoulders. His head, still wearing spectacles, poked through the hole and he was finally crowned with a 'pee pot'. 'All in fun I suppose', he wrote lugubriously in his diary. 'Far & away a better Xmas & new year than last year & hope is definitely reviving in the hearts of the men. One could feel it in the air. Out this year? Let us hope so anyway.'

'Home' Again: Changi Gaol

Once the railway was completed, thousands of POWs retraced their five-day journey down the Malayan peninsula to Singapore. For many it felt like coming home. Ronald Searle, who returned just before Christmas 1943, later wrote in quasi-religious terms of being 'delivered back' to the island.

They were relieved to leave behind the hard physical labour and the constant supervision by guards and to be back in a more permanent setting where the British Army could at least give the appearance of order. Those who had not been 'upcountry' were shocked by the physical appearance of the returning men. By May 1944, many were on their way to their final prison in the Far East.

On the Thailand–Burma Railway POWs had lived in primitive, makeshift huts. When it rained they waded through muddy paths; often they were surrounded by jungle. Changi Gaol was as starkly modern – if not futuristic – as the camps along the railway were primordial. It was built in 1936 on the eastern side of Singapore, just south of Selarang Barracks, and for most of the war it held civilian internees. It was surrounded by a 'vast unscalable wall with guard-posts incorporated into each angle' and dominated by a great tower on which the flag of the rising sun strained to raise a flutter in the humid weather. The only way in was through a huge metal gate suspended from dome-topped pillars.

Inside the prison, hundreds of metal cell doors opened out onto a spider's web of clattering walkways criss-crossed by steel mesh like a high security penitentiary in America's Deep South where men wait for years on Death Row. Changi had been built to hold 600 criminals; by 1944 an estimated 10,000 POWs were crammed inside or camped outside its walls.

They were mainly British, Australian and Dutch POWs but there were also men from Java and Sumatra, a few American merchant seamen and, bizarrely, some Italians who had stopped at Singapore hoping to refuel their submarine. This last group had arrived in gleaming white uniforms but were soon reduced to the grubby state shared by the other inmates.

Half of the POWs lived in cells where four men shared a room designed for a single occupant. One man slept on the central stone platform with a roommate on the floor either side of him and a fourth lying with his feet or head precariously close to a toilet that no longer worked. The noise, smell and heat were overpowering. The only ventilation came from a small grille window high up near the ceiling and through the doorway that was kept permanently open – a closed door came to represent a signal that a prisoner had given up. If prisoners felt a kind of agoraphobia so far from home in the vast Thai jungle, Changi Gaol represented a similar hopelessness – but underscored with claustrophobia.

James Clavell later used the prison as a backdrop for his bestselling dystopian novel, *King Rat*, which has as its anti-hero a wheeler-dealer American prisoner who runs a ruthless black market within the prison. Although some POWs were outraged at his depiction of the brutal, dog-eat-dog (or man-eat-rat) mentality of inmates, the book and the 1965 film convey the pressure cooker atmosphere of Changi Gaol. The opening scene of the haunting black and white movie, which starred George Segal as the American and James Fox as the naive young British officer, shows a prisoner sitting like a king on the latrine and has a surreal, science fiction quality to it.

As the Allies slowly started to make inroads into the Japanese defences, their efforts had a disastrous effect on Singapore's supply of food. Ronald Searle described their plight with customary understatement: 'the food situation, always precarious, was now verging on the dramatic'. Lower leg muscles became as difficult to control as bowels, teeth loosened and fell out, men struggled to remember the most basic facts – 'Changi Memory' added another phrase to the POW's lexicon of words unique to captivity.

But despite their weakened state, the men were made to carry out heavy labour. Some worked fourteen to sixteen hour shifts in which they flattened the ground for a new military airfield; others unloaded ships at the docks and a few dragged trailers of heavy logs. Those who did not work received half rations. By the end of 1944 the thought of food dominated their every waking moment. In this hopeless, obsessive state anything that took their mind off it gained importance.

James Clavell later said that Changi (although he was probably talking about his collective experience, rather than his time in the gaol) 'became my university instead of my prison. Among the inmates there were experts in all walks of life – the high and the low roads. I studied and absorbed everything I could from physics to counterfeiting, but most of all I learned the art of surviving.'

Ronald Searle arrived at Changi Gaol in May 1944, after a few months recovering at Sime Road. His sketchbook chronicles the overcrowded conditions and the despair of the prisoners. He also drew many of the guards who taunted them with the thought that this was just the beginning of their Hundred Year War. The Japanese faces in his sketches are individuals: smiling, scowling, sleeping, sucking on a cigarette, but always with a gun, bayonet or sword visible or suggested in the background. These faces are so uncomfortably authentic that it is not easy to study them for long or to leave the book of his drawings open at a page on which they feature.

Although a visit from the *Kempeitai* left him terrified that his drawings would be discovered, he occasionally risked taking the Japanese into his confidence. From time to time he was part of small working parties sent to the beach to extract salt from the sea or to repair the Japanese officers' club. During these excursions there was usually only one guard and even he might take the opportunity for a nap, relying on his charges to wake him in time. Searle struck up a relationship with Ikeda whom he recognised was just as bored and homesick as the POWs. He risked showing him a sketch he had made of banana trees and the guard asked him to draw his portrait. Searle kept his first attempt in his sketchbook and the guard sent the final version home on an army issue postcard. In return he allowed Searle leeway to sketch the beach and nearby *kampong*.

The prison's administrator, Captain Takahashi, also took an interest in his work and in July 1944, much to Searle's alarm, asked to see his drawings. He sent a package of sketches that he thought would not prove inflammatory: landscapes, fantasies, portraits of the POWs and 'Prison Headgear', a comic sketch of eighteen different men wearing a motley range of headgear from an RAF type with bristling moustache and peaked cap to a sailor with a hat at a jaunty angle, a smiling POW wearing something like a glengarry and a range of different racial types in homemade and official hats. After three days the interpreter returned the artwork beautifully wrapped in a package and handed over sixty sheets of good quality drawing paper. Takahashi's patronage extended to a brief spell in which Searle worked in the Japanese officers' beach hut where he was left in peace and told to paint a mural. One day Takahashi revealed to him that he had studied in Paris and had ambitions to be an artist. He drew a sketch of a mother and child in Searle's notebook and as he left casually gave him some coloured pencils and wax crayons. A few weeks later Takahashi disappeared from the gaol and Searle's pleasant sojourn came to an abrupt end.

Searle had gained an uncomfortably high profile at Changi through the scenery he had painted for the open-air theatre held in one of the courtyards, posters and programmes he had designed for variety shows and illustrations for the camp magazine *Exile*. All of these activities were ways of taking his mind off food. Another way was smoking anything that might resemble a cigarette for the gratification of ingesting something. In his search for thin paper, he cut out neat squares from carefully chosen pages of his sketchbook and half of *Pickwick Papers* went up in smoke after he had read it five times. He used the whole of Rose Macaulay's *The Minor Pleasures of Life* and made the mistake of telling her when he met her after the war that the experience had brought him a further pleasure. She was not amused.

Sydney Piddington, the young Australian conjuror who had been experimenting with a telepathy act, also provided a diversion for bored, starving men. Eric Lomax remembers him visiting the hospital block with Russell Braddon and asking for volunteers:

> It was eerie, in a darkened prison block, to see them guess the contents of a prisoner's pockets or the name of a man's wife, calling up invisible energies as mysterious as radio waves had been to me as a child. We were probably appallingly credulous, but what they did seemed to us real magic in those last months of the war, as the tension mounted towards a barbaric last stand by the Japanese military rulers.

Piddington had a slight stammer and his 'patter' was not as polished as other performers but he was keeping the sort of company that allowed him to dream of fame and the wider world. His friends included Scott

'Scotty' Russell, a New Zealander whose twin obsessions were moun-taineering – despite his elder brother's death in an avalanche – and botany. Just before the war, Russell had combined postgraduate research at Imperial College, London with exploration. He went to the Arctic and then, in 1939, joined the Karakoram Expedition in northern India. He heard about the outbreak of war on the wireless and allowed himself to explore the Khurdopin Pass before returning to fight for his country. As a POW in Singapore he wrote of that final experience of the mountains: 'As I look back it seems that a gate was then closed – the gate to free planning of our lives, and the key to reopen it is still in an uncertain future.' Russell composed his memoirs – on a stash of military forms – when he was not tending the prison garden and like Bill Murray, who wrote about his Scottish mountains from a European prison, the memory of freedom made captivity more bearable.

Although Piddington had not been sent 'upcountry', his 6ft 2in frame had nevertheless been reduced to under eight stone by tiny rations and the hard physical labour of working on the military airport. The idea of a mind-reading act came to him when he saw an article on telepathy by Doctor J.B. Rhine of Duke University, North Carolina. He began to prac-tise with Russell Braddon. Without Piddington seeing, a third POW would point to one object on a board of possessions and Braddon would attempt to transmit which object it was to Piddington. Gradually they felt confi-dent enough to perform in front of a small audience. At first he would guess colours, numbers and objects thought of by a member of the audi-ence. Then volunteers would write items on a blackboard and Piddington would 'transmit' them to Braddon. Finally, someone wrote a name and address on a scrap of paper and Piddington would use his telepathic powers to convey the information to his blindfolded assistant: 'Winston Churchill, 10 Downing Street, London'. Their act caused enormous debate among POWs and the unwanted interest of General Saito, who demanded to see it for himself. Braddon was convinced that if the telepathy worked, the general would believe their 'turn' involved a hidden radio; conversely, if they failed they would be severely punished. There were spared the per-formance when he went down with a bout of malaria.

In the early days the act was not always successful. For some reason Piddington found it almost impossible to 'read' a Dutch audience. On one occasion, Braddon interpreted a line from Shakespeare, 'And through the instrument his pate made way', as something to do with a bald-headed man being hit with a violin. But when concerts were banned after the Japanese took offence at a song, 'On our Return', the telepathy became even more popular as one of the few remaining forms of entertainment. Piddington's friend, Scotty Russell, added an air of scientific authority by testing them for three hours in a locked cell but Piddington was still able to convey the correct message to Braddon ('Please reserve two rooms immediately at the chalet for two weeks') and pinpoint a line from a book that a doctor had chosen. The scientist provided them with a certificate of what had been achieved but nevertheless maintained that their success could be pure coincidence.

As rations became dangerously short and fears grew about their fate, mind games were one of the very few pastimes left to the POW.

The POW Diaspora

POWs in the Far East had to adapt to a range of different conditions as they were moved from camp to camp, country to country. Each time, they had to find the measure of their guards and make the best of the raw materials available in each new camp. Every time they were moved they did their best to take what possessions they had with them – whether that was Nowell Peach's copy of *Gray's Anatomy*, van Heekeren's precious stones or Tom Boardman's homemade musical instrument.

John Lowe, who had spent the first five months of captivity on Singapore where he entertained his fellow POWs with songs such as 'Rumenough, Dumbenough, Tallenough, Smallenough', was rehearsing on the morning of 24 October 1942 when rumours started that they were soon to leave the island. In the afternoon, Japanese medical orderlies inspected the regiment and tested the men for dysentery by the usual glass rod method before the POWs returned to camp to perform a farewell show in front of a depleted audience.

They boarded the *England Maru*, a ship built on the Clyde in Scotland in 1889 and which he described in his diary as an 'old tub', with no idea where they were going. It was the first of three journeys he would take on board vessels that later became known collectively as 'Hell Ships' due to the horrendous conditions on board. Prisoners were packed into the ship's darkness where they struggled to find space even to lie down among the dead and dying. Guards herded him down into holds divided into coffin-like pigeonholes measuring about 2½ feet square and 6 feet deep.

Sanitary conditions were appalling. Around 1,100 men queued to use three clapboard latrines overhanging the side of the ship. After a few days

most men were suffering from dysentery or diarrhoea and formed a per-
petual queue that weaved through the stifling hold and up the flight of
steps through the hatchway guarded by a sentry who shouted when it was
the next man's turn. Once he had finished his business he rejoined the end
of the queue. He had started the heartbreaking chore of choosing letters
from home to use as latrine paper when someone found some old
American newspapers instead.

To begin with they were allowed out on deck in batches for a few hours
where they washed themselves under a salt-water hose before returning
to the gloom. By the end of October it 'rained like hell' straight down the
hatch and into the hold where they collected it for drinking and washing.
A week later the 'old tub is pitching and rolling madly, bow burying itself
in the waves'. One day the Japanese panicked because they thought they
saw a periscope; the ship – in complete contravention of the Geneva
Convention – carried no Red Cross markings or other indication that it
had POWs on board. The guards were right to fear the threat of attack by
enemy submarine or aircraft: according to one figure 10,800 of the 50,000
prisoners transported by sea in the Far East died during the journey and
one in three of those were killed by friendly fire.

For some POWs, the hell ship ordeal came after they had endured the
terrible hardship of the Thailand–Burma Railway. When Johnny
Sherwood returned from 'upcountry' in June 1944, he worked at first on
the docks in Singapore until a Japanese interpreter told the professional
footballer that he and his mates would soon be going to Japan, the beautiful land of the Rising Sun, where they would rest until the end of the
war. He assumed they would be travelling in ships clearly marked with the
Red Cross symbol but became alarmed when he struck up a conversation
with a friendly Chinese man he met at the docks who warned him that
American submarines were torpedoing every ship on its way to Japan.
When he boarded the *Kachidoki Maru* conditions were even more suffo-
cating than those experienced by John Lowe. There was only one toilet for
all the men but, fortunately for Sherwood, he was told to guard a hold and
make sure that one man came up at a time to use it. The heat below was
intolerable and the POWs, who were only allowed a pint of water a day,
frequently passed out from dehydration. On another hell ship, the *Oryoku
Maru*, prisoners driven mad by thirst were said to have attacked their companions for their blood, although this may be apocryphal.

On the night of 11 September 1944, a pack of American submarines was taking up position to attack the convoy that included Sherwood's ship. About one o'clock in the morning a submarine torpedoed a large oil tanker that then ripped into the hull of the *Kachidoki Maru*, sending the ship listing to one side. Sherwood felt sick as he thought of the men down below and went to give them what water he had. Back on deck he could see ships being sunk 'all over the place', 'the whole sea area seemed to light up with exploding torpedoes, and ammo magazines on the Jap warships'. The Japanese guards were rushing around screaming and cursing. Eventually, what was left of the *Kachidoki Maru* convoy regrouped and set off again. 'I thought to myself how lucky we had been, and maybe we can continue our journey to Japan in peace.'

But the following night the submarine had caught up with the convoy. On deck, he watched as ships all around him were torpedoed. He prayed that they would be saved and after a while commented to a friend that maybe they had been lucky again when there was a loud bang. The ship shuddered and appeared to settle quietly; the engines had stopped. The men in the hold could see nothing. An officer near Sherwood shouted through the hatch that the ship had been torpedoed but that it did not seem about to sink. Some believed him, others were too weak to move but a few escaped through the hatch and hid around the ship. Suddenly the boat tipped up and began to sink fast. An officer screamed through the hold that they were going down and that it was every man for himself. Cold water rushed in, sweeping the weakest further into the depths of the ship and pushing a lucky few up into the open. As the ship tipped to an even crazier angle, someone shouted 'Jump well out, Sergeant' and Johnny leapt as far as he could away from the suction that was dragging men down with the vessel.

He landed with a terrific jolt on top of someone and assumed that he had killed him outright. Then, just as he felt his lungs would burst, he broke the surface and swam as hard as he could for about 30 yards where he floated on his back watching the ship slip gracefully underwater. Around him he saw Japanese and Korean guards in lifeboats and the heads of POWs bobbing in the water, some shouting for help. The guards sang in their boats and shook their swords at any POWs who approached.

Sherwood floated and swam, floated and swam for what seemed hours under the full moon until he found a piece of wood about 6 feet long which he clung to as the swell grew stronger. Six more POWs joined him but only two could hang on at once and he and a Scottish sergeant organised a rota. One man, who was covered in oil and who had obviously swallowed a lot of it, did not have the strength to cling on unaided – every time they thought it was safe to let go of him he started to slide into the water and had to be hauled back onto the wood. The Scottish sergeant told Sherwood that they could no longer support him and they agreed to avert their eyes as he drifted away from them. 'That's what we did, we had no options, survive or die, there were no choices.'

Sherwood was lucky to have a full bottle of water with him that kept their throats moist. By two in the afternoon he was silently preoccupied with the thought of sharks, although they kept up a pretence that an American ship would rescue them; the Scottish sergeant even tried to sing 'I Belong to Glasgow'.

By late afternoon they caught sight of a warship in the distance. Thinking it was American they began to scream with delight but as it drew near it assumed the shape of a Japanese cruiser with its guns trained on them. The ship started to pick up the Japanese and Koreans in the lifeboats and ignored the POWs. With the guns still pointing at the bobbing heads the Japanese sailors and survivors appeared to be arguing about what to do with the men in the water. Then a Japanese officer addressed them through a loud speaker. In perfect English he told them they had fifteen minutes to get aboard. Anyone still in the water after that time would be abandoned. In the scramble that followed some of the ship's crew helped haul them up until the ship's alarm sounded and they were on their way. About twelve men were left behind. Sherwood believes that the reason they did not see a shark in the seventeen hours in which they were in the sea was because the explosions must have frightened them away. Some survivors were picked up by American submarines, which returned to the site of the torpedo attack, and these men provided one of the first accounts of conditions on the Thailand–Burma Railway.

By the time John Lowe's ship had docked in a port that turned out to be in Formosa (modern-day Taiwan) he had recorded the death of two men in his diary. He left the ship in drizzling rain and marched through the streets where gawping crowds threw stones and shouted 'Fuoki!' (prisoners!). They were put on trains with blacked-out windows and taken to a town where reporters photographed them. From here they marched to No. 6

Camp, Taihoku, on the northeastern tip of the island. Their new home was a group of bamboo and wooden huts arranged in four bays. A fixed table and benches divided the room where men slept on platforms about one foot off the ground. The windows were holes with bamboo bars and sliding screens. There was no heating and the weather was turning cold.

The POWs at Camp No. 6 were engaged in a range of tasks, most of which involved hard labour. Some men built a memorial park and lake for the Japanese; others worked on the land or in the railway repair shops. Many of the jobs seemed pointless. He was ordered to dig holes in the blue clay and then fill them in again. Japanese guards with fixed bayonets and Koreans armed with canes watched over them as they laid narrow gauge train tracks or dug out stones from soil that they transported in straw and bamboo baskets. They were given three meals of rice seething with weevils and some leaves – often nettles – floating in hot water. The guards enjoyed torturing them by frying cubes of pork in sugared batter by the roadside as they trailed home from work to their watery dinner. Sometimes the cooks boiled up a sack of horse bones that sent a 'heavy aroma of animal glue' over the camp and which they added to the midday meal before sending the bones on to the next camp.

His friend Danny Goldberg, the tailor who had made costumes at Changi and played the violin in the concert party, was given the job of repairing Japanese and POW uniforms in the camp workshop. The demand was so great that he asked Lowe, who had shown an early aptitude for sewing at school, to join him. He was overjoyed at what he viewed as a comparatively 'cushy' job and soon mastered the heavy treadle sewing machines. He patched shirts and shorts and cut the tails off shirts to make new collars. The workshop also had two saddlers and two carpenters who repaired furniture and the wooden shoes which they wore after the guards took their boots to stop them escaping. In the first few months, a retired Japanese colonel was camp commandant and treated them less fiercely than they were used to and told them there was no need to bow when he entered the workshop. He was soon replaced for not being harsh enough. The first time an enormous sergeant from the new regime entered the workshop, Lowe forgot to bow and the man punched him on the ear with a blow that sent him crashing into the wall.

The death rate rose as men succumbed to disease and malnutrition. Each body was put in an orange box coffin and, following the Japanese tradition, a bowl of fruit placed on top – 'of course had it been given to him earlier [it] might have saved his life'. It was Lowe's job to write the dead man's name on a small wooden cross in black Indian ink and to play the piano accordion, which the POWs bought with camp funds, for the short service before the coffin was taken to the hilltop Chinese cemetery. He still finds it impossible to hear the hymn 'Abide with Me' without wanting to weep for those who died in Formosa.

Occasionally he was one of four men who carried the coffin up the narrow path. At certain points along the way the path became so winding that the guards momentarily lost sight of the coffin and its bearers. During these seconds Lowe and his companions would grab a banana and gobble it down – skin and all. When the guards noticed the empty bowl the POWs said gravely that the dead man's soul must have been hungry. They avoided punishment simply because the guards could not disagree without appearing to dishonour their religious beliefs. However, the gratification was short-lived and led to stomach cramp and diarrhoea.

After a few months a senior officer asked Lowe whether he would give up his place in the workshop to a man who was so sick that he would die unless he had some respite. Although the replacement had no tailoring skills, he agreed. His next job was emptying the *benjos* with another POW, Spud Murphy. They scooped out the filth which was squirming with tapeworm using a wooden bucket fixed to a long bamboo pole and ladled it into one metre tall containers. When this was full they hung it by a rope from a thick piece of bamboo. Each man took one end and rested it on his shoulder to carry half a mile to the guards' vegetable patch. They were supposed to dilute the manure but often they poured it over 'neat' which burnt the tomatoes and other plants and earned them a slapping if they got caught. One day the rope, which had started to rot, snapped and the bucket collapsed – splattering them both with its foul contents. The rope broke a second time and a third time Lowe was knocked over by a water buffalo. Each time they were covered with excrement. The other prisoners found the three accidents hilarious but he believes he was only saved from a beating because the stench kept the guard at a distance. After this he worked as a ploughman, guiding a single share plough behind a buffalo by keeping one foot in the rut until he came to the end of the furrow when he switched to the other foot.

On one occasion he was part of the team ordered to unload the sacks of vegetables, tinned food and bags of sugar that arrived by lorry for the Japanese. The guards watched very carefully to make sure nothing was pilfered but Lowe kept a similarly keen eye on where exactly everything was placed in the storeroom. He discovered that, although the door was padlocked, if he pulled hard enough he could create enough space at the bottom to squeeze through. Spud Murphy agreed to act as a lookout from the nearest latrine and to tap on the door to tell him that the coast was clear. On the allotted night, he scrambled under the doorway and felt in the dark for bags of sugar and a few other items of food that he stuffed into his accordion case. As he stood waiting for the knock he heard a terrible commotion outside. Unable to stand the suspense any longer he pushed his way out and walked as nonchalantly as he could to his hut where he discovered that Spud had left his post because another man had been discovered stealing from the kitchen. The thief was held in a cage so cramped that he could neither stand nor lie down. Lowe shared his food but, again, the bananas and sugar were too much for their weakened stomachs and they suffered terrible pains and diarrhoea.

In the autumn of 1944 the camp was woken by the sound of fighter planes, machine gun fire and bomb blasts. Although the attack on the nearby aerodrome gave them cause for hope, it made the days and weeks that followed with no similar action harder to bear. There were a few paperbacks circulating in the camp and Lowe also read Galsworthy's play about two warring families, *The Skin Game*, and decided to stage it. He borrowed a typewriter that 'Busty' Bowen (whose nickname referred to a time when he had been a chubby clerk) had managed to bring with him and exchanged some of his cigarette ration for two writing pads. He had learnt to touch type before the war and spent every spare moment typing out the parts, a blanket ready to cover his work in case a guard came in. When he had finished he asked the Senior Officer to seek permission from the Japanese to put on the play and whether they could use the 'office' in which to stage it. The Japanese, who were as bored as their charges, agreed – once the script had been vetted.

Lowe made folding screens out of strong brown paper, about a metre wide, glued onto a frame of bamboo poles and pegs. He used charcoal from burnt bamboo and chalk that he found in the office to draw a domestic scene on one side of the screen; on the other he sketched a courtroom.

He took the female lead and Danny Goldberg the main male part. Costumes were basic – the two females wore scarves tied up 'turban fashion' on their heads. Four Japanese officers sat in the front room and a further 150 were squeezed into the office. Lowe had expected whistles and catcalls during the love scenes but found the whole audience was 'enthralled'. The Japanese did not understand everything but they too became sucked into the story. At first they sat rigid on their chairs but as the story unravelled they relaxed and turned their peaked hats sideways for a better view.

The camp also provided Lowe's introduction to classical music. A signals officer, Lieutenant Sowerby, loved classical music and having heard Lowe playing hymns on his accordion, asked him if he would take part in a concert. He was appalled to find he could not read music and had no knowledge of classical pieces. He insisted on teaching him how to play Weber's *Invitation to the Dance*; Lowe had never heard of Weber but was eager for any distraction and learnt the piece as Sowerby sang it. The Japanese allowed him to play it at a concert that Sowerby introduced with a talk about the composer. Lowe remembers: 'I was nervous, but played as if my life depended upon it – as perhaps in a way it did – and my audience did me the honour of hardly breathing while I played.' The Japanese seemed to be 'quite carried away' and Lowe remembers it as one of the best evenings in 'three and a half years of monotonous captivity'.

He kept a diary and made the final volume from a few sheets of airmail paper sewn into a cardboard cover the size of a matchbox that he covered with artificial black silk daringly snipped from the pockets of a Japanese officer's trousers as they hung on a line to dry. The diaries were hidden in a belt that he made from cotton and which had four little pockets for each book. On Wednesday 21 February 1945 he recorded that they left No. 6 Camp, Taihoku, in the pouring rain. They marched to the docks, passing through areas that had been badly damaged by air attacks, to board the *Winchester Maru* – another over-crowded and insanitary ship.

A lieutenant died of meningitis. Water was desperately short and they were not even allowed seawater for washing their utensils and had to resort to licking them clean. The ship was carrying sugar and the POWs scooped up what they could find in the cracks of the hold. Lowe played his accordion and they used their compasses to try to work out their direction but the ship changed course so often – probably to try to outwit any lurking submarines – that they had no idea where they were going. On 6 March Lowe was sent out on the open deck to help the cook peel onions; the ship was rolling and pitching in an icy gale. Although he was too ashamed to record it in his diary, he broke down in tears and the Japanese cook allowed him to retreat down below. He spent the following afternoon doing sewing jobs – 'Jimmy Brennan's fleabag, Cap Martin's suspenders, trousers and hats. Frank's slacks' – and felt much better. The deaths continued and two men died in front of him while he queued for the *benjo*.

On 9 March they disembarked. Over the next few days they travelled by foot, train and ship to the Japanese mainland. They passed through stretches of snow and it was 'fearfully cold'. In his spare time he sewed: he repaired someone's greatcoat and replaced buttons on other pieces of clothing. At a city he believed to be Tokyo they 'strap hung' on an underground train. 'We halted near a barrier and through this hordes of gnome-like people loaded to capacity were stampeding, slithering all over the place and coming through the barrier just like popcorn from an oven.'

Eventually they arrived at Hakodate, the southern-most tip of the island of Hokkaido and on a similar latitude to Vladivostok. The scene was Tolstoyan: the docks were covered in snow and men wearing fur coats rode sleighs pulled by horses. It was so bitterly cold that several POWs collapsed and died on the quayside. Later Lowe helped the medical orderlies put them into crates; by then the bodies were frozen stiff and their limbs had to be bent to fit into the boxes.

Their first camp was a pleasant surprise. It was a wooden, two-storied hut and the commandant was another retired colonel who gave them sugared whitebait, the first bread they had seen in years in the form of a barley loaf the size of a tea cake and a tiny sip of vodka. But, as in Taihoku, he was dismissed within two weeks, presumably for having the wrong attitude.

They were set to work unloading coal from the freight trains at the docks or shovelling sugar from the holds of ships or herring into slings to be lifted onto the quayside. After a few weeks Lowe was among those chosen to work in a coalmine a mile from camp. He was sent with three other men to work in a tunnel about 2 metres high and 2 metres wide where they used a pneumatic drill with a metre long bit to bore holes in the rock face into which they pushed sticks of dynamite connected by cable along the tunnel. The blast sent pieces of rock ricocheting down the walls of the shaft. But the job they hated most was blowing out the bottom strata. This meant lying flat on the icy floor. It took three men to support the drill: one held the middle section on his shoulder, another guided the front and the third controlled its handles. They changed positions often but the vibrating machine cut into their bony bodies that had very little clothing to protect them. Inside the narrow tunnel the noise was deafening and, of course, they had no protection for their ears. They were woken at 5.30 a.m. to start their twelve hour shift, during which time the Japanese insisted that they must cover 2 metres. They were given a bowl of rice to take with them and Lowe cut up his Australian slouch hat to sew a cosy with which to keep his lunch warm.

By August 1945 he had been in captivity for three years and was beginning to run out of hope. On 13 August he went down the mineshaft, bowed to the guard and asked permission to go down the tunnel to relieve himself. He had hidden a small drill pick up his sleeve and when he was out of sight of the guard, he braced himself to smash it down on his leg in the hope that a broken limb would invalid him out of the mine. He lifted the drill three times but each time his nerve failed. Finally, he broke down. The guard came looking for him and he was sent back to work. The next day his luck changed and he was given a new job as a gardener. If he had succeeded in breaking his leg, his future life would have been very different.

Tommy Atkins was still in Thailand in early 1945. His final diary entry reads: '12 Feb Planes came back to finish the bridges [at Tamarkan]. Steel bridge – 2½ spans down, wooden bridge badly mauled. One plane – a Yank – flew over us belching M./G. – strafing the railway I am sure.'

Then silence.

The first Allied aircraft were spotted over Singapore in November 1944. The sight of the great planes droning overhead provided an instant fillip to morale – some men were so confident of an early release that they slept with their boots on. But in the months that followed dejection set in, then, later, in the summer of 1945, fears that the Japanese would never surrender and were planning to massacre all POWs. The rumour mill went into overdrive and produced stories that even the person passing them on found hard to believe. One of the most outlandish – and which few believed – was that the Allies had dropped a new type of bomb over Japan which had destroyed the city of Hiroshima and which might lead to a Japanese surrender.

PART V

Freedom

Somewhere Near the End

Hidden wireless sets, the arrival of recently captured POWs and the jumpy behaviour of some guards gave prisoners in Europe a fairly accurate impression of the progress of the war. But despite, or perhaps, because of this knowledge they continued to organise sporting fixtures, to study and to create. In many cases this activity helped take their mind off the uncertainty of their situation; in other instances their efforts were focussed on how to protect themselves if their guards were tempted to use them as hostages as the Allies approached. For those who were forced to march to other camps, further away from the advancing British, Russian and American troops, preserving notebooks, sketches and other mementos of camp life became a concern to add to the worry of lack of food and disease.

The beginning of the end began in Italy. On a hot and sultry evening on 8 September 1943, Eric Newby was lying in the prison hospital at Fontanellato having broken his ankle while falling downstairs in the new boots his parents had sent him via the Red Cross. The guards had greeted the news of the Fascist leader Benito Mussolini's arrest on 25 July with whoops of joy, hurling his picture out of the window, ripping up propaganda and defacing the party's slogans hung on the end of their huts while announcing, 'Benito Finito!'

Just before seven on that September evening, the music blaring out from the guards' radio stopped abruptly to be replaced by the 'gloomy, subdued' voice of Marshal Pietro Badoglio. He had formed a new government and started secret negotiations with the Allies despite the presence of thousands of German troops in his country. Within the orphanage the cry went up of 'Armistizio!' The Senior British Officer, Lieutenant Colonel Hugo de Burgh, called a parade in the hall, put his own sentries on the gate and sent a party to recce the surrounding area. They did not know how close the Germans were but held the wildly optimistic belief that the Allies were only twenty-four hours away.

What happened next appears in marked contrast to the confusion and inertia at many of Italy's other POW camps. Some Senior British Officers stuck rigidly to an order received from MI9, Britain's secret escape organisation, to 'stay put'. MI9 sent the radio message, unbeknown to Churchill, because they feared that the estimated 79,000 British and American POWs might run amok at the first whiff of freedom and make it harder for the Allies to secure Italy. In contrast, when Churchill negotiated the armistice with Italy he insisted that camp commandants should protect their charges from the Germans and help them on their way to Switzerland or to meet their advancing kinsmen. Only a few Italian commandants received and acted on this order. To add to the confusion MI9's senior officer in the Middle East was trying to set up an escape organisation to help ferry as many POWs as possible to the safety of Allied lines. The lack of consensus about exactly how the men should be treated meant that the days when they had greatest chance of escape – shortly after the armistice and before the Fascists regrouped – were squandered.

The reaction among the POWs varied from camp to camp. Some, encouraged by rumours about Allied landings, obeyed the order to stay put. Their fate was to exchange Italian guards for Germans who transported them deep into the Fatherland. At PG21, Chieti, the Senior British Officer threatened British and American would-be escapers with court martial. About forty ignored his orders and escaped. Over a thousand of those who stayed were transported to Germany. There was confusion at nearby PG 78, Sulmona, where some POWs immediately took to the hills whilst others seemed unwilling to leave the camp. The Canadian doctor, Allen Graham, was one of those who stayed behind:

> About 4 o'clock in the afternoon the Germans came. So there wasn't very long we had to patrol things at all, that was pretty shocking, I guess. But there were about 4,000 left and we couldn't let them out, and of course we got cursed and damned ... It may have saved their

lives to keep the men in when they wanted to get out into the village and see the girls. It was a bit disturbing. It sure was to us.

So we kept everything in good shape for the Germans to arrive – of course, we didn't know they were going to stop off. It was very surprising when they did. We thought they would just move through. But I guess they wanted their captives as a bargaining thing and they took them. They had lots of time. There wasn't that much rush. We were too far ahead, too far in advance of the British coming up.

At other camps the Senior British Officer allowed men to make up their own minds. But these were not natural escapers who had spent months planning their route to freedom. They had no maps, no clothes, no forged papers, no stashes of food. Their physical appearance immediately set them apart: most were pale-skinned, many had blond hair and were taller than the average Italian. Few spoke good Italian and even the way they walked and wore their clothes marked them out. They were released into a terrain that was beautiful but treacherous and which became more so as winter took hold. Nor were they throwing themselves on the mercy of a country like Holland or France that had been subjugated by a foreign power. Italian unification was still so recent that nationalism rarely came before loyalty to family or region.

Fontanellato was unusual, but not unique, in that the SBO and the Italian commandant Colonel Eugenio Vicedomini, who had fought with the British in the First World War, had worked out a plan to give the POWs the best possible chance of escape should the Germans arrive. When Vicedomini's scouts spotted advancing Germans, an Italian bugler sounded three Gs: the signal that the enemy was on its way. A group of guards cut a wide hole in the fence at the bottom of the playing field behind the orphanage where around 600 POWs assembled. Dan Billany took with him pages of drawings and descriptions of life as a POW that he had sewn into a book, as well as nine exercise books that contained the unfinished manuscript of *The Cage* that he and his friend David Dowie had been working on.

De Burgh had kept morale and discipline high that summer by banning beards and telling men to put aside any decent clothes they had and some of their Red Cross rations. They had made extra efforts to keep fit and to learn Italian. Alliances had been forged as men decided who and how they would travel once they were on the other side of the orphanage gates. Newby was the only occupant of the hospital and watched through the window as Italians set up machine guns and prepared slit trenches by the deserted road. He hopped through the empty building to find two burly parachutists, who had been assigned to support him on either arm until a horse could relieve them.

Fontanellato sits in a plain of wheat fields and vineyards. It is the worst possible land in which to hide. The flat landscape punctuated by irrigation ditches exposes anyone walking across it and the first time a Messerschmitt 110 skimmed overhead, it had disappeared before Newby had time to hide. It was obvious that the POWs needed to move fast and that he could not keep up. While the former POWs scattered throughout the countryside he was hidden in a hay loft from where he listened to the distant roar of military machinery on the Via Emilia, the Roman road that leads through the Po valley from Parma to Milan, and the closer popping of motorbikes which he took to be German BMWs with sidecars, each carrying three soldiers armed with grenades and machine guns.

The next day an Italian doctor arrived and examined his ankle. He was given civilian clothes and taken to the maternity ward of a hospital on the outskirts of Fontanellato where he exchanged language lessons with the local girl, Wanda. He realised that he was putting her and other local people at risk and decided he must make his own way. Over the next three months he existed in a primitive, dreamlike world in which he moved from one hiding place to the next. Although the Nazis threatened anyone harbouring the enemy with execution, removal to a concentration camp or the destruction of their property, local people took him in and, in return for work, fed and housed him. At one remote farm he engaged in the Sisyphean task of clearing a field of boulders, returning home at night exhausted and isolated from his employers by an insuperable language barrier. On a day off he went for a ramble and fell asleep in a hollow only to awake to find a German soldier standing over him, carrying a butterfly net. The officer immediately recognised him for what he was but decided not to spoil the day by turning him in. On several occasions he became lost in the dense forest of the Apennines and as winter approached he spent three weeks in a damp cave with another POW.

By November of 1943, Newby was one of around 30,000 former POWs on the loose in Italy. Around 24,000 men were already on their way to camps in Germany having enjoyed a fleeting taste of freedom. Dan Billany and David Downie spent their first few days hiding on a small farm owned by the Meletti family five miles northwest of Fontanellato. At night they slept in a hayloft; during the day they moved to woodland or ditches, often meeting up for meals with other POWs who were also hiding with families in the area. Billany and Downie continued to work on *The Cage*.

By early October the book was complete and they knew they must push forward to reach the Allies. They gave the thirteen exercise books containing *The Cage* and Billany's wartime novel, *The Trap*, to Dino Meletti who promised to post them back to Billany after the war. He and Downie, together with two other POWs, disappeared into the Apennines.

In September 1944 Andrew Hawarden at Stalag 383, at the foot of the Bavarian hills, noted vivid reminders of home: the late flowering of hollyhocks and sunflowers that were over 9 feet tall and with giant, 18-inch faces. But despite this prolific evidence of their success, few gardeners had the heart to carry on. Surely they would not be there to see the fruits of their labour in a year's time?

Hidden radios throughout POW camps in Europe and the Far East were reporting encouraging news. At the beginning of June, Hawarden was thrilled by the Allied landings in Normandy. The Red Army, too, was making progress from the east and by the end of July was within twelve miles of Warsaw. News was never more important and at Colditz prisoners bet large sums of money in a sweepstake based on when towns fell to the Allies. They gathered their information from a radio the French had left behind and which was hidden in the attic. It was driven by a mini power-station built from the church organ motor which the Germans had refused to repair and a wooden wheel, 5 feet in diameter, turned by a relay of POWs who worked like galley slaves in their underpants.

Paris was liberated on 25 August and the US First Army crossed into Luxembourg in September. But there were still setbacks. In late September over 6,000 British soldiers surrendered at Arnhem; a few months later POWs at Stalag 383 were listening to a lecture on the battle by a YMCA representative. Despite the overwhelmingly good news, POWs were caught between elation and fear. The American and British armies to the west and the Russians from the east were pushing the German empire – and its POW camps – into a tighter and tighter corridor. The prisoners began to dare to hope that the war might be near an end but jubilation was tempered with unease. Many started to worry that they would be held as hostages or – to use a late twentieth-century term – used as a human shield.

The guards were becoming increasingly nervous too. In the summer, the Germans had ordered that all pigeons should be shot so that they could not be used to carry messages and when, in November, the Commandant of Stalag 383 spotted some perched on top of the huts, Hawarden noted how he 'went berserk', pulled out his revolver and 'blazed away'. All the pigeons flew off unhurt. The Germans were 'very windy' about the increasing number of air raids and the guards themselves were nearly all 'unfits', many of whom were teetering on the edge of mental collapse. Two were taken away 'puddled' after their behaviour during an air raid. One sentry, who was on duty on a watch-tower, threw his rifle to the ground, raised his hands and shouted: 'Yes, Tommy. Yes, Tommy'. The other guard stared at the floor, mumbling to himself before throwing his rifle down and walking away. 'Possibly these are momentary lapses, but, no doubt, they are all getting fed up,' Hawarden commented sympathetically. At the end of November, one of the guards shot himself whilst on duty, prompting Hawarden to remark: 'It looks as if the Germans are trying to exterminate themselves.'

As well as the agony of guessing how long the war might last, the camp had to contend with dwindling rations and the onset of a bitter winter. November 20 was designated 'rabbit day' and nearly everyone who kept a rabbit as a pet put them into pies or stews – even if they were only a few weeks old. Some hutches were mud and clay but most had been built from Red Cross boxes that would be 'very useful for burning'. By December, wood-gathering parties were liable to be cancelled at a moment's notice and the men became very circumspect about burning fires. It was strictly forbidden to fell trees but the guards, desperate for fuel in their own barrack rooms, often cut one down when they thought no one was looking.

Most POW huts had surrendered at least one beam from the roof to the stove. In many the floors had been taken up, leaving mud and dirt. The coldest were the ones where the 'innards' had gone up in smoke and which appeared so precarious that Hawarden worried that they would not withstand the winter storms. Just before Christmas a water main burst and they were forced to wash in the snow. Even table legs had been burnt and the tabletop was suspended from the ceiling by Red Cross string. If a man was repatriated his empty bed was immediately burnt. Most men wore balaclavas and what Hawarden called 'stalag knitted hats'. 'What with these and the "boat" footwear, the lads look anything but soldiers.'

From September they were on 'half parcels' of Red Cross supplies and there were fears that they might run out by Christmas. What parcels they had were hidden from the Germans, who had started to open tins surreptitiously – even those destined for the sick ward – and in December they raided the camp looking for parcels. In January 1945 the POWs resorted to cooking a cat and the Man of Confidence issued repeated warnings about NCOs who were tempted to work for the enemy in return for extra food. His words about the retribution that awaited miscreants must have been oddly cheering: 'all such can expect to meet an intensive enquiry at the end of the show.'

Andrew Hawarden's respiratory problems were becoming more acute in the bitter cold and damp. He had chronic bronchitis and suffered three bouts of pneumonia. He was a frequent visitor to the hospital where there were rumours that patients were about to have their beds stripped of sheets and that they were one of the few British wards left to enjoy such luxuries. Several men were suffering from asthma attacks. Supplies of adrenaline were running low and some sufferers had to endure as many as five bouts in a twenty-four hour period. There were four cases of TB.

As their well-ordered world appeared to be collapsing around them, the POWs clung to the pastimes that had punctuated so much of their captivity. Hawarden received an award from the YMCA in recognition of all he had done for football and some POWs still managed to summon enough energy to skate or play ice hockey on the frozen pool and basketball court. Hawarden still went to see plays, bands and choirs at the National Theatre and Ofladium when he was well enough. The farce *Charley's Aunt* was 'even funnier than at home ... This is because the humour can be added to and one isn't strangled by the script and humour in all forms is appreciated more than anything in this life'. Performances were often disturbed by the crump of distant bombs but were no less ambitious: the Ofladium staged *The Yeoman of the Guard* and the National Theatre followed with *Red Riding Hood* at Christmas. Hawarden was too ill to see the pantomime but its principal actors visited the hospital on the first day of 1945. Despite his illness he was feeling optimistic:

Now we enter another year – the last one of the war – this is my opinion and the opinion of practically all of us here. Although cooped up, we get information of how the people inside Germany are existing and how they do it and put up with it is one of the surprises of the war but to us there is every evidence of a crack in the ice and the recent push on the western front can be put down to one of their last efforts to bolster the waning of the German spirit.

By the end of January his health had deteriorated. He had a continuous headache and was vomiting blood; he had lost 9kg (19¾lb) since he had been in hospital and now weighed 67.7kg (10½ stone). But he was immensely cheered by the arrival of 1,500 invalid parcels from the Red Cross. The radio news and information passed on by the Red Cross representative was also lifting morale. 'The news these days [18 January] is helping the lads a great deal to get over these bad times, with Warsaw going and Joe on the borders of Silesia, we are looking forward to big things in the future.'

And a few days later:

The most important thing nowadays is the news we are getting out of the Russian Forces' advance on Berlin. We have got the news that Joe [Stalin] is only 60 kilos [sic] from Berlin. From what we have seen of the *Volkssturm*, we cannot imagine these non-descripts holding the Russians back, so how well they may fight on their own doorstep. I think a bit of a stand will be put up before Berlin is taken, but there's no doubt about it, its fate is sealed.

The POW population was on the move too – although Hawarden could have no sense of the true scope of the mass movement of prisoners who were being marched in circuitous routes away from the Soviets and then the British and Americans. In February, 1,700 POWs arrived at Stalag 383 from Moosberg (Stalag VIIA). Some had been captured at Arnhem; others were long-term POWs. A few men from Stalag 383 were reunited with old friends. Hawarden heard that the staff at Fort 15, in Thorn, Poland, was moving to Stalag 357. What he did not know was that the POWs at Stalag 357, also at Thorn, were being moved west to

Fallingbostel, a camp on the flat heathland between Hamburg and Hanover. My father was among those men being marched west to escape the advancing Russians.

The months after he was captured in Italy in February 1944 later merged into one seamless period of time linked together by a jumble of three POW camps. He spoke of being held at Stalag IVB at Mühlberg, which, as one of the older camps, was in a sorry state of repair – windows lacked glass and the wind whistled through the patched roofs. He may have stopped there on his way to Stalag 357 which was where, according to the records of the International Committee of the Red Cross, he was in March 1944. The 'Certificate of Merit' he received as a member of Barrack 88's seven-aside inter-barrack rugby tournament shows he was there in May 1944. At that time Stalag 357 was still at Thorn. It was a drab camp of around 3,500 men living in a familiar setting of barbed wire, barrack blocks and 'goon boxes'.

On the night of 13 February 1945, two waves of hundreds of Lancaster bombers attacked Dresden, a stately city of wedding cake churches, parks and boulevards, but also an important German military transport hub, with a ferocity that sparked a great fire-storm that swept through the city. Temperatures soared to over 1,000°C causing a vacuum that uprooted trees and tossed furniture and other debris into the air. Around 50,000 people – many of them civilians – were incinerated or suffocated in the attack. The figure is still disputed and because of the large numbers of refugees who perished, the final number will probably never be known for sure. Kurt Vonnegut, an American prisoner of war who had been captured at the Battle of the Bulge, spent the night of the attack in an abattoir's underground meat locker. After the war the experience inspired his novel, *Slaughterhouse 5, or The Children's Crusade – A Duty-dance with Death*.

In the camp where my father was held, the destruction of Dresden exposed another side to the guards. Until then, they had always seemed half afraid of their charges, viewing them as unstable and unpredictable. But the bombing of Dresden reminded them that they were enemies and the guards retaliated by stripping the POWs of their blankets, leaving them to shiver in the bitter winter night.

The Red Army was pushing west into Poland and East Prussia. On 17 January it had taken Warsaw and by the end of the month had liberated the concentration camp of Auschwitz and was less than a hundred miles from Berlin. And as the Russians advanced so the POWs were ordered onto the road in a series of evacuations that became known as the 'The Long March' or 'The Death March' but which might have been more appropriately named 'The Long Trudge'. The thrill of being on the other side of the barbed wire soon gave way to the despair of struggling through blizzards and temperatures that at times fell to seventeen degrees below zero in Germany's worst winter for fifty years. They dragged makeshift sledges carrying supplies and what possessions they could not bear to part with until they had no more strength to carry them. Every man wore as much clothing as he could pile on. Some even raided their Red Cross and YMCA sports supplies and put on wicket-keeping gloves and pads or fashioned leather hats from rugby balls and footballs that made them look like they were wearing pilots' helmets. But still the cold and wind found a way through. They slept in barns, factories or sometimes by the side of the road, not knowing whether they would wake up in the morning. There was very little food and rarely a chance to heat up rations or to boil water. Frostbite and other illnesses – many of which had ruled the lives of POWs in the Far East for years – began to set in. Poor hygiene, cold and a weakened immune system led to jaundice, scurvy, dysentery, pneumonia, boils and ulcers. It was not uncommon for men to follow a trail of bloody faeces left by men suffering from dysentery.

They were joined on the road by local people who were also fleeing from the Russians; sometimes German troops passed them heading for the Front. Often in these series of marches the guards themselves did not seem to know where they were going and the POWs harboured a nagging worry that they were being taken away to be shot – especially since rumours about the extermination camps were starting to leak out.

Under these conditions some POWs covered hundreds of miles. One of the most arduous journeys was the trek from Stalag Luft IV at Gross Tychow in northern Germany, close to the Baltic Sea, which ended some 500 miles later at Fallingbostel, south of Hamburg. Some of the 10,000 men on it had been held since 1940 and now had to cope with the shock of being outside the routine of everyday prison life. There is no way of verifying how many men died on this march but one figure suggests 150 perished.

About 100,000 POWs marched through the narrow corridor next to the Baltic Sea still held by the Nazis; a further 60,000 prisoners moved through central Germany and 80,000 were driven out of southern Germany. This last group faced the added risk of being strafed by Allied planes. But what my father dreaded most was lack of food. He was convinced that if he did not try to escape he would starve to death – it was as simple as that. I had always thought this reasoning was pure exaggeration and that it was more likely that he had lost patience with captivity and, always an impetuous man, had decided to take matters into his own hands. But looking at photos of some of the emaciated bodies of POWs at Fallingbostel at the point of liberation in April 1945 starvation was a genuine and terrible possibility. These men are as gaunt and skeletal as concentration camp survivors. In one particularly disturbing photo, a man perches on the edge of his bed, as weightless as a sprite. The only thing that appears to tether him to the ground is his right foot – toeless and bulbous with the effects of gangrene.

My father's escape plan was simple and one that several men who faced the forced marches of the last months of the war resorted to. It did not involve tunnelling, disguise or bribery. He and a friend agreed that once the POWs were on the move they would – at a given signal – simply fall into a roadside ditch and lie there until the column had passed by. When they reached a suitable stretch of road the two men exchanged glances. My father tumbled into the undergrowth and lay there. His friend marched on. My father – from a large, close-knit family and having spent the last four years in the army and the latter part of that in POW camps – was alone for the first time in his life. And in a foreign country where he spoke only a handful of words – and those with a thick Scottish accent.

Although the British prisoners at Colditz were not forced onto the road, there was nevertheless a growing unease about their possible use as hostages and, in particular, the fate of the *Prominente* – well-connected POWs such as Haig and relatives of the royal family and of Winston Churchill. The atmosphere was further soured by the dilemma of whether it was still worth trying to escape. Men who had devoted their every waking hour to finding a way out of the castle now had to face the possibility that the end of the war was so tantalisingly close that their best way of reaching home was likely to be with the help of the Red Army or General Patton. For some, the knowledge that this would probably be their final autumn and winter at Colditz made these months hardest to bear. At the end of September, Mike Sinclair, or 'The Red Fox', who had in previous escape bids got as far as Cologne and the Swiss and Dutch borders, shook hands with a fellow POW and started to climb the perimeter wire. He was shot dead as he ran from the castle. He had been a prisoner since 1940.

His was a straightforward, last ditch bid for freedom. At the other extreme, four POWs worked on a way of leaving the castle that – even by Colditz's standards – was breathtakingly bold and inventive. The idea of building a glider came to one of them as he watched snowflakes swirling up over the castle roof. The plan required in-depth knowledge of aerodynamics and engineering to enable them to construct a structure capable of floating two men off the castle's roof at a point that was visible only from the village below. But – just as importantly – they needed a workshop that would be completely invisible to the ever-vigilant Colditz guards. Finding a secret place in a castle which was already riddled with tunnels and other evidence of previous escape bids and which was under constant scrutiny was as much a challenge as actually constructing the glider.

Tony Rolt's pre-war life made him an ideal member of the team: he understood mechanics and he enjoyed danger. He was eighteen and still at Eton when he first competed in a motor racing contest in 1936. Before the war interrupted his career he was considered one of the country's most promising drivers. After he was captured in 1940 he made seven attempts to escape from various camps before arriving at Colditz.

Bill Goldfinch brought engineering skill. He was known for his habit of 'tinkering' and was a second lieutenant in the Royal Engineers (TA) before his twin interests of flying and aircraft design led him to the RAF. He had already started to think about the possibilities of a 'giroplane' or a glider at Stalag Lufts I and III. He met the third member of the glider team, Jack Best, when they were both recovering in a military hospital having just been captured. They tunnelled their way out of Stalag Luft III together and had hoped to steal an aircraft but found the planes were all securely locked up. They were finally picked up rowing the wrong way up the River Oder. When they were reunited at Colditz they were soon known as 'the two old crows' or 'the wicked uncles'. When Goldfinch started work on the glider, he was able to consult a helpful two-volume book called *Aircraft Design* by C.H. Latimer, which included a detailed diagram of a wing section. It appears that the book slipped through the censor's net because the thought of trying to build a plane seemed just too fanciful – even at Colditz. Geoffrey Wardle, a submarine officer nicknamed 'Stooge', completed the four-man team.

It was not immediately obvious that the escape committee would agree that work on the glider, which became known as the 'Colditz Cock', should go ahead. The castle was becoming increasingly crowded as the Germans moved more POWs in – including more *Prominente* – and the chances of its success seemed remote. But the Senior British Officer, Willie Tod, recognised that the project would give POWs who might otherwise resort to dangerous 'goon baiting' a purpose in life.

The team built their secret workshop, which would allow them to work undisturbed and without the need to pack away the parts, behind a false wall in the long, dark attic above the chapel. It took twelve men working through the night to install the fake wall made from palliasse covers tacked to cardboard and three-ply wood. At first, the outer layer of plaster, which was made from the remains of a French tunnel, looked far too dark and patchy but as it dried out it blended in with the colour of the genuine walls. The only way in or out of the workshop was through a trapdoor in the floor; anyone leaving had to cover their footprints back to the trapdoor with bellows full of soot and dust.

The workshop had a bench, tables for the complicated diagrams they were following and racks for their extensive array of tools which included saws, squares, planes and drills bought on the black market or made from bits of beech bedboards, gramophone springs and needles and a cupboard bolt. The main spar of each wing was a solid 18ft-long floorboard. Blue and white check cotton sleeping bags formed the glider's skin which was strengthened with a 'dope' solution made from finely ground millet boiled for four hours to make a paste. Pieces of iron taken from the senior officers' bedsteads were used for reinforcement and the glider's control wires came from field telephone wire.

The men worked under cover of a complicated series of lookouts. One man sat in the attic eaves from where he could see the British quarters. A white towel in the window meant it was safe to carry on working. If it was replaced with a blue towel there were Germans in the building and the workshop needed to fall silent. A green mustard pot warned of imminent danger and a red-painted metal tin was notice to leave the workshop immediately.

The take-off was scheduled for spring 1945 when air raids were expected over Berlin and Leipzig, which would provide cover, and when the flooded meadows where it was hoped the glider would land, 300 feet below and 200 yards away, should have drained. They would knock a hole in the attic wall and the 19ft 9in-long glider would be catapulted on its way from the roof by a pulley system running through holes made in each of the castle's six floors and weighted by a bath full of cement.

But by March the Front was edging closer to Colditz. Twelve hundred French officers arrived after an eighty-five mile march away from the advancing Russians and more *Prominente*, including John Winant Junior, son of the US ambassador to England, moved in. Tod ordered that the glider should be kept in its hiding place until the castle was liberated or another purpose found for it. On April 10 the dull thud of bombs falling on Leipzig and the Leuna synthetic oil plant was replaced with the distinct 'crump' of artillery. The normal routine of prison life was breaking down. *Appels*, which were often called four times a day, ceased altogether and an uneasy calm fell on the castle. Tod and the Commandant held almost constant talks. An SS division moved into the town of Colditz overnight and there were rumours that they had massacred nearby Jewish slave labourers. Tod considered his options. If the POWs attempted a mass breakout they risked being captured by the SS and taken deeper behind the German lines. But if the SS took the castle, they still faced the threat of being used as a human shield. If this happened the glider would be used to send a plea for help to the outside world.

Over the days that followed the POWs watched from on high as the SS mined the bridge and the town's population – women as well as children – helped to dig trenches. German soldiers barricaded themselves into houses and armoured vehicles rattled through the streets. POWs strained to look through telescopes they had made over the years from ground spectacle glass. On Friday 13 April the *Prominente* were taken away in buses. By dusk that same day, the POWs could hear machine-gun fire in the town which continued on and off during the night.

On Saturday American troops started to shell the castle, piercing the roof and sending shards of glass over the cobbles; fire broke out in several places. Douglas Bader was knocked off his tin legs by one blast and the prisoners were ordered to the ground floor. The Commandant tried to persuade them to leave but Tod refused. Eventually a compromise was reached in which the Commandant agreed to hand over the inside of the castle to the POWs in return for a promise that he would not be delivered to the Russians and that the prisoners would not wave flags from windows or betray any other sign to the SS that the castle had surrendered. Tod gambled that as the Americans were concentrating on shelling the town they must realise that there were prisoners in the castle. The battle continued for two days and nights. The electricity supply was cut and the castle was bathed in an eerie moonlight but the POWs maintained their wireless link with the outside world through the hand-cranked power station.

On Sunday 15 April one of the French generals decided to sit for his portrait. When the Germans tried to blow the bridge, the jolt caused artist John Watton to leave a white streak of chalk under his subject's chin. The general refused to allow him to remove the record of the Germans' failure. By late morning American tanks were ambling through the town, soldiers and mine clearers by their sides. The infantrymen shouldered their way through the doors of wrecked houses and white sheets appeared at windows.

Inside the castle, the raggle-taggle of POWs waited in the courtyard, chatting or reading books. Finally, a tall GI, bristling with ammunition and toting a submachine gun, pushed open the castle's gate and stood in the sunshine. The men inside stopped talking or looked up from their books to stare blankly at the stranger. He was equally baffled and gazed up at the forbidding walls, the faces at the barred windows and the cobbles at his feet. After about a minute an officer approached him with outstretched hand. The GI shook his hand and, grinning, was reported to have said: 'Any doughboys here?' – a reference to the lack of ordinary soldiers. His words seemed to confirm that he was real and the POWs rushed forward to greet him; some men burst into tears and others hugged and – it seems only in the case of the French – kissed each other.

Just as the POWs at Colditz could not stop planning ways to escape, so Andrew Hawarden at Stalag 383 clung to his footballing dreams as conditions around him deteriorated. In February a 'lad' died of pneumonia and as his body was being carried out of the hospital another POW – who had been with Hawarden since the start – died of the same illness and meningitis. Surrounded by these tragedies Hawarden escaped by planning an England versus Scotland football match to be played at Newcastle United's St James' Park ground in aid of the Red Cross with ex-POWs making up the teams.

He had contacted the Red Cross, Newcastle and the Football Association at the end of 1944. 'We realise that a definite date could not yet be fixed,' he told the FA, 'but it would be our intention to play the match about 3 weeks after arriving home, when it would be possible to get the lads together before being sent out on any other service.'

The camp's POW leader added a note confirming that Hawarden was genuine and praising his contribution to sport: 'the games played [in camp] have been most keen and have played a great part in providing entertainment for a large number of Prisoners of War'. Newcastle gave their approval and a reply from the FA's representative arrived two months after Hawarden's request: 'I much hope that it will not be long before the proposed game can be staged'.

More POWs were arriving in the camp short of both bedding and clothing – some shared one blanket between two – and the established prisoners gave up their own supplies to help them. The contingent also brought lice with them and Hawarden moaned about the delousing programme. When he was discharged from hospital at the end of February he was shocked at the state of his fellow POWs and of the camp. 'I know that the lads have been pulling down their huts little by little, but I didn't know that the huts were so bad. How some of them are left standing is a miracle.'

In early February a German sentry box was stolen and used for fuel. The theft was even more remarkable because the box had been guarded by 'POW police' charged with keeping law and order as the situation became more desperate.

As the bombing intensified, the huts seemed even more precarious and shook after each blast. In January there were twenty-eight air raid alarms; this grew to fifty in February and by the end of March they had endured seventy-three in one month. The air raids were so frequent that they provided a constant wall of sound that proved easier to sleep through.

Several men had lost 10 to 15 kilos in a month. 'Coffee' was now made by adding boiling water to burnt toast that had been rolled or crushed with a bottle. Flour (brought in by the 'froggies') and cigarettes were the most valuable commodities. A gold ring would fetch twenty cigarettes, a watch thirty; some desperate men swapped shirts, vests, pants or pullovers for flour from the French.

At the beginning of March another 'lad' died and it was quite common for POWs to stay in bed all day to conserve energy. Few wrote to their families, feeling there was no point because they would be home before their letters. The Ofladium closed, there was no roll-call and it was too cold to venture out. A few gardeners planted seeds but were convinced they would not see the benefit of their labour. In the middle of March an Australian died – malnutrition was believed to be the culprit.

Hawarden received letters from home asking about the proposed match at Newcastle and telling him that it was being talked about in the British press. The Football Association sent him an encouraging letter and at the end of March he organised a meeting between the players who were hoping to compete. On March 27 he wrote:

> The lads are beginning to show a little excitement with the continued good news which we keep getting. It is known that every our [sic] that passes our troops (or rather the Yanks) are getting that bit nearer here. If the Germans decide to move us, I cannot see which direction they will take us. In any case it won't be far, because in each direction they are being pressed by allied forces and if they decide to move us, it will mean using troops for which they can hardly spare. What fighting troops they have are needed on the Russian front.

Scouts were posted on the 'Gerry office' ready to go in if the Germans refused to surrender but most believed this would not be necessary. The lads started to pack – sorting out what they would take home and what they would leave behind. To pass the time they played a match against men who had been held at Lamsdorf camp. 'We reckon that another fortnight should see us relieved,' Hawarden wrote.

Correspondence concerning the charity match continued to arrive. As excitement mounted about the Americans – 'Our reckonings are that General Patton's men are within a hundred miles from this Stalag' – so did Hawarden's enthusiasm for the Scotland–England charity match to be held at Newcastle. It was as if the thought of freedom was so overwhelming that he needed something familiar with which to occupy his mind. He held meetings with all the club presidents and secretaries and put out a request for an artist to design a suitable poster and programme. Sergeant Bill Williams received a letter from Barclays Bank's Newcastle branch and a letter from Newcastle United's secretary.

Hawarden began his entry for Sunday 1 April: 'And what we think is the last month of the war'. But four days later there was concern that they were about to be moved, although the Russians and Americans were thought to be about 180 miles away. Four Red Cross vehicles arrived. The trucks, which were nicknamed 'white ladies' or 'white angels', had battled through roads clogged with refugees and were bringing vital supplies to POWs throughout a chaotic Europe. Over the next few days there were a few desultory games of football that were often stopped by air raids and Hawarden discussed the importance of guarantors for the Newcastle game. The radio told them that Patton was less than seventy-five miles away.

They stored cases of their possessions in the Ofladium but Hawarden was convinced that little of it would reach home safely: 'There will be too many people on the loose whenever these camps are evacuated.' On April 15 the Germans said one third of the camp would leave that evening but the medical orderlies argued that three quarters of the POWs were not fit to march. The next day they were told that they must leave for their own safety. They had run out of food and water and if they stayed they risked attack by 'werewolves' – 'These are extreme Nazis with bandit and bludgeon ways, who wouldn't think twice about pressing a trigger.' The first party left at midnight; 400 sick men, including Hawarden, stayed behind. He was among 1,000 men put into the compound where the French had once been held.

'How the number has grown so large is because of the rackets and gate-crashing and it's surprising how many the Gerry guards let in at a few fags per head. The guards themselves are all fed up and as time goes on they are showing great nervousness about their own position.'

The sentries stood down and the POWs were allowed to come and go as they pleased. A few raided the German stores and came back carrying peas, beans, sugar and dried vegetables to share. Other men who had been hiding under the huts to avoid being forced to leave the camp emerged and 'knocked about quite openly. No-one, not even the Gerries, took any notice of them'.

A high-ranking German officer arrived but when he saw the state of affairs allowed them to carry on. Most of the time the main gate was guarded by two British military police who allowed salvage parties to bring in blankets, bowls, jugs, beds and palliasses. Two or three lads cycled down to the closest town, Hohenfels.

> They took a big risk, but it looked as if it was worth it when they came back with half a sheep and a goose. They said that nobody at all bothered them and the Gerry soldiers themselves only say a kind of 'how do you do?' It is noticed that a few of our lads are actually living in civvie houses in Hohenfels and small places round about. The advice given by our Camp authorities is to stay put in Camp.

By April 18 Hawarden believed Allied troops were just 20 miles southwest of Nuremburg but that the Germans still held two thirds of the city. 'Now had it been twenty miles South East of Nuremburg we should be packing our kit again.' Nevertheless, he and the other POWs enjoyed watching their fighter planes strafing a road just outside the camp. As they soared away after the attack they waggled their wings in a jaunty acknowledgement of the POWs.

Some of the prisoners were taking greater and greater risks by visiting nearby towns and villages right under the Germans' noses in search of eggs, meat, flour and bread, which they exchanged with local people for chocolate, soap, cocoa, blankets, underwear and pullovers. The German authorities even had to ask the British military police to fetch back POWs who had moved in with local civilians. Hawarden stayed put – even though it would have been the 'easiest thing in the world to walk through the wire which is cut in umpteen places and if the guard happens to see you, he only asks you not to go as he might get into trouble'. Both water and power had been cut off and water was being brought in, in baths, butts and buckets. The Americans were believed to be ten miles away.

April 20 1945: 'Another couple of days should see the Yanks here.'

Both the German and English authorities grew concerned about looting. 'Almost every nationality' was on the loose, many from concentration camps and foreign workers' camps desperate for food and clothing. 'The people are proving to be a hazard to the advancing American troops.'

Sunday, 22 April 1945 started with machine gun and rifle fire only a few kilometres away. 'We knew automatically that the Yanks were here. We had previously seen Gerry soldier cyclists pedalling away as fast as they could go towards Regensburg.'

'This afternoon, the word went round, "they're here". Then there was a rush to the roadway. First of all I saw a small car in which there were a couple of Yanks and they were talking to Major Neill.'

In the distance he could see a convoy of tanks and cars. He found it impossible to express the feelings of someone 'who has been surrounded by wire for almost five years, then to find himself suddenly freed by a couple of Yanks in a jeep'.

The Americans handed round cigarettes and the POWs draped themselves in union flags. Hawarden seemed to be in a state of shock and disbelief. Perhaps he felt too frail to join in the celebrations or slightly too old for the exuberance that some of the younger POWs showed.

'Meanwhile, the lads have been having a picnic, going through the Gerry barracks and have been fitting themselves up with souvenirs of all descriptions.' He watched 'our lads' taking to horses, motor bikes, push bikes, cars and horse-drawn carts. Some decided to try to make their own way to the British lines; others stood guard over the 'Gerries' who were held in a large hut and made to do some of their fatigues.

> It seems funny to see our lads carrying the rifle and Gerry being the
> prisoner. The Yanks seem to ignore the Germans altogether. They
> have no time for them. One of their remarks to one of our lads was
> 'wait until you boys see what damage has been done to your country
> by the Luftwaffe and Flying Bombs, then you will despise them.'

Fastidious as ever, he was shocked that the 'Yanks' did not bother to dig gun pits but he was impressed by their hardware: 'guns and vehicles were an ey[sic]-opener'.

On the whole, the British and Americans got on well. 'There was a great deal of fraternising between the Yanks and lads. It was like a meeting between long lost brothers with the Yanks being very free with their cigarettes, sweets, biscuits and other grub out of their rations. We even saw white bread and cigars. Our lads were soon taking them to tea, but they favour coffee.'

They discovered that the German quarters offered the luxury of spring beds and linen and a respite from fleas which Hawarden could not help blaming on the French, quoting a POW saying: 'wherever there's a Frenchman, there's fleas'.

But in some cases it was also a time to settle old scores. A French POW had been shot by a German the previous winter over a dispute; now the Frenchman's friend recognised the guard and reported him to the American authorities. There was an instant court martial in which the German confessed. The friend dug a trench near the scene of the killing and the prisoner was marched away. Later two or three shots were heard. A few days afterwards three members of the SS were also shot – 'They had been guilty of some very cruel behaviour.'

As the Germans – now POWs – left, Hawarden was aware of the pressure the American in charge was under: 'May he find some hidden strength in the toe of his boot if any one of the Gerries wants to rest, or requires a drink of water. Many of our lads got shot. The Yanks can go the full limit as far as we are concerned.'

Andrew Hawarden was in the last party to leave Stalag 383. He marvelled at his first sight of oranges and white bread and noticed how 'many lads' gathered souvenirs such as hats, helmets, even weapons. As usual he preferred to observe this final exuberance. At last the train, which in Stalag 383's Crazy Week had only ever been imaginary, was finally leaving for Blighty.

Victory in the Far East

On 21 July 1945 Fergus Anckorn received a postcard from home telling him that his brother-in-law was 'somewhere near Helene's home'. The note, written in June 1944, conveyed much more than family news. Since his brother-in-law was an army captain and Helene had been the family's French governess, he knew that its hidden meaning told him that the Allies had landed in France.

Clandestine wirelesses throughout camps in the Far East kept POWs up-to-date with developments in Europe; soon prisoners had visual proof that the Japanese no longer held the upper hand. In Singapore, Allied reconnaissance planes started to appear and more Japanese combat troops arrived on the island. On 25 February 1945 Allied planes bombed Singapore docks – an event which might have been encouraging had they not destroyed several food stores, which had a disastrous effect on rations.

Friendly fire became a danger for Anckorn who left Chungkai and moved south down the railway to its very start at Nong Pladuk. The camp was made out of the usual bamboo and thatch huts but its main difference was its proximity to the large engineering works of Hashimoto's and to railway sidings. The POWs knew that both were bound to attract the attention of the RAF. Anckorn's experience of the battle for Singapore had left him with a great fear of air raids and because he was in a hut just ten yards from the works, he became convinced that an Allied bomb would kill him.

During the day he and the other POWs worked in the engineering yard where they carried loads or drilled holes. It was not as gruelling as work-ing on the railway but the guards were just as prone to violent outbursts.

To lighten the days at the camp, a few performers started a concert party. Anckorn joined a Jewish comedian and a duo called Hank and Frank. Other POWs played the trumpet, penny whistle and guitar and performed on sets drawn by talented artists. Anckorn listened to a talk on embalming and himself gave a lecture to the officers on Houdini.

He remembers the first air raid one moonlit night in September 1944 when the drone of bombers sent him scuttling from his hut to an air raid trench by the bamboo perimeter fence. His friends tried to persuade him that it was safer to stay in the hut but he preferred to take his chances outside where he shared the trench with guards until a Japanese officer arrived in his pyjamas and ordered him to leave. He lay on the ground by the fence listening to the bombs explode with even greater ferocity as they hit the fuel and ammunition at the railway. A herd of startled, bellowing buffaloes stampeded dangerously close to him, their thundering hooves providing a percussive background to the firework display produced by the RAF. The raid was over by three in the morning by which time the camp was on fire.

The bombardment was a terrible psychological blow. Men who had survived years of ill treatment were now laid out waiting for burial because they had been deliberately made vulnerable to an attack by their own side. Anckorn joined a working party that day to avoid being asked to bury the bodies. When he arrived home the corpses, which had been left in the sun, were still unburied. As one of the few fit men, he was asked to carry them on stretchers made from rice sacks and bamboo poles to a mass grave a mile from the camp. As they left, it started to rain and the stretcher-bearers found it difficult to keep their footing and to prevent the dead slipping to the ground.

On 20 October 1944 he was cheered to receive a postcard from home. His mother had written it a year before and in it she told him that Lucille was 'going strong'. But what pleased him more than anything was the last line – 'Also still smiling!' – which showed she had received his postcard and spotted the coded shorthand.

In early 1945 he was moved back to Kanburi where he worked in a soap factory outside the camp. Here he made blue and white bars in what was probably the sweetest smelling time of his whole captivity. From here he was sent to Bangkok and then to Ubon, a camp set up to build an aerodrome close to the Thai border with what is now Laos and then was known as French Indo-China. His duties were comparatively light – he helped in the sick ward and fetched and carried for those officers running the camp. He joined the concert party and watched plays performed on a circular stage that revolved to reveal three different backdrops.

They were acutely conscious that their position near the aerodrome put them at risk of being bombed and decided to alert the RAF to their existence with an aerial calling card. A pilot taking aim over the camp might well have looked down to see the letters 'P', 'O' and half of 'W' emphasised in a double layer of ash in the markings for the goalmouths and centre circle of the POWs' football pitch and the right-hand side of the 'W' in the abutting basketball court. Allied planes flew over Ubon but the camp was never bombed – it is impossible to know whether this was because the pilots got the hint or not.

But as the signs of an Allied victory grew stronger, so did the prospect that their captors would not allow them to live to see it. They were told to dig a large square pit – its use could only be as a mass grave. Then they were told to switch to digging a moat around the camp and machines guns were mounted at points where their fire could be directed at the huts. Work stopped on the aerodrome and, even more significantly, they were made to dig trenches in the landing strip so that it could not be used for enemy landings. Anckorn started to fantasise about stealing a plane or escaping to Saigon but knew both were ridiculous flights of fancy. In order to keep up with what was happening outside, he took it in turns to break out of the camp and meet up with local Thais who spoke French. He paid them for news and then broke back into camp to disseminate it through a small group of French-speaking Dutch POWs. But after one particularly dangerous news-gathering trip in August he decided it was not worth the risk: 'Tonight they told me that a *bombe atomique* had landed on Hiroshima and wiped it out and I said this is clearly ridiculous. I know that *atomique* means something damned small and Hiroshima is the size of London. So we discounted it.'

News of this mysterious weapon caused puzzlement among POWs who could have no inkling of its terrible strength. A prisoner who was being transported to Bangkok caught sight of a train with the words 'BIG BOMB – WAR OVER – ALL GO HOME' chalked on the side of the engine and was unsure whether or not to believe the message:

*

Footballer Johnny Sherwood had a ringside view of its power but was ignorant of the significance of what he was watching. Having been plucked from the sea by a Japanese ship after the sinking of the *Kachidoki Maru*, he and the other POWs were transferred to an oil tanker. They were given so little water that when a storm blew up they rushed on deck to collect rainwater in any container they could find which, as they had very few possessions, was not much. They cupped their hands out as if in supplication, stood with their mouths wide open and upturned or pressed their faces to the ship's superstructure in an effort to capture the rain as it trickled down the side.

Next they were moved to a whaler and lived in the hold where fishermen normally cut up their mammoth catch. Despite another American submarine attack they eventually reached Fukuoka No. 25 POW Camp in Kyushu, on the southern tip of Japan – 'a lovely little camp with about twenty-five rooms in it' which Sherwood guessed had at one time probably housed Japanese sailors. From here they worked twelve-hour shifts at a local carbon and chemical factory. One of the first signs that the war was nearing an end was that rations dwindled to starvation levels. The men were so desperate that they looked forward to the arrival of traders who twice weekly appeared at the camp with satsumas that the prisoners ate by the dozens before toasting the peel and eating that.

Air raids became more frequent but when the siren went at the factory, the guards scrambled for their shelter leaving the POWs to crawl to their doorless dug-out overlooking Nagasaki Bay from where they yelled encouragement at the waves of B29s: 'Go on, you beauties! Let 'em have it!'

On 6 August a specially equipped B29 plane carried the first atomic bomb to Hiroshima, at the southern end of Honshu. This most deadly of weapons killed between 70,000 and 80,000 people and injured over 70,000 – many of them fatally. A second bomb, dropped on 9 August on Nagasaki, caused widespread destruction and killed an estimated 73,884 people and left 74,909 suffering from the after-effects of radiation.

Sherwood remembers hearing a rumble in the distance and looking over the bay to see a black cloud that turned to grey and then rose into a mushroom shape with 'lots of pretty colours on it'. He assumed that the B29s had dropped their bombs on a chemical factory.

After the all-clear was sounded, rather than being ordered back to work, they were sent to their camp and told they would have the next few days off. The following morning was even stranger. When they paraded, all the guards were there too and the camp commandant and interpreter stood on a platform in front of the POWs. He was 'in a filthy temper' and started shouting and gesticulating at them for several minutes until foam appeared from his mouth and he fell silent. When the interpreter took over he told them about a 'Death Ray Bomb' that had killed thousands of Japanese people, including women and children, and that they would be made to pay for the massacre. If any American set foot on Japanese soil they would be shot.

After the announcement the POWs sat around in groups whispering and wondering. They were shocked by the news of the bomb and terrified that after all they had been through they might be killed at the very end of the war. Everyone was on their guard and restless at lights-out at 10 p.m.

The days after the bombs were dropped were amongst the most uneasy for POWs in the Far East. Fergus Anckorn wrote later to his 'folks' about those last tense moments:

> It had been rumoured for a long time but we could see by the behaviour of the Nips what was in the air. Working parties were stopped, in fact I was out on the last one! We went out to build pill boxes & had just arrived & were about to start when the Nips started shouting through the jungle at the top of their voices 'All men stop' . . . '(war) finish!' We were put on lorries & taken back! My friend Bill . . . and Frans were on my bed drinking coffee to celebrate & saying what a pity I was not there – & in I came to celebrate! Oh the excitement . . . The next day one of our bombers dropped leaflets, what a wonderful sight, the first time we hadn't felt sick with fear & had to grovel in trenches at the sound! We have had a hell of a time: torture, starved, beaten, sweated, in fact we've been slaves. All my friends but one have died foul deaths. I have seen the worst deaths possible, 15 a day for months, each time wondering if I could last.

Jack Chalker was experiencing a similar unease at Nakhon Pathom. In May a Korean guard told him that the war in Europe was over; a month later, machine guns were erected in each corner of the bund surrounding the camp and which overlooked a deep trench. Aware of what the Japanese might be planning, Weary Dunlop organised a secret defence group of the fittest POWs and a desperate plan to try to overthrow the guards if it looked as if they were about to be exterminated. Then in the early evening of 16 August, just when tension seemed to be at breaking point, several senior officers met the Japanese commandant and then assembled POWs in the area by the camp theatre. They told them the war was over. Union, Dutch and American flags appeared from nowhere and were hoisted on bamboo flagpoles. Men cried, cheered and walked around in a daze.

It was deathly quiet at Fergus Anckorn's camp of Ubon. All the 3,000 men had been told to stay in their huts and do nothing to enrage their guards. Eventually the commandant emerged to stand on an orange box and told them the same news. After three years, captors and prisoners changed places with great ease.

The Australians started a giant conga that zigzagged its way through the huts and the next day a plane dropped containers of supplies. One POW was crushed in a tragedy that was repeated in several camps where men were killed by the boxes sent to save them. The concert party put on a show that ended with a grand finale of a mock-up bomber descending from the stage with turning propellers and four men inside it to the sound of 'Out of the Blue came Freedom'. The starving men were warned not to eat too much rich food.

At John Lowe's camp at Hakodate, 1,000 miles north of Hiroshima, he had no idea that an atomic bomb had been dropped. His diary entry for 15 August is headed: 'Has it really happened?' 'Things began to buzz': the radio in the office blared out the 'Nip National Anthem', there was a 'big speech' followed by the anthem again and they were told that all mine work was finished; even the night shift was dismissed. Both POWs and guards found it difficult to believe that the war was over but small changes – like the fact that they could see lights shining from the nearest town – indicated that maybe it was.

Thursday, 16th August 1945. Rations if anything are better – on a Yasume day [rest day], which is unheard of and the swines have issued all kinds of musical instruments, games and books; they have made a library and officers' mess available! And once more I have an accordion to play.

17th August 1945

For exercise, everybody does an hour's 'gardening'. I am told that the Japs have burnt all the medical records. I am very run down now, but the weather is glorious, and I am no longer down the mine.

The Library is opened at last; lots of good books, du Maurier, W.W. Jacobs: I believe we are waiting for an Allied Commission to arrive. It turned out to be a wonderful day: the Japs issued each man with a tooth brush and razor blade: and to be shared by the Camp 32 Red Cross parcels from the hundreds they had stored away for years. As usual with the Japs they then vied with each other to give us more rations than we could eat.

Monday, 20th August 1945

We are sure now that the war is over, that more Red Cross is on the way, and that we are to be moved south within a week. [This turned out to be a false rumour] Had a glorious old sing-song last night. To keep myself occupied I am making two pairs of shorts from an old sheet that I found: I have also been asked to make fly-screens for the *suiji* [cook house].

Tuesday, 21st August 1945

I am 26 today, and for a wonderful birthday present I learned that a secret radio had been smuggled in by an American, and was being operated by a British Signals Officer, and was now broadcasting freely.

Also, Red Cross overcoats have been issued: I have a beautiful nigger-brown one – what swine the Nips are not to have given us this stuff before . . . . it would have saved many lives. This evening's meal contained a small battered pork steak, so I've had a good birthday.

It was not until Friday 24 August that the Japanese commandant made a speech telling them that the war was over. By this stage the POWs paid little attention to the guards – even though they were still fully armed.

The swine [the commandant] was trembling: he continued that he hoped we would forgive grudges, and saké was brought out for us to drink. Later, Col. Emoto, the only Jap officer who had ever tried to be kind to us, and was therefore dismissed, made a speech for which he was clapped: he told us that Red Cross supplies would be dropped by air tomorrow.

The next few days were a mental torture as they scanned the skies for planes. Food improved and became more plentiful after the Japanese handed over the stores. Lowe spent his days reading, writing and sewing. He learnt to play 'The Star Spangled Banner', even though very few of the 'Yanks' seemed to know the words. On Sunday he spotted planes in the distance three times but they seemed to be dropping supplies at other camps. On Monday the visibility was too bad for any to arrive and then on Tuesday, huge B29s circled the camp flying small coloured flags from their open bomb doors. As he gazed up at them canisters dropped trailing parachutes behind them followed by great drums welded together. But the parachutes failed to open and the heavy containers crashed to the ground like bombs. One landed two metres from him but he escaped with only a bamboo splinter above his eye; in the nearby Chinese labour camp ten men were killed.

The supplies included boots and corned beef but their stomachs were unable to cope with such rich food and several men were gripped by acute diarrhoea. The next day he gathered a crop of sweets and chocolates. When the planes arrived again, a proper zone had been marked out on the ground for them and the drop went much more smoothly. Then began a waiting game in which the POWs were repeatedly told they were leaving, only to have their hopes dashed. A jeep arrived carrying British and American marine officers who told them they had to sit tight because there were no Allied troops nearby to protect them. Lowe was suffering from an abscess on the back of his leg but still managed to visit the nearby village to barter for eggs. Later he was treated with penicillin – 'apparently a new wonder drug'.

He gathered coloured silks and used a sewing machine he found in the Japanese quarters to make a union flag that he hoped to take home with him. On 11 September naval planes appeared to amuse them with a display – 'zooming up and down and in and out – most exhilarating'. Then they started to jettison food containers. Tragically, one skidded as it hit the ground and decapitated two Americans who had strayed into the drop zone. Lowe's flag was used to cover their bodies. 'How awful to have survived all those years and then be killed by one of their own planes on a mercy mission,' he wrote in his diary.

He spent his mornings in the tailor's shop and then in the afternoon, explored the surrounding countryside. One day he visited a local seamstress and made a 'side-hat' on her machine. Finally, on Saturday 15 they left the camp by truck for the railway station and then they boarded a Curtis Commando D3 plane. They circled Tokyo – 'Oh boy! What a mess!' He began to reconnect with his old world: when they transferred to a ship he played the piano for the first time in four years and at Manila he saw a white woman again. Lady Mountbatten and a team of helpers visited them – 'Among these women were tobacco-spitting Texans who looked very tough babies indeed'. One crushed his tentative attempts to flirt with her with a biting rebuff. Letters from home caught up with him: his mother had escaped injury in a bomb blast and his brother and sister both had a daughter each. A dockers' strike at San Francisco meant they landed at Vancouver where they were greeted by ships' sirens. 'At last, everybody gave vent to their emotions and wept: it took a long time before we recovered.'

When Johnny Sherwood woke up the morning after his commandant had threatened the POWs with mass execution there was not a guard in sight. 'Was this it, had this terrible war ended, were the guards lying in wait for us, to shoot us all?' They had breakfast and chattered amongst themselves until two American B29s flew so low over the camp that they could see one of the pilots waving to them. It was 'the greatest thrill of our lives'. One of the planes then dropped leaflets telling them that Japan had surrendered and that, in Sherwood's words, 'we were Free-Free-Free'. Other leaflets told them to mark out their camp very clearly and they would return with food, medical supplies and clothing. He went with five other POWs and marked out 'Fukuoka No.25' with strips of white sheets. Despite warnings from a medical officer, when they found a tin of American chocolate had burst open on impact they gorged themselves on it and most suffered severe diarrhoea.

But they only really felt safe when the camp bell rang at midday and they rushed to the main gate to see an American armoured jeep and several US officers and NCOs. Like children they threw themselves at their saviours, hugging them and crying. 'This was the first time in three and a half years that we had been in the company of people who were going to treat us as friends and human beings.'

In June 1945 Nowell Peach was at Landsop in Java when he tasted the contents of a Red Cross parcel for the first time in nearly four years of captivity. Peach, who had lost over three stone in weight, shared the parcel with eleven others. The contents, though welcome, were a long way from his dream meal of fried eggs and sizzling bacon. The package contained a tin of Spam, creamed rice (which he devoured for its sugar content), coffee powder and a small bar of chocolate. The coffee was a shock to his system and kept him up all night.

Landsop had a hidden radio and rumours started to emerge about the end of the war by early August. These gathered momentum and then, on 28 August, their Japanese commandant – who was very short – stood on a table and announced very solemnly that the war had ended. He omitted to say who had won. Even when they had been reassured about the result there was a sense of anticlimax after so long and Peach remembers feeling 'very flat'.

At James Wakefield's camp in Hong Kong, the POWs found themselves in the awkward position of knowing that the Japanese emperor had surrendered before their guards did. K.M.A. Barnett was able to decipher the arcane imperial language used to announce the end in the newspaper they received in the camp. Rather than risk telling the guards himself he simply handed his translation over to the Japanese interpreters. The guards disappeared almost immediately and the POWs put their own men in charge. Wakefield left the camp two days later to act as a liaison officer between the incoming British troops and the local Chinese and the Japanese. 'I had the pleasure of going into the Peninsula Hotel and telling the few Japanese who were in there, "Pack your bags and out you go."'

Nowell Peach returned to Batavia but was threatened by nationalist rebels who sensed this was their moment to make a strike for independence. His most joyous memory of the end of the war was the luxury of sleeping in a hotel where he experienced crisp white sheets for the first time in several years. He had an uncomfortable journey to Singapore in a Hudson aeroplane where he sat on the floor as the plane climbed to 10,000 feet leaving him feeling dizzy from the lack of oxygen. Luckily, the rest of the journey home was by ship which gave him the chance to acclimatise to his freedom and to put on weight from double rations. By the time he reached England he was pleased to see cellulite on his legs but was dismayed to arrive in a drizzly, austere Liverpool at the end of October. It was a stark taste of what was to come.

Homecoming

The end of the war caught up with Terry Frost when he was being held at a remote farm. Unlike Andrew Hawarden, who was too sick to leave Stalag 383, he had been marched out of the camp with other POWs and away from the advancing Allies. The group of POWs were staying at the farm on their journey deeper into Nazi Germany when news reached them that they were free. He was sitting on a log that formed part of a communal toilet, listening to the wireless with the elderly farmer's wife next to him when he heard the Prime Minister's familiar voice. 'I thought here I am having a crap with the old lady next to me, and Churchill's talking about non-fraternisation.'

They were liberated by American troops who stumbled across them at the farm and who took them in trucks to an airfield where they flew home in Dakotas. Back in Britain the May blossom was just emerging.

As it became obvious that the war was nearing its end Clive Dunn came 'out of the smoke'. His files were found and he was no longer a 'non person' and was sent to work on a farm near the Yugoslavian border. Whereas a few years earlier he might have considered escape, now there seemed little point. One day the guard took him and about sixty other POWs to a small hill and waved them off with a cheery 'Auf Wiedersehen!' They headed west, not sure exactly where they were going but hopeful that they would eventually meet up with their own lines. They marched for six weeks, sleeping rough or in barns and avoiding main roads and railway lines for fear of being bombed or strafed. In this twilight period they were not quite free, nor were they still prisoners. They met up with other POWs and German guards tagged along; they lived off nettles and dandelion leaves. When they bumped into members of the SS, their 'guards' reassured them that the POWs were being moved to another stalag. They ended up at camp in Markt Pongau near Salzburg where they raided an unguarded warehouse and lived off the sugar they found inside for three days. About a week later the Americans arrived.

After my father threw himself into the ditch and lay there waiting for the line of men to pass, time stood still. He lived off vegetables he found in the fields and when he became desperate for something more sustaining he approached a farmhouse. I imagine him hiding in the outbuildings, biding his time till he was sure that the only occupant was the farmer's wife and then approaching the kitchen with a mixture of fear and shame at the sheer impoliteness of what he was about to do. He told me later that when he entered the house the woman was understandably terrified. He must have looked like a wild man: dirty, dressed in rags and desperate. In an attempt to calm her, and in return for the food he took, he pressed on her the signet ring his parents had given him as a birthday present. This crazily unbalanced exchange must have confirmed just how *verrückt* he was.

After this, he hid during the day and walked at night. One evening he sat on a hill gazing up at the stars. The sheer loneliness of his circumstances produced an epiphany – a word, of course, that he would never have used. For the first time during his time as a POW the sheer insignificance of his existence hit him. No one knew where he was; if he died his parents would not have a body over which to grieve and, besides, with three other children they would learn to live with their grief. The world would keep on turning.

But he was lucky. The loneliness might eventually have forced him to do something rash but at some point he met up with members of the Polish Resistance who gave him false papers and clothes and – most challenging of all – ordered him not to speak. He worked briefly in a factory. A Canadian and a group of Polish soldiers who were also on the run joined him. My father formed a close bond with one Pole in particular, Josef, who was about the same age as him. They lived in a forest with other displaced people who had reason to flee the Germans until one day the sound of battle was too close for them to consider escaping. In a typically theatrical gesture and with typically blind confidence my father put his ear to the ground and listened. After a few minutes he stood up and reassured the anxious men that the rumble he had felt through the earth was definitely the sound of 'Shermans' – Allied tanks.

His bold pronouncement was proved right when a great, armoured monster ambled towards them. My father leapt in front of it waving his arms in the air and shouting, 'I'm a jock, I'm a jock!' The tank's anonymous gun fixed the tramp-like figure in its sights and, after a few long moments, a head popped up from its turret. 'What the hell are you doing here?' it said, or words to that effect.

J.O.N. Vickers, who had managed to be so studious and yet so troublesome to the Germans, had a similar experience. He had escaped and was hiding in woods near Kassel until he saw an American tank and approached it with his hands in the air. He described it as the most dangerous moment of his entire war. Later he was able to use the Russian he had learnt in camp to interpret what a Russian general was saying to the Americans.

My father was taken to the nearest Allied camp and debriefed and deloused. In one of those astonishing quirks of war that seem to occur so frequently, he met up with a close friend from school. Then he was put on a plane home and flown over a landscape that bore the scars of recent fighting. It was the first flight ever for a boy from Dumbarton and he did not enjoy the sudden bumps and jolts of a military plane. The pilot assumed it would be a treat for him to take a closer look at the foreign scenery and moved the plane closer to the ground until my father, understandably anxious to see Britain again, could stand it no longer and snapped, 'Let's just go home, eh?'

His sister, Ruby, answered the telephone when he was finally able to ring home. She was bewildered by the unfamiliar yet familiar voice, the voice from beyond the grave. When she told their father, 'It's Donnie,' he snatched the receiver from her, angry at what appeared to be a prank before breaking down in tears.

Some days later he went with his other son to meet the returning soldier at the railway station. My father's father was all dressed up in his best suit and hat but to my father's dismay they walked straight past him – unable to recognise the emaciated, shaven-headed Scots Guard. At some point during the celebrations that followed his homecoming, the girlfriend who had sent my father the Dear John letter reappeared and told him that she had made a terrible mistake and that she did want to marry him after all. But my father had grown used to the idea that she would not be his bride and was not about to readjust his vision of the future once more. He had first met my mother at a Scots Guards dance in London before he was posted abroad and sought her out soon after his return in 1945. They married in April 1946 and when he took her up to Scotland made a point of introducing her to his first fiancée. My mother made an effort to look 'as good as she could on coupons'.

A medical inspection in June 1945 showed that his health had slipped from A1 to B1 due to a 'mental breakdown after escape'. His company commander added the remarks: 'At the moment is suffering from bad nerves . . . In time will probably make a useful NCO again.' A year later he had recovered sufficiently for the officer who wrote his testimonial on release from the army to comment: 'I have known CSM [company sergeant major] Gillies for five years and I have the highest opinion of him. He has served six years in the Regiment with an exemplary record. He has a natural ability to handle men, absolutely reliable and I can confidently recommend him for any position of trust and responsibility.' Although on the face of it he had recovered from his experience of captivity, he would still wake in the night, his pyjamas drenched in sweat after he had relived some ordeal from his time in the camp or on the run.

Victory in Europe was celebrated on 8 May 1945 but the relatives of men held in the Far East still had months to wait until they were reunited. On 23 August 1945 Luce wrote to Fergus:

> My knees are knocking together at the very thought of your return. I keep wondering whether you are still my Ferg or whether I shall have to get to know you all over again. I don't mind, we shall have many happy thoughts together.
>
> I haven't changed, just a few more grey hairs and I've just become a bit older, regarding you I haven't changed, I still love you and I would have waited forever, you know that I'm sure by now . . .
>
> Well, my Darling we are anxiously awaiting news of you, ready to welcome you home, and when eventually you arrive, you must forget the past years and we shall begin anew and I shall try to make up to you the awful lonely years you've had.
>
> Goodbye Darling
> All my love, all my life,
> Yours always
> Luce xxxx

Slowly, they began to let their guard down as the more regular letters allowed them to get to know one another again. In October she wrote joyously:

> I'm getting married in about two years too, did you know? Yes, some great guy I've dug up from somewhere, he's rather cute and I'm crazy about him!!

But she was aware that they had experienced different wars.

> Darling, I shall never ask you about all you've been through and unless you feel you want to tell me I shall quite understand. I hope so very much that you'll settle down again & be the same old Ferg, I'm quite sure you will, with everyone to help you.
> By the way, I haven't kissed anyone while you've been away either! ...

She had been 'glamorising' herself but had yet to have her face 'lifted!!' She admitted that she had had 'several offers' but had resolved not to marry if he did not return, adding: 'God how wonderful it will be to have you again it makes my heart turn over'. He told her how he could not bear noise or traffic but she reassured him: 'I'm not so hot myself since I was doodled [in a V-1 flying bomb/Doodlebug raid], however you'll soon be OK.' Now she felt she could tell him that Lambeth Hospital had been badly bombed and that she had suffered a knock on the head – 'I'll let you feel it if you're very good!!!' They began to gain some inkling of the other's life. She told him how she had delivered 180 babies while he had been away. But a talk on the radio gave her some clue as to what he had been through. In it an Australian POW spoke about working on the Thailand–Burma Railway – 'I didn't like it much!' she told Fergus.

When she knew he was on his way home she urged him, 'Darling for heaven's sake enjoy yourself take the girls out & have a fling, God knows you deserve it'. She reassured him that when his general condition improved, his hand would stop shaking '& any way I can always hold it'.

The last few weeks before they were reunited were agony: 'I keep wondering if I shall be shy with you (imagine me shy) but I am quite often these days, perhaps you will be too. Still, mother will stir us up a bit.' She could not decide what to wear. 'I'm still trying to glamorous [sic] myself but it's a hell of a job. I'm not very satisfied with the finished article!'

He arrived at Liverpool on 9 November 1945 to the sound of sirens and hoots from the other ships they passed. A huge crowd was waiting at the docks, faces eagerly scanning the decks for their loved ones. But he knew that he would not be reunited with Luce and his family until the next day when he arrived at Charing Cross. He was shocked by the devastation he saw all around him in London – shops and houses with no windows, gaps where buildings once stood. But nothing could detract from the excitement of his reunion with Luce and his family.

It took him a long time to readjust to life as a free man. The first time he went to London by himself he walked into a Lyons Corner House and was overwhelmed by his new surroundings:

> They had this lovely orchestra all playing, white tie and tails, beautiful table with damask Irish linen table cloth and knife, fork, spoon – all silver. I'd ordered my food and my head flopped onto the table and I started crying my eyes out. I thought, 'Look where I am. I'm in this glorious place.' The waiter came over and said 'Are you alright sir' and I said, 'yes, thank you.' I just walked out.

On another trip to London he suddenly 'flipped' when he was at Charing Cross station and could not remember who he was. He stumbled into a phone box and started scanning the telephone directory, hoping a name would mean something to him. As he flicked through the 'A's his memory began to slide back to normality and when he reached 'Anckorn' he was able to phone his father to tell him to collect him.

PART VI

Ex-POWs

Aftermath

The experience of being a prisoner of war affected each individual in different ways, but it also produced ripples for the generation after the war and beyond. The intensity of the experience was unique. Never again would men feel so bored, so hungry, so watched, so uncertain of their future. These special circumstances led some to study, write and think with an ascetic zeal that never left them.

As well as the many POWs who went into academic life – a form of safe captivity in itself – many wrote books that either looked back on their experience or were composed during captivity. Five years after the end of the war, John Buxton's book, *The Redstart*, based on his painstaking research at Eichstätt and Laufen, was published as part of Collins' prestigious *New Naturalist* series. Its style displays Buxton's skill as a poet. It contains the usual ornithological illustrations but also a map of redstart territories which show how the POW camp influenced the birds: the area between the creek and River Salzach was quieter because it was often out of bounds to prisoners, whereas the patrol ground would have been much noisier because it was where 2,000 men exercised. The book's acknowledgements include a poignant reminder of what it meant to be married to a POW as Buxton thanks his wife for responding to requests for information about the redstart – requests which took up precious space on his cards home to her. As recently as 2009 a newspaper article described *The Redstart* as 'arguably the best single species study ever written'; the Poet Laureate, Andrew Motion, referred to it as a 'masterpiece'. On release Buxton retreated back into the academic life, as an English don, which he had left to become a POW.

Birdwatching behind barbed wire transformed Peter Conder's career. Before the war he had been a self-confessed loner and academic failure who had settled into a job at the family advertising firm. When he returned home he abandoned his safe job to become warden of Skokholm Bird Observatory off the Welsh Coast. A paper by him, Waterston and Buxton, 'Rook and Jackdaw Migrations Observed in Germany, 1942–1945', was published in the journal of the British Ornithologists' Union, *Ibis*, in 1949. Later he became director of the Royal Society for the Protection of Birds and during his thirteen years in this position, membership increased from 20,000 to 200,000.

Waterston also made use of his wartime studies and worked for the Rook and Woodpigeon Investigations at the Agricultural Research Council. But his more lasting legacy was the POW mentality he brought to Loch Garten in Speyside, where, as director of the RSPB in Scotland, he helped to safeguard the return of the osprey that the Victorian passion for egg collecting and hunting had driven to near-extinction. When a pair returned to nest in Speyside in 1954 Waterston set up 'Operation Osprey' to protect them from egg hunters. Studying old film of the site, the pinewoods decked with barbed wire and round-the-clock surveillance look eerily like a Scottish version of a POW camp. But Waterston's legacy was not his ability to protect the birds through stalag security but his daring and highly controversial decision to throw the site open to the public whose presence, he believed, would protect the nests from robbers. He was right. In the summer of 1959, 14,000 visited Loch Garten where eggs had just hatched for the first time. Since then two million people have been to the reserve; two hundred pairs of osprey nested in Scotland in 2008 and Waterston is often credited with inventing 'eco tourism'.

H.R. van Heekeren, who had found archaeological treasure in Thailand, spent the last year or so of the war digging in a Japanese coal mine. Half of it was underwater and the shafts regularly collapsed. Despite constant drilling and dynamiting they only ever found substandard coal. The rest of the mine contained stone and poisonous gas.

When news that the war was over arrived, Dutch, British and American flags appeared from their secret hiding places and someone drew a life-size portrait of Queen Wilhelmina from a silver guilder he had hung on to for all those years. Van Heekeren's interest in archaeology remained undimmed by his ordeal and while the rest of his camp waited to be liberated by the Americans he and a friend risked missing their lift home by embarking on an ambitious trip to climb a volcano near Nagasaki.

As soon as he was certain the war was over he took his precious stones from their hiding place and wrote an article about their discovery. This, together with sketches by a fellow POW, were sent to the *Illustrated London News* and appeared on 5 April 1947. He left the stones with a professor at Manila and a priest later took them by ship to America where they are still held in the Peabody Museum at Harvard University. 'And there they are in a glass case, after all their travels. Seven old stones.'

Van Heekeren returned to the Far East after the war where he held various positions in historical institutions and worked on digs in the region. His discoveries included evidence of an extinct form of pig which was named after him, *Celebochoerus heekereni*, and which he referred to as his 'god child'. Unrest in the region led him to move back to Holland where he collated much of the prehistory findings of the region into two major books, *The Stone Age of Indonesia* (1957) and *The Bronze-Iron Age of Indonesia* (1958), that were later described as 'the foundation of all future prehistoric research in Indonesia'. In the 1960s he was conservator of the prehistory collection at the Rijksmuseum voor Volkenkunde in Leiden and led or took part in three major overseas expeditions to follow up points raised from his POW discoveries. He joined two Thai–Danish expeditions that returned to Thailand and was awarded two honorary degrees by the Rijksuniversity of Leiden and the University of Copenhagen.

In April 1944 a German medical board agreed to Harold Montgomery Belgion's repatriation on health grounds. At home a British doctor confirmed that he was suffering from some sort of nervous problem, as well as a bilateral hernia and that he was fit for home service only. While he was on his way to England via Sweden, Jonathan Cape sent the manuscript of *Reading for Profit* to Geoffrey Faber, who scribbled a note on the covering letter to T.S. Eliot asking him to look at it as Cape had wanted to publish but were short of paper.

It was then passed to Allen Lane at Penguin, where Jonathan Cape negotiated on Belgion's behalf and secured an advance of £75 which rose to £100. They agreed an initial print-run of between 50,000 and 60,000 copies. *Reading for Profit* was to be Belgion's most successful book. The English edition sold over a hundred thousand copies; an American edition appeared and it was translated into French. In May 1947 it even featured in a *Punch* cartoon in which a prim librarian holds up an over-due copy of *Reading for Profit* while pointing to a notice behind her about fines. 'That will be ten shillings to pay on this one,' she tells the borrower.

Belgion married Gladys Helan Mattock in 1945, when he was fifty-three. She had founded Westwood House School, near Peterborough, and over-saw its rapid expansion. When it became a trust Belgion took on the role of secretary. He remained a prolific author, reviewer and lecturer and also campaigned – unsuccessfully – for the release of the American poet Ezra Pound, who was held in a lunatic asylum because the Fascist broadcasts he made from wartime Italy were deemed to show he was mentally unsound. Belgion died in 1973.

A.N.L. Munby went on to be librarian at King's College, Cambridge, for twenty-seven years, a college where his literary hero M.R. James had once been provost. The ghost stories he wrote at Eichstätt were pub-lished in a collection called *The Alabaster Hand* in 1949. The book sold 10,000 copies in hardback and, in a pleasing coincidence, the printer who dealt with the book was Elliott Viney (of Hazell, Watson & Viney) who had worked on *Touchstone*, the POW magazine where three of the sto-ries first appeared.

Terence Prittie's experience at Oflag IX A/H, where he had sent home articles about cricket, also shaped his postwar career. In 1946 he published his first book, *South To Freedom*, that he wrote with Captain W.E. Edwards and in which he drew on his six escape attempts. As his memories of being a POW became less raw he drew on his intimate understanding of Germany to produce more considered writing on its postwar future. After a brief spell as the *Guardian*'s cricketing correspondent, he became its Chief Correspondent in Germany for sixteen years and its diplomatic cor-respondent. He wrote sixteen books, including respected biographies of the German statesmen, Konrad Adenauer and Willy Brandt.

The London bookseller, Hatchards, devoted a whole window of its Piccadilly shop to *Mountain Prospect* by Scott Russell when it was pub-lished after the war. The book, which he wrote on a thick pad of military forms in Changi Gaol in between tending a small plot of land, told of his experience of climbing in Scotland, the Lake District, New Zealand and Switzerland as well as more challenging expeditions to the Arctic and Northern India, when he climbed and studied plants in a brief moment before war changed his life. Back in Britain he returned to plant biology and set up the Agricultural Research Council Radiobiological Laboratory.

Mountain Prospect may have been the first climbing book to be published after the war but its distinctive cover of a soaring snow-clad peak is now a rare collector's piece. *Mountaineering in Scotland*, which Bill Murray finished after the Gestapo destroyed the first draft, was published in 1947 and is still in print. It appeals to both climbers and readers who enjoy his elegiac descriptions of landscape. It was the first of twenty books he wrote, including a biography of Rob Roy, thrillers and several on mountaineering. His final book, *The Evidence of Things Not Seen*, was published after his death and edited by his widow, a poet. In it he discusses the mystical awakening he experienced as a POW.

Eric Newby was finally captured on 29 December 1943 after nearly four months on the run. He spent the rest of the war in Germany but was reunited with Wanda, who had helped him when he first broke his ankle, and they married in 1946. He combined a job in the fashion industry with travel writing. *A Short Walk in the Hindu Kush* was his first success but for many people *Love and War in the Apennines*, which is both comic and deeply moving, remains his finest work and one of the most authentic books about the life of a European POW.

Longmans published Dan Billany and David Dowie's journal, *The Cage*, in 1949 and Faber brought out Billany's novel, *The Trap*, in 1950 but while their manuscripts made it back to Britain, the authors did not. They were last heard of in Mantua in December 1943. Billany may have been killed in an encounter with an informer or they may have died from exposure on the mountains that concealed so many POWs. Neither body has been found. Dino Meletti, the farmer who had sheltered the two men, remained true to his word and in March 1946 the notebooks containing the manuscripts of both books arrived at Billany's parents' house.

The Happiness Book, produced as a present for interned children at Changi that first Christmas of 1942, was miraculously dug up from its hiding place and returned to David Griffin. The front was slightly squashed and some of the illustrations had been transferred to the opposite page. Nevertheless, its fame spread and Lord Mountbatten, who was in the Far East immediately after the war, asked to see it. He remarked that the king would be very interested in it and asked whether he could take it back with him to Britain. Griffin refused, saying he wanted to show his wife. The original is in the State Library of New South Wales but the story has been published professionally.

Captivity exposed men to different social classes, beliefs, cultures and startlingly new ideas they would not have encountered in civilian life. Adrian Heath and Terry Frost grew up in different worlds and yet their chance meeting led to a lifelong friendship that changed both their career paths. Frost said later that learning to paint in a POW camp was 'the best education I could have had before becoming a professional painter' because it taught him to see things around him for the first time.

He returned to a part of the country that had been badly bombed and to a family which viewed being an artist as a 'sissy' occupation. He took up his old job in Birmingham but went to art school at night. He was told he was ineligible for an ex-serviceman's grant to go to art school full-time because he did not have his School Certificate. Out of frustration he hitched to London (it took two days), ostensibly to meet up with his POW friend, Adrian Heath, but he also bumped into Fred Mulley and some other ex-POWs from Stalag 383 in a pub. One of them told him there was an exemption clause that would allow him to obtain a grant, while Heath advised him to move as far away as possible from his family and, thinking back to his pre-war days in Cornwall, suggested St Ives, which had a burgeoning artists' community. Frost took his advice and moved down there with his new wife, Kath, and then between 1947 and 1950 studied at Camberwell School of Art which, together with Heath's studio, was a focus for the new Constructivist movement. He held his first one-man show in London at the Leicester Galleries in 1952. Over the years he abandoned realism and developed an abstract style. Just as flowers placed in a Canadian butter tin had inspired him at Stalag 383 so the Cornish landscape guided his work, such as the rise and fall of boats in a harbour at twilight, in *Blue Movement*. He was knighted in 1998 and died in Cornwall in 2003.

Adrian Heath was moved from Stalag 383 and in his final camp used his artistic talents to forge documents for escapers. Like Frost, he was marched north, away from the advancing Russians, but unlike Frost he was liberated by them, not the Americans. The Russians gave the ex-POWs weapons and urged them to join them but Heath, who was starving and jaundiced, preferred to wait to be taken home. One of the first things he did in

London was to walk up and down Bond Street looking at the galleries and art dealers. He used his army back-pay to buy a Sickert drawing and paintings by Wyndham Lewis and Victor Pasmore. He resumed his studies at the Slade where he felt 'rather old'. After graduation he spent a year in Paris. His abstract style of interlocking planes bounded by curves, acute angles and boxes was inspired by landscape and the female form. Just as he had influenced Frost at Stalag 383 so he proved a charismatic teacher throughout his life.

For other artists, being a POW taught them practical skills and provided a lifelong inspiration. From his studio in an old mill overlooking the snow-topped Mendip Hills and from the distance of seventy years, Jack Chalker can look back to his time as a POW with no bitterness. When he first returned he wanted to share his experiences but found that as soon as he started talking he would begin to shake until he was unable to speak. With time this wore off.

He considers himself lucky that he has been able to pursue the two strands of art that he finds most interesting. His work as a medical orderly and as an artist in the camps gave him a deep anatomical knowledge. His ability to draw quickly and under pressure completed the battery of skills he needed to become a surgical illustrator. Until a few years ago he would sit in on brain and other micro surgery to provide a visual record of the operation in a way that a camera could not. While a photo captures 'the seething mass of greasy, sparkling bits of tissue', the medical team also needs a sparer record. A drawing can provide a clearer sequence of the operation and of which instruments are used and when. His apprenticeship with Marko gave him an appreciation of the work and his postwar expertise was recognised when he became a Fellow of the Society of Medical Artists of Great Britain.

He continued his art studies once he returned to Britain and graduated from the Royal College of Art in 1951. Soon he became part of the thriving Cornish arts scene and helped to set up the new Falmouth College of Art and became its Principal.

'We associated with people like Ben Nicholson and Barbara Hepworth and all these people at that time and it was in the early days then, when the place wasn't swamped with old ladies painting dogs and fishermen's huts.'

He combined teaching with his own creative achievements and later became Principal of the West of England College of Art.

The drawings and paintings he created as a POW, or shortly after release, are exhibited around the world. There is considerable interest in his work in Japan. A permanent gallery devoted to his art was opened in Thailand in 2002. His book, *Burma Railway, Images of War*, was published in 2007 and three years later a Japanese edition appeared.

In 2010 the Cartoon Museum in London held a retrospective of Ronald Searle's work to celebrate his ninetieth birthday. The publicity described him as a 'Graphic Master' and he has influenced a new generation of artists such as Gerald Scarfe and Ralph Steadman. His work represents so much more than the St Trinian's cartoons which he first drew in Changi and which, by virtue of Hollywood adaptations, kept him supplied with the champagne he loved. He emerged from the war with a very different style. The dystopian boarding school of St Trinian's is a sanitised POW camp and some of Searle's postwar drawings echo images he drew as a prisoner – the men hauling logs became school girls dragging a lawn-mower before sports day, the heads of Chinese victims stacked on shelves cropped up again as decapitated teaching staff. Searle has said that he viewed these drawings as 'baby stuff' but that the experience made him a good draughtsman.

Captivity, in a roundabout way, also led him to his wife, Kaye Webb, who was working on *Lilliput*, a magazine which had been launched in 1937 and whose light-hearted style helped it to out-sell *Punch*. Although he had glimpsed his first St Trinian's cartoon in the midst of the battle for Singapore, the staff of *Lilliput* had assumed he had not survived and it was not until the summer of 1945 that Webb knew he was alive. The follow-ing year *Punch* and *Lilliput* both published cartoons he had drawn in Changi Gaol. When Webb and Searle finally met they were instantly attracted to each other, although she was still married to her second hus-band. She quickly fell pregnant with twins – much to Searle's astonishment since he had been told that, as an ex-POW, he might have problems pro-ducing offspring.

Their marriage lasted until the 1960s when he left her quite suddenly. According to his first biographer, Russell Davies, Searle viewed marriage and the noisy social life of his wife as a new form of imprisonment. He obviously found his propulsion straight into the role of father so quickly after his release from Changi difficult to adapt to. When he appeared on *Desert Island Discs* he explained his decision to leave his family and start a new life in France. 'It didn't worry me, because I'd been to zero before. When you've been the lowest of the low, you can never go down lower.' He added that he did not care what people said about him because it was 'a question of survival'.

After the war George Sprod returned to Australia and started to make a living from his art by selling some of his Changi cartoons to the *Sydney Morning Herald* and then submitting new work to other publications. In 1949 he moved to London where he worked as a freelance cartoonist and was reunited with Searle on the *News Chronicle*. He became a highly successful cartoonist for *Punch* before returning to Australia in the 1960s. His work has been exhibited round the world and his admirers have included Sir John Gielgud and the Duke of Edinburgh. He continued to use the same pen and ink methods he perfected in Thailand.

Stanley Gimson, who had sketched such precise views of Changi and Thailand, was inspired by lectures he had attended whilst a POW to study law at Glasgow University. He was called to the Scottish Bar and had a distinguished career as a lawyer, as well as working for several charities.

The 2nd Earl Haig studied at Camberwell School of Art and preferred to stick to realism. He painted landscapes – particularly of the Scottish borders where he spent the rest of his life in his fourteenth-century house near Melrose – and had his first London exhibition at the Redfern Gallery in 1949 and his first north of the border in Edinburgh the same year.

Stanley Warren, who had created the Changi Murals, became an art teacher in Camden, North London, and faded back into civilian life until 1958 when the paintings were rediscovered by members of the RAF living in their barracks in Changi. The *Daily Mirror* launched a hunt for the artist and Warren was eventually discovered when a colleague remembered that he had been a POW in the Far East and brought the cutting into the staff room to show him. The RAF asked him to restore the murals but he was at first reluctant to return to a place that had such painful memories. He was eventually persuaded and made three trips back to work on the paintings.

In 1986 the British Parliament discussed trying to move the Changi Murals to Britain after Singapore won its independence. But the original building is now part of Singapore Ministry of Defence's Changi Airbase Camp, and for security reasons, it is very difficult to visit. A copy of the murals is on display at Changi Museum.

I was fortunate enough to see the originals at Roberts Barracks in the summer of 2008. After a brief walk from the army minibus to the old colonial building, the blast of heat was enough to remind me of how enervating it must have been to live permanently in such temperatures whilst also enduring illnesses such as dysentery. St Luke's Chapel is cool and peaceful, a breeze flitting like a spirit through the room. The murals dominate, their incongruity making them feel like guardian angels. It was difficult to know what to do amongst such powerful historical memories – or ghosts. A quiet prayer seemed to be called for but not expected by the tourism official who was constantly at my side, fanning himself with the Changi Murals information sheet.

Captivity gave artists like Terry Frost the freedom to discover unacknowledged talents. The same was true of men who realised they could hold the attention of a POW audience, had a capacity for learning languages or for teaching. The bumper crop of war films that followed the end of hostilities offered the chance of method acting for many ex-POWs. In real life Donald Pleasance was shot down in August 1944 and later played Flight Lt. Colin Blythe, the prisoner who tries to conceal his blindness so that he can join the other tunnellers in *The Great Escape*. But he also became James Bond's most feared villain, Blofeld, and Heinrich Himmler in *The Eagle Has Landed*. Denholm Elliott had the strange experience of portraying a POW in a different continent in the film adaptation of James Clavell's *King Rat*. Derek Bond, who was held at Moosburg, appeared in one of the earliest – and most darkly convincing – POW films, *The Captive Heart*. Sam Kydd, who was at Stalag XXA at Thorn, was in the same film, although listed only as 'POW in Top Bunk' – at least it was the top. Kydd went on to become a familiar face in British films and TV programmes such as *Dixon of Dock Green*, *Z Cars* and *Robin Hood*.

When Talbot Rothwell returned to Britain he knew that he wanted to make a career from writing. At first he supplied material for the Crazy Gang and Arthur Askey until he broke into the *Carry On* films. He is credited with giving them their trademark lacing of *double entendres* and wrote the scripts for the most famous – including *Carry On up the Khyber* (1968) that many *aficionados* agree is the best. Butterworth, whom he had first met in Stalag Luft III, became a familiar face in the films. He made his debut in *Carry on Cowboy* (1965) and, among many roles, played Citizen Bidet in *Carry on Don't Lose your Head* (1966), about the French Revolution, and Brother Belcher in *Up the Khyber*. It is said that he auditioned for *The Wooden Horse* about the Stalag Luft III escape but failed to win the part on the grounds that he did not look the part.

Roy Dotrice was still a teenager when he became a POW in 1942 and had yet to start his acting career. But imprisonment gave him the chance to perform next to professionals such as Rupert Davies, who would later take the part of the French detective in the highly successful television series, *Maigret*. In July 1945 Dotrice performed in a revue put on by former RAF POWs called *Back Home* that raised money for the Red Cross. He has barely stopped working since and in his eighties was touring with *Brief Lives*, his one-man play about author John Aubrey. When, in 2000, he received a Tony Award for his performances on the New York stage he remembered his POW days: 'It was there that I had my first contact with Americans. I found that they had a unique ability: the ability not to envy, but to applaud other people's successes. And it was then that I fell in love with Americans and America.'

Once Clive Dunn was demobbed, he resumed his acting and variety career. The parts were the familiar comic characters he had played before the war but the part of Corporal Jones in *Dad's Army* offered a release after his years of 'working for Hitler . . . mountain side digging and God knows what else'. Jonesy's twitchy outbursts against the Germans and his pent-up desire to 'let them have it' was a direct result of Dunn's wartime experience. 'It was like a wonderful happy revenge for that.'

In one of his last professional jobs he made his opera debut as Frosch, the drunken jailor in *Die Fledermaus*. 'My few years' experience of old Austrian soldiers in prison camps helped me to create the atmosphere I wanted, and I sang a little Viennese drinking song for good measure.'

But being a POW also made him feel more strongly about the abuse of power; not just the obvious abuses perpetrated by the Nazis but the way those in authority hold sway over those without. This strong feeling of justice has remained with him into his nineties.

As a POW Cy Grant, the black airman who was shot down over The Netherlands, had enjoyed opportunities to study and perform but when he returned to Britain he found his horizons clouded by racial inequality. He experienced very little racism in camp – perhaps, he reasoned, because he was mainly with Canadians. The only time he was called a 'nigger' was by an American airman from the Deep South.

Grant decided that if he survived the war he would study to become a barrister and use this to try to fight colonialism: 'Being a prisoner of war taught me a lot about myself. It gave me, at a crucial point in my life, time to reflect and look at myself and society. It taught me many lessons. How to live with other people, even when one did not particularly care for them; that there were always individuals that one could respect.'

After the war he succeeded in becoming a barrister but show business proved a much more certain way of earning a living. In 1957 he began to appear regularly on BBC's *Tonight* programme, where he performed calypso songs about news items, sometimes with words provided by Bernard Levin. It was the first time British TV audiences had seen a black performer playing a key part in a successful show. He gave up the role to avoid being typecast and played several other parts on TV, in the theatre and in films, although he was always frustrated by the lack of roles for black actors. Ironically, one of his most successful parts was the voice of the puppet Lieutenant Green in the highly successful TV show *Captain Scarlet and the Mysterons*. Its creator, Gerry Anderson, had lost his own brother over The Netherlands in the Second World War and detected in Grant's voice the perfect qualities for a black hero capable of saving planet earth. His character provided an early positive black role model in children's TV and fitted Grant's later writing, theatre work and human rights campaigning – all of which celebrated and explored racial differences.

Far fewer POWs in the Far East achieved the level of fame of performers held in Europe. Perhaps the physical and mental effects of captivity in Japanese hands robbed them of the energy required to inspire an audience. It may be significant that the most famous performers, Sydney Piddington and Slim de Grey, remained in Changi and did not work on the Thailand–Burma Railway.

Piddington the shy conjuror who had perfected his mind-reading act with Russell Braddon in Changi Gaol, was the exception. According to Braddon the war changed Piddington, who became 'forceful, confident, knew what he wanted to do, knew how he thought he ought to do it'. As so often happened with Far Eastern POWs, Piddington stayed in close contact with the friends he had made in the camps, and in particular with members of the Australian concert party. Many of these POWs were still talking about the 'thought transference' act they had seen in Changi and Piddington was asked to perform it on the wireless. But this time his partner was his new wife, Lesley Pope, a well known radio actress; Russell Braddon helped to promote the act and ex-POWs like Leslie Greener vouched for the act's authenticity. In one of the earliest performances Piddington told members of the audience he had not met before what they were thinking and his wife read a line from a book that had been 'telepathically transmitted' by her husband. The act was soon attracting attention around the world and caused a sensation in London where they appeared as part of an eight-programme contract with the BBC. Ronald Searle helped by introducing them to journalists. Twenty million listeners tuned in to one of their most ambitious mind-reading feats. Sydney, who was in a BBC studio in Piccadilly, relayed by telepathy a message that someone had chalked on a board. Lesley, who was held at the Tower of London, successfully revealed the sentence as: 'Be abandoned as the electricians said that they would have no current.' 'To do a Piddington' became an expression for guessing what someone was about to say.

When they appeared at the London Palladium, *The Times* described them as 'modest and inscrutable, two casually performing sphinxes'. After one underwater demonstration they appeared in a print advertisement for Ronson lighters. 'No need to concentrate with a Ronson,' Lesley comments as she lights her cigarette, while her husband replies: 'Lesley's taken the words right out of my mind!' Their act provoked concern among church leaders but the Piddingtons never claimed that what they were doing was genuine telepathy and pointed critics to their catchphrase, 'You are the judges'. Even when they retired in 1954 newspapers were still offering the couple £10,000 to reveal their secret.

Few ex-POWs became as famous as Sydney Piddington but many went on to have distinguished careers. In most cases they struggled to make a living in countries now battling against austerity, rather than bombs. Many found that while their lives had changed, so had the lives of the families they returned to. Jon Vickers, who had spent his fives years as a POW studying to be a teacher, translating broadcasts on a hidden radio and helping with escape attempts, was reunited with his wife at Baker Street station. But like many returning POWs he was to discover that families at home had also suffered while they were away. In his case he learnt that his wife had lost both her legs in an air raid three years before.

He became warden of Wedgwood Memorial College at Barlaston Hall, Staffordshire, and was proud of the fact that it attracted industrial workers such as potters and miners. From here he joined the Electrical Trades Union research department and became its education officer. When Soviet troops invaded Hungary he left the Communist Party for Labour. In the 1960s he joined the Civil Service Union, which represented workers mainly in lower grade jobs, and rose to be its General Secretary. One of his proudest moments was resolving the women night cleaners' recognition dispute of 1972 and after his retirement he continued to sit on an employment appeals tribunal. He also taught for the Workers' Educational Association (WEA) and believed that the teaching he had done behind barbed wire had been a useful preparation for this. He had two children, James and Salley. His daughter is the author of several novels, including *Miss Garnet's Angel* that has sold over three hundred and fifty thousand copies. She treasures her father's copy of *Moby Dick* which has 'Oflag IX' stamped on the front.

John Phillips, who had written hopefully to his family friend, Philippa Cook, from the lower camp at Oflag IX A/H in Spangenberg, returned home to discover that she had succumbed to one of the eligible young men who were 'kicking about in England while we're caged up in monastic seclusion'. She met her future husband, Peter Forwood, a dashing major who in civilian life had been a stockbroker, on a drafty gun site in south Wales while he was waiting to go to Normandy. He proposed to her in a letter he wrote from Holland.

However, the two families remained close friends all their lives and John Phillips managed to put the languages he learnt in Oflag IX A/H to good use after the war when he joined the Sudan Political Service and then became ambassador to Southern Yemen, Jordan and Sudan.

James Wakefield was also able to make use of the languages he learnt in camp and decided to make his future in Hong Kong. He went back with his wife and one of his first jobs was to work with another ex-POW to set up a district office on one floor of the Peninsula Hotel. He rose to the position of Commissioner of Labour and ended his career as Senior Officer in the Secretariat.

For many POWs captivity left them with an attitude of mind – sometimes this was a desire simply to be happy, or, as in my father's case, to enjoy the simple pleasures. Setting up the University of Kuching taught

Frank Bell how study, and language learning in particular, could promote international harmony.

His train journey from Huyton in Liverpool to Euston, London, in 1945 was the 'greatest day' of his life. He could not sit still and rubbed his hands together, not knowing where to look. After the war, learning and teaching languages, which had helped him to get through his experience as a POW, allowed him to start a new life as a free man, but now it was tempered with a need for reconciliation. He returned to Cambridge where he became Assistant Secretary in the university's Department of Extra-Mural Studies. He lectured German POWs who were held in camps in East Anglia and helped to select German students to study at Cambridge. When the university showed no interest in teaching English as a foreign language he decided to borrow money from a friend and set up his own school in a Victorian house in the city in 1955. Other Bell language schools followed in Norwich, Bath and Saffron Walden in Essex, and in 1968 he bought Concord College where teachers prepared overseas students for university. He was a pioneer in Teaching English as a Foreign Language but he saw TEFL as much more than education. He believed that the route to worldwide co-operation and understanding lay in learning and he had no hesitation in welcoming Japanese students to his schools. In 1972, he established an educational charity – the Bell Educational Trust that promotes international understanding and intercultural exchange.

Lucille's patience and compassion helped to restore Fergus Anckorn and, like many other Far Eastern POWs, he found returning to the Far East allowed him to confront his demons. He visited Japan in 1995 but it was only after a trip to Singapore with his son in 2005 that the nightmares he had been experiencing for fifty years stopped. He believes seeing the sparklingly clean, modern island helped him to accept that the dark days of Japanese occupation were over for good. He visited Alexandra Hospital with his daughter, Deborah, in 2007.

His trip to Japan was one of four goals he promised himself he would achieve if he survived. The others were to learn to speak Japanese, to be able to read a compass well and to learn to fly. These last two were born out of a desire to be able to escape from the jungle and, while he does not own a pilot's licence, he has had enough lessons to feel confident that he could take off and land a plane. 'I learnt to use a compass and I've got a fetish about it, I never go anywhere without a compass. I must have ten compasses in this house and I also brought one in the car – I'm not talking about the Sat Nav. I've always got one because it could have saved my life. I thought how important it is to know where you are.'

He has learnt Japanese, although he quickly discovered that his existing vocabulary was made up of coarse 'soldier's language' which startled his polite Japanese teacher. Surviving the war left him with an ambition simply to be happy. For most of his career he taught and continued to perform magic in the evenings. He is now the oldest member of the Magic Circle.

Although Tommy Atkins's diary stopped abruptly in February 1945 he survived the war, despite shrinking from his usual weight of around fifteen stone to six. His family – he had a son, John, and a daughter, Sandra – never knew why he stopped writing the journal to his wife, Bunty. Perhaps the secret activity became too risky or he simply ran out of paper. Like most Far Eastern POWs he found returning to normal life extremely hard and soon after tried to commit suicide.

The army kept him on a repeatedly renewed short commission right up until his retirement in 1964, by which time he had become a major. He remained troubled by what he saw as the slow career progression of men like himself who had risen through the ranks, compared to regular officers. This distinction brought back painful memories of his time on the railway. On leaving the army he became the first civilian police fleet manager in the country. He never spoke with any bitterness against the Japanese, arguing that it was better to have them as friends than enemies.

Curiosity about the country that had started the war guided John Lowe's career. He returned to Islington restless, 'like a bouncing ball', and drifted into several jobs before going to art school and eventually becoming a teacher. A chance conversation with a friend in 1955 led him to apply for a job at a British Forces Education Service north of Hamburg. One of his motivations was that he had never met a German, although Germany's history had shaped his early twenties. John and his family have moved often and lived in several different countries. Throughout his career he has continued to use the skills that had helped him survive as a POW. Wherever he lived or worked he became involved in amateur dramatics, making stage sets or helping with costumes – often improvised out of bits and pieces. In the German boarding school where he worked, he made a set of angel's wings out of a member of staff's bra, three mousetraps and two Perspex rulers. He became the first manager of Strode Theatre, which was attached to a Technical College in Somerset, and later gave an annual lecture at Bristol University to amateur drama groups called 'Making Scenery from Nothing'. When his daughter got married he hammered flat a length of aluminium garden edging to make the baking tin for the top tier of her wedding cake.

I first met him in my daughter's ballet class. When I asked her who the elderly man was amongst the eight-year-olds it took a moment for her to realise whom I was talking about, as if there was nothing unusual about an eighty-eight-year-old joining a class of primary school children. He took up ballet when he was seventy-nine and when, ten years later, he appeared in an amateur production at Ely in Cambridgeshire he was interviewed for national newspapers and television channels around the world. He has a barre and trapeze in his front room where he stretches his muscles and practises ballet movements. He is careful what he eats, not wanting to put on extra pounds that might affect his dance, and when he feels like it he pushes back the furniture and rollerskates round the room. He is dismayed by the thought of 'couch potatoes'.

His experience of being a POW remains with him in small, but significant, ways. He remembers his PIN numbers by writing them down in Japanese script and he regularly talks to young people about the war. The painting he created from memory of the hold of the *England Maru* and the 'cosy' he made from an Australian's hat to keep his rice warm are both part of the Imperial War Museum's exhibition about the 'Forgotten War' at Duxford in Cambridgeshire. He counts himself lucky that his nerve failed him when he tried to smash his leg in a Japanese mine because he would not have taken up ballet and would not have celebrated his ninetieth year by dancing in Ely Cathedral.

Andrew Hawarden returned to Bolton where he worked as a warehouse man and clerk. He died in July 1978.

Back in Britain Doctor Nowell Peach was allowed to join an anatomy course – even though he would be starting half way through. He passed his Part One Fellowship in April 1946 – an astonishing feat after such a short period of study. He is convinced that his copy of *Gray's Anatomy*, which he still has, helped him to resume his studies with such apparent ease. Finding a job as a surgeon was not so easy in postwar Britain when thousands of returning doctors were looking for work. Although he never achieved the position of consultant surgeon he had dreamt of, he became a GP surgeon in Sussex in 1954 and used his surgical knowledge in the local cottage hospital.

Many of the doctors, including Jacob Markowitz, were honoured after the war for their miraculous work in saving lives in jungle operating theatres. The returning POWs contributed to medical knowledge in other ways. Although their terrible suffering was plainly far too high a price to pay, their experiences have nevertheless been of invaluable help to doctors studying tropical illnesses and the psychological effects of war. Far Eastern POWs have helped medical researchers to understand a whole plethora of illnesses such as strongyloidiasis worm infestation that was prevalent among POWs who worked on the railway. The long-term mental effects of their captivity have also added to knowledge of what is now recognised as Post-Traumatic Stress Disorder. Their brave testimonies and willingness to confront terrible memories, still raw after seventy years, continue to add to the knowledge of researchers at the Liverpool School of Tropical Medicine and Queen Mary's Hospital, Roehampton.

When Johnny Sherwood tucked into a long-dreamed-of Sunday lunch of roast beef and Yorkshire pudding prepared by his wife, he felt on 'top of the world'. He cleared his plate but a few hours later was writhing around in agony, convinced he was about to die. Eventually the pain subsided but he had learnt his lesson – his stomach had been permanently damaged by the effect of a starvation diet. Amazingly, he managed to regain enough of his former fitness so that, after a year at home, he was able to return to professional football, playing for Reading, Aldershot and Crystal Palace. He admitted that he could only really play well for three quarters of a game.

E.W. 'Jim' Swanton went on to be one of the most well known and outspoken writers about cricket, both as cricket correspondent for the *Daily Telegraph* and as a summariser on *Test Match Special* for the BBC. He died aged ninety after thirty years as a broadcaster, during which his distinctive, upper class baritone became familiar to cricket fans around the world.

Like John Lowe, my father 'bounced around' after the war. He worked on building projects in what was then Persia, and ran two grocer's shops and a launderette with my mother, among many other jobs. For seventeen years it seemed that he had succumbed to one of the POW's greatest fears – infertility – until my mother fell pregnant at the then uncommonly advanced age of forty. He put their success down to the fact that 1962 was a good year for malt whisky.

He showed no rancour towards the Germans. He was pleased when I learnt the language and fond of my exchange student from Hamburg who herself was deeply embarrassed at what had happened to him during the war. In his sixties he suddenly wanted to visit Germany and when we went there on holiday he repeatedly told anyone who asked that it was his first visit to their country – the only time I ever heard him lie.

My father died whilst I was writing this book. During his final months he was constantly amazed by the stories I told him of what POWs had achieved during their time 'in the bag' and would mutter, 'There were some awfully clever blokes inside.' When he finally left he had by his side his wife of sixty-two years, his daughter and son-in-law. But during his final hours there were other people gathered round his hospital bed and its locker with a photo of his granddaughter on top. They were people we had never met and could not see. My father greeted them with enthusiasm, calling names that we recognised from POW reunions. Perhaps this final gathering proved more than anything else that lifelong friendship was what my father took from his time as a prisoner.

As I prepare to wrap up my interview with Fergus Anckorn in his little home with ten compasses hidden around it, I make a mental note not to forget to take my digital recorder home with me. Fergus, now in his nineties, is tall, white-haired, avuncular. He loves to talk – but not just about the past; he is fascinated by the origin of words, has strong feelings on the perfect way to bake a Victoria sponge and is intrigued by the tiny machine recording our conversation. He bears no obvious signs of the physical suffering he has gone through. He thinks nothing of driving the 160 miles from his home in Kent to a conference about the history of Far Eastern POWs, and, after apologising about his lack of mobility, bounds up the stairs so that I struggle to keep up with him.

Fergus is idly playing with my digital recorder, moving it round and round on the edge of the armchair with the hand he very nearly lost. I wonder vaguely whether this shuffling movement will distort the recording.

The interview is over and I rise from my chair to retrieve the recorder. It is nowhere to be seen. For a moment I'm flummoxed. Then he smiles. 'I suppose I'd better give this back,' and the tiny machine magically reappears.

Acknowledgements

A dusty, scorching hot afternoon in July in a town outside Parma in Italy and a family holiday is not going well. We should be at the seaside, but instead we stand forlornly outside a building which – as POW camp PG49 – was once home to writers Eric Newby and Dan Billany but which is now a hospital that appears to have tighter security than it ever did as a camp. The windows of the austere, terracotta brick façade are hidden behind rust-coloured iron blinds and we gaze through the high railings strung with security cameras; automated gates sweep open for cars to glide through to an underground car park. I press what looks like an intercom and mutter something polite in English, wondering whether anyone is watching me and perhaps laughing at the English tourists. We turn to go but just as we do the gates buzz open and we scamper through. Maybe all that any researcher needs to enter an impregnable stronghold is to hold by the hand an over-heated eight-year-old girl.

Prisoners of war have always been part of my life. They entered my daughter's world in a big way when I started researching this book. Thank you, Rosa, for your forbearance; I hope the swimming pools and ice-cream made up for the occasional POW detours on hot summer days. I am very grateful, too, that my husband, Jim Kelly, and my mother, Renee Gillies, were with me every step of the way.

I had long wanted to write about POWs; my editor, Graham Coster, opened the door and his intelligence, insight and encouragement have guided me as this book took shape. My agent, Faith Evans, provided her usual steadying influence. I am also grateful for the care and enthusiasm of the book's copy-editor, Ljiljana Baird.

We would not have visited the former orphanage at Fontanellato without the encouragement of Steve and Gabrielle Bennett. Being able to stay in their home in Patigno for three summer holidays was a memorable treat. I would also like to thank my cousin, Sandra McGregor, and her husband, Peter, and their daughter, Alice, for making me so welcome in Singapore.

I am very grateful to my kind and clever friends who helped in so many ways during the years it has taken to write this book. Adrian Dunn, Veronica Forwood, Bridie Pritchard and Jenny Burgoyne read early drafts and offered extremely useful suggestions and, together with Sarah Mnatazaganian, Ann-Janine Murtagh, Kathryn Hughes, Andrew Balmford and Sarah Blakeman, have been a huge source of encouragement. Rosy Thornton, Mike Gross, Bill Kirkman, Naomi Needs, Louise Fryer, Clare and Paul Horrell, and Kay Willmott have helped in a myriad of ways – from sending cuttings, lending rare books, putting me in touch with archivists, offering specialist advice and cooking me dinner. Jay Sivell's tenacity as a researcher and her skill as a linguist brought H.R. van Heekeren to life and I am grateful to Justyna Kita and Michael Houten for their efforts to trace the Polish people who helped my father.

Katherine Roddwell, Adrian Barlow and Gilly Carr at Cambridge University's Institute of Continuing Education have been extremely encouraging. The students I have taught while writing this book have been a constant inspiration.

I have been privileged to meet many former Prisoners of War as part of my research. I am extremely grateful to them for sharing their memories and would like to thank: Fergus Anckorn, David Arkush, Tom Boardman, Steve Cairns, Jack Chalker, Clive Dunn, the late Cy Grant, John Lowe, Maurice Naylor, Nowell Peach, Charles Peall, Geoff Stott, Alistair Urquhart and James Wakefield. I would also like to thank the friends and relatives of POWs who have been so supportive: John Atkins, Elisabeth Bell, Ron Boardman, Clio Brisco, Leslie Gent, Sandra Hawarden-Lord, Giles Munby, Gordon O'Brien, Bob Sherwood, Brian Spittle, Martin and Audrey Vaughan, Salley Vickers, Danny and Anthony Frost and other members of the Frost family. I warmly thank all those who have been kind enough to allow me to quote from their relatives' papers.

Past and present members of the committee for Researching FEPOW History have been incredibly helpful and supportive: Keith Andrews (whose indefatigable research shed light on Johnny Sherwood's time as a POW), Sarah Edwards, Jonathan Moffatt, Meg and Mike Parkes, Martin

Percival, Stephen Rockcliffe, Julie Summers and Erica Toosey. In particular, I feel extremely lucky to have met Meg who has been so kind, good-humoured and generous in sharing her extensive knowledge.

I have visited many archives whilst researching this book and I am grateful to everyone who has helped me. In particular, I would like to thank Rod Suddaby, Keeper of Documents at the Imperial War Museum, who, from the very start of this project, has been most helpful in recommending books and collections and in sharing his immense knowledge of the subject. Rod has also been kind enough to read the proofs of this book, although, of course, any errors that slip through are entirely my responsibility. Stephen Walton, Senior Curator in the Documents & Sound Section (IWM Duxford repository), has also been generous in sharing his knowledge of German POW camps and the German language. Claire Wilson, Exhibitions Manager (Special Exhibitions Gallery), Imperial War Museum North, was extremely helpful in answering my queries about the *Captured* exhibition.

Yet again, Peter Elliott, Senior Keeper, Department of Research & Information Services, Royal Air Force Museum, has gone out of his way to answer my queries and to supply me with information that has always been enlightening. Chris Jakes, Principal Librarian Local Studies, has once more guided me round the Cambridgeshire Collection. Emily Oldfield, Information Assistant, British Red Cross Museum and Archives, has been tireless in her attempts to help me find the answers to so many questions. I am extremely grateful to Jeremy Crow, Head of Literary Estates at the Society of Authors, for his advice about tracing copyright holders.

In Singapore, Jeya Ayadurai, Director of the Changi Museum, was helpful and welcoming. Michael Ng, Public Relations Branch, MINDEF Public Affairs, made a memorable trip to Singapore even more remarkable by arranging for me to see the Changi Murals. I am grateful to Verity FitzGerald for allowing me to read her dissertation on FEPOW art.

The knowledge and passion of Rod Beattie, Director, Thailand-Burma Railway Centre, Kanchanaburi, ensure that the history of the railway will never be forgotten. Raoul Kramer's startling photos offer a modern perspective on the tragedy. I enjoyed talking to him about H.R. van Heekeren and to Sears Eldredge, Professor Emeritus in the Theatre and Dance

Department at Macalester College in St. Paul, Minnesota, about entertainment in the Thai camps.

This book has taught me that there was no end to the ingenuity and will to survive among POWs. I am deeply indebted to everyone who confirmed that realisation.

Museums and Archives
As well as the organisations already mentioned I am grateful to the following museums and archives, and to their staff:

Julie Lamara, Local Studies Librarian, Bolton History Centre, Bolton Museum and Archive

Max Taylor, Historian of the British Music Hall Society

Dr Nicholas Clark, Librarian, The Britten–Pears Foundation

Jacqueline Cox, Deputy Keeper of the University Archives, Cambridge University Library

The Gordon Highlanders Museum

David Smith, Senior Local Studies Librarian, Hull Local Studies Library

Tracy Wilkinson. Assistant Archivist, Archive Centre, King's College, Cambridge

Martin Cherry, Librarian, The Library and Museum of Freemasonry

Adele Allen, Archive Assistant, Lambeth Palace Library

The National Archives of Singapore

Anne McKeage, Archivist/History of Health and Medicine Librarian, Health Sciences Library, McMaster University

Joan Self, Archive Information Officer, Met Office, National Meteorological Archive

Netherlands Institute for Advanced Study in the Humanities and Social Sciences

Netherlands Institute for War Documentation (NIOD)

Leamington Spa Art Gallery & Museum

Frances Bellis, Assistant Librarian, Lincoln's Inn Library

Liverpool School of Tropical Medicine

Peabody Museum of Archaeology and Ethnology, Harvard University

Jean Rose, Library Manager, Random House Group Archive & Library

Royal Academy Library

Brent Elliott, Royal Horticultural Society

HQ Scots Guards
Karen Begg, College Librarian, Queens' College, Cambridge
University Library, Cambridge
Wellcome Library, London

Permissions

I am very grateful to the Trustees of the Imperial War Museum for allowing access to their collections and for the copyright holders for their permission to quote extracts from the following papers:

Fergus Anckorn for permission to quote from his papers (87/58/1);

Lida McCallum for permission to quote from the papers of John Gordon McCallum (114/2009);

P.R.D. Millns for permission to quote from the papers of J. G. Brian Millns (07/54/1)

Nicholas Wood for permission to quote from the papers of Lieutenant Richard Wood (90/33/1A);

Sandra Hawarden-Lord for permission to quote from the papers of Battery Sergeant Major Andrew Hawarden (66/132/1).

In addition, I am grateful to the Trustees for permission to quote from the following IWM Sound Archives: Terry Frost (961) and Ernest William Swanton (4777).

The interviews with Adrian Heath and Sir Terry Frost are reproduced with permission of the British Library and are extracts from life story interviews recorded for the National Life Stories project Artists' Lives, in 1992 and 1994 respectively. There are over 300 audio interviews in Artists' Lives, which has been running for over twenty years. All the interviews are available to listen to at the British Library – for more details see www.bl.uk/oralhistory and also the Sound Archive catalogue www.cadensa.bl.uk, catalogue reference C466.

I am extremely grateful to the Syndics of Cambridge University Library for permission to quote from 'Papers relating to examinations taken by British prisoners of war in Germany', Reference UA EDUC 19/119.

I acknowledge the Master, Fellows and Scholars of Churchill College, Cambridge for their kind permission to quote from the Belgion Papers at the Churchill Archives Centre.

Extracts from the correspondence of C.S. Lewis are reproduced with kind permission of C.S. Lewis Pte. Ltd. and I have quoted from letters written by Jonathan Cape to Belgion with the kind permission of his estate and the co-operation of the Random House Group Ltd. Extracts from John Hayward's letters are reproduced with the permission of Henry Oakeley.

Extracts from the letters of Benjamin Britten are © Britten-Pears Foundation.

Nella Last's Diary is reproduced with permission of Curtis Brown Group Ltd, London, on behalf of the Trustees of the Mass Observation Archive: copyright © The Trustees of the Mass Observation Archive; *Nella Last's War*, selection and editorial matter copyright © Richard Broad and Suzie Fleming and Falling Wall Press Ltd 1981, 2006.

I am grateful to John and Veronica Forwood and to Mary Phillips for allowing me to quote from John Phillips' letters. Brian Spittle has been most generous in allowing me to quote from his father's writings and I am grateful to Lesley Gent for permission to quote from her father's diary. John Lowe very kindly allowed me to use parts of his unpublished memoir and diary and the family of Johnny Sherwood have been extremely generous in allowing me to quote from his unpublished account of his time as a POW.

The quotation from *Wisden Cricketers' Almanack* 1946 is by kind permission of John Wisden & Co Ltd.

Every effort has been made to trace copyright holders. The publishers will be glad to rectify in future editions any errors or omissions brought to their attention.

Abbreviations

AWM – Australian War Memorial.
BL – British Library.
IWM – Imperial War Museum.

Notes

The number on the left indicates the
page number referred to.

Preface

xiii 'You see the point is – Sir Terry Frost,
interviewed by Tamsyn Woollcombe,
1994, Artists' Lives, British Library
Sound Archive reference: C466/22.
Tape F4315, side A.

xvi Only one German managed to escape
from England back to Germany. A total
of more than 33,000 British,
Commonwealth and American fighting
men managed escapes or evasions the
other way. *The Oxford Companion to
World War II*, I.C.B. Dear and M.R.D.
Foot, (Editors), Oxford University
Press, 2001, *Oxford Reference Online*.

PART I: EUROPE

Chapter 1: Becoming a POW

3 Sergeant George Booth – Booth
featured in the *Yorkshire Post*, Kriegie
Edition, May 1944, which was produced
in Stalag Luft VI. A profile of him
appeared under the caption 'No.1
POW'. See also
http://www.rafmuseum.org.uk/milest
ones-of-
flight/british_military/1939_2.cfm. I
am indebted to Peter Elliott, Senior
Keeper, Department of Research &
Information Services, Royal Air Force
Museum, for additional information
concerning Booth.

3 an estimated 170,000 to 200,000 British,
Commonwealth and Empire – Adrian

Gilbert, *POW, Allied Prisoners in Europe
1939–1945*, London, 2006, p.xi.

3 90,000 Allied prisoners who were held in
a thousand camps – Julie Summers, *The
Colonel of Tamarkan, Philip Toosey & The
Bridge on the River Kwai*, London, 2006.
p.129 *Report of the International
Committee of the Red Cross on its activities
during the Second World War* (September
1, 1939–June 30, 1947), Volume One –
General Activities, Geneva, May 1948,
cites 1002 camps, p.451.

4 abandon over 50,000 men – *The Oxford
Companion to World War II*. Eds I.C.B.
Dear and M.R.D. Foot, Oxford
University Press, 2001. *Oxford Reference
Online*.

4 the battle for Crete after which 11,370
Allied troops were captured – *The
Oxford Companion to World War II*, Eds
I.C.B. Dear and M.R.D. Foot, Oxford
University Press, 2001. *Oxford Reference
Online*.

4 the garrison's 35,000 men – *The Oxford
Companion to World War II*. Eds I.C.B.
Dear and M.R.D. Foot, Oxford
University Press, 2001. *Oxford Reference
Online*.

4 62,000 of her soldiers – Adrian Gilbert,
POW, Allied Prisoners in Europe 1939–1945,
London, 2006, p.23.

4 The Germans captured over 6,000 men
in September 1944 – *The Oxford
Companion to World War II*. Eds I.C.B.
Dear and M.R.D. Foot, Oxford
University Press, 2001. *Oxford Reference
Online*.

4 led to around 23,000 Americans
becoming POWs. – Adrian Gilbert,
POW, Allied Prisoners in Europe 1939–1945,
London, 2006, p.52.

4 about 5,500 from each category – Gabe Thomas, *Milag: Captives of the Kriegsmarine*, Glamorgan, [1995?], p.viii; Adrian Gilbert, *POW, Allied Prisoners in Europe 1939–1945*, London, 2006, p.37.

4 Around 13,000 British and Commonwealth airmen – *Royal Air Force personnel statistics for the period 3rd September 1939 to 1st September 1945* compiled by the Air Ministry (ADM (Stats)) and dated May 1946. Department of Research & Information Services, RAF Museum, accession number: 012885.

4 Of the 10,000 members of Bomber Command – *The Oxford Companion to World War II*, Eds I.C.B. Dear and M.R.D. Foot, Oxford University Press, 2001. *Oxford Reference Online*. Oxford University Press.

4 the peak year for Bomber Command – my thanks to the RAF Museum for this information.

5 Battery Sergeant Major Andrew Hawarden – his papers are held at the Imperial War Museum, 66/132/1.

5 As a teenager he had worked in a Bolton cotton mill – 1911 census.

6 'Above it all – David Wild, *Prisoner of Hope*, Sussex, 1992, p.22.

7 the Germans took nearly three million soldiers prisoners – Adrian Gilbert, *POW, Allied Prisoners in Europe 1939–1945*, London, 2006, p.65.

7 nearly six million Russian – 5.7 million in Adrian Gilbert, *POW, Allied Prisoners in Europe 1939–1945*, London, 2006, p.211.

7 600,000 of her former ally's troops to POW camps – Adrian Gilbert, *POW, Allied Prisoners in Europe 1939–1945*, London, 2006, p.65.

7 Germany had thirty-one POW camps – Adrian Gilbert, *POW, Allied Prisoners in Europe 1939–1945*, London, 2006, p.66.

7 nearly 79,000 Allied prisoners – Adrian Gilbert, *POW, Allied Prisoners in Europe 1939–1945*, London, 2006, p.287. Roger Absalom, *A strange alliance: aspects of escape and survival in Italy, 1943–45*, says that at the start of September 1943 there were about 72 camps and 12 hospitals being used in Italy for POWs.

From mid August 1943 there were around 79,543 Allied POWS in Italy.

7 50,000 had been taken to Germany – John Nichol & Tony Rennell, *The Last Escape*, London, 2003, p.42.

8 'a patch of stump-studded – Paul Brickhill, *The Great Escape*, London, 2004, p.27.

8 Appell – parade.

8 'gaunt pines with skinny – Paul Brickhill, *The Great Escape*, London, 2004, p.29.

9 'We arrived at the small town of Colditz – P.R. Reid, *The Colditz Story*, 2004, London, p.62.

10 'Welcome to Colditz' – quoted in S.P. Mackenzie, *The Colditz Myth*, Oxford, 2006, p.217.

10 'For some, this was probably the most degrading moment of their lives,' – Clive Dunn, *Permission to Speak, An Autobiography*, London, 1986, p.86.

10 Details of Clive Dunn's capture are taken from *Permission to Speak* and from an interview with the author.

11 'more ridiculous than ever' – Clive Dunn, *Permission to Speak, An Autobiography*, London, 1986, p.86.

11 'staggered' – Clive Dunn, *Permission to Speak, An Autobiography*, London, 1986, p.87.

11 'The surrendering of physical privacy – Clive Dunn, *Permission to Speak, An Autobiography*, London, 1986, p.88.

11 feeling like a 'traitor' – Eric Newby, *Love and War in the Apennines*, London, 1996, p. 29.

11 'I find no difficulty – Eric Newby, *Love and War in the Apennines*, London, 1996, Preface.

12 'How I hate shells,' – David Erskine, *The Scots Guards*, 1919–1955, London, 1956, pages 143–144.

12 'stonks' – David Erskine, *The Scots Guards, 1919–1955*, London, 1956, p.143.

Chapter 2: Settling In and Getting By

15 Lieutenant R.G.M. Quarrie – R.G.M. Quarrie, *Oflag*, Durham, 1995, p.11.

15 British stores – R.G.M. Quarrie, *Oflag*, Durham, 1995, p.5.

15 *Terrorflieger* – Charles Rollings,

Prisoner of War, Voices from Captivity during the Second World War, London, 2007, p.51.

15 *Mörderschwein* – Charles Rollings, *Prisoner of War, Voices from Captivity during the Second World War*, London, 2007, p.53.

15 on the bottom tier of a bunk bed – interview with R.C.A. Hunter, Archives of Hamilton Health Sciences and the Faculty of Health Sciences, McMaster University. Dr Charles Roland Oral History Collection. 1994.44. HCM 27–82.

16 Navigator Cy Grant – *A Member of the RAF of Indeterminate Race, WW2 experiences of a former RAF Navigator & POW*, West Sussex, 2006.

17 whether there were any Jews – R.G.M. Quarrie, *Oflag*, Durham, 1995, p22.

18 *Kriegie* – slang for *Kriegsgefangene*n (Prisoner of War in German)

18 like solidified Vim – Sam Kydd, *For you the war is over*, London, 1973, p.108.

18 'RIF' – http://www.jewishvirtuallibrary.org

18 smelling of cyanide fumes' – Sam Kydd, *For you the war is over*, London, 1973, p.109.

21 What to tell him – *The Prisoner of War* magazine.

22 used a code when writing – W.H. Murray, *The Evidence of Things Not Seen, A Mountaineer's Tale*, London, 2002, p.87.

22 'Dear Buddy – Clive Dunn, *Permission to Speak, An Autobiography*, London, 1986, p.116.

22 Robin Hunter – Archives of Hamilton Health Sciences and the Faculty of Health Sciences, McMaster University. Dr Charles Roland Oral History Collection. 1994.44. HCM 27–82.

23 Tom Swallow – obituary, *The Independent*, Tuesday, 12 February 2008.

24 John Phillips correspondence with Philippa Cook – reproduced with kind permission of Veronica and John Forwood and Mary Phillips.

24 What he could not say – obituary *Daily Telegraph*, 5 June 1998.

25 My Arab tutor – February 25, 1942.

27 Flight Sergeant Charnock –

Department of Research & Information Services, RAF Museum.

28 Flight Lieutenant Kenyon – Department of Research & Information Services, RAF Museum.

Chapter 3: Uses for a Red Cross Parcel Number 1 – String

31 It was 31cm wide – I am grateful to the British Red Cross Museum and Archives for this information.

31 2,500 pairs of spectacles – P.G. Cambray and G.G.B. Brigg, *Red Cross & St John, the official record of the humanitarian services of the War Organisation of the British Red Cross Society and Order of St John of Jerusalem 1939–1947*, p.164.

31 bagpipes – RAF Museum, Department of Research & Information Services, B18080, Sq Leader Philip Jacobs.

31 One elderly major – R.G.M. Quarrie, *Oflag*, Durham, 1995, p. 29.

31 finding a train set – Adrian Gilbert, *POW, Allied Prisoners in Europe 1939–1945*, London, 2006, p.100.

31 lost his false teeth – Hilary St George Saunders, *The Red Cross and the White*, London, 1949, p.32.

31 bakeries in Denmark – P.G. Cambray and G.G.B. Brigg, *Red Cross & St John, the official record of the humanitarian services of the War Organisation of the British Red Cross Society and Order of St John of Jerusalem 1939–1947*, p.137.

32 five and a half million – P.G. Cambray and G.G.B. Brigg, *Red Cross & St John, the official record of the humanitarian services of the War Organisation of the British Red Cross Society and Order of St John of Jerusalem 1939–1947*, p.148.

32 raised £50 – this was at a time when a man working in manufacturing would earn around 111 shillings and 5 pennies or £5.11s. 5d. a week (Source: *Fighting with Figures*).

32 'Such a happy worthwhile day – Richard Broad and Suzie Fleming (editors), *Nella Last's War, The Second World War Diaries of Housewife, 49*, London, 2006, p. 207. Her story was dramatised for television as *Housewife, 49*, starring Victoria Wood.

33 'a marvellous thing – Richard Broad and Suzie Fleming (editors), *Nella Last's War, The Second World War Diaries of Housewife, 49*, London, 2006, p.208.

33 'fantastic' prices – Richard Broad and Suzie Fleming (editors), *Nella Last's War, The Second World War Diaries of Housewife, 49*, London, 2006, p.208.

33 'We put the wireless on – Richard Broad and Suzie Fleming (editors), *Nella Last's War, The Second World War Diaries of Housewife, 49*, London, 2006, Sunday 5 December, 1943.

33 Darts players – Hilary St George Saunders, *The Red Cross and the White*, London, 1949, p.23.

33 Hutchinson gave £500 royalties – Hilary St George Saunders, *The Red Cross and the White*, London, 1949, p.24.

33 Cost of building a bomber and Spitfire – Malcolm Brown, *Spitfire Summer, When Britain Stood Alone*, London, 2000, pp.110–11.

34 'They might have been packed – M. N. McKibbin, *Behind Barbed Wire, Memories of Stalag 383*, London, 1947, p.31.

34 Protecting power – a neutral state (first the USA but after their entry into the war, Switzerland) whose representatives inspected the camps.

35 emergency packing sites – P.G. Cambray and G.G.B. Brigg, *Red Cross & St John, the official record of the humanitarian services of the War Organisation of the British Red Cross Society and Order of St John of Jerusalem 1939–1947*, p.155.

35 three-stranded sisal – Arthur H. Bird, MBE, *Farewell Milag*, p.86.

35 'Very hard on the fingers,' – Robert Holland, *Adversis Major, A short history of the Educational Books Scheme of the Prisoners of War Department of the British Red Cross Society and Order of St John of Jerusalem*, London, 1949, p.18.

36 where it swung 'dizzily' – M N McKibbin, *Behind Barbed Wire, Memories of Stalag 383*, London, 1947, p.14. See also Andrew Hawarden, January 8, 1945.

36 When he took the lead – Clive Dunn,

Permission to Speak, An Autobiography, London, 1986, p.120.

36 created a wig – Eric Fearnside, *The Joy of Freedom, A graphic account of Life in a Prisoner of War Camp during the Second World War*, 1996, p.54.

36 At Marlag und Milag Nord – Arthur H. Bird, *Farewell Milag*, p. 86.

36 String was also used to make wigs at Stalag 383, M.N. McKibbin, *Behind Barbed Wire, Memories of Stalag 383*, London, 1947, p.12, see also Andrew Hawarden, June 10, 1943.

37 'I say, would you mind – Susan Elliott with Barry Turner, *Denholm Elliott, Quest for Love*, London, 1994, p.34.

37 to stitch together balls – Pat Ward-Thomas, *Not only Golf*, London, 1981, p.31; Dale Concannon, *Spitfire on the Fairway: And Other Unexpected Hazards of Golf in Wartime*, London, 2003, pp.101–2.

37 Size of golfball – *The Guardian*, Monday 17 December 2001.

38 Another ball is in the Museum of the New United States Golf Association in New Jersey.

38 After the war – Pat Ward-Thomas, *Not Only Golf*, London, 1981, p.32.

Chapter 4: Friendships and Feuds

39 Ray Beal – private collection, my thanks to Lesley Gent for allowing me to reproduce extracts from his diary.

40 'In the camp the members – Eric Newby, *Love and War in the Apennines*, London, 1996, p.41.

41 Other cliques – S.P. Mackenzie, *The Colditz Myth*, Oxford, 2006, p.136-7.

41 'pigs whisker pullovers – Eric Newby, *Love and War in the Apennines*, London, 1996, p.44.

41 Freemasonry flourished in Stalag 383 – Keith Flynn, *Behind the Wire*, Cardiff, 2004, pp.36–40.

43 When Col. D.P. Iggulden – Col. D.P. Iggulden, *Freemasonry in Oflag 79* by (call number BE 177 PRI fol), The Library and Museum of Freemasonry.

43 F.S. Payne – F.S. Payne, *Freemasonry in Stalag 18 A (Wolfsberg) and Stalag 383* (call number BE177 FRI fol.), The

Library and Museum of Freemasonry.

44 Discussion today hinged – these and subsequent entries are 1943.

45 'He came here as my lackey – Henry Chancellor, *Colditz, The Definitive History*, London, 2001, p. 252.

45 War Substantive Sergeant – A rank held for the duration of the war, after which he would revert to his previous rank.

46 A farmer, butcher or 'food sorter' – Clive Dunn, *Permission to Speak*, London, 1986, p.91.

46 At Stalag XXA Sam Kydd – Sam Kydd, *For You the War is Over*, London, 1973, p.148.

46 Clive Dunn's fellow POWs – Clive Dunn, *Permission to Speak*, 1986, p.112.

47 'I was up a mountain – interview with the author, 8 June 2009.

47 'Gute Nacht, goodnight, sweetheart.' – Clive Dunn, *Permission to Speak*, 1986, p.98.

48 When the guard marched them back – Clive Dunn, *Permission to Speak*, 1986, p.105.

48 Newby was highly unusual – 'How we met: 45. Eric and Wanda Newby', Sunday, 2 August 1992, *Independent on Sunday*.

49 Clive Dunn was sent to hospital – Clive Dunn, *Permission to Speak*, 1986, p.112.

49 Allen Graham – interview with R.C.A. Hunter, Archives of Hamilton Health Sciences and the Faculty of Health Sciences, McMaster University. Dr Charles Roland Oral History Collection. 1994.44. HCM 5–81.

49 But William E. Tucker – interview with R.C.A. Hunter, Archives of Hamilton Health Sciences and the Faculty of Health Sciences, McMaster University. Dr Charles Roland Oral History Collection. 1994.44. HCM–R. 33–83.

49 Sam Kydd remembers one POW claiming – Sam Kydd, *For You the War is Over*, 1973, p.232.

50 'pulling our puddings' – Eric Newby, *Love and War in the Apennines*, London, 1996, p.37.

50 Doctor Allen Graham – Interview with R.C.A. Hunter, Archives of Hamilton Health Sciences and the Faculty of Health Sciences, McMaster University.

50 Robin Hunter remembered – Interview with R.C.A. Hunter, Archives of Hamilton Health Sciences and the Faculty of Health Sciences, McMaster University.

51 'What they shared was a warmth – Susan Elliott with Barry Turner, *Denholm Elliott, Quest for Love*, London, 1994, p.31.

51 'In truth, I suppose – Susan Elliott with Barry Turner, Denholm *Elliott, Quest for Love*, London, 1994, pp.77–78

51 A review in *The Sunday Times* – Valerie Reeves and Valerie Showan, *Dan Billany, Hull's Lost Hero*, 1999, p.76.

51 T.S. Eliot – Valerie Reeves and Valerie Showan, *Dan Billany, Hull's Hero*, 1999, p.82.

51 He gave lectures – Valerie Reeves and Valerie Showan, *Dan Billany, Hull's Hero*, 1999, p.115.

51 'Mrs Unbeeton's cookery – Valerie Reeves and Valerie Showan, *Dan Billany, Hull's Hero*, Hull, 1999, p.116.

51 he wrote to his sister – Valerie Reeves and Valerie Showan, *Dan Billany, Hull's Hero*, Hull, 1999, p.126.

52 See original ms of *The Cage* by Dan Billany, IWM, 4562 96/14/1.

54 a wounded young crow – Clive Dunn, Clive Dunn, *Permission to Speak*, London, 1986, p108.

54 a tame kestrel – W.H. Murray, *The Evidence of Things Not Seen, A Mountaineer's Tale*, London, 2002, p.94.

Chapter 5: Sport

57 Cricket has been – *The Cricketer*, January 1944.

59 Golf – See Dale Concannon, *Spitfire on the Fairway*, London, 2003.

60 'Abort Annie' – Pat Ward-Thomas, *Not Only Golf: An Autobiography*, London, 1981, p.33.

60 Feel it longingly – Pat Ward-Thomas, *Not Only Golf: An Autobiography*, London, 1981, page 33.

61 Germans became used – *The Prisoner of War Magazine*, October 1944.

61 Par of twenty-nine – 'Golfers go to great lengths in times of war', *The Independent*, June 6, 2004.

61 A few mounds – *The Prisoner of War Magazine*, October 1944.

62 'the roughest game' – P.R. Reid, *The Colditz Story*, 1952, p.75.

66 David Wild, a padre at Stalag XXA – David Wild, *Prisoner of Hope*, 1992, p.214.

66 Arsenal Football Club – *Daily Telegraph*, 22 August 2005

66 Guest players – Anton Rippon, *Gas Masks for Goal Posts – Football in Britain during the Second World War*, 2007, pp.60–73.

67 It seems that at least one of the men – David Wild, *Prisoner of Hope*, Sussex, 1992, p.213.

Chapter 6: Uses for a Red Cross Parcel Number 2 – Cigarettes

71 'Let it suffice to note – Paul Fussell, *Wartime: Understanding and behavior in the Second World War*, Oxford, 1989, p.145.

71 (although throwing away) – Eric Newby, *Love and War in the Apennines*, London, 1996, p.170.

71 When Andrew Hawarden was in hospital – February 25, 1945.

72 dried leaves – S.P. Mackenzie, *Colditz Myth*, Oxford, 2006, p.158; Adrian Gilbert, *POW: Allied Prisoners in Europe 1939–1945*, London, 2006, p.107.

72 Soon switched – August, 1940, Adrian Gilbert, *POW: Allied Prisoners in Europe 1939–1945*, 2006, p.107.

72 aimed to send each man a – P.G. Cambray and G.G.B. Briggs, *Red Cross & St John, the official record of the humanitarian services of the War Organisation of the British Red Cross Society and Order of St John of Jerusalem 1939–1947*, London, 1949, p.201.

72 From the beginning of 1941 – P.G. Cambray and G.G.B. Briggs, *Red Cross & St John, the official record of the humanitarian services of the War Organisation of the British Red Cross Society and Order of St John of Jerusalem 1939–1947*, London, 1949, p.202.

73 Allen Graham – interview with R.C.A. Hunter, Archives of Hamilton Health Sciences and the Faculty of Health Sciences, McMaster University. Dr Charles Roland Oral History Collection. 1994.44, HCM 5–81.

73 buy a Luger for 500 cigarettes – M.N. McKibbin, *Behind Barbed Wire, Memories of Stalag 383*, London, 1947, p.42.

73 Economist R.A. Radford – Samuelson, Paul, Bishop, Robert, Coleman, John (editors). *Readings in Economics*, The Economic Organization of a POW Camp by R.A. Radford, New York, McGraw-Hill, 1955.

74 a sunny Whitsun carnival in 1944 – 'Stalag VIIIB – Lamsdorf – And the Red Cross', British Red Cross Archive, Ref. G61, DOM.

74 Australians would sit – Adrian Gilbert, *POW: Allied Prisoners in Europe 1939–1945*, London, 2006, pp.165–6.

74 raced corks – Eric Newby, *Love and War in the Apennines*, London, 1996, p.43.

74 Terry Frost – IWM, Sound Archive, Terry Frost (961/3).

74 At Barth men bet – S.P. Mackenzie, *Colditz Myth*, Oxford, 2006, p.158; Adrian Gilbert, *POW: Allied Prisoners in Europe 1939–1945*, London, 2006, p.203.

74 'Flieger Jockey Club' – *Yorkshire Post, Kriegie edition, Stalag Luft VI*, 1944, p.29.

74 miniature race tracks – see John Worsley's drawing, *Saturday Night Racing; Milag Jockey Club*, IWM ART LD 5119.

75 Long enough – Cy Grant, *A Member of the RAF of Indeterminate Race, WW2 experiences of a former RAF Navigator & POW*, West Sussex, 2006, p.70.

75 At Hawarden's second camp, Stalag 383, bookies – M.N. McKibbin, *Behind Barbed Wire, Memories of Stalag 383*, London, 1947, p.76.

75 for their next of kin as cheques – Eric Newby, *Love and War in the Apennines*, London, 1996, p.43.

75 Craven A – *Captured!* IWM North exhibition, 2009.

75 An Ajax Chessman – *Captured!* IWM North exhibition, 2009.

75 According to family tradition – *Daily Telegraph* obituary, Brigadier Jock Hamilton-Baillie, 23 May 2003.

Chapter 7: 'Stalag Happy': Imaginary Worlds and Other Ways of Escape

76 'What do you think of my duck?' – British Library Sound Archive, NLSC: Artists' Lives, Tape 4, F4315, Side A.

77 'This is a queer gaol – M.N. McKibbin, *Behind Barbed Wire, Memories of Stalag 383*, London, 1947, p.69.

77 'assumed the status of attendants – M.N. McKibbin, *Behind Barbed Wire, Memories of Stalag 383*, London, 1947, p.69.

77 One elaborate charade – M.N. McKibbin, *Behind Barbed Wire, Memories of Stalag 383*, London, 1947, p.76.

77 'It was wonderful to go to Blighty' – British Library Sound Archive, NLSC: Artists' Lives, Tape 4, F4315, Side A.

77 A similar event was staged at BAB 21 at Blechhammer where a whole room of men would decide to set out on a day's outing to somewhere like Bournemouth. They would form a line by holding on to the man in front and choo-choo their way round the camp. Adrian Gilbert, *POW: Allied Prisoners in Europe 1939–1945*, London, 2006, p.169.

78 'It was wonderful stalag happiness' – British Library Sound Archive, NLSC: Artists' Lives, Tape 4, F4315, Side A.

78 they got dressed to walk an imaginary dog – Adrian Gilbert, *POW: Allied Prisoners in Europe 1939–1945*, London, 2006, p.169.

78 Lunacy School – S.P. Mackenzie, *Colditz Myth*, Oxford, 2006, p.342; Adrian Gilbert, *POW: Allied Prisoners in Europe 1939–1945*, London, 2006, p.258.

79 When an eye specialist from Liverpool – Lord Normanby, Archives of Hamilton Health Sciences and the Faculty of Health Sciences, McMaster University. Dr Charles Roland Oral History Collection. 1994.44. HCM 16–86.

79 Robin Hunter – Archives of Hamilton Health Sciences and the Faculty of Health Sciences, McMaster University, Dr Charles Roland Oral History Collection. 1994.44. HCM 27–82.

79 Suicide – See P.R. Reid, *The Colditz*

Story, London, 1952, p.166. Two men were kept under permanent guard so that they did not try to kill themselves.

Chapter 8: Uses for a Red Cross Parcel Number 3 – Tins

82 to make frying pans – Hilary St George Saunders, *The Red Cross and the White*, London, 1949, p.58.

82 The Metal Box Company – P.G. Cambray and G.G.B. Briggs, *Red Cross & St John, the official record of the humanitarian services of the War Organisation of the British Red Cross Society and Order of St John of Jerusalem*, London, 1949, p.140; *Useful Articles from Empty Tins*, Barclay & Fry, (The Metal Box Company), London.

82 hold more than a pint of liquid – Eric Newby, *Love and War in the Apennines*, London, 1996, p.49.

82 to make clogs – M.N. McKibbin, *Behind Barbed Wire, Memories of Stalag 383*, London, 1947, p.13.

83 'There was nobody who wasn't wanted – IWM Sound Archive, Sir Terry Frost (Catalogue Number 961).

83 barometer – William Turcotte, *A Saga of Sagan and Moosburg*, 1995, Department of Research & Information Services, RAF Museum.

83 'kept horrible time, but it did work' – Audio tape interview with Alex Cassie at Stalag Luft III, *Captured!* IWM North exhibition, 2009.

83 John Worsley – obituary in the *Daily Telegraph*, 7 October, 2000, John Worsley.

Chapter 9: POW Artists

84 See Grove Art Online – http://www.oxfordartonline.com

84 According to Heath's Liberation Questionnaire completed on 23 May 1945 (National Archives WO344/140) he was captured on 29/11/41. In his BL interview he says Jan 42, just before fall of Singapore.

85 'Van Gogh peasant' – Adrian Heath, interviewed by Norbert Lynton, 1992, Artists' Lives, British Library Sound

Archive reference: C466/11. Tape One Side B F2905.

86 'Take no notice – Adrian Heath, interviewed by Norbert Lynton, 1992, Artists' Lives, British Library Sound Archive reference: C466/11. Tape One Side B, F2905.

86 'for the ladies over the road.' – IWM Sound Archive, Sir Terry Frost (Catalogue Number 961).

87 'Never having had any real action – IWM Sound Archive, Sir Terry Frost (Catalogue Number 961).

87 'I think that something quite permanently – IWM Sound Archive, Sir Terry Frost (Catalogue Number 961).

88 'There were these beautiful bare arses – IWM Sound Archive, Sir Terry Frost (Catalogue Number 961).

88 'whipped back' to 'Alex' where, 'The Crete job came up' – IWM Sound Archive, Sir Terry Frost (Catalogue Number 961).

89 Hobo Challis – David Lewis, Terry Frost, A Personal Narrative, Aldershot, 1994, p.30.

89 'Why don't you put it on?' – David Lewis, Terry Frost, A Personal Narrative, Aldershot, 1994, p.30.

89 'And that was the start – British Library Sound Archive, NLSC: Artists' Lives, F4315, Side A.

90 'They don't draw that well.' – IWM Sound Archive, Sir Terry Frost (Catalogue Number 961).

90 'university' – IWM Sound Archive, Sir Terry Frost (Catalogue Number 961).

90 Revelation – David Lewis, Terry Frost, A Personal Narrative, Aldershot, 1994, p.30.

90 'the bagpipes,' – IWM Sound Archive, Sir Terry Frost (Catalogue Number 961).

91 'I got the big toe in my eye – Sir Terry Frost, interviewed by Tamsyn Woollcombe, 1994, Artists' Lives, British Library Sound Archive reference C466/22. Tape 4, F4315, Side A.

91 'You can do it in anything – British Library Sound Archive, NLSC: Artists' Lives, Tape 4, F4315, Side A.

91 'Mick Moore would get you anything – IWM Sound Archive, Sir Terry Frost (Catalogue Number 961).

92 'I used to come back and tell all the boys – IWM Sound Archive, Sir Terry Frost (Catalogue Number 961).

92 'I used to write little poem things – IWM Sound Archive, Sir Terry Frost (Catalogue Number 961).

92 '. . . I couldn't take the going out – IWM Sound Archive, Sir Terry Frost (Catalogue Number 961).

93 George Milne – Lord Milne, obituary in Daily Telegraph, 18 February 2005

94 Tom Swallow – See Tom Swallow, Flywheel, Memories of the Open Road, London, 1987 and obituary The Independent, 12 February 2008.

94 One edition was badly damaged by spilt cocoa and had to be redone – Tom Swallow, Flywheel, Memories of the Open Road, London, 1987, p.8. Stalag VIIIB, Lamsdorf also had a car and motor cycle club. Its 80 members met every Sunday evening to listen to lectures on theory and to hold discussions based on catalogues of cars and motorcycles supplied by Germans. See British Red Cross Archive, (Ref. G61, DOM).

94 Wall newspaper – The Education of British prisoners of war in German captivity, 1939–1945 by David Rolf, p.263. Other camp newsletters include: POW WOW (Luft I) and The Yorkshire Post, Kriegie Edition at Stalag Luft VI.

95 James Woolcock – Sam Kydd, For you the war is over, London, 1973, p.218.

96 'And Adrian was still left down . . .' British Library Sound Archive, NLSC: Artists' Lives, Tape 4, F4315, Side A.

96 'Adrian was the bravest – David Lewis, Terry Frost, A Personal Narrative, Aldershot, 1994, p.31.

96 'For myself I was able' – Earl Haig, My Father's Son, The Memoirs of Major the Earl Haig, London, 2000, p.107.

PART II: THE WAR IN THE EAST

Chapter 10: Surrender

100 Greater East Asia Co-Prosperity Sphere – Julie Summers, The Colonel of Tamarkan, Philip Toosey & The Bridge on the River Kwai, London, 2006, p.77.

100 38 per cent of the world's rubber –
'Malaya' entry, Eds I.C.B. Dear and
M.R.D. Foot, *The Oxford Companion to
World War II*, Oxford, 2001.

100 its mines produced – 'Malaya' entry,
Eds I C.B. Dear and M.R.D. Foot, *The
Oxford Companion to World War II*,
Oxford, 2001.

100 14,000 Australians – 'Singapore, fall
of' – Eds I.C.B. Dear and M.R.D. Foot,
The Oxford Companion to World War II,
Oxford, 2001.

101 93,000 of the Royal Netherlands East
Indies Army – 'Netherlands East
Indies', Eds I.C.B. Dear and M.R.D.
Foot, *The Oxford Companion to World
War II*, Oxford, 2001.

102 A quarter of the 50,000 British service
men –
http://www.researchingfepowhistory.
org.uk

102 Of the 94,000 Americans held in
Europe only one percent died in
captivity – Robert C. Doyle 'Prisoners
of War', *The Oxford Companion to
American Military History*. John
Whiteclay Chambers II, ed., Oxford,
1999.

102 the 10,650 American POWs who died
in the Far East – nearly 45 per cent –
Robert C. Doyle 'Prisoners of War',
*The Oxford Companion to American
Military History*. John Whiteclay
Chambers II, ed., Oxford, 1999.

102 the total of 25,600 Americans were
held – Robert C. Doyle 'Prisoners of
War', *The Oxford Companion to American
Military History*. John Whiteclay
Chambers II, ed., Oxford, 1999.

102 While only 265 Australian prisoners –
Joan Beaumont, 'Prisoners of War' –
*The Oxford Companion to Australian
Military History*, Eds Peter Dennis,
Jeffrey Grey, Ewan Morris, Robin Prior
and Jean Bou. Oxford University Press,
2009. *Oxford Reference Online*. Oxford
University Press.

102 Between 7,000 and 10,000 out of
78,000 American and Filipino POWs –
Robert C. Doyle 'Prisoners of War',
*The Oxford Companion to American
Military History*. John Whiteclay
Chambers II, ed., Oxford, 1999.

102 Of the 61,000 Australian, British, and
Dutch POWs who were made to work
on the Thailand–Burma Railway about
12,000 perished. – 'Burma–Thailand
railway', I.C.B. Dear and M.R.D. Foot
(eds), *The Oxford Companion to World
War II*, Oxford, 2001.

103 *The Singapore Grip* – J.G. Farrell, *The
Singapore Grip*, London, 1978, p.4.

103 in 'a mixture of garlic' – *The Other Side
of Tenko*, Len Baynes, p.9.

104 'heady mixture of tamarind – Alistair
Urquhart, *The Forgotten Highlander*,
London, 2010, p.51.

104 There were the vivid colours – Russell
Braddon, *The Naked Island*, London,
1981, p.39.

104 worn at the relief of Mafeking' – Jack
Chalker, *Burma Railway, Images of War*,
Frome, 2007, p.16.

104 'idiotic'. – Jack Chalker, *Burma Railway,
Images of War*, Frome, 2007, p.17.

105 'We were fed ridiculous propaganda –
John Lowe, unpublished memoirs.

105 confidently told his audience –
Charles A. Fisher, *Three Times a Guest,
Recollections of Japan and the Japanese,
1942–1969*, London, 1979, p.16.

105 A British newspaper reported – *The
World at War* DVD; Alistair Urquhart,
The Forgotten Highlander, London, 2010,
p.81.

105 the Japanese suffered – Colin Smith,
*Singapore Burning, Heroism and
Surrender in World War II*, Penguin,
London, 2006, p.45.

105 Nor was this all.' – Russell Braddon,
The Naked Island, 1981, London, p.37.

106 Another Australian soldier, Billy
Young – National Archives of
Singapore.

106 The Zero – Colin Smith, *Singapore
Burning, Heroism and Surrender in World
War II*, Penguin, London, 2006, p.46.

106 'like driving a pick-up truck '. – Colin
Smith, *Singapore Burning, Heroism and
Surrender in World War II*, Penguin,
London, 2006, p.47.

106 'BEWARE OF THE SHARKS'. – Jack
Chalker, *Burma Railway, Images of War*,
Frome, 2007, p.20.

106 'No matter how much training –
interview with the author.

106 like exhausted miners – Colin Smith, *Singapore Burning, Heroism and Surrender in World War II*, Penguin, London, 2006, p.483.

107 'After a while the car hulk – Jack Chalker, *Burma Railway, Images of War*, Frome, 2007, p. 21.

Chapter 11: Changi

109 'walking upright and careless' – Stephen Alexander, *Sweet Kwai Run Softly*, Bristol, 1995, p.63.

109 Sometimes high-ranking Japanese officers – Charles A. Fisher, *Three Times a Guest, Recollections of Japan and the Japanese, 1942–69*, London, 1979, pp.40–41.

109 Changi – For a detailed assessment of Changi see R.P.W. Havers, *Reassessing the Japanese Prisoner of War Experience, The Changi POW Camp, Singapore, 1942–5*, RoutledgeCurzon, London, 2003.

110 Quilts – see Bernice Archer, *The internment of Western civilians under the Japanese 1941–45: a patchwork of internment*, RoutledgeCurzon, London, 2004, Australian War Memorial at: http://www.awm.gov.au/encyclopedia/quilt/history.asp and British Red Cross: http://www.redcross.org.uk/About-us/Who-we-are/Museum-and-archives/Historical-factsheets/The-Changi-quilt

111 around 45,562 POWs on Singapore – see R.P.W. Havers, *Reassessing the Japanese Prisoner of War Experience, The Changi POW Camp, Singapore, 1942–5*, RoutledgeCurzon, London, 2003, p.11.

111 Demand for workers – Havers, Ibid.

112 *The Fenman* – A copy is held in the Cambridgeshire Collection and is reproduced with kind permission of the Cambridgeshire Regiment.

115 'so small as – Charles A. Fisher, *Three Times a Guest, Recollections of Japan and the Japanese, 1942-69*, London, 1979, p.49.

115 Jack Chalker – interview with the author.

115 'odd kind of normality' – Eric Lomax, *The Railway Man*, London, 1996, p.73.

115 Alexandra Hospital – These figures are according to a plaque erected by Singapore's National Heritage Board, although they are not definitive.

116 'like Hallowe'en fright masks' – Eric Lomax, *The Railway Man*, London, 1996, p 74.

Chapter 12: Turned Out Rice Again: Food and Cooking

118 'That's another I learnt . . .' interview with the author.

119 '. . . for the first time . . .' IWM Sound Archive, E.W. Swanton (Catalogue Number 4777).

119 officers would relive – Stephen Alexander, *Sweet Kwai Run Softly*, Bristol, 1995, p.69.

119 a description of a feast – Stephen Alexander, *Sweet Kwai Run Softly*, Bristol, 1995, p.77.

119 chocolate éclairs – Russell Braddon, *The Naked Island*, London, 1981, p.37.

119 'rent, rice and rags' – Sibylla Jane Flower, 'Captors and captives on the Burma–Thailand Railway' in *Prisoners of War and their Captors in World War II* edited by Bob Moore and Kent Fedorowich, Oxford, 1996, p.243.

121 a burnt crust – this is described as 'Kring' in Meg Parkes, '*Notify Alec Rattray . . .*', Wirral, 2002, p.169; the process of extracting the burnt edging is referred to as 'quaning' (see Meg Parkes, '*– A.A. Duncan is OK*', Wirral, 2003, p,109 Dec 1–10th). My thanks to Meg Parkes for pointing out both these references.

121 Stanley Chown – Michael Bentinck, *A Will to Live*, 1996.

121 marmalade – J.D.F. Jones, *Storyteller, The Many Lives of Laurens van der Post*, London, 2001, p.40.

121 Eric Lomax used a 44-gallon drum – Eric Lomax, *The Railway Man*, London, 1996, p.88.

121 'We were counting – interview with the author.

122 'Well, I thought – interview with the author.

122 taps, basins – Oliver Lindsay, *At the Going Down of the Sun, Hong Kong and*

South-East Asia 1941–45, London, 1981, p.26.

122 It looked, to one eye witness – Tony Banham, Not the Slightest Chance, The Defence of Hong Kong, 1941, Hong Kong, 2003, p.285.

123 In his diary – The War Diaries of Weary Dunlop, Viking Books, 1989.

124 'Do you know – interview with the author.

124 'happy feet' – Slim de Grey, Changi, The Funny Side, c.1991, p.105; Alistair Urquhart, The Forgotten Highlander, London, 2010, p.154.

124 POWs in Hong Kong complained of 'electric feet' – Oliver Lindsay. At the Going Down of the Sun, Hong Kong and South-East Asia 1941–45, London, 1981, p.180.

124 After the war doctors recognised a condition among FEPOWs called 'bamboo heart', in which the heart dilates and the valves leak, and which was caused by a lack of protein in the diet. – Julie Summers, The Colonel of Tamarkan, Philip Toosey & The Bridge on the River Kwai, London, 2006, p.355.

124 'Java balls' – interview with Nowell Peach.

124 'camp eyes' – Alistair Urquhart, The Forgotten Highlander, London, 2010, p.159.

124 Beriberi – Frederick L. Dunn, 'Deficiency Diseases.' Cambridge World History of Food. Ed. Kenneth F. Kiple and Kriemhild Coneè Ornelas, Cambridge, 2000.

125 Heavy drinkers – Charles A. Fisher, Three Times a Guest, Recollections of Japan and the Japanese, 1942–1969, London, 1979, p.45.

126 Many artists – Dr Nigel Stanley, lecture, 'Medical aspects relating to FEPOW and civilian internees', Researching FEPOW History Group's 2nd International Conference at the National Memorial Arboretum (NMA), Staffordshire, 31 May–1 June, 2008.

127 800 men from the AIF – R.P.W. Havers, Reassessing the Japanese Prisoner of War Experience, The Changi POW Camp, Singapore, 1942–5, p.44.

128 when Eric Lomax returned to Singapore – Eric Lomax, The Railway Man, London, 1996, p.194.

129 dogs, cats, mice, cockroaches, strips of army blanket – Sir David Griffin, Changi Days, The Prisoner as Poet, Australia, 2002, p.32.

129 'a maternity ward.' – Stephen Alexander, Sweet Kwai Run Softly, Bristol, 1995, p.66.

129 the slime they exuded. – Russell Braddon, The Piddingtons, London, 1950, p.102.

129 Java lizard – J.D.F. Jones, Storyteller, The Many Lives of Laurens van der Post, London, 2001, p.44.

129 'That night I hardly slept – L.L. Baynes, The Other Side of Tenko, 1985, pp.70–71.

129 'How different life now – L.L.Baynes, The Other Side of Tenko, 1985, p.71.

129 invited to the Dutch sector – Monty Parkin, Surviving by Magic, Kent, 2009, p.33.

129 rabbits – J.D.F. Jones, Storyteller, The Many Lives of Laurens van der Post, London, 2001, p.44.

130 Bobby Greene – Stephen Alexander, Sweet Kwai Run Softly, Bristol, 1995, p.94.

130 'Dog Lovers' Club' – Slim de Grey, Changi, The Funny Side, c.1991, p.138 and 148.

130 'It was monsoon – interview with the author.

131 Private Albert Nuttall – Digest of Narrative of Private Nuttall, 2nd Loyal Regiment, papers of Sir Cecil Charles Hughes-Hallett (GBR/0014/HUHT), Churchill Archives Centre.

132 'which of course meant we got almost nothing – Johnny Sherwood, Football, Fame, Fear, 'Pro Player's Story, I Saw the Nagasaki Atom Bomb, p.177.

132 Until almost the end of the war the – Hilary St George Saunders, The Red Cross and the White, London, 1949, p.75.

132 Committee of the International Red Cross – International Committee of the Red Cross, Report of the International Committee of the Red Cross on its activities during the Second World War (September 1, 1939–June 30, 1947), Volume One – General Activities, Geneva, May, 1948, p.444.

133 provisions locally – Hilary St George Saunders, *The Red Cross and the White*, London, 1949, p.151.

Chapter 13: Make Do and Mend

134 Gas cape – a cape designed to protect against poison gas but also used as a groundsheet because of its waterproof properties.

134 Malayan Volunteer Forces – see Rosemary Fell, 'The Malayan Volunteer Forces', http://www.cofepow.org.uk/pages/armedforces_r_malayan_volunteers.htm.

135 John Clemetson – Captain J.G. Clemetson. *Don't Ever again say, 'It can't be done', The story of Changi Industries Inc*, Singapore, 2005.

136 latex – Changi Industries was not the only place where rubber was used. Frank Bell records how latex was used to make cricket balls and in other parts of Asia POWs rebound books which had been attacked by termites and humidity using latex and other materials such as palm leaf or rags.

138 Frank Bell – see Frank Bell, *Undercover University*, Cambridge, 1990.

139 Lifting the lid – Private Papers of F.E. Bell, IWM, 8224 93/15/3.

140 they also stripped the hard spine – Russell Braddon, *The Naked Island*, London, 1981, p.245.

140 A toothbrush – Changi Museum.

140 Les Poidevin – Leslie Poidevin, *Samurais and Circumcisions*, 1985, p.99.

141 Shower – see AWM, ART25085 – 'The shower, Changi, early days', Murray Griffin, brush and brown ink and wash over pencil on paper, 1944.

141 houses for poultry – L.L. Baynes, *The Other Side of Tenko*, 1985, p.70. Len Baynes built a duck run that attracted many admiring visitors.

141 Chess – Jack Cosford, *Yasumi Ni*, 1959, p.21.

141 engraved 'Rolex Waterproof' – Russell Braddon, *Naked Island*, London, 1981, p.246.

141 rice sacks – *Captured!* IWM North exhibition, 2009.

141 'I have a whole lot of boots' –

Captured! IWM North exhibition, 2009.

142 Major Denis Houghton – *Captured!* IWM North exhibition, 2009.

142 Kenneth Trigg – see *Woodworking International*, February–March 1990. He also made a Davy lamp from a small tin, glass bottle with top and bottom cut off and 'devilishly clever ratchet device' to control height of wick. It burnt coconut oil which was so rancid it was inedible.

143 to apply the rosin – my thanks to Sarah Mnatzaganian for this insight.

143 Gunner Charles Woodhams – *Captured!* IWM North exhibition, 2009.

Chapter 14: Entertainment: 'You'll Never Get Off this Island!'

145 'No matter how much – interview with the author.

147 The Optimists – Professor Sears Eldredge, lecture 'Civilian Internee & FEPOW Concert Parties', Researching FEPOW History Group's 2nd International Conference, National Memorial Arboretum (NMA), Staffordshire, 31 May–1 June, 2008.

147 Hellsabuzzin' – R.P.W. Havers, *Reassessing the Japanese Prisoner of War Experience, The Changi POW Camp, Singapore, 1942–5*, RoutledgeCurzon, London, 2003, p.61.

147 'Turned out rice again.' – R.P.W. Havers, *Reassessing the Japanese Prisoner of War Experience, The Changi POW Camp, Singapore, 1942–5*, RoutledgeCurzon, London, 2003, p.43.

148 'lorry loads of dead Indians and Chinese' – John Lowe, unpublished memoir.

149 'a quiet, most unassuming' – John Lowe, unpublished memoir.

149 They performed – interview with the author.

150 'The rash of concert parties – Russell Braddon, *The Naked Island*, 1981, p.172.

150 'a beauteous female' – Russell Braddon, *The Piddingtons*, London, 1950, p.92.

150 'fearful old bags' – Russell Braddon, *The Piddingtons*, London, 1950, p.92.

150 You're sweeter than all I know etc. –
     Changi Souvenir Song Book, Ray Tullipan
     and Slim de Grey.

151 Terai – Russell Braddon, *The Naked
     Island*, 1981, p.183.

151 Joey – AWM RELAWM30623.

152 'Black Jack' – His nickname came
     from his complexion, glowering brown
     eyes under bushy black eyebrows and
     his dark hair. He was a stern
     commander who insisted that the men
     at Changi were soldiers, not prisoners
     and later refused to join any ex-POW
     associations.

152 You can't exaggerate the
     importance. – Singapore National
     Archives.

153 *Dover Road* – Charles A. Fisher, *Three
     Times a Guest, Recollections of Japan and
     the Japanese, 1942–1969*, London, 1979,
     p.55.

153 Dennis East – Professor Sears
     Eldredge, lecture 'Civilian Internee &
     FEPOW Concert Parties', Researching
     FEPOW History Group's 2nd
     International Conference, National
     Memorial Arboretum (NMA),
     Staffordshire, 31 May–1 June, 2008.

153 Nitwits – Diary entry, November 22,
     1944, Jack Farrow, *Darkness before Dawn*,
     Peterborough.

Chapter 15: Sport

154 Football and cricket were popular at
     the start – IWM Sound Archive, E.W.
     Swanton (Catalogue Number 4777).

154 *Sportsman's Paper – Captured!* IWM
     North exhibition, 2009.

155 give mock commentaries – IWM
     North's 2004 exhibition, 'The Greater
     Game', *Daily Telegraph*, 29 July 2004.

155 twelve hours – Cricket pundit
     Swanton dies,
     http://news.bbc.co.uk/2/hi/sport/cri
     cket/614842.stm

156 Footballers – Anton Rippon, *Gas
     Masks for Goal Posts – Football in Britain
     during the Second World War*, Stroud,
     2007, p.116.

157 'Those who have never – Doris
     Lessing, *Under My Skin*, London, 1995,
     p.125.

157 forty-five deaths at Changi – quoted in
     R.P.W. Havers, *Reassessing the Japanese
     Prisoner of War Experience, The Changi
     POW Camp, Singapore, 1942–5*,
     RoutledgeCurzon, London, 2003, p.64.

157 the going rate was ten cigarettes –
     quoted in R.P.W. Havers, *Reassessing
     the Japanese Prisoner of War Experience,
     The Changi POW Camp, Singapore,
     1942–5*, RoutledgeCurzon, London,
     2003, p.46.

158 to swat flies. Patients at Tamarkan of
     the Thai Railways were encouraged to
     do this – Julie Summers, *The Colonel of
     Tamarkan, Philip Toosey & The Bridge on
     the River Kwai*, London, 2006, p.191.

158 'Not knowing – Johnny Sherwood,
     *Football, Fame, Fear, 'Pro Player's Story, I
     Saw the Nagasaki Atom Bomb*, p.58.

158 'rolled in' – Johnny Sherwood,
     *Football, Fame, Fear, 'Pro Player's Story, I
     Saw the Nagasaki Atom Bomb*, p.58.

158 'down in the dumps' – Johnny
     Sherwood, *Football, Fame, Fear, 'Pro
     Player's Story, I Saw the Nagasaki Atom
     Bomb*, p. 59.

158 'I must admit – Johnny Sherwood,
     *Football, Fame, Fear, 'Pro Player's Story, I
     Saw the Nagasaki Atom Bomb*, p.61.

159 banned soccer and boxing – R.P.W.
     Havers, *Reassessing the Japanese Prisoner
     of War Experience, The Changi POW
     Camp, Singapore, 1942–5*,
     RoutledgeCurzon, London, 2003, p.108.

Chapter 16: Recording Captivity Through Art and Photography

161 '(albeit self-appointed) participator-
     recorder'. – Ronald Searle, *To the Kwai –
     and Back, War Drawings 1939–1945*,
     London, 1986, p.9.

161 Circumstances were too basic –
     Ronald Searle, *To the Kwai – and Back,
     War Drawings 1939–1945*, London, 1986,
     p.10.

161 'During my captivity I had – Ronald
     Searle, *To the Kwai – and Back War
     Drawings 1939–1945*, London, 1986, p.9.

162 Lilliput – Russell Davies, *Ronald Searle,
     A Biography*, London, 2003, p.54.

162 'Of all things – interview with the
     author.

163 Murray Griffin – see AWM – http://www.awm.gov.au/people/artist_profiles/griffin.asp.

164 'I didn't have any grand design – Tim Bowden, *Changi Photographer, George Aspinall's Record of Captivity*, Australia, 1984, p.46.

165 close physical contact – Tim Bowden, *Changi Photographer, George Aspinall's Record of Captivity*, Australia, 1984, p.94.

166 'At that time – Tim Bowden, *Changi Photographer, George Aspinall's Record of Captivity*, Australia, 1984, p.68.

167 Captain Mohan Singh — R.P.W. Havers, *Reassessing the Japanese Prisoner of War Experience, The Changi POW Camp, Singapore, 1942–5*, RoutledgeCurzon, London, 2003, p.190, footnote 141, and p.58.

167 as 'changelings', – Jack Chalker, *Burma Railway, Images of War*, Frome, p.29.

167 two platforms – Jack Chalker, *Burma Railway, Images of War*, Frome, p.26.

168 'homosexual assaults' – Jack Chalker, *Burma Railway, Images of War*, Frome, p.29.

168 R.P.W. Havers, *Reassessing the Japanese Prisoner of War Experience, The Changi POW Camp, Singapore, 1942–5*, RoutledgeCurzon, London, 2003, provides probably the fullest description of events at Selarang.

169 Accounts vary as to how many water taps were working; some say just one, others three.

170 the third anniversary – Eric Lomax, *The Railway Man*, London, 1996, p.80.

170 'For God's sake shoot me – quoted in R.P.W. Havers, *Reassessing the Japanese Prisoner of War Experience, The Changi POW Camp, Singapore, 1942–5*, RoutledgeCurzon, London, 2003, p.71.

171 Galleghan climbed – Tim Bowden, *Changi Photographer, George Aspinall's Record of Captivity*, Australia, 1984, p.90.

171 For Eric Lomax – *The Railway Man*, London, 1996, p.81.

Chapter 17: POW Doctor

172 The quotes from Doctor Peach are taken from an interview with author; additional information was supplied by telephone and letter.

174 *Gray's Anatomy* – See *Sunday Telegraph*, March 30, 2008, 'The book that changed the course of medical history'.

177 Lecture – Weary Dunlop referred to this lecture on 'bird photography' in a diary entry of 9 May 1942.

177 Les Poidevin – After the war he wrote about his experiences in *Samurais and Circumcisions*.

178 Miraculous – Leslie Poidevin, *Samurais and Circumcisions*, 1985, p.43.

178 'This was a great experience – Leslie Poidevin, *Samurais and Circumcisions*, 1985, p.43.

179 'not only a stimulus' – Leslie Poidevin, *Samurais and Circumcisions*, 1985, p.75.

179 'Making good progress – Meg Parkes, 'Notify Alec Rattray. . .', Wirral, 2002, p.22.

Chapter 18: Taking Flight: Escape Through Birdwatching

184 'an inveterate note taker' – by email.

185 'No doubt . . .' by email.

186 For more about the remarkable life of Jack Spittle, and examples of his note-taking and sketches, see http://bspittle.wordpress.com/

Chapter 19: Survival Teams

187 'I had at this moment in time – 'Football, Fame, Fear, 'Pro Player's Story, I Saw the Nagasaki Atom Bomb*, p.98.

187 'I always seemed – 'Football, Fame, Fear, 'Pro Player's Story, I Saw the Nagasaki Atom Bomb*, p.111.

187 a group of three – Julie Summers, *Stranger in the House*, London, 2008, p.86.

188 elaborate ritual – Meg Parkes, '– A.A. Duncan is OK', Wirral, 2003, p.46.

188 some grated coconut – Russell Braddon, *The Naked Island*, London, 1981, p.184.

188 a small lump of gulah Malacca – Russell Braddon, *The Naked Island*, London, 1981, p.168.

188 exotic tattoos – Stephen Alexander, *Sweet Kwai Run Softly*, Bristol, 1995, p.119; – Charles A. Fisher, *Three Times a*

Guest, Recollections of Japan and the Japanese, 1942–1969, London, 1979, p.85.

188 go into politics. – R.P.W. Havers, *Reassessing the Japanese Prisoner of War Experience, The Changi POW Camp, Singapore, 1942–5,* RoutledgeCurzon, London, 2003, p.121.

188 as 'griff' or 'icecream' – Russell Braddon, *The Piddingtons,* London, 1950, p.112.

189 R.P.W. Havers suggests – R.P.W. Havers, *Reassessing the Japanese Prisoner of War Experience, The Changi POW Camp, Singapore, 1942–5,* pp.139–140.

189 The officers' mess at Bukit Timah – Julie Summers, *The Colonel of Tamarkan, Philip Toosey & The Bridge on the River Kwai,* London, 2006, p.105.

189 the official insistence – Russell Braddon, *The Naked Island,* London, 1981, p.172.

189 Sad Case of the Disappearing Cocktail – Stephen Alexander, *Sweet Kwai Run Softly,* Bristol, 1995, p.93.

189 By the start of 1943 – Sibylla Jane Flower, 'Captors and Captives on the Burma–Thailand Railway,' *Prisoners of war and their captors in World War II* by Bob Moore and Kent Fedorowich, p.242. British officers were more likely to arrive on the Burma–Thai Railway with a mixture of men from different regiments, compared to the Australians who had fewer units and were not obliged to break them up in this way. p.240. On Christmas Day 1942, for example, officers were told that they would have to start work at Chungkai – Charles A. Fisher, *Three Times a Guest, Recollections of Japan and the Japanese, 1942–1969,* London, 1979, pp.68–70.

190 Colonel Philip Toosey – Julie Summers, *The Colonel of Tamarkan, Philip Toosey & The Bridge on the River Kwai,* London, 2006, p.146 and p.149.

190 'The peace and tranquillity of those meetings – Transactions of The Research Lodge of Otago. July 30, 1958, Masonic Experiences at the Japanese Prisoner-of-war camp at Changi, Malayan Peninsula. From an address by W. Bro. H.W. Wylie, PGD

to the Essex Masters' Lodge, NO 3256 and published in the transactions of that Lodge, Freemasons' Library, London.

191 'Many men – *The Broken Column* by W.A.G. Edwards.

191 Most groups of Masons kept detailed – for example, The Roberts Hospital, Changi, Singapore Prisoner of War Masonic Association, Changi, Singapore, Freemasons' Library, London.

191 For details of Masons in the Far East see *Behind the Wire* by Keith Flynn.

192 whether red-headed women – J.D.F. Jones, *Storyteller, The Many Lives of Laurens van der Post,* London, John Murray, 2001, p.48. Van der Post mentions this in his diary of 20 December 1942.

192 debated whether it was preferable to be stuck in captivity – J.D.F. Jones, *Storyteller, The Many Lives of Laurens van der Post,* London, John Murray, 2001, p.48. L.V.D diary entry, 6 January 1943.

192 a 'camp giggle' – J.D.F. Jones, *Storyteller, The Many Lives of Laurens van der Post,* London, John Murray, 2001, p.47.

192 a prolonged and heated debate was whether single or double beds – Frank Bell, *Undercover University,* Cambridge, 1990, p.76.

192 'intellectual link with the world from which we were separated' – Frank Bell, *Undercover University,* Cambridge, 1990, p.54.

192 ski-ing, crime, big game hunting – Russell Braddon, *The Naked Island,* London, 1981, p.135.

192 'Scents and Perfumes', 'A Holiday in a Lunatic Asylum', 'Hollywood' and 'Murder and Robbery in Shanghai – Oliver Lindsay, *At the Going Down of the Sun, Hong Kong and South-East Asia 1941–45,* London, 1981, p.86.

193 Bartram and Dart – Russell Braddon, *The Naked Island,* London, 1981, p.272.

193 'Evidently this time – D.F. Jones, *Storyteller, The Many Lives of Laurens van der Post,* London, John Murray, 2001.

194 'gave the old memory – Meg Parkes, 'Notify Alec Rattray. . .', Wirral, 2002, p.III.

195 'The Things That Annoy Me' – Frank Bell, Undercover University, Cambridge, 1990, p.45.

Chapter 20: Escape Through Study

197 a prison university at Landsop camp – D.F. Jones, Storyteller, The Many Lives of Laurens van der Post, London, John Murray, 2001, p.41.

197 taught navigation – D.F. Jones, Storyteller, The Many Lives of Laurens van der Post, London, John Murray, 2001, p.41.

197 By Sept 42 1,200 students were engrossed in 30 subjects, – D.F. Jones, Storyteller, The Many Lives of Laurens van der Post, London, John Murray, 2001, p.41.

198 'two POW universities' – Charles A. Fisher, Three Times a Guest, Recollections of Japan and the Japanese, 1942–1969, London, 1979, p.55.

198 'senior school teachers' – Charles A. Fisher, Three Times a Guest, Recollections of Japan and the Japanese, 1942–1969, London, 1979, p.55.

198 'at least comparable' – Charles A. Fisher, Three Times a Guest, Recollections of Japan and the Japanese, 1942–1969, London, 1979, p.56.

198 Phd thesis – Charles A. Fisher, Three Times a Guest, Recollections of Japan and the Japanese, 1942–1969, London, 1979, pp. 99–100. He did not say what the subject was.

198 18th Division's University – Stephen Alexander, Sweet Kwai Run Softly, Bristol, 1995, p.78.

198 in a small mosque – Stephen Alexander, Sweet Kwai Run Softly, Bristol, 1995, p.79.

198 S.C. Irons – Cambridgeshire Collection.

199 at its peak, as many as 9,000 POWs – R.P.W. Havers, Reassessing the Japanese Prisoner of War Experience, The Changi POW Camp, Singapore, 1942–5, RoutledgeCurzon, London, 2003, p.60.

199 Oppie – obituary, The Independent,
Monday, 15 December 1997.

200 'You don't know Obituary Antony Easthope, The Guardian, Friday 17 December 1999.

200 Captain Leslie Greener – David Griffin, Changi Days, The Prisoner as Poet, Australia, 2002, p.16.

201 400 Australians learned to read and write at Changi – Brian MacArthur, Surviving the Sword, Prisoners of the Japanese 1942–45, London, p.189.

201 'each man created – David Griffin, Changi Days, The Prisoner as Poet, Australia, 2002, p.12.

201 The Happiness Box – David Griffin, The Happiness Box, Singapore, 2002.

202 20,000 books – Brian MacArthur, Surviving the Sword, Prisoners of the Japanese 1942–45, London, 2007, p.189.

202 J.G.B. Millns – IWM J.G.B. Millns, catalogue number: 15371 07/54/1.

203 David Piper – see David Piper, I Am Well, Who Are You?, Wytham, 1998.

204 Stephen Alexander read – Stephen Alexander, Sweet Kwai Run Softly, Bristol, 1995, p.76. He was probably referring to William Shirer's Berlin Diary: The Journal of a Foreign Correspondent 1934–41.

204 To my surprise – Stephen Alexander, Sweet Kwai Run Softly, Bristol, 1995, p.146.

204 resumed the literary studies – Stephen Alexander, Sweet Kwai Run Softly, Bristol, 1995, p.169.

204 'on the solemn side with a strong whiff of Fabianism' – Stephen Alexander, Sweet Kwai Run Softly, Bristol, p.120.

204 Terence Charley – Stephen Alexander, Sweet Kwai Run Softly, Bristol, 1995, p.170.

204 Frank Bell – Frank Bell, Undercover University, Cambridge, 1990, p.23.

205 Vicarious pleasure – Frank Bell, Undercover University, Cambridge, 1990, p.23.

205 The Wind in the Willow – Jack Chalker, Burma Railway, Images of War, Frome, 2007 p.63.

205 Alice's Adventures – Julie Summers, The Colonel of Tamarkan, Philip Toosey & The Bridge on the River Kwai, London, 2006, p.191.

205 *Winnie the Pooh* – Russell Braddon, *The Naked Island*, London, 1981, p.179.

Chapter 21: University of Kuching

206 '[It was the] nearest approach – Frank Bell, *Undercover University*, Cambridge, 1990, p16.
207 'I envisaged it as the cultural centre – Ibid., p.17.
208 'such as I had never met before! – Ibid., p.24.
208 'to make this period of captivity – Ibid., p.25.
209 'too far gone in mental decay – Ibid., p.78.
209 'reasonable – Ibid., p.64.
210 'To be at a desk – Ibid., p.31.
210 'Nip in camp – Ibid., p.29.
211 'In my dreams – Ibid., p.59.
212 'one large and excellent dictionary – Ibid., p.167.
212 'highly dangerous – Ibid., p.62.

Chapter 22: Languages and Communicating with the Outside World

216 Esperanto – Russell Braddon, *The Naked Island*, London, 1981, p.253.
216 'neat columns – Eric Lomax, *The Railway Man*, London, 1996, p.103.
216 Jim Wakefield – interview with the author.
217 surrounded by a high electrified fence – Oliver Lindsay, *At the Going Down of the Sun, Hong Kong and South-East Asia 1941-45*, London, 1981, p.74.
219 100 soldiers with them as batmen – Oliver Lindsay, *At the Going Down of the Sun, Hong Kong and South-East Asia 1941-45*, London, 1981, p.74.
219 Taipan – a foreign manager or head of a firm.
220 While he was a POW he passed the time by translating – Derek Davies in *Far Eastern Economic Review*, 3 December 1987. By the time of his death in 1987 he was believed to be fluent in at least 20 languages.
220 Solomon Bard – *South China Morning Post*, 20 November 1987.
220 Every six months the Red Cross's representative – Oliver Lindsay, *At the Going Down of the Sun, Hong Kong and South-East Asia 1941-45*, London, 1981, p.78.
220 By 1944 his flat and office – Oliver Lindsay, *At the Going Down of the Sun, Hong Kong and South-East Asia 1941-45*, London, 1981, p.144.

Chapter 23: Hidden Wireless Sets

223 British Army Aid Group – Oliver Lindsay, *At the Going Down of the Sun, Hong Kong and South-East Asia 1941-45*, London, 1981, pp.89-90.
223 It made contact – Oliver Lindsay, *At the Going Down of the Sun, Hong Kong and South-East Asia 1941-45*, London, 1981, p.110.
223 Information about shipping – Oliver Lindsay, *At the Going Down of the Sun, Hong Kong and South-East Asia 1941-45*, London, 1981, p.111.
223 Medicine and other items – Oliver Lindsay, *At the Going Down of the Sun, Hong Kong and South-East Asia 1941-45*, London, 1981, p.112.
223 'The Pipe' – Sir Charles David Griffin, National Archives of Singapore.
224 Eric Lomax writes – Eric Lomax, *The Railway Man*, London, 1996, pp.89-91.
224 The set was eventually discovered – Eric Lomax, *The Railway Man*, London, 1996, p.108.
224 in a broom head, – David Griffin, *Changi Days, The prisoner as Poet*, Australia, 2002, p.96.
224 a water bottle – For example, from May 1944, Captain Charles Wells hid his diary in a water bottle in Thailand that he kept casually slung over his bed space where it survived many searches. *Captured!* IWM North exhibition, 2009.
224 Sack of rice – Russell Braddon, *The Naked Island*, London, 1981, p.181.
224 a pair of clogs – J.D.F. Jones, *Storyteller, The Many Lives of Laurens van der Post*, London, 2001, p.50.
224 a xylophone – Russell Braddon, *The Piddingtons*, London, 1950, p.124.
224 Stage – Slim de Grey, *Changi, The Funny Side*, c.1991, p.114.
224 Mosquito netting – Stephen Alexander, *Sweet Kwai Run Softly*,

Bristol, 1995, p.156.

224 The Second Cambridgeshire regiment smuggled in a radio – Stephen Alexander, *Sweet Kwai Run Softly*, Bristol, 1995, p.91.

224 George Aspinall stole a set from a building – Tim Bowden, *Changi photographer George Aspinall's Record of Captivity*, Australia, 1984, p.76

224 Wall cavity – Tim Bowden, *Changi photographer George Aspinall's Record of Captivity*, Australia, 1984, p.79.

224 Boreholes– Jack Chalker, *Burma Railway, Images of War*, Frome, 2007, p.25.

224 boiler – Russell Braddon, *The Naked Island*, London, 1981, p.268.

224 packed in a bully beef tin – Stephen Alexander, *Sweet Kwai Run Softly*, Bristol, 1995, p.102.

224 Prematurely dark – Brian MacArthur, *Surviving the Sword, Prisoners of the Japanese 1942–1945*, London, 2007, p.144.

224 as a guard sat on a chair in – J.D.F. Jones, *Storyteller, The Many Lives of Laurens van der Post*, London, 2001, p.50.

225 Sydney Piddington – Russell Braddon, *The Piddingtons*, London, 1950, pp. 89–91.

225 Allied forces launched a seaborne attack on the German-occupied French port of Dieppe on 19 August 1942. Around 4,000 men were killed, injured or taken prisoner.

225 At Batu Lintang in Kuching a professional actor – Frank Bell, *Undercover University*, 1990, Cambridge, p.30.

225 'Have you had any icecream today?' – *Cambridge Evening News*, 14 August 1985.

225 As a precaution – Ewart Escritt, *Beyond the Three Pagodas Pass*, Oxford, 1988, p.37.

225 'larding' it with 90% of false information – Griffin, National Archives of Singapore.

226 His hands and arms were bound – Oliver Lindsay, *At the Going Down of the Sun, Hong Kong and South-East Asia 1941–45*, London, 1981, p.128.

226 Colonel L.A. Newnham – Oliver Lindsay, *At the Going Down of the Sun, Hong Kong and South-East Asia 1941–45*,

London, 1981, p.131, Internees and some local Chinese people were also executed for their involvement, p.119.

226 'for fortitude as a POW' – George Cross.

Chapter 24: Religion

227 Harvest thanksgiving – David Allen, *Jim, The Life of E.W. Swanton*, London, 2004, p.107.

227 Proselytising stance – David Allen, *Jim, The Life of E.W. Swanton*, London, 2004, p.125.

227 Noel Duckworth – Cambridgeshire Collection, *The Times*, Monday, December 1, 1980.

228 as many as fifteen funerals – Julie Summers, *The Colonel of Tamarkan, Philip Toosey & The Bridge on the River Kwai*, London, 2006, p.216.

228 A British padre – Julie Summers, *The Colonel of Tamarkan, Philip Toosey & The Bridge on the River Kwai*, London, 2006, p.194.

229 'I was disgusted – Monty Parkin, *Surviving by Magic*, Kent, 2009, p.66.

229 'One thing I discovered – Julie Summers, *The Colonel of Tamarkan, Philip Toosey & The Bridge on the River Kwai*, London, 2006, p.195.

229 American POWS – Paul Fussell, *Wartime: understanding and behavior in the Second World War*, Oxford, 1989, pp.233–234.

229 Moffat edition – Eric Lomax, *The Railway Man*, London, 1996, p.102.

229 Russell Braddon read a copy of the Bible – Russell Braddon, *The Naked Island*, London, 1981, p.144.

229 Frank Bell witnessed a similar interest in the Bible – Frank Bell, *Undercover University*, Cambridge, 1990, p.61.

230 Louis Zamperini – Laura Hillenbrand, *Unbroken, A World War II Story of Survival, Resilience, and Redemption*, New York, 2010.

230 'Religion comes up – Singapore National Archives.

230 'formal religion – Jack Chalker, *Burma Railway, Images of War*, Frome, 2007, p.48.

230 'Another thing – Monty Parkin,

Surviving by Magic, Kent, 2009, p.107.

Chapter 25: The Magic of Letters from Home

231 These letters are held at the Imperial War Museum, the papers of Fergus Anckorn (catalogue number: 213 87/58/1).

Chapter 26: The Changi Murals

238 An interview with Stanley Warren is held at the National Archives of Singapore.

239 G.J.M. Chambers – *Crockford's Clerical Directory*, 1941. Extra information kindly supplied by Adele Allen, Archive Assistant, Lambeth Palace Library.

239 See also Peter W. Stubbs, *The Changi Murals, The Story of Stanley Warren's War* and *The Changi Murals*, Singapore, c.2003, by Wally Hammond, Changi University Series, Singapore, 2002.

239 a skit on the film *The Dancing Years* called *The Dancing Tears* – *The Guardian*, February 27, 1992.

240 Stephen Alexander saw the murals – Stephen Alexander, *Sweet Kwai Run Softly*, Bristol, 1995, p.88.

PART III: EUROPE

Chapter 27: Reading for Profit

248 The Papers of (Harold) Montgomery Belgion Reference GBR/0014/BLGN are held at the Churchill Archives Centre. Many of his papers were destroyed in a German bombing raid and details about his life 1918–39 are therefore sparse. See *Who Was Who*, A & C Black, 1920–2008.

249 He wrote two other books – *The Human Parrot* (OUP, 1931) and *News from the French* (Faber, 1938, also translated into German). *Our Present Philosophy of Life* was translated into French.

249 *The Criterion*, A Literary Review, Vol XV, No. LXI July 1936, p.759.

249 Until in the 1990s – see 'T.S.Eliot is innocent' by Craig Raine, *The Observer*, 8 September 1996.

250 Postcard sent from the Athenaeum – September 1941.

251 One estimate suggested that about ten per cent – Hilary St George Saunders, *The Red Cross and the White: A short history of the joint war organization of the British Red cross Society and the Order of St John of Jerusalem during the war 1939–1945*, London, 1949, p.36.

251 embroidered 'V' for victory – Hilary St George Saunders, *The Red Cross and the White: A short history of the joint war organization of the British Red cross Society and the Order of St John of Jerusalem during the war 1939–1945*, London, 1949, p.36.

252 The United States and Canada allowed some food.

252 average 1,300 next-of-kin parcels a day – P.G. Cambray and G.G.B. Briggs, *Red Cross & St John, the official record of the humanitarian services of the War Organisation of the British Red Cross Society and Order of St John of Jerusalem 1939–1947*, London, 1949, p.188.

253 During the 1920s Belgion had acted – Michael Howard, *Jonathan Cape, Publisher*, London, 1971, p.151.

254 Margaret and David – his two children from his second marriage to Vida – were sent to New York for safety.

255 Auden – The poet left Britain to live in America in 1939.

255 Hayward was the original 'Man in White Spats' in *Old Possum's Book of Practical Cats* – Graham Chainey, *A Literary History of Cambridge*, Cambridge CUP, 1995, p.265; P.G. Cambray and G.G.B. Briggs, *Red Cross & St John, the official record of the humanitarian services of the War Organisation of the British Red Cross Society and Order of St John of Jerusalem 193–1947*, London, 1949, p.214.

256 it had sent out 71,000 volumes to POW and internment camps in Europe. When the war ended it had sent out 239,500 volumes – P.G. Cambray and G.G.B. Briggs, *Red Cross & St John, the official record of the humanitarian services of the War*

Organisation of the British Red Cross Society and Order of St John of Jerusalem 1939–1947, London, 1949, p.202.

257 or to a holding reserve in Geneva – P.G. Cambray and G.G.B. Briggs, *Red Cross & St John, the official record of the humanitarian services of the War Organisation of the British Red Cross Society and Order of St John of Jerusalem 1939–1947*, London, 1949, p.204.

258 'It is hard to describe – The Rev. David H.C. Read, 'Books in Prison II. Further Reflections of a POW chaplain', *Chambers' Journal*, October 1947, No. 43, p.657.

259 'like the Dutch painters – Paul Fussell, *Wartime: understanding and behavior in the Second World War*, Oxford, 1989, p.237.

259 Eric Newby, *Love and War in the Apennines*, 1996, London, 1996, p.64.

259 Decline and Fall of the Roman Empire – Eric Newby, *Love and War in the Apennines*, London, 1996, p.182.

259 'It was extraordinary how the hero – The Rev. David H.C. Read, 'Books in prison I. Reflections of a POW chaplain,' *Chambers' Journal*, October 1947, 593–5.

260 'One could settle peacefully – Pat Ward-Thomas, *Not only golf, an autobiography*, London, 1981, p.21.

260 Barbed-Wire University – Robert Holland, *Adversis Major, A short history of the Educational Books Scheme of the Prisoners of War Department of the British Red Cross Society and Order of St John of Jerusalem*, London, 1949, p.90.

260 Six thousand – Adrian Gilbert, *POW, Allied Prisoners in Europe, 1939–1945*, London, 2007, p.77.

260 an incredible collection of fifteen thousand books, as well as sixty thousand privately owned books – Robert Holland, *Adversis Major, A short history of the Educational Books Scheme of the Prisoners of War Department of the British Red Cross Society and Order of St John of Jerusalem*, London, 1949, p.47.

260 Censorship – Robert Holland, *Adversis Major, A short history of the Educational Books Scheme of the Prisoners of War Department of the British Red Cross*

Society and Order of St John of Jerusalem, London, 1949, pp.47–48.

260 As a result any book that – Robert Holland, *Adversis Major, A short history of the Educational Books Scheme of the Prisoners of War Department of the British Red Cross Society and Order of St John of Jerusalem*, London, 1949, p.46.

260 Rubbed out any marks – P.G. Cambray and G.G.B. Briggs, *Red Cross & St John, the official record of the humanitarian services of the War Organisation of the British Red Cross Society and Order of St John of Jerusalem 1939–1947*, London, 1949, p.214.

260 Jewish authors – P.G. Cambray and G.G.B. Briggs, *Red Cross & St John, the official record of the humanitarian services of the War Organisation of the British Red Cross Society and Order of St John of Jerusalem 1939–1947*, London, 1949, p.214; Hilary St George Saunders, *The Red Cross and the White: A short history of the joint war organization of the British Red cross Society and the Order of St John of Jerusalem during the war 1939–1945*, London, 1949, p.41.

261 *Lady Chatterley's Lover* – Adrian Gilbert, *POW, Allied Prisoners in Europe, 1939–1945*, London, 2007, p.186.

262 Holiday camps – see S.P. Mackenzie, *The Colditz Myth*, Oxford, 2006, pp.251–2 and Adrian Gilbert, *POW, Allied Prisoners in Europe, 1939–1945*, London, 2007, p.247.

263 *Decline and Fall* – 'Books in prison I. Reflections of a POW chaplain,' by The Rev. David H.C. Read, *Chambers' Journal*, October 1947, p.593.

Chapter 28: Gardening and Birdwatching

264 '... I determined that these birds – quoted in Stephen Moss, *A Bird in the Bush, A Social History of Birdwatching*, London, 2005, p.156.

265 *Touchstone* – REL/17, *Touchstone*, No. 8, Bobby Loder Collection, Archive Centre, King's College, Cambridge.

265 'inhabited another world – quoted in Stephen Moss, *A Bird in the Bush, A Social History of Birdwatching*, London,

2005, p.157.

265 Peter Conder – see Mark Cocker,
     Crow Country, London, 2007. Archives
     of Peter. J. Conder (1919–1993): A
     HANDLIST. I., Zoology Library
     Services – Oxford University Library
     Services.

265 'as near paradise – quoted in Mark
     Cocker, *Crow Country*, London, 2007,
     p.203, footnote 102.

265 German toilet paper – Stephen Moss,
     *A Bird in the Bush, A Social History of
     Birdwatching*, London, 2005, p.158.

265 their own special interests – Adrian
     Gilbert, *POW, Allied Prisoners in Europe,
     1939–1945*, London, 2007, p.170.

266 air raids – Mark Cocker, *Crow
     Country*, London, 2007, p.180.

266 'newly spread with human
     excrement'. – quoted Mark Cocker,
     Crow Country, London, 2007, p.180.

266 *Birdwatching – The Song of the
     Redstart* by A.N.L. Munby is kindly
     reproduced with the permission of
     Giles Munby.

267 an excellent lookout during escape
     attempts – Stephen Moss, *A Bird in the
     Bush, A Social History of Birdwatching*,
     London, 2005, p.158.

267 German ornithologist – John Buxton,
     The Redstart, London, 1950, p.144.

267 'God Save the King!' Stephen Moss, *A
     Bird in the Bush, A Social History of
     Birdwatching*, London, 2005, p.158.

267 Robert Warren – BBC WW2 People's
     War, contributed 29 January 2005,
     Article ID, A3592389.

268 Penguins – Paul Brickhill, *The Great
     Escape*, London, 2004, p.40 and p.41.
     Alex Lees became famous as one of the
     gardeners who helped The Great
     Escape. See his obituary in *The Times*,
     April 30, 2009.

268 Marlag – P.G. Cambray and G.G.B
     Briggs, *Red Cross & St John, the official
     record of the humanitarian services of the
     War Organisation of the British Red Cross
     Society and Order of St John of Jerusalem
     1939–1947*, London, 1949. p.209.

268 Even at Colditz – S.P. Mackenzie, *The
     Colditz Myth*, Oxford, 2006, p.178.

269 lupins and tulips – Adrian Gilbert,
     *POW, Allied Prisoners in Europe,
     1939–1945*, London, 2007, pp.169–170.

269 traditional horticultural show – See
     Squadron Leader Philip Jacobs at Stalag
     VIIIB, RAF Museum.

269 RHS – Bent Elliott, *The Royal
     Horticultural Society: A History 1804–2004*,
     Chichester, 2004.

269 Ministry of Economic Warfare – P.G.
     Cambray and G.G.B. Briggs, *Red Cross
     & St John, the official record of the
     humanitarian services of the War
     Organisation of the British Red Cross
     Society and Order of St John of Jerusalem
     1939–1947*, London, 1949, p.209.

269 By early 1943 the Red Cross – *The
     Prisoner of War*, February 1943.

269 Gardeners at Stalag Luft III – see
     Logbook of Squadron Leader C. I.
     Rolfe, 1943, IWM, Catalogue number:
     228 90/13/1.

Chapter 29: Study

271 'in the middle of a plain – Sandy
     Hernu, *Q: The biography of Desmond
     Llewelyn*, Seaford, 1999, p.51.

271 encouraged by the arrival of a Red
     Cross parcel sent from America –
     Charles Rollings, *Prisoner of War, Voices
     from Captivity during the Second World
     War*, London, 2007, p.239.

272 spelling bee – Fred Henson, War log,
     Red Cross Archives.

272 Douglas Bader – Charles Rollings,
     *Prisoner of War, Voices from Captivity
     during the Second World War*, London,
     2007, p.110.

272 Six different faculties – P.G. Cambray
     and G.G.B. Briggs, *Red Cross & St John,
     the official record of the humanitarian
     services of the War Organisation of the
     British Red Cross Society and Order of St
     John of Jerusalem 1939–1947*, London,
     1949, p.215.

272 'a method of escape from the
     immediate circumstances of prison
     life' – Robert Holland, *Adversis Major, A
     short history of the Educational Books
     Scheme of the Prisoners of War
     Department of the British Red Cross
     Society and Order of St John of Jerusalem*,
     London, 1949, p.16.

272 'Nostalgia is the Gulf Stream –

Terence Prittie, *Mainly Middlesex*, London, 1947, p.73.

272 'In the evening light Lord's – Terence Prittie, *Mainly Middlesex*, London, 1947, p16.

273 'I came in the end – W.H. Murray, *The Evidence of Things Not Seen, A Mountaineer's Tale*, London, 2002, p.88.

273 'I no longer – W.H. Murray, *The Evidence of Things Not Seen, A Mountaineer's Tale*, London, 2002, p.98.

274 Tim's Old Funnies – A.N.L. Munby, *The Alabaster Hand and Other Ghost Stories*, Chester, 1995, p.xvi.

274 The Alabaster Hand – *The Alabaster Hand and Other Ghost Stories*, Chester, 1995.

274 'Most other ranks' – Montgomery Belgion, *Reading for Profit*, London, 1951.

274 Some POWs made their own candles – Robert Holland, *Adversis Major, A short history of the Educational Books Scheme of the Prisoners of War Department of the British Red Cross Society and Order of St John of Jerusalem*, London, 1949, p.68.

274 'accidie' – 'Books in prison I. Reflections of a POW chaplain,' by The Rev. David H.C. Read, B.D., *Chambers' Journal*, October 1947, p. 593.

275 'its power to provide' – Robert Holland, *Adversis Major, A short history of the Educational Books Scheme of the Prisoners of War Department of the British Red Cross Society and Order of St John of Jerusalem*, London, 1949, preface.

276 The Educational Book Section – P.G. Cambray and G.G.B. Briggs, *Red Cross & St John, the official record of the humanitarian services of the War Organisation of the British Red Cross Society and Order of St John of Jerusalem 1939–1947*, London, 1949, p.224.

277 The King and Queen – Hilary St George Saunders, *The Red Cross and the White: A short history of the joint war organization of the British Red cross Society and the Order of St John of Jerusalem during the war 1939–1945*, London, 1949, p.204.

277 By the end of May 1942 she had received – Hilary St George Saunders, *The Red Cross and the White: A short history of the joint war organization of the British Red cross Society and the Order of St John of Jerusalem during the war 1939–1945*, London, 1949, p.212.

277 By the end of the war the Educational Book Section had dispatched 263,000 volumes – *Institute Examinations Behind Barbed Wire 1939–1945* by John Freear (unpublished c.1979).

277 Pointed to career ambitions after the war – Robert Holland, *Adversis Major, A short history of the Educational Books Scheme of the Prisoners of War Department of the British Red Cross Society and Order of St John of Jerusalem*, London, 1949, p.50.

277 Oflag V-A – Robert Holland, *Adversis Major, A short history of the Educational Books Scheme of the Prisoners of War Department of the British Red Cross Society and Order of St John of Jerusalem*, London, 1949, p.116.

278 C.S. Lewis said he looked forward – quoted in *Christian News Letter* (4 February 1942).

278 bulky works on criticism – Robert Holland, *Adversis Major, A short history of the Educational Books Scheme of the Prisoners of War Department of the British Red Cross Society and Order of St John of Jerusalem*, London, 1949, p.66.

278 Twenty-one POWs sat it – P.G. Cambray and G.G.B. Briggs, *Red Cross & St John, the official record of the humanitarian services of the War Organisation of the British Red Cross Society and Order of St John of Jerusalem 1939–1947*, London, 1949, p.220.

278 Eventually the British Red Cross approved – Robert Holland, *Adversis Major, A short history of the Educational Books Scheme of the Prisoners of War Department of the British Red Cross Society and Order of St John of Jerusalem*, London, 1949, p.61.

279 sent rulers, mathematical instruments, – Booklet produced by New Bodleian Educational Books Section, *Results of POW Exams, 1st July – 31 December 1943*.

279 *Electra* – Robert Holland, *Adversis*

Major, *A short history of the Educational Books Scheme of the Prisoners of War Department of the British Red Cross Society and Order of St John of Jerusalem*, London, 1949, p.101.

279 Clow Ford – Robert Holland, *Adversis Major, A short history of the Educational Books Scheme of the Prisoners of War Department of the British Red Cross Society and Order of St John of Jerusalem*, London, 1949, pp.56–58.

280 Many merchant seamen – Robert Holland, *Adversis Major, A short history of the Educational Books Scheme of the Prisoners of War Department of the British Red Cross Society and Order of St John of Jerusalem*, London, 1949, p.78.

281 temperatures were included in supervisors' reports – Robert Holland, *Adversis Major, A short history of the Educational Books Scheme of the Prisoners of War Department of the British Red Cross Society and Order of St John of Jerusalem*, London, 1949, p.97.

281 interrupting an accountancy – *Institute Examinations Behind Barbed Wire 1939–1945* by John Freear (unpublished c.1979).

281 'normal air raid' – *Institute Examinations Behind Barbed Wire 1939–1945* by John Freear (unpublished c.1979).

281 The Educational Section sent exam papers to just under 17,000 candidates and recorded a pass rate of 78.5 per cent. – Robert Holland, *Adversis Major, A short history of the Educational Books Scheme of the Prisoners of War Department of the British Red Cross Society and Order of St John of Jerusalem*, London, 1949, p.129.

281 Nearly 11,000 exams – P.G. Cambray and G.G.B. Briggs, *Red Cross & St John, the official record of the humanitarian services of the War Organisation of the British Red Cross Society and Order of St John of Jerusalem 1939–1947*, London, 1949, p.221.

281 for further details of Gee see EDUC 19/119, Cambridge University Archives.

282 'We have several prisoners of war writing thesis – October 27, 1943, EDUC 19/119, Cambridge University Archives.

282 Captain P.N. Bartlett – EDUC 19/119, Cambridge University Archives.

282 J.O.N. Vickers – obituary, *The Guardian*, 23 June 2008.

283 'as it will, obviously, save a lot of time – EDUC 19/119, Cambridge University Archives. Written on 14.5.43.

284 Harvey answered some of his concerns – He also suggested he might ask the University of London School of Slavonic and European Studies (at present evacuated to Regent's Park College, Pusey Street, Oxford) if they need any more staff.

284 After the exam Vickers wrote to Harvey – on 11 November 1943, received 8 January 1944.

285 'The criticisms of inadequacy of reading – 23 April 1944.

285 'it would save a valuable year in peacetime – 29. September 1944.

286 Dennistoun-Sword – *The Times*, 22 June 1944; The Gordon Highlanders Museum; *Life of a Regiment*; *Regimental Journal*, September/October 1977, *Burkes' Peerage*. My thanks to Lincoln's Inn.

286 Tony Barber – obituary, *The Independent*, 19 December 2005.

286 'no women, no drinks and no distractions of any kind.'– *Daily Telegraph*, 19 December 2005.

287 Fred Mulley – *The Independent*, 16 March 1995.

287 Worcestershire Regiment (http://www.worcestershireregiment.com/wr.php?main=inc/pow_F_W_Mulley)

287 Lord Thomas of Gwydir – Daily*Telegraph*, February, 2008.

288 qualified as a chartered accountant whilst at Colditz – S.P. Mackenzie, *The Colditz Myth*, Oxford, 2006, p.80.

288 by the end of the year relatives and close friends could submit their letters – P.G. Cambray and G.G.B. Briggs, *Red Cross & St John, the official record of the humanitarian services of the War Organisation of the British Red Cross*

Society and Order of St John of Jerusalem 1939–1947, London, 1949, p.163.

288 They sent items such as a Braille watch – P.G. Cambray and G.G.B. Briggs, *Red Cross & St John, the official record of the humanitarian services of the War Organisation of the British Red Cross Society and Order of St John of Jerusalem 1939–1947*, London, 1949, p.162.

289 'The real difficulty in the rehearsing – Lord Normanby, Archives of Hamilton Health Sciences and the Faculty of Health Sciences, McMaster University. Dr Charles Roland Oral History Collection, 1994.44. HCM 16–86.

289 'Then we really settled down – Lord Normanby. Archives of Hamilton Health Sciences and the Faculty of Health Sciences, McMaster University. Dr Charles Roland Oral History Collection, 1994.44. HCM 16–86.

289 a masseur received – P.G. Cambray and G.G.B. Briggs, *Red Cross & St John, the official record of the humanitarian services of the War Organisation of the British Red Cross Society and Order of St John of Jerusalem 1939–1947*, London, 1949, p.163.

290 'Please accept our hearty congratulations – February 28 1944.

290 Began well & was – Letter 4 May 1944, H.B. Everard to Belgion.

290 let me acknowledge the courtesy – Churchill Archives, January 1944.

Chapter 30: Music and Theatre

291 The camp had five bands – S.P. Mackenzie, *The Colditz Myth*, Oxford, 2006, p.209.

291 only ten sets of bagpipes – RAF Museum, Department of Research & Information Services, B18080, Sq Leader Philip Jacobs.

291 By the end of 1941 – P.G. Cambray and G.G.B. Briggs, *Red Cross & St John, the official record of the humanitarian services of the War Organisation of the British Red Cross Society and Order of St John of Jerusalem 1939–1947*, London, 1949, p.205.

292 kettle drums – *The R.C.M. Magazine*, vol. 41.(Royal College of Music)

magazine, Summer term, 1945, 'Music in Prisoners of War Camps' by Emily Daymond.

292 the Red Cross had provided 100 camps – P.G. Cambray and G.G.B. Briggs, *Red Cross & St John, the official record of the humanitarian services of the War Organisation of the British Red Cross Society and Order of St John of Jerusalem 1939–1947*, London, 1949, 206.

292 16,000 musical instruments – *The R.C.M. Magazine*, vol. 41. (Royal College of Music) magazine, Summer term, 1945, 'Music in Prisoners of War Camps' by Emily Daymond.

292 'For me being a prisoner of war for two years – Cy Grant, *A Member of the RAF of Indeterminate Race, WW2 experiences of a former RAF Navigator & POW*, West Sussex, 2006, p.60.

292 at its peak, 10,000 British POWs – Adrian Gilbert, *POW, Allied Prisoners in Europe, 1939–1945*, London, 2007, p.83.

293 One POW remembered how 14,000 – British Red Cross Archive, Stalag VIIIB – Lamsdorf – And the Red Cross (Ref. G61, DOM).

293 'found a talent emerging that I hadn't really felt when I was at RADA'– Susan Elliott with Barry Turner, *Denholm Elliott, Quest for Love*, London, 1994, p.29.

293 'Denny was totally engrossed – Susan Elliott with Barry Turner, *Denholm Elliott, Quest for Love*, London, 1994, p.30.

293 'they were so different from the rest of us hunger-hardened, predatory PoWs that – Susan Elliott with Barry Turner, *Denholm Elliott, Quest for Love*, London, 1994, p.32.

293 Peter Butterworth and Talbot Rothwell – Webber, Richard. *50 Years of Carry On*, Century, 2008, London, p.77 and p.91.

294 'I pulled funny faces – Dunn interview with the author.

294 to apply Vaseline to wounds – Clive Dunn, *Permission to Speak, An Autobiography*, London, 1986, p122.

294 a wet towel – Clive Dunn, *Permission to Speak, An Autobiography*, London, 1986, p.122 and Eric Fearnside, *The Joy of*

Freedom, 1996, p.43.

294 exotic complaints – Eric Fearnside, The Joy of Freedom, 1996, p.43.

295 did not damage his hands – Eric Fearnside, The Joy of Freedom, 1996, p.47.

295 'mixed grills' – The R.C.M. Magazine, vol.41,(Royal College of Music) magazine, Summer term, 1945, 'Music in Prisoners of War Camps' by Emily Daymond.

295 'Nebuchadnezzar's Band' – The R.C.M. Magazine, vol.41,(Royal College of Music) magazine, Summer term, 1945, 'Music in Prisoners of War Camps' by Emily Daymond.

296 At Chieti he scored – The Galpin Society Journal, vol. 52, (Apr. 1999), pp.11–26).

296 performed in black tie at a POW nightclub – http://thebrunswickclub.org.uk/arthu rroyall.htm.

296 Herb Perry – http://living.scotsman.com/features/-Leader-of-the-band.4008754.jp.

296 The clothes went straight to the escape committee – http://living.scotsman.com/features/-Leader-of-the-band.4008754.jp.

296 Rolled up map – http://living.scotsman.com/features/-Leader-of-the-band.4008754.jp. Published Date: 23 April 2008.

296 Pat Reid hid his small saw – P.R. Reid, The Colditz Story, London, 1952, p.185.

296 Douglas Bader used a baton to conduct – Adrian Gilbert, Allied Prisoners in Europe, 1939–1945, London, 2007, p.252.

296 a male voice choir – Paul Brickhill, The Great Escape, London, 2004, p.49.

297 'Harry' was hidden under the theatre – Paul Brickhill, Great Escape, London, 2004, p.138.

297 gramophone records – S.P. Mackenzie, The Colditz Myth, Oxford, 2006, p.221.

297 and ENSA made monthly recordings that the YMCA delivered – P.G. Cambray and G.G.B. Briggs, Red Cross & St John, the official record of the humanitarian services of the War

Organisation of the British Red Cross Society and Order of St John of Jerusalem 1939–1947, London, 1949, p.207.

297 'massively built palace of Mozart's Salzburg archbishop' – Making Music magazine, May 1947, 'Music in POW Camps in Germany', Part 1.

297 But professional actors had standards – Adrian Gilbert, Allied Prisoners in Europe, 1939–1945, London, 2007, p.173.

298 By February 1941 Wood had given up his own studies – Letter home, 11 Feb 41, IWM, Papers of Lieutenant R Wood (IWM 90/33/1A).

298 The Gala all-Schubert – letter from Wood to Beryl, 18 February 1941, IWM, Papers of Lieutenant R.Wood (IWM 90/33/1A).

298 wanted to pay off the 2,000 marks – 'Music in POW Camps in Germany – One' by Richard Wood in Making Music, The official journal of the Rural Music Schools Association, May 1947. (Wood remembers that they charged five and three marks a seat).

298 'I threw myself seriously – Sandy Hernu, Q: The biography of Desmond Llewelyn, Seaford, 1999, p.58.

298 entire cast and back-stage – Desmond Llewelyn obituary, The Guardian, 20 December 1999.

298 'a poor play, well-acted'. – Letters, 24.1.43, IWM, Papers of Lieutenant R. Wood (IWM 90/33/1A).

298 See Goodliffe website. http://www.mgoodliffe.co.uk/.

298 'The play splutters to an end like a badly made firework, with bursts of sharp emotion – Philip Hoare, Noel Coward, London, 1995, p.219.

298 For extra detail about productions at Eichstatt see: Bobby Loder Collection, Archive Centre, King's College, Cambridge and POWs in Pantomime at: http://www.kings.cam.ac.uk/archive-centre/archive-month/december-2009.html.

299 God save the king! – Hilary St George Saunders, The Red Cross and the White, London, 1949, p.57.

299 called Ballet Nonsense – P.R. Reid, The

Colditz Story, London, 1952, p.72.

300 Jock Hamilton-Baillie –
http://www.telegraph.co.uk/news/ob
ituaries/1430972/Brigadier-Jock-
Hamilton-Baillie.html

300 a special kind of head-dress – Adrian
Gilbert, *Allied Prisoners in Europe,
1939–1945*, London, 2007, p.173.

301 its seventy-six costumes – *The R.C.M.
Magazine*, Vol. 41,(Royal College of
Music) magazine, Summer term, 1945,
'Music in Prisoners of War Camps' by
Emily Daymond.

301 See Gilbert and Sullivan in Stalag 383
by Trevor Hills in *Gilbert & Sullivan
News*, Summer 2004. My thanks to
Tony Joseph for drawing this to my
attention.

301 Olivier Messiaen composed the
Quartet for the End of Time while he was
held at a POW camp at Görlitz in
Silesia in the winter of 1940–41. It was
first performed a violinist, cellist and
clarinettist who were also held there.
Oxford Music Online.

302 During the winter of 1942–43 records
of Britten's *Michelangelo Sonnets* –
Letter: 21/4/74 from Wood to Grigg,
IWM Papers of Lieutenant R. Wood
(IWM 90/33/1A) and programme notes
to First performance of Ballad in
England at Wigmore Hall, March 7,
1951.

302 'That brings us to the present – *Letters
from a Life: The Selected Letters and
Diaries of Benjamin Britten,
1913–1976*,Volume two, 1939–45, p.1173.

303 Eichstätt Festival – 'Music in POW
Camps in Germany' in *Making Music*,
Part 2, October 1947.

PART IV THE FAR EAST

Chapter 31: 'Upcountry': The
Thailand–Burma Railway

307 The Bridge on the River Kwai – see
'The Bridge on the River Kwai: Novel,
Film and Reality', pp.5–28 in Julie
Summers, *The Colonel of Tamarkan,
Philip Toosey & The Bridge on the River
Kwai*, London, 2006. The film departs

from reality in countless ways: the
men at Tamarkan did not whistle
'Colonel Bogey' and there were no
Americans at this point on the
railway.

308 'Alec Guinness saying to the Japs –
Monty Parkin, *Surviving by Magic*, Kent,
2009, p.38.

308 270,000 native labourers – *The Oxford
Companion to World War II*.

308 Figures vary but one authority, Louis
Allen, has estimated that 12,000 Allied
prisoners and 90,000 native labourers
perished. – *The Oxford Companion to
World War II*.

308 A base camp – Sibylla Jane Flower,
'Captors and captives on the
Burma–Thailand Railway' in *Prisoners
of War and their Captors in World War II*
edited by Bob Moore and Kent
Fedorowich, Oxford, 1996, p.231.

310 Tommy Atkins – my thanks to John
Atkins for allowing me to read the
original manuscript of his father's
diary. A copy is held at the IWM,
Private Papers of A F Atkins, 4599
81/32/1.

310 Sawah – irrigated rice-field.

313 'The jungle is full'/ 'pianola roller'/
'good, hard stopper' – Jack Chalker
interview with the author.

Chapter 32: Art and Medicine on the
Railway

315 'the blessing' – interview with the
author.

315 'I think art' – interview with the
author.

316 'I was just incredibly lucky.' –
interview with the author.

316 'I was dragged off' – interview with
the author.

317 'It was better there – interview with
the author.

318 'It was not an encouraging – Jack
Chalker, *Burma Railway, Images of War*,
Frome, 2007, p.70.

318 'sweet-foul' – Jack Chalker, *Burma
Railway, Images of War*, Frome, 2007,
p.71.

318 'Just before sundown – Jack Chalker,
Burma Railway, Images of War, Frome,

2007, p.74.

319 ' Sale [?] – Unable to decipher the handwriting.

321 M&B 693 was a form of sulfanilamide developed by the drug firm, May and Baker, to treat a variety of infections.

322 Captain Jacob Markowitz – 'I was a knife, fork, and spoon Surgeon' – by Dr J. Markowitz, *Magazine Digest*, June 1946.

322 as Associate Professor of Physiology at the University of Toronto where he – Brian MacArthur, *Surviving the Sword, Prisoners of the Japanese 1942–45*, London, p.226.

322 from one warm-blooded animal – *National Post* http://network.nationalpost.com/np/ blogs/fullcomment/archive/2008/11/1 0/bernie-m-farber-jungle-surgeon-canadian-hero.aspx

322 'Marko had removed' – interview with the author.

323 'It helped one's survival' – interview with the author.

323 'They didn't want to admit' – interview with the author.

324 artificial limbs –http://www.sciencemuseum.org.uk/ broughttolife/objects/display.aspx?id= 5792 - accessed 21 May 2010.

324 One made in Germany in 1940 –http://www.sciencemuseum.org.uk/ broughttolife/objects/display.aspx?id= 4901 - accessed 21 May 2010.

324 'sufficient to give' – interview with the author.

325 'I was sure' – interview with the author.

326 'Something terribly funny' – interview with the author.

327 'attap stare' – Alistair Urquhart, *The Forgotten Highlander, My Incredible Story of Survival During the War in the Far East*, London, 2010, p.157.

327 'Survive this day.' – Alistair Urquhart, *The Forgotten Highlander, My Incredible Story of Survival During the War in the Far East*, London, 2010, p.157.

327 'camp giggle' – J.D.F. Jones, *Storyteller, The Many Lives of Laurens van der Post*, London, John Murray, 2001, p.47.

327 the POWs' favour as two privates in

the Argyll and Sutherland – Ewart Escritt, *Beyond the Three Pagodas Pass*, Oxford, 1988, p.44.

328 'great fireworks display' – interview with the author.

328 'He went home' – interview with the author.

Chapter 33: Archaeologist on the 'Death Railway'

329 'On many occasions ' – Ronald Searle, *To the Kwai – and Back, War Drawings 1939–1945*, London, 1986, p.113.

330 he wrote later in his memoir – H.R. van Heekeren, *De Onderste Steen Boven, Belevenissen van een Globetrotter*, Van Gorcum, Prakke & Prakke, Assen, 1969.

330 'I threw myself with enthusiasm' – chapter two, H.R. van Heekeren, *De Onderste Steen Boven, Belevenissen van een Globetrotter*, Van Gorcum, Prakke & Prakke, Assen, 1969.

330 'an enthusiastic, competent amateur' – from his CV, Netherlands Institute for Advanced Study in the Humanities and Social Sciences (NIAS).

331 Something in the air – 'Zeven oude stenen' ('Seven old stones') in the magazine *Tong Tong*, May 1967.

331 Bankao – for a modern photograph of the site of his findings see Raoul Kramer, *Lost Track – A Search along the Burma-Thailand Railway 65 Years Later*, Neo Lux, Amsterdam, 2010, pp.84–85.

331 Dr Harold Churchill remembers a Dutchman, 'glad of his opportunities for finding flint arrowheads and other Neolithic tools while working on the railroad near Chungkai,' – Dr Sue Palmer, *Prisoners on the Kwai, Memoirs of Dr Harold Churchill*, Dereham, 2005, p.35. See also: Ewart Escritt, *Beyond the Three Pagodas Pass*, Oxford, 1988, pp.27–28

331 'I took it in my hands – 'Zeven oude stenen' ('Seven old stones') in the magazine *Tong Tong*, May 1967.

331 'I felt immediately – 'Zeven oude stenen' ('Seven old stones') in the magazine *Tong Tong*, May 1967.

332 'Lots of people – 'Zeven oude stenen'

('Seven old stones') in the magazine *Tong Tong*, May 1967.

332 I am indebted to Jay Sivell for her painstaking translation of several documents and for her tenacity in uncovering more information about van Heekeren. I am also very grateful to Netherlands Institute for War Documentation (NIOD), Netherlands Institute for Advanced Study in the Humanities and Social Sciences (NIAS) and to Raoul Kramer.

Chapter 34: Entertainment and Ingenuity on the 'Death Railway'

333 For a detailed assessment of entertainment among POWs see Sears Eldredge, 'Captive Audiences/Captive Performances: Music and Theatre as Strategies for Survival on the Burma-Thai Railway, 1942–1945. http://digitalcommons.macalester.edu /thdabooks/1

335 'I was so pleased – interview with the author.

336 'avoided being trampled' – Ewart Escritt, *Beyond the Three Pagodas Pass*, Oxford, 1988, p.26.

336 'Where they all came from – Johnny Sherwood, *Football, Fame, Fear, 'Pro Player's Story, I Saw the Nagasaki Atom Bomb*, p.105.

337 Gordon McCallum, IWM, Accession Number 114/2009.

338 'It was this useless – Lieutenant J.G.B. Millns, word processed memoir, IWM, 15371 07/54/1, p.6.

339 'The paper factory – Lieutenant J.G.B. Millns, word processed memoir, IWM, 15371 07/54/1, p.9.

339 'We got every hour' – interview with author.

341 guitars from scraps – Jack Chalker, *Burma Railway, Images of War*, Frome, 2007, p.91.

341 Tom Boardman – interview with author.

341 many 'reserving' their seat – Monty Parkin, *Surviving by Magic*, Kent, 2009, p.57.

342 Pearl Fishers – Charles Fisher, *Three Times a Guest, Recollections of Japan and the Japanese, 1942–1969*, London, 1979, p.83.

342 'more than we knew they could' – Leslie Poidevin, *Samurais and Circumcisions*, 1985, p.79.

342 chalk to use as make-up – Oliver, Lindsay. *At the Going Down of the Sun, Hong Kong and South-East Asia 1941–45*, London, 1981, p.86.

342 *Thai Diddle Diddle* – see Doctor Hardie, *The Times*, October 18, 1983; Han Samethini Remembered (http://hansamethini.blogspot.com/20 09/04/10-prison-camp-musician-december-1944.html.), and Charles Fisher, *Three Times a Guest, Recollections of Japan and the Japanese, 1942–1969*, London, 1979, p.82.

342 'the ability – Charles Fisher, *Three Times a Guest, Recollections of Japan and the Japanese, 1942–1969*, London, 1979, p.83.

343 bigger wings, a bamboo drop-curtain . . . – Jack Chalker, *Burma Railway, Images of War*, Frome, 2007, p.110.

343 craniotomy – Jack Chalker, *Burma Railway, Images of War*, Frome, 2007, p.104.

344 silk cami-knickers – Jack Chalker, *Burma Railway, Images of War*, 2007, p.111, and Professor Sears Eldredge, lecture 'Civilian Internee & FEPOW Concert Parties', Researching FEPOW History Group's 2nd International Conference, National Memorial Arboretum (NMA), Staffordshire, 31 May–1 June, 2008.

344 But the trouble – interview with author.

344 'It was astonishing – Charles Fisher, *Three Times a Guest, Recollections of Japan and the Japanese, 1942–1969*, London, 1979, p.81.

345 'Clearly some of our – Charles Fisher, *Three Times a Guest, Recollections of Japan and the Japanese, 1942–1969*, London, 1979, p.81.

345 Stephen Alexander noticed – Stephen Alexander, *Sweet Kwai Run Softly*, Bristol, 1995, p.202.

345 'It was he – Jack Cosford, *Yasumi Ni*,

Reprinted from *The Woodbridge Reporter & Wickham Market Gazette*, p.33.

346 ' – died at sea – the ship transporting him to Japan was torpedoed by an Allied submarine.

346 'It played an enormous part – interview with the author.

346 Babes in the Wood – December 29, 2007, *The Times*.

347 Jim Swanton – David Rayvern Allen, *Jim, The Life of E.W. Swanton*, London, 2004, pp.112–3

348 Weary Dunlop's diary – December 19–25, 1943.

Chapter 35: 'Home' Again: Changi Gaol

350 coming home – Russell Braddon, *The Piddingtons*, London, 1950, p.77.

350 'delivered back' – Ronald Searle, *To the Kwai – and Back, War Drawings 1939–1945*, London, 1986, p.128.

350 'vast unscalable wall' – Ronald Searle, *To the Kwai – and Back, War Drawings 1939–1945*, London, 1986, p.132.

351 'some Italians' – Ronald Searle, *To the Kwai – and Back, War Drawings 1939–1945*, London, 1986, p.137.

351 'the food situation – Ronald Searle, *To the Kwai – and Back, War Drawings 1939–1945*, London, 1986, p.140.

351 'Changi Memory – Ronald Searle, *To the Kwai – and Back, War Drawings 1939–1945*, London, 1986, p.140.

352 'became my university – obituary, *New York Times*, 8 September 1994.

352 Hundred Year War – Ronald Searle, *To the Kwai – and Back, War Drawings 1939–1945*, London, 1986, p.138.

352 *kampong* – Malay village.

353 made the mistake – Ronald Searle, *To the Kwai – and Back, War Drawings 1939–1945*, London, 1986, p.158.

353 It was eerie – Eric Lomax, *The Railway Man*, London, 1996, p.194.

353 Piddington was also friends with the artist and traveller, Leslie Greener and the Australian ski champion Tom Mitchell.

354 'As I look back – Scott Russell, obituary, *The Independent*, 1 September 1999.

354 mind-reading – The *Journal of the*

Society for Psychical Research provided lengthy discussion of their work (Vol. 35, pp. 83–85, 116–19, 187, 244–45, 316–18; Vol. 42, p. 250).

355 'Please reserve – Russell Braddon, *The Piddingtons*, London, 1950, p.128.

Chapter 36: The POW Diaspora

357 'rained like hell' – John Lowe diary, 30 October 1942.

357 'old tub is pitching' – John Lowe diary, 8 November 1942.

357 10,800 of the 50,000 prisoners – Brian MacArthur, *Surviving the Sword, Prisoners of the Japanese 1942–45*, London, 2007, p.325.

357 said to have attacked – Brian MacArthur, *Surviving the Sword, Prisoners of the Japanese 1942–45*, London, 2007, p.331.

358 'all over the place – Johnny Sherwood, *Football, Fame, Fear, 'Pro Player's Story, I Saw the Nagasaki Atom Bomb*, pp.186–7.

358 'the whole sea area – Johnny Sherwood, *Football, Fame, Fear, 'Pro Player's Story, I Saw the Nagasaki Atom Bomb*, p.187.

358 'I thought to myself – Johnny Sherwood, *Football, Fame, Fear, 'Pro Player's Story, I Saw the Nagasaki Atom Bomb*, p.187.

359 'That's what we did' – Johnny Sherwood, *Football, Fame, Fear, 'Pro Player's Story, I Saw the Nagasaki Atom Bomb*, p.196.

363 'I was nervous – John Lowe, unpublished memoir, p.44.

364 'Jimmy Brennan's fleabag – John Lowe diary, Wednesday, 7th March 1945.

364 'We halted near a barrier – John Lowe diary, Saturday, 11th March 1945.

365 slept with their boots on – see R.P.W. Havers, *Reassessing the Japanese Prisoner of War Experience, The Changi POW Camp, Singapore, 1942–45*, RoutledgeCurzon, London, 2003, p.148.

PART V: FREEDOM

Chapter 37: Somewhere Near the End

369 'gloomy, subdued – Eric Newby, Love and War in the Apennines, London, 1996, p.47.

370 'about 4 o'clock' – Allen Graham – interview with R.C.A. Hunter, Archives of Hamilton Health Sciences and the Faculty of Health Sciences, McMaster University. Dr Charles Roland Oral History Collection. 1994.44. HCM 5–81.

373 Large sums of money – P.R. Reid, The Latter Days at Coldtiz, London, 2003, p.159.

373 Colditz power station – P.R. Reid, The Latter Days, pp.158–9.

374 'went beserk' – 21 November 1944.

374 'Yes, Tommy.' – 26 November 1944.

375 'stalag knitted hats' – 27 November 1944.

375 'all such can expect' – 12 January 1945.

376 'Now we enter another year – 1 January 1945.

376 'The most important thing – 21 January 1945.

377 Dresden – The Times, commentary, March 18, 2010.

378 seventeen degrees below zero – John Nichol and Tony Rennell, The Last Escape, The Untold Story of Allied Prisoners of War in Germany 1944–45, London, Penguin, 2003, p.69.

378 jaundice, scurvy, dysentery – John Nichol and Tony Rennell, The Last Escape, The Untold Story of Allied Prisoners of War in Germany 1944–45, London, Penguin, 2003, p.77.

378 Gross Tychow – John Nichol and Tony Rennell, The Last Escape, The Untold Story of Allied Prisoners of War in Germany 1944–45, London, Penguin, 2003, p.105.

378 a line of bloody faeces – John Nichol and Tony Rennell, The Last Escape, The Untold Story of Allied Prisoners of War in Germany 1944–45, London, Penguin, 2003, p.136.

378 100,000 POWs – John Nichol and Tony Rennell, The Last Escape, The Untold Story of Allied Prisoners of War in Germany 1944–45, London, Penguin, 2003, p.155.

378 60,000 prisoners – John Nichol and Tony Rennell, The Last Escape, The Untold Story of Allied Prisoners of War in Germany 1944–45, London, Penguin, 2003, p.156.

378 80,000 – John Nichol and Tony Rennell, The Last Escape, The Untold Story of Allied Prisoners of War in Germany 1944–45, London, Penguin, 2003, p.157.

378 Some even raided their Red Cross and YMCA sports supplies – John Nichol and Tony Rennell, The Last Escape, The Untold Story of Allied Prisoners of War in Germany 1944–45, London, Penguin, 2003, p.167.

378 See http://www.raf.mod.uk/longmarch/gallery/

380 he watched snowflakes – The Times, February 8, 2008.

380 Tony Rolt – see obituaries; – The Independent, Monday, 11 February 2008; The Times, February 8, 2008; The Guardian (sport) Saturday 9 February 2008.

380 'tinkering' – P.R. Reid, Colditz, The Latter Days, London, 1952, p.208.

380 'the two old crows' or 'the wicked uncles' – 12 October 2007, The Telegraph.

384 He had contacted the Red Cross – The Red Cross closed the fund, for which the POWs were hoping to raise money, in June 1945 before the game could be played.

Chapter 38: Victory in the Far East

392 Tonight they told me – interview with author.

392 'BIG BOMB – WAR OVER – ALL GO HOME' – IWM notes, 07/54/1 Lieutenant J.G.B. Millns, p.11.

393 'a lovely little camp' – Johnny Sherwood, Football, Fame, Fear, 'Pro Player's Story, I Saw the Nagasaki Atom Bomb, p.213.

393 'Go on you beauties' – Johnny Sherwood, Football, Fame, Fear, 'Pro Player's Story, I Saw the Nagasaki Atom Bomb, p.228

393 'lots of pretty colours on it' – Johnny Sherwood, *Football, Fame, Fear, 'Pro Player's Story, I Saw the Nagasaki Atom Bomb*, p.219.

394 'in a filthy temper' – Johnny Sherwood, *Football, Fame, Fear, 'Pro Player's Story, I Saw the Nagasaki Atom Bomb*, p.230.

394 'Death Ray bomb' – Johnny Sherwood, *Football, Fame, Fear, 'Pro Player's Story, I Saw the Nagasaki Atom Bomb*, p.230.

394 'They put us in a lorry' – interview with the author.

396 *suiji* – cookhouse.

398 'was this it' – Johnny Sherwood, *Football, Fame, Fear, 'Pro Player's Story, I Saw the Nagasaki Atom Bomb*, p.232.

398 'we were Free-Free-Free' – Johnny Sherwood, *Football, Fame, Fear, 'Pro Player's Story, I Saw the Nagasaki Atom Bomb*, p.233.

398 'This was the first time' – Johnny Sherwood, *Football, Fame, Fear, 'Pro Player's Story, I Saw the Nagasaki Atom Bomb*, p.237.

399 'I had the pleasure – interview with the author.

Chapter 39: Homecoming

401 'I thought here I am – Sir Terry Frost, interviewed by Tamsyn Woollcombe, 1994, Artists' Lives, British Library Sound Archive reference: C466/22. Tape 4 (F4315), Side A.

403 J.O.N. Vickers – *The Guardian*, Monday 23 June 2008; obituary, *The Observer*, 12 December 2010, p.15.

404 August 1945 Luce wrote to Fergus at No. 1 Camp, Thailand, Siam.

405 'I'm getting married – written 9 October 1945.

405 'Darling, I shall never ask – written 9 October 1945.

405 'By the way – written 9 October 1945.

405 'glamorising – written 4 October 1945.

405 'several offers' – written 4 October 1945.

405 'God how wonderful – written 4 October 1945.

405 'I'm not so hot – written 4 October 1945.

405 'I'll let you feel it – written 31 October 1945.

405 'I didn't like it much!' – 3 November 1945.

405 'Darling for heaven's sake enjoy – written 11 November 1945.

405 'I keep wondering – 6 November 1945.

405 'I'm still trying – 6 November 1945.

406 'They had this lovely orchestra – interview with the author.

PART VI: EX-POWS

Chapter 40: Aftermath

409 John Buxton –'John Buxton, author of what is arguably the best single species study ever written: *The Redstart – The Guardian*, Saturday 17 October 2009. Andrew Motion described it as 'a masterpiece' – *Daily Telegraph*, 09 Feb 2009. Buxton also wrote poetry while he was a POW; *Westward* was later published by Faber.

410 Operation Osprey – BBC4, *Birds Britannia, Waterbirds*, broadcast November 14, 2010.

410 For van Heekeren's career see: *Het Vaderland*, 26 October 1961, *Algemeen Handelsblad*, 25 January 1968, *Haarlems Dagblad* (obituary), 16 September 1974, 'The Death of Dr. H. R. van Heekeren', *Indonesia and the Malay World*, 2:5, 6–7, 1977.

411 Van Heekeren wrote about his findings after the war in: *The Illustrated London News*, April 5, 1947; *Journal of the Siam Society*, 49 (2), 1961 ('A Preliminary Note on the Excavation of the Sai-Yok Rock-Shelter'); The Prehistoric Society, No.2, 1948, ('Prehistoric Discoveries in Siam, 1943–44').

411 'Will you look at this?' – The Papers of (Harold) Montgomery Belgion, GBR/0014/BLGN, Churchill Archives Centre.

411 Belgion's advance – This was at a time when a man working in manufacturing would earn around 111 shillings and 5 pence or £5.11s 5d. a week (Source: *Fighting with Figures*).

412 Terence Prittie obituary – *The Times*, Wednesday May 29, 1985.

413 Review of *The Evidence of Things Not Seen* in *The Observer*, Sunday 23 June 2002.

414 'the best education I could have had before becoming a professional painter' David Lewis, *Terry Frost, A Personal Narrative*, Scolar Press, 1994, Aldershot, p.32.

414 'sissy' – David Lewis, *Terry Frost, A Personal Narrative*, Scolar Press, 1994, Aldershot, p.32.

415 'rather old' – Adrian Heath, interviewed by Norbert Lynton, 1992, Artists' Lives, British Library Sound Archive reference: C466/11. Tape One Side B, F2905.

415 'The seething mass' – interview with the author.

415 'We associated with people' – interview with the author.

416 According to his first biographer, Russell Davies, – Valerie Grove, *So Much to Tell*, London, 2010, p.125.

416 'baby stuff' – Valerie Grove, *So Much to Tell*, London, 2010, p.61.

417 'It didn't worry me – quoted in Valerie Grove, *So Much to Tell*, London, 2010, p.270.

417 George Sprod – see obituary, *The Independent*, April 16, 2003.

417 Stanley Gimson – see obituary, *The Times*, October 17, 2003.

419 *Back Home – The Times*, July 17, 1945.

419 It was there that I had – *Insight on the News*, July 31, 2000 by Woody West.

419 'working for Hitler . . . mountain side digging and god know's what else' – *Don't Panic! The Dad's Army Story* (repeated on 2 August 2008).

419 'It was like a wonderful happy revenge for that.' – *Don't Panic! The Dad's Army Story* (repeated on 2 August 2008).

419 My few years' experience – Dunn, Clive. *Permission to Speak, An Autobiography*, London, 1986, p.238.

420 The only time he was called a 'nigger' – Cy Grant, *A Member of the RAF of Indeterminate Race, WW2 experiences of a former RAF Navigator & POW*, West Sussex, 2006, p.64.

420 'Being a prisoner of war taught me a lot about myself – Cy Grant, *A Member of the RAF of Indeterminate Race, WW2 experiences of a former RAF Navigator & POW*, West Sussex, 2006, p.104.

420 Cy Grant obituary – 17 February 2010, *The Guardian*.

420 'forceful, confident, knew what he wanted to do, knew how he thought he ought to do it – Russell Braddon, *The Piddingtons*, London, 1950, p.152.

421 J.O.N. Vickers – obituary. *The Guardian*, 23 June 2008; *The Observer*, 12 December 2010, p.15.

422 John Phillips – obituary, *Daily Telegraph*, 5 June 1998.

Bibliography

Books

Absalom, Roger, *A Strange alliance: aspects of escape and survival in Italy, 1943–4*, Firenze: Olschki, 1991

Adams, Guy, Backwater, Oflag IX A/H, Lower Camp, Frederick Muller, London, 1944

Alexander, Stephen, *Sweet Kwai Run Softly*, Merriotts Press, Bristol, 1995

Allen, David and Rayvern, Jim, *The Life of E.W. Swanton*, Aurum, London, 2004

Archer, Bernice, *The internment of Western civilians under the Japanese 1941–1945: a patchwork of internment*, RoutledgeCurzon, London, 2004

Audus, Leslie, *Spice Island Slaves: A History of Japanese Prisoner-of-War Camps in Eastern Indonesia, May 1943–August 1945*, Alma, Richmond, 1996

Ballard, J. G., *Miracles of Life, Shanghai to Shepperton, An Autobiography*, Fourth Estate, London, 2008

Banham, Tony, *Not the Slightest Chance, The Defence of Hong Kong, 1941*, Hong Kong University Press, 2003

Baynes, L.L., *The Other Side of Tenko*, W.H. Allen, London, 1985

Beattie, Rod, *The Death Railway, A Brief History*, Image Makers Company, Bangkok, 2005

Belgion, Montgomery, *Reading for Profit*, London, Cresset Press, 1951

Bell, Frank, *Undercover University*, Elisabeth Bell, Cambridge, 1990

Bennett, Alan, *Forty Years On and Other Plays*, Faber, London, 1985

Bentinck, Michael, *My Dad, My Hero*, Print–Out, Histon, 1994

Bentinck, Michael, *A Will to Live: Three True Stories*, Michael Bentinck, Cambridge, 1996

Billany, Dan, *The Cage*, in collaboration with David Dowie, Longmans, Green & Co, London, 1949

Bird, Arthur H., *Farewell Milag*, self-published, 1995

Boulle, Pierre, *The Bridge on the River Kwai*, Secker & Warburg, London, 1954

Bowden, Tim, *Changi Photographer, George Aspinall's Record of Captivity*, ABC Enterprises and William Collins, for Australian Broadcasting Corporation, 1984

Braddon, Russell, *The Naked Island*, Michael Joseph, London, 1981

Braddon, Russell, *The Piddingtons*, Werner Laurie, London, 1950

Brazier, Roy, *Spurs at War 1939–46*, Romary, Haverhill, 1999

Brickhill, Paul, *The Great Escape*, Cassell Military Paperbacks edition, 2004

British Red Cross Society & Order of St John of Jerusalem, *Useful Articles from Empty Tins*, Barclay & Fry, (The Metal Box Company), London

Broad, Richard and Fleming, Suzie, (editors), *Nella Last's War, The Second World War Diaries of Housewife, 49*, Profile Books, London, 2006

Brown, Malcolm, *Spitfire Summer, When Britain Stood Alone*, Carlton, London, 2000

Brownlow, Kevin, *David Lean, A Biography*, Faber, London, 1997

Buxton, John, *The Redstart*, Collins, London, 1950

Cambray, P.G. and Briggs, G.G.B., *Red Cross & St John, the official record of the humanitarian services of the War Organisation of the British Red Cross Society and Order of St John of Jerusalem 1939–1947*, Sumfield and Day, London, 1949

Carpenter, Humphrey, *Benjamin Britten, A Biography*, Faber, London, 1992

Carver, Tom, *Where the hell have you been?* Short Books, London, 2009

Chainey, Graham, *A Literary History of Cambridge*, Cambridge University Press, 1995

Chalker, Jack Bridger, *Burma Railway, Images of War*, Mercer Books, Frome, 2007

Chambers II, John Whiteclay (ed.), *The Oxford Companion to American Military History*, Oxford University Press, Oxford, 1999

Chancellor, Henry, *Colditz, The Definitive History*, Hodder & Stoughton, London, 2001

Clemetson, Captain J.G., *Don't ever again say, "It can't be done", The Story of Changi Industries Inc*, Changi University Press Publication, Singapore, 2005

Cocker, Mark, *Crow Country, a Meditation on Birds, Landscape and Nature*, Jonathan Cape, London, 2007

Concannon, Dale, *Spitfire on the Fairway: And Other Unexpected Hazards of Golf in Wartime*, Aurum, London, 2003

Cosford, Jack, *Yasumi ni*, reprinted from The Woodbridge Reporter & Wickham Market Gazette, 1959

Davis, Russell, *Ronald Searle, a biography*, Chris Beetles, London, 2003

Dear, C.B. and Foot, M.R.D. (editors), *The Oxford Companion to World War II*, Oxford University Press, 2001

Dennis, Peter, Grey Jeffrey, Morris, Ewan, Prior, Robin and Bou, Jean, *The Oxford Companion to Australian Military History*, Oxford University Press, 2009

Doyle, Peter, *Prisoner of War in Germany*, Oxford, Shire Library, 2008

Dunlop, E.E., *The War Diaries of Weary Dunlop*, Harmondsworth, Viking, 1989

Dunn, Clive, *Permission to Speak, An Autobiography*, Century, London, 1986

Elliott, Brent, *The Royal Horticultural Society: a History 1804–2004*, Chichester, Phillimore, 2004

Elliott, Susan, with Barry Turner, *Denholm Elliott, Quest for Love*, Headline, 1994

Erskine, David, *The Scots Guards, 1919–1955*, William Clowes, London, 1956

Escritt, Ewart, *Beyond the Three Pagodas Pass*, Oxford, 1988

Farrow, Jack, *Darkness before Dawn*, Stamford House Publishing, Peterborough

Fearnside, Eric, *The joy of freedom / a graphic account of life in a prisoner of war camp during the Second World War, including some unique photographs and a selection of humorous short stories*, The Real Time Factory, 1996

Fisher, Charles, *Three times a guest, Recollections of Japan and the Japanese, 1942–1969*, Cassell, London, 1979

Fletcher-Cooke, John, *The Emperor's Guest, 1942–45*, Leo Cooper, London, 1971

Flynn, Keith, *Behind the Wire*, Gareth P. Jenkins, Wales, 1998

Fussell, Paul, *Wartime: understanding and behavior in the Second World War*, Oxford University Press, 1989

Gilbert, Adrian, *POW, Allied Prisoners in Europe, 1939–1945*, John Murray, London, 2007

Gillies, Midge, *Waiting for Hitler, Voices from Britain on the Brink of Invasion*, Hodder & Stoughton, London, 2006

Grant, Cy, *A Member of the RAF of Indeterminate Race, WW2 experiences of a former RAF Navigator & POW*, Woodfield Publishing, West Sussex, 2006

Grey de, Slim, *Changi, The Funny Side*, Peter Hall (Tobago Pty Ltd), c.1991

Griffin, David, *Changi Days, The Prisoner as Poet*, Kangaroo Press, Australia, 2002

Griffin, David, *The Happiness Box*, Media Masters, Singapore, 2002

Grove, Valerie, *So Much to Tell*, Viking, London, 2010

Haig, Earl, *My Father's Son, The Memoirs of Major the Earl Haig*, London, Leo Cooper, 2000

Hammond, Wally, *The Changi Murals*, Changi University Series, Singapore, 2002

Havers, R.P.W., *Reassessing the Japanese Prisoner of War Experience, The Changi POW Camp, Singapore, 1942–5*, RoutledgeCurzon, London, 2003

Hayes, Dean, *Bolton Wanderers, an A–Z*, Palatine, Preston, 1994

Hayes, Dean, *Bolton Wanderers*, Sutton, Stroud, 1999

Hayward, J.B., *Prisoners of war, British Army, 1939–1945*, in association with the Imperial War Museum, Department of Printed Books, Polstead, 1990

Hayward, J.B., *Prisoners of war, naval and air forces of Great Britain and the Empire, 1939–1945*, in association with the Imperial War Museum, Department of Printed Books, Polstead, 1990

Hayward, J.B., *Prisoners of war, armies and other land forces of the British Empire, 1939–1945*, in association with the Imperial War Museum, Department of Printed Books, Polstead, 1990

Heekeren, H.R. Van, *De Onderste Steen Boven, Belevenissen van een Globetrotter*, Van Gorcum, Prakke & Prakke, Assen, 1969

Hernu, Sandy, Q: *The biography of Desmond Llewelyn*, S.B. Publications, Seaford, 1999

Hillenbrand, Laur, *Unbroken, A World War II Story of Survival, Resilience, and Redemption*, Random House, New York, 2010

Hoare, Philip, *Noël Coward: A Biography*, Sinclair-Stevenson, London, 1995

Holland, Robert. W., *Adversis Major, A short history of the Educational Books Scheme of the Prisoners of War Department of the British Red Cross Society and Order of St John of Jerusalem*, Staples Press in conjunction with the British Red Cross, London, 1949

Holmes, Richard, *The Oxford Companion to Military History*, Oxford University Press, 2004

Howard, Michael S., *Jonathan Cape, Publisher*, Cape, London, 1971

Howlett, Peter, *Fighting with Figures, A Statistical Digest of the Second World War* prepared by the Central Statistical Office, HMSO, London, 1995

Hutching, Megan (ed.), *Inside Stories, New Zealand Prisoners of War Remember*, HarperCollins in association with the History Group, Ministry for Culture and Heritage, Auckland, 2002

Hutt, Denis E., *The Cambridgeshire Regiment 1920–61*, the author, Cambridge, 1990

International Committee of the Red Cross, *Report of the International Committee of the Red Cross on its activities during the Second World War (September 1, 1939–June 30, 1947), Volume One – General Activities*, Geneva, May, 1948

Jones, J.D.F., *Storyteller, The Many Lives of Laurens van der Post*, London, John Murray, 2001

Kiple, F. and Kriemhild Coneè Ornelas (ed.), *The Cambridge World History of Food*, Cambridge University Press, Cambridge, 2000

Kirby, S. Woodburn, *The War against Japan*, H.M.S.O., London, 1957–69

Kramer, Raoul, *Lost Track – A Search along the Burma–Thailand Railway 65 Years Later*, Neo Lux, Amsterdam, 2010

Kydd, Sam, *For you the war is over*, Bachman & Turner, London, 1973

Lessing, Doris, *Under My Skin, Volume One of My Autobiography, to 1949*, Flamingo, London, 1995

Lewis, David, *Terry Frost, A Personal Narrative*, Scolar Press, Aldershot, 1994

Lindsay, Oliver, *At the Going Down of the Sun, Hong Kong and South-East Asia 1941–45*, Hamish Hamilton, London, 1981

Lomax, Eric, *The Railway Man*, Vintage, London, 1996

MacArthur, Brian, *Surviving the Sword, Prisoners of the Japanese 1942–45*, Abacus, London, 2007

Mackenzie, S.P., *The Colditz Myth*, Oxford University Press, 2006

Mason, W. Wynne, *Prisoners of War*, War History Branch, Dept of Internal Affairs, Wellington, 1954

McCann, Graham, *Dad's Army, The Story of a Classic Television Show*, Fourth Estate, London, 2001

McKibbin, M.N., *Behind Barbed Wire, Memories of Stalag 383*, Staple Press, London, 1947

Mitchell, D. (ed.), *Letters from a Life: The Selected Letters and Diaries of Benjamin Britten, 1913–1976*, Volume two, 1939–45, Faber, London, 1991

Moffatt, Jonathan and McCormick, Audrey Holmes, *Moon over Malaya: a tale of Argylls and Marines*, Coombe, 1999

Mogg, R.P.L., *For This Alone*, Basil Blackwell, Oxford, 1944

Moore, Bob and Federowich, *Kent, Prisoners of War and Their Captors in World War II*, Berg, Oxford, 1996

Moss, Stephen, *A Bird in the Bush: A Social History of Birdwatching*, Aurum, London, 2005

Munby, A.N.L., *The Alabaster Hand and Other Ghost Stories*, Ash-Tree Press, Penyffordd, Chester, 1995

Murray, W.H., *The Evidence of Things Not Seen, A Mountaineer's Tale*, Baton Wicks, London, 2002

Murray, W.H., *Mountaineering in Scotland*, J.M. Dent, London, 1947

Nelson, David, *The Story of Changi, Singapore*, Changi Publication Co., West Perth, Australia, 1973

Newby, Eric, *Love and War in the Apennines*, Picador, London, 1996

Nichol, John and Rennell, Tony, *The Last Escape, The Untold Story of Allied Prisoners of War in Germany 1944–45*, Penguin, London, 2003

Palmer, Sue, *Prisoners on the Kwai, Memoirs of Dr Harold Churchill*, Larks Press, Dereham, 2005

Pape, R.B., *The Yorkshire Post: P.O.W. edition. Stalag Luft VI*, Kriegie edition, 1944

Patten, Marguerite, *Victory Cookbook*, Hamlyn, London, 1995

Parkes, Meg, 'Notify Alec Rattray…', Kranji, Wirral, 2002

Parkes, Meg, '– A.A. Duncan is OK', Kranji, Wirral, 2003

Parkin, Monty, *Surviving by Magic*, A.M. Parkin, Kent, 2009

Paterson, Sarah, *Tracing your Family History – Army*, Imperial War Museum, London, 2006

Pavillard, Stanley, *Bamboo Doctor*, Macmillan, London, 1960

Peachey, Philip, *Jeweller's Rouge: Survival by the River Kwai*, The Springfield Leisure-Art Collection, Wroxall, 2002

Philps, Richard, *Prisoner Doctor: an Account of the Experiences of a Royal Air Force Medical Officer during the Japanese Occupation of Indonesia, 1942 to 1945*, Book Guild, Lewes, 1996

Piper, David, *I am well, who are you?*, Anne Piper, Wytham, 1998

Prittie, Terence, *Mainly Middlesex*, Hutchinson's Library of Sports and Pastimes, London, 1947

Purcell, Tim and Gething, Mike, *Wartime Wanderers, A Football Team at War*, Mainstream Publishing, London, 1996

Quarrie, R.G.M., *Oflag*, The Pentland Press, Durham, 1995

Ramachandra, Guha, *A Corner of a Foreign Field: the Indian history of a British sport*, Picador, London, 2003

Reeves, Valerie A. and Showan, Valerie, *Dan Billany, Hull's Lost Hero*, Kingston Press, Kingston-upon-Hull, 1999

Reid, P.R., *The Colditz Story*, Cassell Military Paperbacks, London, 1952

Reid, P.R., *The Latter Days at Colditz*, Cassell Military, London, 2003

Rippon, Anton, *The Tottenham Hotspur Story*, Moorland Publishing, Ashbourne, 1980

Rippon, Anton, *Gas Masks for Goal Posts – Football in Britain during the Second World War*, Sutton Publishing, Stroud, 2007

Rollings, Charles, *Prisoner of War, Voices from Captivity during the Second World War*, Ebury Press, London, 2007

Ross, Alan, *Ranji, Prince of Cricketers*, London, Collins, 1983

Samuelson, Paul, Bishop, Robert, Coleman, John (editors), *Readings in Economics*, 'The Economic Organization of a POW Camp' by R.A. Radford, New York, McGraw-Hill, 1955

Saunders, Hilary St George, *The Red Cross and the White: A Short History of the Joint War Organisation of the British Red Cross Society and the Order of St John of Jerusalem during the War 1939–1945*, Hollis & Carter, London, 1949

Searle, Ronald, *To the Kwai – and Back, War Drawings 1939–1945*, Collins in association with the Imperial War Museum, London, 1986

Smith, Colin, *Singapore Burning, Heroism and Surrender in World War II*, Penguin, London, 2006

Stubbs, Peter, W., *The Changi Murals, The Story of Stanley Warren's War*, Landmark Books, Singapore, c.2003

Summers, Julie, *Stranger in the House, Women's Stories of Men Returning from the Second World War*, Simon & Schuster, London, 2008

Summers, Julie, *The Colonel of Tamarkan, Philip Toosey & The Bridge on the River Kwai*, Pocket Books, London, 2006

Swallow, Tom, *Flywheel, Memories of the Open Road*, Webb & Bower, Exeter, 1987

Taylor, William, *With the Cambridgeshires at Singapore*, Trevor Allen Bevis, March, 1971

Terkel, Studs, *'The Good War', An Oral History of World War Two*, Pantheon Books, New York, 1984

Thomas, Gabe, *Milag: Captives of the Kriegsmarine*, The Milag Prisoner of War Association, Glamorgan, 1995

Towle, Philip, Kosuge, Margaret and Kibata,Yoichi (editors), *Japanese Prisoners of War*, Hambledon and London, London, 2000

Urquhart, Alistair, *The Forgotten Highlander, My Incredible Story of Survival During the War in the Far East*, Little, Brown, London, 2010

Ward-Thomas, Pat, *Not Only Golf: An Autobiography*, Hodder and Stoughton, London, 1981

Webber, Richard, *50 years of Carry On*, Century, London, 2008

Wild, David, *Prisoner of Hope*, The Book Guild, Sussex, 1992

Wild, Simon, *Ranji, A Genius Rich and Strange*, The Kingswood Press, London, 1991

Selected Fiction

Ballard, J.G., *Empire of the Sun*, Harper Perennial, 2006

Boulle, Pierre (translated from the French by Xan Fielding), *The Bridge on the River Kwai*, Fontana, London, 1978

Clavell, James, *King Rat*, Flame, London, 1999

Farrell, J.G., *The Singapore Grip*, Weidenfeld and Nicolson, London, 1978

Kennedy, A.L., *Day*, Vintage, London, 2008

Post, Laurens van der, *The Seed and the Sower*, Hogarth Press, London, 1963

Selected Periodicals

The British Red Cross Quarterly Review, January 1946

The British Red Cross Quarterly Review, October 1946

Bulletin of the Raffles Museum, Jack Spittle's "Nesting Habits of Some Singapore Birds", 1950.

Chambers' Journal, October 1947, pp.593–5, "Books in prison I. Reflections of a POW chaplain", by The Rev. David H.C. Read

Chambers' Journal, No. 43 p.657. "Books in Prison II. Further Reflections of a POW chaplain", by The Rev. David H.C. Read

The Criterion, A Literary Review, Vol XV, No. LXI, July 1936, p.759

The Galpin Society Journal, Vol. 52, (Apr., 1999), Anthony Cuthbert Baines, A biographical memoir by Joan Rimmer

The Guardian, interview with Clive Dunn, 10 June 2002

History of Education, editor Dr Roy Lowe, published by Taylor & Francis, London, Vol. 18, No. 3, September 1989, 'The Education of British prisoners of war in German captivity, 1939–1945' by David Rolf

Illustrated London News, April 5, 1947

Journal of the Siam Society 49 (2): 99–108, 1961, A preliminary note on the excavation of the Sai-Yok Rock-shelter

The Library Quarterly, Volume 76, Number 4 (October 2006): 420–37, 'Finding "Another Great World": Australian Soldiers and Wartime Libraries' by Amanda Laugesen

Making Music magazine (official journal of rural music schools association), May 1947, 'Music in Pow Camps in Germany,' Parts 1 and 2

The R.C.M. Magazine, vol. 41, (Royal College of Music) magazine, 'Music in Prisoners of War Camps' by Emily Daymond

The Prisoner of War magazine

Proceedings of the Prehistory Society Cambridge 14:24–32, 1948, 'Prehistoric discoveries in Siam, 1943–1944'

Saga Magazine, February 2002, interview with Clive Dunn

Tong Tong magazine, May 1967

Wisden Cricketers' Almanack, 1946, London, "Cricket Under the Japs" by Major E.W. Swanton, R.A. (pp. 48–51)

Woodworking International, Feb., March 1990

Miscellaneous

Brewer, Frank, *Prisoners of the Japanese, A Record of Certain Camps in the Palembang Area of Sumatra*

Fitzgerald, Verity, *Analysis of the Visual Arts of Japanese Prisoners of War in the Far East During World War II*, Dissertation submitted for the Oxford Brookes BA in History of Art, 2010

Freear, John, *Institute Examinations Behind Barbed Wire 1939–1945*, c.1979

Poidevin, Leslie, *Samurais and Circumcisions*, self-published, 1985

Sherwood, H.W. 'Johnny' – *Football, Fame, Fear, 'Pro Player's Story, I Saw the Nagasaki Atom Bomb* (unpublished)

Who Was Who, A & C Black, 1920–2008

Discography

The Bridge on the River Kwai (1957)
The Captive Heart (1946)
The Great Escape (1963)
King Rat (1965)
La Grande Illusion (1937)
Stalag 17 (1953)
The Wooden Horse (1950)
The World at War (2005)

Sound Archives

Imperial War Museum:
Sir Terry Frost (961)
Birendra Nath Mazumdar (16800)

Ernest William Swanson (4777)

British Library:
Sir Terry Frost, interviewed by Tamsyn Woollcombe, 1994, Artists' Lives, British
    Library Sound Archive reference: C466/22. Tape F4315, side A
Adrian Heath, interviewed by Norbert Lynton, 1992, Artists' Lives, British Library
    Sound Archive reference: C466/11. Tape One Side B F2905

Selected Websites

Australian War Memorial – http://www.awm.gov.au/
British Red Cross – http://www.redcross.org.uk/
Children of and Families of FEPOWs: http://www.cofepow.org.uk/
Eldredge, Sears A., "Captive Audiences/Captive Performers: Music and Theatre
    as Strategies for Survival on the Burma-Thai Railway 1942–1945" (2010). *Books*.
    Book 1.
http://digitalcommons.macalester.edu/thdabooks/1/#
International Committee of the Red Cross – http://www.icrc.org
http://www.hongkongwardiary.com/
http://www.mansell.com/search-helps.html
http://www.researchingfepowhistory.org.uk/

Index

Professor of Linguistics at Georgetown University in Washington DC, Deborah Tannen is currently McGraw Distinguished Lecturer at Princeton University. She received her Ph.D. in linguistics from the University of California, Berkeley and has been awarded fellowships and grants from many organisations including The Rockefeller Foundation, The National Endowment for the Humanities, and the National Science Foundation. With eleven books and over seventy articles to her credit, she has been invited to lecture all over the world. She is Associate Editor of the journal *Text* and is on the editorial boards of all the major journals in her field.

You Just Don't Understand: Women and Men in Conversation has been a phenomenal bestseller in the UK, the USA, Canada, Australia, Germany and Holland. Virago also publish her widely acclaimed *That's Not What I Meant!:* How Conversational Style Makes or Breaks Your Relations With Others.

YOU JUST DON'T UNDERSTAND

Women and Men in Conversation

Deborah Tannen

Published by VIRAGO PRESS Limited 1992
20–23 Mandela Street, Camden Town, London NW1 0HQ

First published in Great Britain in hardback by Virago Press in 1991
First published in the United States of America by William Morrow and Company, Inc, 1990

A CIP catalogue record for this book is available from the British Library.

Printed in Great Britain by Cox & Wyman Ltd, Reading, Berkshire

TO MY FATHER AND MOTHER
SOURCE AND SUSTENANCE

CONTENTS

ACKNOWLEDGMENTS

No usual thanks are sufficient to acknowledge my debt to the generous colleagues who read drafts of this book and improved it with their comments. For these gifts of time and attention, I am grateful to A. L. Becker, Penelope Eckert, Ralph Fasold, Michael Geis, Karl Goldstein, Robin Lakoff, Neal Norrick, Susan Philips, Naomi Tannen, Barrie Thorne, and David Wise.

My debt to Robin Lakoff goes further back. The pioneer in linguistic research on language and gender, she provided a starting point for me, and for a generation of scholars, by blazing a trail that has since branched into many diverging paths of inquiry. Her course at the 1973 Linguistic Institute largely inspired me to become a linguist and to choose as my training ground the University of California, Berkeley, where she was one of my teachers. She has remained a friend, a generous supporter, and a model of a scholar who pursues theoretical research without losing sight of its practical implications.

My gratitude to Ralph Fasold is also far ranging. He has been a continuing and cherished source of intellectual support and challenge, engaging me in dialogue on my research and offering illuminating perspectives, examples, and sources from his own—as well as invaluable computer consulting. I am grateful to Georgetown University for providing me with this perfect colleague and friend.

Also at Georgetown, I thank James Alatis, dean of the School of Languages and Linguistics; my colleagues in the sociolinguistics program; and the students who have listened and contributed to my developing ideas.

Many others were helpful in vital ways, including reading and commenting on parts of drafts, giving examples from their

ACKNOWLEDGMENTS

own experience, or discussing ideas with me. Although I list them together, each person's contribution is individually appreciated: Katherine Abramovitz, Steve Barish, Niko Besnier, Tom Brazaitis, Bruce Brigham, Marjorie Brigham, Penelope Brown, Jocelyn Burton, Caroline Celce-Murcia, Andrew Cohen, Bronwyn Davies, Bambi Evans-Murray, Paul Friedrich, Allen Furbeck, Jim Garofallou, John Goldsmith, Paul Goldstein, Marjorie Harness Goodwin, John Guarnaschelli, Annie Hawkinson, Ray Hays, Paul Hopper, Deborah James, Christina Kakava, Judith Katz-Schwartz, Carolyn Kinney, Mark Kohut, Helen Kotsonis, Addie Macovski, Joseph Mahay, Alan Marx, Rachel Myerowitz, Susie Napper, Myriam Nastase, Mandana Navid-Tabrizi, Rebekah Perks, Molly Peterson, PuaPua Ponafala, Dennis Preston, Lucy Ray, Dan Read, Chuck Richardson, Celia Roberts, Joanna Robin, Elif Rosenfeld, Cynthia Roy, Pamela Saunders, Deborah Schiffrin, Gail Schricker, Tom Schricker, Amy Sheldon, Wendy Smith, Kyong Sook Song, Carola Sprengel, Jana Staton, Dorothy Tannen, Eli Tannen, Gary Weaver, Bob Webb, Etsuko Yamada, and Haru Yamada.

I thank Bruce Dorval for the opportunity to analyze his videotapes and transcripts of friends talking and for permission to use excerpts from them. I also thank Suzanne Gluck, who is everything anyone could wish for in an agent and more, and the entire staff of William Morrow and Company, but especially my editor, Maria Guarnaschelli, who has believed passionately in the book from its inception and has lavished on it her boundless enthusiasm and energy.

To my husband, thank you for everything.

PREFACE

Each person's life is lived as a series of conversations. Analyzing everyday conversations, and their effects on relationships, has been the focus of my career as a sociolinguist. In this book I listen to the voices of women and men. I make sense of seemingly senseless misunderstandings that haunt our relationships, and show that a man and a woman can interpret the same conversation differently, even when there is no apparent misunderstanding. I explain why sincere attempts to communicate are so often confounded, and how we can prevent or relieve some of the frustration.

My book *That's Not What I Meant!* showed that people have different conversational styles. So when speakers from different parts of the country, or of different ethnic or class backgrounds, talk to each other, it is likely that their words will not be understood exactly as they were meant. But we are not required to pair off for life with people from different parts of the country or members of different ethnic groups, though many choose to. We *are* expected to pair off with people of the other gender, and many do, for long periods of time if not for life. And whereas many of us (though fewer and fewer) can spend large portions of our lives without coming into close contact with people of vastly different cultural backgrounds, few people—not even those who have no partners in life or whose primary relationships are with same-sex partners—can avoid close contact with people of the other gender, as relatives and co-workers if not as friends.

That's Not What I Meant! had ten chapters, of which one dealt with gender differences in conversational style. But when I received requests for interviews, articles, and lectures, 90 percent wanted me to focus on 10 percent of the book—the chapter on male-female differences. Everyone wanted to know more about gender and conversational style.

I too wanted to find out more. Indeed, I had decided to become a linguist largely because of a course taught by Robin Lakoff that included her research on gender and language. My first major linguistic study was of gender and cultural differences in indirectness, and I was fairly familiar with others' research on the topic. But although I had always inhabited the outskirts of gender research, I had not leaped into its inner circle, partly because the field is so controversial.

Whenever I write or speak about conversational style differences between women and men, sparks fly. Most people exclaim that what I say is true, that it explains their own experience. They are relieved to learn that what has caused them trouble is a common condition, and there is nothing terribly wrong with them, their partners, or their relationships. Their partners' ways of talking, which they had ascribed to personal failings, could be reframed as reflecting a different system. And their own ways of talking, which their partners had been hounding them about for years, could be defended as logical and reasonable.

But although most people find that my explanation of gender differences in ways of talking accounts for their own experience—and they are eager to offer their own examples to prove it—some people become agitated as soon as they hear a reference to gender. A few become angry at the mere suggestion that women and men are different. And this reaction can come from either women or men.

Some men hear any statement about women and men, coming from a woman, as an accusation—a fancy way of throwing up her hands, as if to say, "You men!" They feel they are being objectified, if not slandered, by being talked about at all.

But it is not only men who bridle at statements about women and men. Some women fear, with justification, that any observation of gender differences will be heard as implying that it is women who are different—different from the standard, which is whatever men are. The male is seen as normative, the female as departing from the norm. And it is only a short step—maybe an inevitable one—from "different" to "worse."

Furthermore, if women's and men's styles are shown to be different, it is usually women who are told to change. I have seen this happen in response to my own work. In an article I wrote for *The Washington Post,* I presented a conversation that had taken place between a couple in their car. The woman had asked, "Would you like to stop for a drink?" Her husband had answered, truthfully, "No," and they hadn't stopped. He was later frustrated to learn that his wife was annoyed because she had wanted to stop for a drink. He wondered, "Why didn't she just say what she wanted? Why did she play games with me?" The wife, I explained, was annoyed not because she had not gotten her way, but because her preference had not been considered. From her point of view, she had shown concern for her husband's wishes, but he had shown no concern for hers.

My analysis emphasized that the husband and wife in this example had different *but equally valid* styles. This point was lost in a heavily edited version of my article that appeared in the *The Toronto Star,* which had me advising: "The woman must realize that when he answers 'yes' or 'no' he is not making a non-negotiable demand." The *Star* editor had deleted the immediately preceding text, which read: "In understanding what went wrong, the man must realize that when she asks what he would like, she is not asking an information question but rather starting a negotiation about what both would like. For her part, however, the woman must realize that . . ." Deft wielding of the editorial knife had transformed my claim that women and men should *both* make adjustments into a claim that women must make a unilateral effort to understand men. Informing women of what they alone must "realize" implies that the man's way is right and the woman's wrong. This edited version was reprinted in a textbook, and the error proliferated.

We all know we are unique individuals, but we tend to see others as representatives of groups. It's a natural tendency, since we must see the world in patterns in order to make sense of it; we wouldn't be able to deal with the daily onslaught of people and objects if we couldn't predict a lot about them and feel that we know who and what they are. But this natural and useful ability to see patterns of similarity has unfortunate consequences. It is offensive to reduce an individual to a category, and it is also misleading. Dividing women and men into categories risks reinforcing this reductionism.

Generalizations, while capturing similarities, obscure differences. Everyone is shaped by innumerable influences such as ethnicity, religion, class, race, age, profession, the geographical regions they and their relatives have lived in, and many other group identities—all mingled with individual personality and predilection. People are apt to sum up others by reference to one category or a few, such as "southern belle," "New York Jewish intellectual," "Boston Brahmin," or "hot-tempered Italian." Although these categories might predict some of the behaviors of the people so described, they miss far more about them than they capture. In innumerable ways, every person is utterly unlike anyone else—including anyone else from many of the same categories.

Despite these dangers, I am joining the growing dialogue on gender and language because the risk of ignoring differences is greater than the danger of naming them. Sweeping something big under the rug doesn't make it go away; it trips you up and sends you sprawling when you venture across the room. Denying real differences can only compound the confusion that is already widespread in this era of shifting and re-forming relationships between women and men.

Pretending that women and men are the same hurts women, because the ways they are treated are based on the norms for men. It also hurts men who, with good intentions, speak to women as they would to men, and are nonplussed when their words don't work as they expected, or even spark resentment and anger.

This paradox is expressed by an American Indian woman, Abby Abinanti, describing why she found law school a difficult and alienating experience:

People did not like or accept the idea of Indians or women being lawyers. Some people could not decide which idea they hated more. Some pretended that it didn't make any difference, that we were all the same. I, too, could be "one of the boys," "one of the white boys." Not likely. Both of these approaches created problems for me.

It is easy to see how people who hate the idea of women or Indians being lawyers would create problems for an Indian woman in law school. It is harder to see how those who wanted to accept her as an equal also created problems for her. Assuming she was the same was destructive, because she was not the same; the assumptions, values, and styles that reflected and validated their identities undercut hers.

The desire to affirm that women are equal has made some scholars reluctant to show they are different, because differences can be used to justify unequal treatment and opportunity. Much as I understand and am in sympathy with those who wish there were no differences between women and men—only reparable social injustice—my research, others' research, and my own and others' experience tell me it simply isn't so. There *are* gender differences in ways of speaking, and we need to identify and understand them. Without such understanding, we are doomed to blame others or ourselves—or the relationship—for the otherwise mystifying and damaging effects of our contrasting conversational styles.

Recognizing gender differences frees individuals from the burden of individual pathology. Many women and men feel dissatisfied with their close relationships and become even more frustrated when they try to talk things out. Taking a *sociolinguistic* approach to relationships makes it possible to explain these dissatisfactions without accusing anyone of being crazy or wrong, and without blaming—or discarding—the relationship. If we recognize and understand the differences beween us, we can take them into account, adjust to, and learn from each other's styles.

The sociolinguistic approach I take in this book shows that

many frictions arise because boys and girls grow up in what are essentially different cultures, so talk between women and men is cross-cultural communication. A cross-cultural approach to gender differences in conversational style differs from the work on gender and language which claims that conversations between men and women break down because men seek to dominate women. No one could deny that men as a class are dominant in our society, and that many individual men seek to dominate women in their lives. And yet male dominance is not the whole story. It is not sufficient to account for everything that happens to women and men in conversations—especially conversations in which both are genuinely trying to relate to each other with attention and respect. The effect of dominance is not always the result of an intention to dominate. That is the news that this book brings.

In this era of opening opportunity, women are beginning to move into positions of authority. At first we assumed they could simply talk the way they always had, but this often doesn't work. Another logical step is that they should change their styles and talk like men. Apart from the repugnance of women's having to do all the changing, this doesn't work either, because women who talk like men are judged differently—and harshly. We have no choice but to examine our choices and their effects. Only by understanding each other's styles and our own options can we begin to realize our opportunities and escape the prison of a monolithic conversational style.

Conversational style differences do not explain all the problems that arise in relationships between women and men. Relationships are sometimes threatened by psychological problems, true failures of love and caring, genuine selfishness—and real effects of political and economic inequity. But there are also innumerable situations in which groundless allegations of these failings are made, simply because partners are expressing their thoughts and feelings, and their assumptions about how to communicate, in different ways. If we can sort out differences based on conversational style, we will be in a better position to confront real conflicts of interest—and to find a shared language in which to negotiate them.

In opening the preface to *That's Not What I Meant!*, I told of a student who said that taking a course I taught at Georgetown University had saved her marriage. Not long ago, the same woman—now a professor, and still married—wrote me a letter. She said that she and her husband had been talking, and somehow the conversation had turned into an argument. In the middle of it he said in exasperation, "Dr. Tannen had better hurry up and write that new book, because this business of men and women talking has got to be the biggest problem around!" In closing this preface, I offer this book to him, and to women and men everywhere who are trying their best to talk to each other.

You Just Don't Understand

ONE

Different Words, Different Worlds

Many years ago I was married to a man who shouted at me, "I do not give you the right to raise your voice to me, because you are a woman and I am a man." This was frustrating, because I knew it was unfair. But I also knew just what was going on. I ascribed his unfairness to his having grown up in a country where few people thought women and men might have equal rights.

Now I am married to a man who is a partner and friend. We come from similar backgrounds and share values and interests. It is a continual source of pleasure to talk to him. It is wonderful to have someone I can tell everything to, someone who understands. But he doesn't always see things as I do, doesn't always react to things as I expect him to. And I often don't understand why he says what he does.

At the time I began working on this book, we had jobs in different cities. People frequently expressed sympathy by making comments like "That must be rough," and "How do you stand it?" I was inclined to accept their sympathy and say things like "We fly a lot." Sometimes I would reinforce their concern: "The worst part is having to pack and unpack all the time." But my husband reacted differently, often with irritation. He might respond by de-emphasizing the inconvenience: As academics, we had four-day weekends together, as well as long vacations throughout the year and four months in the summer. We even benefited from the intervening days of uninterrupted time for work. I once overheard him telling a dubious man that we were lucky, since studies have shown that married couples who live together spend less than half an hour a week talking to each other; he was implying that our situation had advantages.

I didn't object to the way my husband responded—everything he said was true—but I was surprised by it. I didn't understand why he reacted as he did. He explained that he sensed condescension in some expressions of concern, as if the questioner were implying, "Yours is not a real marriage; your ill-chosen profession has resulted in an unfortunate arrangement. I pity you, and look down at you from the height of complacence, since my wife and I have avoided your misfortune." It had not occurred to me that there might be an element of one-upmanship in these expressions of concern, though I could recognize it when it was pointed out. Even after I saw the point, though, I was inclined to regard my husband's response as slightly odd, a personal quirk. He frequently seemed to see others as adversaries when I didn't.

Having done the research that led to this book, I now see that my husband was simply engaging the world in a way that many men do: as an individual in a hierarchical social order in which he was either one-up or one-down. In this world, conversations are negotiations in which people try to achieve and maintain the upper hand if they can, and protect themselves from others' attempts to put them down and push them around. Life, then, is a contest, a struggle to preserve independence and avoid failure.

I, on the other hand, was approaching the world as many women do: as an individual in a network of connections. In this world, conversations are negotiations for closeness in which people try to seek and give confirmation and support, and to reach consensus. They try to protect themselves from others' attempts to push them away. Life, then, is a community, a struggle to preserve intimacy and avoid isolation. Though there are hierarchies in this world too, they are hierarchies more of friendship than of power and accomplishment.

Women are also concerned with achieving status and avoiding failure, but these are not the goals they are *focused* on all the time, and they tend to pursue them in the guise of connection. And men are also concerned with achieving involvement and avoiding isolation, but they are not *focused* on these goals, and they tend to pursue them in the guise of opposition.

Discussing our differences from this point of view, my husband pointed out to me a distinction I had missed: He reacted the way I just described only if expressions of concern came from men in whom he sensed an awareness of hierarchy. And there were times when I too disliked people's expressing sympathy about our commuting marriage. I recall being offended by one man who seemed to have a leering look in his eye when he asked, "How do you manage this long-distance romance?" Another time I was annoyed when a woman who knew me only by reputation approached us during the intermission of a play, discovered our situation by asking my husband where he worked, and kept the conversation going by asking us all about it. In these cases, I didn't feel put down; I felt intruded upon. If my husband was offended by what he perceived as claims to superior status, I felt these sympathizers were claiming inappropriate intimacy.

INTIMACY
AND INDEPENDENCE

Intimacy is key in a world of connection where individuals negotiate complex networks of friendship, minimize differences, try to reach consensus, and avoid the appearance of superiority, which would highlight differences. In a world of status, *independence* is key, because a primary means of establishing status is to tell others what to do, and taking orders is a marker of low status. Though all humans need both intimacy and independence, women tend to focus on the first and men on the second. It is as if their life-blood ran in different directions.

These differences can give women and men differing views of the same situation, as they did in the case of a couple I will call Linda and Josh. When Josh's old high-school chum called him at work and announced he'd be in town on business the following month, Josh invited him to stay for the weekend. That evening he informed Linda that they were going to have a houseguest, and that he and his chum would go out together the first night to shoot the breeze like old times. Linda was upset. She was going to be away on business the week before, and the Friday night when Josh would be out with his chum would be her first night home. But what upset her the most was that Josh had made these plans on his own and informed her of them, rather than discussing them with her before extending the invitation.

Linda would never make plans, for a weekend or an evening, without first checking with Josh. She can't understand why he doesn't show her the same courtesy and consideration that she shows him. But when she protests, Josh says, "I can't say to my friend, 'I have to ask my wife for permission'!"

To Josh, checking with his wife means seeking permission, which implies that he is not independent, not free to act on his own. It would make him feel like a child or an underling. To

Linda, checking with her husband has nothing to do with permission. She assumes that spouses discuss their plans with each other because their lives are intertwined, so the actions of one have consequences for the other. Not only does Linda not mind telling someone, "I have to check with Josh"; quite the contrary—she likes it. It makes her feel good to know and show that she is involved with someone, that her life is bound up with someone else's.

Linda and Josh both felt more upset by this incident, and others like it, than seemed warranted, because it cut to the core of their primary concerns. Linda was hurt because she sensed a failure of closeness in their relationship: He didn't care about her as much as she cared about him. And he was hurt because he felt she was trying to control him and limit his freedom.

A similar conflict exists between Louise and Howie, another couple, about spending money. Louise would never buy anything costing more than a hundred dollars without discussing it with Howie, but he goes out and buys whatever he wants and feels they can afford, like a table saw or a new power mower. Louise is disturbed, not because she disapproves of the purchases, but because she feels he is acting as if she were not in the picture.

Many women feel it is natural to consult with their partners at every turn, while many men automatically make more decisions without consulting their partners. This may reflect a broad difference in conceptions of decision making. Women expect decisions to be discussed first and made by consensus. They appreciate the discussion itself as evidence of involvement and communication. But many men feel oppressed by lengthy discussions about what they see as minor decisions, and they feel hemmed in if they can't just act without talking first. When women try to initiate a freewheeling discussion by asking, "What do you think?" men often think they are being asked to decide.

Communication is a continual balancing act, juggling the conflicting needs for intimacy and independence. To survive in the world, we have to act in concert with others, but to survive as ourselves, rather than simply as cogs in a wheel, we have to act alone. In some ways, all people are the same: We all eat and sleep and drink and laugh and cough, and often we eat, and laugh at, the same things. But in some ways, each person is different, and individuals' differing wants and preferences may conflict with each other. Offered the same menu, people make different choices. And if there is cake for dessert, there is a chance one person may get a larger piece than another—and an even greater chance that one will *think* the other's piece is larger, whether it is or not.

ASYMMETRIES

If intimacy says, "We're close and the same," and independence says, "We're separate and different," it is easy to see that intimacy and independence dovetail with connection and status. The essential element of connection is symmetry: People are the same, feeling equally close to each other. The essential element of status is asymmetry: People are not the same; they are differently placed in a hierarchy.

This duality is particularly clear in expressions of sympathy or concern, which are all potentially ambiguous. They can be interpreted either symmetrically, as evidence of fellow feeling among equals, or asymmetrically, offered by someone one-up to someone one-down. Asking if an unemployed person has found a job, if a couple have succeeded in conceiving the child they crave, or whether an untenured professor expects to get tenure can be meant—and interpreted, regardless of how it is meant— as an expression of human connection by a person who understands and cares, or as a reminder of weakness from someone who is better off and knows it, and hence as condescending. The latter view of sympathy seems self-evident to many men. For example, a handicapped mountain climber named Tom Whittaker, who leads groups of disabled people on outdoor expeditions, remarked, "You can't feel sympathetic for someone you admire"— a statement that struck me as not true at all.

The symmetry of connection is what creates community: If two people are struggling for closeness, they are both struggling for the same thing. And the asymmetry of status is what creates contest: Two people can't both have the upper hand, so negotiation for status is inherently adversarial. In my earlier work, I explored in detail the dynamics of intimacy (which I referred to as involvement) and independence, but I tended to ignore the force of status and its adversarial nature. Once I identified these dynamics, however, I saw them all around me. The puzzling behavior of friends and co-workers finally became comprehensible.

Differences in how my husband and I approached the same situation, which previously would have been mystifying, suddenly made sense. For example, in a jazz club the waitress recommended the crab cakes to me, and they turned out to be terrible. I was uncertain about whether or not to send them back. When the waitress came by and asked how the food was, I said that I didn't really like the crab cakes. She asked, "What's wrong with them?" While staring at the table, my husband answered, "They don't taste fresh." The waitress snapped, "They're frozen! What do you expect?" I looked directly up at her and said, "We just don't like them." She said, "Well, if you don't like them, I could take them back and bring you something else."

After she left with the crab cakes, my husband and I laughed because we realized we had just automatically played out the scripts I had been writing about. He had heard her question "What's wrong with them?" as a challenge that he had to match. He doesn't like to fight, so he looked away, to soften what he felt was an obligatory counterchallenge: He felt instinctively that he had to come up with something wrong with the crab cakes to justify my complaint. (He was fighting for me.) I had taken the question "What's wrong with them?" as a request for information. I instinctively sought a way to be right without making her wrong. Perhaps it was because she was a woman that she responded more favorably to my approach.

When I have spoken to friends and to groups about these

differences, they too say that now they can make sense of previously perplexing behavior. For example, a woman said she finally understood why her husband refused to talk to his boss about whether or not he stood a chance of getting promoted. He wanted to know because if the answer was no, he would start looking for another job. But instead of just asking, he stewed and fretted, lost sleep, and worried. Having no others at her disposal, this wife had fallen back on psychological explanations: Her husband must be insecure, afraid of rejection. But then, everyone is insecure, to an extent. Her husband was actually quite a confident person. And she, who believed herself to be at least as insecure as he, had not hesitated to go to her boss to ask whether he intended to make her temporary job permanent.

Understanding the key role played by status in men's relations made it all come clear. Asking a boss about chances for promotion highlights the hierarchy in the relationship, reminding them both that the employee's future is in the boss's hands. Taking the low-status position made this man intensely uncomfortable. Although his wife didn't especially relish taking the role of supplicant with respect to her boss, it didn't set off alarms in her head, as it did in his.

In a similar flash of insight, a woman who works in sales exclaimed that now she understood the puzzling transformation that the leader of her sales team had undergone when he was promoted to district manager. She had been sure he would make a perfect boss because he had a healthy disregard for authority. As team leader, he had rarely bothered to go to meetings called by management and had encouraged team members to exercise their own judgment, eagerly using his power to waive regulations on their behalf. But after he became district manager, this man was unrecognizable. He instituted more regulations than anyone had dreamed of, and insisted that exceptions could be made only on the basis of written requests to him.

This man behaved differently because he was now differently placed in the hierarchy. When he had been subject to the authority of management, he'd done all he could to limit it. But when the authority of management was vested in him, he did all he could to enlarge it. By avoiding meetings and flouting regulations, he had evidenced not disregard for hierarchy but rather discomfort at being in the subordinate position within it.

Yet another woman said she finally understood why her fiancé, who very much believes in equality, once whispered to her that she should keep her voice down. "My friends are downstairs," he said. "I don't want them to get the impression that you order me around."

That women have been labeled "nags" may result from the interplay of men's and women's styles, whereby many women are inclined to do what is asked of them and many men are inclined to resist even the slightest hint that anyone, especially a woman, is telling them what to do. A women will be inclined to repeat a request that doesn't get a response because she is convinced that her husband would do what she asks, if he only understood that she *really* wants him to do it. But a man who wants to avoid feeling that he is following orders may instinctively wait before doing what she asked, in order to imagine that he is doing it of his own free will. Nagging is the result, because each time she repeats the request, he again puts off fulfilling it.

THE MIXED METAMESSAGES OF HELP

Emily and Jacob were planning their wedding themselves, but Emily's parents were footing a large part of the bill. Concerned that things come out right, her parents frequently called and asked detailed questions about the prices they were paying and the service they were getting: What hors d'oeuvres would be served? How many pieces would be provided per guest? What did dinner include? Would celery and olives be placed on each table? What flowers would be on the tables? Had all this been put in writing? Emily and Jacob heard the detailed questions as implying that the wedding was poised on the brink of disaster because they were not competent to arrange it. In response to Emily's protests, her mother explained, "We want to be part of the planning; we want to help."

As with offers of sympathy, there is always a paradox entailed in offering or giving help. Insofar as it serves the needs of the one helped, it is a generous move that shows caring and builds rapport. But insofar as it is asymmetrical, giving help puts one person in a superior position with respect to the other. Borrowing the terminology of Gregory Bateson, we may regard the help as the *message*—the obvious meaning of the act. But at the same time, the act of helping sends *metamessages*—that is, information about the relations among the people involved, and their attitudes toward what they are saying or doing and the people they are saying or doing it to. In other words, the message of helping says, "This is good for you." But the fact of giving help may seem to send the metamessage "I am more competent than you," and in that sense it is good for the helper.

In interpreting the metamessages of status and connection in a particular instance of giving help, or any communication act, much depends on how things are done and said. For example, in an expression of sympathy, how comments are worded, in what tone of voice they are spoken, accompanied by what facial expressions and gestures all determine the impression made. All these signals send metamessages about how the communication is meant. A "soothing" pat might reinforce the impression of condescension; a look of great concern might intensify the impression that the other person is in deep trouble; an offhand smile might suggest instead that a question is intended as concern between equals.

The conflicting metamessages inherent in giving help become especially apparent when people are in a hierarchical relationship to each other by virtue of their jobs. Just as parents are often frustrated in attempts to be their children's "friends," so bosses who try to give friendly advice to subordinates may find that their words, intended symmetrically, are interpreted through an asymmetrical filter. For example, the director of a residential facility for retarded people was sympathetic to complaints by staff members about their low wages, so he spoke at a meeting with what he thought was forthrightness and concern. He leveled with them by admitting that their jobs would never pay enough to support a family. He also told them they would not be able to advance to higher-paying jobs if they did not have graduate degrees. As their friend, he advised that if they wanted jobs that could lead to more lucrative careers, they would have to find different jobs. The staff did not appreciate their director's candor, because they did not receive his communication as an expression of concern for their welfare coming from a peer. Rather, they heard it as a threat from a boss: "If you don't like it here, you can jolly well leave."

FRAMING

Another way to think about metamessages is that they *frame* a conversation, much as a picture frame provides a context for the images in the picture. Metamessages let you know how to interpret what someone is saying by identifying the activity that is going on: Is this an argument or a chat? Is it helping, advising, or scolding? At the same time, they let you know what position the speaker is assuming in the activity, and what position you are being assigned.

Sociologist Erving Goffman uses the term *alignment* to express this aspect of framing. If you put me down, you are taking a superior alignment with respect to me. Furthermore, by showing the alignment that you take with regard to others, what you say frames you, just as you are framing what you say. For example, if you talk to others as if you were a teacher and they were your students, they may perceive that your way of talking frames you as condescending or pedantic. If you talk to others as if you were a student seeking help and explanations, they may perceive you as insecure, incompetent, or naïve. Our reactions to what others say or do are often sparked by how we feel we are being framed.

THE MODERN FACE
OF CHIVALRY

Framing is key in the following commonplace scene. A car is moving slowly down the street while another is edging out of a parking spot. The driver of the parked car hesitates, but the driver of the other car stops and signals, with a hand wave, that he is yielding the right-of-way. If the driver of the parked car is a woman, chances are she will smile her thanks and proceed while the gallant man waits. But if the driver of the parked car is a man, he may well return wave for wave and insist on waiting himself, even if, under other circumstances, he might try to move out quickly before an advancing car got in his way.

The chivalrous man who holds a door open or signals a woman to go ahead of him when he's driving is negotiating both status and connection. The status difference is implied by a me-tamessage of control: The woman gets to proceed not because it is her right but because he has granted her permission, so she is being framed as subordinate. Furthermore, those in a position to grant privileges are also in a position to change their minds and take them away. This is the dimension to which some women respond when they protest gallant gestures as "chauvinist." Those who appreciate such gestures as "polite" see only the connection: He's being nice. And it is also the dimension the man performing the generous gesture is likely to see, and the reason he may be understandably incensed if his polite gesture sparks protest rather than thanks.

But if being allowed to proceed in traffic is simply a polite gesture that gives one an advantage, why do so many men decline the gift of the right-of-way and gesture the other car, or a pedestrian, to proceed ahead of them instead? Because waving another person on in traffic also preserves independence: The driver is deciding on his own course of action, rather than being told what to do by someone else.

THE PROTECTIVE FRAME

A protective gesture from a man reinforces the traditional alignment by which men protect women. But a protective gesture from a woman suggests a different scenario: one in which women protect children. That's why many men resist women's efforts to reciprocate protectiveness—it can make them feel that they are being framed as children. These underlying dynamics create sense out of what otherwise seem to be senseless arguments between women and men.

Here is an example of a momentary gesture that led to momentous frustration. Sandra was driving, and Maurice was sitting in the seat beside her. When she had to brake suddenly, she did what her father had always done if he had to stop suddenly when Sandra was sitting beside him: At the moment she braked, she extended her right arm to protect the person beside her from falling forward.

This gesture was mostly symbolic. Sandra's right arm was not strong enough to restrain Maurice. Perhaps its main function was simply to alert him that she was stopping unexpectedly. In any case, the gesture had become for her, as it was for her father, automatic, and it made her feel competent and considerate. But it infuriated Maurice. The explanation he gave was that she should keep both hands on the wheel for reasons of safety. She knew she did not lose control of the car when she extended her arm, so they never could settle this difference. Eventually she trained herself to resist this impulse with Maurice to avoid a fight, but she felt sadly constrained by what she saw as his irrational reaction.

Though Maurice explained his reaction in terms of safety,

he was actually responding to the framing implied by the gesture. He felt belittled, treated like a child, because by extending her arm to break his fall, Sandra was protecting him. In fact, Maurice was already feeling uncomfortable about sitting passively while Sandra was driving, even though it was her car. Many men and women who feel they have achieved equality in their relationship find that whenever they get into a car together, she automatically heads for the passenger seat and he for the driver's; she drives only when he is not there.

The act of protecting frames the protector as dominant and the protected as subordinate. But the status difference signaled by this alignment may be more immediately apparent to men. As a result, women who are thinking in terms of connection may talk and behave in ways that accept protection, unaware that others may see them as taking a subordinate position.

DIFFERENT MEANS TO THE SAME END

Both status and connection can be used as means to get things done by talking. Suppose you want to get an appointment with a plumber who is fully booked for a month. You may use strategies that manipulate your connections or your differences in status. If you opt for status, you may operate either as one-down or one-up. For example, one-up: You let it be known that you are an important person, a city official who has influence in matters such as licensing and permits that the plumber has need of. Or one-down: You plaintively inform the receptionist that you are new in town, and you have no neighbors or relatives to whom you could turn to take a shower or use the facilities. You hope she will feel sorry for you and give you special consideration. Whether you take a one-up or one-down stance, both these approaches play on differences in status by acknowledging that the two people involved are in asymmetrical relation to each other.

On the other hand, you could try reinforcing your sameness.

If you are from the same town as the plumber's receptionist, or if you are both from the same country or cultural group, you may engage her in talk about your hometown, or speak in your home dialect or language, hoping that this will remind her that you come from the same community so she will give you special consideration. If you know someone she knows, you may mention that person and hope this will create a feeling of closeness that will make her want to do something special for you. This is why it is useful to have a personal introduction to someone you want to meet, to transform you from a stranger into someone with whom there is a personal connection.

The example of talking to a plumber's receptionist illustrates options that are available whenever anyone tries to get something done. Ways of talking are rarely if ever composed entirely of one approach or the other, but rather are composed of both and interpretable as either. For example, many people consider name-dropping to be a matter of status: "Look how important I am, because I know important people." But it is also a play on intimacy and close connections. Claiming to know someone famous is a bit like claiming to know someone's mother or cousin or childhood friend—an attempt to gain approval by showing that you know someone whom others also know. In name-dropping they don't actually know the people named, but they know *of* them. You are playing on connections, in the sense that you bring yourself closer to the people you are talking to by showing you know someone they know of; but to the extent that you make yourself more important by showing you *know* someone they have *only heard* of, you are playing on status.

Much—even most—meaning in conversation does not reside in the words spoken at all, but is filled in by the person listening. Each of us decides whether we think others are speaking in the spirit of differing status or symmetrical connection. The likelihood that individuals will tend to interpret someone else's words as one or the other depends more on the hearer's own focus, concerns, and habits than on the spirit in which the words were intended.

WHO'S DECEPTIVE?

In regarding these varying but related approaches to human relationships, people tend to sense that one or the other is the real dynamic. One man, on hearing my analysis of ways of talking to the plumber, commented, "Wouldn't using solidarity be deceptive?" If, like many men, one believes that human relations are fundamentally hierarchical, then playing on connection rather than status amounts to "pretending" there is no status—in other words, being deceptive. But those who tend to regard connection as the basic dynamic operating between people see attempts to use status differences as manipulative and unfair.

Both status and connection are ways of being involved with others and showing involvement with others, although those who are focused on one may not see the other as a means of involvement. Men are more often inclined to focus on the jockeying for status in a conversation: Is the other person trying to be one-up or put me down? Is he trying to establish a dominant position by getting me to do his bidding? Women are more often attuned to the negotiation of connections: Is the other person trying to get closer or pull away? Since both elements are always present, it is easy for women and men to focus on different elements in the same conversation.

MIXED JUDGMENTS
AND MISJUDGMENTS

Because men and women are regarding the landscape from contrasting vantage points, the same scene can appear very different to them, and they often have opposite interpretations of the same action.

A colleague mentioned that he got a letter from a production editor working on his new book, instructing him to let her know if he planned to be away from his permanent address at any time in the next six months, when his book would be in production. He commented that he hadn't realized how like a parole officer a production editor could be. His response to this letter surprised me, because I have received similar letters from publishers, and my response is totally different: I like them, because it makes me feel important to know that my whereabouts matter. When I mentioned this difference to my colleague, he was puzzled and amused, as I was by his reaction. Though he could understand my point of view intellectually, emotionally he could not imagine how one could not feel framed as both controlled and inferior in rank by being told to report one's movements to someone. And though I could understand his perspective intellectually, it simply held no emotional resonance for me.

In a similar spirit, my colleague remarked that he had read a journal article written by a woman who thanked her husband in the acknowledgments section of her paper for helpful discussion of the topic. When my colleague first read this acknowledgment, he thought the author must be incompetent, or at least insecure: Why did she have to consult her husband about her own work? Why couldn't she stand on her own two feet? After hearing my explanation that women value evidence of connection, he reframed the acknowledgment and concluded that the author probably valued her husband's involvement in her work and made reference to it with the pride that comes of believing one has evidence of a balanced relationship.

If my colleague's reaction is typical, imagine how often women who think they are displaying a positive quality—connection— are misjudged by men who perceive them as revealing a lack of independence, which the men regard as synonymous with incompetence and insecurity.

IN PURSUIT OF FREEDOM

A woman was telling me why a long-term relationship had ended. She recounted a recurrent and pivotal conversation. She and the man she lived with had agreed that they would both be free, but they would not do anything to hurt each other. When the man began to sleep with other women, she protested, and he was incensed at her protest. Their conversation went like this:

SHE: How can you do this when you know it's hurting me?
HE: How can you try to limit my freedom?
SHE: But it makes me feel awful.
HE: You are trying to manipulate me.

On one level, this is simply an example of a clash of wills: What he wanted conflicted with what she wanted. But in a fundamental way, it reflects the difference in focus I have been describing. In arguing for his point of view, the key issue for this man was his independence, his freedom of action. The key issue for the woman was their interdependence—how what he did made her feel. He interpreted her insistence on their interdependence as "manipulation": She was using her feelings to control his behavior.

The point is not that women do not value freedom or that men do not value their connection to others. It is rather that the desire for freedom and independence becomes more of an issue for many men in relationships, whereas interdependence and connection become more of an issue for many women. The difference is one of focus and degree.

In a study of how women and men talk about their divorces, Catherine Kohler Riessman found that both men and women mentioned increased freedom as a benefit of divorce. But the word *freedom* meant different things to them. When women told her they had gained freedom by divorce, they meant that they had gained "independence and autonomy." It was a relief for them

40

not to have to worry about how their husbands would react to what they did, and not have to be "responsive to a disgruntled spouse." When men mentioned freedom as a benefit of divorce, they meant freedom from obligation—the relief of feeling "less confined," less "claustrophobic," and having "fewer responsibilities."

Riessman's findings illuminate the differing burdens that are placed on women and men by their characteristic approaches to relationships. The burden from which divorce delivered the women was perceived as internally motivated: the continual preoccupation with how their husbands would respond to them and how they should respond to their husbands. The burden from which it delivered the men was perceived as externally imposed: the obligations of the provider role and a feeling of confinement from having their behavior constrained by others. Independence was not a gift of divorce for the men Riessman interviewed, because, as one man put it, "I always felt independent and I guess it's just more so now."

The Chronicle of Higher Education conducted a small survey, asking six university professors why they had chosen the teaching profession. Among the six were four men and two women. In answering the question, the two women referred to teaching. One said, "I've always wanted to teach." The other said, "I knew as an undergraduate that I wanted to join a faculty. . . . I realized that teaching was the thing I wanted to do." The four men's answers had much in common with each other and little in common with the women's. All four men referred to independence as their main motive. Here are excerpts from each of their responses:

I decided it was academe over industry because I would have my choice of research. There's more independence.

I wanted to teach, and I like the freedom to set your own research goals.

I chose an academic job because the freedoms of academia

outweighed the money disadvantages—and to pursue the research interest I'd like to, as opposed to having it dictated.

I have a problem that interests me. . . . I'd rather make
$30,000 for the rest of my life and be allowed to do basic
research than to make $100,000 and work in computer
graphics.

Though one man also mentioned teaching, neither of the women
mentioned freedom to pursue their own research interests as a
main consideration. I do not believe this means that women are
not interested in research, but rather that independence, freedom
from being told what to do, is not as significant a preoccupation
for them.

In describing what appealed to them about teaching, these
two women focused on the ability to influence students in a positive way. Of course, influencing students reflects a kind of power
over them, and teaching entails an asymmetrical relationship, with
the teacher in the higher-status position. But in talking about their
profession, the women focused on connection to students, whereas
the men focused on their freedom from others' control.

MALE-FEMALE CONVERSATION IS CROSS-CULTURAL COMMUNICATION

If women speak and hear a language of connection and intimacy,
while men speak and hear a language of status and independence,
then communication between men and women can be like cross-
cultural communication, prey to a clash of conversational styles.
Instead of different dialects, it has been said they speak different
genderlects.

The claim that men and women grow up in different worlds
may at first seem patently absurd. Brothers and sisters grow up
in the same families, children to parents of both genders. Where,

then, do women and men learn different ways of speaking and hearing?

IT BEGINS AT THE BEGINNING

Even if they grow up in the same neighborhood, on the same block, or in the same house, girls and boys grow up in different worlds of words. Others talk to them differently and expect and accept different ways of talking from them. Most important, children learn how to talk, how to have conversations, not only from their parents but from their peers. After all, if their parents have a foreign or regional accent, children do not emulate it; they learn to speak with the pronunciation of the region where they grow up. Anthropologists Daniel Maltz and Ruth Borker summarize research showing that boys and girls have very different ways of talking to their friends. Although they often play together, boys and girls spend most of their time playing in same-sex groups. And, although some of the activities they play at are similar, their favorite games are different, and their ways of using language in their games are separated by a world of difference.

Boys tend to play outside, in large groups that are hierarchically structured. Their groups have a leader who tells others what to do and how to do it, and resists doing what other boys propose. It is by giving orders and making them stick that high status is negotiated. Another way boys achieve status is to take center stage by telling stories and jokes, and by sidetracking or challenging the stories and jokes of others. Boys' games have winners and losers and elaborate systems of rules that are frequently the subjects of arguments. Finally, boys are frequently heard to boast of their skill and argue about who is best at what.

Girls, on the other hand, play in small groups or in pairs; the center of a girl's social life is a best friend. Within the group, intimacy is key: Differentiation is measured by relative closeness. In their most frequent games, such as jump rope and hopscotch, everyone gets a turn. Many of their activities (such as playing house) do not have winners or losers. Though some girls are certainly more skilled than others, girls are expected not to boast about it, or show that they think they are better than the others. Girls don't give orders; they express their preferences as suggestions, and suggestions are likely to be accepted. Whereas boys say, "Gimme that!" and "Get outta here!" girls say, "Let's do this," and "How about doing that?" Anything else is put down as "bossy." They don't grab center stage—they don't want it—so they don't challenge each other directly. And much of the time, they simply sit together and talk. Girls are not accustomed to jockeying for status in an obvious way; they are more concerned that they be liked.

Gender differences in ways of talking have been described by researchers observing children as young as three. Amy Sheldon videotaped three- to four-year-old boys and girls playing in threesomes at a day-care center. She compared two groups of three—one of boys, one of girls—that got into fights about the same play item: a plastic pickle. Though both groups fought over the same thing, the dynamics by which they negotiated their conflicts were different. In addition to illustrating some of the patterns I have just described, Sheldon's study also demonstrates the complexity of these dynamics.

While playing in the kitchen area of the day-care center, a little girl named Sue wanted the pickle that Mary had, so she argued that Mary should give it up because Lisa, the third girl, wanted it. This led to a conflict about how to satisfy Lisa's (invented) need. Mary proposed a compromise, but Sue protested:

MARY: I cut it in half. One for Lisa, one for me, one for me.
SUE: But, Lisa wants a *whole* pickle!

Mary comes up with another creative compromise, which Sue also rejects:

MARY: Well, it's a whole *half* pickle.
SUE: No, it isn't.

MARY: Yes, it is, a whole *half* pickle.
SUE: *I'll* give her a whole half. I'll give her a *whole whole*. I gave her a whole one.

At this point, Lisa withdraws from the alliance with Sue, who satisfies herself by saying, "I'm pretending I gave you one."

On another occasion, Sheldon videotaped three boys playing in the same kitchen play area, and they too got into a fight about the plastic pickle. When Nick saw that Kevin had the pickle, he demanded it for himself:

NICK: [Screams] Kevin, but the, oh, I *have* to cut! I want to cut it! It's mine!

Like Sue, Nick involved the third child in his effort to get the pickle:

NICK: [Whining to Joe] Kevin is not letting me cut the pickle.
JOE: Oh, I know! I can pull it away from him and give it back to you. That's an idea!

The boys' conflict, which lasted two and a half times longer than the girls', then proceeded as a struggle between Nick and Joe on the one hand and Kevin on the other.

In comparing the boys' and girls' pickle fights, Sheldon points out that, for the most part, the girls mitigated the conflict and preserved harmony by compromise and evasion. Conflict was more prolonged among the boys, who used more insistence, appeals to rules, and threats of physical violence. However, to say that these little girls and boys used *more* of one strategy or another is not to say that they didn't use the other strategies at all. For example, the boys did attempt compromise, and the girls did attempt physical force. The girls, like the boys, were struggling for control of their play. When Sue says by mistake, "*I'll* give her a whole half," then quickly corrects herself to say, "I'll give her a *whole whole*," she reveals that it is not really the size of the portion that is important to her, but who gets to serve it.

While reading Sheldon's study, I noticed that whereas both

Nick and Sue tried to get what they wanted by involving a third child, the alignments they created with the third child, and the dynamics they set in motion, were fundamentally different. Sue appealed to Mary to fulfill someone else's desire; rather than saying that *she* wanted the pickle, she claimed that Lisa wanted it. Nick asserted his own desire for the pickle, and when he couldn't get it on his own, he appealed to Joe to get it for him. Joe then tried to get the pickle by force. In both these scenarios, the children were enacting complex lines of affiliation.

Joe's strong-arm tactics were undertaken not on his own behalf but, chivalrously, on behalf of Nick. By making an appeal in a whining voice, Nick positioned himself as one-down in a hierarchical structure, framing himself as someone in need of protection. When Sue appealed to Mary to relinquish her pickle, she wanted to take the one-up position of serving food. She was fighting not for the right to *have* the pickle, but for the right to *serve* it. (This reminded me of the women who said they'd become professors in order to teach.) But to accomplish her goal, Sue was depending on Mary's desire to fulfill others' needs.

This study suggests that boys and girls both want to get their way, but they tend to do so differently. Though social norms encourage boys to be openly competitive and girls to be openly cooperative, different situations and activities can result in different ways of behaving. Marjorie Harness Goodwin compared boys and girls engaged in two task-oriented activities: The boys were making slingshots in preparation for a fight, and the girls were making rings. She found that the boys' group was hierarchical: The leader told the others what to do and how to do it. The girls' group was egalitarian: Everyone made suggestions and tended to accept the suggestions of others. But observing the girls in a different activity—playing house—Goodwin found that they too adopted hierarchical structures: The girls who played mothers issued orders to the girls playing children, who in turn sought permission from their play-mothers. Moreover, a girl who was a play-mother was also a kind of manager of the game. This study shows that girls know how to issue orders and operate in a hierarchical structure, but they don't find that mode of behavior appropriate when they engage in task activities with their peers. They do find it appropriate in parent-child relationships, which they enjoy practicing in the form of play.

These worlds of play shed light on the world views of women and men in relationships. The boys' play illuminates why men would be on the lookout for signs they are being put down or told what to do. The chief commodity that is bartered in the boys' hierarchical world is status, and the way to achieve and maintain status is to give orders and get others to follow them. A boy in a low-status position finds himself being pushed around. So boys monitor their relations for subtle shifts in status by keeping track of who's giving orders and who's taking them.

These dynamics are not the ones that drive girls' play. The chief commodity that is bartered in the girls' community is intimacy. Girls monitor their friendships for subtle shifts in alliance, and they seek to be friends with popular girls. Popularity is a kind of status, but it is founded on connection. It also places popular girls in a bind. By doing field work in a junior high school, Donna Eder found that popular girls were paradoxically—and inevitably—disliked. Many girls want to befriend popular girls, but girls' friendships must necessarily be limited, since they entail intimacy rather than large group activities. So a popular girl must reject the overtures of most of the girls who seek her out—with the result that she is branded "stuck up."

THE KEY IS UNDERSTANDING

If adults learn their ways of speaking as children growing up in separate social worlds of peers, then conversation between women and men is cross-cultural communication. Although each style is valid on its own terms, misunderstandings arise because the styles are different. Taking a cross-cultural approach to male-female conversations makes it possible to explain why dissatisfactions are justified without accusing anyone of being wrong or crazy.

Learning about style differences won't make them go away,

but it can banish mutual mystification and blame. Being able to understand why our partners, friends, and even strangers behave the way they do is a comfort, even if we still don't see things the same way. It makes the world into more familiar territory. And having others understand why we talk and act as we do protects us from the pain of their puzzlement and criticism.

In discussing her novel *The Temple of My Familiar*, Alice Walker explained that a woman in the novel falls in love with a man because she sees in him "a giant ear." Walker went on to remark that although people may think they are falling in love because of sexual attraction or some other force, "really what we're looking for is someone to be able to hear us."

We all want, above all, to be heard—but not merely to be heard. We want to be understood—heard for what we think we are saying, for what we know we meant. With increased understanding of the ways women and men use language should come a decrease in frequency of the complaint "You just don't understand."

TWO

Asymmetries: Women and Men Talking at Cross-purposes

E ve had a lump removed from her breast. Shortly after the operation, talking to her sister, she said that she found it upsetting to have been cut into, and that looking at the stitches was distressing because they left a seam that had changed the contour of her breast. Her sister said, "I know. When I had my operation I felt the same way." Eve made the same observation to her friend Karen, who said, "I know. It's like your body has been violated." But when she told her husband, Mark, how she felt, he said, "You can have plastic surgery to cover up the scar and restore the shape of your breast."

Eve had been comforted by her sister and her friend, but she was not comforted by Mark's comment. Quite the contrary, it upset her more. Not only didn't she hear what she wanted, that he understood her feelings, but, far worse, she felt he was asking her to undergo more surgery just when she was telling him how much this operation had upset her. "I'm not having any more surgery!" she protested. "I'm sorry you don't like the way it looks." Mark was hurt and puzzled. "I don't care," he protested. "It doesn't bother me at all." She asked, "Then why are you telling me to have plastic surgery?" He answered, "Because you were saying *you* were upset about the way it looked."

Eve felt like a heel: Mark had been wonderfully supportive and concerned throughout her surgery. How could she snap at him because of what he said—"just words"—when what he had done was unassailable? And yet she had perceived in his words metamessages that cut to the core of their relationship. It was self-evident to him that his comment was a reaction to her complaint, but she heard it as an independent complaint of his. He thought he was reassuring her that she needn't feel bad about her scar because there was something she could *do* about it. She heard his suggestion that she do something about the scar as evidence that *he* was bothered by it. Furthermore, whereas she wanted reassurance that it was normal to feel bad in her situation, his telling her that the problem could easily be fixed implied she had no right to feel bad about it.

Eve wanted the gift of understanding, but Mark gave her the gift of advice. He was taking the role of problem solver, whereas she simply wanted confirmation for her feelings.

A similar misunderstanding arose between a husband and wife following a car accident in which she had been seriously injured. Because she hated being in the hospital, the wife asked to come home early. But once home, she suffered pain from having to move around more. Her husband said, "Why didn't you stay in the hospital where you would have been more comfortable?" This hurt her because it seemed to imply that he did not want her home. She didn't think of his suggestion that she should have stayed in the hospital as a response to her complaints about the pain she was suffering; she thought of it as an independent expression of his preference not to have her at home.

"THEY'RE MY TROUBLES—NOT YOURS"

If women are often frustrated because men do not respond to their troubles by offering matching troubles, men are often frustrated because women do. Some men not only take no comfort in such a response, they take offense. For example, a woman told me that when her companion talks about a personal concern— for example, his feelings about growing older—she responds, "I know how you feel; I feel the same way." To her surprise and chagrin, he gets annoyed; he feels she is trying to take something away from him by denying the uniqueness of his experience.

A similar miscommunication was responsible for the following interchange, which began as a conversation and ended as an argument:

> HE: I'm really tired. I didn't sleep well last night.
> SHE: I didn't sleep well either. I never do.
> HE: Why are you trying to belittle me?
> SHE: I'm not! I'm just trying to show that I understand!

This woman was not only hurt by her husband's reaction; she was mystified by it. How could he think she was belittling him? By "belittle me," he meant "belittle my experience." He was filtering her attempts to establish connection through his concern with preserving independence and avoiding being put down.

"I'LL FIX IT FOR YOU"

Women and men are both often frustrated by the other's way of responding to their expression of troubles. And they are further hurt by the other's frustration. If women resent men's tendency to offer solutions to problems, men complain about women's refusal to take action to solve the problems they complain about. Since many men see themselves as problem solvers, a complaint or a trouble is a challenge to their ability to think of a solution, just as a woman presenting a broken bicycle or stalling car poses a challenge to their ingenuity in fixing it. But whereas many women appreciate help in fixing mechanical equipment, few are inclined to appreciate help in "fixing" emotional troubles.

The idea that men are problem solvers was reinforced by the contrasting responses of a husband and wife to the same question on a radio talk show. The couple, Barbara and William Christopher, were discussing their life with an autistic child. The host asked if there weren't times when they felt sorry for themselves and wondered, "Why me?" Both said no, but they said it in different ways. The wife deflected attention from herself: She said that the real sufferer was her child. The husband said, "Life is problem solving. This is just one more problem to solve."

This explains why men are frustrated when their sincere attempts to help a woman solve her problems are met not with gratitude but with disapproval. One man reported being ready to tear his hair out over a girlfriend who continually told him about problems she was having at work but refused to take any of the advice he offered. Another man defended himself against his girlfriend's objection that he changed the subject as soon as she recounted something that was bothering her: "What's the point of talking about it any more?" he said. "You can't do anything about it." Yet another man commented that women seem to wallow in their problems, wanting to talk about them forever, whereas he and other men want to get them out and be done with them, either by finding a solution or by laughing them off.

Trying to solve a problem or fix a trouble focuses on the message level of talk. But for most women who habitually report problems at work or in friendships, the message is not the main point of complaining. It's the metamessage that counts: Telling about a problem is a bid for an expression of understanding ("I know how you feel") or a similar complaint ("I felt the same way when something similar happened to me"). In other words, troubles talk is intended to reinforce rapport by sending the metamessage "We're the same; you're not alone." Women are frustrated when they not only don't get this reinforcement but, quite the opposite, feel distanced by the advice, which seems to send the metamessage "We're not the same. You have the problems; I have the solutions."

Furthermore, mutual understanding is symmetrical, and this symmetry contributes to a sense of community. But giving advice is asymmetrical. It frames the advice giver as more knowledgeable, more reasonable, more in control—in a word, one-up. And this contributes to the distancing effect.

The assumption that giving advice can be oneupmanship underlies an observation that appeared in a book review. In commenting on Alice Adams's *After You've Gone,* reviewer Ron Carlson explained that the title story is a letter from a woman to a man who has left her for a younger woman. According to Carlson, the woman informs her former lover about her life "and then steps up and clobbers him with sage advice. Here is clearly a superior woman. . . ." Although we do not know the intention of the woman who wrote the story, we see clearly that the man who reviewed it regards giving advice as a form of attack and sees one who gives advice as taking a superior position.

PARALLEL TRACKS

These differences seem to go far back in our growing up. A sixteen-year-old girl told me she tends to hang around with boys rather than girls. To test my ideas, I asked her whether boys and girls both talk about problems. Yes, she assured me, they both do. Do they do it the same way? I asked. Oh, no, she said. The girls go on and on. The boys raise the issue, one of them comes up with a solution, and then they close the discussion.

Women's and men's frustrations with each other's ways of

dealing with troubles talk amount to applying interpretations based on one system to talk that is produced according to a different system. Boys and men do not respond to each other the way women respond to each other in troubles talk. The roots of the very different way that men respond to talk about troubles became clear to me when I compared the transcript of a pair of tenth-grade boys talking to each other to the transcripts of girls' conversations from videotapes of best friends talking, recorded as part of a research project by psychologist Bruce Dorval.

Examining the videotaped conversations, I found that the boys and girls, who expressed deep concerns to each other, did it in different ways—ways that explain the differences that come up in daily conversations between women and men. The pairs of girls at both the sixth grade and tenth grade talked at length about one girl's problems. The other girl pressed her to elaborate, said, "I know," and gave supporting evidence. The following brief excerpts from the transcripts show the dramatic difference between the girls and boys.

The tenth-grade girls are talking about Nancy's problems with her boyfriend and her mother. It emerges that Nancy and Sally were both part of a group excursion to another state. Nancy suddenly left the group and returned home early at her mother's insistence. Nancy was upset about having to leave early. Sally reinforces Nancy's feelings by letting her know that her sudden departure was also upsetting to her friends:

NANCY: God, it was *bad.* I couldn't believe she made me go home.

SALLY: I thought it was kind of weird though, I mean, one minute we were going out and the next minute Nancy's going, "Excuse me, gotta be going." [Both laugh] I didn't know what was going *on,* and Judy comes up to me and she whispers (the whole place knows), "Do you know that Nancy's going home?" And I go, "What?" [Both laugh] "Nancy's going home." I go, *"Why?"* She goes, "Her mom's mak-

> ing her." I go [makes a face], "Ah." She comes back and goes, "Nancy's left." Well, I said, "WELL, that was a fine thing TO DO, she didn't even come and say goodbye." And she starts boiling all over me. I go [mimicking yelling], *"All right!!"* She was upset, Judy. I was like "God"—

Sally's way of responding to her friend's troubles is to confirm Nancy's feelings of distress that her mother made her leave the trip early, by letting her know that her leaving upset her friends. In contrast, examining the transcript of a conversation between boys of the same age shows how differently they respond to each other's expressions of troubles.

The tenth-grade boys also express deep feelings. Theirs too is troubles talk, but it is troubles talk with a difference. They don't concentrate on the troubles of one, pursuing, exploring, and elaborating. Instead, each one talks about his own troubles and dismisses the other's as insignificant.

In the first excerpt from these boys' conversation, Richard says he feels bad because his friend Mary has no date for an upcoming dance, and Todd dismisses his concern:

> RICHARD: God, I'm going to feel so bad for her if she stays home.
>
> TODD: She's not going to stay home, it's ridiculous. Why doesn't she just ask somebody?

Yet Todd himself is upset because he has no date for the same dance. He explains that he doesn't want to ask Anita, and Richard, in turn, scoffs at his distress:

> TODD: I felt so bad when she came over and started talking to me last night.
>
> RICHARD: Why?
>
> TODD: I don't know. I felt uncomfortable, I guess.
>
> RICHARD: **I'll never understand that.** [Laugh]

Far from trying to show that he understands, Richard states flatly that he doesn't, as shown in boldface type.

Richard then tells Todd that he is afraid he has a drinking problem. Todd responds by changing the subject to something that is bothering him, his feelings of alienation:

RICHARD: When I took Anne home last night she told me off.

TODD: Really?

. . .

RICHARD: You see when she found out what happened last Thursday night between Sam and me?

TODD: Mhm.

RICHARD: She knew about that. And she just said— and then she started talking about drinking. You know? . . . And then she said, you know, "You, how you hurt everybody when you do it. You're always cranky." And she just said, "I don't like it. You hurt Sam. You hurt Todd. You hurt Mary. You hurt Lois."

. . .

I mean, when she told me, you know I guess I was kind of stunned. [Pause] I didn't really drink that much.

TODD: **Are you still talking to Mary, a lot, I mean?**

RICHARD: Am I still talking to Mary?

TODD: Yeah, 'cause that's why— that's why I was mad Friday.

RICHARD: Why?

TODD: Because.

RICHARD: 'Cause why?

TODD: 'Cause I didn't know why you all just wa- I mean I just went back upstairs for things, then y'all never came back. I was going, "Fine. I don't care." I said, "He's going to start this again."

As the lines printed in boldface show, when Richard says that he is upset because Anne told him he behaved badly when he was drunk, Todd responds by bringing up his own concern: He feels left out, and he was hurt when Richard disappeared from a party with his friend Mary.

Throughout the conversation, Todd expresses distress over feeling alienated and left out. Richard responds by trying to argue Todd out of the way he feels. When Todd says he felt out of place at a party the night before, Richard argues:

RICHARD: **How could you feel out of place? You knew Lois, and you knew Sam.**

TODD: I don't know. I just felt really out of place and then last night again at the party, I mean, Sam was just running around, he knew everyone from the sorority. There was about five.

RICHARD: **Oh, no, he didn't.**

TODD: He knew a lot of people. He was— I don't know.

RICHARD: **Just Lois. He didn't know everybody.**

. . .

TODD: I just felt really out of place that day, all over the place. I used to feel, I mean—

RICHARD: **Why?**

TODD: I don't know. I don't even feel right in school anymore.

RICHARD: **I don't know, last night, I mean—**

TODD: I think I know what Ron Cameron and them feels like now. [Laugh]

RICHARD: **[Laugh] No, I don't think you feel as bad as Ron Cameron feels.**

TODD: I'm kidding.

RICHARD: **Mm-mm. Why should you? You know more people—**

TODD: I can't talk to anyone anymore.

RICHARD: **You know more people than me.**

By telling Todd that his feelings are unjustified and incomprehensible, Richard is not implying that he doesn't care. He clearly means to comfort his friend, to make him feel better. He's implying, "You shouldn't feel bad because your problems aren't so bad."

MATCHING TROUBLES

The very different way that women respond to the telling of troubles is dramatized in a short story, "New Haven," by Alice Mattison. Eleanor tells Patsy that she has fallen in love with a married man. Patsy responds by first displaying understanding and then offering a matching revelation about a similar experience:

> "Well," says Patsy. "I know how you feel."
> "You do?"
> "In a way, I do. Well, I should tell you. I've been sleeping with a married man for two years."

Patsy then tells Eleanor about her affair and how she feels about it. After they discuss Patsy's affair, however, Patsy says:

> "But you were telling me about this man and I cut you off. I'm sorry. See? I'm getting self-centered."
> "It's OK." But she is pleased again.

The conversation then returns to Eleanor's incipient affair. Thus Patsy responds first by confirming Eleanor's feelings and matching her experience, reinforcing their similarity, and then by encouraging Eleanor to tell more. Within the frame of Patsy's similar predicament, the potential asymmetry inherent in revealing personal problems is avoided, and the friendship is brought into balance.

What made Eleanor's conversation with Patsy so pleasing to Eleanor was that they shared a sense of how to talk about troubles, and this reinforced their friendship. Though Eleanor raised the matter of her affair, she did not elaborate on it until Patsy pressed her to do so. In another story by the same author, "The Knitting," a woman named Beth is staying with her sister in order to visit her sister's daughter Stephanie in a psychiatric hospital. While there, Beth receives a disturbing telephone call from her boyfriend, Alec. Having been thus reminded of her troubles, she wants to talk about them, but she refrains, because her sister doesn't ask. She feels required, instead, to focus on her sister's problem, the reason for her visit:

> She'd like to talk about her muted half-quarrels with Alec of the last weeks, but her sister does not ask about the phone call. Then Beth thinks they should talk about Stephanie.

The women in these stories are balancing a delicate system by which troubles talk is used to confirm their feelings and create a sense of community.

When women confront men's ways of talking to them, they judge them by the standards of women's conversational styles. Women show concern by following up someone else's statement of trouble by questioning her about it. When men change the subject, women think they are showing a lack of sympathy—a failure of intimacy. But the failure to ask probing questions could just as well be a way of respecting the other's need for independence. When Eleanor tells Patsy that she is in love with Peter, Patsy asks, "Are you sleeping with him?" This exploration of Eleanor's topic could well strike many men—and some women—as intrusive, though Eleanor takes it as a show of interest that nourishes their friendship.

Women tend to show understanding of another woman's feelings. When men try to reassure women by telling them that their situation is not so bleak, the women hear their feelings being belittled or discounted. Again, they encounter a failure of intimacy just when they were bidding to reinforce it. Trying to trigger a symmetrical communication, they end up in an asymmetrical one.

A DIFFERENT SYMMETRY

The conversation between Richard and Todd shows that although the boys' responses are asymmetrical if looked at separately—each dismisses the other's concerns—they are symmetrical when looked at together: Todd responds to Richard's concern about his drinking in exactly the same way that Richard responds to Todd's feeling of alienation, by denying it is a problem:

RICHARD: Hey, man, I just don't feel— I mean, after what Anne said last night, I just don't feel like doing that.

TODD: **I don't think it was that way. You yourself knew it was no big problem.**

RICHARD: Oh, Anne— Sam told Anne that I fell down the levee.

TODD: **It's a lie.**

RICHARD: I didn't fall. I slipped, slid. I caught myself.

TODD: **Don't worry about it.**

RICHARD: But I do, kind of. I feel funny in front of Sam. I don't want to do it in front of you.

TODD: **It doesn't matter 'cause sometimes you're funny when you're off your butt.**

Todd denies that Richard was so drunk he was staggering ("It's a lie") and then says that even if he was out of control, it wasn't bad; it was funny.

In interpreting this conversation between tenth-grade boys, I initially saw their mutual reassurances and dismissals, and their mutual revelations of troubles, in terms of connection and sameness. But another perspective is possible. Their conversation may be touching precisely because it was based on asymmetries of status—or, more precisely, a deflecting of such asymmetries. When Todd tells his troubles, he puts himself in a potentially one-down position and invites Richard to take a one-up position by disclaiming troubles and asymmetrically offering advice or sympathy. By offering troubles of his own, Richard declines to take the superior position and restores their symmetrical footing, sending the metamessage "We're just a couple of guys trying to make it in a world that's tough on both of us, and both of us are about equally competent to deal with it."

From this perspective, responding as a woman might—for example by saying, "I can see how you feel; you must feel awful; so would I if it happened to me"—would have a totally different meaning for boys, since they would be inclined to interpret it through the lens of status. Such a response would send a meta-message like "Yes, I know, you incompetent jerk, I know how awful you must feel. If I were as incompetent as you, I'd feel the same way. But, lucky for you, I'm not, and I can help you out here, because I'm far too talented to be upset by a problem like that." In other words, refraining from expressing sympathy is generous, insofar as sympathy potentially condescends.

Women are often unhappy with the reactions they get from men when they try to start troubles talk, and men are often unhappy because they are accused of responding in the wrong way when they are trying to be helpful. But Richard and Todd seem satisfied with each other's ways of reacting to their troubles. And their ways make sense. When men and women talk to each other, the problem is that each expects a different kind of response. The men's approach seeks to assuage feelings indirectly by attacking their cause. Since women expect to have their feelings supported, the men's approach makes them feel that they themselves are being attacked.

"Don't Ask"

Talking about troubles is just one of many conversational tasks that women and men view differently, and that consequently cause trouble in talk between them. Another is asking for information. And this difference too is traceable to the asymmetries of status and connection.

A man and a woman were standing beside the information booth at the Washington Folk Life Festival, a sprawling complex of booths and displays. "You ask," the man was saying to the woman. "I don't ask."

Sitting in the front seat of the car beside Harold, Sybil is fuming. They have been driving around for half an hour looking for a street he is sure is close by. Sybil is angry not because Harold does not know the way, but because he insists on trying to find it himself rather than stopping and asking someone. Her anger stems from viewing his behavior through the lens of her own: If she were driving, she would have asked directions as soon as she realized she didn't know which way to go, and they'd now be comfortably ensconced in their friends' living room instead of driving in circles, as the hour gets later and later. Since asking directions does not make Sybil uncomfortable, refusing to ask makes no sense to her. But in Harold's world, driving around until he finds his way is the reasonable thing to do, since asking for help makes him uncomfortable. He's avoiding that discomfort and trying to maintain his sense of himself as a self-sufficient person.

Why do many men resist asking for directions and other kinds of information? And, it is just as reasonable to ask, why is it that many women don't? By the paradox of independence and intimacy, there are two simultaneous and different metamessages implied in asking for and giving information. Many men tend to focus on one, many women on the other.

When you offer information, the information itself is the message. But the fact that you have the information, and the person you are speaking to doesn't, also sends a metamessage of superiority. If relations are inherently hierarchical, then the one who has more information is framed as higher up on the ladder, by virtue of being more knowledgeable and competent. From this perspective, finding one's own way is an essential part of the independence that men perceive to be a prerequisite for self-respect. If self-respect is bought at the cost of a few extra minutes of travel time, it is well worth the price.

Because they are implicit, metamessages are hard to talk about. When Sybil begs to know why Harold won't just ask someone for directions, he answers in terms of the message, the information: He says there's no point in asking, because anyone he asks may not know and may give him wrong directions. This is theoretically reasonable. There are many countries, such as, for example, Mexico, where it is standard procedure for people to make up directions rather than refuse to give requested information. But this explanation frustrates Sybil, because it doesn't make sense to her. Although she realizes that someone might give faulty directions, she believes this is relatively unlikely, and surely it cannot happen every time. Even if it did happen, they would be in no worse shape than they are in now anyway.

Part of the reason for their different approaches is that Sybil believes that a person who doesn't know the answer will say so, because it is easy to say, "I don't know." But Harold believes that saying "I don't know" is humiliating, so people might well take a wild guess. Because of their different assumptions, and the invisibility of framing, Harold and Sybil can never get to the bottom of this difference; they can only get more frustrated with each other. Keeping talk on the message level is common, because it is the level we are most clearly aware of. But it is unlikely to resolve confusion since our true motivations lie elsewhere.

To the extent that giving information, directions, or help is of use to another, it reinforces bonds between people. But to the extent that it is asymmetrical, it creates hierarchy: Insofar as giving information frames one as the expert, superior in knowledge, and the other as uninformed, inferior in knowledge, it is a move in the negotiation of status.

It is easy to see that there are many situations where those who give information are higher in status. For example, parents explain things to children and answer their questions, just as teachers give information to students. An awareness of this dynamic underlies one requirement for proper behavior at Japanese dinner entertainment, according to anthropologist Harumi Befu. In order to help the highest-status member of the party to dominate the conversation, others at the dinner are expected to ask him questions that they know he can answer with authority.

Because of this potential for asymmetry, some men resist receiving information from others, especially women, and some women are cautious about stating information that they know, especially to men. For example, a man with whom I discussed these dynamics later told me that my perspective clarified a comment made by his wife. They had gotten into their car and were about to go to a destination that she knew well but he did not know at all. Consciously resisting an impulse to just drive off and find his own way, he began by asking his wife if she had any advice about the best way to get there. She told him the way, then added, "But I don't know. That's how I would go, but there might be a better way." Her comment was a move to redress the imbalance of power created by her knowing something he didn't know. She was also saving face in advance, in case he decided not to take her advice. Furthermore, she was reframing her directions as "just a suggestion" rather than "giving instructions."

"I'LL FIX IT IF IT KILLS ME"

The asymmetry implied in having and giving information is also found in having and demonstrating the skill to fix things—an orientation that we saw in men's approaches to troubles talk. To further explore the framing involved in fixing things, I will present a small encounter of my own.

Unable to remove the tiny lid that covers the battery compartment for the light meter on my camera, I took the camera to a photography store and asked for help. The camera salesman tried to unscrew the lid, first with a dime and then with a special instrument. When this failed, he declared the lid hopelessly stuck. He explained the reason (it was screwed in with the threads out of alignment) and then explained in detail how I could take pictures without a light meter by matching the light conditions to shutter settings in accordance with the chart included in rolls of film. Even though I knew there wasn't a chance in the world I would adopt his system, I listened politely, feigning interest, and assiduously wrote down his examples, based on an ASA of 100, since he got confused trying to give examples based on an ASA of 64. He further explained that this method was actually superior to using a light meter. In this way, he minimized the significance of not being able to help by freeing the battery lid; he framed himself as possessing useful knowledge and having solved my problem even though he couldn't fix my camera. This man wanted to help me—which I sincerely appreciated—but he also wanted to demonstrate that he had the information and skill required to help, even though he didn't.

There is a kind of social contract operating here. Many women not only feel comfortable seeking help, but feel honor-bound to seek it, accept it, and display gratitude in exchange. For their part, many men feel honor-bound to fulfill the request for help whether or not it is convenient for them to do so. A man told me about a time when a neighbor asked him if he could fix her car, which was intermittently stalling out. He spent more time than he could spare looking at her car, and concluded that he did not have the equipment needed to do the repair. He felt bad about not having succeeded in solving her problem. As if sensing this, she told him the next day, and the next, that her car was much better now, even though he knew he had done nothing to improve its performance. There is a balance between seeking help and showing appreciation. Women and men seem equally bound by the requirements of this arrangement: She was bound to show appreciation even though he hadn't helped, and he was bound to invest time and effort that he really couldn't spare, in trying to help.

Another example of the social contract of asking for help and showing appreciation occurred on a street corner in New York City. A woman emerged from the subway at Twenty-third Street and Park Avenue South, and was temporarily confused about which direction to walk in to reach Madison Avenue. She knew that Madison was west of Park, so with a little effort she could have figured out which way to go. But without planning or thinking, she asked the first person to appear before her. He replied that Madison did not come down that far south. Now, she knew this to be false. Furthermore, by this time she had oriented herself. But instead of saying, "Yes, it does," or "Never mind, I don't need your help," she found a way to play out the scene as one in which he helped her. She asked, "Which way is west?" and, on being told, replied, "Thank you. I'll just walk west."

From the point of view of getting directions, this encounter was absurd from start to finish. The woman didn't really need help, and the man wasn't in a position to give it. But getting directions really wasn't the main point. She had used the commonplace ritual of asking directions of a stranger not only—and not mostly—to find her way on emerging from the subway, but to reinforce her connection to the mass of people in the big city by making fleeting contact with one of them. Asking for help was simply an automatic way for her to do this.

"I'LL HELP YOU IF IT KILLS YOU"

Martha bought a computer and needed to learn to use it. After studying the manual and making some progress, she still had many questions, so she went to the store where she had bought it and asked for help. The man assigned to help her made her feel like the stupidest person in the world. He used technical language in explaining things, and each time she had to ask what a word meant she felt more incompetent, an impression reinforced by the tone of voice he used in his answer, a tone that sent the metamessage "This is obvious; everyone knows this." He explained things so quickly, she couldn't possibly remember them. When she went home, she discovered she couldn't recall what he had demonstrated, even in cases where she had followed his explanation at the time.

Still confused, and dreading the interaction, Martha returned to the store a week later, determined to stay until she got the information she needed. But this time a woman was assigned to help her. And the experience of getting help was utterly transformed. The woman avoided using technical terms for the most part, and if she did use one, she asked whether Martha knew what it meant and explained simply and clearly if she didn't. When the woman answered questions, her tone never implied that everyone should know this. And when showing how to do something, she had Martha do it, rather than demonstrating while Martha watched. The different style of this "teacher" made Martha feel like a different "student": a competent rather than stupid one, not humiliated by her ignorance.

Surely not all men give information in a way that confuses and humiliates their students. There are many gifted teachers who also happen to be men. And not all women give information in a way that makes it easy for students to understand. But many women report experiences similar to Martha's, especially in dealing with computers, automobiles, and other mechanical equipment; they claim that they feel more comfortable having women explain things to them. The different meanings that giving help entails may explain why. If women are focusing on connections, they will be motivated to minimize the difference in expertise and to be as comprehensible as possible. Since their goal is to maintain the appearance of similarity and equal status, sharing knowledge helps even the score. Their tone of voice sends metamessages of support rather than disdain, although "support" itself can be experienced as condescension.

If a man focuses on the negotiation of status and feels someone must have the upper hand, he may feel more comfortable when he has it. His attunement to the fact that having more information, knowledge, or skill puts him in a one-up position comes through in his way of talking. And if sometimes men seem intentionally to explain in a way that makes what they are explaining difficult to understand, it may be because their pleasant feeling of knowing more is reinforced when the student *does not* understand. The comfortable margin of superiority diminishes with every bit of knowledge the student gains. Or it may simply be that they are more concerned with displaying their superior knowledge and skill than with making sure that the knowledge is shared.

A colleague familiar with my ideas remarked that he'd seen evidence of this difference at an academic conference. A woman delivering a paper kept stopping and asking the audience, "Are you with me so far?" My colleague surmised that her main concern seemed to be that the audience understand what she was saying. When he gave his paper, his main concern was that he not be put down by members of the audience—and as far as he could tell, a similar preoccupation was motivating the other men presenting papers as well. From this point of view, if covering one's tracks to avoid attack entails obscuring one's point, it is a price worth paying.

This is not to say that women have no desire to feel knowledgeable or powerful. Indeed, the act of asking others whether they are able to follow your argument can be seen to frame you as superior. But it seems that having information, expertise, or skill at manipulating objects is not the primary measure of power for most women. Rather, they feel their power enhanced if they can be of help. Even more, if they are focusing on connection rather than independence and self-reliance, they feel stronger when the community is strong.

"TRUST ME"

A woman told me that she was incredulous when her husband dredged up an offense from years before. She had been unable to get their VCR to record movies aired on HBO. Her husband had looked at the VCR and declared it incapable of performing this function. Rather than accepting his judgment, she asked their neighbor, Harry, to take a look at it, since he had once fixed her VCR in the past. Harry's conclusion was the same as that of her husband, who was, however, incensed that his wife had not trusted his expertise. When he brought it up years later, the wife exclaimed in disbelief, "You still remember that? Harry is dead!" The incident, though insignificant to the wife, cut to the core of the husband's self-respect, because it called into question his knowledge and skill at managing the mechanical world.

Trust in a man's skill is also at issue between Felicia and Stan, another couple. Stan is angered when Felicia gasps in fear while he is driving. "I've never had an acident!" he protests. "Why can't you trust my driving?" Felicia cannot get him to see her point of view—that she does not distrust *his* driving in particular but is frightened of driving in general. Most of all, she cannot understand why the small matter of involuntarily sucking in her breath should spark such a strong reaction.

"BE NICE"

Having expertise and skill can reinforce both women's and men's sense of themselves. But the stance of expert is more fundamental to our notion of masculinity than to our concept of femininity. Women, according to convention, are more inclined to be givers of praise than givers of information. That women are expected to praise is reflected in a poster that was displayed in every United States post office branch inviting customers to send criticism, suggestions, questions, and compliments. Three of these four linguistic acts were represented by sketches of men; only compliments were represented by a sketch of a woman with a big smile on her face, a gesture of approval on her fingers, and a halo around her head. The halo is especially interesting. It shows that the act of complimenting frames the speaker as "nice."

Giving praise, like giving information, is also inherently asymmetrical. It too frames the speaker as one-up, in a position to judge someone else's performance. Women can also be framed as one-up by their classic helping activities as mothers, social workers, nurses, counselors, and psychologists. But in many of these roles—especially mothers and nurses—they may also be seen as doing others' bidding.

OVERLAPPING MOTIVATIONS

When acting as helpers, women and men typically perform different kinds of tasks. But even the same task can be approached with eyes on different goals, and this difference is likely to result in misjudgments of others' intentions. The end of my camera story underlines this. At a family gathering, I brought the camera to my brother-in-law, who has a reputation in the family for mechanical ability. He took it to his workshop and returned an hour and a half later, having fixed it. Delighted and grateful, I commented to his daughter, "I knew he would enjoy the challenge." "Especially," she pointed out, "when it involves helping someone." I felt then that I had mistaken his displayed concern with the mechanics of the recalcitrant battery cover as reflecting his ultimate concern. But fixing the camera was a way of showing concern for me, of helping me with his effort. If women directly offer help, my brother-in-law was indirectly offering help, through the mediation of my camera.

A colleague who heard my analysis of this experience thought I had missed an aspect of my broken-camera episode. He pointed out that many men get a sense of pleasure from fixing things because it reinforces their feeling of being in control, self-sufficient, and able to dominate the world of objects. (This is the essence of Evelyn Fox Keller's thesis that the conception of science as dominating and controlling nature is essentially masculine in spirit.) He told me of an incident in which a toy plastic merry-go-round, ordered for his little boy, arrived in pieces, having come apart during shipping. His wife gave the toy to her uncle, renowned in the family as a fixer and helper. Her uncle worked for several hours and repaired the toy—even though it was probably not worth more than a few dollars. The uncle brought this up again the next time he saw them, and said he would have stayed up all night rather than admit he couldn't put it together. My colleague was convinced that the motivation to gain dominion over the plastic object had been stronger than the motivation to help his sister and nephew, though both had been present.

Furthermore, this man pointed out that he, and many other men, take special pleasure in showing their strength over the world of objects for the benefit of attractive women, because the thanks and admiration they receive is an added source of pleasure and satisfaction. His interpretation of my revised analysis was that my niece and I, both women, would be inclined to see the helping aspect of an act as the "real" or main motive, whereas he still was inclined to see the pleasure of demonstrating skill, succeeding where the camera expert had failed, and whacking the recalcitrant battery lid into line as the main ones.

The element of negotiating status that characterizes many men's desire to show they are knowledgeable and skillful does not negate the connection implied in helping. These elements coexist and feed each other. But women's and men's tendencies to place different relative weights on status versus connection result in asymmetrical roles. Attuned to the metamessage of connection, many women are comfortable both receiving help and giving it, though surely there are many women who are comfortable only in the role of giver of help and support. Many men, sensitive to the dynamic of status, the need to help women, and the need to be self-reliant, are comfortable in the role of giving information and help but not in receiving it.

THE VIEW FROM A DIFFERENT MOUNTAIN

In a story by Alice Mattison, "The Colorful Alphabet," a man named Joseph invites another man, Gordon, to visit his family in the country, because Gordon's wife has just left him. During the visit, they all climb a mountain. On the way down, they stop to rest, and Gordon realizes that he left his beloved old knapsack on the mountaintop. Joseph volunteers to climb back up to get it, because Gordon is not used to climbing and his feet are sore. Joseph's wife goes with him, but she is too tired to climb all the way to the top, and he leaves her on the path to complete the mission himself. When he finds her again, he is empty-handed: The bag wasn't there. He says then that he knew it wouldn't be, because he had seen a man carrying the bag pass them when they all stopped to rest. He explains why he didn't just say that he had seen someone go by with the bag: "I couldn't tell him I'd seen it and hadn't been smart enough to get it back for him." Instead, he says, "I had to *do* something."

Exhausted and frustrated, the wife is not so much angry as incredulous. She can't understand how he could have preferred reclimbing the mountain (and making her reclimb it too) to admitting that he had seen someone carrying Gordon's bag. "I would never have done that," she says, but she speaks "more in wonder than anger." She explains, "I'd have just blurted it out. I'd have been upset about making the mistake—but not about people *knowing*. That part's not a big deal to me." Her husband says, "Oh, is it ever a big deal to me."

This story supports the view of men's style that I have been proposing. Joseph wanted to help Gordon, and he did not want to let it be known that he had done something he thought stupid. His impulse to do something to solve the problem was stronger than his impulse not to climb a mountain twice. But what struck me most strongly about the story was the wife's reflections on the experience. She thinks:

> It was one of the occasional moments when I'm certain I haven't imagined him: I would never have done what he'd done, wouldn't have dreamt it or invented it—Joseph was, simply, *not me*.

This excerpt reflects what may be the subtlest yet deepest source of frustration and puzzlement arising from the different ways that women and men approach the world. We feel we know how the world is, and we look to others to reinforce that conviction. When we see others acting as if the world were an entirely different place from the one we inhabit, we are shaken.

We look to our closest relationships as a source of confirmation and reassurance. When those closest to us respond to events differently than we do, when they seem to see the same scene as part of a different play, when they say things that we could not imagine saying in the same circumstances, the ground on which we stand seems to tremble and our footing is suddenly unsure. Being able to understand why this happens—*why* and *how* our partners and friends, though like us in many ways, are *not* us, and different in other ways—is a crucial step toward feeling that our feet are planted on firm ground.

THREE

"Put Down That Paper and Talk to Me!": Rapport-talk and Report-talk

I was sitting in a suburban living room, speaking to a women's group that had invited men to join them for the occasion of my talk about communication between women and men. During the discussion, one man was particularly talkative, full of lengthy comments and explanations. When I made the observation that women often complain that their husbands don't talk to them enough, this man volunteered that he heartily agreed. He gestured toward his wife, who had sat silently beside him on the couch throughout the evening, and said, "She's the talker in our family."

Everyone in the room burst into laughter. The man looked puzzled and hurt. "It's true," he explained. "When I come home from work, I usually have nothing to say, but she never runs out.

If it weren't for her, we'd spend the whole evening in silence." Another woman expressed a similar paradox about her husband: "When we go out, he's the life of the party. If I happen to be in another room, I can always hear his voice above the others. But when we're home, he doesn't have that much to say. I do most of the talking."

Who talks more, women or men? According to the stereotype, women talk too much. Linguist Jennifer Coates notes some proverbs:

A woman's tongue wags like a lamb's tail.

Foxes are all tail and women are all tongue.

The North Sea will sooner be found wanting in water than a woman be at a loss for a word.

Throughout history, women have been punished for talking too much or in the wrong way. Linguist Connie Eble lists a variety of physical punishments used in Colonial America: Women were strapped to ducking stools and held underwater until they nearly drowned, put into the stocks with signs pinned to them, gagged, and silenced by a cleft stick applied to their tongues.

Though such institutionalized corporal punishments have given way to informal, often psychological ones, modern stereotypes are not much different from those expressed in the old proverbs. Women are believed to talk too much. Yet study after study finds that it is men who talk more—at meetings, in mixed-group discussions, and in classrooms where girls or young women sit next to boys or young men. For example, communications researchers Barbara and Gene Eakins tape-recorded and studied seven university faculty meetings. They found that, with one exception, men spoke more often and, without exception, spoke for a longer time. The men's turns ranged from 10.66 to 17.07 seconds, while the women's turns ranged from 3 to 10 seconds. In other words, the women's longest turns were still shorter than the men's shortest turns.

When a public lecture is followed by questions from the floor, or a talk show host opens the phones, the first voice to be heard asking a question is almost always a man's. And when they ask questions or offer comments from the audience, men tend to talk longer. Linguist Marjorie Swacker recorded question-and-answer sessions at academic conferences. Women were highly visible as speakers at the conferences studied; they presented 40.7 percent of the papers at the conferences studied and made up 42 percent of the audiences. But when it came to volunteering and being called on to ask questions, women contributed only 27.4 percent. Furthermore, the women's questions, on the average, took less than half as much time as the men's. (The mean was 23.1 seconds for women, 52.7 for men.) This happened, Swacker shows, because men (but not women) tended to preface their questions with statements, ask more than one question, and follow up the speaker's answer with another question or comment.

I have observed this pattern at my own lectures, which concern issues of direct relevance to women. Regardless of the proportion of women and men in the audience, men almost invariably ask the first question, more questions, and longer questions. In these situations, women often feel that men are talking too much. I recall one discussion period following a lecture I gave to a group assembled in a bookstore. The group was composed mostly of women, but most of the discussion was being conducted by men in the audience. At one point, a man sitting in the middle was talking at such great length that several women in the front rows began shifting in their seats and rolling their eyes at me. Ironically, what he was going on about was how frustrated he feels when he has to listen to women going on and on about topics he finds boring and unimportant.

RAPPORT-TALK AND REPORT-TALK

Who talks more, then, women or men? The seemingly contradictory evidence is reconciled by the difference between what I call *public* and *private speaking*. More men feel comfortable doing "public speaking," while more women feel comfortable doing "private" speaking. Another way of capturing these differences is by using the terms *report-talk* and *rapport-talk*.

For most women, the language of conversation is primarily a language of rapport: a way of establishing connections and negotiating relationships. Emphasis is placed on displaying similarities and matching experiences. From childhood, girls criticize peers who try to stand out or appear better than others. People feel their closest connections at home, or in settings where they *feel* at home—with one or a few people they feel close to and comfortable with—in other words, during private speaking. But even the most public situations can be approached like private speaking.

For most men, talk is primarily a means to preserve independence and negotiate and maintain status in a hierarchical social order. This is done by exhibiting knowledge and skill, and by holding center stage through verbal performance such as storytelling, joking, or imparting information. From childhood, men learn to use talking as a way to get and keep attention. So they are more comfortable speaking in larger groups made up of people they know less well—in the broadest sense, "public speaking." But even the most private situations can be approached like public speaking, more like giving a report than establishing rapport.

PRIVATE SPEAKING: THE WORDY WOMAN AND THE MUTE MAN

What is the source of the stereotype that women talk a lot? Dale Spender suggests that most people feel instinctively (if not consciously) that women, like children, should be seen and not heard, so any amount of talk from them seems like too much. Studies have shown that if women and men talk equally in a group, people think the women talked more. So there is truth to Spender's view. But another explanation is that men think women talk a lot because they hear women talking in situations where men would not: on the telephone; or in social situations with friends, when they are not discussing topics that men find inherently interesting; or, like the couple at the women's group, at home alone—in other words, in private speaking.

Home is the setting for an American icon that features the silent man and the talkative woman. And this icon, which grows out of the different goals and habits I have been describing, explains why the complaint most often voiced by women about the men with whom they are intimate is "He doesn't talk to me"—and the second most frequent is "He doesn't listen to me."

A woman who wrote to Ann Landers is typical:

> My husband never speaks to me when he comes home from work. When I ask, "How did everything go today?" he says, "Rough . . ." or "It's a jungle out there." (We live in Jersey and he works in New York City.)
>
> It's a different story when we have guests or go visiting. Paul is the gabbiest guy in the crowd—a real spellbinder. He comes up with the most interesting stories. People hang on every word. I think to myself, "Why doesn't he ever tell *me* these things?"
>
> This has been going on for 38 years. Paul started to go quiet on me after 10 years of marriage. I could never figure out why. Can you solve the mystery?
>
> —The Invisible Woman

Ann Landers suggests that the husband may not want to talk because he is tired when he comes home from work. Yet women who work come home tired too, and they are nonetheless eager to tell their partners or friends everything that happened to them during the day and what these fleeting, daily dramas made them think and feel.

Sources as lofty as studies conducted by psychologists, as down to earth as letters written to advice columnists, and as sophisticated as movies and plays come up with the same insight: Men's silence at home is a disappointment to women. Again and again, women complain, "He seems to have everything to say to everyone else, and nothing to say to me."

The film *Divorce American Style* opens with a conversation in which Debbie Reynolds is claiming that she and Dick Van Dyke don't communicate, and he is protesting that he tells her everything that's on his mind. The doorbell interrupts their quarrel, and husband and wife compose themselves before opening the door to greet their guests with cheerful smiles.

Behind closed doors, many couples are having conversations like this. Like the character played by Debbie Reynolds, women feel men don't communicate. Like the husband played by Dick Van Dyke, men feel wrongly accused. How can she be convinced that he doesn't tell her anything, while he is equally convinced he tells her everything that's on his mind? How can women and men have such different ideas about the same conversations?

When something goes wrong, people look around for a source to blame: either the person they are trying to communicate with ("You're demanding, stubborn, self-centered") or the group that the other person belongs to ("All women are demanding"; "All men are self-centered"). Some generous-minded people blame the relationship ("We just can't communicate"). But underneath, or overlaid on these types of blame cast outward, most people believe that something is wrong with them.

If individual people or particular relationships were to blame, there wouldn't be so many different people having the same problems. The real problem is conversational style. Women and men have different ways of talking. Even with the best intentions, trying to settle the problem through talk can only make things worse if it is ways of talking that are causing trouble in the first place.

BEST FRIENDS

Once again, the seeds of women's and men's styles are sown in the ways they learn to use language while growing up. In our culture, most people, but especially women, look to their closest relationships as havens in a hostile world. The center of a little girl's social life is her best friend. Girls' friendships are made and maintained by telling secrets. For grown women too, the essence of friendship is talk, telling each other what they're thinking and feeling, and what happened that day: who was at the bus stop, who called, what they said, how that made them feel. When asked who their best friends are, most women name other women they talk to regularly. When asked the same question, most men will say it's their wives. After that, many men name other men with whom they do things such as play tennis or baseball (but never just sit and talk) or a chum from high school whom they haven't spoken to in a year.

When Debbie Reynolds complained that Dick Van Dyke didn't tell her anything, and he protested that he did, both were right. She felt he didn't tell her anything because he didn't tell her the fleeting thoughts and feelings he experienced throughout the day—the kind of talk she would have with her best friend. He didn't tell her these things because to him they didn't seem like anything to tell. He told her anything that seemed important—anything he would tell his friends.

Men and women often have very different ideas of what's important—and at what point "important" topics should be raised. A woman told me, with lingering incredulity, of a conversation with her boyfriend. Knowing he had seen his friend Oliver, she asked, "What's new with Oliver?" He replied, "Nothing." But later in the conversation it came out that Oliver and his girlfriend had decided to get married. "That's nothing?" the woman gasped in frustration and disbelief.

For men, "Nothing" may be a ritual response at the start of a conversation. A college woman missed her brother but rarely called him because she found it difficult to get talk going. A typical conversation began with her asking, "What's up with you?" and his replying, "Nothing." Hearing his "Nothing" as meaning "There is nothing personal I want to talk about," she supplied talk by filling him in on her news and eventually hung up in frustration. But when she thought back, she remembered that later in the conversation he had mumbled, "Christie and I got into another fight." This came so late and so low that she didn't pick up on it. And he was probably equally frustrated that she didn't.

Many men honestly do not know what women want, and women honestly do not know why men find what they want so hard to comprehend and deliver.

"TALK TO ME!"

Women's dissatisfaction with men's silence at home is captured in the stock cartoon setting of a breakfast table at which a husband and wife are sitting: He's reading a newspaper; she's glaring at the back of the newspaper. In a Dagwood strip, Blondie complains, "Every morning all he sees is the newspaper! I'll bet you don't even know I'm here!" Dagwood reassures her, "Of course I know you're here. You're my wonderful wife and I love you very much." With this, he unseeingly pats the paw of the family dog, which the wife has put in her place before leaving the room. The cartoon strip shows that Blondie is justified in feeling like the woman who wrote to Ann Landers: invisible.

Another cartoon shows a husband opening a newspaper and asking his wife, "Is there anything you would like to say to me before I begin reading the newspaper?" The reader knows that there isn't—but that as soon as he begins reading the paper, she will think of something. The cartoon highlights the difference in what women and men think talk is for: To him, talk is for information. So when his wife interrupts his reading, it must be to inform him of something that he needs to know. This being the case, she might as well tell him what she thinks he needs to know before he starts reading. But to her, talk is for interaction. Telling things is a way to show involvement, and listening is a way to show interest and caring. It is not an odd coincidence that she always thinks of things to tell him when he is reading. She feels the need for verbal interaction most keenly when he is (unaccountably, from her point of view) buried in the newspaper instead of talking to her.

Yet another cartoon shows a wedding cake that has, on top, in place of the plastic statues of bride and groom in tuxedo and gown, a breakfast scene in which an unshaven husband reads a newspaper across the table from his disgruntled wife. The cartoon reflects the enormous gulf between the romantic expectations of marriage represented by the plastic couple in traditional wedding costume, and the often disappointing reality represented by the two sides of the newspaper at the breakfast table—the front, which he is reading, and the back, at which she is glaring.

These cartoons, and many others on the same theme, are funny because people recognize their own experience in them. What's not funny is that many women are deeply hurt when men don't talk to them at home, and many men are deeply frustrated by feeling they have disappointed their partners, without understanding how they failed or how else they could have behaved.

Some men are further frustrated because, as one put it, "When in the world am I supposed to read the morning paper?" If many women are incredulous that many men do not exchange personal information with their friends, this man is incredulous that many women do not bother to read the morning paper. To him, reading the paper is an essential part of his morning ritual, and his whole day is awry if he doesn't get to read it. In his words, reading the newspaper in the morning is as important to him as putting on makeup in the morning is to many women he knows. Yet many women, he observed, either don't subscribe to a paper or don't read it until they get home in the evening. "I find this very puzzling," he said. "I can't tell you how often I have picked up a woman's morning newspaper from her front door in the evening and handed it to her when she opened the door for me."

To this man (and I am sure many others), a woman who objects to his reading the morning paper is trying to keep him from doing something essential and harmless. It's a violation of his independence—his freedom of action. But when a woman who expects her partner to talk to her is disappointed that he doesn't, she perceives his behavior as a failure of intimacy: He's keeping things from her; he's lost interest in her; he's pulling away. A woman I will call Rebecca, who is generally quite happily married, told me that this is the one source of serious dissatisfaction with her husband, Stuart. Her term for his taciturnity is *stinginess of spirit*. She tells him what she is thinking, and he listens silently. She asks him what he is thinking, and he takes a long time to answer, "I don't know." In frustration she challenges, "Is there nothing on your mind?"

For Rebecca, who is accustomed to expressing her fleeting thoughts and opinions as they come to her, *saying* nothing means *thinking* nothing. But Stuart does not assume that his passing thoughts are worthy of utterance. He is not in the habit of uttering his fleeting ruminations, so just as Rebecca "naturally" speaks her thoughts, he "naturally" dismisses his as soon as they occur to him. Speaking them would give them more weight and significance than he feels they merit. All her life she has had practice in verbalizing her thoughts and feelings in private conversations with people she is close to; all his life he has had practice in dismissing his and keeping them to himself.

WHAT TO DO WITH DOUBTS

In the above example, Rebecca was not talking about any particular kind of thoughts or feelings, just whatever Stuart might have had in mind. But the matter of giving voice to thoughts and feelings becomes particularly significant in the case of negative feelings or doubts about a relationship. This difference was highlighted for me when a fifty-year-old divorced man told me about his experiences in forming new relationships with women. On this matter, he was clear: "I do not value my fleeting thoughts, and I do not value the fleeting thoughts of others." He felt that the relationship he was currently in had been endangered, even permanently weakened, by the woman's practice of tossing out her passing thoughts, because, early in their courtship, many of her thoughts were fears about their relationship. Not surprisingly, since they did not yet know each other well, she worried about whether she could trust him, whether their relationship would destroy her independence, whether this relationship was really right for her. He felt she should have kept these fears and doubts to herself and waited to see how things turned out.

As it happens, things turned out well. The woman decided that the relationship was right for her, she could trust him, and she did not have to give up her independence. But he felt, at the time that he told me of this, that he had still not recovered from the wear and tear of coping with her earlier doubts. As he put it, he was still dizzy from having been bounced around like a yo-yo tied to the string of her stream of consciousness.

In contrast, this man admitted, he himself goes to the other extreme: He never expresses his fears and misgivings about their relationship at all. If he's unhappy but doesn't say anything about it, his unhappiness expresses itself in a kind of distancing coldness. This response is just what women fear most, and just the reason they prefer to express dissatisfactions and doubts—as an antidote to the isolation and distance that would result from keeping them to themselves.

The different perspectives on expressing or concealing dissatisfactions and doubts may reflect a difference in men's and women's awareness of the power of their words to affect others. In repeatedly telling him what she feared about their relationship, this woman spoke as though she assumed he was invulnerable and could not be hurt by what she said; perhaps she was underestimating the power of her words to affect him. For his part, when he refrains from expressing negative thoughts or feelings, he seems to be overestimating the power of his words to hurt her, when, ironically, she is more likely to be hurt by his silence than his words.

These women and men are talking in ways they learned as

children and reinforced as young adults and then adults, in their same-gender friendships. For girls, talk is the glue that holds relationships together. Boys' relationships are held together primarily by activities: doing things together, or talking about activities such as sports or, later, politics. The forums in which men are most inclined to talk are those in which they feel the need to impress, in situations where their status is in question.

MAKING ADJUSTMENTS

Such impasses will perhaps never be settled to the complete satisfaction of both parties, but understanding the differing views can help detoxify the situation, and both can make adjustments. Realizing that men and women have different assumptions about the place of talk in relationships, a woman can observe a man's desire to read the morning paper at the breakfast table without interpreting it as a rejection of her or a failure of their relationship. And a man can understand a woman's desire for talk without interpreting it as an unreasonable demand or a manipulative attempt to prevent him from doing what he wants to do.

A woman who had heard my interpretations of these differences between women and men told me how these insights helped her. Early in a promising relationship, a man spent the night at her apartment. It was a weeknight, and they both had to go to work the next day, so she was delighted when he made the rash and romantic suggestion that they have breakfast together and report late for work. She happily prepared breakfast, looking forward to the scene shaped in her mind: They would sit facing each other across her small table, look into each other's eyes, and say how much they liked each other and how happy they were about their growing friendship. It was against the backdrop of this heady expectation that she confronted an entirely different scene: As she placed on the table an array of lovingly prepared eggs, toast, and coffee, the man sat across her small table—and opened the newspaper in front of his face. If suggesting they have breakfast together had seemed like an invitation to get closer, in her view (or obstructing her view) the newspaper was now erected as a paper-thin but nonetheless impenetrable barrier between them.

Had she known nothing of the gender differences I discuss, she would simply have felt hurt and dismissed this man as yet another clunker. She would have concluded that, having enjoyed the night with her, he was now availing himself of her further services as a short-order cook. Instead, she realized that, unlike her, he did not feel the need for talk to reinforce their intimacy. The companionability of her presence was all he needed, and that did not mean that he didn't cherish her presence. By the same token, had he understood the essential role played by talk in women's definition of intimacy, he could have put off reading the paper—and avoided putting her off.

THE COMFORT OF HOME

For everyone, home is a place to be offstage. But the comfort of home can have opposite and incompatible meanings for women and men. For many men, the comfort of home means freedom from having to prove themselves and impress through verbal display. At last, they are in a situation where talk is not required. They are free to remain silent. But for women, home is a place where they are free to talk, and where they feel the greatest need for talk, with those they are closest to. For them, the comfort of home means the freedom to talk without worrying about how their talk will be judged.

This view emerged in a study by linguist Alice Greenwood of the conversations that took place among her three preadolescent children and their friends. Her daughters and son gave different reasons for their preferences in dinner guests. Her daughter Stacy said she would not want to invite people she didn't know well because then she would have to be "polite and quiet" and put on good manners. Greenwood's other daughter, Denise, said she liked to have her friend Meryl over because she could act crazy with Meryl and didn't have to worry about her manners, as she would with certain other friends who "would go around talking to people probably." But Denise's twin brother, Dennis, said nothing about having to watch his manners or worry about how others would judge his behavior. He simply said that he liked to have over friends with whom he could joke and laugh a lot. The girls' comments show that for them being close means being able to talk freely. And being with relative strangers means having to watch what they say and do. This insight holds a clue to the riddle of who talks more, women or men.

PUBLIC SPEAKING: THE TALKATIVE MAN AND THE SILENT WOMAN

So far I have been discussing the private scenes in which many men are silent and many women are talkative. But there are other scenes in which the roles are reversed. Returning to Rebecca and Stuart, we saw that when they are home alone, Rebecca's thoughts find their way into words effortlessly, whereas Stuart finds he can't come up with anything to say. The reverse happens when they are in other situations. For example, at a meeting of the neighborhood council or the parents' association at their children's school, it is Stuart who stands up and speaks. In that situation, it is Rebecca who is silent, her tongue tied by an acute awareness of all the negative reactions people could have to what she might say, all the mistakes she might make in trying to express her ideas. If she musters her courage and prepares to say something, she needs time to formulate it and then waits to be recognized by the chair. She cannot just jump up and start talking the way Stuart and some other men can.

Eleanor Smeal, president of the Fund for the Feminist Majority, was a guest on a call-in radio talk show, discussing abortion. No subject could be of more direct concern to women, yet during the hour-long show, all the callers except two were men. Diane Rehm, host of a radio talk show, expresses puzzlement that although the audience for her show is evenly split between women and men, 90 percent of the callers to the show are men. I am convinced that the reason is not that women are uninterested in the subjects discussed on the show. I would wager that women listeners are bringing up the subjects they heard on *The Diane Rehm Show* to their friends and family over lunch, tea, and dinner. But fewer of them call in because to do so would be putting themselves on display, claiming public attention for what they have to say, catapulting themselves onto center stage.

I myself have been the guest on innumerable radio and television talk shows. Perhaps I am unusual in being completely at ease in this mode of display. But perhaps I am not unusual at all, because, although I am comfortable in the role of invited expert, I have never called in to a talk show I was listening to, although I have often had ideas to contribute. When I am the guest, my position of authority is granted before I begin to speak. Were I to call in, I would be claiming that right on my own. I would have to establish my credibility by explaining who I am, which might seem self-aggrandizing, or not explain who I am and risk having my comments ignored or not valued. For similar reasons, though I am comfortable lecturing to groups numbering in the thousands, I rarely ask questions following another lecturer's talk, unless I know both the subject and the group very well.

My own experience and that of talk show hosts seems to hold a clue to the difference in women's and men's attitudes toward talk: Many men are more comfortable than most women in using talk to claim attention. And this difference lies at the heart of the distinction between report-talk and rapport-talk.

REPORT-TALK IN PRIVATE

Report-talk, or what I am calling public speaking, does not arise only in the literally public situation of formal speeches delivered to a listening audience. The more people there are in a conversation, the less well you know them, and the more status differences among them, the more a conversation is *like* public speaking or report-talk. The fewer the people, the more intimately you know them, and the more equal their status, the more it is like private speaking or rapport-talk. Furthermore, women feel a situation is more "public"—in the sense that they have to be on good behavior—if there are men present, except perhaps for family members. Yet even in families, the mother and children may feel their home to be "backstage" when Father is not home, "onstage" when he is: Many children are instructed to be on good behavior when Daddy is home. This may be because he is not home often, or because Mother—or Father—doesn't want the children to disturb him when he is.

The difference between public and private speaking also explains the stereotype that women don't tell jokes. Although some women are great raconteurs who can keep a group spellbound by recounting jokes and funny stories, there are fewer such personalities among women than among men. Many women who do tell jokes to large groups of people come from ethnic backgrounds in which verbal performance is highly valued. For example, many of the great women stand-up comics, such as Fanny Brice and Joan Rivers, came from Jewish backgrounds.

Although it's not true that women don't tell jokes, it is true that many women are less likely than men to tell jokes in large groups, especially groups including men. So it's not surprising that men get the impression that women never tell jokes at all. Folklorist Carol Mitchell studied joke telling on a college campus. She found that men told most of their jokes to other men, but they also told many jokes to mixed groups and to women. Women, however, told most of their jokes to other women, fewer to men, and very few to groups that included men as well as women. Men preferred and were more likely to tell jokes when they had an audience: at least two, often four or more. Women preferred a small audience of one or two, rarely more than three. Unlike men, they were reluctant to tell jokes in front of people they didn't know well. Many women flatly refused to tell jokes they knew if there were four or more in the group, promising to tell them later in private. Men never refused the invitation to tell jokes.

All of Mitchell's results fit in with the picture I have been drawing of public and private speaking. In a situation in which there are more people in the audience, more men, or more strangers, joke telling, like any other form of verbal performance, requires speakers to claim center stage and prove their abilities. These are the situations in which many women are reluctant to talk. In a situation that is more private, because the audience is small, familiar, and perceived to be members of a community (for example, other women), they are more likely to talk.

The idea that telling jokes is a kind of self-display does not imply that it is selfish or self-centered. The situation of joke telling illustrates that status and connection entail each other. Entertaining others is a way of establishing connections with them, and telling jokes can be a kind of gift giving, where the joke is a gift that brings pleasure to receivers. The key issue is asymmetry: One person is the teller and the others are the audience. If these roles are later exchanged—for example, if the joke telling becomes a round in which one person after another takes the role of teller—then there is symmetry on the broad scale, if not in the individual act. However, if women habitually take the role of appreciative audience and never take the role of joke teller, the asymmetry of the individual joke telling is diffused through the larger interaction as well. This is a hazard for women. A hazard for men is that continually telling jokes can be distancing. This is the effect felt by a man who complained that when he talks to his father on the phone, all his father does is tell him jokes. An extreme instance of a similar phenomenon is the class clown, who, according to teachers, is nearly always a boy.

RAPPORT-TALK IN PUBLIC

Just as conversations that take place at home among friends can be like public speaking, even a public address can be like private speaking: for example, by giving a lecture full of personal examples and stories.

At the executive committee of a fledgling professional organization, the outgoing president, Fran, suggested that the organization adopt the policy of having presidents deliver a presidential address. To explain and support her proposal, she told a personal anecdote: Her cousin was the president of a more established professional organization at the time that Fran held the same position in this one. Fran's mother had been talking to her cousin's mother on the telephone. Her cousin's mother told Fran's mother that her daughter was preparing her presidential address, and she asked when Fran's presidential address was scheduled to be. Fran was embarrassed to admit to her mother that she was not giving one. This made her wonder whether the organization's professional identity might not be enhanced if it emulated the more established organizations.

Several men on the committee were embarrassed by Fran's reference to her personal situation and were not convinced by her argument. It seemed to them not only irrelevant but unseemly to talk about her mother's telephone conversations at an executive committee meeting. Fran had approached the meeting—a relatively public context—as an extension of the private kind. Many women's tendency to use personal experience and examples, rather than abstract argumentation, can be understood from the perspective of their orientation to language as it is used in private speaking.

A study by Celia Roberts and Tom Jupp of a faculty meeting

at a secondary school in England found that the women's arguments did not carry weight with their male colleagues because they tended to use their own experience as evidence, or argue about the effect of policy on individual students. The men at the meeting argued from a completely different perspective, making categorical statements about right and wrong.

The same distinction is found in discussions at home. A man told me that he felt critical of what he perceived as his wife's lack of logic. For example, he recalled a conversation in which he had mentioned an article he had read in *The New York Times* claiming that today's college students are not as idealistic as students were in the 1960s. He was inclined to accept this claim. His wife questioned it, supporting her argument with the observation that her niece and her niece's friends were very idealistic indeed. He was incredulous and scornful of her faulty reasoning; it was obvious to him that a single personal example is neither evidence nor argumentation—it's just anecdote. It did not occur to him that he was dealing with a different logical system, rather than a lack of logic.

The logic this woman was employing was making sense of the world as a more private endeavor—observing and integrating her personal experience and drawing connections to the experiences of others. The logic the husband took for granted was a more public endeavor—more like gathering information, conducting a survey, or devising arguments by rules of formal logic as one might in doing research.

Another man complained about what he and his friends call women's "shifting sands" approach to discussion. These men feel that whereas they try to pursue an argument logically, step by step, until it is settled, women continually change course in midstream. He pointed to the short excerpt from *Divorce American Style* quoted above as a case in point. It seemed to him that when Debbie Reynolds said, "I can't argue now. I have to take the French bread out of the oven," she was evading the argument because she had made an accusation—"All you do is criticize"— that she could not support.

This man also offered an example from his own experience. His girlfriend had told him of a problem she had because her boss wanted her to do one thing and she wanted to do another. Taking the boss's view for the sake of argumentation, he pointed out a negative consequence that would result if she did what she wanted. She countered that the same negative consequence would result if she did what the boss wanted. He complained that she was shifting over to the other field of battle—what would happen if she followed her boss's will—before they had made headway with the first—what would happen if she followed her own.

SPEAKING FOR THE TEAM

A final puzzle on the matter of public and private speaking is suggested by the experience I related at the opening of this chapter, in which a woman's group I addressed had invited men to participate, and a talkative man had referred to his silent wife as "the talker in our family." Following their laughter, other women in the group commented that this woman was not usually silent. When their meetings consisted of women only, she did her share of talking. Why, then, was she silent on this occasion?

One possibility is that my presence transformed the private-speaking group into a public-speaking event. Another transformation was that there were men in the group. In a sense, most women feel they are "backstage" when there are no men around. When men are present women are "onstage," insofar as they feel they must watch their behavior more. Another possibility is that it was not the presence of men in general that affected this woman's behavior, but the presence of *her husband*. One interpretation is that she was somehow cowed, or silenced, by her husband's presence. But another is that she felt they were a team. Since he was talking a lot, the team would be taking up too much time if she spoke too. She also may have felt that because he was representing their team, she didn't have to, much as many women let their husbands drive if they are in the car, but do the driving themselves if their husbands are not there.

Obviously, not every woman becomes silent when her husband joins a group; after all, there were many women in the group who talked a lot, and many had brought spouses. But several other couples told me of similar experiences. For example, when one couple took evening classes together, he was always an active participant in class discussion, while she said very little. But one semester they had decided to take different classes, and then she found that she was a talkative member of the class she attended alone.

Such a development can be viewed in two different ways. If talking in a group is a good thing—a privilege and a pleasure—then the silent woman will be seen as deprived of her right to speak, deprived of her voice. But the pleasures of report-talk are not universally admired. There are many who do not wish to speak in a group. In this view, a woman who feels she has no need to speak because her husband is doing it for her might feel privileged, just as a woman who does not like to drive might feel lucky that she doesn't have to when her husband is there—and a man who does not like to drive might feel unlucky that he has to, like it or not.

AVOIDING MUTUAL BLAME

The difference between public and private speaking, or report-talk and rapport-talk, can be understood in terms of status and connection. It is not surprising that women are most comfortable talking when they feel safe and close, among friends and equals, whereas men feel comfortable talking when there is a need to establish and maintain their status in a group. But the situation is complex, because status and connection are bought with the same currency. What seems like a bid for status could be intended as a display of closeness, and what seems like distancing may have been intended to avoid the appearance of pulling rank. Hurtful and unjustified misinterpretations can be avoided by understanding the conversational styles of the other gender.

When men do all the talking at meetings, many women—including researchers—see them as "dominating" the meeting, intentionally preventing women from participating, publicly flexing their higher-status muscles. But the *result* that men do most of the talking does not necessarily mean that men *intend* to prevent women from speaking. Those who readily speak up assume that others are as free as they are to take the floor. In this sense, men's speaking out freely can be seen as evidence that they assume women are at the same level of status: "We are all equals," the metamessage of their behavior could be, "competing for the floor." If this is indeed the intention (and I believe it often, though not always, is), a woman can recognize women's lack of participation at meetings and take measures to redress the imbalance, without blaming men for intentionally locking them out.

The culprit, then, is not an individual man or even men's styles alone, but the difference between women's and men's styles. If that is the case, then both can make adjustments. A woman can push herself to speak up without being invited, or begin to speak without waiting for what seems a polite pause. But the adjustment should not be one-sided. A man can learn that a woman who is not accustomed to speaking up in groups is *not* as free as he is to do so. Someone who is waiting for a nice long pause before asking her question does not find the stage set for her appearance, as do those who are not awaiting a pause, the moment after (or before) another speaker stops talking. Someone who expects to be invited to speak ("You haven't said much, Millie. What do you think?") is not accustomed to leaping in and claiming the floor for herself. As in so many areas, being admitted as an equal is not in itself assurance of equal opportunity, if one is not accustomed to playing the game in the way it is being played. Being admitted to a dance does not ensure the participation of someone who has learned to dance to a different rhythm.

FOUR

Gossip

The impression that women talk too freely and too much in private situations is summed up in a word: *gossip*. Although gossip can be destructive, it isn't always; it can serve a crucial function in establishing intimacy—especially if it is not "talking against" but simply "talking about."

The label "gossip" casts a critical light on women's interest in talking about the details of people's lives. Evidence that the negativity of the term reflects men's interpretation of women's ways of talking can be seen in the following excerpt from Marge Piercy's novel *Fly Away Home*. Daria falls in love with Tom partly because he differs from her former husband, Ross, in this respect:

> It surprised her what he knew about the people around him. Ross would never have known that Gretta disliked her

son's teacher, or that Fay had just given walking papers to her boyfriend because he drank too much in front of her boys. For a man, Tom had an uncommon interest in the details of people's lives. Gossip, Ross would call it, but she thought it was just being interested in people.

Not only men disparage an interest in the details of people's lives as "gossip." The great southern writer Eudora Welty, remembering her Mississippi childhood, writes that her mother tried to keep a talkative seamstress from telling stories about local people in front of her little girl: " 'I don't want her exposed to gossip,' " Welty recalls her mother saying, "as if gossip were the measles and I could catch it." But far from having a bad influence on the child, the gossipy stories about people that Welty loved to hear inspired her to become a writer. When people talk about the details of daily lives, it is gossip; when they write about them, it is literature: short stories and novels.

Mary Catherine Bateson draws another parallel—between gossip and anthropology, the academic discipline that makes a career of documenting the details of people's lives. She recalls that her mother, Margaret Mead, told her she would never make an anthropologist because she wasn't interested enough in gossip.

IN GOSSIP BEGINS FRIENDSHIP

Telling details of others' lives is partly the result of women's telling their friends details of their own lives. These details become gossip when the friend to whom they are told repeats them to someone else—presumably another friend. Telling what's happening in your life and the lives of those you talk to is a grown-up version of telling secrets, the essence of girls' and women's friendships.

In Alice Mattison's story "New Haven," which I quoted in Chapter Two, Eleanor tells Patsy that she is falling in love with a married man. As soon as these words are out, Eleanor feels "a little ashamed to lack her secret suddenly," but "she also feels pleased; she doesn't have to guard it, for once. And it's exhilarating to talk about Peter." I was struck by Mattison's phrasing—"to lack her secret"—which captures the way that *having* a secret makes a person feel enhanced, and telling it is giving something away—in the sense of possession as well as the idiomatic sense of revelation. Mattison also captures the pleasure in not having to hide something, and being able to talk about what's really on your mind.

Not only is telling secrets evidence of friendship; it *creates* a friendship, when the listener responds in the expected way. Eleanor does not know Patsy well, but she would like to. There is an affinity and a budding friendship between them; they have taken to going together for coffee and ice cream following the rehearsals of the musical group in which they both play. By telling Patsy what was going on in her life, telling her secret, Eleanor promoted Patsy from acquaintance to friend.

Keeping friends up to date about the events in one's life is not only a privilege; for many women it is an obligation. One woman explained that she didn't enjoy telling the story of her breakup with her boyfriend over and over, but she had to, because if she had failed to inform any of her close friends about such an important development, they would have been deeply hurt when they found out. They would have taken her secrecy as a sign that she was curtailing their friendship, clipping its wings. The woman, furthermore, was incredulous when she learned that her boyfriend had not told anyone at all about their breakup. He had gone to work, gone to his gym, and played squash with his friends, all as if nothing had happened to change his life.

Because telling secrets is an essential part of friendship for most women, they may find themselves in trouble when they have no secrets to tell. For example, a woman I'll call Carol had several women friends she talked to every few days, exchanging stories about dates with men. They would share their excitement before a new date, and after the date took place, they would report in detail what had been said and done. So when Carol fell in love and formed a lasting relationship with a man, she ran out of material for talks with her friends. She also had less time to talk on the phone, since she now spent most of her free time with the man. This put a strain on her friendships; it was as if she had gathered up her marbles, reneging on her part in the partnership of talk that constituted the friendship.

Situations in which one person feels abandoned because the other forms a permanent relationship are not limited to women friends. In the story "Mendocino" by Ann Packer, the narrator, Bliss, finds it sad to visit her brother, who now lives with a woman, because his intimacy with the woman has diminished his intimacy with her. Bliss recalls their former closeness, when

> they would exchange work stories, and, into a second bottle of wine, confide in each other the news of their most recent failures at love. It amazes Bliss that until this moment she never once realized it was because they were failures that they talked about them. Now Gerald has his success, and it is as if the two of them had never been anything but what they are now: wary, cordial.

Because they are not exchanging secrets about relationships in one-on-one conversation, Bliss perceives her conversations with Gerald, now taking place in a group of three, to be wary and cordial—in a way, more like public speaking.

Many things conspire to separate people from their single friends if they find a stable relationship. I had a friend, a man, who had been single for many years and had developed a wide and strong network of women friends to whom he talked frequently. When he developed a stable relationship with a woman and they moved in together, his friends complained that he did not tell them anything anymore. "It's not that I'm keeping things from them," he told me. "It's just that Naomi and I get along fine and there's nothing to tell." By saying this, he did, however, tell me about a problem in his relationships—although it involved not his partner but his friends.

RAPPORT-TALK AS LAMENT

A folklorist, Anna Caraveli, studied women's laments in the villages of Greece. Laments are spontaneous, ritualized, oral poems that some Greek women chant to express grief over the loss of loved ones to expatriation or death. According to Caraveli, women typically recite laments in the company of other women. Even more significant, women feel they *need* other women to participate for the lament to be successful. One woman who performed a lament for Caraveli to tape remarked that she could have done it better if she'd had other women there to help her.

When the Greek women gather to share laments, each one's expression of grief reminds the others of their own suffering, and they intensify each other's feelings. Indeed, both Caraveli and anthropologist Joel Kuipers, who has studied a similar lament tradition in Bali, note that women judge each other's skill in this folk art by their ability to move others, to involve them in the experience of grieving. Expressing the pain they feel in losing loved ones bonds the women to each other, and their bonding is a salve against the wound of loss. According to anthropologist Joel Sherzer, the performance of "tuneful weeping" over dead loved ones is the exclusive domain of women in vastly differing societies all over the world.

Folk rituals of lament are parallel to the less formal but equally widespread ritual by which modern American and European women get together for troubles talk. They too bond in pain. This may explain why troubles make such good talk. Bonding through troubles is widespread among women and common between women and men. It seems to be far less common between men.

Some of the men I interviewed said they did not discuss their problems with anyone. Most of those who said they did told me they tended to discuss them with women friends. Some men said that they had a man friend with whom they discussed problems. But there were differences that indicated they were somewhere farther on the continuum from the pole of intimacy than most women. First of all, they had one friend, at most two, with whom they discussed problems, not several, or even many, as was the case with many women I talked to. Second, they often said they had not spoken to that friend in a while—days, weeks, months, or even longer—but they knew that if they needed him, he would be there. Most women were in constant touch with their closest friends, and frequently discussed even minor decisions and developments in their lives. One man told me he does have a friend that he tells his troubles to, but if he does not have a serious problem, he does not call his friend; that's why so much time can pass without their talking.

One woman, whom I will call Shirley, told me of her surprise at receiving a call from a man who had broken her heart; he said he wanted to come over and talk. It turned out that what he wanted to talk about was that he had just had his heart broken—by another woman. Shirley asked why he had come to her. He said there was no one else he could talk to about how he felt. What about his friends? He just didn't feel comfortable talking to them about something like this.

When most men talk to their friends on the phone, they may discuss what's happening in business, the stock market, the soccer match, or politics. They do gossip (although they may not call it that) in the sense of talking about themselves and other people. But they tend to talk about political rather than personal relationships: institutional power, advancement and decline, a proposal that may or may not get through the committee, a plan for making money. If men do mention their wives and families, the mention is likely to be brief, not belabored and elaborated in depth or detail. If they make reference to a difficult personal situation, it will likely be minimal and vague ("It's been rough").

A man described his Thanksgiving to me. Three generations of his wife's family had gathered: brothers and sisters, their children, and their parents. The men went outside to play football, while the women stayed inside and talked. The older women ended up telling the youngest granddaughter she was too young to get married.

Earlier we saw that women's inclination to engage in troubles talk is confusing to men, who mistake the ritual lament for a request for advice. Now we can see that troubles talk is just one aspect of the ongoing intimate conversation that can be called gossip. Not only is providing solutions to minor problems beside the point, but it cuts short the conversation, which *is* the point. If one problem is solved, then another must be found, to keep the intimate conversation going.

SMALL TALK
SERVES A BIG PURPOSE

Small talk is crucial to maintain a sense of camaraderie when there is nothing special to say. Women friends and relatives keep the conversational mechanisms in working order by talking about small things as well as large. Knowing they will have such conversations later makes women feel they are not alone in life. If they do not have someone to tell their thoughts and impressions to, they *do* feel alone. This is dramatized in a short story by Ursula Le Guin titled "In and Out." A woman who is becoming interested in doing ceramics gets some help and advice from a local potter. He gives her more attention than she sought, and she finds it difficult to get away. When she finally drives off, he calls after her, saying that

> if she wanted to try bringing pots up on his wheel she could come over any evening, which left her really wishing she was at the office, where she could tell somebody. "He said, 'Come over and bring pots up on my wheel'!"

Like a writer who sees small events in her life as material for a story, Le Guin's character sees her life as material for conversations.

Students in my class on gender differences recorded casual conversations between women friends and men friends. It was easy to get recordings of women friends talking, partly because most of the students were women, but also because the request to "record a conversation with your friend" met with easy compliance from the students' female friends and family members. But asking men to record conversations with their friends had mixed results. One woman's mother agreed readily, but her father insisted that he didn't have conversations with his friends. "Don't you ever call Fred on the phone?" she asked, naming a man she knew to be his good friend. "Not often," he said. "But if I do, it's because I have something to ask, and when I get the answer, I hang up."

Another woman's husband delivered a tape to her with great satisfaction and pride. "This is a good conversation," he announced, "because it's not just him and me shooting the breeze, like 'Hi, how are you? I saw a good movie the other day,' and stuff. It's a problem-solving task. Each line is meaningful." When the woman listened to the tape, she heard her husband and his friend trying to solve a computer problem. Everything they said was technical and impersonal. Not only did she not consider it "a good conversation," she didn't really regard it as a conversation at all. His idea of a good conversation was one with impersonal, factual, task-focused content. Hers was one with personal content.

These differences also show up in relations between parents and children. My students tell me that when they talk to "their parents" on the phone, they spend most of the time talking to their mothers. Their fathers typically join the conversation only when they have a business matter to discuss or report. This happens in writing as well as in speaking, and apparently it is not limited to American families. A German student showed me a card she had received that her mother had covered with handwritten "conversation" inquiring about her daughter's life and health and filling her in on family news. Folded into the card was a brief typewritten note from her father, telling her to go to the university registrar and obtain a form that he needed for tax purposes.

In response to an article I had written, a journalist remarked that my claim that many men have little use for small talk, since they believe talk is designed to convey information, rang a bell with him. He deplores chit-chat and believes that talk should have significant content, be interesting and meaningful. This is fine so long as there is a business meeting with lots of substance to discuss. But he finds himself verbally hamstrung when the meeting breaks up, and he has to embark on the long walk down the hall with a stranger. Opposed in principle to, and simply unpracticed in, making small talk, he is at a loss when there is no "big talk" available.

For most women, getting together and telling about their feelings and what is happening in their lives is at the heart of friendship. Having someone to tell your secrets to means you are not alone in the world. But telling secrets is not an endeavor without risks. Someone who knows your secrets has power over you: She can tell your secrets to others and create trouble for you. This is the source of the negative image of gossip.

WHEN GOSSIP IS RUMOR

The most negative image of gossip reflects a situation in which destructive rumors that have no basis in fact are spread. An extreme illustration of such a situation is described in Edna O'Brien's story "The Widow." In this story, a woman named Biddy, whose beloved husband has drowned, finally finds happiness in a new relationship. The people of the town watch her every move and criticize her new love interest, predicting disaster, but she has what she thinks is the last laugh when she becomes engaged. A week before the wedding, the happy couple visit the local pub and stand everyone to drinks.

Then Biddy, being a little tipsy, tapped her glass with her engagement ring and said she was going to give a little recitation. Without further ado, she stood up, smiled that sort of urchin smile of hers, ran her tongue over her lips, another habit, and recited a poem entitled "People Will Talk." It was a lunge at all those mischievous, prurient people who begrudged her her little flourish. It may have been—indeed, many people said that it was—this audacious provocation that wreaked the havoc of the next weeks. Had she confided in a few local women, she might have been saved, but she did not confide; she stood aloof with her man, her eyes gleaming, her happiness assured.

Far from assured, Biddy's happiness is doomed. She is undone by malicious and unfounded gossip. The rumor is spread that her first husband committed suicide because she made his life intolerable. Biddy tries desperately to prevent her fiancé from hearing the false rumors, and one of her efforts in this regard leads to her death. O'Brien implies that spreading the malicious rumor was the townspeople's way of punishing Biddy for thumbing her nose at the power of their tongues, and for holding herself aloof from them by not confiding in other women—in other words, they undid her with gossip because she had not shown the proper respect for it.

In many ways, our society is becoming more private than public in orientation, more gossiplike in public domains. Most forms of public communication, such as television news and public officials' press conferences, are becoming more informal in style, with remarks being made (or made to seem) off the cuff rather than prepared. One result of this is the need for frequent public apologies, and even resignations, by people who have spoken off the cuff, making the kinds of comments that are common in private conversations but unacceptable in public. Another aspect of this development is increased interest in the private lives of public people. It is perhaps not surprising that an aspect of this interest—perhaps a byproduct of it—is the role of rumor in public life.

A *Washington Post* article headlined THE PUBLIC POLITICS OF RUMOR notes that whereas rumors have long been "a staple of politics," only recently have they been readily reported by the media, whether or not the reporter has been able to confirm their truth. The incident that sparked this article was one in which the Republican National Committee's communication director resigned after having written and distributed a memo implying— not stating—that the newly installed Democratic Speaker of the House was homosexual. The *Post* writer comments that rumors are effective even if they are later disproved and retracted; the damage is done by their mere existence, because most people assume "where there's smoke, there's fire." The American public arena has become a little more like the Irish community of Edna O'Brien's story.

THE USES OF GOSSIP

These are dramatic examples of the destructive potential of gossip. Nora Ephron describes the more circumscribed danger of telling one's secrets to friends in her novel *Heartburn*. The heroine, Rachel, runs into her friend Meg Roberts on a plane to Washington from New York. Meg mentions their friend Betty's birthday party, and Rachel is aghast to realize she forgot all about the party. She has an unassailable excuse: She left her husband and flew to New York because she had learned that he was passionately in love and having an affair with another woman. Now, however, she is on her way back home with her husband, intending to resume her marriage. She doesn't want to make use of her excellent excuse because it would be too good as gossip:

> The only way Betty would ever forgive me would be for me to tell her why, and if I told her why she'd tell everyone in Washington, and then everyone in town would know something about our marriage that I didn't want them to know. I know all about Meg Roberts' marriage, for example, because Meg confides in her friend Ann, who confides in Betty, who confides in me.

True friends, everyone feels, do not repeat their friends' secrets to others. Revealing a secret can be the basis for the end of a friendship. And yet people do often repeat what is told to them in confidence by their friends. Why is this so?

Penelope Eckert, an anthropologist, spent time with high school girls and got to know their social worlds. Donna Eder, a sociologist, did the same in junior high. Both noticed that girls get status by being friends with high-status girls: the cheerleaders, the pretty ones, the ones who are popular with boys. If being friends with those of high status is a way to get status for yourself, how are you to prove to others that a popular girl is your friend? One way is to show that you know her secrets, because it is in the context of friendship that secrets are revealed.

A few high school girls told Eckert that they prefer to have boys as friends because boys don't try to get juicy details and are less likely to spread them around. The girls may think that this demonstrates the moral superiority of boys. But Eckert points out that the reason a boy is less likely to scavenge for gossip and distribute his findings is that he has much less to gain by it. Boys' main access to status is less a matter of whom they are close to than of their achievements and skill, primarily at sports, and their ability to prevail in a fight (though the older a boy gets, the more his fights tend to be verbal rather than physical).

There is yet another way that the desire to forge connections may be at work in creating gossip. Talking about someone who is not there is a way of establishing rapport with someone who *is* there. By agreeing about their evaluation of someone else, people reinforce their shared values and world views.

GOSSIP AS SOCIAL CONTROL

The reinforcement of values by talking about other people also works in another way. We measure our behavior against the potential for gossip, hearing in our minds how others are likely to talk about us. In trying to decide what to do, we automatically project contemplated actions onto the backdrop of this imagined dialogue, and our decisions about how to act are influenced by what we think others would say about them. Having decided, we hide, adjust or display our behavior to prevent criticism and ensure being praised. Those who are of a rebellious nature and age may defy expectations evidenced in gossip. Regardless of the stance taken toward them, the assumptions underlying "what people will say" plant in us an image of what a good person is and does. Hearing people praised for being generous and self-effacing, we get the idea that these are good things to be. Hearing people criticized for being stingy, disloyal, or ugly, we get the idea that these are not good things to be.

Girls and women feel it is crucial that they be liked by their peers, a form of involvement that focuses on symmetrical connections. Boys and men feel it is crucial that they be respected by their peers, a form of involvement that focuses on asymmetrical status. Being disliked is a more devastating punishment for girls and women, because of their need for affiliation. Marjorie Harness Goodwin, in her study of teen and preteen boys and girls at play, found that when a girl's behavior was strongly disapproved, the other girls ostracized her for a month and a half—the ultimate means of social control. In contrast, although boys sometimes left the group when they felt they were insulted too much, Goodwin did not find boys excluded for an extended period of time.

LETTING IT SHOW

The need to be liked and approved of can be at odds with the neeed to reveal secrets, since secrets expose one's weaknesses. In an example I gave earlier, a woman's former boyfriend had his heart broken and he wanted to talk about it—so much that he went to her, even though he had left her long before. Why didn't he feel comfortable talking to his friends about problems? Maybe for the same reason that many men interviewed by Catherine Kohler Riessman did not talk to anyone about their divorce. One of the men told her, "I think everybody hates to have anybody know that they have problems. . . . You always try and keep your problems to yourself." These men, like many others, are keenly aware of the imbalance in power that can result from telling secrets. For one thing, those who show weakness can feel they have put themselves in a one-down position. For another, they are giving away information that could be used against them.

Women are aware of this danger too. Robinette Kennedy, a psychologist who studied women's friendships in a village in Crete, found that women are keenly aware of the danger of malicious gossip resulting from exchanging secrets. She asked twelve schoolgirls to write what qualities they valued in a friend, and every single one wrote: not betraying secrets. Kennedy found that some women actually avoided having friendships for this reason, but they missed having friends. In a society where women and men lived in separate spheres and had to take clearly defined roles in relation to each other, having a woman friend meant that there was at least one relationship in which a woman could be completely herself, and be understood and accepted. If she had no one to whom she could tell her true feelings, she felt painfully isolated.

The women and girls in the Greek village and the American schoolgirls that Eder and Eckert studied had the same dilemma: They needed friends to talk to, but they knew that talking to friends is risky. Girls and women, more often than boys and men, are willing to take the risk, because their eyes are on the payoff in rapport. The possibilities of appearing vulnerable and of losing independence are in the corner of the eye. Men are less likely to take the risk because for them preventing vulnerability and protecting their independence are in the foreground, and issues of intimacy in the background.

Many men resent their wives' or girlfriends' talking about their relationships to friends. To these men, talking about a personal relationship to others is an act of disloyalty. One man I interviewed waxed eloquent on this point. He said he regarded telling intimate details about a relationship—especially those that showed a partner's weaknesses—as a breach of trust, pure and simple. He expressed disdain for anyone who would need to stoop to such a level in order to create rapport with friends. Such strong reactions support the claim by anthropologist Jill Dubisch (writing about Greek culture) that talking about family matters to nonfamily members is taboo because it destroys a sacred boundary between inside and outside, taking outside the home what properly belongs inside it.

Dubisch also points out the symbolic connection between verbal and sexual pollution: Allowing strangers into the house by telling them the family's secrets is like "illicit sexual penetration." This seems to capture the dilemma of widows in Greece as seen in a line from a lament that Caraveli recorded: "Widow in the house, gossips at the door." The widow is confined to the house, because if she steps outside, anything she does will expose her to the sexual accusations of gossip.

To say that many men do not exchange secrets about their own and others' lives for the purpose of establishing intimacy is certainly not to say that they do not have a need and a way to bond with others through talk. If women's source of involvement, talking about personal lives, is an irritant to men, then to find a source of men's involvement, we can inspect an aspect of their behavior that is an irritant to women: the daily newspaper.

NEWS AS GOSSIP

A retired professor met daily with several retired male friends at a local diner. He and his friends referred to their gatherings as "solving the world's problems"—and this gives a good indication of what they talked about.

Men's interest in the details of politics, news, and sports is parallel to women's interest in the details of personal lives. If women are afraid of being left out by not knowing what is going on with this person or that, men are afraid of being left out by not knowing what is going on in the world. And exchanging details about public news rather than private news has the advantage that it does not make men personally vulnerable: The information they are bartering has nothing to do with them.

In a book about the history of news, Mitchell Stephens points out that men have long been obsessed with exchanging details about current events. He does not actually say he is talking about "men" but rather "the English"; however, it is clear from his description that it is English *men* to whom his comments apply.

It might be surprising to learn that more than 275 years ago, the English—though they had no radio, television, satellites or computers, they obtained much of their news at the coffeehouse—thought *their* era was characterized by an obsession with news. The condition was described in a newspaper written in 1712 as "the furious itch of novelty," and it was said to have "proved fatal to many families; the meanest of shopkeepers and handicrafts spending whole days in coffee-houses, to hear news and talk politicks, whilst their wives and children wanted bread at home. . . ." Similar behavior had been noted in the mid-seventeenth century in Cambridge. "Scholars are so Greedy after news . . . that they neglect all for it," one concerned observer complained.

If "the English" are gathering in coffeehouses to "talk politicks" while their wives and children are at home, then "the English" are actually "English men." But how similar this picture of men gathering to exchange news is to the stereotype of women neglecting their household duties to gossip on the phone or meet over coffee in their kitchens.

THE POWER OF DETAILS

Discussing details about the news and exchanging details about private lives are coming together, as newspapers report more about the private lives of people in the news. The phenomenal success of *People* magazine is only the most extreme instance. Consider this article opening:

> Charles and Jeanne Atchison live near the Cowboy City dance bar on a gravel street in a peeling white and gold mobile home. Weeds sway in the breeze out front. It's a street with a melancholy down-on-one's-luck feel about it. The town is Azle, Tex., a tiny speck on the periphery of Fort Worth.
>
> A few years ago, the picture was a far prettier one. Charles (Chuck) Atchison was all set. He made good money— more than $1,000 a week—enough to pay for a cozy house, new cars, fanciful trips. But all that is gone. He's six months behind on rent for his land, and don't even ask about the legal bills.
>
> "It's sort of like I was barreling along and I suddenly shifted into reverse," Mr. Atchison said with a rueful smile. "Well, welcome to whistle blower country."
>
> Chuck Atchison is 44, with a stony face and a sparse mustache.

These lines are not from a short story or magazine article. The excerpt is from the front page of the "Business" section of *The New York Times*—that soberest section of the soberest of American newspapers. In reporting what happened to Atchison, a quality control inspector who exposed safety violations at a nuclear plant, the journalist gives a personal view of the whistle-blower: what he looked like, what his house looked like—details that involve the reader.

According to columnist Bob Greene, journalists began turning their attention to such mundane details in 1963, when Jimmy Breslin wrote a column entitled "A Death in Emergency Room One" describing the last moments of John Kennedy's life. Greene says Breslin's column "literally took his readers into the corridors and operating rooms of Parkland Hospital on that day." Greene observes, "Journalists today are trained to get those telling details quickly. . . ." The same brand of journalism is said to have established the career of columnist Russell Baker, whose coverage of Queen Elizabeth's coronation focused not on the public pageantry but on the backstage details—for example, as a reviewer noted, the "long lines of colonial potentates in animal skins and gold braid forming to use Westminster Abbey's toilets."

Why would readers want to feel that they were in the corridors and operating rooms of the hospital in which Kennedy lay? Why would they be interested in the lines outside the toilets at a coronation? Because such details give them a pleasurable sense of involvement, of being part of something, just as gossip does for women who talk about the details of their own and others' lives.

THE JOY OF INVOLVEMENT

Despite the growing appreciation of details in news stories, the usefulness of telling details in everyday conversation is not universally recognized. A woman told me that members of her family refer to her grandmother in a phrase that typifies the old woman's conversation: "I had a little ham, I had a little cheese." This affectionate yet disparaging mode of reference reveals that they find it boring when Grandmother tells them what she had for lunch. They wish she would give fewer details, or not report her lunch at all.

My great-aunt, for many years a widow, had a love affair when she was in her seventies. Obese, balding, her hands and legs misshapen by arthritis, she did not fit the stereotype of a woman romantically loved. But she was—by a man, also in his seventies, who lived in a nursing home but occasionally spent weekends with her in her apartment. In trying to tell me what this relationship meant to her, my great-aunt told of a conversation. One evening she had had dinner out, with friends. When she returned home, her male friend called and she told him about the dinner. He listened with interest and asked her, "What did you wear?" When she told me this, she began to cry: "Do you know how many years it's been since anyone asked me what I wore?" When my great-aunt said this, she was saying that it had been years since anyone had cared deeply—intimately—about her. The exchange of relatively insignificant details about daily life sends a metamessage of rapport and caring.

Attention to details associated with a person is often a sign of romantic interest. In a novel titled *The Jealous One,* by Celia Fremlin, a woman sends her husband, Geoffrey, next door to deliver a dinner invitation to their new neighbor, who has moved in that day. Geoffrey returns full of excitement, bubbling with admiration for and details about the new neighbor. He announces, starry-eyed, that the neighbor has invited *them* to dinner in her not-yet-furnished home, and he asks his wife if she has a red ribbon for Shang Low, the neighbor's Pekingese, explaining that *Shang Low* is the opposite of *Shang High.* The wife responds with irony, but Geoffrey is slow to join in her ironic denigration of the neighbor's airs in ribboning her dog:

> She giggled in terrible solitude for a fraction of a second; and then Geoffrey joined in, a tiny bit too late and a tiny bit too loud. And the joke did not lead to another joke. Murmuring something about "having promised . . .", Geoffrey hurried away out of the kitchen and out of the house, without any red ribbon. And this piece of red ribbon, which they didn't look for, didn't find, and probably hadn't got, became the very first of the objects which couldn't ever again be mentioned between them.

Geoffrey's romantic interest in the new neighbor leaks out in his enthusiastic, uncritical recounting of details about her, such as the breed and name of her dog.

If recalling a detail or name is a sign of caring, failure to recall a name can be seen as a sign of lack of caring. Complaints are frequent from people whose parents disapprove of their partners or friends and seem to display their disapproval subtly by habitually referring to them by the wrong names or failing to recall their names. The same phenomenon can be manipulated for positive ends. This was the case with a woman who remained friends with the wife of an acquaintance of her former husband's.

Her friend persisted in referring to the former husband's new wife as "what's her name." The divorced woman took the metamessage of this to be "Even though I see her occasionally, I don't really care about her. You are still the one who counts to me." Not remembering the new wife's name was offered as evidence of lack of caring about her—and, consequently, loyalty to the first wife.

Paying attention to details of a person's appearance can be a means of flirting. A woman had an appointment to meet a man she had met only once before, briefly. They were both married; the purpose of the meeting was business. But the man began their conversation by observing that she looked younger than he recalled, and her hair was different. "You were wearing a hat, then, weren't you?" he said. "And you were dressed in white then too." Simply saying that he had noticed her appearance the first time they had met was a kind of flirtation. It was not a displeasing one to her, though her husband found it displeasing when she recounted it to him.

The noticing of details shows caring and creates involvement. Men, however, often find women's involvement in details irritating. Because women are concerned first and foremost with establishing intimacy, they value the telling of details.

Conversely, many women complain that men don't tell enough details. A woman thus frustrated is Laura in Alice Mattison's story "Sleeping Giant." Laura and Dan are both troubled by their son-in-law's plan to buy an old, run-down house. In the past, when Laura tried to talk to her daughter about it, the daughter defended her husband. But Dan now assures Laura that their daughter sees her point of view, because she said as much to him. "Believe me," he says, "she's not happy about this." Laura wants more details about the conversation, but Dan won't supply them. Laura asks:

> "Well, why doesn't she tell him so?"
> He doesn't answer.
> "What did she say *exactly*?" Laura is searching in her

canvas bag for her car keys. She's chilly after all, and there's a flannel shirt in the trunk of the car. She waits, holding the keys and the bag, but Dan still doesn't answer, and she drops the bag on the bench. "What did she *say?*"

"Oh, I don't remember. General things."

"What did *you* say?"

"Oh, I don't know, Laura." Laura turns aside abruptly, opens the trunk, and stares into it for a moment, annoyed that Dan won't tell her more.

Laura sounds like innumerable flesh-and-blood women I've talked to. As one put it, "Men don't tell the whole story—who said what." Another complained of her husband: "It's like pulling teeth to get him to tell me, 'What did she *say?* What did he *say?*' "

Yet another woman recalled a time that her best friend's husband tried unsuccessfully to take part in one of their conversations. Breaking with tradition, he tried to tell about an experience that he thought was similar to the ones they were discussing. The two women plied him with questions he couldn't answer about exactly what had been said and how and why. He backed off from the story, and didn't try to tell any more. Perhaps he was wondering to himself why the women were interested in all these unimportant details.

"SKIP THE DETAILS"

Though many women value the recounting of subtle nuances in conversations with close friends, there are situations in which everyone feels oppressed by being told, or asked for, what seem like too many details. If interest in details is a sign of intimacy, a woman will resist such interest if it comes from someone she doesn't want to be intimate with. And everyone has had the experience of being told unwanted details—so many that they seem pointless, or demand longer or more intimate attention than one wants to give. Many of the examples I have collected of people piling on details in conversation involve old people. This may be because old people often want more involvement with young people than young people want with them, or because old people frequently cannot hear well, so they tell detailed stories to maintain interaction. Old people are also more inclined to reminisce about the past, consequently telling stories that are likely to include details.

It is a tenet of contemporary American psychology that mental health requires psychological separation from one's parents. One way of resisting overinvolvement, for some people at least, is resisting telling details. For example, one woman told me that her mother sought overinvolvement with her and had succeeded in achieving overinvolvement with her sister Jane. To support her claim, she said, "It's amazing, the details of Jane's life my mother knows." Later, she was explaining how she resists her mother's attempts to get overly involved in her life. As an example of her mother's prying, she said, "She's hungry for details. If I tell her I went somewhere, she asks, 'What did you wear?' "

The question that offended this woman was the same one that had brought my great-aunt such happiness. The difference is that my great-aunt was seeking involvement with the man who asked her what she wore. This woman was resisting what she perceived as the excessive involvement her mother sought with her. Presumably, however, when her sister Jane talks to their mother, she does not feel that the question "What did you wear?" is inappropriate. Perhaps, like my great-aunt, Jane values the show of caring and resulting involvement.

MIXING BUSINESS WITH GOSSIP

Many women mix talk about relatively important things, like business, with talk about relatively unimportant things, like clothes. On Monday morning, Marjorie walks into Beatrice's office to ask her opinion about a contract. After they have settled their business, or perhaps before, they bring each other up to date on their personal lives: Marjorie has her hands full with her ailing mother-in-law; Beatrice is feeling optimistic about a new relationship.

A woman who runs a counseling center noted that when she meets with women on her staff, it is not unusual for them to spend 75 percent of the time in personal talk and then efficiently take care of business in the remaining 25 percent. To men on the staff, this seems like wasting time. But the director places value on creating a warm, intimate working environment. She feels that such personal talk contributes to a sense of rapport that makes the women on her staff happy in their jobs and lays a foundation for the working relationship that enables them to conduct business so efficiently.

The mutual knowledge and trust that grows out of personal talk can precede a business relationship as well as grow out of it. A magazine article described a partnership between two women who own a construction company. The seed of their working relationship had been planted years before the business was founded, when the two women met regularly to exchange coffee and talk. When one of them decided to start a business, her working relationship with her partner was already in place.

For women who engage in frequent, regular social talk with friends, the machinery is up and running when a significant decision needs to be made. Elizabeth Loftus, a psychologist specializing in eyewitness testimony, was confronted with a moral dilemma when she was asked to testify on behalf of the man accused of being "Ivan the Terrible"—a notoriously sadistic Nazi war criminal. To be consistent, Loftus felt she should testify in this case as she had in many others. But her relatives and friends argued against it, and she recoiled at the prospect of undermining the testimony of the few witnesses who were alive to tell what Ivan had done—a mere fifty survivors of an estimated million of Ivan's victims. The dilemma was resolved when a friend dropped by for tea. Loftus recalls, "My friend, quoting Emerson, reminded me that 'A foolish consistency is the hobgoblin of little minds.' " With this comfort, Loftus decided not to testify. If women and men have different habits for social talk, they also make different use of it.

Differences in uses of social talk also begin early. One couple I talked to had different perspectives on their son's relationship with his best friend. The mother thought it odd that, despite the significant amount of time the boys spent together, for example playing football, their son found out what college his best friend was going to by reading it in their yearbook. One day a girl called him to ask whether his friend had a date for the prom. She was calling for *her* friend, who wanted to ask his friend, but not if he already had a date. Not only did their son not know whether his best friend had a date for the prom, but he was annoyed that the girl thought he should know. He gave her his friend's phone number and suggested she call to find out directly. He later commented that had he known his friend was going to the prom, he might have planned to go himself; not keeping up with such personal information deprived him of a chance to go.

All of this seemed very strange to the boy's mother, who could not imagine what it meant to be best friends if it didn't include knowing the basic developments in the other's life. To the boy's father, however, it seemed unremarkable.

TALKING-ABOUT VERSUS TALKING-AGAINST

The relatively positive or negative value that is placed on talking about personal details—of one's own life or others'— is reflected in the positive and negative views of gossip. One man commented that he and I seemed to have different definitions of gossip. He said, "To you it seems to be discussion of personal details about people known to the conversationalists. To me, it's a discussion of the weaknesses, character flaws, and failures of third persons, so that the participants in the conversation can feel superior to them. This seems unworthy, hence gossip is bad."

This man's view parallels that of a woman who told me she was troubled by one of the women in her child care co-op who gossiped too much. But it turned out that this woman's gossip was all negative: putting down other members of the co-op and criticizing them. It was not the talking-*about* that was disturbing, but the talking-*against*. This distances the speakers from those they are talking about, rather than bringing them closer. Furthermore, it is natural to assume that someone who has only negative things to say about others will also say negative things about you when you aren't there.

Gossip as talking-against is related to a verbal game that Christine Cheepen calls "scapegoat." In conversations she analyzed, Cheepen found that speakers talked against someone who wasn't there to redress imbalances of power that had erupted. "Scapegoat" was a way for speakers to achieve parity with each other by teaming up against someone else.

In Cheepen's examples, however, the third party whom the conversationalists teamed up against wasn't just anyone—it was their boss. And this brings us back to the view of the man who told me why he considers gossip to be bad. To the extent that talking about someone who is not there brings an absent party into the room, the effect is to establish connection. But if that party is brought into the room to be *put down,* then the effect is negotiation of status. As always, connection and status are operating at once, so both views are valid. They are different takes on the same scene.

WOMEN AND MEN ON THEIR OWN TERMS

What is the solution, then, if women and men are talking at cross-purposes, about gossip as about other matters? How are we to open lines of communication? The answer is for both men and women to try to take each other on their own terms rather than applying the standards of one group to the behavior of the other. This is not a "natural" thing to do, because we tend to look for a single "right" way of doing things. Understandably, experts are as liable to do this as anyone else.

A national audience-participation talk show featured a psychologist answering questions about couples' relationships. A woman in the audience voiced a complaint: "My husband talks to his mother, but he won't talk to me. If I want to know how his day was, I listen to his conversation with his mother." The psychologist told this woman, "He probably trusts his mother more than he trusts you."

This comment reinforced the woman's own suspicions and worst fears. And what the psychologist said was perfectly legitimate and reasonable—within the framework of talk in women's friendships: The friend to whom you talk daily, telling all the little experiences you had, is your best friend. But how reasonable an interpretation is it from the man's point of view? I would wager that her husband did not think he needed to do anything special to create intimacy with his wife, because he was with her every day. But because his mother was alone, he humored her by telling her unimportant little things that she seemed to want to hear. His mother's need to hear such details would make sense to her son because she was alone and needed them as a substitute for the real thing, like watching life from her window. He wouldn't understand why his wife would want and need to hear such talk. Although it is possible that this man trusts his mother more than his wife, the evidence given does not warrant such a conclusion.

This therapist was judging the man's way of talking by women's standards. In a sense, the values of therapy are those more typically associated with women's ways of talking than with men's. This may be why a study showed that among inexperienced therapists, women do better than men. But over time, with experience, this gender difference disappears. Eventually, perhaps, men therapists—and men in therapy—learn to talk like women. This is all to the good. Assertiveness training, on the other hand, teaches women to talk more like men, and this too is to the good. Women and men would both do well to learn strategies more typically used by members of the other group—not to switch over entirely, but to have more strategies at their disposal.

Habitual ways of talking are hard to change. Learning to respect others' ways of talking may be a bit easier. Men should accept that many women regard exchanging details about personal lives as a basic ingredient of intimacy, and women should accept that many men do not share this view. Mutual acceptance will at least prevent the pain of being told you are doing something wrong when you are only doing things your way.

FIVE

"I'll Explain It to You": Lecturing and Listening

A t a reception following the publication of one of my books, I noticed a publicist listening attentively to the producer of a popular radio show. He was telling her how the studio had come to be built where it was, and why he would have preferred another site. What caught my attention was the length of time he was speaking while she was listening. He was delivering a monologue that could only be called a lecture, giving her detailed information about the radio reception at the two sites, the architecture of the station, and so on. I later asked the publicist if she had been interested in the information the producer had given her. "Oh, yes," she answered. But then she thought a moment and said, "Well, maybe he did go on a bit." The next day she told me, "I was thinking about what you asked. I couldn't have cared less about what he was saying. It's just that I'm so used to listening to men go on about things I don't care about, I didn't even realize how bored I was until you made me think about it."

I was chatting with a man I had just met at a party. In our conversation, it emerged that he had been posted in Greece with the RAF during 1944 and 1945. Since I had lived in Greece for several years, I asked him about his experiences: What had Greece been like then? How had the Greek villagers treated the British soldiers? What had it been *like* to be a British soldier in wartime Greece? I also offered information about how Greece had changed, what it is like now. He did not pick up on my remarks about contemporary Greece, and his replies to my questions quickly changed from accounts of his own experiences, which I found riveting, to facts about Greek history, which interested me in principle but in the actual telling left me profoundly bored. The more impersonal his talk became, the more I felt oppressed by it, pinned involuntarily in the listener position.

At a showing of Judy Chicago's jointly created art work *The Dinner Party*, I was struck by a couple standing in front of one of the displays: The man was earnestly explaining to the woman the meaning of symbols in the tapestry before them, pointing as he spoke. I might not have noticed this unremarkable scene, except that *The Dinner Party* was radically feminist in conception, intended to reflect women's experiences and sensibilities.

While taking a walk in my neighborhood on an early summer evening at twilight, I stopped to chat with a neighbor who was walking his dogs. As we stood, I noticed that the large expanse of yard in front of which we were standing was aglitter with the intermittent flickering of fireflies. I called attention to the sight, remarking on how magical it looked. "It's like the Fourth of July," I said. He agreed, and then told me he had read that the lights of fireflies are mating signals. He then explained to me details of how these signals work—for example, groups of fireflies fly at different elevations and could be seen to cluster in different parts of the yard.

In all these examples, the men had information to impart

and they were imparting it. On the surface, there is nothing surprising or strange about that. What is strange is that there are so many situations in which men have factual information requiring lengthy explanations to impart to women, and so few in which women have comparable information to impart to men.

The changing times have altered many aspects of relations between women and men. Now it is unlikely, at least in many circles, for a man to say, "I am better than you because I am a man and you are a woman." But women who do not find men making such statements are nonetheless often frustrated in their dealings with them. One situation that frustrates many women is a conversation that has mysteriously turned into a lecture, with the man delivering the lecture to the woman, who has become an appreciative audience.

Once again, the alignment in which women and men find themselves arrayed is asymmetrical. The lecturer is framed as superior in status and expertise, cast in the role of teacher, and the listener is cast in the role of student. If women and men took turns giving and receiving lectures, there would be nothing disturbing about it. What is disturbing is the imbalance. Women and men fall into this unequal pattern so often because of the differences in their interactional habits. Since women seek to build rapport, they are inclined to play down their expertise rather than display it. Since men value the position of center stage and the feeling of knowing more, they seek opportunities to gather and disseminate factual information.

If men often seem to hold forth because they have the expertise, women are often frustrated and surprised to find that when they have the expertise, they don't necessarily get the floor.

FIRST ME, THEN ME

I was at a dinner with faculty members from other departments in my university. To my right was a woman. As the dinner began, we introduced ourselves. After we told each other what departments we were in and what subjects we taught, she asked what my research was about. We talked about my research for a little while. Then I asked her about her research and she told me about it. Finally, we discussed the ways that our research overlapped. Later, as tends to happen at dinners, we branched out to others at the table. I asked a man across the table from me what department he was in and what he did. During the next half hour, I learned a lot about his job, his research, and his background. Shortly before the dinner ended there was a lull, and he asked me what I did. When I said I was a linguist, he became excited and told me about a research project he had conducted that was related to neurolinguistics. He was still telling me about his research when we all got up to leave the table.

This man and woman were my colleagues in academia. What happens when I talk to people at parties and social events, not fellow researchers? My experience is that if I mention the kind of work I do to women, they usually ask me about it. When I tell them about conversational style or gender differences, they offer their own experiences to support the patterns I describe. This is very pleasant for me. It puts me at center stage without my having to grab the spotlight myself, and I frequently gather anecdotes I can use in the future. But when I announce my line of work to men, many give me a lecture on language—for example, about how people, especially teenagers, misuse language nowadays. Others challenge me, for example questioning me about my research methods. Many others change the subject to something they know more about.

Of course not all men respond in this way, but over the years I have encountered many men, and very few women, who do. It is not that speaking in this way is *the* male way of doing things, but that it is *a* male way. There are women who adopt such styles, but they are perceived as speaking like men.

IF YOU'VE GOT IT, FLAUNT IT—
OR HIDE IT

I have been observing this constellation in interaction for more than a dozen years. I did not, however, have any understanding of *why* this happens until fairly recently, when I developed the framework of status and connection. An experimental study that was pivotal in my thinking shows that expertise does not ensure women a place at center stage in conversation with men.

Psychologist H. M. Leet-Pellegrini set out to discover whether gender or expertise determined who would behave in what she terms a "dominant" way—for example, by talking more, interrupting, and controlling the topic. She set up pairs of women, pairs of men, and mixed pairs, and asked them to discuss the effects of television violence on children. In some cases, she made one of the partners an expert by providing relevant factual information and time to read and assimilate it before the videotaped discussion. One might expect that the conversationalist who was the expert would talk more, interrupt more, and spend less time supporting the conversational partner who knew less about the subject. But it wasn't so simple. On the average, those who had expertise did talk more, but men experts talked more than women experts.

Expertise also had a different effect on women and men with regard to supportive behavior. Leet-Pellegrini expected that the one who did not have expertise would spend more time offering agreement and support to the one who did. This turned out to be true—*except* in cases where a woman was the expert and her nonexpert partner was a man. In this situation, the women experts showed support—saying things like "Yeah" and "That's right"—far *more* than the nonexpert men they were talking to. Observers often rated the male nonexpert as more dominant than the female expert. In other words, the women in this experiment

127

not only didn't wield their expertise as power, but tried to play it down and make up for it through extra assenting behavior. They acted as if their expertise were something to hide.

And perhaps it was. When the word *expert* was spoken in these experimental conversations, in all cases but one it was the man in the conversation who used it, saying something like "So, you're the expert." Evidence of the woman's superior knowledge sparked resentment, not respect.

Furthermore, when an expert man talked to an uninformed woman, he took a controlling role in structuring the conversation in the beginning *and* the end. But when an expert man talked to an uninformed man, he dominated in the beginning but not always in the end. In other words, having expertise was enough to keep a man in the controlling position if he was talking to a woman, but not if he was talking to a man. Apparently, when a woman surmised that the man she was talking to had more information on the subject than she did, she simply accepted the reactive role. But another man, despite a lack of information, might still give the expert a run for his money and possibly gain the upper hand by the end.

Reading these results, I suddenly understood what happens to me when I talk to women and men about language. I am assuming that my acknowledged expertise will mean I am automatically accorded authority in the conversation, and with women that is generally the case. But when I talk to men, revealing that I have acknowledged expertise in this area often invites challenges. I *might* maintain my position if I defend myself successfully against the challenges, but if I don't, I may lose ground.

One interpretation of the Leet-Pellegrini study is that women are getting a bum deal. They don't get credit when it's due. And in a way, this is true. But the reason is not—as it seems to many women—that men are bums who seek to deny women authority. The Leet-Pellegrini study shows that many men are inclined to jockey for status, and challenge the authority of others, when they are talking to men too. If this is so, then challenging a woman's authority as they would challenge a man's could be a sign of respect and equal treatment, rather than lack of respect and discrimination. In cases where this is so, the inequality of the treatment results not simply from the men's behavior alone but from the differences in men's and women's styles: Most women lack experience in defending themselves against challenges, which they misinterpret as personal attacks on their credibility.

Even when talking to men who are happy to see them in positions of status, women may have a hard time getting their due because of differences in men's and women's interactional goals. Just as boys in high school are not inclined to repeat information about popular girls because it doesn't get them what they want, women in conversation are not inclined to display their knowledge because it doesn't get them what they are after. Leet-Pellegrini suggests that the men in this study were playing a game of "Have I won?" while the women were playing a game of "Have I been sufficiently helpful?" I am inclined to put this another way: The game women play is "Do you like me?" whereas the men play "Do you respect me?" If men, in seeking respect, are less liked by women, this is an unsought side effect, as is the effect that women, in seeking to be liked, may lose respect. When a woman has a conversation with a man, her efforts to emphasize their similarities and avoid showing off can easily be interpreted, through the lens of status, as relegating her to a one-down position, making her appear either incompetent or insecure.

A SUBTLE DEFERENCE

Elizabeth Aries, a professor of psychology at Amherst College, set out to show that highly intelligent, highly educated young women are no longer submissive in conversations with male peers. And indeed she found that the college women did talk more than the college men in small groups she set up. But what they said was different. The men tended to set the agenda by offering opinions, suggestions, and information. The women tended to react, offering agreement or disagreement. Furthermore, she found that body language was as different as ever: The men sat with their legs stretched out, while the women gathered themselves in. Noting that research has found that speakers using the open-bodied position are more likely to persuade their listeners, Aries points out that talking more may not ensure that women will be heard.

In another study, Aries found that men in all-male discussion groups spent a lot of time at the beginning finding out "who was best informed about movies, books, current events, politics, and travel" as a means of "sizing up the competition" and negotiating "where they stood in relation to each other." This glimpse of how men talk when there are no women present gives an inkling of why displaying knowledge and expertise is something that men find more worth doing than women. What the women in Aries's study spent time doing was "gaining a closeness through more intimate self-revelation."

It is crucial to bear in mind that both the women and the men in these studies were establishing camaraderie, and both were concerned with their relationships to each other. But different aspects of their relationships were of primary concern: their place in a hierarchical order for the men, and their place in a network of intimate connections for the women. The consequence of these disparate concerns was very different ways of speaking.

Thomas Fox is an English professor who was intrigued by the differences between women and men in his freshman writing classes. What he observed corresponds almost precisely to the experimental findings of Aries and Leet-Pellegrini. Fox's method of teaching writing included having all the students read their essays to each other in class and talk to each other in small groups. He also had them write papers reflecting on the essays and the discussion groups. He alone, as the teacher, read these analytical papers.

To exemplify the two styles he found typical of women and men, Fox chose a woman, Ms. M, and a man, Mr. H. In her speaking as well as her writing, Ms. M. held back what she knew, appearing uninformed and uninterested, because she feared offending her classmates. Mr. H spoke and wrote with authority and apparent confidence because he was eager to persuade his peers. She did not worry about persuading; he did not worry about offending.

In his analytical paper, the young man described his own behavior in the mixed-gender group discussions as if he were describing the young men in Leet-Pellegrini's and Aries's studies:

> In my sub-group I am the leader. I begin every discussion by stating my opinions as facts. The other two members of the sub-group tend to sit back and agree with me. . . . I need people to agree with me.

Fox comments that Mr. H reveals "a sense of self, one that acts to change himself and other people, that seems entirely distinct from Ms. M's sense of self, dependent on and related to others."

Calling Ms. M's sense of self "dependent" suggests a negative view of her way of being in the world—and, I think, a view more typical of men. This view reflects the assumption that the alternative to independence is dependence. If this is indeed a male view, it may explain why so many men are cautious about becoming intimately involved with others: It makes sense to avoid humiliating dependence by insisting on independence. But there is another alternative: *inter*dependence.

The main difference between these alternatives is symmetry. Dependence is an asymmetrical involvement: One person needs the other, but not vice versa, so the needy person is one-down. Interdependence is symmetrical: Both parties rely on each other, so neither is one-up or one-down. Moreover, Mr. H's sense of self is also dependent on others. He requires others to listen, agree, and allow him to take the lead by stating his opinions first.

Looked at this way, the woman and man in this group are both dependent on each other. Their differing goals are complementary, although neither understands the reasons for the other's behavior. This would be a fine arrangement, except that their differing goals result in alignments that enhance his authority and undercut hers.

DIFFERENT INTERPRETATIONS— AND MISINTERPRETATIONS

Fox also describes differences in the way male and female students in his classes interpreted a story they read. These differences also reflect assumptions about the interdependence or independence of individuals. Fox's students wrote their responses to "The Birthmark" by Nathaniel Hawthorne. In the story, a woman's husband becomes obsessed with a birthmark on her face. Suffering from her husband's revulsion at the sight of her, the wife becomes obsessed with it too and, in a reversal of her initial impulse, agrees to undergo a treatment he has devised to remove the birthmark—a treatment that succeeds in removing the mark, but kills her in the process.

Ms. M interpreted the wife's complicity as a natural response to the demand of a loved one: The woman went along with her husband's lethal schemes to remove the birthmark because she wanted to please and be appealing to him. Mr. H blamed the woman's insecurity and vanity for her fate, and he blamed her for voluntarily submitting to her husband's authority. Fox points out that he saw her as individually responsible for her actions, just as he saw himself as individually responsible for his own actions. To him, the issue was independence: The weak wife voluntarily took a submissive role. To Ms. M, the issue was interdependence: The woman was inextricably bound up with her husband, so her behavior could not be separated from his.

Fox observes that Mr. H saw the writing of the women in the class as spontaneous—they wrote whatever popped into their heads. Nothing could be farther from Ms. M's experience as she described it: When she knew her peers would see her writing, she censored everything that popped into her head. In contrast, when she was writing something that only her professor would read, she expressed firm and articulate opinions.

There is a striking but paradoxical complementarity to Ms. M's and Mr. H's styles, when they are taken together. He needs someone to listen and agree. She listens and agrees. But in another sense, their dovetailing purposes are at cross-purposes. He misinterprets her agreement, intended in a spirit of connection, as a reflection of status and power: He thinks she is "indecisive" and "insecure." Her reasons for refraining from behaving as he does—firmly stating opinions as facts—have nothing to do with her attitudes toward her knowledge, as he thinks they do, but rather result from her attitudes toward her relationships with her peers.

These experimental studies by Leet-Pellegrini and Aries, and the observations by Fox, all indicate that, typically, men are more comfortable than women in giving information and opinions and speaking in an authoritative way to a group, whereas women are more comfortable than men in supporting others.

IS ANYBODY LISTENING?

In Jules Feiffer's play *Grown Ups*, a woman, Marilyn, tries to tell her parents, Jack and Helen, about something that happened to her, but she never succeeds in getting them to listen. Her explicit attempts to tell her story are highlighted by boldface type.

MARILYN: **This you gotta hear! I was coming home Wednesday on the bus from Philadelphia—**

JACK: Nobody said a word to me about Philadelphia.

HELEN: Marilyn, you want me to check the chicken for you?

MARILYN: Leave it, Mama.

HELEN: The old lady's trying to give a hand.

MARILYN: I'm like you; if somebody starts to help I forget what I'm doing. **Sit down, you'll love this: I was coming home from Philadelphia—**

JACK: [To Helen] Did you know she was out of town?

MARILYN: Two days!

JACK: Who took care of my grandchildren?

MARILYN: How should I know? Out of sight, out of mind. No, Rudy was here. He got them out of bed in the morning and back in bed at night. In between I don't even want to know what happened. **Am I ever going to be able to tell you this or not?**

HELEN: [Returning to table] You're going out of town, Marilyn?

Marilyn can't get her parents to pay attention to her story. They continually sidetrack the narration with comments about her cooking, her housekeeping, her family, her safety, and her brother, Jake:

HELEN: Where's Jake?

MARILYN: On the way. **So I caught the last bus back to the city—**

JACK: I don't like you taking a last bus, it's dangerous.

MARILYN: **It's not nearly as dangerous as trying to tell a story around here.**

Like the woman who wrote to Ann Landers that her husband doesn't talk to her, Marilyn feels invisible. She sees her parents' lack of interest in listening to her as symbolic of their inability to see and value her as a person, as she explains to Jake:

MARILYN: You at least, they know you're alive. No matter what I do you know how it feels? I'll put it this way: If *you* take them some place in your car, you're this wonderful success who can afford his own car; if I take them some place in my car, I'm the chauffeur. More than anything, you know what kills me? The thing I loved most was you and Mama in the kitchen with your stories. She'd tell one, you'd tell one, she'd tell one, you'd tell one. I thought someday I'll be old enough to have my

own real experiences and then *I'll* have stories!
To this day they will not allow me to tell a story.
Isn't it crazy that I should still be bothered by
that?

JAKE: I told my stories to get away from her stories.

Jake's explanation of why he told stories as a child shows his
impulse to avoid being in the listening position. Whereas Marilyn
loved listening to their mother's stories, Jake says he learned to
hold the floor with his own stories in order to avoid listening to
hers.

Just as Marilyn believed that she would have stories to tell
when she grew up, I recall that when I was a child, there were
two skills I thought all adults had that I didn't have: whistling
and snapping their fingers. I assumed I would acquire these abilities with age and eagerly awaited the development. But I grew
up, and I still can't whistle or get my fingers to produce a snap
worth listening to. It never occurred to me when I was a child
that these skills did not magically appear, like the physical changes
of puberty. I realized too late that if I wanted to know how to
whistle and snap my fingers, I had to practice. The grown daughter in *Grown Ups* could not tell stories in a way to command
attention partly because she hadn't gotten any practice as a child.
What she'd done as a child was listen attentively and appreciatively as her mother and brother told stories. While Jake was
getting practice in commanding attention through verbal performance, Marilyn was getting practice in listening.

The skills Marilyn and Jake honed as children provided the
basis for their adult vocations. Jake became a journalist at *The
New York Times:* He made a career of writing news stories that
millions would read, another form of verbal display to an audience. Marilyn became a social worker: She made a career of sitting and listening to other people talk.

In Feiffer's play, Marilyn really is not as good a storyteller
as Jake—she gets bogged down in unimportant details and interrupts herself to fuss about accuracy when it doesn't make any

difference to the story. The scene ends with Jake triumphantly holding forth, retelling to a rapt audience a story that Marilyn has just botched. This implies that her own storytelling deficiencies are the cause of her failing to command attention. But it could well be that even if Marilyn had been able to tell a good story, her family wouldn't have listened, because they had long since come to assume that Jake tells stories and Marilyn doesn't. By the same process, since more men than women are comfortable holding forth to a crowd, it may well be that it is difficult for women to get center stage, regardless of how articulate they are, because a norm is established by which most people expect men, and not women, to command attention.

GROWING UP INVISIBLE

Anthropologists Frederick Erickson and Susan Florio recorded a real-life conversation that could have been a blueprint for the family created by Jules Feiffer in *Grown Ups*. Erickson studied the videotape they made of a dinner table conversation of an Italian family in Boston. The youngest boy in the family had fallen off his bicycle and he had a bruise to prove it. To comfort him, his father and brothers told him—and everyone present—about times they had fallen off their bikes. In their stories, they didn't just fall off, they "wiped out" their bikes, lending an air of glamour and daring to their accidents. The longest and most impressive story was told by the father, who had the biggest bike: a motorcycle. In this way, the older boys and men in the family gave the youngest brother a lesson in fearlessness as well as storytelling. Not only was doing dangerous things part of being a man, but so was crashing—and telling about it before an audience of other men and appreciative women.

Throughout this portion of the conversation, the boys and men told stories, while the women—the mother, the sister, and Susan Florio, the researcher-guest—took the role of audience. Florio was a particularly important member of the audience, because it was partly for her, an attractive young woman, that the young men were displaying their prowess at riding bikes, weathering crashes, and telling stories. When the daughter, the little boy's sister, tried to tell about falling off her bike, nobody paid any attention to her, and she never got past the first line, which is highlighted in the excerpt with boldface type.

FATHER: [About youngest brother Jimmy's bruise] That's really a good one, huh?

MOTHER: Yeah.

JIMMY: Yeah, and a scrape near the—

FATHER: You should keep a patch on that.

BROTHER 2: Go get the patch—

BROTHER 3: The patching kit. Scrape down— [Kidding Jimmy by analogy with a tire-patching kit]

SISTER: **I wiped out my bike on the hill.**

BROTHER 1: Last time I did it. That was a good wipeout.

BROTHER ?: /??/ was the last time I did this.

FATHER: I'll have to get you a helmet too.

BROTHER 1: [To brother 2] I think one of my best, my best wipeouts, was when I hit you when I was doing about twenty.

The little brother's wipeout—falling off his bike—is the object of a lot of attention. But the little girl's attempt to tell about her wipeout is completely ignored, just as Marilyn finds her attempts to tell about her experience ignored by her family in Feiffer's play.

There are many reasons this could happen. It could be that the way the little girl goes about getting a turn is different. After announcing that she wiped out her bike on the hill, she may have waited to be encouraged to continue, whereas the boys just pressed on until they got to tell their stories. She may have spoken too quietly and tentatively. Or it may simply be that the family is not interested in girls' stories in general, or girls' wipeouts in particular.

In his paper, Erickson shows that the wipeout stories are lessons in male behavior. Through attention to their stories, the boys are learning, and demonstrating for the youngest boy, that risking danger in riding a bike is good, getting hurt is unavoidable, sustaining injury bravely is commendable, technical knowledge and skill can be useful (there is a lot of talk about the mechanics of brakes and the engineering of roads), and telling about risking danger, sustaining injury, and applying and displaying technical expertise is a good way to get attention and impress people. Perhaps none of these lessons are deemed relevant for the sister. In any event, the net effect is that the boys in the family are learning to hold center stage by talking; the girl in the family is learning to listen.

LISTENER AS UNDERLING

Clearly men are not always talking and women are not always listening. I have asked men whether they ever find themselves in the position of listening to another man giving them a lecture, and how they feel about it. They tell me that this does happen. They may find themselves talking to someone who presses information on them so insistently that they give in and listen. They say they don't mind too much, however, if the information is interesting. They can store it away for future use, like remembering a joke to tell others later. Factual information is of less interest to women because it is of less use to them. They are unlikely to try to pass on the gift of information, more likely to give the gift of being a good audience.

Men as well as women sometimes find themselves on the receiving end of a lecture they would as soon not hear. But men tell me that it is most likely to happen if the other man is in a position of higher status. They know they have to listen to lectures from fathers and bosses.

That men can find themselves in the position of unwilling listener is attested to by a short opinion piece in which A. R.

Gurney bemoans being frequently "cornered by some self-styled expert who harangues me with his considered opinion on an interminable agenda of topics." He claims that this tendency bespeaks a peculiarly American inability to "converse"—that is, engage in a balanced give-and-take—and cites as support the French observer of American customs Alexis de Tocqueville, who wrote, "An American . . . speaks to you as if he was addressing a meeting." Gurney credits his own appreciation of conversing to his father, who "was a master at eliciting and responding enthusiastically to the views of others, though this resiliency didn't always extend to his children. Indeed, now I think about it, he spoke to us many times as if he were addressing a meeting."

It is not surprising that Gurney's father lectured his children. The act of giving information by definition frames one in a position of higher status, while the act of listening frames one as lower. Children instinctively sense this—as do most men. But when women listen to men, they are not thinking in terms of status. Unfortunately, their attempts to reinforce connections and establish rapport, when interpreted through the lens of status, can be misinterpreted as casting them in a subordinate position—and are likely to be taken that way by many men.

WHAT'S SO FUNNY?

The economy of exchanging jokes for laughter is a parallel one. In her study of college students' discussion groups, Aries found that the students in all-male groups spent a lot of time telling about times they had played jokes on others, and laughing about it. She refers to a study in which Barbara Miller Newman found that high school boys who were not "quick and clever" became the targets of jokes. Practical joking—playing a joke *on* someone—is clearly a matter of being one-up: in the know and in control. It is less obvious, but no less true, that *telling* jokes can also be a way of negotiating status.

Many women (certainly not all) laugh at jokes but do not

later remember them. Since they are not driven to seek and hold center stage in a group, they do not need a store of jokes to whip out for this purpose. A woman I will call Bernice prided herself on her sense of humor. At a cocktail party, she met a man to whom she was drawn because he seemed at first to share this trait. He made many funny remarks, which she spontaneously laughed at. But when she made funny remarks, he seemed not to hear. What had happened to his sense of humor? Though telling jokes and laughing at them are both reflections of a sense of humor, they are very different social activities. Making others laugh gives you a fleeting power over them: As linguist Wallace Chafe points out, at the moment of laughter, a person is temporarily disabled. The man Bernice met was comfortable only when he was making her laugh, not the other way around. When Bernice laughed at his jokes, she thought she was engaging in a symmetrical activity. But he was engaging in an asymmetrical one.

A man told me that sometime around tenth grade he realized that he preferred the company of women to the company of men. He found that his female friends were more supportive and less competitive, whereas his male friends seemed to spend all their time joking. Considering joking an asymmetrical activity makes it clearer why it would fit in with a style he perceived as competitive.

"WHO DO YOU THINK YOU'RE TALKING TO?"

Subtle asymmetries in listening and speaking may also shed light on the common complaint that men often don't talk to women at home. Gerry Philipsen is an anthropologist who spent two and a half years working among teenage boys in an urban Italian working-class neighborhood. These boys were loud and loquacious when hanging around with each other on the street corner or in the local bar. But they did not talk to superiors or inferiors.

If they wanted to get something from a person in a position of authority, they relied on intermediaries, just as they prayed to a saint for intercession rather than praying directly to God. To those in a subordinate position—children, women, or boys of lower status—they got their way by a show of physical power and, if necessary, violent action. To talk to someone of higher status would be cheeky, bold, out of order. To talk to someone of lower status would be weak, ineffectual, and inviting subordination.

There are two ways in which the culture of these "macho" teenage boys is similar to the culture of girls and women. Like girls, these boys gain status by affiliation: The more influential people they know, the more status they have. But the point of affiliation for them is power—they use their connections to get things done. For girls, affiliation is an end in itself: Their status goes up if they're friends with high-status girls. These boys are like girls in that they talk only when they feel comfortable, among peers. But why don't they want to talk to girls? It may be that they assume that the girls are lower in status, whereas the girls feel—or want to feel—that a partner, even a male one, is a peer.

Class differences may play a larger role in conversational styles than we think. Sociologist Mirra Komarovsky, in her classic study *Blue Collar Marriage,* found that the more middle class a couple was, the more the husband and wife considered each other friends. Among high school graduates, there was an expectation that a husband should talk to his wife. Among those who had not graduated from high school, wives who wanted their husbands to talk to them were thought to be inappropriately demanding. The expectation was that wives should talk to their female relatives and leave their husbands alone.

MUTUAL ACCUSATIONS

Considering these dynamics, it is not surprising that many women complain that their partners don't listen to them. But men make the same complaint about women, although less frequently. The accusation "You're not listening" often really means "You don't understand what I said in the way that I meant it," or "I'm not getting the response I wanted." Being listened to can become a metaphor for being understood and being valued.

In my earlier work I emphasized that women may get the impression men aren't listening to them even when the men really are. This happens because men have different habitual ways of showing they're listening. As anthropologists Maltz and Borker explain, women are more inclined to ask questions. They also give more listening responses—little words like *mhm, uh-uh,* and *yeah*—sprinkled throughout someone else's talk, providing a running feedback loop. And they respond more positively and enthusiastically, for example by agreeing and laughing.

All this behavior is doing the work of listening. It also creates rapport-talk by emphasizing connection and encouraging more talk. The corresponding strategies of men—giving fewer listener responses, making statements rather than asking questions, and challenging rather than agreeing—can be understood as moves in a contest by incipient speakers rather than audience members.

Not only do women give more listening signals, according to Maltz and Borker, but the signals they give have different meanings for men and women, consistent with the speaker/audience alignment. Women use "yeah" to mean "I'm with you, I follow," whereas men tend to say "yeah" only when they agree. The opportunity for misunderstanding is clear. When a man is confronted with a women who has been saying "yeah," "yeah," "yeah," and then turns out not to agree, he may conclude that she has been insincere, or that she was agreeing without really listening. When a woman is confronted with a man who does *not* say "yeah"—or much of anything else—she may conclude that *he* hasn't been listening. The men's style is more literally focused on the message level of talk, while the women's is focused on the relationship or metamessage level.

To a man who expects a listener to be quietly attentive, a woman giving a stream of feedback and support will seem to be talking too much for a listener. To a woman who expects a listener to be active and enthusiastic in showing interest, attention, and support, a man who listens silently will seem not to be listening at all, but rather to have checked out of the conversation, taken his listening marbles, and gone mentally home.

Because of these patterns, women may get the impression that men aren't listening when they really are. But I have come to understand, more recently, that it is also true that men listen to women less frequently than women listen to men, because the act of listening has different meanings for them. Some men really *don't* want to listen at length because they feel it frames them as subordinate. Many women do want to listen, but they expect it to be reciprocal—I listen to you now; you listen to me later. They become frustrated when they do the listening now and now and now, and later never comes.

MUTUAL DISSATISFACTION

If women are dissatisfied with always being in the listening position, the dissatisfaction may be mutual. That a woman feels she has been assigned the role of silently listening audience does not mean that a man feels he has consigned her to that role—or that he necessarily likes the rigid alignment either.

During the time I was working on this book, I found myself at a book party filled with people I hardly knew. I struck up a conversation with a charming young man who turned out to be a painter. I asked him about his work and, in response to his answer, asked whether there has been a return in contemporary art to figurative painting. In response to my question, he told me a lot about the history of art—so much that when he finished and said, "That was a long answer to your question," I had long since forgotten that I had asked a question, let alone what it was. I had not minded this monologue—I had been interested in it— but I realized, with something of a jolt, that I had just experienced the dynamic that I had been writing about.

I decided to risk offending my congenial new acquaintance

in order to learn something about his point of view. This was, after all, a book party, so I might rely on his indulgence if I broke the rules of decorum in the interest of writing a book. I asked whether he often found himself talking at length while someone else listened. He thought for a moment and said yes, he did, because he liked to explore ideas in detail. I asked if it happened equally with women and men. He thought again and said, "No, I have more trouble with men." I asked what he meant by trouble. He said, "Men interrupt. *They* want to explain to *me*."

Finally, having found this young man disarmingly willing to talk about the conversation we had just had and his own style, I asked which he preferred: that a woman listen silently and supportively, or that she offer opinions and ideas of her own. He said he thought he liked it better if she volunteered information, making the interchange more interesting.

When men begin to lecture other men, the listeners are experienced at trying to sidetrack the lecture, or match it, or derail it. In this system, making authoritative pronouncements may be a way to begin an *exchange* of information. But women are not used to responding in that way. They see little choice but to listen attentively and wait for their turn to be allotted to them rather than seizing it for themselves. If this is the case, the man may be as bored and frustrated as the woman when his attempt to begin an exchange of information ends in his giving a lecture. From his point of view, she is passively soaking up information, so she must not have any to speak of. One of the reasons men's talk to women frequently turns into lecturing is *because* women listen attentively and do not interrupt with challenges, sidetracks, or matching information.

In the conversations with male and female colleagues that I recounted at the outset of this chapter, this difference may have been crucial. When I talked to the woman, we each told about our own research in response to the other's encouragement. When I talked to the man, I encouraged him to talk about his work, and he obliged, but he did not encourage me to talk about mine. This may mean that he did not want to hear about it—but it also may not. In her study of college students' discussion groups, Aries found that women who did a lot of talking began to feel uncomfortable; they backed off and frequently drew out quieter members of the group. This is perfectly in keeping with women's desire to keep things balanced, so everyone is on an equal footing. Women expect their conversational partners to encourage them to hold forth. Men who do not typically encourage quieter members to speak up, assume that anyone who has something to say will volunteer it. The men may be equally disappointed in a conversational partner who turns out to have nothing to say.

Similarly, men can be as bored by women's topics as women can be by men's. While I was wishing the former RAFer would tell me about his personal experiences in Greece, he was probably wondering why I was boring him with mine and marveling at my ignorance of the history of a country I had lived in. Perhaps he would have considered our conversation a success if I had challenged or topped his interpretation of Greek history rather than listening dumbly to it. When men, upon hearing the kind of work I do, challenge me about my research methods, they are inviting me to give them information and show them my expertise—something I don't like to do outside of the classroom or lecture hall, but something they themselves would likely be pleased to be provoked to do.

The publicist who listened attentively to information about a radio station explained to me that she wanted to be nice to the manager, to smooth the way for placing her clients on his station. But men who want to ingratiate themselves with women are more likely to try to charm them by offering interesting information than by listening attentively to whatever information the women have to impart. I recall a luncheon preceding a talk I delivered to a college alumni association. My gracious host kept me entertained before my speech by regaling me with information about computers, which I politely showed interest in, while inwardly screaming from boredom and a sense of being weighed down by irrelevant information that I knew I would never remember. Yet I am sure he thought he was being interesting, and it is likely that at least some male guests would have thought that he was. I do not wish to imply that all women hosts have entertained me in the perfect way. I recall a speaking engagement before which I was taken to lunch by a group of women. They were so attentive to my expertise that they plied me with questions, prompting me to exhaust myself by giving my lecture over lunch before the formal lecture began. In comparison to this, perhaps the man who lectured to me about computers was trying to give me a rest.

The imbalance by which men often find themselves in the role of lecturer, and women often find themselves in the role of audience, is not the creation of only one member of an interaction. It is not something that men do to women. Neither is it something that women culpably "allow" or "ask for." The imbalance is created by the difference between women's and men's habitual styles.

HAMPERED BY STYLE

"War with Japan," a story by Frederick Barthelme, shows a man retreating into lecturing his son not because he wants to, but because it's familiar and safe. The story begins with the narrator announcing that he is going to move out of the house and into an apartment over the garage, because he and his wife have "been having a kind of trouble." He thinks about asking their twelve-year-old son to help him move his things:

> I think I'll take the opportunity to explain why I'm switching out to the garage, and then I think maybe I won't, because it won't come out clear. I don't know why I want to explain stuff to him—I guess I want to win him. . . .

When the narrator approaches his son and tells him he wants to have a talk with him, this is what he says:

> "What I want to tell you is that there are all these things wrong now, and they didn't use to be wrong. I'm figuring

you're going to notice that they're wrong and start wondering *why,* so I thought I'd get a step up, you know? Doing my duty."

He looks uncertain, so I say, "Let me give you an example. I was sitting inside here thinking about a war with the Japanese. Now, Charles, we're not about to have any war with the Japanese, you understand that, right?"

The father ends up lecturing his son about the Japanese, the Russians, the American government, and society. He makes jokes. He does not say anything about himself, his feelings, his move out of the house, or his relationship with the boy's mother and the boy. The story is ironic and sad because it is clear that this father will not "win" his son this way. The lecture he gives about war with Japan is of no interest to the boy, nor is it what the father really wanted to say. He slipped into explaining what was going on in the world because he found it more familiar, and hence easier to talk about, than explaining what was going on in the family.

This father seems to have succumbed to his fear that if he tried to explain why he was moving to the garage, it wouldn't "come out clear." He feels he should have precise answers and explanations, as he does about politics. Perhaps he would feel freer to say what is on his mind if he gave up the belief that he can't speak unless he has everything all worked out. His son would have benefited more from hearing his father's personal thoughts and feelings, even if they weren't perfectly clear. The man in this story was handicapped by his habitual style.

On the other hand, always taking the role of respondent rather than initiator is limiting to women. This tendency has significant consequences in sexual relations. Philip Blumstein and Pepper Schwartz, in their study *American Couples,* found that lesbians have sex less often than gay men and heterosexual couples. The sociologists believe that this happens because, as they found, in heterosexual couples the man almost always initiates sex, and the woman either complies or exercises veto power. Among gay men, at least one partner takes the role of initiator. But among lesbians, they found, often neither feels comfortable taking the role of initiator, because neither wants to be perceived as making demands.

HOPE FOR THE FUTURE

What is the hope for the future? Must we play out our assigned parts to the closing act? Although we tend to fall back on habitual ways of talking, repeating old refrains and familiar lines, habits can be broken. Women and men both can gain by understanding the other gender's style, and by learning to use it on occasion.

Women who find themselves unwillingly cast as the listener should practice propelling themselves out of that position rather than waiting patiently for the lecture to end. Perhaps they need to give up the belief that they must wait for the floor to be handed to them. If they have something to say on a subject, they might push themselves to volunteer it. If they are bored with a subject, they can exercise some influence on the conversation and change the topic to something they would rather discuss.

If women are relieved to learn that they don't always have to listen, there may be some relief for men in learning that they don't always have to have interesting information on the tips of their tongues if they want to impress a woman or entertain her. A journalist once interviewed me for an article about how to strike up conversations. She told me that another expert she had interviewed, a man, had suggested that one should come up with an interesting piece of information. I found this amusing, as it seemed to typify a man's idea of a good conversationalist, but not a woman's. How much easier men might find the task of conversation if they realized that all they have to do is listen. As a woman who wrote a letter to the editor of *Psychology Today* put it, "When I find a guy who asks, 'How was your day?' and really wants to know, I'm in heaven."

SIX

Community and Contest: Styles in Conflict

When two people's paths cross, there is bound to be a conflict of interest: We can't both stand on the same spot without one of us standing on the other's foot. If no one steps aside, someone will get stepped on. You and I are not the same person, so some of our wants will be different and conflict is inevitable. Because we can't both get our way, we may find ourselves in a power struggle.

It may seem at first that conflict is the opposite of rapport and affiliation. Much of what has been written about women's and men's styles claims that males are competitive and prone to conflict whereas females are cooperative and given to affiliation. But being in conflict also means being involved with each other. Although it is true that many women are more comfortable using language to express rapport whereas many men are more comfortable using it for self-display, the situation is really more complicated than that, because self-display, when part of a mutual struggle, is also a kind of bonding. And conflict may be valued as a way of creating involvement with others.

To most women, conflict is a threat to connection, to be avoided at all costs. Disputes are preferably settled without direct confrontation. But to many men, conflict is the necessary means by which status is negotiated, so it is to be accepted and may even be sought, embraced, and enjoyed.

Walter Ong, a scholar of cultural linguistics, shows in his book *Fighting for Life* that "adversativeness"—pitting one's needs, wants, or skills against those of others—is an essential part of being human, but "conspicuous or expressed adversativeness is a larger element in the lives of males than of females." He demonstrates that male behavior typically entails contest, which includes combat, struggle, conflict, competition, and contention. Pervasive in male behavior is ritual combat, typified by rough play and sports. Females, on the other hand, are more likely to use intermediaries or to fight for real rather than ritualized purposes. Friendship among men often has a large element of friendly aggression, which women are likely to mistake for the real thing.

Ong demonstrates the inextricable relationship between oral performance and "agonistic" relations. Oral disputation—from formal debate to the study of formal logic—is inherently adversative. With this in mind, we can see that the inclination of many men to expect discussions and arguments in daily conversation to adhere to rules of logic is a remnant of this tradition. Furthermore, oral performance in self-display—what I have been calling report-talk—is part of a larger framework in which many men approach life as a contest.

Because their imaginations are not captured by ritualized combat, women are inclined to misinterpret and be puzzled by the adversativeness of many men's ways of speaking and miss the *ritual* nature of friendly aggression. At the same time, the enactment of community can be ritualized just as easily as the enactment of combat. The appearance of community among women may mask power struggles, and the appearance of sameness may mask profound differences in points of view. Men can be as confused by women's verbal rituals as women are by men's. Such confusions abound in the verbal lives of couples.

"DON'T TELL ME WHAT TO DO"

A woman I'll call Diana often begins statements with "Let's." She might say, "Let's go out for brunch today," or "Let's clean up now, before we start lunch." This makes Nathan angry. He feels she is ordering him around, telling him what to do. Diana can't understand why he takes it that way. It is obvious to her that she is making suggestions, not demands. If he doesn't feel like doing what she proposes, all he has to do is say so. She would not press her preference if she knew it wasn't what he wanted.

Loraine frequently compliments Sidney and thanks him for doing things such as cleaning up the kitchen and doing the laundry. Instead of appreciating the praise, Sidney resents it. "It makes me feel like you're demanding that I do it all the time," he explains. Another man made a similar comment about his mother. She praised him for calling her, saying, "You're a very good person." He felt she was trying to ensure that he call her regularly by implying that if he neglected to call, he would be a bad person.

In their study of the private lives of American couples, Philip Blumstein and Pepper Schwartz quote a young man who, in discussing his sexual relationship with his girlfriend, told them, "We were in bed and she was saying, 'Do this lighter,' or 'Do this softer,' and I just told her that I was making love to her and she was going to have to let me do it my own way. . . . You don't want to feel bossed around. . . .'"

In all these examples, men complained that their independence and freedom were being encroached on. Their early warning system is geared to detect signs that they are being told what to do—even in so apparently affiliative an activity as making love. Such complaints surprise and puzzle women, whose early warning systems are geared to detect a different menace. Being on the lookout for threats to independence makes sense in the framework of an agonistic world, where life is a series of contests that test a man's skill and force him to struggle against others who are trying to bend his will to theirs. If a man experiences life as a fight for freedom, he is naturally inclined to resist attempts to control him and determine his behavior.

This world view has given rise to the concept of the henpecked husband: Many men resent any inkling that their wives want to get them to do things. Women's lives have historically been hemmed in at every turn by the demands of others—their families, their husbands—and yet, though individual women may complain of overbearing husbands, there is no parallel stereotype of a "roosterpecked wife." Why not? Seeing people as interdependent, women expect their actions to be influenced by others, and they expect people to act in concert. Their struggle is to keep the ties strong, keep everyone in the community, and accommodate to others' needs while making what efforts they can at damage control with respect to their own needs and preferences. If a man struggles to be strong, a woman struggles to keep the community strong.

LET'S GO BACK TO THE CHILDREN

The misunderstanding between Diana and Nathan can be traced to habitual conversational styles typical of women and men—styles that take shape with the first words children learn to use at play. Diana's tendency to make proposals beginning with "Let's" is not just idiosyncratic. Researchers who study children at play have found that girls of all ages tend to speak in this way.

Psychologist Jacqueline Sachs and her colleagues, studying

preschoolers between the ages of two and five, found that girls tended to make proposals for action by saying "Let's," whereas boys often gave each other commands. For example, in playing doctor, the little boys said things like:

"Lie down."

"Get the heart thing."

"Gimme your arm."

"Try to give me medicine."

When girls played doctor, they said things like "Let's sit down and use it."

Marjorie Harness Goodwin found exactly the same pattern in a completely different group—black children between the ages of six and fourteen, playing on the streets of a Philadelphia neighborhood. The boys, who were (agonistically) making sling-shots in preparation for a fight, gave each other orders:

"Gimme the pliers!"

"Man, don't come *in* here where I *am*."

"Give me that, man. After this, after you chop 'em, give 'em to me."

"Get off my steps."

The girls, who were making glass rings out of bottle necks, didn't issue commands. They made proposals beginning with "Let's":

"Let's go around Subs and Suds [a corner bar/restaurant]."

"Let's ask her, 'Do you have any bottles?' "

"Come on. Let's go find some."

"Come on. Let's turn back, y'all, so we can safe keep 'em."

"Let's move *these* out *first*."

Other ways the girls proposed activities were with "We gonna" ("We gonna make a *whole* display of rings"), "We could" ("We *could* use a sewer" [to sand down the glass surfaces of the rings]), "Maybe" ("Maybe we can slice them like that"), and "We gotta"

("We gotta find some more bottles"). All these are attempts to influence what the others do without telling them what to do. At the same time, they reinforce the identities of the girls as members of a community.

Children may be influenced by their parents' styles, just as adults are influenced by what they learned as children. Psycholinguist Jean Berko Gleason studied how parents talk to their young children, and found that fathers issue more commands to their children than mothers do, and they issue more commands to their sons than to their daughters. Sociolinguist Frances Smith observed a similar pattern in a public-speaking situation. Examining the practice sermons of male and female students at a Baptist seminary, she found that when referring to chapters and verses in their exegesis, the men frequently gave the audience orders, such as "Listen carefully as I read Luke, chapter seventeen." The women, on the other hand, rarely uttered imperatives but rather tended to invite the audience to participate, as in "Let's go back to verses fifteen and sixteen."

Given this pattern, Nathan is not far off the mark when he hears "Let's" as equivalent to a command. It *is* a way of getting others to do what someone wants. And yet Diana is also right when she says he should not feel coerced. The difference lies in the fundamentally different social structures of girls and boys, and women and men. In the hierarchical order that boys and men find or feel themselves in, status is indeed gained by telling others what to do and resisting being told what to do. So once Nathan has deciphered Diana's "Let's" as her way of saying what she wants him to do, his next step is to resist her. But girls and women find or feel themselves in a community that is threatened by conflict, so they formulate requests as proposals rather than orders to make it easy for others to express other preferences without provoking a confrontation. Not accustomed to having others try to bend their will simply to solidify a dominant position, girls do not learn to resist others' demands on principle and don't expect others to resist theirs on principle either.

It is not that women do not want to get their way, but that they do not want to purchase it at the cost of conflict. The irony of interactions like those between Diana and Nathan is that the differences between men's and women's styles doom their efforts. The very moves that women make to avoid confrontation have the effect of sparking it in conversation with some men. Insofar as men perceive that someone is trying to get them to do something without coming right out and saying so, they feel manipulated and threatened by an enemy who is all the more sinister for refusing to come out in the open.

"I'LL BE THE DOCTOR AND YOU BE THE BABY"

These differences in approaches to conflict have many other ramifications in ways of talking as well. In her study of preschoolers at play, Sachs found that when little boys played doctor, "I'll be the doctor" was the normal stance. Boys wanted to take the doctor role 79 percent of the time, and they often got into long arguments about which boy would get this high-status role. Others have found similar patterns. Linguist Elaine Anderson had preschoolers play out doctor-patient scenes with hand puppets. She too found that the boys wanted to take the high-status role of doctor and generally refused to be the patient or baby. The girls wanted to be the doctor only a third of the time; they often wanted to be the patient, the baby, or the mother.

In Sachs's study, in the vast majority of cases, boys told each other what role to take ("Come on, be a doctor"). Girls, on the other hand, usually asked each other what role they wanted ("Will you be the patient for a few minutes?") or made a joint proposal ("I'll be the nurse and you be the doctor"; "Now we can both be doctors"; "We both can be sick"; or "Okay, and I'll be the doctor for my baby and you be the doctor for your baby"). Many of these proposals, in addition to avoiding confrontation or telling others what to do, are creative ways of keeping the girls equal in status.

Do these experimental studies, in which children played in a laboratory setting, accurately reflect how children play in natural settings? Evidence that they do appears in an article written by a father, Rodger Kamenetz, that begins:

> My daughter Anya, six, and her friend Rosemary, seven, were playing together in Anya's room. The door was ajar, and when I heard some cooing noises, I peeked in and saw that each child was holding a Cabbage Patch doll, cradling it in her arms. "Now you change your baby," said Rosemary to Anya, "and I'll change mine."

In reading this I was struck by the symmetry of the girls' play. Rosemary was proposing that they both engage in the same activity at the same time. Instead of trying to cast Anya in the low-status role of baby, she reserved that role for the unprotesting Cabbage Patch dolls.

DIFFERENT SOCIAL STRUCTURES

Girls' and boys' different ways of trying to influence each other's behavior reflect—and create—different social structures. In getting ready for their slingshot fight, the boys in Goodwin's study evidenced a hierarchical organization: The leaders told the others what to do. Giving orders and getting others to follow them was the way that certain boys got to be and stay leaders. A command, by definition, distinguishes the speaker from the addressee and frames him as having more power. In contrast, the girls' groups were organized in an egalitarian way; according to Goodwin, "In accomplishing a task activity even among four- and five-year-olds, all participate jointly in decision making with minimal negotiation of status." By framing proposals with "Let's" and "We," the girls implied that their group was a community, and the results of compliance would increase the power of the community, not the individual power of the person making the suggestion.

Furthermore, the boys typically did not give reasons for their demands, other than their desires. For example, a boy who took a leadership role made demands like:

"PLIERS. I WANT THE PLIERS!"
"Look, man. I want the wire cutters right now."

But the girls gave reasons for their suggestions:

SHARON: We gotta *clean* 'em first. You know.
PAM: I know.
SHARON: 'Cause they got germs.
PAM: Wash 'em and stuff 'cause just in case they got germs on 'em.

Not giving reasons for their demands, the boys reinforced their orders as moves in a contest. Compliance indicated submission to the authority of the leader, although submission is an act of cooperation insofar as it reinforces the smooth working of the group. But the girls' methods of getting their way worked differently. Not only did they give reasons, but the reasons were for the general good: The bottles should be cleaned so no one would be harmed by germs. When Pam collaborated by echoing Sharon's suggestion and also her reason, she appeared to be participating in the decision making rather than following orders. This does not, however, mean that there may not be a pattern in whose suggestions tend to be taken up, or that someone whose suggestions are frequently taken up may not feel personal satisfaction and gain prestige in the group.

The different social structures that boys and girls maintained went along with the sorts of activities they preferred. Boys particularly liked to play openly competitive games, such as football and basketball. Even for activities that were not competitive by nature, the boys often broke into teams to facilitate competition. Girls were not much interested in organized sports or games. They preferred whole-group activities such as jump rope or hopscotch.

Goodwin found that the boys ranked themselves according to skill at different activities and often boasted and bragged about their abilities and possessions. Like the little boys in Sachs's study, arguing over who would get to be the doctor, the preteen and teenage boys in Goodwin's study argued about status—about relative skill and who had the power to tell whom what to do. The girls argued about their relative appearance, their relationships to others, and what others said about them. Whereas boys boasted that they were better, a girl who acted as if she was better than the others was criticized for "bragging" or "showing off."

Boys not only commanded but also insulted and threatened each other. If they had a complaint about another boy, they tended to voice it in his presence. Girls' complaints, however, were typically voiced in the absence of the accused.

The girls' preference to avoid direct confrontation resulted in behavior that is traditionally thought of in a negative way—talking behind someone's back. Expressing this negative view, one man remarked that girls sacrifice sincerity for harmony. The accusation of "insincerity" is commonplace in cross-cultural communication, because culturally different individuals don't talk in ways that seem obviously appropriate. Sparking direct confrontation by expressing criticism may seem "sincere" to those who believe that confrontation reinforces camaraderie. But in a system where confrontation causes rifts, it would not be "sincere" at all, since directly expressing criticism and sparking a fight would send a metamessage that one wants to weaken the bonds of friendship.

"YOU DIDN'T SAY WHY"

These differences in children's experience result in divergent expectations, assumptions, and attitudes that confuse adult conversations. For example, the following argument arose because the woman expected to hear reasons from a man who was not in the habit of giving them. Maureen and Philip were trying to set a date for a dinner party.

MAUREEN: The only weekend we seem to have free is October tenth.

PHILIP: That's the opening of hunting season.

MAUREEN: Well, let's do it Saturday or Sunday evening.

PHILIP: Okay, make it Saturday.

MAUREEN: Wouldn't you want to be able to hunt later on the first day of hunting?

PHILIP: [Annoyed] I *said* Saturday, so obviously that's the day I prefer.

MAUREEN: [Now also annoyed] I was just trying to be considerate of you. You didn't give a reason for choosing Saturday.

PHILIP: I'm taking off Thursday and Friday to hunt, so I figure I'll have had enough by Saturday night.

MAUREEN: Well, why didn't you say that?

PHILIP: I didn't see why I had to. And I found your question very intrusive.

MAUREEN: I found your response very offensive!

Since Philip didn't give a reason for choosing Saturday, Maureen assumed he might be accommodating to what he perceived to be her preference, as she might have done—indeed, as she was doing. She wanted to let him know that it wasn't necessary, and she was hurt by his objecting when she was being considerate. To Philip, being asked to explain his reasons feels like having to give an account of his time. He assumes that individuals watch out for their own interests, so her poking around in his interests is intrusive. Her attempts to ameliorate a potential conflict of interests actually sparked a conflict.

A GOOD KNOCK-DOWN DRAG-OUT FIGHT

Differences in attitudes toward conflict itself show up in daily conversations. Gail hates to argue. If Norman becomes angry and raises his voice, she is deeply upset. "I can't talk to you if you're yelling," she says. "Why can't we discuss this like mature people?" Norman can never figure this out. To him, being able to fight with someone is evidence of intimacy. In contrast, the endless monotonous discussions that she values as a sign of intimacy are anathema to him. They just wear him down, whereas he feels fine after a good knock-down, drag-out fight—which leaves her feeling weary and defeated. He regards such fighting as a form of ritual combat and values it as a sign of involvement, since only those who are intimately involved with each other argue.

Many cultures of the world see arguing as a pleasurable sign of intimacy, as well as a game. Americans in Greece often get the feeling that they are witnessing an argument when they are over-hearing a friendly conversation that is more heated than such a conversation would be if Americans were having it. Linguist Deborah Schiffrin showed that in the conversations of working-class Eastern European Jewish speakers—both male and female—in Philadelphia, friendly argument was a means of being sociable. Linguist Jane Frank analyzed the conversation of a Jewish couple who tended to polarize and take argumentative positions in social situations. But they were not fighting. They were staging a kind of public sparring, where both fighters were on the same side.

Greeks often show caring by telling people what to do. A Greek woman studying in the United States surprised and annoyed her dorm-mates by asking them questions like "Why are you keeping the refrigerator door open so long?" and "Why are you eating so little? You have to eat more than that." These questions would be common among friends in Greece and would be valued as a show of concern and involvement. To Americans, they are intrusive and critical. Her American dorm-mates responded by calling the Greek woman "Mom." What she intended as a sign of intimate caring was taken as a show of status characteristic of mothers talking to children.

Sociologists William Corsaro and Thomas Rizzo studied children in American and Italian nursery schools between the ages of two and four. They found that one of the Italian children's favorite activities was engaging in the kind of heated debate that Italians call *discussione* but Americans would regard as arguing. The researchers describe a typical instance of a routine that was

played out several times a week, when the children were supposed to be quietly drawing with felt marking pens: A boy, Rob-
erto, makes a display of searching for a red marker. Making sure
everyone at his table is watching, he tries and discards all the red
markers at his table, then gets up and takes one from another
table. The children at the other table either don't notice or, more
likely, pretend not to notice. But before long, a girl at that table,
Antonia, asks loudly, "Where's red?" and *she* makes a show of
searching for a red marker and displaying dissatisfaction with all
those she and her tablemates can find.

Then the drama begins. This is how Corsaro and Rizzo describe it:

> Antonia slaps her forehead with the palm of her hand and
> shouts, "They robbed us!"
>
> This exclamation sets several things in motion simulta-
> neously. Roberto looks up from his work and smiles at the
> other children at his table. They all catch his eye and smile
> back, signaling that they know what is about to happen. At
> the same time, several of the children at the third table look
> over to Antonia's table and then quickly over to Roberto's.
> Finally, at Antonia's table Maria jumps up, points to Ro-
> berto and shouts: "It was Roberto!" Immediately Antonia,
> Maria and several other children march over to Roberto's
> table. Just as they arrive, a girl at the table, Luisa, grabs
> seven or eight markers (including the one Roberto took) and
> hides them in her lap under the table. Once at the table An-
> tonia accuses Roberto of stealing the red marker. He denies
> it, challenging Antonia and the others to find the stolen
> marker. As Antonia and Maria begin to look for the red
> marker, Bruna, backed by several other children from the
> third table, enters the dispute, claiming that Roberto did in-
> deed steal the marker and that Luisa is hiding it. Luisa shouts,
> "No, it's not true!" But Antonia reaches under the table and
> grabs the markers that Luisa is hiding. At this point there
> is a great deal of shouting, gesturing, pushing and shov-

ing and the teachers must once again intervene and settle the dispute.

These children are not squabbling over a red marker; there are more than enough markers to go around. As Corsaro and Rizzo put it, they would simply rather argue than draw. And this seems to go for girls as well as boys in the Italian preschool.

FIGHTING FOR FRIENDSHIP

Though *discussione*—loudly arguing for the fun of it—is enjoyed by both girls and boys in the Italian preschool, American boys and girls are less well matched in their attitudes toward conflict. Boys are far more likely to express and create affiliation by opposition. Teasing is a way that boys show affection to girls by taking an agonistic stance. A common example is the classic scene in which a boy pulls the braids of a girl he likes. I don't know any girls who liked having their braids pulled, but if she likes the boy, a girl might prefer aggression to being ignored. This was the case with a Polish girl, Eva Hoffman, who recalls her childhood companion Marek in her book *Lost in Translation*:

> I'm in love with him. I can't stay away from him, even though sometimes he plays boyishly mean pranks on me: he drops an enormous tome on my head when I pass in front of his window, and once, he tries to stuff me into a hole in the forest, which turns out to have been left there by the Germans, and might still have some mines in it.

Marek's playfulness was potentially lethal. Nonetheless, Hoffman recalls, "We talk to each other ceaselessly, and in games with other kids we're a team." In fact, "in spite of these risky games we play with each other, I have a deep belief that his greater physical strength is there to protect me."

For boys and men, aggression does not preclude friendship. Quite the contrary, it is a good way to start interaction and create involvement. A woman told me of her surprise when she was a member of a mixed group of students attending a basketball game at the University of Michigan. Although their tickets had seat assignments, the usual practice among students at this university was for spectators to take any seats they found—first come, first served. Following these unwritten rules, the students took seats in the front row of the balcony. Before long, a group of men from Michigan State University arrived, assuming they were entitled to the seats shown on their tickets. Finding people in their seats, they ordered them out. When the University of Michigan students refused to vacate the seats, a loud argument ensued in which the men of the two groups denounced and threatened each other, and the women sank down in their seats. After a while, the visitors settled for the seats adjoining the disputed ones. Then the men who had just been engaged in an angry verbal fight began a friendly chat about the teams and the schools and the game about to begin. The women were dumbfounded. They would never have engaged in such an argument, but they assumed that if they had it would have made them enemies for life, not friends in the wink of an eye.

The possibility that a fight could be a way of initiating rather than precluding friendship struck me as a revelation when I read the transcripts in Corsaro and Rizzo's study. For me, observing the peer culture of the nursery school boys was like glimpsing a foreign world. Here, for example, is an episode they describe among American preschool boys:

Two boys (Richard and Denny) have been playing with a Slinky on the stairway leading to the upstairs playhouse in the school. During their play two other boys (Joseph and Martin) enter and stand near the bottom of the stairs.

DENNY: Go!

[Martin now runs off, but Joseph remains and he eventually moves halfway up the stairs.]

JOSEPH: These are big shoes.

RICHARD: **I'll punch him right in the eye.**

JOSEPH: **I'll punch you right in the nose.**

DENNY: **I'll punch him with my big fist.**

JOSEPH: **I'll—I—I—**

RICHARD: **And he'll be bumpety, bumpety and punched out all the way down the stairs.**

JOSEPH: **I—I—I'll—I could poke your eyes out with my gun. I have a gun.**

DENNY: **A gun! I'll—I—I—even if—**

RICHARD: **I have a gun too.**

DENNY: **And I have guns too and it's bigger than yours and it's poo-poo down. That's poo-poo.**

[All three boys laugh at Denny's reference to poo-poo.]

RICHARD: **Now leave.**

JOSEPH: **Un-uh. I gonna tell you to put on—on the gun on your hair and the poop will come right out on his face.**

DENNY: **Well—**

RICHARD: **Slinky will snap right on your face too.**

DENNY: **And my gun will snap right—**

Up to this point, Richard and Denny seem to be engaged in a bitter fight with Joseph, who has tried to disrupt their Slinky game. Denny introduces a humorous tone by mentioning poo-poo, which makes all the boys laugh. But they are still threatening each other. Corsaro and Rizzo describe what happened next:

At this point a girl (Debbie) enters, says she is Batgirl, and asks if they have seen Robin. Joseph says he is Robin, but she says she is looking for a different Robin and then runs off. After Debbie leaves, Denny and Richard move into the playhouse and Joseph follows. From this point to the end of the episode the three boys play together.

After an angry fight in which they threatened to punch and shoot each other and snap the Slinky in each other's faces, the three boys play together amicably. Not only did the altercation not prevent their playing together; it facilitated it. I suspect that picking a fight was Joseph's way of making contact with the other boys, and engaging Joseph in the fight was Denny and Richard's method of easing his way into their play.

MAKING NICE

Also intriguing in this preschool episode is the part played by the girl, Debbie. It is her appearance in the guise of Batgirl that occasions the end of the boys' verbal fight and their shift to playing together peacefully. Debbie seems to swoop down like Batgirl on a peace mission.

If the boys were creating an argument, the girl manages not to say she disagrees even though she really does. When Debbie says she is looking for Robin, and Joseph says he is Robin, she does not reply, "No, you're not!" Instead, she accepts his premise and says she is looking for a different Robin.

The role of the female as peacemaker crops up again and again. In the following scene from the story "Volpone" by Jane Shapiro, a daughter takes the role of peacemaker in a fight between her mother and brother. The fight erupts because of the mother's and son's differing focuses on intimacy and independence in the act of showing concern.

In this story, the narrator is visiting her son, Zack, at college. He has been taking part in a demonstration against the university's investments in South Africa by sleeping in one of a number of shanties the students have built on campus. At dinner with his visiting family (which includes his sister Nora, his father, William, and his grandfather Pep) Zack explains that he's frustrated because, in contrast to the administrators of other universities where students "*routinely* get their heads smashed," the president of his college tolerates and even supports the student protesters, but does not exert pressure on the trustees to divest.

Here is the voice of Zack's mother, who is narrating the story:

> After a pause, I said, "Well, I'm sorry you're not making more of an impression on the trustees, but, speaking as a mother, there are times when I'm really glad you're not at Berkeley, or wherever, getting your head routinely smashed."
>
> Zack gave me a curious look, and Nora sat back and gave me an amused one. *"As a mother,"* she said. "You usually try not to say that."

By sitting back and reminding her mother that she usually tries not to speak "as a mother," Nora seems to be trying to divert her mother from the conversational path she has embarked on. But the narrator continues, with disastrous results:

> I said, "Well, I mean, I'm torn. Obviously I support you and I'm proud of you, and I think it's important you stand by your convictions, and obviously I *don't* believe in trying to keep my kids from operating independently and doing what they think is right. At the same time there's a part of me that says I really don't want you getting smashed in the head." Although stagy, this sounded so reasonable to me as to be unassailable. William was supportively, absently nodding. "It's a conflict I've not resolved," I said, "and—"
>
> "It's kind of irrelevant, Mom, whether *you want* to try to keep us from 'operating' in a certain way," Zack said. "We're people. We're already 'operating.' It's nice that you make an effort to frame it in a 'liberal' way. But your idea, Mom, about whether you should *let us* do it is kind of—I don't know, not exactly germane."

William then moves in to discipline his son in his wife's defense, and father and son are both angered. Nora steps in to defuse the anger and make everyone friends again:

> Nora leaned and set her hand on Pep's forearm. She said, "Come on, guys."

There was a silence, in which Nora reached across to Zack's plate and picked up his last curled shrimp and said to him in a warm voice, "You want this?" He moved his head back and forth. Nora held the shrimp up in her fingers before popping it in her mouth and said, "This is undeniably a Vermont shrimp." She grinned at Pep. She said, "This shrimp regrets everything."

When joking doesn't do the trick, Nora tries a direct appeal, softened with the use of a nickname that calls on her bond with Zack: "Come on, Z."

Zack's angry reaction comes as a surprise to his mother. She thinks she is showing concern for him in the spirit of connection and caring, but he interprets her comments in the spirit of status and control: If she is allowing him to act on his own, then his autonomy is not real, but granted by her. Picking up on the superiority implied by protection, Zack reacts to his mother's framing him as her child. His father tried to settle this conflict by a show of power, reinforcing Zack's lower status: He tells the boy not to talk to his mother that way. But the daughter takes the role of peacemaker, trying to nuzzle Zack out of his anger by a show of bonding.

"DON'T YOU AGREE?"

The role of peacemaker reflects the general tendency among women to seek agreement. When Marge tells John something she thought of or a comment someone else made, John often responds by pointing out a weakness in the position or an alternative perspective. This makes Marge vaguely uncomfortable. One day she repeated someone's comment that echoed a point of view John himself had argued only a few days before. She was sure he would say, "Oh, yes. That's right." In fact, her main reason for repeating the remark was to please John by offering support for his position. But, to Marge's surprise and distress, John pointed out the other side. Even when she was sure she was sowing agreement, she reaped a harvest of disagreement. To John, raising a different point of view is a more interesting contribution to make than agreeing. But Marge finds his disagreeing disagreeable, because it introduces a note of contentiousness into the conversation.

For Marge, disagreement carries a metamessage of threat to intimacy. John does not see disagreement as a threat. Quite the opposite, he regards being able to express disagreement as a sign of intimacy. One man explained to me that he feels it is his duty, when someone expresses a view, to point out the other side; if someone complains of another's behavior, he feels he should explain what that person's motives might be. When someone takes a position, he feels he ought to help explore it by trying to poke holes in it, and playing devil's advocate for the opposing view. In all this, he feels he is being supportive, and in a way he is, but it is support modeled on an adversative stance—a stance that is more expected and appreciated by men than by women.

ENTER THE CHALLENGER

This difference in approach to agreement versus challenge comes up in educational settings too. A colleague had the students in his linguistics class read my book *That's Not What I Meant!* as a course text. He then set them the assignment of composing questions for me and sent me a dozen to answer. Of the twelve students whose questions I received, ten were women and two were men. All ten women's questions were supportive or exploring, asking for clarification, explanation, or personal information. For example, they asked: "Can you explain further . . . ? "Can you give another example?" "Are differences biological or social?" "Where do you get your examples?" "How will society change if everyone accepts your ideas?" "Why did you marry your husband?" The two questions from men were challenging. One asked, in essence, "Your book deals a lot with psychology;

why did you reject the way a psychologist interrogated you at your seminar?" The other asked, "Doesn't much of the material in your book fall more easily into the realm of rhetoric and communication than linguistics?"

The women's questions seemed charming to me, but the men's seemed cheeky. I remarked on the pattern to my husband. "Well, it was a setup," he commented. "How so?" I asked. "Well," he said, "their professor told them, 'Here's your chance—here's the expert.' It's a setup to challenge you." So there it was again: He too thought it natural to challenge an expert. I, like the women in this class, think that access to an expert is a chance to learn inside information and make personal contact.

What then is the "meaning" of a challenge? I heard the men's questions as attempting to undercut my authority. Both seemed to be saying, "You aren't really a linguist," and one further questioned my interpretation of my own example. I didn't like this. I liked the women's questions better: I felt they reinforced my authority. I didn't even mind the intrusive one about my marriage, which allowed me to be wry and amusing in my response. But challenging can be a form of respect. A male colleague commented that "softball" questions are pointless when there is a serious issue involved. Making a similar point, another male colleague commented, with regard to a somewhat critical book review he had written, "In a way you honor someone by grappling with him (yes, her too)." I was intrigued that both chose adversative metaphors—from sports and combat—to explain why challenging is obviously (to them) constructive in an academic interchange. I doubt I am unusual among women in seeing challenges as somewhat more real than ritual, and to take them personally as attempts to undercut my authority rather than to bolster it by "grappling" with me.

It seems likely to me now that the young men who asked challenging questions were trying to engage me on an intellectual level. But they fell into a "cross-cultural" gap: I do not enjoy "grappling" when I feel personally challenged, though I certainly enjoy intellectual discussion if I feel my authority is respected. I would have valued their questions had they been phrased differently: "Could you explain further why you objected to the behavior of the psychologist in your example?" and "Could you expand on the relationship between your work and the fields of rhetoric and communication?" A way similar questions have been posed to me is "I agree with you, but I have trouble answering people who ask me why what I do is linguistics. How do you answer people like that?" Someone who phrases questions this way elicits the same information but takes the footing of an ally rather than an adversary.

FIGHTING TO BE NICE

Since recognizing these patterns, I have been amazed at how often men invoke the theme of aggression to accomplish affiliative ends. For example, a guest speaker in one of my classes wanted to make the point that seemingly odd behavior could have many different explanations. To illustrate, he said, "Now take this young lady here in the first row. Suppose she suddenly stood up and began strangling this other young lady sitting next to her." In reaching for an example of unexpected behavior, he just happened to think of attack.

Another man was about to begin a workshop for about thirty people in a room that was large enough to hold fifty. The audience had taken seats in the back, leaving a moat of empty rows around the speaker. When his initial request that they move forward produced no response, the speaker resorted to a teasing threat: "If you don't move forward, when you leave, I'll follow you out and kill you."

A hypnotist was trying to help a woman retrieve her knowledge of Japanese, which she had once known well but had forgotten since becoming fluent in Chinese. After inducing a light trance, he suggested, "Imagine that someone is speaking to you in Japanese, trying to push you around. Yell at them in Japanese: 'Get out of here!'" In trying to suggest an emotionally engaging situation, he hit upon one that is pivotal to most men. But I wondered—and doubted—if this would be particularly compelling for the woman. Later, in explaining his approach, he said, "Let's see if we can get the Japanese to arm-wrestle the Chinese and win."

WOLF WORDS
IN SHEEP'S CLOTHING

If boys and men often use opposition to establish connections, girls and women can use apparent cooperation and affiliation to be competitive and critical. Goodwin found, for example, that girls particularly liked a jump-rope rhyme that allowed them to count how many jumps they were making. Gossip too can be competitive, if one vies to be the first to know the news.

Developmental psychologist Linda Hughes shows the subtle balancing of cooperation and competition among fourth- and fifth-grade girls playing a game called foursquare. In this game, each of four children stands in a square drawn on the ground, as they bounce a ball among them. Anyone who misses the ball, hits it out of the square, or bounces it twice is out: She leaves the game and the next child in line comes in. Although in principle the game is played by individuals, in practice these girls played as if they were on teams: They tried to get their friends in and others out.

Hughes explains that the girls played within a complex system that required them to be, in their own terms, "nice" and not "mean." Getting people out was mean, but it wasn't *really* mean if it was done for the purpose of being nice to someone else—getting a friend in. The girls had to be competitive; always being nice and never getting anyone out would be mean to all the children waiting in line who would never get in. But they had to enact competition within a framework of cooperation. So, for example, a girl who was about to hit a ball hard and get someone out might call to her friend, "Sally, I'll get you in!" This announced for all to hear that she was not trying to be mean to the girl she was getting out; she was just being nice to her friend.

The girls referred to this required behavior as being "nice-mean." They told Hughes they didn't like playing with boys, because the boys just tried to get everybody out.

Anthropologist Penelope Brown presents dramatic examples of how Tenejapa women use apparent agreement to disagree. Women in this Mayan Indian community in Mexico do not openly express anger or fight. If they feel angry, they show it by refusing to speak or smile or touch. How, then, do they enact conflict when the situation requires it—for example, in court? Brown filmed a court case that took place following an unusual and scandalous incident in which a young bride abandoned her new husband and married another man. The groom's family sued the runaway bride's family for the return of gifts that they had, in accordance with custom, given the bride.

The two families were represented in court by the mothers of the bride and groom. In presenting their cases, the two women argued angrily—by agreeing with each other in ironic and sarcastic tones. For example, when the groom's mother claimed she had given the bride a belt worth two hundred pesos, the bride's mother responded, "Perhaps it wasn't one hundred or so?" This ironically implied, "It was only worth one hundred pesos." She also denigrated a skirt her daughter had received by saying, "Perhaps it's that it's real wool then, perhaps!"—ironically claiming that the skirt was not made of real wool. The groom's mother countered, "Perhaps it's not that it was expensive then," implying, "It was expensive!" The other retorted, "Really expensive, [it is] itself then, perhaps, eh?"—sarcastically implying, "It was cheap!"

Forbidden to express anger and disagreement directly, these peasant women expressed themselves in the manner that was available to them—the vocabulary of politeness and agreement. This example from an exotic culture may seem extreme, but the pattern is not so different from the ways modern women sometimes accomplish negative ends with apparently positive means. All the verbal ways of being "nice" that are expected of women can be used to hurt as well as to heal.

A common way of hurting someone without seeming to intend to is to repeat a critical remark made by someone else, with the for-your-own-good introduction "I think you should know." For example, Hilda told Annemarie that Annemarie's sister-in-law had regaled a roomful of women with stories about problems Annemarie was having with her teenage son. Annemarie was mortified to learn that her family problems were the topic of public discussion. Since she wouldn't tell her husband not to confide in his sister, and she didn't want to pick a fight with her sister-in-law, she felt there was nothing she could do but stew. Annemarie would not have been hurt had she not been told, so it was her "friend" Hilda who had hurt her, not her sister-in-law.

To make matters worse, every time Annemarie met Hilda thereafter, Hilda gazed at her, brimming with concern, and asked, "How *are* you? How are things working *out*?" This made Annemarie feel like an emotional basket case rather than a normal parent whose children had normal problems. All forms of support can be used to undercut. Showing elaborate concern for others' feelings can frame you as the social worker who has it all together, and them as your patients.

Offering helpful suggestions can also indirectly imply criticism. For example, a woman named Sarah suggested to her friend Phyllis that Phyllis might ease her parents' next visit by having them stay in a hotel instead of in Phyllis's one-bedroom apartment. Instead of appreciating the advice, Phyllis correctly perceived that Sarah thought she was too involved with her parents.

Praise can pack a wallop if it's hiding criticism in its pockets. For example, "Your new beau is fabulous—he's not boring, like the last one" seems to be praising your new beau, yet you walk away smarting from the slap to your old one. Similarly, the compliment "Your presentation was excellent. It was much easier to follow than your last one," leaves you with a vision of your audience scratching their heads over your last presentation.

Another way that criticism can leak out without its author taking responsibility for it is in speculating about others' motives. For example, Patricia was wondering aloud why a man she had met had not called her. Nadine had an idea: "Maybe he thought you were stuck up because you told him you want to be called Patricia instead of Patty." Though Patricia still had no idea about the man's thoughts, she had learned what Nadine thought of her using her full name.

MESSAGES AND METAMESSAGES IN FIGHTS

Though women may be reluctant to fight openly, and men may be inclined to fight playfully, there are many occasions when men and women do engage in conflict—openly, seriously, and with each other. Often such arguments lead to frustration not only about the subject of dissension but also about the other's way of arguing. Once again the difference between messages and metamessages is key.

A man told me about the following conversation, which he felt typified why he found it frustrating to argue with a woman. The encounter began with her waking him up in the middle of the night.

> HE: What's wrong?
> SHE: You were taking up too much of the bed.
> HE: I'm sorry.
> SHE: You're always doing that.
> HE: What?
> SHE: Taking advantage of me.
> HE: Wait a minute. I was asleep. How can you hold me responsible for what I do when I'm asleep?
> SHE: Well, what about the time . . .

She then took him to task for past offenses.

It was hard for this couple to find a meeting ground in their dispute because they were moving on different levels. He was talking on the message level: He took up too much of the bed.

But she was focused on the metamessage level: The way he was sleeping showed that he took advantage of her generally, took up "too much space" in their relationship. She took the opportunity of this concrete offense to discuss the pattern of behavior that it represented. He felt it was unfair to pull a string of past events out of the hat of this inadvertent transgression, like so many colored handkerchiefs in a magician's trick.

Exactly the same points of view, similarly allotted, characterize a conversation in Anne Tyler's novel *The Accidental Tourist*. Macon and Muriel have been living together, but Macon is still legally married to someone else. Macon makes a casual remark about Alexander, Muriel's son:

> "I don't think Alexander's getting a proper education," he said to her one evening.
> "Oh, he's okay."
> "I asked him to figure what change they'd give back when we bought the milk today, and he didn't have the faintest idea. He didn't even know he'd have to subtract."
> "Well, he's only in second grade," Muriel said.
> "I think he ought to switch to a private school."
> "Private schools cost money."
> "So? I'll pay."
> She stopped flipping the bacon and looked over at him. "What are you saying?" she said.
> "Pardon?"
> "What are you saying, Macon? Are you saying you're committed?"

Muriel goes on to tell Macon that he must make up his mind whether he wants to divorce his wife and marry her: She can't put her son in a new school and then have to pull him out when and if Macon returns to his wife. The conversation ends with Macon saying, incredulously, "But I just want him to learn to subtract!"

Like the man and woman who were arguing in the middle of the night, Macon is concerned with the message, the simple matter of Alexander's learning math. But Muriel is concerned with the metamessage: What would it say about their relationship if he began paying for her son's education?

An argument that arose between a real-life husband and wife shows the same pattern. In this argument, which was recorded and analyzed (from a different point of view) by Jane Frank, a husband returned home and called his wife to arms: "How would you like to eat humble crow?" She had said it would be impossible to find a painting of a particular size and type that he wanted; now he had found one and he wanted her to admit that she had been wrong. Instead, the wife claimed that she had said it would be difficult, not impossible, to find. She proposed a compromise: She hadn't meant her remark as he interpreted it. But he would have none of that. She had said it; he had proved her wrong; she should admit defeat. Their argument, which became very heated, could not be resolved, because he never wavered from the message level—the literal accuracy of what she had said—but she soon moved on to what seemed far more important to her, the metamessage that his position sent about their relationship: "Why do you always want to prove me wrong and rank me out?"

"THAT REMINDS ME OF A STORY"

These different world views shape every aspect of our ways of talking. One aspect that has been studied by linguists and anthropologists is storytelling—the accounts of personal experiences that people exchange in conversation. And the stories we hear and tell in conversation shape our views. Through hearing people tell what happened to others, we form assumptions about the right way to behave. And the ways that women and men talk about events in their lives reflect and create their different worlds.

Each year, students in my classes record ordinary conversations that they happen to take part in, and transcribe a segment where people tell about personal experiences. One year, two students analyzed all the stories transcribed by class members to compare the ones told by women and those told by men. They found differences that fit in with the patterns I have been describing.

The fourteen stories that men had told were all about themselves. Of the twelve stories told by women, only six were about themselves; the others were about incidents that happened to other people. The men, but not the women, had told stories in which there were protagonists and antagonists. For the most part, the stories that men told made them look good. For example, two men told about times when they had won a game for their team by their extraordinary performance. Many of the women told stories that made them look foolish. For example, one woman told of not having realized she had broken her nose until a doctor informed her of the fact years later. Another told of having been so angry at losing her hubcap to a pothole that she stopped the car, searched in vain among a pile of hubcaps that had found a similar fate, and, not wanting to leave empty-handed, took a Mercedes hubcap that was of no use to her.

My students' informal comparison of the men's and women's stories had results similar to those of a study by Barbara Johnstone of fifty-eight conversational narratives recorded by her students. Johnstone found that

the women's stories tend to be about community, while the men's tend to be about contest. The men tell about human contests—physical contests such as fights as well as social contests in which they use verbal and/or intellectual skill to defend their honor. They tell about contests with nature—hunting and fishing. Stories about contests with people or animals can take the form of tall tales, which are themselves a kind of contest between a teller and his audience. When a male storyteller is not the protagonist in his story, the protagonist is a man; men rarely tell stories involving women.

The women's stories, on the other hand, revolve around the norms of the community, and joint action by groups of people. The women tell about incidents in which they violate social norms and are scared or embarrassed as a result; about people helping other people out of scrapes; about sightings of apparent ghosts which are then explained by others; about meeting their mates and acquiring their cats. The women tell about peculiar people, dramatizing their abnormal behavior and setting it implicitly in contrast with social norms. They tell stories about themselves, about other women, and about men.

In Johnstone's study, not only did men more often tell about experiences in which they had acted alone, but when men and women told about acting alone, the outcomes tended to be different. The vast majority of men who reported acting alone also reported a happy outcome. The majority of women who reported acting alone portrayed themselves as suffering as a result. Only a very small number of stories told by men (four out of twenty-one) had the protagonist receiving help or advice from someone. In a much larger proportion of the women's stories (eleven of twenty-six), the protagonist received help or advice from others.

Johnstone concludes that men live in a world where they see power as coming from an individual acting in opposition to others and to natural forces. For them, life is a contest in which they are constantly tested and must perform, in order to avoid the risk of failure. For women, Johnstone claims, the community is the source of power. If men see life in terms of contest, a struggle against nature and other men, for women life is a struggle against the danger of being cut off from their community.

MUTUAL MISJUDGMENTS

These patterns provide a new context in which to place Thomas Fox's observations of the men and women in his writing class. Mr. H tried to exert influence on the group. Ms. M tried to avoid standing out and offending. A large part of Mr. H's self-definition revealed his view of the world as an arena for competition and conflict. According to Fox, Mr. H's writing described "competition and conflict with fellow cadets at West Point where he spent a year, with basketball teams and officials, with school-mates, and most importantly, according to Mr. H, with his brother."

If Mr. H appeared confident, his essays reveal the anguish he has experienced as a result of the agonistic world he inhabits. Since he is always in hierarchies, he has suffered badly in situations where he felt one-down: in his brief military experience, where everyone conspired to make entering cadets feel "like shit," and in his family, where he believed that his brother and sister were favored. Fox explains:

> Mr. H's essays are a litany of hierarchies, from the grada-tions of classmates at West Point, to his description of a bas-ketball game where the official unjustly penalizes the player, to the way he presents his family as a hierarchy of privilege with his parents at the top, followed by his brother, then his sister, and finally Mr. H at the bottom. All of these hierar-chies work to Mr. H's disadvantage, and as he states, in a marvelously appropriate misspelling, they "inferiorate" him.

In other words, what emerges as male confidence can be as much the result of past pain as what appears as female insecurity.

Women and men are inclined to understand each other in terms of their own styles because we assume we all live in the same world. Another young man in Fox's writing class noticed that his female peers refused to speak with authority. He imag-ined the reason to be that they feared being wrong. For him, the point was knowledge, a matter of individual ability. It did not occur to him that what they feared was not being wrong, but being offensive. For them, the point was connection: their rela-tion to the group.

Both Mr. H and Ms. M expressed dissatisfaction with the roles they learned to play. Ms. M traced hers to her father, who cautioned her not to let on how much she knew. Mr. H blamed the agonistic world for casting him in his role:

> I personally used to be an open and very nice and sensitive person: deep down I still am. However, through competition

with my family and relationships at school, I changed my personality, "toughening up" and shutting others out.

Though opposition can be a means to affiliative ends, the hierarchical, competitive world of boys can also cause emotional pain and interfere with establishing connections.

DIFFERENT COMPLEXITIES

In responding to the differences between women and men described in this chapter, people frequently ask or tell me which style is better. Even researchers sometimes make value judgments. In comparing fifth-grade boys and girls—ten- and eleven-year-olds—at play, Janet Lever concludes that the boys' games better prepare them for life in the world of work because boys' games involve more complex rules and roles. But girls' games also involve complexity—in verbally managing interpersonal relations. Penelope Eckert, who observed boys and girls in high school, points out that boys define their social status in a simple and straightforward way—their individual skill and achievement, especially at sports—but girls "must define theirs in a far *more complicated* way, in terms of their overall character."

Lever describes a game the fifth-grade girls played that seemed "monotonous" to her. A large number of girls stood in a circle and together performed prescribed movements and recited a chant called "Doctor Knickerbocker Number Nine." One girl twirled in the center with her eyes closed, stopping with her arm extended. The girl to whom she pointed had to join her in the center, where she then twirled and picked another girl in the same way. When nine girls were in the center, the ninth became the new number one, and the other eight returned to the circle.

Why was this fun? Lever explains: "Shouts of glee were heard from the circle's center when a friend had been chosen to join them. Indeed, a girl could gauge her popularity by the loudness of these shouts." In other words, the game is fun because it manipulates and plays off the commodity that is important to girls—

the strength of their affiliations—just as the boys' games play off their valued commodity—skill. The girls' game is an experiment in shifting alliances. Their game is indeed a contest, but not one of skill; it is, rather, a popularity contest.

Majorie Harness Goodwin and Charles Goodwin describe an elaborate verbal routine that is one of the main preoccupations of the preteen and teenage girls in the working-class black neighborhood where they lived and worked. Called "He-Said-She-Said" by the girls themselves, this verbal routine is "instigated" when one girl tells another that a third was talking about her behind her back. The Goodwins remark that "the males studied had no structure for extended debate of comparable complexity."

So it is not that the boys' behavior is more complex in general. Rather, boys and girls are learning to handle complexity in different arenas—boys in terms of complex rules and activities, girls in terms of complex networks of relationships, and complex ways of using language to mediate those relationships.

WHOSE WAY IS BETTER?

Is it true that boys' games better prepare men for success in the work world? Surely the conviction that they cannot and should not act alone can be a hindrance to women who need to make quick decisions. But the conviction that they *must* act independently, and always find their way without help, is a hindrance to men, for there are times when they do not have all the information needed to make a decision. Furthermore, studies show that women *and men* who have been successful in the traditionally male fields of business and science are *not* very competitive. Rather, they excel in "work competence" or "work mastery." They simply do their jobs extremely well.

Women's inclination to seek agreement may even be an advantage in management. Many people feel that women make better managers because they are more inclined to consult others and involve employees in decision making, and everyone agrees that employees are more likely to implement a policy efficiently if they feel they have played a part in making it. One man described his wife's small business as an open arena in which people called her by first name, felt free to enter her office unannounced, and felt themselves to be a part of a group endeavor rather than underlings. In his own business, he said, his employees addressed him as "Mr." and never entered without knocking—and, he felt, were less satisfied with their work situation.

Though maintaining an atmosphere of community rather than hierarchy may have advantages in some settings, people who are not afraid of conflict have an advantage in innumerable inevitable situations where others try to get their way. Being willing to make a scene can be an effective form of power. Here's a trivial but telling example.

The audience was sparse at a concert in a large concert hall. Many people were seated in the farthest balcony, but entire sections much closer to the stage were empty, so some of those in the last balcony got up and moved into the closer empty seats. An usher came in just as the crowd was resettling and the concert beginning. She chose a couple she saw reseating themselves, shined her flashlight in their faces, and told them to return to their own seats. The woman was ready to do as they were told, but the man began to shout angrily at the usher, who disappeared instantly, the only way she could put an immediate end to the loud disturbance.

In another instance, a salesman boasted to his colleagues that he was one of the most powerful members of the sales staff. When he spoke at meetings, he was rarely crossed. He was proud of this, attributing it to his high status. In fact, no one crossed him because he was well known to have a quick temper and a nasty tongue, and no one wanted to be on the receiving end of his outbursts. The effect of fear is sometimes indistinguishable from the effect of respect.

Women who are incapable of angry outbursts are incapable of wielding power in this way. Far worse, their avoidance of confrontation opens them up to exploitation. In a word, they don't stand up for themselves. Celebrity women are not immune to this pattern. Oprah Winfrey, for example, has said, "My biggest flaw is my inability to confront people. After all the shows I've done, the books I've read, the psychologists I've talked to, I still allow myself to get ripped off to the nth degree. It takes me days and days of procrastinating and agonizing before I can work up the nerve to say anything. Sometimes I think I'd rather just run out and get hit by a truck than confront someone who is ripping me off."

This is not Oprah Winfrey's idiosyncratic flaw; it's a problem that innumerable women experience. In fact, it is not so much a flaw as a strength that is not working in oppositional contexts. Successful women may be especially prone to this weakness because they are likely to have achieved success by getting along with people—not by fighting with them. In order to get along with people and be liked, many women learn to avoid confrontation. But it is easier to rip off a person who is trying to avoid confrontation than someone who regards the world from an oppositional stance.

One Sunday I received a telephone call at home from a student who asked me a slew of questions about the dissertation she was writing. After spending a great deal of time answering her questions, I pointed out that she should really be putting these questions to her "mentor," my colleague who had primary responsibility (and got primary credit) for guiding her research. The student replied that she had to have answers to her questions that day, and she didn't want to disturb him at home.

Why was it all right to disturb me at home on Sunday, and not him, even though it was his job she was asking me to do? People find most women more approachable than most men. There are many possible reasons for this. Perhaps women's time does not seem as valuable as men's. Many of us can recall the feeling that our mother's time was at our disposal, but our father's time was reserved for more important pursuits outside the home; we had to wait for him to have time for us—so his time felt more valuable when we got it. But another reason for the greater approachability of women is their avoidance of conflict, which means they are less likely to respond harshly if displeased.

Always taking an adversative stance can result in avoiding situations one might really enjoy. And always accommodating can result in accepting situations one would really rather avoid. One man described to me what he and his former wife called the I-like-chicken-backs phenomenon. When his family ate a chicken for dinner, someone had to eat the back, and in his family it was always his wife, who assured the others, "I like chicken backs." But, as this man commented to me, nobody really likes chicken backs. She had convinced herself that she liked chicken backs—and broken egg yolks and burned toast—to be accommodating. But years of accommodating built up to mounting frustration that they both believed had contributed to their eventual divorce.

Even among couples who do not divorce, accommodation can take a toll. Again, a celebrity provides an example. The actress Jayne Meadows said in an interview that early in their marriage, her husband, comedian Steve Allen, had "manipulated" her into turning down major offers. For example, she said, "Steve kept me from the lead in *Will Success Spoil Rock Hunter?*" When questioned about this on a talk show, Allen said he had simply remarked, "It's a little gamey, that opening scene," and Meadows herself decided to turn the role down. Jayne Meadows apparently inferred—probably correctly—that her husband preferred that she not take the part. But did she have to honor his preference? At the time she felt she did, but looking back she wished she hadn't.

AND NOW FOR SOMETHING COMPLETELY DIFFERENT

For many women, openly opposing the will of others—or what they perceive to be others' will—is unthinkable. Ironically, it may be easier for some to think of leaving. This was the case with a woman I will call Dora, who did not realize, until it was too late, that opposing her husband's will would not bring the house down. But the cumulative frustration of never getting her way did.

A source of frustration for Dora was a series of used automobiles. It was she who drove to work, and she who took the car to the garage, but her husband, Hank, who chose the cars they would buy. Hank always went for cars that were cheap, interesting, and continually in need of repair. After Dora was nearly killed by a run-down Renault with unfixable brakes, they were in the market for yet another used car.

Hank fixed his sights on a fifteen-year-old Alfa Romeo that a mechanic he knew was getting ready to sell. Dora wanted to take advantage of the chance to buy a late-model VW from a friend who was leaving the country. Determined to reach a decision by consensus, she tried every verbal resource she could think of to convince Hank that it made sense to buy the boring but dependable VW rather than the dashing old Alfa Romeo, but he would not be convinced.

If this had happened at any previous time, Dora would have acceded to her husband's wishes and cursed him in her heart each time she drove the Alfa Romeo to work—or to the garage for repair. But this incident occurred when their marriage was already on the rocks. With so little to lose, she bought the VW from her friend and steeled herself for the torrent of anger she was sure she'd incur. To her amazement, Hank never spoke a word of remonstrance. When she told him what she had expected, he told her she had been foolish: She should have just done what she wanted from the start if she felt that strongly about it. He couldn't understand why she felt she had to have his blessing to do what she was certain was right.

The most extreme example I have encountered of the conviction that accommodation is the best way to achieve domestic harmony came from a woman who talked to me about her very early marriage to a man so violent that she had feared for the lives of her children and herself. In explaining to me why she had tolerated his beatings, she said that her husband had had a difficult childhood, deprived of love, and she had felt she could heal his wounds—and those of their relationship—by providing him unconditional love. One time he beat her so badly that she was knocked unconscious. When she came to, he said, "I guess it's over." She replied, "I still love you." What he saw as a blow so vicious that it would surely drive her away, she saw as a chance to prove once and for all that her love was truly unconditional. Even with such provocation, she did not consider defiance or challenge to be an available response.

No matter how dissatisfied people are with the results they are getting, they rarely question their way of trying to get results. When what we are doing is not working, we do not try doing something totally different. Instead, we try harder by doing more of what seems self-evidently the right way to proceed. But when styles differ, more of the same is usually met with more of the same from the other party as well. As a result, far from solving the problem, our efforts only make things worse.

This came out in the account of a couple, Molly and George. Molly can't bear it when George yells. But yelling seems only natural to him, since he grew up in a home where he, his two brothers, and his father were always opposing each other, struggling and tussling and arguing. Occasionally Molly surprises George by shouting back. She hates this, but he likes it. George explained, "When I get angry about something and I attack, I expect resistance. If I don't get resistance, I get frustrated, and then I get really angry."

As this example shows, attempts to avoid conflict can actually spark it with someone for whom conflict is a valued means of involvement. An earnest American exchange student discovered this in conversation with his Spanish host in Seville. The host liked to talk against Catalans, members of an ethnic group living in northeast Spain, and she knew that her American guest did not share her views. Once she tried to provoke him by saying, "The Catalans are sons of bitches." The young American tried to be conciliatory: "Well, you have your opinion and I have mine, so let's not worry about it." Far from avoiding an argument, this refusal to engage in debate infuriated her and sparked an angry attack. They had to talk for an hour before coming to a partial understanding—not about attitudes toward Catalans, but about attitudes toward verbal conflict.

IN SEARCH OF FLEXIBILITY

When one's habitual style is not working, trying harder by doing more of the same will not solve problems. Instead, men and women could both benefit from flexibility. Women who avoid conflict at all costs would be better off if they learned that a little conflict won't kill them. And men who habitually take oppositional stances would be better off if they broke their addiction to conflict.

Because people are different, not only in gender but in cultural background, differences in attitudes toward verbal opposition will persist among friends, lovers, and strangers. But they are particularly likely—and particularly troubling—in long-term relationships, which are by nature affected by issues of control and conflicting desires. Playing the relationship game together is harder if you're playing by different rules—or playing different games. Since the meaning of conflict, and the means that seem natural to deal with it, are fundamentally different for women and men, this is an arena where men's and women's styles are especially likely to come into conflict. Simply realizing that what seems like unfair or irrational behavior may be the result of a different style helps to reduce frustration. Conflicts will still arise, but at least you'll be arguing about real conflicts of interest rather than fighting styles.

SEVEN

Who's Interrupting?
Issues of Dominance
and Control

H ere is a joke that my father likes to tell.

A woman sues her husband for divorce. When the judge asks her why she wants a divorce, she explains that her husband has not spoken to her in two years. The judge asks the husband, "Why haven't you spoken to your wife in two years?" He replies, "I didn't want to interrupt her."

This joke reflects the commonly held stereotype that women talk too much and interrupt men.

In direct contradiction of this stereotype, one of the most widely cited findings to emerge from research on gender and language is that men interrupt women. I have never seen a popular article on the subject that does not cite this finding. It is deeply satisfying because it refutes the misogynistic stereotype that accuses women of talking too much, and it accounts for the experience reported by most women, who feel they are often cut off by men.

Both claims—that men interrupt women and that women interrupt men—reflect and bolster the assumption that an interruption is a hostile act, a kind of conversational bullying. The interrupter is seen as a malevolent aggressor, the interrupted an innocent victim. These assumptions are founded on the premise that interruption is an intrusion, a trampling on someone else's right to the floor, an attempt to dominate.

The accusation of interruption is particularly painful in close relationships, where interrupting carries a load of metamessages—that a partner doesn't care enough, doesn't listen, isn't interested. These complaints strike at the core of such a relationship, since that is where most of us seek, above all, to be valued and to be heard. But your feeling interrupted doesn't always mean that someone set out to interrupt you. And being accused of interrupting when you know you didn't intend to is as frustrating as being cut off before you've made your point.

Because the complaint "You interrupt me" is so common in intimate relationships, and because it raises issues of dominance and control that are fundamental to the politics of gender, the relationship between interruption and dominance bears closer inspection. For this, it will be necessary to look more closely at what creates and constitutes interruption in conversation.

DO MEN INTERRUPT WOMEN?

Researchers who report that men interrupt women come to their conclusion by recording conversation and counting instances of interruption. In identifying interruptions, they do not take into account the substance of the conversations they studied: what was being talked about, speakers' intentions, their reactions to each other, and what effect the "interruption" had on the conversation. Instead, mechanical criteria are used to identify interruptions. Experimental researchers who count things need operational criteria for identifying things to count. But ethnographic researchers—those who go out and observe people doing naturally whatever it is the researchers want to understand—are as wary of operational criteria as experimenters are wedded to them. Identifying interruptions by mechanical criteria is a paradigm case of these differences in points of view.

Linguist Adrian Bennett explains that "overlap" is mechanical: Anyone could listen to a conversation, or a tape recording of one, and determine whether or not two voices were going at once. But interruption is inescapably a matter of interpretation regarding individuals' rights and obligations. To determine whether a speaker is violating another speaker's rights, you have to know a lot about both speakers and the situation. For example, what are the speakers saying? How long has each one been talking? What has their past relationship been? How do they feel about being cut off? And, most important, what is the content of the second speaker's comment, relative to the first: Is it a reinforcement, a contradiction, or a change in topic? In other words, what is the second speaker trying to *do*? Apparent support can subtly undercut, and an apparent change of topic can be an indirect means of support—as, for example, when an adolescent boy passes up the opportunity to sympathize with his friend so as not to reinforce the friend's one-down position.

All these and other factors influence whether or not anyone's speaking rights have been violated and, if they have been, how significant the violation is. Sometimes you feel interrupted but you don't mind. At other times, you mind very much. Finally, different speakers have different conversational styles, so a speaker might *feel* interrupted even if the other did not *intend* to interrupt.

Here is an example that was given by Candace West and Don Zimmerman to show a man interrupting a woman. In this case I think the interruption is justified in terms of interactional rights. (The vertical lines show overlap.)

> FEMALE: So uh you really can't bitch when you've got all
> those on the same day (4.2) but I uh asked my
> physics professor if I couldn't chan|ge that|
> MALE: |Don't |touch
> that
> (1.2)
> FEMALE: What?
> (pause)
> MALE: I've got everything jus'how I want it in that note-
> book, you'll screw it up leafin' through it like that.

West and Zimmerman consider this an interruption because the second speaker began while the first speaker was in the middle of a word (*change*). But considering what was being said, the first speaker's rights may not have been violated. Although there are other aspects of this man's talk that make him seem like a conversational bully, interrupting to ask the woman to stop leafing through his notebook does not in itself violate her right to talk. Many people, seeing someone handling their property in a way that was destroying their painstaking organization of it, would feel justified in asking that person to stop immediately, without allowing further damage to be done while waiting for the appropriate syntactic and rhetorical moment to take the floor.

Sociologist Stephen Murray gives an example of what he regards as a prototypical case of interruption—where someone cuts in to talk about a different topic when the first speaker has not even made a single point. Here is his example:

> H: I think |that
> W: |Do you want some more salad?

This simple exchange shows how complex conversation can be. Many people feel that a host has the right, if not the obligation, to offer food to guests, whether or not anyone is talking. Offering food, like asking to have salt or other condiments passed, takes priority, because if the host waited until no one was talking to offer food, and guests waited until no one was talking to ask for platters beyond their reach, then the better the conversation, the more likely that many guests would go home hungry.

This is not to say that any time is the right time to interrupt to offer food. If a host *habitually* interrupts to offer food *whenever* a partner begins to say something, or interrupts to offer food just when a speaker reaches the climax of a story or the punchline of a joke, it might seem like a violation of rights or the expression of mischievous motives. But the accusation of interrupting cannot be justified on the basis of a single instance like this one.

Conversational style differences muddy the waters. It may be that one person grew up in a home where conversation was constant and all offers of food overlapped ongoing talk, while another grew up in a home where talk was sparse and food was offered only when there was a lull in the conversation. If two such people live together, it is likely that one will overlap to offer food, expecting the other to go on speaking, but the overlap-aversant partner will feel interrupted and maybe even refuse to resume talking. Both would be right, because interruption is not a mechanical category. It is a matter of individual perceptions of rights and obligations, as they grow out of individual habits and expectations.

INTERRUPTION WITHOUT OVERLAP

In these examples, an overlap—two voices talking at once—is not necessarily an interruption, that is, a violation of someone's speaking rights. There are also instances where speakers do feel that their rights have been infringed on, and may even feel interrupted, when there is no overlap. An example of such an instance appears in Alice Greenwood's analysis of dinner table conversations among her three children (twins Denise and Dennis, twelve, and Stacy, eleven) and their friends. In the following example, Denise and Stacy have performed a verbal routine for the benefit of their brother's dinner guest, Mark, fourteen. This dialogue, which Greenwood calls the Betty routine, is one the sisters often perform together. Before they start, they get Mark's attention: Denise says, "Listen to this. Mark, listen to this." Then Denise and Dennis announce, "It's so funny." But Mark doesn't agree:

DENISE: [In Betty voice] Excuse me, are you Betty?
      . . .
STACY: Oh, yes.
DENISE: [In Betty voice] Betty who?
STACY: [In Betty voice] Bettybitabitabittabuttabut—
    [Dennis, Denise, and Stacy laugh.]
MARK: Whaaaat?
    [Dennis, Denise, and Stacy laugh hysterically.]

Although this routine sparks delighted laughter from the three siblings, and on other occasions also sparked laughter among friends, Mark did not laugh and claimed not to get the joke. Denise and Stacy tried to explain it to him:

DENISE: I said, "Betty who?," like you say "Betty Jones." Then she says, "Bettybitabitabitta—"
→DENNIS: Did anyone eat from this yet?
MARK: No. Actually, what I was going to say was can I try that soup? It looks quite good.
DENISE: Listen, listen, listen, listen.
MARK: Say it in slow motion, okay?
STACY: Betty bought a bit of bitter butter and she said, "This butter's bitter. If I put it in my batter, it will make my batter bitter." So Betty bought a bit of better butter to—
→DENISE: You never heard that before?
MARK: No. Never.
DENISE: Mark, seriously?
MARK: Seriously.
DENISE: It's like the famous to— |
→STACY: | tongue twister.

MARK: No. The famous tongue twister is
Peterpiperpicked—
→DENISE: Same thing. It's like that. It's
like that one.
MARK: **You keep interrupting me.**

In this excerpt, Denise and Stacy repeatedly cut each other off, as shown by the arrows and vertical lines, but there is no indication that either resents it. They do seem to mind their brother Dennis's overlapping to ask about the food ("Did anyone eat from this yet?") because he's interrupting their explanation (Denise protests, "Listen, listen, listen, listen"). The girls are supporting each other, talking on the same team.

Most striking is Mark's complaint, "You keep interrupting me." This is intriguing because what Mark was saying when he got interrupted ("No. The famous tongue twister is Peterpiperpicked—") was actually an interruption of the girls' explanation, even though his voice did not overlap theirs. The same is true for the previous time they "interrupted" him: Just as Denise said, "All right. Watch this," Mark began to ask, "Is it as funny as a—" but he didn't get to finish because Dennis laughed and Denise launched the routine, as announced. So Mark's protest seems like a real-life instance of the humorous line "Don't talk while I'm interrupting you."

Mark also took an oppositional stance, even though he was really supporting rather than disagreeing. The girls just said that their tongue twister was "*like* the famous tongue twister." If Mark had simply offered "the famous tongue twister" (Peter Piper picked a peck of pickled peppers), then his interruption would have been supportive, furnishing the end of Denise's explanation. Instead, he began by saying "No," as if they had been claiming that theirs *was* the famous tongue twister.

In this conversation, the girls were trying to include Mark in their friendly banter. Greenwood found, in studying her children's conversations with their friends, that the more interruptions a conversation contained, the more comfortable the children felt in it and the more they enjoyed it. But Mark refused to be part of their fun by insisting on his right to hold the floor without interruption. Perhaps his being a few years older was a factor. Perhaps he did not like being cast in the role of audience. Perhaps he felt he was being put down when Denise asked, "You never heard that before? . . . Mark, seriously?" Whatever the reason, Denise, Stacy, and Dennis were doing rapport-talk, and Mark wanted to do something more like report-talk. It is not surprising that Denise later told her mother that she didn't like Mark.

Although Denise did "interrupt" Mark to tell him he had the idea ("Same thing. It's like that"), there is no evidence that she was trying to dominate him. Furthermore, though Denise and Stacy interrupted each other, there is no evidence that they were trying to dominate each other. There is, however, some evidence that Mark might have been trying to dominate Stacy and Denise, for example by refusing to laugh at their jokes and rejecting their explanation of their verbal routine, even though he did not overlap their speech. So it is not the interruption that constitutes dominance but what speakers are trying to do when they talk to each other.

OVERLAP WITHOUT INTERRUPTION

Claiming that an interruption is a sign of dominance assumes that conversation is an activity in which one speaker speaks at a time, but this reflects ideology more than practice. Most Americans *believe* one speaker *ought* to speak at a time, regardless of what they actually do. I have recorded conversations in which many voices were heard at once and it was clear that everyone was having a good time. When I asked people afterward their impressions of the conversation, they told me that they had enjoyed themselves. But when I played the tape back for them, and they heard that people had been talking all together, they were embarrassed and made comments like "Oh, God, do we really do that?" as if they had been caught with their verbal pants down.

In a book entitled *Conversational Style*, I analyzed two and a half hours of dinner table conversation among six friends. Looking back on the conversation, some of the friends told me they had felt that others had "dominated" the conversation—and when I first listened to the tape, I too thought that it looked that way. But the accused pleaded innocent: They claimed they had not intended to dominate; in fact, they wondered why the others had been so reticent. Only by comparing different parts of the conversation to each other was I able to solve the puzzle.

The inadvertent interruptions—and the impression of domination—came about because the friends had different conversational styles. I call these styles "high considerateness" and "high involvement," because the former gave priority to being considerate of others by not imposing, and the latter gave priority to showing enthusiastic involvement. Some apparent interruptions occurred because high-considerateness speakers expected longer pauses between speaking turns. While they were waiting for the proper pause, the high-involvement speakers got the impression they had nothing to say and filled in to avoid an uncomfortable silence.

Other unintended interruptions resulted when high-involvement speakers chimed in to show support and participation: High-considerateness speakers misinterpreted the choral support as attempts to yank the floor away from them, and they stopped, to avoid what to them would have been a cacophony of two voices at once. Ironically, these interruptions were not only the interpretations of the apparent victims—they were their creations. When high-involvement speakers used exactly the same techniques with each other, the effect was positive rather than negative: Chiming in with speakers didn't stop anybody from talking. It greased the conversational wheels and enlivened spirits.

Here are two examples from my study that illustrate these two contrasting situations, and the different effects of overlap on conversation. The first example shows overlapping that had a positive effect, in a segment of conversation among three high-involvement speakers. The second shows overlapping between high-involvement and high-considerateness speakers that disrupted the conversation. Though gender is not a factor in the overlap patterns in these conversations, understanding how overlap can work—or fail to work—is fundamental to making sense of the relationship between gender and interruption.

SUCCESSFUL COOPERATIVE OVERLAPPING

The first example took place in the context of a discussion about the impact of television on children. Only three of the six friends were talking here, the three high-involvement speakers: Steve (the host), Peter (Steve's brother, who was a guest), and Deborah (the author, who was also a guest). Steve made the statement that television has been bad for children, and I responded by asking whether Steve and Peter had grown up with television. It might not be a coincidence that I, the woman, shifted the focus from an abstract, impersonal statement to a personal one.

> STEVE: I think it's basically done damage to children. That what good it's done is outweighed by the damage.|
> →DEBORAH: |Did you two grow up with television?
> PETER: Very little. We had a TV in the Quonset—|
> →DEBORAH: |How old were you when your parents got.it?|
> →STEVE: |We had a TV, but we didn't watch it all the time. We were very young. I was four when my parents got a TV.|
> →DEBORAH; |You were four?
> PETER: I even remember that. |I don't remember /??/
> →STEVE: |I remember they got a TV before we moved out of the Quonset huts. In 1954.

→PETER: │I remember we got it in the Quonset huts.

DEBORAH: [Chuckle] You lived in Quonset huts? When you were how old?

STEVE: You know my father's dentist said to him, "What's a Quonset hut?" And he said, "God, you must be younger than my children." He was. Younger than both of us.

As indicated by vertical lines and arrows, this conversation includes many overlaps and "latchings"—instances where a second speaker begins speaking without leaving any perceptible pause. Yet the speakers show no evidence of discomfort or annoyance. All three speakers take turns that latch onto or intrude into others' turns. In this conversation, Peter and Steve, who are brothers, operate as a duet, much as Denise and Stacy did in the earlier example.

This example contains a clue to why high-involvement speakers don't mind being overlapped. These speakers yield to an intrusion if they feel like it, but if they don't feel like it, they put off responding, or ignore the intrusion completely. For example, when Peter is saying, "We had a TV in the Quonset [huts]," I interrupt to ask, "How old were you when your parents got it?" Steve doesn't answer my question right away. Instead, he first finishes Peter's statement: "We had a TV, but we didn't watch it all the time." Only then does he turn to answering my question: "We were very young. I was four when my parents got a TV." At another point, Steve ignores my question. I ask, "You lived in Quonset huts? When you were how old?" Without even acknowledging my question, Steve simply offers a vignette about his father that the topic of Quonset huts called to his mind. Part of the reason Steve does not find my questions intrusive is that he does not feel compelled to answer them—exactly the assumption that frees me to toss them out exuberantly. Another reason that the overlaps are cooperative is that they do not change the topic but elaborate on it.

UNSUCCESSFUL COOPERATIVE OVERLAPPING

The success of this brief conversation had nothing to do with whether or not speakers overlapped or interrupted; it was successful because the speakers had similar habits and attitudes about overlapping speech. The next example shows a segment of the same dinner table conversation that was not successful. Peter and I appear again here, but, instead of Steve, we are talking to David, who has a high-considerateness style.

David, an American Sign Language interpreter, is telling us about ASL. As listeners, Peter and I use overlap and latching to ask supportive questions, just as I asked supportive, overlapping questions of Peter and Steve in the previous example. Here too our questions show interest in what the speaker is saying rather than shifting focus. But the effect is very different:

DAVID: So, and this is the one that's Berkeley. This is the Berkeley sign for |Christmas.

→DEBORAH: |Do you figure out those, those, um, correspondences? Or do—

DAVID: | /?/ |

when you learn the signs, does somebody tell you?

DAVID: Oh, you mean |watching it? Like—

→DEBORAH: |'Cause I can imagine knowing that sign, and not figuring out that it had anything to do with the decorations.

DAVID: No. Y-you know that it has to do with the decorations. |

→DEBORAH: |'Cause somebody tells you? Or you figure |it out? |

→DAVID: |No. |Oh. You, you talking about me?

199

DEBORAH: Yeah.

DAVID: Or a deaf person?|

→DEBORAH: |You. You.

DAVID: Me? Uh, someone tells me, usually. But a lot of them I can tell. I mean they're obvious. The better I get, the more I can tell. The longer I do it the more I can tell what they're talking about.| Without| knowing what the

→DEBORAH: |Huh |That's interesting.

DAVID: sign is. |

→PETER: |But how do you learn a new sign?

DAVID: How do I learn a new sign? |

PETER: |Yeah. I mean supposing Victor's talking and all of a sudden he uses a sign for Thanksgiving, and you've never seen it before.

All Peter's and my comments are latched or overlapped on David's, as the arrows show. But only two of David's seven comments overlap ours. Furthermore, these two utterances—one that was inaudible (shown by a question mark in slashes) and one in which David said, "No"—are probably both attempts to answer the first parts of my double-barreled questions ("Do you figure out those—those, um, correspondences?" and " 'Cause somebody tells you?"). David shows evidence of discomfort in his pauses, hesitations, repetitions, and circumlocutions. When I played the segment back for him, he told me that the fast pace of the conversation in general and the questions in particular had caught him off guard and made him feel borne in upon.

It is difficult for me to regard this conversation in merciless print, because it makes me look overbearing. Yet I recall my goodwill toward David (who remains one of my closest friends) and my puzzlement at the vagueness of his answers. Comparing this effect on David to the effect of my "machine-gun questions" on Steve and Peter, I was relieved to see that "machine-gun questions" had exactly the effect I had intended when used with other high-involvement speakers: They were taken as a show of interest and rapport; they encouraged and reinforced the speaker. But when such questions were used with high-considerateness speakers, they created disruptions and interruptions. It was not the overlapping or fast pacing that created the interruption and discomfort *but the style difference*. Style differences are the very basis of such terms as *fast pacing* and *pausing*. Characteristics such as "fast pacing" are not inherent, but result from the styles of speakers *relative to each other*. I might add that as a result of doing this research, I learned not to use machine-gun questions or cooperative overlapping with people who don't respond well— a tangible benefit of understanding conversational style.

CULTURAL DIFFERENCES

In my study of dinner table conversation, the three high-involvement speakers were New York City natives of Jewish background. Of the three high-considerateness speakers, two were Catholics from southern California and one was from London, England. Although a sample of three does not prove anything, nearly everyone agrees that many (obviously not all) Jewish New Yorkers, many New Yorkers who are not Jewish, and many Jews who are not from New York have high-involvement styles and are often perceived as interrupting *in conversations with speakers from different backgrounds,* such as the Californians in my study. But many Californians expect shorter pauses than many midwesterners or New Englanders, so in conversations between them, the Californians end up interrupting. Just as I was considered extremely polite when I lived in New York but was sometimes perceived as rude in California, a polite Californian I know was shocked and hurt to find herself accused of rudeness when she moved to Vermont.

The cycle is endless. Linguists Ron and Suzanne Scollon show that midwestern Americans, who may find themselves interrupted in conversations with easterners, become aggressive interrupters when they talk to Athabaskan Indians, who expect much longer pauses. Many Americans find themselves interrupting when they talk to Scandinavians, but Swedes and Norwegians are perceived as interrupting by the longer-pausing Finns, who are themselves divided by regional differences with regard to length of pauses and rate of speaking. As a result, Finns from certain parts of the country are stereotyped as fast talking and pushy, and those from other parts of the country are stereotyped as slow talking and stupid, according to Finnish linguists Jaakko Lehtonen and Kari Sajavaara.

Anthropologists have written about many cultures in the world where talking together is valued in casual conversation. This seems to be the norm in more parts of the world than the northern European norm of one-speaker-speaks-at-a-time. Karl Reisman coined the term *contrapuntal conversations* to describe the overlapping style he observed in Antigua. Karen Watson borrowed his term to describe Hawaiian children's verbal routines in which they jointly joke and engage in "talk story." Watson explains that for these children, taking a turn is not a matter of individual performance but "partnership in performance." Michael Moerman makes similar observations about Thai conversation. Reiko Hayashi finds far more simultaneous speech among Japanese speakers in casual conversation than among Americans. Jeffrey Shultz, Susan Florio, and Frederick Erickson found that an Italian-American boy who was considered a serious behavior problem at school was simply chiming in as was appropriate and normal in his home. All of these researchers document overlapping speech that is not destructive, not intended to exercise dominance and violate others' rights. Instead, it is cooperative, a means of showing involvement, participation, connection. In short, simultaneous talk can be rapport-talk.

WOMEN AS COOPERATIVE
OVERLAPPERS

Paradoxically (in light of the men-interrupt-women research), and most important for our discussion here, another group that has been found to favor conversations in which more than one person speaks at a time is women. Folklorist Susan Kalčik was one of the first to observe women's use of overlapping talk by taping a women's group. In reviewing studies that compared all-male and all-female interaction, linguists Deborah James and Janice Drakich found that, of those reporting differences, the great majority observed more interruptive talk among the females.

Linguist Carole Edelsky inadvertently uncovered women's preference for overlapping talk when she set out to determine who talked more at a series of faculty committee meetings. She found that men talked more than women if one person was speaking while the others listened silently, but women talked as much as men during periods when more than one voice was heard at the same time. In other words, women were less likely to participate when the situation felt more like report-talk, more likely to do so when it felt like rapport-talk. Cooperative overlapping framed parts of the meeting as rapport-talk.

Following is an example of women in casual conversation overlapping in a highly cooperative and collaborative way. It comes from a conversation recorded at a kitchen table by linguist Janice Hornyak, who was a party to the conversation. Jan and her mother, Peg, who are from a southern state, were visiting relatives in the North, where Jan got to see snow for the first time. Peg and Marge, who are sisters-in-law, reminisce, for Jan's benefit, about the trials of raising small children in a part of the country where it snows. (Jan's mother raised her older children in the North but moved to the South before Jan was born.)

PEG: The part I didn't like was putting everybody's snow pants and boots |and

→MARGE: |Oh yeah, that was the worst part,

PEG: |and scarves

→MARGE: |and get them all bundled up in boots and everything and they're out for half an hour and then they come in and they're all covered with this snow and they get that *shluck* all over |

→PEG: |All that wet stuff and

→JAN: That's why adults don't like snow, huh?

MARGE: That's right.

PEG: Throw all the stuff in the dryer and then they'd come in and sit for half |an hour

MARGE: |And in a little while they'd want to go back out again.

PEG: Then they want to go back out again.

As in the conversation among Steve, Peter, and myself presented above, all three speakers in this example initiate turns that either latch onto or intrude into other speakers' turns. Like Denise and Stacy and like Steve and Peter in earlier examples, Peg and Marge play a conversational duet: They jointly hold one conversational role, overlapping each other without exhibiting (or reporting) resentment at being interrupted.

Hornyak points out the even more intriguing fact that these speakers often end a comment with the conjunction *and,* creating the appearance of interruption when there is none, as when Peg says, "All that wet stuff and." Hornyak claims that this strategy is used by many speakers in her family, and is satisfying and effective when used with each other. She is criticized, however, for using this same strategy among others, who protest that it confuses them. They may even get the impression that someone who ends a sentence with *and* doesn't know whether or not she is finished.

Why would anyone want to create the impression of inter-ruption when there is none? One reason that speakers from some cultural groups leave little or no pause between turns is that they see silence in friendly conversation as a sign of lack of rapport. Overlapping is a way to keep conversation going without risking silence. I should note, though, that Hornyak and the family mem-bers she taped do not speak loudly or quickly or all at once. Their overlaps, though frequent, are brief; ending sentences with *and* is a way to achieve the appearance of interruption when there is minimal overlap.

Though Hornyak feels the strategy of creating the appear-ance of overlap by ending a sentence with *and* is peculiar to her family, others have commented that they know people who do this. At least one man I spoke to said that his mother (to his father's chagrin) regularly ends her comments with *and uh,* and that *her* mother and all her sisters do it too—but her father and brother don't. This man also considered this a family style. Al-though it clearly does run in families, the style seems to result from a combination of gender and culture.

Gender and culture also dovetail in another example of the false appearance of interruption. William Labov and David Fan-shel, in a study of a psychotherapy session between a nineteen-year-old patient called Rhoda and a social worker, show that Rhoda never ended a speaking turn by falling silent. Instead, when she had said all she wanted to say, she began to repeat herself. Her repetitions were an invitation to the therapist to begin speak-ing by interrupting her. Both client and therapist were New Yorkers, Jewish, and women.

CULTURAL EXPLANATIONS: A MIXED BLESSING

The realization that people with similar cultural backgrounds have similar ways of talking often comes as a revelation and a relief to people who thought they had personal quirks or even psychological problems. For example, a Greek-American man I interviewed for a study of indirectness in conversation had been told by friends and lovers throughout his life that there was something wrong with him, because he always beat around the bush instead of coming out and saying what was on his mind. He told me that his parents spoke that way, and I told him that I had found that Greeks often tended to be more indirect than Americans, and Greek-Americans were somewhere in the middle. This man was enormously relieved, saying that my explanation rang a bell. He went on to say:

> I see it as either something heroically different or a real impediment. . . . Most of the time I think of it as a problem. And I can't really sort it out from my family and background. . . . I don't know if it's Greek. I just know that it's me. And it feels a little better to know that it's Greek.

Viewing his "family" style as an ethnic style relieved this man of the burden of individual pathology otherwise implied by being different from most of the people he communicated with.

But the tendency of people from similar cultural backgrounds to have habitual ways of speaking that are similar to each other's and different from those of people from other cultural backgrounds, has had unfortunate, even tragic consequences. When people who are identified as culturally different have different conversational styles, their ways of speaking become the basis for negative stereotyping. As I mentioned earlier, anti-Semitism classically attributes loudness, aggressiveness, and "pushiness" to Jewish people—making a leap from ways of speaking to character. For example, in a letter to Henry Miller, Lawrence Durrell described a Jewish fellow writer: "He is undependable, erratic, has bad judgment, loud-mouthed, pushing, vulgar, thoroughly Jewish . . ."

The perception that Jews (or New Yorkers—the categories are often fused in many people's minds) are loud and pushy simply blames the minority group for the effect of their style *in in-*

teraction with others who use a different style. Anthropologist Thomas Kochman shows that a parallel style difference underlies the stereotyping of "community" blacks as inconsiderate, overbearing, and loud. When members of one group have the power to persecute members of the other, the results of such misjudgments are truly tragic.

If cultural differences are likely to cause misjudgment in personal settings, they are certain to do so in international ones. I would wager that the much-publicized antipathy between Nancy Reagan and Raisa Gorbachev resulted from cultural differences in conversational style. According to Nancy Reagan, "From the moment we met, she talked and talked and *talked*—so much that I could barely get a word in, edgewise or otherwise." I suspect that if anyone asked Raisa Gorbachev, she would say she'd been wondering why her American counterpart never said anything and made her do all the conversational work.

Of course not all Russians or Jews or New Yorkers or blacks are high-involvement speakers. Many use the style in some situations but not others. Some have erased, modified, or never used such styles at all. No group is homogeneous; for example, the high-involvement style I describe is more common among East European than German Jewish speakers. But many Jewish speakers do use some variety of high-involvement style in some situations, as do many Italian, Greek, Spanish, South American, Slavic, Armenian, Arab, African, and Cape Verdean speakers—and members of many other groups I have not mentioned.

A WORD OF CAUTION

The juxtaposition of these two lines of inquiry—gender and interruption on the one hand, and ethnicity as conversational style on the other—poses a crucial and troubling dilemma. If it is theoretically wrongheaded, empirically indefensible, and morally insidious to claim that speakers of particular ethnic groups are pushy, dominating, or inconsiderate because they appear to interrupt in conversations with speakers of different, more "mainstream" ethnic backgrounds, can it be valid to embrace research that "proves" that men dominate women because they appear to interrupt them in conversation? If the researchers who have found men interrupting women in conversation were to "analyze" my audiotapes of conversations among New York Jewish and California Christian speakers, they would no doubt conclude that the New Yorkers "interrupted" and "dominated"—the impression of the Californians present. This was not, however, the intention of the New Yorkers, and—crucially—not the result of their behavior alone. Rather, the pattern of apparent interruption resulted from the *difference* in styles. In short, such "research" would do little more than apply the ethnocentric standards of the majority group to the culturally different behavior of the minority group.

In a parallel way, claims that men dominate women because they interrupt them in conversation accept the assumption that conversation is an enterprise in which only one voice should be heard at a time. This erroneous assumption has significant negative consequences for women. Many women, when they talk among themselves in situations that are casual, friendly, and focused on rapport, use cooperative overlapping: Listeners talk along with speakers to show participation and support. It is this practice, when overheard, that has led men to stereotype women as noisily clucking hens. And women who enjoy such conversations when they have them may later feel embarrassed and guilty, because they accept the one-speaker-at-a-time ethic that is more appropriate to men's "public speaking" conversational style, or report-talk, than it is to women's "private speaking" style, which emphasizes rapport-talk.

Juxtaposing research claiming that men interrupt women with my study of dinner table conversation provides a linguistic parallel but a political contrast. Jews are a minority in the United States, as are blacks and members of the other groups that I mentioned as having high-involvement style. Minorities are at a disadvantage. But in the male-female constellation, it is women who are at a social and cultural disadvantage. This transforms the political consequences of blaming one group for dominating the other.

Most people would agree that women as a class are dominated by men as a class in our culture, as in most if not all cultures of the world. Therefore many would claim that viewing gender differences as cross-cultural communication is copping out, covering up real domination with a cloth of cultural difference. Though I am sympathetic to this view, my conscience tells me that we cannot have it both ways. If we accept the research in one paradigm—the men-interrupt-women one—then we are forced into a position that claims that high-involvement speakers, such as blacks and Jews and, in many circumstances, women, are pushy, aggressive, or inconsiderately or foolishly noisy.

The consequences of such a position are particularly dangerous for American women of ethnic or regional backgrounds that favor high-involvement conversational styles. The United States witnessed a dramatic example of just such consequences when Geraldine Ferraro, a New Yorker of Italian extraction, ran for vice president and was labeled a bitch by Barbara Bush, a woman of more "mainstream" background. The view of high-involvement style as dominance, taken from the men-interrupt-women paradigm, yields the repugnant conclusion that many women (including many of us of African, Caribbean, Mediterranean, South American, Levantine, Arab, and East European backgrounds) are dominating, aggressive, and pushy—qualities that are perceived as far more negative in women than in men.

As a woman who has personally experienced the difficulty many women report in making themselves heard in some interactions with men (especially "public" situations), I am tempted to embrace the studies that men interrupt women: It would allow me to explain my experience in a way that blames others. As a high-involvement-style speaker, however, I am offended by the labeling of a feature of my conversational style as loathsome, based on the standards of those who do not share or understand it. As a Jewish woman raised in New York who is not only offended but frightened by the negative stereotyping of New Yorkers and women and Jews, I recoil when scholarly research serves to support the stereotyping of a group of speakers as possessing negative intentions and character. As a linguist and researcher, I know that the workings of conversation are more complex than that. As a human being, I want to understand what is going on.

WHO'S INTERRUPTING?

The key to understanding what is going on, at least in part, is the distinction between rapport-talk and report-talk—the characteristic ways that most women use language to create a community and many men use it to manage contest. As a result, though both women and men complain of being interrupted by each other, the behaviors they are complaining about are different.

In many of the comments I heard from people I interviewed, men felt interrupted by women who overlapped with words of agreement and support and anticipation of how their sentences and thoughts would end. If a woman supported a man's story by elaborating on a point different from the one he had intended, he felt his right to tell his own story was being violated. He interpreted the intrusion as a struggle for control of the conversation.

For example, a man was telling about some volunteer work he had done as a cashier at a charity flea market. At the end of the day, there had been a shortfall in his cash register, which he had to make up from his own pocket. A woman listening to him kept overlapping his story with comments and expressions of sympathy, elaborating on how unfair it was for him to have to pay when he had been volunteering his time. As a matter of fact, the man had not been telling his experience in order to emphasize the injustice of it, and he felt interrupted and "manipulated" by the woman, whom he saw as trying to take over his story. Her offense was an excess (in his view) of rapport-talk.

This brings me back to my father, and why he might take particular relish in telling the joke about the man who didn't talk to his wife because he didn't want to interrupt her. My father believes that only one person should speak at a time. As a result, he often has a hard time getting the floor in conversations involving my mother, my two sisters, and me, since we overlap and do not leave pauses between our comments. He also feels that once he begins to talk, he should be permitted to continue until he is satisfied that he has explained his ideas completely. My mother and sisters and I feel that in a casual conversation among friends or family, it is acceptable to chime in when you think you know what others are getting at; if you're wrong, they are free to correct you, but if you're right, everyone prefers the show of connection and rapport that comes from being understood without having to spell everything out.

My father's view of this situation surfaced some years ago when he was talking and my mother chimed in. He wistfully sighed and said to my mother, "You have an advantage, dear. If I want to say something, I have to wait until no one else is talking. But you can say what you want whenever you think of it." For her part, my mother can't understand why my father needs special privileges to say something—why doesn't he just jump in like the rest of us? And I can recall feeling as a teenager that listening to my father, who is an attorney, explain something to me was like hearing a summation to the jury.

So both the man and the women in my family feel oppressed, at times, by others' ways of talking—he because he is interrupted and doesn't find the pauses he needs to enter the conversation, and we because he forbids and eschews overlaps and won't just take part like everyone else. The women in the family value overlaps and interruptions as shows of involvement in rapport-talk, and the man in the family values not being imposed on in report-talk. And he approaches casual conversations at home more like report-talk than the women do.

Then what is the source of women's complaints that they are interrupted by men? Just as my sisters, my mother, and I expect my father to toss out brief comments like the rest of us, men who approach conversation as a contest in which everyone

211

competes for the floor might be treating women as equals, expecting them to compete for the floor like everyone else. But women are far less likely to do so, since they do not regard conversations as contests and have little experience in fighting for the right to be heard. Quite the opposite, Elizabeth Aries found that women who talked a lot in discussion groups often invited quieter group members to speak.

UNCOOPERATIVE OVERLAPPING

Whereas women's cooperative overlaps frequently annoy men by seeming to co-opt their topic, men frequently annoy women by usurping or switching the topic. An example of this kind of interruption is portrayed in "You're Ugly, Too," a short story by Lorrie Moore. The heroine of this story, a history professor named Zoë, has had an ultrasound scan to identify a growth in her abdomen. Driving home after the test, she looks at herself in the rearview mirror and recalls a joke:

> She thought of the joke about the guy who visits his doctor and the doctor says, "Well, I'm sorry to say, you've got six weeks to live."
> "I want a second opinion," says the guy. . . .
> "You want a second opinion? O.K.," says the doctor. "You're ugly, too." She liked that joke. She thought it was terribly, terribly funny.

Later in the story, at a Halloween party, Zoë is talking to a recently divorced man named Earl whom her sister has fixed her up with. Earl asks, "What's your favorite joke?" This is what happens next:

> "Uh, my favorite joke is probably—O.K., all right. This guy goes into a doctor's office, and—"
> "I think I know this one," interrupted Earl, eagerly. He

wanted to tell it himself. "A guy goes into a doctor's office, and the doctor tells him he's got some good news and some bad news—that one, right?"

"I'm not sure," said Zoë. "This might be a different version."

"So, the guy says, 'Give me the bad news first,' and the doctor says, 'O.K. You've got three weeks to live.' And the guy cries, 'Three weeks to live! Doctor, what is the good news?' And the doctor says, 'Did you see that secretary out front? I finally fucked her.'"

Zoë frowned.

"That's not the one you were thinking of?"

"No." There was accusation in her voice. "Mine was different."

"Oh," said Earl. He looked away and then back again. "What kind of history do you teach?"

When Earl interrupts Zoë, it is not to support her joke but to tell her joke for her. To make matters worse, the joke he tells isn't just different; it's offensive. When he finds out that his joke was not the same as hers, he doesn't ask what hers was. Instead, he raises another topic entirely ("What kind of history do you teach?").

Most people would agree that Earl's interruption violated Zoë's speaking rights, because it came as Zoë was about to tell a joke and usurped the role of joke teller. But Zoë yielded quickly to Earl's bid to tell her joke. As soon as he said "some good news and some bad news," it was obvious that he had a different joke in mind. But instead of answering "No" to his question ". . . that one, right?" Zoë said, "I'm not sure. This might be a different version," supporting his bid and allowing for agreement where there really was disagreement. Someone who viewed conversation as a contest could have taken back the floor at this point, if not before. But Zoë seemed to view conversation as a game requiring each speaker to support the other's words. If they had known each other well enough to argue about this later, Earl might have challenged, "Why didn't you stop me when you saw I was going to tell a different joke, instead of letting me go on and then getting mad?"

Another part of the same story shows that it is not overlap that creates interruption but conversational moves that wrench a topic away from another speaker's course. Zoë feels a pain in her stomach, excuses herself, and disappears into the bathroom. When she returns, Earl asks if she's all right, and she tells him that she has been having medical tests. Rather than asking about her health, Earl gives her some food that was passed around while she was in the bathroom. Chewing, she says, "With my luck it'll be a gallbladder operation." Earl changes the subject: "So your sister's getting married? Tell me, really, what you think about love." Zoë begins to answer:

"All right. I'll tell you what I think about love. Here is a love story. This friend of mine—"

"You've got something on your chin," said Earl, and he reached over to touch it.

Like offering food, taking something off someone's face may take priority over talk, but doing so just as Zoë starts to tell a story seems like a sign of lack of interest in her story, and lack of respect for her right to continue it. Furthermore, this is not an isolated incident, but one in a series. Earl did not follow up Zoë's revelation about her health with questions or support, didn't offer advice, and didn't match her revelation with a mutual one about himself. Instead, he shifted the conversation to another topic—love—which he might have felt was more appropriate than a gallbladder operation for initiating a romantic involvement. For the same reason, taking something off her chin may have been too good an opportunity for touching her face to pass up. Indeed, many of his moves seem to be attempts to steer the conversation in the direction of flirting.

WHO'S DRIVING?

Interruption, then, has little to do with beginning to make verbal sounds while someone else is speaking, though it does have to do with issues of dominance, control, and showing interest and caring. Women and men feel interrupted by each other because of the differences in what they are trying to accomplish with talk. Men who approach conversation as a contest are likely to expend effort not to support the other's talk but to lead the conversation in another direction, perhaps one in which they can take center stage by telling a story or joke or displaying knowledge. But in doing so, they expect their conversational partners to mount resistance. Women who yield to these efforts do so not because they are weak or insecure or deferential but because they have little experience in deflecting attempts to grab the conversational wheel. They see steering the conversation in a different direction not as a move in a game, but as a violation of the rules of the game.

Being blamed for interrupting when you know you didn't mean to is as frustrating as feeling interrupted. Nothing is more disappointing in a close relationship than being accused of bad intentions when you know your intentions were good, especially by someone you love who should understand you, if anyone does. Women's effusion of support can be irritating to men who would rather meet with verbal sparring. And a left jab meant in the spirit of sparring can become a knockout if your opponent's fists are not raised to fight.

EIGHT

Damned If You Do

Morton, a psychologist on the staff of a private clinic, has a problem with the clinic director, Roberta. At staff meetings, Roberta generally opens discussion of issues by asking all staff members for their opinions. She invites debate about the pros and cons of proposals, but somehow, when the meeting ends, they always end up deciding—by consensus—to do what Roberta thinks best. The women on the staff are happy with Roberta as a director. They feel she listens to their points of view, and they like the rule by consensus rather than fiat. But Morton feels Roberta is manipulative. If they are going to do what she wants anyway, why does she make them waste their breath expressing opinions? He would prefer she just lay down the law, since she is the boss.

Morton's impression that Roberta does not act like a boss is the result of style differences. She *is* acting like a boss—a woman boss. She prefers to rule by consensus, and the women on her staff like it that way. But he is frustrated by her indirectness; he thinks she should rule by fiat.

Style differences may also be partly responsible for the observation that some women who have achieved high status or positions of authority do not behave in ways appropriate to their positions. But there may be another factor at work too. Since Matina Horner's pioneering research, many psychologists have observed that women seem to fear success. Again, the research on children's play sheds light.

Take Marjorie Harness Goodwin's research on verbal routines by which the preteen and teenage girls in her study criticized each other behind their backs. Significantly, and sadly, the examples Goodwin mentions are based on success: Girls are criticized for appearing better than the others in the group. Of two disputes that Goodwin describes, one girl's offense was to skip a grade in school and get straight A's on her report card; the other girl incurred the wrath of her peers by wearing newer and more expensive clothes than they.

In my own study of videotaped conversations among friends, a similar complaint is lodged by the sixth-grade girls against another girl:

SHANNON: She's gotta wear a Polo every *day*.
JULIA: I know, well I like *Polo*, but *God*!
SHANNON: Every *day*!?
JULIA: Really!
SHANNON: Just think how much— and sh-she's putting herself *up*.

Appearing better than others is a violation of the girls' egalitarian ethic: People are supposed to stress their connections and similarity.

In light of these and many other studies of girls' real conversations, it is no wonder that girls fear rejection by their peers if they appear too successful and boys don't. Boys, from the earliest age, learn that they can get what they want—higher status—by displaying superiority. Girls learn that displaying superiority will not get them what they want—affiliation with their peers. For this, they have to appear the same as, not better than, their friends.

The appearance of similarity does not mean actual sameness. Penelope Eckert, who spent several years with high school students in a midwestern city, explains how complex the girls' system of masked status can be. For example, the popular girls are the ones who must determine when to switch from the clothes of one season to the clothes of the next—for example, from winter to spring clothing. If less popular girls show up wearing cotton clothes while the popular girls are still wearing wool, they have committed a gaffe, shown themselves to be outsiders. If they switch after the popular girls have appeared in cotton, they mark themselves as followers, limited to public information. The goal is to dress in unison: If they make the switch on the same day as the popular girls, they are gloriously the same—and have subtly proven that they are in the know.

NEVER BOAST OR BRAG

Another aspect of the pressure on girls not to appear better than their peers is the injunction not to boast. Gender differences in attitudes toward boasting are the cause of much mutual judgment and misjudgment between women and men—and some odd verbal behavior on the part of women.

For example, a college student named Connie was telling her friends that a high school adviser had tried to talk her out of applying to the college they were all now attending. The adviser had felt that Connie's applying would hurt the chances of another girl from the same high school, Sylvia. In explaining the adviser's thinking, Connie said, "Sylvia's grades weren't—I mean—it sounds so pompous of me, but Sylvia's grades weren't as good as mine." Connie could barely bring herself to make a simple factual statement about her grades, because it smacked of boasting.

Margaret and Charles are both successful lawyers. Though they get along perfectly well when alone, they occasionally find themselves arguing after dinner engagements with new acquaintances, especially people who have status and connections in tax law, Charles's specialty. Margaret feels that Charles boasts: He lets it be known how important he is by mentioning recognition he has received, cases he has won, and important people he knows (in Margaret's view, name-dropping). In his eagerness to impress, he sometimes embellishes what he has done and implies that he knows people he has actually met only once or twice. For her part, Margaret tries to hide her success. She deliberately avoids letting on if she knows important people whose names arise in the conversation, and she never alludes to her many accomplishments.

Charles is as frustrated by Margaret's behavior as she is by his. If she will not let on how important she is, he does it for her. This upsets her even more. She feels his boasting for her is as impolite as her doing it herself, and all the alternatives she can imagine are unappealing: She can ignore or disrupt Charles's attempts to speak for her, which seems rude to him and violates what she feels is an obligation to support him; she can let him talk for her, which frames her as a child who cannot speak for herself; or she can participate, and speak in a way she does not want to speak—boasting.

Margaret feels people will not like her if she boasts; she would rather they learn from others how successful she is, and she feels they will approve of her modesty when they do. She also fears people will not like Charles if he boasts, and this is upsetting to her because she is affiliated with Charles, so what people think of him is a reflection on her. Charles, on the other hand, feels that people will not respect him unless he lets them know he merits respect. He also feels they will respect Margaret more if they know that she is an accomplished attorney, not just his wife.

Both Margaret and Charles judge each other's ways of talking in terms of personality characteristics—and each also places moral value on style. Margaret assumes that a good person is modest and self-effacing. Charles considers displaying accomplishments to be a requirement, not a liability, and he regards Margaret's (to him, false) modesty as foolishly self-denigrating, evidence of insecurity. Each one thinks he or she is simply expecting the other to be a good person, but their definitions of a good person vary because of the differing expectations for a good girl and a good boy.

The reluctance of girls and women to boast in certain situations shows up in two strikingly similar examples that I encountered in vastly different contexts. Ingmar Bergman's *Scenes from a Marriage* opens with a couple being interviewed for a magazine by a woman named Mrs. Palm. Marianne and Johan respond very differently to Mrs. Palm's question "How would you describe yourselves in a few words?" This is Johan's answer:

> It might sound conceited if I described myself as extremely intelligent, successful, youthful, well-balanced, and sexy. A man with a world conscience, cultivated, well-read, popular, and a good mixer. Let me see, what else can I think of . . . friendly. Friendly in a nice way even to people who are worse off. I like sports. I'm a good family man. A good son. I have no debts and I pay my taxes. I respect our government whatever it does, and I love our royal family. I've left the state church. Is this enough or do you want more details? I'm a splendid lover. Aren't I, Marianne?

This is Marianne's answer:

> Hmm, what can I say . . . I'm married to Johan and have two daughters.

Even with prodding Marianne doesn't add much information:

> MARIANNE: That's all I can think of for the moment.
> MRS. PALM: There must be something . . .

MARIANNE: I think Johan is rather nice.

JOHAN: Kind of you, I'm sure.

MARIANNE: We've been married for ten years.

JOHAN: I've just renewed the contract.

MARIANNE: I doubt if I have the same natural appreciation of my own excellence as Johan. But to tell the truth, I'm glad I can live the life I do. It's a good life, if you know what I mean. Well, what else can I say . . . Oh dear, this is difficult!

JOHAN: She has a nice figure.

MARIANNE: You're joking. I'm trying to take this thing seriously. I have two daughters, Karin and Eva.

JOHAN: You've already said that.

I was reminded of this fictional conversation when I read the following real-life dialogue in Carol Gilligan's *In a Different Voice*. As part of her research exploring children's moral development, Gilligan interviewed two 11-year-old children named Amy and Jake. Among the questions she asked them was "How would you describe yourself to yourself?" I heard loud echoes of Johan and Marianne in Jake's and Amy's responses. First, here is how Jake answered:

Perfect. That's my conceited side. What do you want—any way that I choose to describe myself? *(Interviewer: If you had to describe the person you are in a way that you yourself would know it was you, what would you say?)* I'd start off with eleven years old. Jake [last name]. I'd have to add that I live in [town], because that is a big part of me, and also that my father is a doctor, because I think that does change me a little bit, and that I don't believe in crime, except for when your name is Heinz [a reference to a previous question Jake was asked]; that I think school is boring, because I think that kind of changes your character a little bit. I don't sort of know how to describe myself, because I don't know how to read my personality. *(If you had to describe the way you actually would describe yourself, what would you say?)* I like corny jokes. I don't really like to get down to work, but I can do all the stuff in school. Every single problem that I have seen in school I have been able to do, except for ones that take knowledge, and after I do the reading, I have been able to do them, but sometimes I don't want to waste my time on easy homework. And also I'm crazy about sports. I think, unlike a lot of people, that the world still has hope . . . Most people that I know I like, and I have the good life, pretty much as good as any I have seen, and I am tall for my age.

This is how the girl, Amy, answered the question:

You mean my character? *(What do you think?)* Well, I don't know. I'd describe myself as, well, what do you mean? *(If you had to describe the person you are in a way that you yourself would know it was you, what would you say?)* Well, I'd say that I was someone who likes school and studying, and that's what I want to do with my life. I want to be some kind of a scientist or something, and I want to do things, and I want to help people. And I think that's what kind of person I am, or what kind of person I try to be. And that's probably how I'd describe myself. And I want to do something to help other people. *(Why is that?)* Well, because I think that this world has a lot of problems, and I think that everybody should try to help somebody else in some way, and the way I'm choosing is through science.

What struck me about these two children's answers to the same question was, first, how much longer Jake's was (and I assume the ellipsis after "hope" indicates even more words were omitted), and how boastful it was—in contrast to Amy's statement, which was not boastful at all. Jake says he's perfect, his father is a doctor, he can solve "every single problem" at school even though he finds school boring, he has the best life he has seen, and he's tall. It is possible that his comment "sometimes I don't want to waste my time on easy homework" might be a defense of less-than-superior achievement at school. In contrast, Amy says she likes school and studying but doesn't say if she does well at it, and that she wants to help people through science.

Both Johan in Bergman's screenplay and Jake in Gilligan's interview are aware that they sound "conceited" and make a joke of it. Indeed, Johan's entire answer seems tongue-in-cheek, like his comments interspersed in Marianne's answer. But Johan and Jake say what they do nonetheless. Though Amy has a bit more to say than Marianne, it isn't that much more. Both Amy and Marianne repeat themselves rather than fulfill the request in a way that might sound like bragging. Marianne does not mention that she is a lawyer. Amy says she plans to be a scientist, but she emphasizes that her purpose will be to help others rather than to achieve money, fame, or status.

Women's feelings that they should not boast come from explicit training as well as peer pressure in childhood. Such training is described in the alumnae newsletter of one of the most academically challenging girls' high schools in the country. In this newsletter a woman wrote an epitaph to her sister, who had been the very top student in her graduating class and who had recently died. A brilliant woman, her sister had had a moderately successful career that did not reflect her spectacular ability. The writer comments that her sister "took too much to heart her mother's admonitions: Stay in the background; never brag; always do your best."

These examples demonstrate that women are expected not to boast in relatively public situations, but it would be misleading to imply that women never boast at all. I return to the couple I dubbed Margaret and Charles for an example of a context in which she boasted but he felt he would not have. In the situation described earlier, Margaret felt Charles should not "show off" to new acquaintances. On another occasion, Charles felt that Margaret was inappropriately boasting. In complaining to close friends that she had not been promoted to partner as quickly as men in her firm who had brought in much less business and had far fewer billable hours, Margaret enumerated her early successes. Charles told her later that he thought this had been insensitive, since one of their listening friends was a young lawyer who was not advancing quickly at all. To Charles, self-aggrandizing information is to be used in public to achieve status, appropriately displayed when first meeting people or with people who have, or seem to be claiming, superior status. But to Margaret, self-aggrandizing information is to be used only in private, appropriately revealed in rapport-talk—conversations with people she knows and trusts, who will not judge her for her pride. When dealing with close friends, she forgets about their relative status—an aspect of relationships that Charles never forgets.

The different lenses of status and connection may once more work against women. Women are reluctant to display their achievements in public in order to be likable, but regarded through the lens of status, they are systematically underestimated, and thought self-deprecating and insecure. It is tempting to recommend that women learn to display their accomplishments in public, to ensure that they receive the respect they have earned. Unfortunately, however, women are judged by the standards of women's behavior.

This was evident, for example, at a faculty meeting devoted to promotions, at which a woman professor's success was described: She was extremely well published and well known in the field. A man commented with approval, "She wears it well." In other words, she was praised for not acting as successful as she was. By implication, if she had acted in a way consonant with her achievement, she would not have been praised—and perhaps would not have been liked.

HIS POLITENESS IS HER POWERLESSNESS

There are many kinds of evidence that women and men are judged differently even if they talk the same way. This tendency makes mischief in discussions of women, men, and power. If a linguistic strategy is used by a woman, it is seen as powerless; if it is done by a man, it is seen as powerful. Often, the labeling of "women's language" as "powerless language" reflects the view of women's behavior through the lens of men's.

Because they are not struggling to be one-up, women often find themselves framed as one-down. Any situation is ripe for misinterpretation, because status and connections are displayed by the same moves. This ambiguity accounts for much misinterpretation, by experts as well as nonexperts, by which women's ways of talking, uttered in a spirit of rapport, are branded powerless. Nowhere is this inherent ambiguity clearer than in a brief comment in a newspaper article in which a couple, both psychologists, were jointly interviewed. The journalist asked them the meaning of "being very polite." The two experts responded simultaneously, giving different answers. The man said, "Subservience." The woman said, "Sensitivity." Both experts were right, but each was describing the view of a different gender.

Experts and nonexperts alike tend to see anything women do as evidence of powerlessness. The same newspaper article quotes another psychologist as saying, "A man might ask a woman, 'Will you please go to the store?' where a woman might say, 'Gee, I really need a few things from the store, but I'm so tired.' " The woman's style is called "covert," a term suggesting negative qualities like being "sneaky" and "underhanded." The reason offered for this is power: The woman doesn't feel she has a right to ask directly.

Granted, women have lower status than men in our society. But this is not necessarily why they prefer not to make outright demands. The explanation for a woman's indirectness could just as well be her seeking connection. If you get your way as a result of having demanded it, the payoff is satisfying in terms of status: You're one-up because others are doing as you told them. But if you get your way because others happened to want the same thing, or because they offered freely, the payoff is in rapport. You're neither one-up nor one-down but happily connected to others whose wants are the same as yours. Furthermore, if indirectness is understood by both parties, then there is nothing covert about it: That a request is being made is clear. Calling an indirect communication covert reflects the view of someone for whom the direct style seems "natural" and "logical"—a view more common among men.

Indirectness itself does not reflect powerlessness. It is easy to think of situations where indirectness is the prerogative of those in power. For example, a wealthy couple who know that their servants will do their bidding need not give direct orders, but can simply state wishes: The woman of the house says, "It's chilly in here," and the servant sets about raising the temperature. The man of the house says, "It's dinner time," and the servant sees about having dinner served. Perhaps the ultimate indirectness is getting someone to do something without saying anything at all: The hostess rings a bell and the maid brings the next course; or a parent enters the room where children are misbehaving and stands with hands on hips, and the children immediately stop what they're doing.

Entire cultures operate on elaborate systems of indirectness. For example, I discovered in a small research project that most Greeks assumed that a wife who asked, "Would you like to go to the party?" was hinting that she wanted to go. They felt that she wouldn't bring it up if she didn't want to go. Furthermore, they felt, she would not state her preference outright because that would sound like a demand. Indirectness was the appropriate means for communicating her preference.

Japanese culture has developed indirectness to a fine art. For example, a Japanese anthropologist, Harumi Befu, explains the delicate exchange of indirectness required by a simple invitation to lunch. When his friend extended the invitation, Befu first had to determine whether it was meant literally or just *pro forma*, much as an American might say, "We'll have to have you over for dinner some time" but would not expect you to turn up at the door. Having decided the invitation was meant literally and having accepted, Befu was then asked what he would like to eat. Following custom, he said anything would do, but his friend, also following custom, pressed him to specify. Host and guest repeated this exchange an appropriate number of times, until Befu deemed it polite to answer the question—politely—by saying that tea over rice would be fine. When he arrived for lunch, he was indeed served tea over rice—as the last course of a sumptuous meal. Befu was not surprised by the feast, because he knew that protocol required it. Had he been given what he had asked for, he would have been insulted. But protocol also required that he make a great show of being surprised.

This account of mutual indirectness in a lunch invitation may strike Americans as excessive. But far more cultures in the world use elaborate systems of indirectness than value directness. Only modern Western societies place a priority on direct communication, and even for us it is more a value than a practice.

Evidence from other cultures also makes it clear that indirectness does not in itself reflect low status. Rather, our assumptions about the status of women compel us to interpret anything they do as reflecting low status. Anthropologist Elinor Keenan, for example, found that in a Malagasy-speaking village on the island of Madagascar, it is women who are direct and men who are indirect. And the villagers see the men's indirect way of speaking, using metaphors and proverbs, as the better way. For them, indirectness, like the men who use it, has high status. They regard women's direct style as clumsy and crude, debasing the beautiful subtlety of men's language. Whether women or men are direct or indirect differs; what remains constant is that the women's style is negatively evaluated—seen as lower in status than the men's.

IT'S DIFFERENT
COMING FROM A MAN

Research from our own culture provides many examples of the same behavior being interpreted differently depending on whether it's done by women or men. Take, for example, the case of "tag questions"—statements with little questions added onto the end, as in "It's a nice day, isn't it?" Linguist Robin Lakoff first pointed out that many women use more tag questions than men. Though studies seeking to test Lakoff's observation have had somewhat mixed results, most support it. Jacqueline Sachs, observing the language of children as young as two to five, found that girls used more than twice as many tag questions as boys. And research has shown that people *expect* women to use tags. Psychologists David and Robert Siegler conducted an experiment asking adults to guess the sex of speakers. Sure enough, the stereotype held: Subjects guessed a woman was speaking when tags were used, a man when they weren't. The stereotype can actually be more compelling than reality: In another experiment, psychologists Nora Newcombe and Diane Arnkoff presented adults with communications in which women and men used equal numbers of tag questions, and found that their subjects thought the women had used more.

Most troubling of all, women and men are judged differently even if they speak the same way. Communications researcher Patricia Hayes Bradley found that when women used tag questions and disclaimers, subjects judged them as less intelligent and knowledgeable *than men who also used them.* When women did not give support for their arguments, they were judged less intelligent and knowledgeable, *but men who advanced arguments without support were not.* In other words, talking in ways that are associated with women causes women to be judged negatively, but talking the same way does not have this effect on men. So it is not the ways of talking that are having the effect so much as people's attitudes toward women and men.

Many other studies have similar results. Psychologists John and Sandra Condry asked subjects to interpret why an infant was crying. If they had been told the baby was a boy, subjects thought he was angry, but if they had been told it was a girl, they thought she was afraid. Anne Macke and Laurel Richardson, with Judith Cook, discovered that when students judged professors, generating more class discussion was taken to be a sign of incompetence—only if the professor was female.

SILENCE IS GOLDEN—OR LEADEN

Research itself has fallen prey to this double standard. In studies claiming that men exert power by talking more than women, women's silence is cited as evidence that they have no power. At the same time, other studies claim that men's use of silence and refusing to speak is a show of their power. A theme running through Mirra Komarovsky's classic study *Blue Collar Marriage* is that many of the wives interviewed said they talked more than their husbands ("He's tongue-tied," one woman said of her husband; "My husband has a great habit of not talking," said another). More of the wives want to talk, and have their husbands talk, about problems. In contrast, more husbands withdraw in the face of troubles ("When I don't feel good, I light out and don't dump my load on them"), emotional stress, or a wife's "demands." Yet there is no question but that these husbands are "dominant" in their marriages. Taciturnity itself can be an instrument of power. Komarovsky quotes a mother who says of her husband, "He doesn't say much but he means what he says and the children mind him."

Jack Sattel believes men use silence to exercise power over women, and he illustrates with the following scene from Erica Jong's novel *Fear of Flying*. The first line of dialogue is spoken by Isadora, the second by her husband, Bennett.

> "Why do you always have to do this to me? You make me feel so lonely.
> "That comes from you."
> "What do you mean it comes from me? Tonight I wanted to be happy. It's Christmas Eve. Why do you turn on me? What did I do?"
> Silence.
> "What did I do?"
> He looks at her as if her not knowing were another injury.

"Look, let's just go to sleep now. Let's just forget it."

"Forget what?"

He says nothing.

"Forget the fact that you turned on me? Forget the fact that you're punishing me for nothing? Forget the fact that I'm lonely and cold, that it's Christmas Eve and again you've ruined it for me? Is that what you want me to forget?"

"I won't discuss it."

"Discuss what? *What* won't you discuss?"

"Shut up! I won't have you screaming in the hotel."

"I don't give a fuck what you won't have me do. I'd like to be treated civilly. I'd like you to at least do me the courtesy of telling me why you're in such a funk. And don't look at me that way . . ."

"What way?"

"As if my not being able to read your mind were my greatest sin. I *can't* read your mind. I *don't* know why you're so mad. I *can't* intuit your every wish. If that's what you want in a wife you don't have it in me."

"I certainly don't."

"Then what is it? Please tell me."

"I shouldn't have to."

"Good God! Do you mean to tell me I'm expected to be a mind reader? Is that the kind of mothering you want?"

"If you had any empathy for me . . ."

"But I *do*. My God, you don't give me a chance."

"You tune out. You don't listen."

"It was something in the movie, wasn't it?"

"What, in the movie?"

"The quiz again. Do you have to quiz me like some kind of criminal? Do you have to *cross-examine* me? . . . It was the funeral scene. . . . The little boy looking at his dead mother. Something got you there. That was when you got depressed."

Silence.

"Well, *wasn't* it?"

Silence.

"Oh come on, Bennett, you're making me *furious*. Please tell me. Please."

(He gives the words singly like little gifts. Like hard little turds.) "What was it about that scene that got me?"

"Don't quiz me. Tell me!" (She puts her arms around him. He pulls away. She falls to the floor holding onto his pajama leg. It looks less like an embrace than like a rescue scene, she sinking, he reluctantly allowing her to cling to his leg for support.)

"Get up!"

(Crying) "Only if you tell me."

(He jerks his leg away.) "I'm going to bed."

This painful scene does seem to support Sattel's claim that Bennett uses silence as a weapon against his wife. Each successive refusal to tell her what's bothering him is like a blow laying her lower and lower—until she is literally on the floor. But would our intepretation change if we reversed the genders in this scene?

With genders reversed, the scene seems impossible. It is hard to imagine a man begging his wife to tell him what he did wrong. What leaped to my mind, when I tried to reverse genders, was a scene in which the man withdraws, disabling her silence as a weapon. What makes Bennett's silence so punishing is Isadora's insistence on making him talk to her. It is the interaction of the two styles—his withdrawal and her insistence that he tell her what she did wrong—that is devastating to both. If Bennett shared Isadora's belief that problems should be talked out, or she shared his practice of withdrawing when problems arise, they would not have found themselves in this devastating scene.

"I'M SORRY, I'M NOT APOLOGIZING"

There are many ways that women talk that make sense and are effective in conversations with women but appear powerless and self-deprecating in conversations with men. One such pattern is that many women seem to apologize all the time. An apology is a move that frames the apologizer as one-down. This might seem obvious. But the following example shows that an apparent apology may not be intended in that spirit at all.

A teacher was having trouble with a student widely known to be incorrigible. Finally, she sent the boy to the principal's office. Later the principal approached her in the teachers' lounge and told her the student had been suspended. The teacher replied, "I'm sorry," and the principal reassured her, "It's not your fault." The teacher was taken aback by the principal's reassurance, because it had not occurred to her that the student's suspension might be her fault until he said it. To her, "I'm sorry" did not mean "I apologize"; it meant "I'm sorry to hear that." "I'm sorry" was intended to establish a connection to the principal by implying, "I know you must feel bad about this; I do too." She was framing herself as connected to him by similar feelings. By interpreting her words of shared feeling as an apology, the principal introduced the notion that she might be at fault, and framed himself as one-up, in a position to absolve her of guilt.

The continuation of this story indicates that these different points of view may be associated with gender. When this teacher told her grown daughter about the incident, the daughter agreed that the principal's reaction had been strange. But when she told her son and husband, they upbraided her for apologizing when she had not been at fault. They too interpreted "I'm sorry" as an apology.

There are several dynamics that make women appear to apologize too much. For one thing, women may be more likely to apologize because they do not instinctively balk at risking a one-down position. This is not to say that they relish it, just that it is less likely to set off automatic alarms in their heads. Yet another factor is that women are heard as apologizing when they do not intend to do so. Women frequently say "I'm sorry" to express sympathy and concern, not apology.

This confusion is rooted in the double meaning of the word *sorry*. This double meaning is highlighted in the following anecdote. A twelve-year-old Japanese girl living in the United States was writing a letter of condolence to her grandmother in Japan because her grandfather had died. The girl was writing in Japanese, but she was more accustomed to English. She began in the appropriate way: "I'm so sorry that Grandfather died." But then she stopped and looked at what she had written. "That doesn't sound right," she said to her mother. "I didn't kill him." Because she was writing in a language that was not second nature to her, this girl realized that an expression most people use automatically had a different meaning when interpreted literally. "I'm sorry," used figuratively to express regret, could be interpreted literally to mean "I apologize."

The difference between ritual and literal uses of language is also at play in the following example. A businesswoman named Beverly returned from an out-of-town trip to find a phone message on her answering machine from her division head. The message explained that he had found an enormous number of errors in a report written by her assistant. He told her that he had indicated the errors, returned the report to the assistant, and arranged for the deadline to be extended while she typed in the corrections. Beverly was surprised, since she had read and approved the report before leaving on vacation, but she said, "I'm sorry"—and was offended when he said, "I'm not blaming anyone." This seemed to imply that he *was* blaming her, since he introduced the idea.

"PLEASE DON'T ACCEPT MY APOLOGY"

Beverly asked her assistant to show her the lengthy corrected report and became angry when she saw that half the pages had "errors" marked, but few were actually errors. Nearly all involved punctuation, and most were matters of stylistic preference, such as adding commas after brief introductory phrases or before the conjunction *and*. In a large number of cases, she felt that her division head had introduced punctuation errors into sentences that were grammatically correct as they stood.

Later that day she encountered the division head at an office party and announced as soon as she saw him that she was angry at him and told him why. She realized by his reaction that she had offended his sensibilities by raising the matter in front of someone else. She immediately apologized for having blurted out her anger rather than expressing it more diplomatically, and she later visited him in his office to apologize again. She was sure that if she apologized for having confronted him in the wrong way at the wrong time, he would counterapologize for having overcorrected the report and for going directly to the assistant instead of through her. Instead, he generously said, "I accept your apology," and affably changed the subject to office politics.

Now accepting an apology is arguably quite rude. From the point of view of connection, an apology should be matched. And from the perspective of status, an apology should be deflected. In this view, a person who apologizes takes a one-down position, and accepting the apology preserves that asymmetry, whereas deflecting the apology restores balance. Although she felt immediately uncomfortable, Beverly did not realize until after she had left the office, all smiles and goodwill, that not only had her division head rudely accepted her apology, but he had not offered a balancing one.

Women's and men's differential awareness of status may have been the cause of Beverly's problem in a more fundamental way too. She felt quite friendly with her division head; she liked him; she had come to think of him as a friend. For her, as for many women, being friends means downplaying if not obliterating status differences. When she blurted out her anger, she was not thinking of herself as upbraiding a superior in front of others. To the extent that he remained aware of the difference in their status despite their friendly relationship, to accept her criticism would have amounted to public humiliation. Had she focused on their status differences rather than their friendship, she would not have approached him as she did. She would not, for example, have taken that tack with the company president.

WOMEN ADAPT TO MEN'S NORMS

In all these examples, the styles more typical of men are generally evaluated more positively and are taken as the norm. In a related and perhaps even more distressing asymmetry, when women and men are in groups together, the very games they play are more likely to be men's games than women's.

In Ursula Le Guin's story "In and Out," a former secretary recalls an all-women meeting:

> Like when the group of secretaries met to plan a meeting to talk about women in the city government, and the meeting had been so terrific, people saying things they didn't even know they thought, and ideas coming up, and nobody pushing anybody around.

By implication, an interchange in which people got to say what they were thinking and nobody was pushing anybody around was not the norm for meetings she had participated in or observed, but a quality that distinguished this meeting, in which only women participated.

A professor commented on how pleasant she found it to work on all-women committees, as compared to the mixed-gender committees she was more used to. But when she made this observation at a mixed-gender dinner party, a man strenuously objected. He said he had noticed no difference between all-male committees and those that included women. This man was surely telling the truth as he experienced it, because when women and men get together they interact according to men's, not women's, norms. So being in a mixed rather than a same-gender meeting makes less difference to men than to women.

Research in a range of disciplines shows that women make more adjustments than men in mixed groups. Elizabeth Aries found, in comparing the body postures of young men and women in all-male, all-female, and mixed discussion groups, that the men sat more or less the same way whether or not there were women present: They sprawled out in "relaxed" positions, taking up a large amount of space around them. The women in her study, however, drew themselves in, assuming "ladylike" postures, when there were men in the group, but relaxed and sprawled out when there weren't. In other words, the men took the same physical positions whether or not there were women present, but the women seemed to feel they were onstage when men were there, backstage when they found themselves with women only.

A similar point emerges from a study by Alice Deakins of the topics that women and men talk about. Deakins did what is called an eavesdropping study: While seated alone in a dining room where bank officers had lunch, she noted what people at adjacent tables were talking about. This was not a situation where the men were executives and the women their wives and secretaries. The men and women in Deakins's study were all bank officers, meeting as equals at work. Deakins found that when there were no women present, the men talked mostly about business and never about people, not even people at work. Their next most often discussed topic was food. Another common topic was sports and recreation. When women talked alone, their most frequent topic was people—not people at work so much as friends, children, and partners in personal relationships. The women discussed business next, and third, health, which included weight control.

When women and men got together, they tended to avoid the topics that each group liked best and settle on topics of interest to both. But in discussing those topics, *they followed the style of the men alone.* They talked about food the way men did, focusing on the food they were eating and about restaurants rather than diet and health. They talked about recreation the way men did, focusing on sports and vacations rather than exercising for diet or health, as the women did when they were alone. And they talked about housing in the way men did, focusing on location, property values, and commuting time, rather than the way women did, focusing on the interiors of houses (for example, layout and insulation) and what goes on among people inside houses (for example, finding cleaning help).

In analyzing tape recordings of private conversations among teenagers, Deborah Lange found a similar pattern. When the girls were alone, they talked about problems in their relationships with friends; when boys were alone, they talked about activities and plans, and made comments about friends. When boys and girls were together, they talked about activities and plans, and made comments about friends. In other words, when boys and girls talked together, they talked more or less the way boys talked when there were no girls present. But when girls got together with no boys present, they talked very differently.

All these (and many other) studies show that male-female conversations are more like men's conversations than they are like women's. So when women and men talk to each other, both make adjustments, but the women make more. Women are at a disadvantage in mixed-sex groups, because they have had less practice in conducting conversation the way it is being conducted in these groups. This may help to explain why girls do better at single-sex schools, whereas boys do about the same whether they go to boys' schools or coeducational ones. It may also explain why the women, but not the men, in Aries's study of college discussion groups said they preferred the same-gender group. All of these studies help to answer the question of why women are dissatisfied with communication in their relationships with men, while men who are parties to the same conversations express less dissatisfaction with them.

The talk that takes place at meetings and discussion groups is relatively more public, more like report-talk. Considering their preference for rapport-talk, it is not surprising that many women find it hard to get the floor at meetings, even though many men have a hard time getting the floor in conversations with women who are overlapping to build rapport. One reason many women find it difficult to get and keep the floor at meetings with men is that they won't compete for it. However, this chapter has presented only a few of many studies showing that even when women do behave the same way as men, they get different responses. This raises the question of how much women's difficulty in getting heard at meetings results from their ways of talking, and how much from their being women. This question also throws into relief the asymmetry of options available to women and men.

EQUAL DISCRIMINATION

Many women tell of having made a comment at a meeting or conference that is ignored. Later a man makes the same comment and it is picked up, approved or discussed, attributed to him rather than to her. Most women feel that this happens because people are less likely to pay attention to an idea that is raised by a woman, and the studies mentioned above indicate that there is truth to that. But the *way* ideas are raised may be a factor too. The following experience indicates this, but it also indicates that women and men do not have the same options available.

Professor A, a biochemist who teaches at a major university and is well known in his field, told me of the following experience. Having a diffident style, and being timid about speaking in public, he geared up his courage to speak following a public lecture in the biology department. He phrased his observation as a question: "Have you considered this chemical influence on the biological process you just described?" The lecturer responded, in effect, "No, I haven't," and the point was dropped. Soon after, however, another man, Professor B, spoke up. He began, "I would like to return to the point made by my colleague Professor A, because I think it is very important." He then repeated the point in a long-winded way. The idea then became the focus of extended discussion, and everyone who spoke to the issue began by saying, "I'd like to comment further on the important point raised by Professor B."

Had Professor A been a woman, it would have been natural to assume that the idea was first ignored because it was expressed by a woman, and later taken up because it was expressed by a man. But in this case, both speakers were men, so their gender could not have been the cause of the different responses they received. What was different was the way the two men expressed the "same" idea. Perhaps Professor A had not explained his idea in enough detail to allow others to see its importance. More likely, the way he spoke—diffidently, briefly, and phrasing his point as a question—framed his idea as not important, whereas the way Professor B spoke—at length and in a loud, declamatory voice—framed the same idea with a different metamessage: "This is important. Take note!"

This example is important because it sheds light on the role played by *how* people speak, regardless of their gender. But it also shows that women are at a disadvantage, since women are more likely than men to phrase their ideas as questions, take up less time with their questions, and speak at lower volume and higher pitch. The example shows that men who do not use the forceful strategies associated with masculinity are also at a disadvantage. In this sense, Professor A was in the same position as a woman who speaks in the same way.

UNEQUAL REMEDIES

But in another sense, Professor A's position is very different from that of a woman who has a similar conversational style. If Professor A decided to adjust his style to be more like Professor B's, he would find himself commanding more attention in public, if that is what he wants. And in the process, he would better fit the model of masculinity in our culture. But women who attempt to adjust their styles by speaking louder, longer, and with more self-assertion will also better fit the model of masculinity. They may command more attention and be more respected, but they may also be disliked and disparaged as aggressive and unfeminine.

Indeed, a woman need not be particularly aggressive to be criticized. A professor who invited a prominent woman researcher to speak to his students was shocked to hear some of his students—both female and male—comment later that they had found her arrogant. He had seen nothing arrogant about her at all. She simply hadn't engaged in any of the womanly behavior they had come to expect, such as continually smiling, qualifying her statements, or cocking her head in a charming way.

Ways of talking associated with masculinity are also associated with leadership and authority. But ways of talking that are considered feminine are not. Whatever a man does to enhance his authority also enhances his masculinity. But if a woman adapts her style to a position of authority that she has achieved or to which she aspires, she risks compromising her femininity, in the eyes of others.

As a woman who has achieved a high level of status in my profession, I grapple with this contradiction daily. When I go to academic conferences, I often meet colleagues from other universities who know me only by my scholarly publications and reputation. Not infrequently, new acquaintances say that they are surprised that I am so nice or so feminine. "You're not what I expected," I have repeatedly been told. "You're not aggressive at all." Others have remarked, "I thought you'd be cold," or "hard," or "competitive." When I press them about why they expected that of me, I am told, "I just figured that any woman who is as successful as you would have to be that way."

Just such assumptions emerge from a study by Harriet Wall and Anita Barry of college students' expectations about male and female professors. The researchers gave students identical materials on prospective professors—information about their academic backgrounds, publications, and letters of recommendation—and asked the students to predict how well the candidates would do if hired, including their chances to win a distinguished teaching award. Some who read the materials under a woman's name predicted that she would not win the award because, as one writer put it, "Too much business, not enough personality."

No one made inferences like this when exactly the same "file" was read under a man's name.

Another reason women professors may be judged more harshly than men, Wall and Barry found, is that students expect more of women. Those who thought they were evaluating a woman expected her to be more nurturing and to devote more time to her students outside of class than those who thought they were evaluating a man. The researchers point out that in evaluating real professors, students might have more praise for a male professor than for a female who actually devotes more time to them, because the woman is, after all, just doing what's expected, while the man is doing more than expected. In reading this study, I was, of course, reminded of the graduate student who had called me at home on Sunday because she didn't want to bother her dissertation director at home.

LANGUAGE KEEPS WOMEN IN THEIR PLACE

Nowhere is the conflict between femininity and authority more crucial than with women in politics. The characteristics of a good man and a good candidate are the same, but a woman has to choose between coming across as a strong leader *or* a good woman. If a man appears forceful, logical, direct, masterful, and powerful, he enhances his value as a man. If a woman appears forceful, logical, direct, masterful, or powerful, she risks undercutting her value as a woman.

As Robin Lakoff shows in *Language and Woman's Place*, language comes at women from two angles: the words they speak, and the words spoken about them. If I wrote, "After delivering the acceptance speech, the candidate fainted," you would know I was talking about a woman. Men do not faint; they pass out. And these terms have vastly different connotations that both reflect and affect our images of women and men. *Fainting* conjures up a frail figure crumpling into a man's rescuing arms, the back of her hand pressed to her forehead—probably for little reason, maybe just for dramatic effect. *Passing out* suggests a straightforward fall to the floor.

An article in *Newsweek* during the 1984 presidential campaign quoted a Reagan aide who called Ferraro "a nasty woman" who would "claw Ronald Reagan's eyes out." Never mind the nastiness of the remark and of the newsmagazine's using it to open its article. Applied to a man, *nasty* would be so tame as to seem harmless. Furthermore, men don't claw; they punch and sock, with correspondingly more forceful results. The verb *claw* both reflects and reinforces the stereotypical metaphor of women as cats. Each time someone uses an expression associated with this metaphor, it reinforces it, suggesting a general "cattiness" in women's character.

Even when seeming to praise Ferraro, the article used terms drenched in gender. She was credited with "a striking gift for tart political rhetoric, needling Ronald Reagan on the fairness issue and twitting the Reagan-Bush campaign for its reluctance to let Bush debate her." If we reversed subject and object, *needling* and *twitting* would not sound like praise for Reagan's verbal ability—or any man's. (I will refrain from commenting on the connotations of *tart,* assuming the word's double meaning was at least consciously unintended.)

In his book *The Language of Politics,* Michael Geis gives several examples of words used to describe Ferraro that undercut her. One headline called her "spunky," another "feisty." As Geis observes, *spunky* and *feisty* are used only for creatures that are small and lacking in real power; they could be said of a Pekingese but not a Great Dane, perhaps of Mickey Rooney but not of John Wayne—in other words, of any average-size woman, but not of an average-size man.

I am sure that the journalists who wrote these descriptions of Ferraro came to praise her, not to bury her. Perhaps they felt they were choosing snappy, eye-catching phrases. But their words bent back and trivialized the vice presidential candidate, high-

lighting, even if unintentionally, the incongruity between her images as a woman and as a political leader. When we think we are
using language, our language is using us.

It's not that journalists, other writers, or everyday speakers
are deliberately, or even unintentionally, "sexist" in their use of
language. The important point is that gender distinctions are built
into language. The words available to us to describe women and
men are not the same words. And, most damaging of all, through
language, our images and attitudes are buttressed and shaped.
Simply by understanding and using the words of our language,
we all absorb and pass on different, asymmetrical assumptions
about men and women.

BOUND BY BODY LANGUAGE

Body language is eloquent too. Political candidates necessarily
circulate photographs of their families. In the typical family photograph, the candidate looks straight out at the camera, while his
wife gazes up at him. This leads the viewer's eye to the candidate
as the center of interest. In a well-publicized family photograph,
Ferraro was looking up at her husband and he was looking straight
out. It is an appealing photo, which shows her as a good woman,
but makes him the inappropriate center of interest, just as his
finances became the center of interest in candidate Ferraro's financial disclosure. Had the family photograph shown Ferraro
looking straight out, with her husband gazing adoringly at her, it
would not have been an effective campaign photo, because she
would have looked like a domineering wife with a namby-pamby
for a husband.

Ironically, it is probably more difficult for a woman to hold
a position of authority in a relatively egalitarian society like that
of the United States than in more hierarchical ones. An American
woman who owned and edited an English-language magazine in
Athens told me that when Greeks came to the magazine to do

business, as soon as they realized that she was the boss, they focused their attention on her. But if her male assistant editor was in the room, Americans were irresistibly drawn to address themselves to him. It seems that Greeks' sensitivity to the publisher's status overrode their awareness of her gender, but Americans, who are less intimidated by status than Greeks, could not rise above their awareness of gender.

Much of this book has shown that women's and men's style differences are symmetrically misleading. Men and women learn to use language in the different worlds of boys and girls, and each group interprets the other's ways of talking in terms of its own. But in many ways, differences between women's and men's styles are not symmetrical. When men and women get together in groups, they are likely to talk in ways more familiar and comfortable to the men. And both women's and men's ways of talking are typically judged by the standards of men's styles, which are regarded as the norm. Most distressing in a society where equality is the agreed-upon goal, and where more and more women are entering high-status positions, women in authority find themselves in a double bind. If they speak in ways expected of women, they are seen as inadequate leaders. If they speak in ways expected of leaders, they are seen as inadequate women. The road to authority is tough for women, and once they get there it's a bed of thorns.

NINE

"Look at Me When I'm Talking to You!": Cross Talk Across the Ages

One source of inspiration for this book was a research project I participated in, dealing with how friends talk to each other at grade levels ranging from second grade to university. Although I had not intended to examine gender differences, when I watched the set of videotapes recorded by Bruce Dorval, I was overwhelmed by the differences that separated the females and males at each age, and the striking similarities that linked the females, on one hand, and the males, on the other, across the vast expanse of age. In many ways, the second-grade girls were more like the twenty-five-year-old women than like the second-grade boys.

The two categories of differences between the male and female speakers in the videotapes that were most striking to me were what the friends talked about and their body language—

how they oriented themselves to each other with their bodies and eyes.

Differences in physical alignment, or body language, leap out at anyone who looks at segments of the videotapes one after another. At every age, the girls and women sit closer to each other and look at each other directly. At every age, the boys and men sit at angles to each other—in one case, almost parallel—and never look directly into each other's faces. I developed the term *anchoring gaze* to describe this visual home base. The girls and women anchor their gaze on each other's faces, occasionally glancing away, while the boys and men anchor their gaze elsewhere in the room, occasionally glancing at each other.

The boys' and men's avoidance of looking directly at each other is especially important because researchers, and conventional wisdom, have emphasized that girls and women tend to be more indirect than boys and men in their speech. Actually, women and men tend to be indirect about different things. In physical alignment, and in verbally expressing personal problems, the men tend to be more indirect.

TEASING AND TELLING STORIES AT SECOND GRADE

The two pairs of second-graders provide the most obvious contrast in physical alignment and in what they talk about. The second-grade boys, Kevin and Jimmy, move so incessantly that it seems the chairs they are sitting on can't contain them. They never look directly at each other. They look around the room, at the ceiling, and at the video camera set up in the room. They squirm, jump out of their chairs, rhythmically kick their feet, make faces at each other and the camera, and point to objects in the room. One boy continually pummels the arms of his chair. They sing, make motor sounds by trilling their lips, and utter nonsense syllables.

246

And what are the boys talking about amid all this hubbub? They make a show of misbehaving by mugging for the camera, saying dirty words, laughing, and then clamping their hands over their giggles and shushing each other up. They tease: Jimmy tells Kevin over and over, "Your hair is standing up! Your hair always sticks up!" and Jimmy tries to smooth his hair, since he has no mirror to see that it looks just fine. They jump from topic to topic, as they try to find "something to do."

"WHAT GAMES DOES HE HAVE?"

For the second-grade boys, "something to do" is "games to play." For example, they look around the room in which they have been placed (Professor Dorval's university office), in search of games:

> JIMMY: Look. You know what the game— what the game is over there? We play— we had that in first grade.

> JIMMY: What games do we— does he have?
> KEVIN: I don't know.
> JIMMY: Probably only that. That's a dumb game, isn't it?
> KEVIN: Looks pretty good though.

> JIMMY: I can't wait until we play games.

Since they can't find any games to play (or don't feel they can help themselves to games they see in the room), they try to think of other things they can do:

> JIMMY: Well, if you have something to do, do it.
> KEVIN: Here he comes back in. What would you like to do?
> JIMMY: Play football.

Though he obviously can't do it right now, Jimmy has no trouble thinking of what he would like to do: play football. He'd like to be outside, running around with a group of boys, not sitting in a chair talking to one friend. Since they can't be physically active now, they talk about being so in the future; Kevin says, "You want to come over to my house one day? Ride my bike?"

The boys do find "something to do," though it is not their first choice. In a tone that shows mock impatience, Jimmy demands that Kevin find something to do and Kevin obliges, making a suggestion that the boys take up:

JIMMY: Would *you* find something to *do*?
KEVIN: Patty cake.
JIMMY: [Laugh] Look. Patty cake. Come on, let's do patty cake. Come on.

All these excerpts give the impression of young children with a lot of energy—much like any young children, I might have thought, until I viewed the videotape of two girls of the same age. The picture the second-grade girls present seems truly to be of another world. Jane and Ellen sit very still, practically nose to nose for much of the time. One or the other or both sit at the edge of their chairs, and they look directly into each other's faces. They calmly look elsewhere in the room only when they are thinking of what to say next. They do not cast about for something to do; they seem satisfied that they are already doing something: talking to each other.

Looking at the two transcripts side by side shows how different these conversations are: Whereas the second-grade boys' transcript is a mass of short spurts of speech, each boy's turn rarely taking more than a line, the transcript of the second-grade girls' conversation shows big blocks of talk, so that a single page of transcript might have one or two turns. This is because the girls are telling each other stories about things that have happened to them and other people. But these are not just any stories. They are about accidents and mishaps, illnesses and hospital visits.

"THAT'S SERIOUS!"

Telling stories about misfortunes seemed to me a rather strange thing to do, until I realized that the girls were strictly following the orders they had been given. Dorval had instructed them, as he did the boys and all the other pairs of friends in his study, to consult with each other and find something serious to talk about. So when he left the room, the girls huddled and whispered and then separated, faced each other, and began to exchange stories about things they considered serious. The stories in the following excerpt are rather short, but otherwise they are typical of the second-grade girls' conversation.

> ELLEN: Remember? What— when I told you about my uncle? He went up the ladder after my grandpa? And he fell and, um, cracked his head open? He's— and you know what? It still hasn't healed.
>
> JANE: One time, my uncle, he was, uh, he has like this bull ranch? In Millworth? And the bull's horns went right through his head.
>
> ELLEN: That's serious.

The way Ellen shows approval of Jane's story, "That's serious," shows that telling stories about disasters was meant to comply with the instructions they had been given.

Comparing the boys and girls of the same age, I had the feeling I was looking at two different species. The request to talk to each other about something serious seemed to make sense to the girls; they were asked to do something they often do by choice: sit together and talk. But the same request was a different one for boys, who are far less likely just to sit together and talk to each other in the course of their play. They are more used to *doing* things together—running around outside or playing games inside.

Looking at the tapes from the perspective of status and connection, or of oppositional versus supportive frameworks, I could see the patterns clearly. The boys, who have identified each other as best friends, show their affection for each other in an oppositional framework. Jimmy's repeated teasing, making Kevin think his hair is standing up when it's not, is one example. Jimmy also pretends to shoot Kevin, saying, "You're under arrest." And he says something intentionally mean: "I know William doesn't like you at all." Both boys play-fight, taking harmless swipes at each other.

FLOUTING AUTHORITY

The boys continually show their awareness of the authority figure who has placed them in this situation, as in the brief example above, where Kevin says, "Here he comes back in." They seek to undercut the experimenter's authority by resisting doing what they have been told (to talk about something serious) and by playful defiance. For example, they jump up and make faces at the camera, then giggle and shush each other, pretending momentarily to look like good little boys. They invoke the experimenter to flout his authority when he is nowhere in sight, as when Jimmy says, ". . . and then made a fart—here he comes!" Here, as elsewhere, their "misbehavior" seems aimed at the adult who has told them what to do.

Since they were instructed to talk about something serious, what better way to avoid compliance than to tell jokes? This the boys do:

KEVIN: Knock knock.
JIMMY: Who's there?
KEVIN: Fruit.
JIMMY: Fruit who?
KEVIN: Fruit bar.
JIMMY: What do you call a sleeping bull?

KEVIN: Bull chase. What?
JIMMY: Well? Well?
KEVIN: I don't know.
JIMMY: Bulldozer. You get it? Bulldozer.

Sometimes the jokes are scatological, and it is clear that they are breaking the rules of decorum with the adult authority in mind:

KEVIN: Knock knock.
JIMMY: Who's there?
KEVIN: [Jumping in his seat] Knock knock knock knock.
JIMMY: Who's there? [Pause] Tu tu. Tu tu who? You got tu tu in your panties.
KEVIN: I don't either.
JIMMY: I wonder if he hears us—he can—just move your mouth. [Both boys proceed to do so.]

This brief example has it all: Jimmy tells a joke; he teasingly puts Kevin down; he refers to a taboo subject; he shows his preoccupation with the authority figure who might object to their breaking these rules; and he defies and mocks the situation by pretending (and getting Kevin to pretend) to talk without producing sound. If telling a joke is a kind of performance that sets the teller at center stage, Jimmy is so exuberant in telling his tu-tu joke that he hogs the stage for the audience participation part as well, speaking all four lines of the knock-knock dialogue. On the other hand, he may simply be filling in for Kevin, who started the routine with "Knock knock," but didn't seem to have a joke in mind to follow through.

PLAYING "INTERVIEW"

Finding themselves sitting together and talking seems to suggest to these boys the hierarchical situation of being questioned by an adult. Playacting and mocking this framework, Jimmy takes the role of interviewer:

JIMMY: I've got four things to say.
KEVIN: Yeah?
JIMMY: I've got four things to say.
KEVIN: Tell me.
JIMMY: You doing good in your schoolwork, huh?
KEVIN: Yeah.
JIMMY: Um, play soccer good?
KEVIN: Uh huh.
JIMMY: You're nice. What was the last one? How are you?
KEVIN: Fine.
JIMMY: It's your turn.

Kevin's and Jimmy's turns are all very short—just a few words—with only two exceptions: one in which Jimmy explains a video game, and another in which he explains how to play patty cake (even though it was Kevin who proposed playing it). In both, he is taking the role of teacher.

A WORLD OF DIFFERENCE

These are just a few examples of what is pervasive in the twenty-minute videotape: The boys are physically restless; their idea of what to do involves physical activities; they are continually aware of the hierarchical framework they are in, and they do what they can to mock and resist it; and they show their affection for each other in an oppositional format. They directly disagree with each other, but then disagreement is a natural response to the put-downs and mock assaults that are initiated. For example, Kevin protests, "I don't either" when Jimmy tells him he has "tu tu" in his panties, and "No, I'm not" when Jimmy tells him he is under arrest.

The second-grade girls' conversation in the same situation includes nothing that resembles any of the ways of talking just described for the boys. The girls too are aware of the authoritarian framework they are in, but they are complying with it rather than defying or mocking it. And, far from playfully attacking each other, they support each other by agreeing with and adding to what the other says. Rather than colluding to defy authority, they reassure each other that they are successfully complying, as when Ellen tells Jane, "That's serious." In contrast to the teasing by which each boy implies that the other is doing things wrong, the girls offer reassurance that they are doing things right.

The brief stories the girls tell in the excerpt above are also typical of the ways the stories are linked to each other and to the girls' shared experience. By starting out with "Remember?" Ellen reminds Jane that Jane was there or has heard the story before. Already, in second grade, these little girls tell stories with the characteristic rising intonation that makes every phrase sound like a question. Like so many ways of talking that are characteristic of girls and women, when looked at from the perspective of status, this rising intonation could be interpreted as a request for approval and therefore evidence of insecurity. But it could also be seen—and, I think, is more accurately seen—as a way of inviting the listener to participate by saying something like "uh huh," or nodding. Jane also begins many of her stories by saying her friend's name—another mark of involvement.

The short example above is also typical of the longer conversation in that Jane follows Ellen's story with a similar story. Jane's story matches Ellen's not only in being about an accident, but also in being about an uncle and a head wound.

The second-grade girls, like the boys, talk about future activities, but what they propose is different from what the boys propose. Whereas Kevin invites Jimmy to come over and ride his bike, Jane tells Ellen that she has just read a Bible story that she liked a lot. She says Ellen can come over to her house so that Jane can read it to her—or she can read it herself. Not only does Ellen propose a talking activity, in contrast to Kevin's suggestion of a physical activity, but Jane also avoids framing Ellen as lower in status by assuring her that she can read the story herself rather than being read to, if she prefers.

Before the investigator entered the room and reminded them

to talk about something serious, the girls were exchanging different kinds of stories. Like women who tell troubles as a kind of rapport-talk, these second-grade girls were exchanging matching complaints. For example, Jane complained that her little brother kept asking her to read stories to him but wouldn't let her finish any of them; he kept bringing out new books for her to start reading. Ellen responded with a matching story about reading to *her* brother, only her problem was that he had chosen a long book, and each time she finished a chapter and thought she was done reading to him, he'd insist on hearing one more. Here they were, in second grade, establishing rapport by complaining about others who were close to them and by matching and supporting each other's stories.

Men and women to whom I showed these videotapes had very different reactions to these second-graders. My reaction was typical of women's: I thought Jane and Ellen were sweet little girls, and I smiled to see them. I was touched by their eagerness to fulfill the experimenter's request. My heart went out to them. But the little boys made me nervous. I wished they'd *sit still*! I thought their joking silly, and I didn't like their teasing and mock attacks. I felt sorry for poor Kevin, who kept trying to smooth down his hair and was told that another little boy didn't like him.

But men I showed the tapes to reacted very differently. They thought the boys cute, and they found their energy and glee touching. They were sympathetic to the boys' impulse to poke fun at the situation and defy the experimenter's authority. The girls seemed to them like a pair of Goody Two Shoes. Some men commented that they didn't trust the girls' behavior; they felt that little children couldn't really enjoy sitting so still—they must be on their best behavior to kiss up to the experimenter.

So there it is: Boys and girls grow up in different worlds, but we think we're in the same one, so we judge each other's behavior by the standards of our own.

LIFE IMITATES EXPERIMENT

Nowhere are the consequences of these differences more striking than in elementary school, where teachers expect children to sit quietly and do as they're told, like the girls in the videotapes I examined, and not to fidget and jump around and tease each other and resist orders, like the boys. While reading a study of teaching style in a kindergarten class, I came across real-life support for the pattern I had noticed and described, as well as a dramatic illustration of the consequences of that pattern. Ethnographer Jane White studied what she calls the "relentless politeness" of primary-school teachers. She begins an article with an excerpt from a lesson in which a kindergarten teacher, Mrs. Bedford, is introducing a social studies lesson. Mrs. Bedford says:

> Oh my, what a nice-looking group of kindergartners. Oh, it makes Mrs. Bedford so *happy* to see such smiling faces. Now, are we all sitting comfortably? [*Pause*] Let's see who is here. Looks like everybody's here. Our line leader for today is Mark W. [*Students talking among themselves*] Oh, I like the way Tammy and Barbara are sitting down. They're so *ready* for first grade. Oh, and Corrie and Heather, how nice . . . and Colleen and Sherrie, you look terrific. Joey, could you turn around so I can see your face? Steven T., would you come sit up here by me? Bobby, find yourself a place there. Stephen S., right there is a good place for you. Is everybody comfortable? Are we ready?

White was not concerned with gender differences in her study; her purpose in presenting this excerpt was to show that the teacher used "polite" ways of speaking, like praising good behavior rather than censuring bad, and phrasing directives as questions. But in reading this wonderfully graphic and familiar example, I noticed that all the children who were being praised for sitting quietly were girls, and all the children who were being (indirectly) criticized for not sitting still were boys.

The same impression leaped out at me from another article as well. To show that elementary-school teachers regard boys and girls as separate social groups, sociologist Barrie Thorne quotes a teacher who said, "The girls are ready and the boys aren't." Both these examples from real classrooms dramatize that school requires behavior that is more "natural" for girls than boys.

In the previously mentioned study by Alice Greenwood of her preteen son and daughters talking to their friends over dinner, I encountered another example of real-life support for the patterns I observed in the videotapes of friends talking. Just as the second-grade girls reassured each other, "That's serious," when the girls in Greenwood's study talked to their friends, a funny story was often supported by the reassurance "That's really funny." Even more, the girls would begin to laugh appreciatively *before* a story was told, as soon as another girl announced her intention to tell a story by saying, "This is so funny." In contrast, the boy said a good conversation was one "where we make jokes and crack on each other"—exactly what the second-grade boys chose to do.

These real-life examples reassured me that the two videotapes I had studied were typical, not exceptional. But my findings are also supported by a battery of research on little girls and boys at play, which has documented the greater physical activity and aggressiveness of little boys, their greater tendency to end up in parallel rather than coordinated play, and their greater tendency to take oppositional stances. Developmental psychologist Campbell Leaper, for example, found that five-year-old girls elaborate on each other's ideas in a "mutually positive" manner, whereas little boys of the same age exhibit "negative reciprocity" by which one boy tries to control and the other withdraws. In her study of three- and four-year-olds in a day-care center, Amy Sheldon found that even when the girls and boys both engaged in individual activities with same-sex threesomes, the girls—unlike the boys— kept each other connected by calling out what they were doing and responding to the others' comments.

If it is fascinating to see the source of adult patterns in second-graders, it boggles the mind to see them in three-year-olds. No wonder it is hard for men and women to understand each other's point of view: We have been looking at the view from different vantage points for as long as we have been looking.

TROUBLE WITH PEOPLE AND THINGS IN SIXTH GRADE

The sixth-grade boys and girls present as stark a contrast as the second-graders. Walt, sitting in a high-backed wooden chair with arms, is also physically restless, but he shows it by squirming rather than jumping up and down and in and out of his seat. Walt twists all over his chair. At one point, he leans to the side and reaches one arm way down the side of the chair as if he were Rubber Man. The other boy, Tom, is physically fairly still, but he doesn't look comfortable either. He stretches his legs out in front of him, and much of the time he has one arm draped over the back of his upholstered chair. He is more stiff than still.

These boys don't look at each other either. Walt rubs his eyes continually, creating a physical barrier to looking at Tom. He plays with his fingers, spending more time looking at them than at Tom. Tom too sits aligned with his chair, at an angle to Walt. They frequently look around, apparently searching for things to talk about and often finding them. For example, they comment on the decorations ("That's a funny-looking picture," and later, "Dang, this is quite a picture"); they notice a sprinkler in the ceiling and one boy explains to the other, "It's in case something catches on fire." Spotting his bag, Walt pulls out a new pair of shoes, which they both look at, handle, and talk about.

Turning to the sixth-grade girls, we are looking at a different scene altogether. Rather than aligning themselves with their chairs, the girls sit across the chairs in order to face each other directly. Shannon sits quite still, at the edge of the wooden chair, with her arms resting on the arms of the chair. Julia sits in the upholstered chair without arms, but rather than spreading out from it like Tom, she draws her legs and arms up onto the chair. She puts her left ankle on her right knee, holds her foot, and plays with her shoelaces. She frequently glances at her foot, but her gaze is anchored on her friend's face, in contrast to Walt, whose gaze is anchored on his fingers.

Julia and Shannon change positions several times during their talk, but the changes are neither abrupt nor frequent, and the girls are always tightly and directly aligned with each other in gaze and posture. The boys at this age exude a sense of energy held in check. Walt's squirming and Tom's motionlessness both seem caused by discomfort. The girls seem comfortable with the level of movement allowed them, but the boys seem to be restraining themselves, as if they have learned that the level of energy they feel should not be expressed. Perhaps this contrast holds a clue to the stony quality of many men's stillness.

What the boys and girls talk about is also as different as can be. In the twenty minutes of conversation, Tom and Walt touch on fifty-five topics. They talk about school, homework, cable TV, sports, sex and violence on TV (they don't approve of it), things in the room, things they want (a motorbike, a computer, a shotgun), other boys at school, Walt's shoes, a rock group they play in, inflation, Nancy Reagan's buying a dress for three thousand dollars (they don't approve), girls, guns, videos, and their friendship. None of these topics is pursued for more than a few turns, and each turn is short.

Like the second-grade boys' conversation, the sixth-grade boys' includes only two extended turns, and they are both report-talk, framing the boys as differently placed in a hierarchy: Tom sings a song he recently composed for their rock group, framing himself as the performer and Walt as his audience, and he tells about a bicycle accident he was in.

"IT *HURTS* WHEN YOU LOSE YOUR BEST FRIEND"

Again, moving from the sixth-grade boys to the girls of the same age is like moving to another planet. The girls spend almost all their time talking about Julia's falling out with a third friend, Mary. Julia says how bad she feels about losing a friend ("It *hurts* when you lose your best friend, a really close friend"). The girls agree that the breakup was Mary's fault. Their talk reveals how central their friendships are to their world. Julia says, "I like getting a friend and keeping it *forever*," and "I couldn't live without a friend." Shannon agrees: "I don't think anybody could live without a friend, either." Julia declares to Shannon that they will "be friends practically *forever*."

Over and over, the sixth-grade girls express their fear that anger disrupts friendships. Julia explains that her friendship with Mary ended because Mary got mad, and was therefore "mean." In contrast, she maintains that she herself does not get mad at people, even when she doesn't like what they do:

SHANNON: Too bad you and Mary are not good friends anymore.

JULIA: I know. God, it's— she's so *mean* sometimes. . . . And then— what was so sad, she just— gets *mad* at you all of a sudden. And like if she does something I don't like, I mean, I just— I don't *like* it, I mean, I don't get *mad* at her!

JULIA: My mom does things that I don't like a lot, and— I just— I mean, I don't get *mad* at her.

Julia feels—and fears—that when people get mad, they fight, and fighting can lead to separation. At one point she introduces what seems like a new and unrelated topic—her worry that her parents might get divorced. But it is really the same topic: She's afraid her parents will get divorced because she sometimes hears them fight, and she believes that one of the reasons Mary is such a difficult person is that her parents are divorced.

Here again I came across independent corroboration for these patterns in real-life dialogue among children of roughly the same age. The issue of "getting mad" turns up in a conversation between teenage girls taped by Deborah Lange. In that conversation, one girl tells about a problem: She would like to get all her friends together, but she can't, because they don't all like each other. As she keeps repeating that she's not mad, she sounds a lot like Julia:

> I'm not mad at Deena or anything. I'm not mad at Millicent or Rita. But I . . . I always . . . It's so hard to make plans with all of them at once.

Instead of being mad at her friends, she makes efforts to placate them all:

> . . . because Rita gets in fights with Millicent and Deena thinks that Millicent's being a bitcher, and it's so mean because it's not fair because, um, I try to, um, I try to, um, I try to make it so I can make plans with all of them but I-I'd rather just that all of them got along than trying to be, um, than trying to, um, you know I mean I myself have to change.

Not only does this excerpt show sixth-grade girls sharing troubles talk about their relationships with friends, but it also shows that they want to avoid conflict and preserve harmony.

"I KNOW"

In the videotape of sixth-grade girls, Shannon and Julia, like the second-grade girls, reinforce each other's feelings. For example, Shannon repeatedly agrees with Julia about Mary. Here is what they say right after the excerpt in which Julia says that Mary gets mad, whereas she doesn't:

SHANNON: She tries to upset people.
JULIA: She *does*. And she just sees me *cry*ing and everything. She just lets me *suf*fer.
SHANNON: And she loves it.
JULIA: I know. She enjoys the *whole thing*.

Shannon supports Julia's complaint about Mary by offering similar observations, and Julia incorporates Shannon's additions into her complaints.

THE SAME TOPIC—WITH A DIFFERENCE

Even when the sixth-grade boys and girls talk about the same thing, what they talk about is different. For example, both pairs of friends begin by reporting what happened the night before, but Julia tells about a problem with her father, while Tom tells about a problem with the television. First, the boys:

TOM: Man, yesterday? We were sitting and watching cable? Some big old jet came flying by, sounded like he was going to land.
WALT: [Laugh]
TOM: And then our cable went out yesterday.
WALT: Ours too.

And that was that. Now, the girls:

JULIA: Um, guess what happened last night.
SHANNON: What?
JULIA: Um, I went, um, okay. Last night, um, my brother, um, by b— Okay, my dad said, "Julia, you gotta pick up, by yourself." And /?/ I said, "Well, if my brother doesn't have to," and so me and my dad got into a big fight and everything, you know? And um, oh God. And I bit him. I couldn't *be*lieve it. Oh God.

SHANNON: Oh my gosh. Did he get mad?

JULIA: Yeah, but not— not right now, just— I went in my room. I locked the door.

Julia told about interacting with a person, her father, and Tom told about interacting with an object, the television. Her story is also longer than any turn produced by the boys at the same age. And it is talk about a fight, a primary female concern, because fights threaten intimacy.

Another aspect of Julia's story that is typical of girls and women is that she recreates the drama of what happened between people by acting out what they said, in dialogue. She takes on her father's voice—"Julia, you gotta pick up, by yourself"— and enacts her protest—"Well, if my brother doesn't have to." Because girls and women are concerned with conveying the emotional impact of what happened between people, they use dialogue to dramatize events more than boys and men do.

"WHEN IT'S TIME *TO* TALK, YOU CAN'T TALK"

Like the second-grade girls, the sixth-grade girls appear completely comfortable sitting and talking. But the sixth-grade boys seem to be struggling—struggling to sit in their chairs, and to find something to talk about. They say as much:

TOM: I tried to think of what to say 'cause we were on film. It's different.

WALT: I know.

TOM: When you're outside you can—

WALT: I know, I can scream but not in an apartment.

TOM: Or you can talk up a storm.

WALT: Uh-huh.

TOM: When it's time *to* talk, you can't talk.

Walt seems to take Tom's mention of being "outside" as a reference to the benefits of playing outside rather than inside, and he supports that idea with the example that it's okay to scream outside. But Tom seems to be referring to the world outside this artificial situation, commenting on the difficulty they are having in finding things to talk about when they are told to talk.

These remarks show that Tom is aware that they are in a situation where they have been told what to do, and he suggests that this is part of the reason they are having trouble finding things to talk about. Though it is not as obvious and pervasive as with the second-grade boys, Tom also mocks the situation with a joke: "Smile, you're on *Candid Camera*." Even more dramatically, when Dorval leaves the boys alone following his brief reminder, Tom salutes—first subtly, and apparently automatically, then in an exaggerated way, apparently mocking his own automatic sign of subordination.

In response to the discomfort of being in the experimental situation, the second-grade boys talk about the games they would like to play. The sixth-grade boys imagine being out of this situation when they're grown up. The following example also shows the way they use the room to shift topics suddenly—something the girls never do.

TOM: Man, I can't wait till I'm grown up.
WALT: Yeah, I know what you mean.
TOM: Get out of college, go to the marines. Get out of the marines, go to the air force. Get out of the air force, get married.
WALT: Yeah, I can't wait till I'm sixteen to get my car.
TOM: I can't wait till I'm seventeen to get married.
WALT: Yeah, me too. **Look at that *thing* over there!**

It is touching to see how the boys yearn to be grown up, even though they are a bit confused about what adult behavior they will undertake, at what age. Nothing like this is said by any of the girls in the videotapes. I interpret it as an expression of the boys' discomfort at being children who can be told what to do, and I suspect it comes up here as a fantasy about a way to escape situations like this one. Although more briefly, a similar impulse is expressed by Kevin, one of the second-graders, in an interchange about their ages. Though he isn't sure exactly what age he is and what that means ("I am almost ten but I'm not eight yet"), Kevin reassures himself, "I'm catching up with big people." The boys show more eagerness to be grown up, so they can get out from under in the hierarchy.

CONTRASTING CONCEPTS OF FRIENDSHIP

Despite the striking differences between the boys' and girls' conversations, it would be misleading to imply that there are no similarities in their styles and concerns. The differences are not absolute, but of degree. For example, all these children are concerned with preserving their friendships. Here is what the sixth-grade boys say about it:

TOM: Seems like me and you do everything together.

WALT: Yeah, we're going hunting this Sunday, right?

TOM: Seems like, if we have something to do, if there's a fight, one of us would be on the same side, or if we have an idea, me and you are automatically in it. And everyone else wants to go against you and everything. It's hard to agree without someone saying something to you.

WALT: I know.

TOM: 'Cause there's *one* group and then there's another. The *good* group is the one who always gets picked on.

Though the boys, like the girls, comment on what good friends they are, there are differences in how they express it. First of all, the boys' discussion of their friendship is brief, and the topic doesn't come up again, whereas the girls' talk about their friendship goes on at length and repeatedly recurs. Tom's remark that he and Walt are good friends focuses on their doing things together ("Seems like me and you do everything together"). And fighting is central to their notion of friendship. Agreement between Walt and him, Tom says, automatically sparks opposition from others. His is an agonistic world, in which friendship is a matter of banding together against others.

In contrast, Julia's claim that she and Shannon are good friends is based on mutual understanding and longevity:

> JULIA: At least me and you have been knowing each other since kindergarten, and we know how each other *are*.

and on not fighting with each other:

> JULIA: Me and you *never* get in fights hardly.

and on communicating:

> JULIA: I mean like if I try to talk to you, you'll say, "Talk to *me*!" And if you try to talk to me, I'll *talk* to you.

Comparing the conversations of these boys and girls in sixth grade, one can see the root of women's and men's complaints about communication in their relationships with each other. The boys do say a bit about their friendships and about other people, but most of their talk is about things and activities and opinions about social issues. The only object the girls handle and discuss is one that symbolizes their friendship. Julia asks Shannon if she has given her a friendship pin, and Shannon says yes. Julia then says she read that if you're really good friends, you give two; she then reaches into her bag and gives Shannon a second friendship pin. All the girls' talk is about friends, friendship, and feelings; they orchestrate this talk at a level of subtlety and complexity that is not seen in the sixth-grade boys' talk.

MERGED AND PARALLEL CONVERSATIONS IN TENTH GRADE

Moving on to tenth grade, we come to a videotape that has been essential to my understanding of men's communication. The girls at this grade level are very much like the sixth-grade girls. They sit drawn up into their chairs, they look straight at each other, and they talk about the problems one of the girls has with her mother and her boyfriend. The tenth-grade boys, however, are different not only from the girls but from the younger boys. Their postures are the most extreme on the videotapes: They are sprawled out, almost reclining against the chairs they are supposed to be sitting in. Richard, like Tom in the sixth grade, is almost motionless, and he looks steadfastly ahead, as if he had been forbidden to look at his friend Todd, as Orpheus was forbidden to look back at Eurydice. Todd uses his feet to drag a swivel chair into place as a footstool and pushes it around with his feet as he looks ahead or around the room, only occasionally glancing at Richard. Someone viewing this tape commented that these boys look like they are riding in a car: Their bodies are parallel rather than facing each other, and they are both looking steadily ahead, one only occasionally glancing as his friend and the other almost never doing so.

But turn up the sound, and this scene is transformed. The boys are not talking about impersonal topics. Far from it. These are the boys whose conversation was presented and discussed in Chapter Two. They are exchanging the most intimate talk that I heard in any of Dorval's videotapes. Whereas the girls talked about problems they had with other people—absent parties—these boys are confronting their relationship to each other, and one is revealing deep feelings of loss and hurt and longing.

"I KNOW WHAT'S BUGGING ME"

As we saw earlier, Todd is feeling alienated: He feels left out at parties; he has no date for an upcoming dance and doesn't want to ask anyone he knows; he doesn't feel right with girls who like him, and he doesn't feel right with his buddies either. He pines for the past when he and Richard spent time alone together and talked more. Todd's complaint can be seen in the following excerpt. To convey the halting quality of the conversation, numbers in parentheses are used to indicate seconds of pause.

TODD: What the hell we supposed to talk about? I mean, I know what's bugging me.

RICHARD: What's bugging you?

TODD: [Snicker] That we don't talk.

RICHARD: Who don't talk?

. . .

TODD: We're doing it again.

RICHARD: What?

TODD: Not talking.

RICHARD: I know. Well, go.

TODD: We're not even making small talk anymore. [Laugh]

RICHARD: Right, okay. (3.4) I mean, you know. What can I say? (3.6) I mean, if you meant everything you said last weekend, and *I* meant everything *I* said. (1.0)

TODD: Well, of course I did. But I mean, I don't know. I guess we're growing up. I mean, I don't know. I guess I live in the past or something. I really enjoyed those times when we used to stay up all night long and just, you know, spend the nights over someone else's house just to talk all night.

RICHARD: Mhm.

TODD: They were kinda fun.

RICHARD: Yeah, that *was* fun. (2.2)

TODD: But now we're lucky if we say anything to each other in the hall.

RICHARD: [With a mock-challenging intonation] Oh, all right!

TODD: I'm serious. I remember walking in the hall and I'd say "Hi" to you and you'd say "Hi there" or sometimes you'll push me in the locker, if I'm lucky. [Laugh] (1.4)

RICHARD: [Protesting] We talk.
 TODD: Not the same way anymore.
   (4.8)
RICHARD: I never *knew* you wanted to *talk*.

Although most men for whom I have played this conversation comment that it is unusual, it nonetheless happened. What is most striking is the stark contrast, almost contradiction, between these boys' words and their body language. Though their words speak of intense involvement, their bodies are in careless, lounging positions.

ARE MEN DISENGAGED?

I told a family therapist about my observation that the girls looked directly at each other and aligned their bodies facing each other, whereas the boys looked anywhere but into each other's faces and positioned themselves at angles to each other. She commented, "That always happens with the families I see. The men won't look at me, and they won't look at their wives. The men are always disengaged." But this pair of tenth-grade boys who are not looking at each other are nothing if not engaged. They are superengaged, even when displaying disengagement nonverbally. For example, Richard stretches and rubs his face in an elaborate yawn when he says, "I never *knew* you wanted to *talk*."

Considering these videotapes of boys and girls at different ages, and the situation described by the family therapist, I was struck by a massive imbalance: When a woman looks at her therapist and her partner, she is simply doing what she has always done, what feels natural and normal and right. But when a man is asked to look directly at his therapist and his wife, he is being asked to do something different—something he has little practice doing, something that might even seem wrong to do. Proclaiming men "disengaged" on the basis of their body language seems premature and unfair. They are being judged by the standards of a different culture. This is not to say that the men might not be disengaged, nor that it might not be beneficial for them to try looking straight at their wives and therapists when they talk to them, just that the interpretation of disengagement is not warranted solely on the basis of indirect physical and visual alignment.

Within the bounds of their own culture, there is plenty of evidence of engagement in the body language of the tenth-grade boys, ample evidence that they are attending and attuning to each other. Their motions are finely coordinated. They make similar movements, in similar directions, at the same time. They are acting in concert, creating ensemble (to borrow a term from Ron Scollon), or (to borrow a concept from A. L. Becker) like two geese preening their feathers, seeming to ignore each other but mirroring each other's movements in coordinated rhythm.

Why would men and boys look outward, away from each other, and around the room, rather than directly at each other? A likely explanation is that looking directly at another man would seem like a hostile action, a display of threat. And looking directly at a woman might seem sexual, a display of flirting. One colleague who made a comment to this effect joined me where I was sitting. Finding a chair facing mine, he pulled the chair farther away and turned it at an angle, so he did not sit facing me directly. We both laughed because this instinctive gesture enabled him to sit at an angle to me—just like the boys and men in the videotapes I had shown him.

Judged by the standards of women, who look at each other when they talk together, men's looking away is a barrier to intimacy, a means of avoiding connection. But if boys and men avoid looking directly at each other to avoid combativeness, then for them it is a way of achieving friendly connection rather than compromising it.

The tenth-grade boys' and girls' physical alignments can be interpreted as different ways of reaching the same goal—involvement—rather than as evidence that the girls are involved and the boys aren't. This symmetry parallels their different ways of accomplishing troubles talk. As we saw in Chapter Two, Nancy and Sally spend most of their time discussing Nancy's problems with her mother and boyfriend, and Sally responds to Nancy's complaints by reinforcing them. In contrast, Richard and Todd both tell of troubles, but they respond to each other's problems by downplaying and dismissing them.

Though different from the girls' ways of responding to each other's problems, the boys' style of reassuring each other has its own logic. Like their postures, the boys' conversation positions them on parallel tracks. Each talks about his own concerns, while the other belittles them or even changes the subject. By women's standards, this shows a lack of caring about the other and his problems. But it can be a way to make the other feel better. Talking about a problem over and over might be a way of expressing concern, but it also might make the problem seem more serious. For example, if Nancy felt bad because she had to leave the party, Sally's telling her that everyone was stunned when she left might make her feel worse. But from another viewpoint, Sally is giving Nancy proof that the girls in the group care about her and missed her when she left.

The tenth-grade girls and boys present a vision of similar goals accomplished in different ways. Both show signs of discomfort with the situation and mock the instructions. (Sally says, "Talk about Jerry. That's serious and/or intimate," and Todd remarks, "Now we have to get intimate.") Both pairs do soon settle down and do just what they were told—though the girls' resistance, expressed as giggling and joking lasts longer than the boys'. In fact, it continues for the first five minutes of the tape, at which point Dorval reminds them of their task. During this time, they tease one another, but a teasing put-down is rescinded as soon as it is uttered: Sally says, laughing, "Dizzy! No, you're not dizzy."

If boys and girls are so different at second, sixth, and tenth grade, what of the men and women in the twenty-four- to twenty-seven-year-old range?

ADULT FRIENDS' CONVERSATION

The videotapes of adult friends talking show a natural development of the young people's styles. Gone is the pressure cooker of emotions concerning themselves and their alliances. Gone is the preoccupation with parents and their authority. But palpably present are the differences in ways of aligning themselves to each other with their bodies and their talk.

Let's look at the twenty-five-year-old women. Although they seem comfortable with the experimental situation, they seem frustrated by their conversation. Their struggle arises because one friend feels the other has pushed the code of agreement too far.

"I KNOW WE'VE HAD ARGUMENTS BEFORE"

The strain of negotiating agreement and similarity is felt throughout the women's dialogue. Intriguingly, traces of a similar strain are found in the sixth-grade girls' conversation too. In her eagerness to espouse harmony and eschew conflict, Julia stresses to Shannon that they never fight. Shannon briefly disagrees, pointing out that they do.

JULIA: Me and you *never* get in fights hardly.
SHANNON: |/?/ to me long
JULIA: |Till we get in arg— We get in *arguments*, but not *fights*. Sometimes we do.
SHANNON: Like when we're playing hopscotch, we get in arguments and fight and—
JULIA: Right. |But we don't get in *fights!*
SHANNON: |But it's— [shrugs]

271

Not all Shannon's words are entirely audible, but it is clear that when Julia says that she and Shannon do not fight, Shannon subtly disagrees. She says, "Like when we're playing hopscotch, we get in arguments and fight." But Julia insists that although they may have arguments, which are trivial, they do not have fights, which are serious, and Shannon quickly gives up the disagreement.

This germ of dissent grows into a recurrent and controlling theme in the conversation between Pam and Marsha, the adult women in Dorval's videotapes. Pam begins the conversation by saying that one thing she likes about Marsha is that Marsha always agrees with her. Pam seems to intend this as a compliment, a statement about why they are friends. Perhaps she is trying to justify why she selected Marsha to join her in the experiment. But Marsha seems to take the remark as a put-down, an implication that she has no mind of her own. As the conversation proceeds, Marsha repeatedly claims that she disagrees with Pam, and Pam tries to dismiss the disagreement, with the result that the conversation becomes an extended disagreement.

> MARSHA: Um, God, Pam, I know we've had arguments before.
>
> MARSHA: We disagree on a lot of things, though. Um, school for instance. And since you've got such a, you have such a positive—
> PAM: |Positive? You saw me a few minutes ago.
> MARSHA: |Um yeah, well no, you've got such— you've got such a positive attitude.
> PAM: No, I don't.
>
> MARSHA: See, that's one thing that we do disagree on. Maybe I'm not a very confident person, I guess, and you've got my share.
> PAM: Well, I— well, what do you think of my computer science attitude right now?

ONEDOWNMANSHIP

One of the ways Marsha tries to prove that she and Pam disagree or are different is to point out that Pam is a better student and has more self-confidence. This sparks an intriguing display of onedownmanship. Pam claims not to be self-confident, and not to be as good a student as Marsha says. On the other hand, she accuses Marsha of being a better student than she admits:

MARSHA: See, that's another thing. You're always, I mean I'm just so bad about this. I get into a class and the highest that I can really hope to get is may— a B, if I can get a B, out of a course, I guess it's just been so long since I have gotten an A.

PAM: That you don't think about it?

MARSHA: Yeah, well, I don't think that it's attainable.

PAM: I don't either.

MARSHA: But Pam, every, you know, every semester when we start school, it's like you talk about it though, that you've got to get an A in this course.

PAM: A's? I get B's. I try but I never get A's. I always get B's. Well, maybe except in my psychology courses, maybe. But not all of 'em.

In this excerpt, Pam reinforces connection by offering Marsha the conclusion of her sentence:

MARSHA: I guess it's just been so long since I have gotten an A.

PAM: That you don't think about it?

And she tries to play "I'm the same":

MARSHA: Yeah, well, I don't think that it's attainable.

PAM: I don't either.

But Marsha does not want to grant Pam this sameness:

MARSHA: But Pam, every, you know, every semester when we start school, it's like you talk about it though, that you've got to get an A in this course.

Pam, however, sticks to her claim, saying that she doesn't really get A's, and if she does, it isn't often:

PAM: A's? I get B's. I try but I never get A's. I always get B's. Well, maybe except in my psychology courses, maybe. But not all of 'em.

Lack of achievement, like similarity and agreement, seems to be the commodity with which Pam is trying to barter for symmetrical connection to Marsha.

As with Marsha's suggestion that Pam is confident, Pam seems to take Marsha's suggestion that she gets good grades as an accusation to be resisted rather than as a compliment to be accepted. As if in counterattack, Pam points out that Marsha did well in a religion class: "You do well on the tests, fifteen out of fifteen," whereas "I hadn't even read those chapters." Symmetrically, Marsha disclaims merit: "It's a lot of common sense." In this regard too, the sixth-grade girls' conversation contains the germs of this verbal game. Early in their conversation, they trade observations about how bad they are at ice skating.

For the women and girls, agreeing and being the same are ways to create rapport. Excelling, being different, and fighting are threats to rapport. The boys are buying rapport too, but they buy it with a different currency: They don't fear disagreement, and they don't seem to need to declare themselves the same. But any strategy can be taken too far, and Marsha seems to resent Pam's assertion that she always agrees.

The game of onedownmanship that these women play is reminiscent of a pattern in Iranian interaction that William Beeman calls getting the lower hand. But this game, Beeman explains, is intensely hierarchical in nature. By portraying himself as lower in status, an Iranian puts himself at the mercy of someone more powerful, who is thereby obligated to do things for him: It invokes a protector schema. Though women may at times take a one-down position so men will take care of them, the game that the women in this videotape play seems to have a very different goal: to reinforce symmetry rather than asymmetry, to keep the scales even by lowering one's own side.

MARRIAGE—
"A SERIOUS ENOUGH TOPIC"

The twenty-five-year-old men present a very different picture. They sit at angles to each other, looking starched or frozen stiff. Timothy almost never looks at Winston. Though Winston looks at Timothy when he's listening, he often looks away, and when he is speaking, he never looks at Timothy at all. The men show a great deal of discomfort and strain in choosing a topic to talk about. They are very earnest about the injunction to talk about something serious, and to them *serious* seems to mean something important in the world, about which they can make a substantive contribution. Here's what they settle on:

> WINSTON: How about marriage?
> TIMOTHY: That's a serious enough topic.
> WINSTON: Serious topic, and it doesn't receive a lot of attention.

In discussing marriage, a potentially personal topic, they speak mainly in the abstract, making general statements without revealing anything personal:

> TIMOTHY: Why do you think, uh, so many marriages ain't making it? That's, uh, you know, a broad question.
> WINSTON: I think most people rush into it, for one thing. (6.0) Just can't wait to get married.

TIMOTHY: I think, uh, I think people, a lot of people, and I'm not saying I *do* but a lot of people don't have an adequate or a mature, you know, definition in their lives of what love is. You know, uh, I don't know, 'cause a lot of the strife, you know, in my opinion, in marriages and relationships is because the person has the, uh, you know, selfish attitude.

There are ways in which these men's conversation conforms to what has been predicted for men, but in other ways it doesn't. According to the stereotype, and the findings of some research, women's talk is more hesitant. But Timothy hesitates and uses fillers like *you know, uh,* and *in my opinion,* giving the impression of insecurity or not being sure of what he is saying. It seems that the situation is making him uncomfortable. Yet by speaking abstractly rather than personally, he conforms to expectations of men's as compared to women's speech.

Later in the conversation, Timothy talks about his relationship with a woman he is dating. He says that he is considering marriage but has gotten no further than that: He is cautious because marriage is forever, and he is wary because women often try to rush men into marriage.

Timothy then says, "You know I don't just want to talk about my situation." After a pause, Winston responds: "Well, mine's with school, and school is just the epitome of being an unsettled person." Winston seems to be implying that he does not have a girl friend because he's a student and therefore his life is unsettled. But he expresses this indirectly, as a general statement about the situation he is in: "mine's with school." Timothy asked him the question indirectly, by making a statement ("I don't just want to talk about my situation") rather than asking directly, "What about you?" In other contexts, for example when trying to negotiate mutual preferences and decisions, women are often more indirect than men. But when it comes to talking about their personal relationships and feelings, many men are more indirect.

"A PRETTY SHY ATTITUDE"

A poignant example of indirectness occurs when Winston says that sometimes men become cautious about relationships because they have been hurt, or, in his words, "torched":

> I think a lot of people start off like maybe when they're young they might have the attitude of what they think is a hundred percent give and then they get torched. Or what they think is torched. And it's liable to just, you know, give them, you know, a pretty shy attitude towards it for a long time.

Winston seems to be implying he has been hurt and that is why he is not in a relationship now. But if this is what he means, he does not say it directly. He does not say anything about any relationships of his own.

FOLLOW THE LEADER

Comparing the videotapes of girls and boys and women and men talking to their friends in this experimental setting provides evidence for the gender differences pattern. These conversations show girls and women working hard to create a community of connection, bonding through talking about troubles in their personal relationships, and struggling to maintain their individuality in the face of pressure to agree. The boys and men are working hard to preserve their independence in a hierarchical world, to achieve intimacy within oppositional frameworks. But it would be misleading to imply that the girls' friendships are entirely egalitarian. An important aspect of these videotapes is the asymmetry in the alignments taken up by the two friends in each conversation.

Among the second-grade boys, Jimmy is clearly a leader: He

has the only extended turns, he gives orders and instructions, he teases, and he initiates most of the conversational moves. Of the sixth-grade boys, Tom is a leader who raises most of the topics, is the main speaker, and takes the performer role in the two instances of report-talk. Of the fifty-five topics covered in their interaction, Tom raises forty. Walt, who generally takes a contributing and supporting role, raises fifteen topics, of which six involve calling attention to objects in the room.

The situation presented by the girls is more complicated. The second-grade girls are the only ones in whom there are no apparent asymmetries in the footings they assume. The alignments taken up by the sixth- and tenth-grade girls are strikingly asymmetrical, even though much of what they say seems intended to achieve the appearance of agreement, support, and connection. Of the sixth-graders, Julia seems to be the leader. Of fourteen topics discussed, she raises twelve. Most of the discussion centers around her relationship with Mary, her concerns about keeping friends, and her anxiety about separation and loss. When the experimenter briefly enters the room at the five-minute mark, Julia is the one who talks to him. Yet it is Shannon who "chooses" the topic of Julia's relationship with Mary by saying, "Too bad you and Mary are not good friends anymore."

Similarly, most of the tenth-grade girls' conversation is about Nancy, but it is Sally who suggests that they talk about Nancy's problems. In response to Nancy's question "Well, what do you want to talk about?" Sally says, "Your mama. Did you talk to your mama?" In terms of the number of topics raised, the girls seem fairly balanced: Sally raises nine topics, Nancy seven. However, all but one of the topics Sally raises are questions focused on Nancy. Much previous research on "topic control" assumes that raising a topic is a sign of dominance in a conversation. From this point of view, Sally "controls" the conversation when she raises topics, although even this is subject to Nancy's collaboration in making it a topic by picking it up. Can she really be said to "dominate," though, if the topics she raises concern Sally?

In some ways, the tenth-grade boys' conversation is more symmetrical than the girls': Nancy and Sally talk entirely about

Nancy's problems, but Richard and Todd both tell about their own troubles, and both respond by dismissing or downplaying the other's. Among the adult men and women, Pam is a kind of leader: She tends to set the themes to which Marsha reacts. Yet the recurrent question of whether or not they disagree becomes a theme because of Marsha's response to Pam's opening observation that Marsha always agrees with her. The adult men present a similar paradox: The topic of marriage is suggested by Winston, and he is the one who talks to Dorval when he comes in. But six of the seven subtopics by which they actually discuss marriage are chosen by Timothy.

Does talking more about her problems put a girl in a higher-status position, since she's taking up more conversational space, or does it put her in a lower one, since she's being portrayed as the one with problems? No one would suggest that the patient has more status or power in a psychotherapy session, even though he or she does most of the talking and raises all the topics. Does raising the topic imply "dominance" in the sense of "controlling" the conversation, if the topic raised is of primary concern to the other girl? I don't know the answers to these questions, but I would know more if I knew whether these girls habitually apportion the roles of troubles teller and supporter in these ways, or if they reverse roles in different conversations. At any rate, it is clear that issues of dominance and control are far more complex than can be captured in surface descriptions such as who raises topics. And although the girls and women are focused on connection, and the boys and men on status, there are nonetheless asymmetries among the women and girls, and symmetries among the men and boys.

In all their complexity, these videotapes show that from the earliest ages through adulthood, boys and girls create different worlds, which men and women go on living in. It is no surprise that women and men who are trying to do things right in relationships with each other so often find their partners wanting, and themselves criticized. We try to talk to each other honestly, but it seems at times that we are speaking different languages— or at least different genderlects.

TEN

Living with Asymmetry: Opening Lines of Communication

An American woman set out for a vacation cruise and landed in a Turkish prison. Reading her book *Never Pass This Way Again*, I could see that Gene LePere's ordeal was an extreme example of the disastrous consequences that can result from cross-cultural differences in what I term conversational style—ways of framing how you mean what you say, and what you think you are doing when you say it. LePere's experience also illustrates, in an unusually dramatic way, the dangers of trying to avoid conflict and say no in a polite way.

LePere left her cruise ship for a brief tour of ancient ruins in Turkey. At an archeological site, she fell behind her group as she became absorbed in admiring the ruins. Suddenly, her path was blocked by a man selling artifacts she had no interest in buying.

280

Yet she found herself holding a stone head, and when she told him politely that she did not want it, he would not take it back. Instead, he thrust forward another one, which she also automatically accepted. Since the man would not take either head back, the only path to escape she could envision was offering to buy them. She cut his price in half and hoped he'd refuse so she could move on. Instead, he agreed to drop the price, and she dropped the two heads into her tote. But as she handed him the money, he handed her a third head. Once more she insisted she did not want it, but he just stepped back to avoid repossessing it. Seeing no alternative, she paid for the third head and stalked off—shaken and angry. When LePere tried to reboard her cruise ship, she showed her purchases to customs officials, who had her arrested and thrown into jail for trying to smuggle out a national treasure. The third head was a genuine antiquity.

Having lived in Greece and observed the verbal art of bargaining, I could see that talking to the vendor and saying she did not want the artifacts would mean to him that she might want them if the price were lower. If she really had no intention of buying, she would not have talked to him at all. She would have pushed her way past him and walked on, never establishing eye contact—and surely not taking possession of any heads, no matter how insistently he proffered them. Each time she accepted a head, he received evidence of her interest and encouragement to offer another. Each step in his increasingly aggressive sales pitch was a response to what likely appeared to him as her bargaining maneuvers. Refusing to look at or talk to him, or, as a last resort, placing the heads on the ground—these were unthinkable alternatives for a polite American woman.

LePere paid dearly for this fleeting breakdown in communication across cultures. Though cross-cultural communication between women and men generally has less drastic consequences, the process of incremental misunderstanding by which it occurs is similar. And in a way, male-female miscommunication is more dangerous, because it is more pervasive in our lives, and we are less prepared for it. We expect differences when we talk to people who come from different countries; we have ways to think about such differences, like "customs" and "cultural assumptions." But we don't expect family, friends, co-workers, and romantic partners who grew up in "the same culture" and speak "the same language" to understand words differently and have different views of the world. But often they do.

WHY THINGS GET WORSE

Gene LePere's experience illustrates the process that Gregory Bateson identified and named complementary schismogenesis—a mutually aggravating spiral by which each person's response to the other's behavior provokes more exaggerated forms of the divergent behavior. LePere's mounting frustration with the vendor's hard-sell practices resulted in behavior that encouraged him to step them up. For example, she offered a low price for the two heads because she had no interest in buying them, but from his point of view this was a show of interest and willingness to participate in the bargaining process. So what she did to escape the situation only further embroiled her in it.

Complementary schismogenesis commonly sets in when women and men have divergent sensitivities and hypersensitivities. For example, a man who fears losing freedom pulls away at the first sign he interprets as an attempt to "control" him, but pulling away is just the signal that sets off alarms for the woman who fears losing intimacy. Her attempts to get closer will aggravate his fear, and his reaction—pulling further away—will aggravate hers, and so on, in an ever-widening spiral. Understanding each other's styles, and the motives behind them, is a first move in breaking this destructive circuit.

INEQUALITY BEGINS
AT HOME

Another reason that gender differences are so much more troubling than other cross-cultural differences is that they occur where the home and hearth are. We all sense that stepping into a vastly foreign culture involves risk; that's why there's a thrill of adventure associated with foreign travel. But we expect to be safe in our own homes. And there we expect to be equal.

Sociologist Erving Goffman points out that inequality due to differences in race and ethnicity disappears when people of the same race or ethnic background close the doors to their own homes. But in private, personal places that we cherish as havens from the outside world, inequality based on gender comes into its own. Not only do we not escape such discrimination in our most intimate relationships, but we can hardly conceive of them apart from gender-based alignments that are inherently asymmetrical—implying differences in status. We cannot take a step without taking stances that are prescribed by society and gender specific. We enact and create our gender, and our inequality, with every move we make.

PHYSICAL CONSTELLATIONS

A woman and a man showing mutual affection cannot do it in the same way. When a man and a woman walk down the street embracing, his arm is around her shoulders, and her arm rests on his waist. If their stance is more casual, his hand may rest in his pocket as she holds on to his arm. These stances are not symmetrical. If a woman walks with her arm around a man's shoulders and his arm around her waist, passersby look back in a double take. If a woman keeps her hands in her pockets while a male hooks his hand onto her arm, or she has her arm on the shoulder of a male who has his hands in his pockets, chances are the woman is a mother and the male is her child..

Some people point out that men put their arms on women's shoulders, not the reverse, because the man is usually taller, so it would be uncomfortable if not impossible for the woman and man to reverse positions. But these rituals are observed even if the man is not taller and must stretch to maintain the protective position. If he is too short to put his arm around the woman's shoulders, they will not reverse positions but settle for holding hands. Moreover, our society expects the man to be taller (and older and richer and smarter) precisely because this frames him as protective—and higher in status.

The asymmetry of women's and men's alignments is epitomized in the positions they take. Even the most intimate moments cannot be imagined without reference to gender. When a woman and man lie down on a blanket or in bed, he typically lies on his back, flat and straight, while she lies on her side with her body curved and nestled against his. Her head rests on his shoulder; his arm is around her. Daily, men and women take these positions automatically, and their ritualized nature is a source of comfort; it feels right and good, partly because it is personally familiar, and partly because it mirrors a configuration we have seen countless times in pictures and in life. But reenacting the ritual also reinforces the asymmetry of the relationship, as he is solid, firm, protecting, and she is off-balance, off-center, protected.

A poet, Cheryl Romney-Brown, created a poem around the recurrent image of a woman burying her face in the crook of a man's neck. She shows that this gesture recurs throughout a woman's life:

IN THE CROOK OF HIS NECK

Fine hairs on his shoulders gleam
like epaulets, reminding me of silk

mulberry threads Penelope used
for tapestries spun waiting
for her hero to come home.
We, women, always long for men
to step out of a myth or a Marlboro ad.

It begins all over again as he
caresses my back. I inhale the scent,
begin to relax. Once more I become
a defenseless girl wanting only
to close my eyes, bury my head
in the crook of his neck.

How old was I the first time,
possibly three? It happened
when Daddy came home. "Please
hold me, protect me, werewolves
are out, their eyes burning hot.
If you don't I know I will die."
I closed my eyes, buried
my head in the crook of his neck.

When I was sixteen, ripe but pure,
down by the arbor on a hot summer night,
my first beau's lips brushed mine. "My hero,
your Juliet's here." Pink tulle bound
my heart. I closed my eyes, buried
my head in the crook of his neck.

I am a grown woman, mother of men.
Experience fades; memory stills.
If only for a moment, I am saved.
My hero is here for maybe an hour,
willing to do battle, kill all my foes.
Illusions, myths, whatever is true.
I close my eyes, bury my head
in the crook of his neck.

Romney-Brown's poem captures the childlike nature of the asymmetrical embrace by which a woman places her head on a man's shoulder, nestling against him, and its protective meaning. The poet traces this delicious feeling of being protected to her relationship to her father when she was a child. Presumably, a little boy might also have nestled against his father or mother, seeking solace and protection. But as an adult, the woman is still taking the child's position in the constellation, while the man has moved into the position taken by the parent.

This poem also captures the automatic way a woman moves into the protected position with men who are not literally protecting her. The standard tableau is immutably in place, ready for the young girl to take her position in it on her first date, and still there, half a lifetime later, for her to step into after divorce. The woman's role in this ritual configuration is resumed even when she has long since proven her ability to protect others, as the "mother of men."

The rigidity of these ritual constellations is portrayed in a pivotal scene in the film *The Accidental Tourist*. The hero, Macon, appears, disheveled and distraught, at the home of Muriel, a woman who has shown a romantic interest in him. Macon tells Muriel the dreadful story of his son's death, and confesses that he has been unable to recover from it. Touched by his confession, Muriel leads Macon to bed, to comfort him for his devastating loss. In bed, Macon lies on his back and lifts his arm to place it around Muriel, who snuggles against him. In choreographing this scene, the director apparently felt that the demands of convention, which require the man to take the physical position of protector and comforter, were stronger than the demands of the immediate scene in which Muriel is comforting Macon.

The physical alignment that women and men take up to each other when they lie down together is just one of a network of asymmetries that enact our genders and simultaneously reinforce status differences between men and women. Goffman is eloquent in describing these asymmetries:

In our society in all classes the tenderest expression of affection involves displays that are politically questionable, the place taken up in them by the female being differentiated from and reciprocal to the place taken up by the male. Cross-sex affectional gestures choreograph protector and protected, embracer and embraced, comforter and comforted, supporter and supported, extender of affection and recipient thereof; and it is defined as only natural that the male encompass and the female be encompassed. And this can only remind us that male domination is a very special kind, a domination that can be carried right into the gentlest, most loving moment without apparently causing strain—indeed, these moments can hardly be conceived of apart from these asymmetries.

Gender is a category that will not go away. As Goffman put it, it is "one of the most deeply seated traits of man"(!). We create masculinity and femininity in our ways of behaving, all the while believing we are simply acting "naturally." But our sense of what is natural is different for women and men. And what we regard as naturally male and female is based on asymmetrical alignments.

In Goffman's terms, gender relations are patterned on the parent-child complex. In other words, the ways we enact our genders as we try to be good women and men take on meaning by analogy with parents and children. Goffman points out that men are to women as adults are to children: loving protectors who will hold open doors, offer the first portion of sweets, reach high shelves, and lift heavy loads. But along with the privileges of childhood come liabilities: Children's activities are interruptible, their time and territory expendable. Along with the privilege of being protected comes the loss of rights, and not being respected and treated like a full-fledged person. Being the protector frames someone as competent, capable, and deserving of respect. Being protected frames one as incompetent, incapable, and deserving of indulgence.

ASYMMETRIES IN CONVERSATION: "I ONLY DID IT FOR YOU"

In talking to couples about communication in their relationships, I was surprised by how often men referred to their role as protectors of women in explaining why they spoke as they did. For example, one couple told me of a recent argument. The woman had noticed that her husband was favoring one arm and asked why. He said that his arm hurt. She asked how long it had been hurting him, and he said, "Oh, a few weeks." To his surprise, she reacted with hurt and anger: "Go ahead, treat me like a stranger!"

To her, intimacy meant telling what's on your mind, including what hurts. By not telling her that his arm hurt, her husband was pushing her away, distancing her with his silence. I instinctively understood this woman's point of view. But I did not immediately understand the man's. In explaining his side of the story, he said, "I guess men learn from the beginning to protect women." This puzzled me. I asked what protection had to do with not telling his wife that his arm hurt. "I was protecting her," he explained. "Why should I worry her by telling her about my pain, since it might be nothing and go away anyway?"

Deciding what to tell his wife reflects this man's perceived role as her protector. But it also grows out of and reinforces the alignment by which he is in a superior position. He is stronger than she, and he has power to cause her worry by the information he imparts. This man does not feel, as his wife perceives, that he is trying to curtail their intimacy. Intimacy is simply not at issue for him. In her world, the imparting of personal information is the fundamental material of intimacy, so withholding such information deprives her of the closeness that is her lifeblood. Their different interpretations of the same information simply reflect their different preoccupations. They are tuned to different frequencies.

It may be that this man was also protecting his autonomy, staving off his wife's excessive show of concern. But this was not the reason he offered in explaining his motives. In his explanatory system, his role as protector was primary. The same was true for another husband whose wife complained about a very different type of behavior.

The wife, whom I will call Michele, objected to the habit her husband, Gary, had of answering her questions by providing information other than what she had requested. Here are two typical exchanges that she recounted:

MICHELE: What time is the concert?
GARY: You have to be ready by seven-thirty.

MICHELE: How many people are coming to dinner?
GARY: Don't worry. There'll be enough food.

Michele gets frustrated because she feels that by withholding information, Gary is holding tight to the reins of power in the relationship. But he maintains that he is "watching out for her" by getting to the real point of her questions. Both points of view are plausible. The cause of their different interpretations of the same conversation resides in the ambiguity inherent in protecting. He sees his attention to her concerns as protective; she sees that the protective stance frames him as one-up in competence and control.

Another man reported similar conversations with his wife. In this case, however, the roles are reversed: It is the wife, Valerie, who gives what she thinks is the relevant information rather than answering the question asked, and it is the husband, Ned, who objects to her doing so. Here are two examples of their dialogues:

NED: Are you leaving now?
VALERIE: You can take a nap if you want.

NED: Are you just about finished?
VALERIE: Do you want to have supper now?

In defending herself against Ned's complaints, Valerie gives an explanation very different from the one given by the husband in the previous example. She says that she is anticipating Ned's desires and concerns.

This man and woman give different explanations for behaving in the same way; they truly seem to think of themselves as doing the same thing for different reasons. Being the protector is central to him; being helpful is central to her.

If women and men sometimes have (or give) different motivations when they behave in similar ways, there are also situations where their different motivations lead them to behave differently. Each individual works out a unique way of balancing status differences and connection to others. But if we think of these motivations as two ends of a continuum, women and men tend to cluster at opposite ends. Because of these differences in points of view, a man and a woman may perceive the same scene in different ways and misinterpret each other's motives. Understanding the differences can deflect the misinterpretation, and make sense where there seemed to be no sense.

SOLVING PUZZLES

A man told me with puzzlement about his most rebellious childhood friend, Henry. Henry flouted authority at every turn: in the way he wore his hair (sticking straight out in all directions), the way he dressed (flamboyantly, absurdly), the things he did (making crank phone calls, publicly ridiculing teachers), the way he planned his future (he refused to go to college; instead, he left the country). But several years later, Henry returned to the United States—transformed into a traditionalist. For example, he insisted that friends who visited him must bring their wives, because wives were supposed to accompany their husbands everywhere. And his political views became more and more conservative.

The rebellious youth who turns into an authoritarian adult is a commonly observed paradox. I recall being surprised at first to hear Charlotte Linde's observation that policemen whose conversations she had studied talked frequently about what "bad boys" they had been, trading stories about their youthful escapades and how cleverly they had broken the law in their wild days. This seeming puzzle returned to me, the pieces now fitting together, as I came to understand the view of the world as a hierarchical social order. "Born rebels" who defy authority are not oblivious of it, but oversensitive to it. Defying authority is a way of asserting themselves and refusing to accept the subordinate position. When they are old enough, or established enough, to take the dominant position, reinforcing authority becomes the way to assert themselves, since the hierarchy is now operating to their advantage.

Another puzzle solved for me was my similarities to and differences from my father. For example, my father passed on to me his love of reading and of words. "What book are you reading?" he regularly asked me when I was a child. But I was disappointed when, as a young adult, I recommended to him some of the novels I loved, and he couldn't get through them. "It's so boring," he'd say. "Nothing ever happens." And he could never get me to read some of the books he loved when he was a child (for example, *The Three Musketeers*) and as an adult (for example, *The Maltese Falcon*). Like most men, my father is interested in action. And this is also why he disappoints my mother when she tells him she doesn't feel well and he offers to take her to the doctor. He is focused on what he can do, whereas she wants sympathy.

TWO PATHS TO INVOLVEMENT

Offering sympathy and offering to do something can be different ways of achieving the same goal—involvement with others. All conversations serve the universal human need for involvement as well as the simultaneous but conflicting need for independence. And just as women and men often have contrasting senses of intimacy, so also do they often have contrasting senses of independence. Those who see relationships as fundamentally hierarchical will feel that to be independent they must be dominant rather than subordinate. But another view is possible. It is possible to avoid being dependent on or subordinate to others, but not dominate them either. In other words, there is a symmetrical rather than asymmetrical independence.

That these two views reflect characteristically male and female views of independence is supported by Philip Blumstein and Pepper Schwartz's study *American Couples*. A husband they quote as typical said he needs to be independent *and to have others dependent on him*. This is an outgrowth of the protector stance that is built into our society's sense of what it means to be masculine. The difference between men's and women's assumptions about independence also emerges in their attitudes toward money. Blumstein and Schwartz found that for men, having money provides a sense of power, but for women, it provides security and autonomy—simply the ability not to be dependent. An intriguing result of their comparison of heterosexual and homosexual couples is that only among lesbian couples did earning more money not establish a partner as relatively more powerful in the relationship. Lesbians, they found, use money to avoid dependence but not to dominate. And only among gay male couples did one partner feel more successful if the other partner's income was lower.

WHEN STRENGTHS BECOME LIABILITIES

These differing understandings of independence grow out of the distinct kinds of relations women and men learn and practice as boys and girls growing up. And these disparate worlds exert distinct pressures on each gender. The pressure to maintain connections with others while appearing skillful and knowledgeable, and while negotiating relative rank, can become a burden for boys and men. The pressure to achieve status while avoiding conflict and appearing no better than anyone else can become a burden for girls and women.

Women sometimes suffer from an overabundance of rapport. For example, their expectation that an expression of troubles should be met with matching troubles can be felt as a stringent requirement to have matching troubles to tell. One woman said of a friend, "Marian tries to rope me into her neuroses, implying I have the same problems she does. I don't like it because I don't have the same problems." A similar frustration was expressed by another woman, Jill, who told me about her friend Elizabeth, who always includes her in her statements: "We have trouble with this," or "That's a problem for us." When Elizabeth issues an inclusive statement, she expects Jill to come up with a matching experience. If Jill says, "That's not a problem for me," Elizabeth feels rejected and accuses Jill of putting her down. "Some women don't let you be different," Jill said. "They don't let you have any individuality."

If women are not always perfectly satisfied by their friendships with women, neither are all men perfectly happy with their friendships with men. Many men told me that they prefer women as friends because they find it harder to talk to men. One man told me it took him two years in a new city to find two men who were willing to talk about how they felt, to admit problems and listen to his, men he did not feel were competitive with him. Men's need to be strong and independent all the time can be felt as a stringent requirement not to have troubles. This was the view expressed to Catherine Kohler Riessman by a divorced man who said, "I think everybody hates to have anybody know that they have problems. . . . You always try and keep your problems to yourself. . . ."

Several men commented to me that it is American men in particular who make friendly conversation into a contest. One British man told me that back home his best friends had been men, but since he emigrated to the United States, most of his friends have been women. On a visit home, he spent time with an old friend who was male. "We yielded to one another," he said, explaining to me what the difference was. "We didn't try to one-up or prevail all the time." An American man expressed a similar opinion. He said he finds European men easier to talk to. "Talking to American men," he commented, "is like a war zone."

And yet, the man who told me it had taken him two years to find men to befriend did find two. And everyone knows women and men who, in some ways, are more "like" the other gender than like their own. This is natural, since individuals develop patterns of behavior based on innumerable influences, such as where they grew up, ethnic background, religious or cultural affiliation, class, and the vast reservoir of personal experience and genetic inheritance that makes each person's life and personality unique. But seeing a pattern against which to evaluate individual differences provides a starting point to develop not only self-understanding but also flexibility—the freedom to try doing things differently if automatic ways of doing them aren't having entirely successful results.

Both women and men could benefit from learning each other's styles. Many women could learn from men to accept some conflict and difference without seeing it as a threat to intimacy, and many men could learn from women to accept interdependence without seeing it as a threat to their freedom.

Women's inclination to preserve intimacy by avoiding conflict also explains the initially surprising finding of Blumstein and Schwartz that women want more time away from their partners than men do. I think there are two reasons for this. First, many women have a kind of communication with their women friends that they don't have with their partners, and that is not possible if their partners are present. Second, when women are with partners, they make more adjustments and accommodations, buying harmony at the cost of their own preferences. Therefore, being with partners is more of a strain on them than it is on men, who are less inclined to accommodate.

If accommodating automatically is a strain, so is automatically resisting others' will. Sometimes it is more effective to take the footing of an ally. The "best" style is a flexible one. The freest person is the one who can choose which strategies to use, not the one who must slavishly replay the same script over and over—as we all tend to do. There is nothing inherently wrong with automatic behavior. If we did not do most things automatically, it would take massive concentration and energy to do anything. But by becoming aware of our ways of talking and how effective they are, we can override our automatic impulses and adapt our habitual styles when they are not serving us well.

IT ALL DEPENDS

In trying to develop such awareness of ways of talking, people often ask me what a particular expression or conversational habit "really means." I always answer that no phrase or device has only one meaning. Like the practice of overlapping—beginning to talk when someone else is already speaking—what looks on the surface like the same way of talking can have varied meanings and effects. A listener may talk along with a speaker to provide support, or to change the topic. Even changing the topic can have a range of meanings. It can show lack of interest, it can be an attempt to dominate the conversation, or it can be a kind of "mutual revelation device"—matching the speaker's experience with the listener's. Even mutual revelation can be done with different motives: either in a spirit of connection, to establish rapport and emphasize sameness, or in a spirit of competition, to top a story and frame oneself as more important.

Evidence that the same behavior can have very different meanings emerges in an article by Lee Cronk comparing gift giving in different cultures. Citing an African example, Cronk describes the custom called *hxaro,* in the words of a !Kung man named !Xoma: "Hxaro is when I take a thing of value and give it to you. Later, much later, when you find some good thing, you give it back to me. When I find something good I will give it to you, and so we will pass the years together." Asked what would count as a fair exchange (for example, how many strings of beads would you have to give if your friend gave you a spear?), !Xoma wouldn't answer. He explained that any return would be acceptable because "we don't trade with things, we trade with people."

In contrast, a New Guinea society has a custom called *moka* by which gifts are given to gain prestige and shame rivals. One legendary *moka* gift given in the 1970s included several hundred pigs, some cows and wild birds, a truck, a motorbike, and thousands of dollars in cash. The person who gave all this is said to have told the person he gave it to, "I have won. I have knocked you down by giving so much."

In these two cultural rituals, the same act—giving gifts—has very different meanings. *Hxaro,* done among friends, is cooperative, whereas *moka,* done among rivals, is competitive. The key difference between these two practices is symmetry versus asymmetry. In *hxaro,* the exchange of gifts is symmetrical, each friend reciprocating with a matching gift. But in *moka,* it is asymmetrical, each rival trying to top the other's gifts so he can come out on top.

Since any statement or action can grow out of widely divergent motives and intentions, it is not safe to trust our instincts about what a comment or action "means." A !Kung person might have a very different instinctive reaction to a gift than a member of the New Guinea tribe that practices *moka.* This awareness can be a key to improving conversations and relationships among women and men. We would all do well to distrust our automatic responses to what others say, especially if our automatic responses are negative. Instead, we should try to see things from the other person's perspective. Once they know that men and women often have different assumptions about the world and about ways of talking, people are very creative about figuring out how this rift is affecting their own relationships.

OPENING LINES OF COMMUNICATION

Many experts tell us we are doing things wrong and should change our behavior—which usually sounds easier than it turns out to be. Sensitivity training judges men by women's standards, trying to get them to talk more like women. Assertiveness training judges women by men's standards and tries to get them to talk more like men. No doubt, many people can be helped by learning to be more sensitive or more assertive. But few people are helped by being told they are doing everything all wrong. And there may be little wrong with what people are doing, even if they are winding up in arguments. The problem may be that each partner is operating within a different system, speaking a different genderlect.

An obvious question is, Can genderlect be taught? Can people change their conversational styles? If they want to, yes, they can—to an extent. But those who ask this question rarely want to change their own styles. Usually, what they have in mind is sending their partners for repair: They'd like to get him or her to change. Changing one's own style is far less appealing, because it is not just how you act but who you feel yourself to be. Therefore a more realistic approach is to learn how to interpret each other's messages and explain your own in a way your partner can understand and accept.

Understanding genderlects makes it possible to change—to try speaking differently—when you want to. But even if no one changes, understanding genderlect improves relationships. Once people realize that their partners have different conversational styles, they are inclined to accept differences without blaming themselves, their partners, or their relationships. The biggest mistake is believing there is one right way to listen, to talk, to have a conversation—or a relationship. Nothing hurts more than being told your intentions are bad when you know they are good, or being told you are doing something wrong when you know you're just doing it your way.

Not seeing style differences for what they are, people draw conclusions about personality ("you're illogical," "you're insecure," "you're self-centered") or intentions ("you don't listen," "you put me down"). Understanding style differences for what they are takes the sting out of them. Believing that "you're not interested in me," "you don't care about me as much as I care about you," or "you want to take away my freedom" feels awful. Believing that "you have a different way of showing you're listening" or "showing you care" allows for no-fault negotiation: You can ask for or make adjustments without casting or taking blame.

If you understand gender differences in what I call conversational style, you may not be able to prevent disagreements from arising, but you stand a better chance of preventing them from spiraling out of control. When sincere attempts to communicate end in stalemate, and a beloved partner seems irrational and obstinate, the different languages men and women speak can shake the foundation of our lives. Understanding the other's ways of talking is a giant leap across the communication gap between women and men, and a giant step toward opening lines of communication.

NOTES

Bibliographical information on research cited below is listed in the References section. If more than one article or book by the same author or authors is included in the References, a note indicates which source is referred to. Bibliographical information for news items and other secondary sources is given in the Notes.

PREFACE

14 My study of indirectness in conversation is "Ethnic Style in Male-Female Conversation."

14 A similar reticence accompanies research on style differences involving minorities. For example, Andrew Hacker ("Affirmative Action: The New Look," *The New York Review of Books,* October 12, 1989, p. 68) discusses an incident in which black organizations demanded the withdrawal of a New York State Department of Education handbook explaining that blacks and whites have different learning styles. Even though the research had been done by a black scholar, Janice Hale-Benson, the protesters branded the findings racist. Hacker explains, "The question, of course, is whether the tendencies Hale-Benson analyzed will be construed not simply as different, but also as inferior." The key word here is *construed.* Readers' reactions may be very different from researchers' intentions.

15 My article "Did You Say What I Just Heard?" appeared in *The Washington Post* on October 12, 1986, p. D3. The *Toronto Star* version appeared (without my knowledge) under the title "Why We Should Also Listen Between the Lines" on November 16, 1986, p. D1. The textbook that includes excerpts from this edited version is *People in Perspective* (second edition), edited by Wayne Sproule (Scarborough, Ontario: Prentice-Hall Canada, 1988). The material appeared as edited by the *Star,* even though I granted permission on condition that the deleted sentence be restored.

16 I have borrowed the metaphor of sweeping things under the

rug from Robin Lakoff. I first heard her use it in her course at the 1973 Linguistic Institute at the University of Michigan.

17 Abby Abinanti, "Lawyer," *Women and Work: Photographs and Personal Writings,* text ed. by Maureen R. Michelson, photographs ed. by Michael R. Dressler and Maureen R. Michelson (Pasadena, CA: NewSage Press 1986), p. 52.

CHAPTER ONE
DIFFERENT WORDS, DIFFERENT WORLDS

25 The term *connection* as a goal motivating women will remind readers of Carol Gilligan's influential work on girls' moral development. I have not cited her in my discussion because, although I may have been unwittingly influenced in my choice of the term, my status-connection framework is a direct outgrowth of the power-solidarity dimension, a fundamental concept in sociolinguistics. This concept was introduced by Roger Brown and Albert Gilman in their 1960 article "The Pronouns of Power and Solidarity," was explored by Paul Friedrich in a 1972 article, "Social Context and Semantic Feature: The Russian Pronominal Usage," and is pervasive in the sociolinguistic literature (see Chapter One, "Address Forms," in Ralph Fasold's *The Sociolinguistics of Language*). The dynamics of this dimension as a motivation for conversation is a theme running through my 1986 book, *That's Not What I Meant!,* which includes a chapter entitled "Power and Solidarity." In this book I use *status* and *connection* in place of the terms *power* and *solidarity* because I realized that the connotations of the latter terms are different for lay readers than for sociolinguists: *Power* in common parlance connotes intentionally wielding power, and *solidarity* has come to suggest Polish politics.

28 The quotation from Tom Whittaker appeared in "A Salute to Everyday Heroes," *Newsweek,* July 10, 1989, p. 46.

33 The term *framing* traces to Gregory Bateson, "A Theory of Play and Fantasy," *Steps to an Ecology of Mind*. Erving Goffman developed the concept in his book *Frame Analysis* and the chapter "Footing" in *Forms of Talk*.

33 Goffman discusses alignment in *Frame Analysis* and "Footing."

40 No page references are given for Riessman because her book was not yet available in print when this book went to press.

41 "The Pros and Cons of an Academic Career: Six Views from Binghamton," *The Chronicle of Higher Education,* January 25, 1989, p. A15.

43 Barrie Thorne has studied extensively the extent to which boys and girls spend their time together and apart. See for example her article "Girls and Boys Together . . . But Mostly Apart: Gender Arrangements in Elementary Schools."

46 The term *positioning* was suggested to me by Bronwyn Davies. See Davies and Harré, "Positioning: Conversation and the Production of Selves."

48 Alice Walker's comment was made in an interview on *The Diane Rehm Show,* WAMU, Washington, DC, August 31, 1989.

CHAPTER TWO
ASYMMETRIES: WOMEN AND MEN TALKING AT CROSS-PURPOSES

52 The Christophers were discussing their book *Mixed Blessings* on *The Diane Rehm Show,* WAMU, Washington, DC, June 6, 1989.

53 I have borrowed the term *troubles talk* from Gail Jefferson. See, for example, her article "On the Sequential Organization of Troubles-Talk in Ordinary Conversation."

53 The quotation is from "Clobbering Her Ex," a review of Alice Adams's *After You've Gone* in *The New York Times Book Review,* October 8, 1989, p. 27.

54 Bruce Dorval videotaped friends talking at a range of ages. He describes the tapes and how he collected them in a book he edited, *Conversational Coherence and Its Development.* That book includes chapters in which scholars from different disciplines analyze selected videotapes. My analysis of gender differences in the videotapes is included in that collection and is also the basis for Chapter Nine of this book.

54 Excerpts are from transcripts originally prepared by Bruce Dorval and his assistants. I have checked and occasionally refined the transcripts, and made a few changes in punctuation to enhance readability for the nonspecialist reader. In transcripts throughout the book, the following conventions apply: Parentheses indicate parenthetical intonation (pitch and loudness are reduced; intonation is flattened). /?/ indicates that something was said but couldn't be deciphered. A dash following a word indicates that the speaker cut off the word or phrase right there. Usually this represents the slight stumbling of a false start rather than an abrupt self-interruption. *Italics* indicate emphatic stress; CAPITAL LETTERS indicate more emphatic stress. Three spaced periods (. . .) are an ellipsis, showing that several lines have been omitted. Three un-

spaced periods (. . .) indicate a pause. **Boldface** type highlights lines that are crucial for the point I am making about the example.

58 "New Haven," like all the other stories by Alice Mattison that I quote, is in *Great Wits* (New York: William Morrow, 1988). This quotation is from p. 63.

58 Mattison, "New Haven," p. 64.

59 Mattison, "The Knitting," p. 36.

60 The alternative interpretation of the boys' dismissal of each other's concerns was pointed out to me by Ralph Fasold.

72 Mattison, "The Colorful Alphabet," p. 125.

CHAPTER THREE
"PUT DOWN THAT PAPER AND TALK TO ME!":
RAPPORT-TALK AND REPORT-TALK

75 Connie Eble (p. 469) cites Gerald Carson (p. 55) for the "cleft stick" reference. In Carson's words, "In East Hampton, New York, cleft sticks were slipped over too-busy tongues. . . ."

Authors who discuss the historical attitude that women talk too much include Dennis Baron, Connie Eble, Alette Hill, and Cheris Kramarae. Deborah James and Janice Drakich have written an article reviewing research that aims to determine who talks more, women or men.

77 The observation that women are thought to talk more if they talk equally has been made by many, including Dale Spender *(Man Made Language)* and Carole Edelsky ("Who's Got the Floor?"). Myra and David Sadker ("Sexism in the Schoolroom of the '80s") report that teachers who were shown a film of classroom discussion overwhelmingly thought the girls were talking more, when in fact the boys were talking three times more.

78 Political scientist Andrew Hacker, reviewing *Husbands and Wives: A Nationwide Survey of Marriage* by Anthony Pietropinto and Jacqueline Simenauer (New York: Times Books, 1979), has also observed that women frequently give lack of communication as a reason for divorce, whereas men who were parties to the same marriages rarely do. (Hacker, "Divorce à la Mode," *The New York Review of Books,* May 3, 1979, p. 24.)

80 Here again I am drawing on Maltz and Borker, who summarize and integrate the research of others, including Marjorie Harness Goodwin, Barrie Thorne, Donna Eder and Maureen Hallinan, Pamela Fishman, and Janet Lever.

80 The observation that men name their wives as their best friends, whereas women name women friends rather than their husbands, is frequently made. See, for example, Robert Sternberg and Susan Grajek, "The Nature of Love."

88 Smeal was a guest on *The Mike Cuthbert Show*, WAMU, Washington DC, January 17, 1989.

88 Rehm's statement is quoted in Patricia Brennan, "Diane Rehm: Making a Foray from Radio to TV," *The Washington Post TV Week*, August 28–September 3, 1988, p. 8.

89 The concept of "backstage" comes from Erving Goffman, *The Presentation of Self in Everyday Life*.

91 Roberts and Jupp presented the findings of their study at the 1985 Linguistic Institute, Georgetown University.

CHAPTER FOUR
GOSSIP

96 Marge Piercy, *Fly Away Home* (New York: Summit, 1984), p. 235.

97 Eudora Welty, *One Writer's Beginnings* (Cambridge, MA: Harvard University Press, 1984), p. 14.

97 Mary Catherine Bateson, p. 193.

98 Mattison, "New Haven," p. 63.

99 Ann Packer, "Mendocino," *The New Yorker*, June 6, 1988, p. 38.

102 Ursula Le Guin, "In and Out," *The New Yorker*, January 16, 1989, p. 30.

104 Edna O'Brien, "The Widow," *The New Yorker*, January 23, 1989, p. 31.

105 Dan Balz, "The Public Politics of Rumor," *The Washington Post*, June 8, 1989, pp. A1, A10.

106 Nora Ephron, *Heartburn* (New York: Pocket Books, 1983), p. 123.

109 Regarding boys' willingness to talk about problems, Penelope Eckert found a difference among the high school students she studied, depending on whether they were "jocks" or "burnouts": The former don't talk; the latter do.

111 Stephens, p. 13.

112 N. R. Kleinfield, "The Whistle Blower's Morning After," *The New York Times*, November 9, 1986, Section 3, p. 1. The discussion of details in this chapter is drawn from my book *Talking Voices: Repetition, Dialogue, and Imagery in Conversational Discourse*.

113 The detail from Russell Baker's book *The Good Times* is taken from "Restless on His Laurels," a review of Baker's book by R. Z. Shepard, *Time,* June 5, 1989, pp. 83–84.

114 Celia Fremlin, *The Jealous One* (Chicago: Academy, 1985), pp. 16–17. Steve Barish called this excerpt to my attention.

116 Mattison, "Sleeping Giant," p. 124.

118 The article about partners Sherry Turner and Linda Rabbitt, written by Randy Reiland, appeared in *The Washingtonian,* June 1988, p. 34.

118 Elizabeth Loftus, "Trials of an Expert Witness," "My Turn" column, *Newsweek,* June 29, 1987, p. 10.

121 The talk show referred to was *Donahue.* I have paraphrased the comments of the audience member and guest, based on my viewing of the show. The transcript of the show is *Donahue* Transcript #031188, available from Multimedia Entertainment, Inc.

121 The study of male and female therapists is reported in *Psychiatry '86,* August 1986, pp. 1, 6.

CHAPTER FIVE
"I'LL EXPLAIN IT TO YOU":
LECTURING AND LISTENING

129 The reference is to Aries (1982).

130 The reference is to Aries (1976).

131 Fox, p. 61.

132 Mr. H's view of female writing reminded me of the comments I encountered by male critics about the novels of a modern Greek writer, Lilika Nakos. Because her novels captured the rhythms of the conversational idiom, some critics mistook Nakos's achievement. For example, one called her masterful prose a "spontaneous outpouring." Another called it "not literature, but conversation." I cite these and other attributions in my book *Lilika Nakos.*

133 Jules Feiffer, *Grown Ups* (New York: Samuel French, 1982), pp. 7–8, 8–9, and 26–27.

139 A. R. Gurney, "Conversation Piece," "My Turn" column, *Newsweek,* June 26, 1989, pp. 10–11.

139 The reference is to Aries (1976).

142 Maltz and Borker did not do the original research, but rather integrated the findings of a number of other researchers. That women ask more questions and give more listening responses is attributed to research by Pamela Fishman and by Lynette Hirschman. That women

respond more positively is also attributed to them, as well as to Fred Strodtbeck and Richard Mann.

145 The reference is to Aries (1976).

146 Frederick Barthelme, "War with Japan," *The New Yorker,* December 12, 1988, pp. 44, 45.

148 The letter, signed Evelyn Aron, Mexico City, Mexico, appeared in *Psychology Today,* May 1988, p. 5.

CHAPTER SIX
COMMUNITY AND CONTEST: STYLES IN CONFLICT

150 Articles by Amy Sheldon and by Campbell Leaper review the research on gender and conflict.

150 The quotation is from Ong, p. 51.

151 Blumstein and Schwartz, p. 212.

153 Sachs, p. 183.

153 No page references are given for Goodwin because her book was not yet available when this one went to press.

155 Sachs, pp. 180–181.

156 Rodger Kamenetz, "Confessions of a Meddling Dad," *Working Mother,* May 1989, p. 224.

157 The vertical line indicates overlap: Both girls are speaking at once.

157 The observation that boys prefer competitive games is made by Janet Lever (1978) as well as Goodwin.

158 These complaints did often come to light, and direct confrontation did take place, instigated by a third girl who repeated the criticism. The fight then centered not around the original complaint, but the offense of talking behind someone's back. The same pattern is reported by Amy Shuman, who also observed black junior-high-school girls in Philadelphia.

161 Corsaro and Rizzo, p. 63.

162 Eva Hoffman, *Lost in Translation: A Life in a New Language* (New York: E. P. Dutton, 1989), pp. 18–19.

163 Corsaro and Rizzo, p. 34.

166 Jane Shapiro, "Volpone," *The New Yorker,* November 30, 1987, p. 39.

175 Anne Tyler, *The Accidental Tourist* (New York: Alfred A. Knopf, 1985), p. 280.

176 The reference is to Frank (1988).

176 The students who observed gender differences in the class narratives were Elizabeth Nowell and Lalzarliani Malsawma.

177 I have taken the title of this chapter, "Community and Contest," from the title of Johnstone's article.

179 The quotations from Fox are from pp. 62, 65, and 61, respectively.

180 The reference is to Lever (1978).

180 The reference is to Eckert (1990).

180 The quotation is from Lever (1978), p. 478.

181 Walter Ong attributes the finding that successful women excel in "work competence" to Beverly and Otis Duncan.

183 The statement by Oprah Winfrey is from Mary-Ann Bendel, "TV's Super-Women," *Ladies' Home Journal,* March 1988, p. 170.

184 Jayne Meadows's comments are from Richard Meryman, "The Jayne Meadows Story," *Lear's,* June 1989, p. 84. Steve Allen expressed his view in an interview on *The Diane Rehm Show,* WAMU, Washington, DC, October 11, 1989.

CHAPTER SEVEN
WHO'S INTERRUPTING?
ISSUES OF DOMINANCE
AND CONTROL

This chapter is adapted from my article "Interpreting Interruption in Conversation."

189 The researchers most often cited for the finding that men interrupt women are Candace West and Don Zimmerman (for example, West and Zimmerman, 1983, 1985; Zimmerman and West, 1975). However, many others have come to similar conclusions (for example, Eakins and Eakins, Greif). Deborah James and Janice Drakich are currently reviewing the literature on interruption.

190 The point that violation of speaking rights is a matter of degree is made by Stephen Murray.

191 The example comes from West and Zimmerman, 1983, p. 105. The numbers in parentheses show seconds of pause. Vertical lines show overlap: two voices speaking at once.

193 Transcription is based on Greenwood's, with minor adjustments for readability and changes of names. Vertical lines show latching: The second speaker began with no overlap but no perceptible pause either.

197 Analyzing conversations in which the researcher participated

is a common practice among sociolinguists. The conviction is that what is lost in objectivity is counterbalanced by two crucial gains: the abilities to tape and analyze naturally occurring conversation, and to understand more deeply what was going on.

198 I have adopted the term *latching* from the work of Sacks, Schegloff, and Jefferson. Jane Falk coined the term *conversational duet* and described the phenomenon in which two speakers share a single conversational role.

204 Janice Hornyak recorded, transcribed, and analyzed this excerpt in conjunction with my course in discourse analysis at Georgetown University, spring 1989.

206 My study of indirectness in Greek and American conversational style is reported in Tannen (1982).

206 The excerpt from Durrell's letter to Miller is taken from Vivian Gornick, "Masters of Self-congratulation," a review of *The Durrell-Miller Letters,* ed. by Ian S. MacNiven, in *The New York Times Book Review,* November 20, 1988, p. 47.

207 The quote from Nancy Reagan is from her book, *My Turn,* as excerpted in *Newsweek,* October 23, 1989, p. 66.

209 The argument that Maltz and Borker and I are covering up real male domination with the cross-cultural hypothesis is cogently argued in a paper by Nancy Henley and Cheris Kramarae.

212 Lorrie Moore, "You're Ugly, Too," *The New Yorker,* July 3, 1989 pp. 34, 38, 40.

CHAPTER EIGHT
DAMNED IF YOU DO

217 The reference to Matina Horner's research is taken from Carol Gilligan.

218 Other studies of girls' real conversations include those by Penelope Eckert and by Donna Eder.

221 Bergman, pp. 2–4; Gilligan, pp. 33–34.

223 The epitaph, written by Jane Hines Reis about her sister, Joyce Hines, appeared in *AlumNotes: Hunter College High School Alumanae/i Association,* Fall 1988, pp. 3–4.

225 The article "Sexes: Who's Talking?" by Carol Krucoff appeared in *The Washington Post,* November 9, 1981, p. D5.

226 The research project I refer to is described in Tannen (1982).

228 Aries (1987) reviews studies that tested Lakoff's observation about tag questions.

228 Thorne, Kramarae, and Henley, in a chapter reviewing articles

that compared women's and men's speech, cite many studies that show that women and men are judged differently if they speak the same way.

229 The quotations from Komarovsky are taken from pp. 13, 162, 158, 159, 162, and 353.

230 Erica Jong, *Fear of Flying* (New York: Holt, Rinehart and Winston, 1973), pp. 118–119.

235 Ursula Le Guin, "In and Out," *The New Yorker,* January 16, 1989, p. 31.

236 The reference is to Aries (1982).

236 "The Case for Girls' Schools" is summed up by Elisabeth Griffith, *The Washington Post Education Review,* August 6, 1989. M. Elizabeth Tidball reviews her own and others' research testifying to the superior achievement of graduates of women's colleges. Myra and David Sadker's research shows that girls become "spectators" to the educational process in co-educational classrooms: They are called on far less; when they do contribute to class discussion, their contributions are less likely to be evaluated or engaged at length; and teachers are more inclined to do things for them rather than show them how to do things for themselves.

237 The reference is to Aries (1976).

241 "Language Keeps Women in Their Place" was the headline given by the *St. Louis Post-Dispatch* to an op-ed piece I wrote that appeared October 12, 1984. The same piece also appeared under the headline "How the Instilled Gender Sense of Words Handicapped Ferraro," *Baltimore Evening Sun,* November 9, 1984, p. A15. The last two sections of this chapter are based on material from this piece.

242 The *Newsweek* article appeared on August 6, 1989, p. 17.

243 The photograph of Ferarro and family appears in *Newsweek,* August 27, 1984, p. 21.

CHAPTER NINE
"LOOK AT ME WHEN I'M TALKING TO YOU!": CROSS TALK ACROSS THE AGES

245 With support from the Society for Research in Child Development, Bruce Dorval invited me, along with scholars from several disciplines, to analyze his videotapes. As observed in a note to Chapter Two, Dorval provides a description of his research design, sample transcripts, and analyses of the same data by other scholars in his edited volume *Conversational Coherence and Its Development.* This chapter includes material adapted from my contribution to that volume, "Gen-

der Differences in Conversational Coherence: Physical Alignment and Topical Cohesion," as well as similar material presented in "Gender Differences in Topical Coherence: Creating Involvement in Best Friends' Talk."

256 Thorne, p. 170.

256 I later observed other tapes in Dorval's study and confirmed that they fit the pattern described here.

272 What appears to be a false start (Marsha: "You've got such— You've got such a positive attitude") was occasioned by an interruption. In between these two phrases, the investigator entered the room, in accordance with the experimental design, and briefly reminded the speakers of the task at hand.

CHAPTER TEN
LIVING WITH ASYMMETRY:
OPENING LINES OF COMMUNICATION

280 Gene LePere, *Never Pass This Way Again* (Bethesda, MD: Adler and Adler, 1987).

282 For numerous examples of complementary schismogenesis in relationships, see Watzlawick, Beavin, and Jackson.

283 Here and throughout the chapter, reference is to Goffman's essay "Gender Display" in his book *Gender Advertisements*.

284 "In the Crook of His Neck" is from *Circling Home* (Washington, DC: Scripta Humanistica, 1989), pp. 27–28.

287 "Gender Display," pp. 8–9, 7.

292 *American Couples*, pp. 73–76, 163.

295 Cronk cites University of Toronto anthropologist Richard Lee for information about the !Kung of the Kalahari desert. He ascribes the *moka* ritual to the Mount Hagen tribes of New Guinea and gives similar examples from the Kwakiutl of British Columbia, noting that anthropologists generally use the Chinook Indian term *potlatch* to refer to property-giving ceremonies. I am grateful to Ralph Fasold for calling my attention to this article.

REFERENCES

Anderson, Elaine S. 1977. *Learning to Speak with Style*. Ph.D. dissertation, Stanford University.

Aries, Elizabeth. 1976. "Interaction Patterns and Themes of Male, Female, and Mixed Groups." *Small Group Behavior* 7:1.7–18.

Aries, Elizabeth. 1982. "Verbal and Nonverbal Behavior in Single-Sex and Mixed-Sex Groups: Are Traditional Sex Roles Changing?" *Psychological Reports* 51.127–134.

Aries, Elizabeth. 1987. "Gender and Communication." *Sex and Gender,* ed. by Phillip Shaver and Clyde Hendrick, 149–176. Newbury Park, CA: Sage.

Baron, Dennis. 1986. *Grammar and Gender*. New Haven, CT: Yale University Press.

Bateson, Gregory. 1972. *Steps to an Ecology of Mind*. New York: Ballantine.

Bateson, Mary Catherine. 1984. *With a Daughter's Eye: A Memoir of Margaret Mead and Gregory Bateson*. New York: William Morrow.

Becker, A. L. 1988. "Attunement: An Essay in Philology and Logophilia." *On the Ethnography of Communication: The Legacy of Sapir*. Essays in honor of Harry Hoijer, 1984, ed. by Paul V. Kroskrity, 109–146. Los Angeles: UCLA Department of Anthropology.

Beeman, William O. 1986. *Language, Status, and Power in Iran*. Bloomington: Indiana University Press.

Befu, Harumi. 1986 [1974]. "An Ethnography of Dinner Entertainment in Japan." *Japanese Culture and Behavior,* ed. by Takie Sugiyama Lebra and William P. Lebra, 108–120. Honolulu: University of Hawaii Press.

Bennett, Adrian. 1981. "Interruptions and the Interpretation of Conversation." *Discourse Processes* 4:2.171–188.

Blumstein, Philip, and Pepper Schwartz. 1984. *American Couples: Money, Work, Sex*. New York: William Morrow.

Bohn, Emil, and Randall Stutman. 1983. "Sex-Role Differences in the Relational Control Dimension of Dyadic Interaction." *Women's Studies in Communication* 6.96–104.

Bradley, Patricia Hayes. 1981. "The Folk-Linguistics of Women's Speech:

An Empirical Examination." *Communication Monographs* 48.73–90.

Brooks-Gunn, Jeanne, and Wendy Schempp Matthews. 1979. *He & She: How Children Develop Their Sex Role Identity*. Englewood Cliffs, NJ: Prentice-Hall.

Brown, Penelope. 1990. "Gender, Politeness, and Confrontation in Tenejapa." *Discourse Processes* 13:1.

Brown, Roger, and Albert Gilman. 1960. "The Pronouns of Power and Solidarity." *Style in Language*, ed. by Thomas Sebeok, 253–276. Cambridge, MA: M.I.T. Press.

Caraveli, Anna. 1986. "The Bitter Wounding: The Lament as Social Protest in Rural Greece." *Gender and Power in Rural Greece*, ed. by Jill Dubisch, 169–194. Princetown, NJ: Princeton University Press.

Carson, Gerald. 1966. *The Polite Americans: A Wide-Angle View of Our More or Less Good Manners over 300 Years*. New York: William Morrow.

Chafe, Wallace. 1987. "Humor as a Disabling Mechanism." *American Behavioral Scientist* 30:3.16–25.

Cheepen, Christine. 1988. *The Predictability of Informal Conversation*. London: Pinter. New York: Columbia University Press.

Coates, Jennifer. 1986. *Women, Men, and Language*. London: Longman.

Condry, John, and Sandra Condry. 1976. "Sex Differences: A Study of the Eye of the Beholder." *Child Development* 47.812–819.

Conley, John M., William M. O'Barr, and E. Allen Lind. 1979. "The Power of Language: Presentational Style in the Courtroom." *Duke Law Journal*, Vol. 1978, no. 6.

Corsaro, William, and Thomas Rizzo. 1990. "Disputes in the Peer Culture of American and Italian Nursery School Children." *Conflict Talk*, ed. by Allen Grimshaw, 21–66. Cambridge: Cambridge University Press.

Cronk, Lee. 1989. "Strings Attached." *The Sciences*, May/June, 2–4.

Davies, Bronwyn, and Rom Harré. 1990. "Positioning: Conversation and the Production of Selves." *Journal for the Theory of Social Behaviour* 20:1.

Deakins, Alice H. 1989. *Talk at the Top: Topics at Lunch*. Ms., English Department, William Paterson College.

Dorval, Bruce (ed.). 1990. *Conversational Coherence and Its Development*. Norwood, NJ: Ablex.

Dubisch, Jill. 1986. "Culture Enters Through the Kitchen: Women, Food, and Social Boundaries in Rural Greece." *Gender and Power in Rural Greece*, ed. by Jill Dubisch, 195–214. Princeton, NJ: Princeton University Press.

Duncan, Beverly, and Otis Dudley Duncan. 1978. *Sex Typing and Social Roles*. With the collaboration of James A. McRae, Jr. New York: Academic Press.

Eakins, Barbara Westbrook, and R. Gene Eakins. 1978. *Sex Differences in Communication*. Boston: Houghton Mifflin.

Eble, Connie C. 1976. "Etiquette Books as Linguistic Authority." *The Second LACUS Forum 1975,* ed. by Peter A. Reich, 468–475. Columbia, SC: Hornbeam.

Eckert, Penelope. 1989. *Jocks and Burnouts*. New York: Teachers College Press.

Eckert, Penelope. 1990. "Cooperative Competition in Adolescent 'Girl Talk.' " *Discourse Processes* 13:1.

Edelsky, Carole. 1981. "Who's Got the Floor?" *Language in Society* 10.383–421.

Eder, Donna. 1990. "Serious and Playful Disputes: Variation in Conflict Talk Among Female Adolescents." *Conflict Talk,* ed. by Allen Grimshaw, 67–84. Cambridge: Cambridge University Press.

Eder, Donna, and Maureen Hallinan. 1978. "Sex Differences in Children's Friendships." *American Sociological Review* 43.237–250.

Eder, Donna, and Stephanie Sanford. 1986. "The Development and Maintenance of Interactional Norms Among Early Adolescents." *Sociological Studies of Child Development,* Vol. 1, ed. by Patricia A. Adler and Peter Adler, 283–300. Greenwich, CT: JAI Press.

Erickson, Frederick. 1990. "Social Construction of Discourse Coherence in a Family Dinner Table Conversation." *Conversational Coherence and Its Development,* ed. by Bruce Dorval, 207–238. Norwood, NJ: Ablex.

Esposito, Anita. 1979. "Sex Differences in Children's Conversations." *Language and Speech* 22, Pt. 3, 213–220.

Falk, Jane. 1980. "The Conversational Duet." *Proceedings of the Sixth Annual Meeting of the Berkeley Linguistics Society,* 507–514. Berkeley, CA: Department of Linguistics, University of California.

Fasold, Ralph W. 1990. *The Sociolinguistics of Language*. Oxford: Basil Blackwell.

Fishman, Pamela M. 1978. "Interaction: The Work Women Do." *Social Problems* 25:4.397–406. Revised version in *Language, Gender and Society,* ed. by Barrie Thorne, Cheris Kramarae, and Nancy Henley, 89–101. Rowley, MA: Newbury House, 1983.

Fox, Thomas. 1990. "Gender Interests in Reading and Writing." *The Social Uses of Writing: Politics and Pedagogy,* 51–70. Norwood, NJ: Ablex.

Frank, Jane. 1988. "A Comparison of Intimate Conversations: Prag-

matic Theory Applied to Examples of Invented and Actual Dialog."
The SECOL Review 12:3.186–208.

Frank, Jane. 1989. "Communicating 'by Pairs': Agreeing and Disagreeing Among Married Couples." Ms., Georgetown University.

Friedrich, Paul. 1972. "Social Context and Semantic Feature: The Russian Pronominal Usage." *Directions in Sociolinguistics*, ed. by John J. Gumperz and Dell Hymes, 270–300. New York: Holt, Rinehart and Winston. Reprint, Oxford: Basil Blackwell.

Geis, Michael L. 1987. *The Language of Politics*. New York: Springer-Verlag.

Gilligan, Carol. 1982. *In a Different Voice: Psychological Theory and Women's Development*. Cambridge, MA: Harvard University Press.

Gleason, Jean Berko. 1987. "Sex Differences in Parent-Child Interaction." *Language, Gender, and Sex in Comparative Perspective*, ed. by Susan U. Philips, Susan Steele, and Christine Tanz, 189–199. Cambridge: Cambridge University Press.

Gleason, Jean Berko, and Esther Blank Greif. 1983. "Men's Speech to Young Children." *Language, Gender and Society*, ed. by Barrie Thorne, Cheris Kramarae, and Nancy Henley, 140–150. Rowley, MA: Newbury House.

Goffman, Erving. 1959. *The Presentation of Self in Everyday Life*. Garden City, NY: Doubleday.

Goffman, Erving. 1967. *Interaction Ritual*. Garden City, NY: Doubleday.

Goffman, Erving. 1974. *Frame Analysis*. New York: Harper and Row.

Goffman, Erving. 1979. "Gender Display." *Gender Advertisements*, 1–9. New York: Harper and Row.

Goffman, Erving. 1981. "Footing." *Forms of Talk*, 124–159. Philadelphia: University of Pennsylvania Press.

Goodwin, Marjorie Harness. In press. *He-Said-She-Said: Talk as Social Organization Among Black Children*. Bloomington: Indiana University Press.

Goodwin, Marjorie Harness, and Charles Goodwin. 1987. "Children's Arguing." *Language, Gender, and Sex in Comparative Perspective*, ed. by Susan U. Philips, Susan Steele, and Christine Tanz, 200–248. Cambridge: Cambridge University Press.

Greenwood, Alice. 1989. *Discourse Variation and Social Comfort: A Study of Topic Initiation and Interruption Patterns in the Dinner Conversation of Preadolescent Children*. Ph.D. dissertation, City University of New York.

Greif, Esther Blank. 1980. "Sex Differences in Parent-Child Conversations." *Women's Studies International Quarterly* 3:2/3.253–258.

Hayashi, Reiko. 1988. "Simultaneous Talk—from the Perspective of Floor Management of English and Japanese Speakers." *World Englishes* 7:3.269–288.

Henley, Nancy, and Cheris Kramarae. Forthcoming. "Miscommunication, Gender and Power." *Handbook of Miscommunication and Problematic Talk,* ed. by Nikolas Coupland, John Wiemann, and Howard Giles. Bristol: Multilingual Matters.

Hill, Alette Olin. 1986. *Mother Tongue, Father Time: A Decade of Linguistic Revolt.* Bloomington: Indiana University Press.

Hirschman, Lynette. 1973. "Female-Male Differences in Conversational Interaction." Paper presented at the annual meeting of the Linguistic Society of America, San Diego, CA.

Hoffman, Eva. 1989. *Lost in Translation: A Life in a New Language.* New York: E. P. Dutton.

Horner, Matina S. 1972. "Toward an Understanding of Achievement-Related Conflicts in Women." *Journal of Social Issues* 28.157–175.

Hughes, Linda A. 1988. " 'But That's Not *Really* Mean': Competing in a Cooperative Mode." *Sex Roles* 19:11/12.669–687.

James, Deborah, and Janice Drakich. 1989. "Understanding Gender Differences in Amount of Talk." Ms., Linguistics Department, University of Toronto, Scarborough Campus.

Jefferson, Gail. 1988. "On the Sequential Organization of Troubles-Talk in Ordinary Conversation." *Social Problems* 35:4.418–441.

Johnstone, Barbara. 1989. "Community and Contest: How Women and Men Construct Their Worlds in Conversational Narrative." Paper presented at Women in America: Legacies of Race and Ethnicity, Georgetown University, Washington, DC.

Kalčik, Susan. 1975. " '. . . Like Ann's Gynecologist or the Time I Was Almost Raped': Personal Narratives in Women's Rap Groups." *Journal of American Folklore* 88:3–11. Reprinted in *Women and Folklore,* ed. by Claire R. Farrer. Austin: University of Texas Press.

Keenan, Elinor. 1974. "Norm-makers, Norm-breakers: Uses of Speech by Men and Women in a Malagasy Community." *Explorations in the Ethnography of Speaking,* ed. by Richard Bauman and Joel Sherzer, 125–143. Cambridge: Cambridge University Press.

Keller, Evelyn Fox. 1985. *Reflections on Gender and Science.* New Haven, CT: Yale University Press.

Kennedy, Robinette. 1986. "Women's Friendships on Crete: A Psychological Perspective." *Gender and Power in Rural Greece,* ed. by Jill Dubisch, 121–138. Princeton, NJ: Princeton University Press.

Kochman, Thomas. 1981. Black and white styles in conflict. Chicago: University of Chicago Press.

Komarovsky, Mirra. 1962. *Blue-Collar Marriage.* New York: Vintage.

Kramarae, Cheris. 1981. *Women and Men Speaking*. Rowley, MA: Newbury House.

Kuipers, Joel C. 1986. "Talking About Troubles: Gender Differences in Weyewa Speech Use." *American Ethnologist* 13:3.448–462.

Labov, William. 1972. "The Linguistic Consequences of Being a Lame." *Language in the Inner City*, 255–292. Philadelphia: University of Pennsylvania Press.

Labov, William, and David Fanshel. 1977. *Therapeutic Discourse*. New York: Academic Press.

Lakoff, Robin. 1975. *Language and Woman's Place*. New York: Harper and Row.

Lange, Deborah. 1988. "Using *Like* to Introduce Constructed Dialogue: How *Like* Contributes to Discourse Coherence." Master's thesis, Georgetown University.

Leaper, Campbell. 1988. "The Sequencing of Power and Involvement in Girls' and Boys' Talk." Ms. submitted for publication, Psychology Department, University of California, Santa Cruz.

Leet-Pellegrini, H. M. 1980. "Conversational Dominance as a Function of Gender and Expertise." *Language: Social Psychological Perspectives*, ed. by Howard Giles, W. Peter Robinson, and Philip M. Smith, 97–104. Oxford: Pergamon.

Leffler, Ann, D. L. Gillespie, and J. C. Conaty. 1982. "The Effects of Status Differentiation on Nonverbal Behavior." *Social Psychology Quarterly* 45:3.153–161.

Lehtonen, Jaakko, and Kari Sajavaara. 1985. "The Silent Finn." *Perspectives on Silence*, ed. by Deborah Tannen and Muriel Saville-Troike, 193–201. Norwood, NJ: Ablex.

Lever, Janet. 1976. "Sex Differences in the Games Children Play." *Social Problems* 23.478–483.

Lever, Janet. 1978. "Sex Differences in the Complexity of Children's Play and Games." *American Sociological Review* 43.471–483.

Linde, Charlotte. 1988. "The Use of Narrative in the Negotiation of Values: Group Identity in an Airborne Police Agency." Paper presented at the annual meeting of the Linguistic Society of America, New Orleans.

Macke, Anne Statham, and Laurel Walum Richardson, with Judith Cook. 1980. *Sex-Typed Teaching Styles of University Professors and Student Reactions*. Columbus: Ohio State University Research Foundation.

Maltz, Daniel N., and Ruth A. Borker. 1982. "A Cultural Approach to Male-Female Miscommunication." *Language and Social Identity*, ed. by John J. Gumperz, 196–216. Cambridge: Cambridge University Press.

REFERENCES

Mitchell, Carol. 1985. "Some Differences in Male and Female Joke-Telling." *Women's Folklore, Women's Culture,* ed. by Rosan A. Jordan and Susan J. Kalčik, 163–186. Philadelphia: University of Pennsylvania Press.

Moerman, Michael. 1987. "Finding Life in Dry Dust." *Talking Culture: Ethnography and Conversation Analysis,* 19–30. Philadelphia: University of Pennsylvania Press.

Murray, Stephen O. 1985. "Toward a Model of Members' Methods for Recognizing Interruptions." *Language in Society* 13.31–41.

Newcombe, Nora, and Diane Arnkoff. 1979. "Effects of Speech Style and Sex of Speaker on Person Perception." *Journal of Personality and Social Psychology* 37.1293–1303.

Newman, Barbara Miller. 1971. *Interpersonal Behavior and Preferences for Exploration in Adolescent Boys: A Small Group Study.* Ph.D. dissertation, University of Michigan.

Ong, Walter J., S. J. 1981. *Fighting for Life: Contest, Sexuality, and Consciousness.* Ithaca, NY: Cornell University Press. Paperback: Amherst, MA: University of Massachusetts Press, 1989.

Philipsen, Gerry. 1975. "Speaking 'Like a Man' in Teamsterville: Culture Patterns of Role Enactment in an Urban Neighborhood." *Quarterly Journal of Speech* 61.13–22.

Reisman, Karl. 1974. "Contrapuntal Conversations in an Antiguan Village." *Explorations in the Ethnography of Speaking,* ed. by Richard Bauman and Joel Sherzer, 110–124. Cambridge: Cambridge University Press.

Riessman, Catherine Kohler. In press. *Divorce Talk: Women and Men Make Sense of Personal Relationships.* New Brunswick, NJ: Rutgers University Press.

Sachs, Jacqueline. 1987. "Young Children's Language Use in Pretend Play." *Language, Gender, and Sex in Comparative Perspective,* ed. by Susan U. Philips, Susan Steele, and Christine Tanz, 178–188. Cambridge: Cambridge University Press.

Sacks, Harvey, Emanuel A Schegloff, and Gail Jefferson. 1974. "A Simplest Systematics for the Organization of Turntaking for Conversation." *Language* 50:4.696–735.

Sadker, Myra, and David Sadker. 1985. "Sexism in the Schoolroom of the '80s." *Psychology Today,* March 1985, 54–57.

Sadker, Myra, and David Sadker. 1986. "Sexism in the Classroom: From Grade School to Graduate School." *Phi Delta Kappan* 67:7.

Sattel, Jack W. 1983. "Men, Inexpressiveness, and Power." *Language, Gender and Society,* ed. by Barrie Thorne, Cheris Kramarae, and Nancy Henley, 119–124. Rowley, MA: Newbury House.

Schiffrin, Deborah. 1984. "Jewish Argument as Sociability." *Language in Society* 13:3.311–335.

Scollon, Ron. 1982. "The Rhythmic Integration of Ordinary Talk." *Analyzing Discourse: Text and Talk. Georgetown University Round Table on Languages and Linguistics 1981,* ed. by Deborah Tannen, 335–349. Washington, DC: Georgetown University Press.

Scollon, Ron, and Suzanne B. K. Scollon. 1981. *Narrative, Literacy and Face in Interethnic Communication.* Norwood, NJ: Ablex.

Sheldon, Amy. 1990. "Pickle Fights: Gendered Talk in Preschool Disputes." *Discourse Processes* 13:1.

Sherzer, Joel. 1987. "A Diversity of Voices: Men's and Women's Speech in Ethnographic Perspective. *Language Gender, and Sex in Comparative Perspective,* ed. by Susan U. Philips, Susan Steele, and Christine Tanz, 95–120. Cambridge: Cambridge University Press.

Shultz, Jeffrey, Susan Florio, and Frederick Erickson. 1982. "Where's the Floor? Aspects of the Cultural Organization of Social Relationships in Communication at Home and at School." *Ethnography and Education: Children in and out of School,* ed. by Perry Gilmore and Alan Glatthorn, 88–123. Washington, DC: Center for Applied Linguistics (distributed by Ablex, Norwood, NJ).

Shuman, Amy. 1986. *Storytelling Rights: The Uses of Oral and Written Texts by Urban Adolescents.* Cambridge: Cambridge University Press.

Siegler, David M., and Robert S. Siegler. 1976. "Stereotypes of Males' and Females' Speech." *Psychological Reports* 39.167–170.

Smith, Frances. 1990. *Gender and the Framing of Exegetical Authority in Sermon Performances.* Ph.D. dissertation, Georgetown University.

Spender, Dale. 1980. *Man Made Language.* London: Routledge and Kegan Paul.

Stephens, Mitchell. 1988. *A History of News: From the Drum to the Satellite.* New York: Viking.

Sternberg, Robert J., and Susan Grajek. 1984. "The Nature of Love." *Journal of Personality and Social Psychology* 47.312–329.

Strodtbeck, Fred L., and Richard D. Mann. 1956. "Sex Role Differentiation in Jury Deliberations." *Sociometry* 19.3–11.

Swacker, Marjorie. 1976. "Women's Verbal Behavior at Learned and Professional Conferences." *The Sociology of the Languages of American Women,* ed. by Betty Lou Dubois and Isabel Crouch, 155–160. San Antonio: Trinity University.

Tannen, Deborah. 1982. "Ethnic Style in Male-Female Conversation." *Language and Social Identity,* ed. by John J. Gumperz, 217–231. Cambridge: Cambridge University Press.

Tannen, Deborah. 1983. *Lilika Nakos*. Boston: G. K. Hall.

Tannen, Deborah. 1984. *Conversational Style: Analyzing Talk Among Friends*. Norwood, NJ: Ablex.

Tannen, Deborah. 1986. *That's Not What I Meant! How Conversational Style Makes or Breaks Your Relations with Others*. New York: William Morrow.

Tannen, Deborah. 1989. "Interpreting Interruption in Conversation." *Papers from the 25th Annual Regional Meeting of the Chicago Linguistic Society. Part Two: Parasession on Language in Context,* ed. by Bradley Music, Randolph Graczyk, and Caroline Wiltshire, 266–287. Chicago: Chicago Linguistic Society.

Tannen, Deborah. 1989. *Talking Voices: Repetition, Dialogue, and Imagery in Conversational Discourse*. Cambridge: Cambridge University Press.

Tannen, Deborah. 1990. "Gender Differences in Conversational Coherence: Physical Alignment and Topical Cohesion." *Conversational Coherence and Its Development,* ed. by Bruce Dorval, 167–206. Norwood, NJ: Ablex.

Tannen, Deborah. 1990. "Gender Differences in Topical Coherence: Creating Involvement in Best Friends' Talk." *Discourse Processes* 13:1.

Thorne, Barrie. 1986. "Girls and Boys Together . . . but Mostly Apart: Gender Arrangements in Elementary Schools." *Relationships and Development,* ed. by Willard W. Hartup and Zick Rubin, 167–184. Hillsdale, NJ: Erlbaum.

Thorne, Barrie, Cheris Kramarae, and Nancy Henley. 1983. "Language, Gender and Society: Opening a Second Decade of Research." *Language, Gender and Society,* ed. by Barrie Thorne, Cheris Kramarae, and Nancy Henley, 7–24. Rowley, MA: Newbury House.

Tidball, M. Elizabeth. 1989. "Women's Colleges: Exceptional Conditions, Not Exceptional Talent, Produce High Achievers." *Educating the Majority: Women Challenge the Tradition,* ed. by Carol S. Pearson, Donna L. Shavlik, and Judith G. Touchton, 157–172. New York: Macmillan.

Wall, Harriet M., and Anita Barry. 1985. "Student Expectations for Male and Female Instructor Behavior." *Women in Higher Education: Traditions, Transitions and Revolutions,* ed. by Roy E. Cheatham, 283–291. Proceedings for Women in Higher Education Conferences. St. Louis: Saint Louis University, Metropolitan College, and SAASS, Inc.

Watson, Karen A. 1975. "Transferable Communicative Routines." *Language in Society* 4.53–72.

Watzlawick, Paul, Janet Helmick Beavin, and Don D. Jackson. 1967. *The Pragmatics of Human Communication.* New York: Norton.

West, Candace, and Don H. Zimmerman. 1983. "Small Insults: A Study of Interruptions in Cross-Sex Conversations Between Unacquainted Persons." *Language, Gender, and Society,* ed. by Barrie Thorne, Cheris Kramarae, and Nancy Henley, 103–117. Rowley, MA: Newbury House.

West, Candace, and Don H. Zimmerman. 1985. "Gender, Language, and Discourse." *Handbook of Discourse Analysis,* Vol. 4: *Discourse Analysis in Society,* ed. by Teun A. van Dijk, 103–124. London: Academic Press.

White, Jane J. 1989. "The Power of Politeness in the Classroom: Cultural Codes That Create and Constrain Knowledge Construction." *Journal of Curriculum and Supervision* 4:4.298–321.

Yamada, Haru. 1989. *American and Japanese Topic Management Strategies in Business Conversations.* Ph.D. dissertation, Georgetown University.

Zimmerman, Don H., and Candace West. 1975. "Sex Roles, Interruptions and Silences in Conversation." *Language and Sex: Difference and Dominance,* ed. by Barrie Thorne and Nancy Henley, 105–129. Rowley, MA: Newbury House.

INDEX

INDEX

Also by Deborah Tannen

THAT'S NOT WHAT I MEANT!
How Conversational Style Makes or Breaks
Your Relations With Others

In this earlier work by this path-breaking linguist, Deborah
Tannen explains the way our relationships with friends,
families, partners, colleagues and bosses are just as
powerfully shaped by how we say something as what we
actually say.

from Deborah Tannen's preface –
"This book is about private speaking: how it works, why it
goes well sometimes and badly at other times. It explains the
invisible processes of conversational style that shape
relationships. Understanding these processes restores a sense
of control over our lives, making it possible to improve
communication and relationships in all the settings in which
people talk to each other: at work, in interviews, in public
affairs, and most important of all, at home."

In revealing the conversational signals and devices we all use
– consciously and unconsciously – to present ourselves to the
world, Deborah Tannen once again helps banish the
misunderstandings that haunt all our lives.

From Virago in autumn 1992.

Other Virago Books of interest

BOYS WILL BE BOYS
Breaking the Link Between Masculinity and Violence
Myriam Miedzian

Most acts of violence are committed by men – boys, after all, will be boys. But why? And how can we begin to raise sons whose sense of self-worth will not be dependent on the masculine mystique of toughness and repressed emotion. In this ground-breaking work, social worker and philosopher Myriam Miedzian brings fascinating new insights to the problems of violent toys, television, sports, parents' and teachers' attitudes, and goes on to suggest concrete ways to overcome them. This essential, transforming book is for anyone who wants to explore and influence the root cause of violence in our society.

SLOW MOTION
Changing Masculinities, Changing Men
Lynne Segal

"Women do not write books about men," wrote Virginia Woolf. Neither, until recently, did men. Throughout the 1980s questions concerning the changing nature of men's lives and experiences have been debated with new passion and concern. From the exploration of sex roles to the study of gender and power, the psychology of men has emerged fraught with strain and crisis. Ironically, the thoughts of those seeking a sexual politics to undermine men's power over women remain consistently gloomy, while the category of masculinity remains deeply obscure.

Slow Motion, by the author of the highly-acclaimed *Is the Future Female?*, approaches the "problem of men" in a new way, by looking not at masculinity, but at specific *masculinities*. From tough guys and martial men to camp, gay, black-macho and anti-sexist men, their competing images and roles are analysed to move beyond cynicism to create a new sexual agenda for the 1990s.

FATHERS
Reflections by Daughters
Edited by Ursula Owen

Of all the shaping human relationships, the one between father and daughter is the least written about, especially from the daughter's point of view. This book is a collage of memoirs and polemic, stories and poems, describing experiences which range from the most intense loyalty and love to the dark and painful areas of paternal tyranny and incest. Every daughter and every father will recognise something of their story here: some will realise, perhaps for the first time, just how deeply this bond has affected their lives. For these writers, whose ages range from thirteen to sixty, have produced fascinating and sometimes shocking insights into what is probably the most unresolved relationship of them all.

Contributions from Anne Boston, Dinah Brooke, Angela Carter, Eileen Fairweather, Elaine Feinstein, Olivia Harris, Cora Kaplan, Doris Lessing, Melanie MacFadyean, Sara Maitland, Julia O'Faolain, Kate Owen, Grace Paley, Adrienne Rich, Rose Rider, Michele Roberts, Sheila Rowbotham, Barbara Taylor.

THE DRAMA OF BEING A CHILD
Alice Miller

"Full of wisdom and perception" – *Anthony Storr*

"Every parent should read Alice Miller's *The Drama of Being a Child*. It might make for fewer casualties in that primal battlefield – the homestead" – *Edna O'Brien, Observer*

"Illuminating and distressingly familiar. The reader has the complex experience of recognising a great truth simultaneously with revelation and the realisation of personal tragedy long and deeply suppressed" – *Ruth Rendell, New Statesman*

Alice Miller's startling insights into child development are shared with us here as she explains her conviction that violence and cruelty in society have their roots in conventional child rearing and in education. She shows how many children, adapted from birth to the needs and ambitions of their parents, lose the ability to experience and express their true feelings, eventually to become estranged from their real selves. In sublimating their full potential in order to fulfil the desires of their parents, they impede the creativity, vitality and integrity that is authentically their own. Many people who have read her books have discovered within themselves the little child they once were. This may explain the strong and deep reactions Alice Miller's books have evoked in so many readers.